RUSSIAN FEDERATION

Siberia

Moscow

Volga

Ob'

Yenisey

Lena

Amur

KAZAKHSTAN

MONGOLIA

Gobi

NE

AVIA

ack Sea

abul

GEORGIA

ARMENIA

UZBEKISTAN

KYRGYZSTAN

URKEY

TURKMENISTAN

TAJIKISTAN

CHINA

Beijing

NORTH
KOREA

JAPAN

Seoul

SOUTH
KOREA

Tokyo

RUS

NON-

RAEL

SYRIA

AZERBAIJAN

AFGHANISTAN

Kabul

AKSAI CHIN
claimed by India,
controlled by China

Yellow River

Shanghai

IRAQ

IRAN

Tehran

PAKISTAN

NEPAL

BHUTAN

Yangtze

*Ryukyu
Islands*

airo

JORDAN

KUWAIT

Delhi

Indus

Ganges

Guangzhou

TAIWAN

GYPT

BAHRAIN

QATAR

SAUDI
ARABIA

UNITED
ARAB
EMIRATES

OMAN

INDIA

Karachi

BANGLADESH

Calcutta

BURMA

LAOS

Hong Kong

Macao
to China 1999

Bombay

The Gulf

Madras

THAILAND

VIETNAM

Mekong

PARACEL
ISLANDS
disputed

Manila

Nile

UDAN

ERITREA

YEMEN

*Socotra
to Yemen*

*Laccadive
Islands*

*Andaman
Islands*

Bangkok

CAMBODIA

PHILIPPINES

DJIBOUTI

SRI LANKA

*Nicobar
Islands*

SPRATLY
ISLANDS
disputed

ETHIOPIA

SOMALIA

MALDIVES

BRUNEI

DA

UGANDA

KENYA

SEYCHELLES

BRITISH INDIAN
OCEAN TERRITORY

MALAYSIA

SINGAPORE

Borneo

BURUNDI

INDIAN OCEAN

Sumatra

INDONESIA

TANZANIA

*Agalega Islands
to Mauritius*

Jakarta

New
Guinea

Java

MALAWI

COMOROS

MAYOTTE

MBIA

Zambezi

*Tromelin
to Réunion*

*Rodrigues
to Mauritius*

Timor

Darling

MBABWE

MADAGASCAR

MAURITIUS

RÉUNION

MOZAMBIQUE

SWAZILAND

LESOTHO

COCOS
ISLANDS

CHRISTMAS
ISLAND

ASHMORE AND
CARTIER ISLANDS

WAKE ISLAND

NORTHERN
MARIANA ISLANDS

GUAM

MARSHALL
ISLANDS

PACIFIC OCEAN

MICRONESIA

PALAU

KIRIBATI

NAURU

PAPUA
NEW GUINEA

SOLOMON
ISLANDS

TUVALU

VANUATU

FIJI

CORAL SEA
ISLANDS

NEW
CALEDONIA

AUSTRALIA

NORFOLK
ISLAND

*Lord Howe
Island*

Sydney

NEW
ZEALAND

CULTURAL
ANTHROPOLOGY

CULTURAL ANTHROPOLOGY

Canadian Edition

Nancy Bonvillain
Simon's Rock College of Bard

Brian Schwimmer
University of Manitoba

PEARSON

Prentice
Hall

Toronto

Library and Archives Canada Cataloguing in Publication

Bonvillain, Nancy, 1945–
    Cultural anthropology / Nancy Bonvillain, Brian Schwimmer.

Includes bibliographical references and index.
ISBN 978-0-13-159681-8

        1. Ethnology—Textbooks.   I. Schwimmer, Brian Ethan   II. Title.

GN316.B66 2009   306   C2008-900722-0

ISBN-13: 978-0-13-159681-8
ISBN-10: 0-13-159681-0

Vice President, Editorial Director: Gary Bennett
Senior Acquisitions Editor: Laura Forbes
Signing Representative: Duncan Mackinnon
Marketing Manager: Sally Aspinall
Developmental Editor: Charlotte Morrison-Reed
Production Editor: Richard di Santo
Copy Editor: Patricia Jones
Proofreader: Nancy Carroll
Production Coordinator: Avinash Chandra
Composition: ICC Macmillan Inc.
Photo and Permissions Research: Terri Rothman
Art Director: Julia Hall
Interior Design: Geoff Agnew
Cover Design: Kerrin Hands
Cover Image: Getty Images/Gary Holscher

3 4 5   14 13 12 11

Printed and bound in Canada.

Brief Contents

Contents

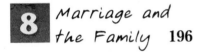

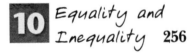

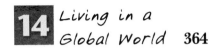

Special Features

case study

Culture Change

Controversies

In Their Own Voices

Anthropology Applied

Preface

We live in a nation and a world in which cultural diversity commands increasing attention. Differences in beliefs, attitudes, and practices challenge our capacity for understanding and tolerance and have raised complex political and moral debates. *Cultural Anthropology* is intended to address these issues of pluralism by introducing students to a systematic consideration of differences among the world's cultures. Its focus is on understanding the importance of culture for human ways of life and how cultures develop, integrate, and change. It seeks to spark excitement about the fascinating diversity of peoples' beliefs and behaviours and about the broader similarities that unite us. This book, therefore, provides a global view of humanity's many facets. It takes a traditional approach in chapter organization, focusing on various aspects of societal organization and expression. But it also emphasizes the processes of culture change that are integral to all societies. In addition to teaching about other peoples, anthropology both as a discipline and as a framework of analysis has the potential to help students appreciate the cultural patterns underlying their own behaviours, beliefs, and attitudes. This book also attempts to present the voices of the peoples who anthropologists study. Through these voices, and through analyses of indigenous and marginalized peoples today, students may come to understand the global processes that affect us all.

An important feature of this text is its focus on culture change and contemporary social issues through general observations about cultural processes with detailed and interrelated case studies. It considers culture not as a static and homogeneous system, but as a field of values and ideas that serve peoples' needs and interests. Culture is flexible and can be contested by different groups within a society, and thus it can serve both to support domination of one class or society over another and to contest subordination and exploitation. In focusing on change and process, this text highlights the notion that the societies and the cultures that people develop are dynamic systems, adapted to new situations and invigorated by new ideas.

CANADIAN CONTENT

This edition of the text has been written specifically for Canadian students. A substantial effort has been made to include ethnographic studies of the various cultures that make up our national mosaic and illustrate how they are interlinked within a wider context of Canadian institutions, policies, practices, and trends. Detailed attention is given to Aboriginal peoples with a particular emphasis on those from the Pacific Northwest Coast, as well as Mohawk and Inuit cultures. Some cases are continued from chapter to chapter to provide a context for considering how different parts of a culture are interrelated and integrated. Continuity of treatment also provides a context for considering how indigenous cultures are affecting and being influenced by contemporary trends such as resource development, land claims, and environmental change that are discussed in the closing chapters of the book. Attention is also given to many Canadian cultures including French Canadians and other ethnicities and immigrant communities. Treatment of local cultures is balanced by a consideration of broader patterns and trends in our society within every chapter. Among other issues, the text details linguistic, ethnic, and religious diversity, family and marriage trends, consumption patterns, gender, and social stratification. We have attempted to explain how these features of our society are linked together, how they affect the various cultural communities, and how both are influenced by basic institutions, most prominently Canadian public policy and political economy. Special attention is given to bilingual and multicultural legislation and the administration of Aboriginal peoples, as well as to broader patterns of inequality and government attempts to mitigate them. The text places these aspects of our society within the wider international context of increasing globalization and economic liberalization.

FORMAT OF THE BOOK

Cultural Anthropology consists of fourteen chapters covering the breadth of the discipline of cultural anthropology. The first two chapters lay the groundwork for the study of human culture. Chapter 1 ("What Is Anthropology?") presents the basic outline of the field of anthropology, describing its development, exemplifying its various subdisciplines, and introduces the concept of culture. It also introduces a key focus of this text—understanding that cultures are dynamic systems of behaviour and belief, ever changing and adjusting to internal and external forces. Chapter 2 ("Studying Culture") takes a closer look at the specific methodologies that anthropologists have developed to analyze cultural behaviour and formulate theories to explain both similarities and differences found throughout the world. It offers an array of theoretical perspectives used to analyze culture. It also takes the reader into the experience of fieldwork, a hallmark of anthropological research.

The next two chapters describe the systems of language and socialization basic to all human societies. Chapter 3 ("Language and Culture") introduces topics in the structure of language but concentrates on the complex relationships between language and other aspects of culture. Chapter 4 ("Learning One's Culture") discusses the various perspectives taken in different societies about the ways that parents and families raise their children and teach them the norms and values of their communities.

The text then proceeds with discussions of specific topics within cultural anthropology. Chapters 5 ("Making a Living") and 6 ("Economic Systems") focus on subsistence practices, ways of making a living, and patterns of production and exchange. Chapters 7 ("Kinship and Descent") and 8 ("Marriage and the Family") describe the various systems of kinship found throughout the world, detailing different ways of reckoning descent and forming marriages and families. In Chapter 9 ("Gender"), we look closely at issues of gender, attempting to understand the conditions under which egalitarian gender relationships and attitudes are sustained, as well as the conditions under which inequality between men and women becomes established. Chapter 10 ("Equality and Inequality") also considers issues of inequality in the realm of social stratification, analyzing social segmentation on the basis of caste, class, race, and ethnicity. Chapter 11 ("Political Systems") furthers this discussion in the analysis of political systems, including ways of establishing leadership, arriving at group decisions, and settling disputes both within a community and between communities.

Chapters 12 ("Religion") and 13 ("The Arts") focus on various aspects of expressive and symbolic culture. Chapter 12 is concerned with the ways that people express religious beliefs and organize religious practice. It relates these beliefs and practices to other aspects of social, economic, and political life. And Chapter 13 is concerned with aesthetic values and their embodiment in artistic production.

Finally, Chapter 14 ("Living in a Global World") is directly concerned with the themes of globalization and culture change that permeate the text and are

In Their Own Voices

Aboriginal Children in Canadian Residential Schools

In the name of "civilization" the Canadian government removed thousands of First Nations children from their families and communities and placed them in Church-run residential schools in order to assimilate them into Canadian culture and society. The author comments on the affects of this system on his family and his cultural heritage.

The defining moment of [my father's] life came when he entered St. Mary's Residential School. Until then, he had been raised as a boy of respectable birth and reliable prospects, in both the Sto:lo community and the non-native world. St. Mary's, founded in 1863, was the pride of the Catholic Oblate order that had established a "mission" to the Indians in the Fraser Valley. From their

to discipline us. If I didn't behave, he told me, I would be sent to a school where children had to rise at 5:00 a.m., say prayers on their knees for hours, and eat thin gruel three times a day. Porridge, porridge, and more porridge was his abiding memory of the school's fare, particularly galling to Sto:lo who thrived on the Fraser River's rich salmon and sturgeon resources.

My father was a fluent Halq'emeylem speaker, and he remembered having his knuckles rapped with a wooden stick or getting whipped for speaking either his language or the Chinook or N'laka'pamuz languages, both of which he spoke well as a child.

St. Mary's, like other Indian residential schools, was designed to strip aboriginal peoples of our culture. My father was at the school to grow up to be a little White man to enter the White world. . . . Some of the priest's words, enforced by the rod, must have stayed with my

Case Study

Language, Politics, and Society in Canada

Language issues have played a prominent role in the formation of Canadian society and have had wide and

has been expressed in terms of a need "to adapt to the new realities, notably the 'Quiet Revolution' in [a growingly militant] Quebec" and "to establish a working relationship between two linguistic communities" (Canadian Heritage website). Similar provisions have been extended within areas of provincial responsibility in all of the provinces, both within the mandated area of education and for other public services. However, New Brunswick is the only officially bilingual province. Alberta and Saskatchewan have passed legislation proclaiming English as their official language, while French is the sole official language of Quebec (Hudon 2007).

Quebec's official language policy has adopted the most notable provisions within the country because of its concern with the preservation of French and the maintenance of francophone identity both within Quebec and the wider Canadian framework. In addition to exclusive recognition of French, laws have been passed to ensure that French is more prominently displayed than English or any other language on all signage. French is also the official language of

Culture Change

CHANGING MALE AND FEMALE SOCIALIZATION AMONG THE INUIT

often continued to go out on the land on periodic hunting and trapping expeditions. This new division of labour affected boys and girls differently. Both genders attended the local schools for at least the primary grades, but high school completion was not common for either group. Boys spent some time accompanying their fathers on hunting and trapping trips, but only occasionally and at their own discretion. They spent most of their adolescence in all-male peer groups and devoted their time to leisure activities, such as playing hockey or other sports or just "hanging out." This pattern was partially based on the adoption of the youth culture prevalent in southern Canada. It represented a clear departure from traditional socialization and sociability, where few people of the same age cohort were in regular daily contact and much of the day was spent with adults in subsistence activities. Girls, on the other hand, tended to be raised according to a more traditional model. Daughters would stay home and take care of the house and their younger siblings while their mothers were at work. They would also sew items for sale or engage in wage employment to earn incomes to support their families. They generally did not perceive their greater responsibility as onerous given attention in every chapter. We look at migration and translocalism that are increasingly affecting the composition and dynamics of Canadian society, and at recent global trends influencing the lives of indigenous peoples in a variety of localities.

SPECIAL FEATURES

In addition to the focus on change, the text is tied together by a number of recurring features. Each chapter begins with a narrative, usually a sacred or secular story, that dramatizes important themes discussed in the chapter. Several of the opening narratives are also selected from historical documents or contemporary interviews and accounts relating to the content of the chapter.

Each chapter also contains a feature, "In Their Own Voices," that presents points of view that highlight and exemplify the chapter's theme or content. Most of these "Voices" are of indigenous peoples whose lives are discussed in the text. Some are from memoirs or novels, and others are excerpted from speeches or conferences.

The Somali Affair and Military Culture

In 1993, the Canadian public was shocked by the actions of Canadian Airborne troops serving in a "peace enforcement" mission in Somalia. Two soldiers had captured a Somali teenager trespassing on their base and tortured him to death. In the wake of a public uproar, a commission of inquiry was formed to investigate the incident and to recommend changes within the army to rectify any problems that were identified. Many possible influences were cited including problems in the chain of command, poor training and discipline, malarial drug trials, "a few bad apples," and the "dark side of human nature." Among the researchers involved in this project, Donna Winslow (1997), an anthropologist from the University of Ottawa, considered the importance of culture in the formation of attitudes and practices that may have led to this act of violence. Her research indicated that the Canadian sol-

semi-autonomous units distinguished by region and collective symbols adopted by each group. Basic training procedures, complemented by hazing rituals, created a strong sense of collective identity and loyalty that cast the group as a single family. This orientation served an important function; it maintained military morale in combat settings. Soldiers were more likely to sacrifice their lives for their "brothers" than for more abstract ideals such as patriotism. In times of peace, however, intense bonding introduces a distinct problem. Both troops and commanders will cover for each other and refuse to report any problems up the chain of command out of loyalty to one another and concern that the unit as a whole bears responsibility for the actions of any of its members. As such, the offenders in the Somali affair proceeded to torture their victim under an assurance that if anyone became aware of their crimes they would look the other way and remain silent. In light of her findings, Winslow recom-

In addition, the text includes numerous case studies that present extended discussions of the processes described in the chapters. These case studies enable students to understand the complex relationships among various aspects of cultural behaviour and attitudes. Many of the case studies focus on aspects of culture change, investigating the intricate consequences of innovation and transformation.

Most chapters also include "Culture Change" items that focus specifically on the ways that features of culture are transformed. They stress the interconnections among material change, behavioural practices, and ideology, demonstrating the complex interactions that result from change.

Many chapters contain a feature on "Anthropology Applied." These features highlight the roles that anthropologists play in applying theory and knowledge to practical concerns. Also, some chapters contain "Controversies" features that present differing opinions about key theoretical or research topics.

The maps in this text were specifically created by Dorling Kindersley, the leading publisher of atlases for educational use and for general consumers. The maps and descriptions illustrate the profound significance of geography as a relevant, essential component to the study of cultural anthropology. They appear throughout the text to help students understand the location of the example or people under discussion.

In addition, there are marginal "globalization icons" throughout the book. These features contribute to and strengthen the emphasis on culture change and put cultural transformations in their global context.

Finally, the book's pedagogical features include a marginal glossary and marginal questions, preview and summary questions, critical thinking questions, and both sectional reviews and chapter summaries. These features help students focus on significant ideas and concepts presented in the chapters.

Controversies

Should Canada Be Part of a North American Union?

For the last several years, the idea of a North America Union modelled on the European Union has been increasingly considered in academic and political circles. At the end of 2004, this interest was made more prominent by the formation of the Independent Task Force on North America under the chairmanship of John Manley, a former cabinet minister in the Chretien government with representation from the United States, Mexico, and Canada. The final report of the task force recommended the closer integration of the three economies through the relaxation of customs and immigration controls to allow the free movement of goods and people across the continent (Council on Foreign

societal violence are lower in Canada (Gagnon 2001), and its military policy stresses peacekeeping. On another level, hockey is closely associated with Canadian identity, while the United States identifies baseball as its "national pastime."

However, a closer degree of continental integration threatens these cherished institutions. The *North American Free Trade Agreement* and the retreat of Canadian government involvement in the economy through the reversal of measures such as the *Foreign Investment Review Act*, government ownership of national transport carriers, and transport subsidies to farmers have led to changes in the Canadian economy, society, and culture. The Canadian Wheat Board monopoly, a pillar of our agricultural policy and important force for stability in rural society, is now under threat and may be history by the time this book goes to

GLOBALIZATION

The increasing prevalence of bilateral descent in the world today is partly an outgrowth of the adaptive functions of bilateral descent groups in industrial societies and partly a result of the globalization of culture based on Euro-American power and influence.

SUPPLEMENTAL RESOURCES

The ancillary materials that accompany *Cultural Anthropology* are part of a compete teaching and learning package that have been carefully created to enhance the topics discussed in the text.

Instructor Supplements

Pearson MyTest. A powerful assessment generation program that helps instructors easily create and print quizzes, tests, and exams, as well as homework or practice hand-outs. Questions and tests can all be authored online, allowing instructors ultimate flexibility and the ability to efficiently manage assessments at any time, from anywhere.

Instructor's Resource CD-ROM (ISBN-13: 978-0-13-813369-6). This resource CD includes the following instructor supplements:

- **Instructor's Resource Manual:** For each chapter in the text, this valuable resource provides a detailed outline, list of objectives, discussion questions, and classroom activities.
- **Test Item File:** This supplement provides all of the test questions included in the MyTest in Word format.
- **PowerPoints:** These presentations cover the important points in each chapter and reproduce selected images from the text.

Most of these instructor supplements are also available for download from a password protected section of Pearson Education Canada's online catalogue (vig.pearsoned.ca). Navigate to your book's catalogue page to view a list of the supplements that are available. See your local sales representative for details and access.

Student Supplements

Companion Website. This online resource supports students with their studies in cultural anthropology. Featuring a variety of learning tools, including online quizzes with immediate feedback and extended case studies, this site is a comprehensive resource organized according to the chapters in *Cultural Anthropology*. It can be found at **www.pearsoned.ca/bonvillain**.

Pearson Advantage. For qualified adopters, Pearson Education Canada is proud to introduce the Pearson Advantage—the first integrated Canadian service program committed to meeting the customization, training, and support needs for your course. Our commitments are made in writing and in consultation with faculty. Your local sales representative can provide you with more details on this service program.

Content Media Specialists. Pearson's Content Media Specialists work with faculty and campus course designers to ensure that Pearson technology products, assessment tools, and online course materials are tailored to meet your specific needs. By assisting in the integration of a variety of instructional materials and media formats, this highly qualified team is dedicated to helping schools take full advantage of a wide range of educational technology.

ACKNOWLEDGEMENTS

I would like to thank the editorial staff at Pearson Canada for all of their encouragement, assistance, and patience in the preparation of this book. I would like to especially acknowledge Charlotte Morrison-Reed, the development editor, for her many suggestions for improvement and for her willingness to always give me the final decision. I would also like to thank Christine Cozens, executive acquisitions editor; Patricia Jones, copy editor; Nancy Carroll, proofreader; Richard di Santo, production editor; Avinash Chandra, production coordinator; and Terri Rothman, photo researcher. They all provided careful guidance that made a long and potentially frustrating process turn out to be an enjoyable and enriching experience.

I would also like to thank the reviewers whose comments and suggestions on drafts of this text were much appreciated.

Terri Aihoshi, *MacEwan College*
Jill Allison, *Memorial University of Newfoundland*
Jacklyn Bate, *Malaspina University College*
Michel Bouchard, *University of Northern British Columbia*
Maureen Bracewell, *Capilano College*
Constance deRoche, *Cape Breton University*
Roberta Robin Dods, *University of British Columbia*
Mathias Guenther, *Wilfred Laurier University*
Douglas R. Hudson, *University College of the Fraser Valley*
Randy Johnson, *Red Deer College*
Thomas McIlwraith, *Douglas College*
Bill Rodman, *McMaster University*
Deidre Rose, *Wilfred Laurier University*
David C. Ryniker, *University of British Columbia*
Pamela Stern, *University of Waterloo*

CULTURAL
ANTHROPOLOGY

What Is Anthropology?

CHAPTER 1

Preview

1. **What is anthropology? What are the core concepts of anthropology?**

2. **How does anthropology overlap with other fields?**

3. **What are the four subfields of anthropology? How is the study of culture integrated into each subfield?**

4. **What is applied anthropology? What contributions can applied anthropologists offer other fields?**

5. **What is culture? With what basic definition of culture do anthropologists tend to agree?**

6. **In what sense can culture be both shared and not shared by members of a society?**

7. **How is culture learned and transmitted?**

8. **In what sense can culture be both adaptive and maladaptive?**

9. **What are some forces of cultural integration?**

10. **In what ways is culture based on symbols?**

11. **How do cultures change?**

12. **How is globalization defined? How can the concepts of culture contact and culture change help us to understand globalization?**

There were villagers at the Middle Place and a girl had her home there at Wind Place where she kept a flock of turkeys.

At the Middle Place they were having a Yaaya Dance.

They were having a Yaaya Dance, and during the first day this girl wasn't drawn to the dance.

She stayed with her turkeys taking care of them.

That's the way she lived: it seems she didn't go to the dance on the first day, that day she fed her turkeys . . . and so the dance went on and she could hear the drum.

When she spoke to her turkeys about this, they said, "If you went it wouldn't turn out well: who would take care of us?" That's what her turkeys told her.

She listened to them and they slept through the night.

Then it was the second day of the dance and night came.

That night with the Yaaya Dance half over she spoke to her big tom turkey:

"My father-child, if they're going to do it again to-morrow why can't I go?" she said. "Well if you went, it wouldn't turn out well." That's what he told her. "Well then I mustn't go." That's what the girl said, and they slept through the night.

. . . The next day was a nice warm day, and again she heard the drum over there.

Then she went around feeding her turkeys, and when it was the middle of the day, she asked again, right at noon. "If you went, it wouldn't turn out well. There's no point in going: let the dance be, you don't need to go, and our lives depend on your thoughtfulness," that's what the turkeys told her.

"Well then, that's the way it will be," she said, and she listened to them.

But around sunset the drum could be heard, and she was getting more anxious to go.

She went up on her roof and she could see the crowd of people. It was the third day of the dance.

That night she asked the same one she asked before and he told her, "Well, if you must go, then you must dress well. . . .

"You must think of us, for if you stay all afternoon, until sunset, then it won't turn out well for you," he told her. . . .

The next day the sun was shining, and she went among her turkeys and spread their feed. When she had fed them she said, "My fathers, my children, I'm going to the Middle Place. I'm going to the dance," she said. "Be *on your way, but think of us. . . ." That's what her children told her.*

And she left. . . .

She went to where the place was, and when she entered the plaza, the dance directors noticed her.

Then they asked her to dance, she went down and danced, and she didn't think about her children.

Finally it was mid-day, and when mid-day came she was just dancing away until it was late, the time when the shadows are very long.

The turkeys said, "Our mother, our child doesn't know what's right."

"Well then, I must go and I'll just warn her and come right back and whether she hears me or not, we'll leave before she gets here," that's what the turkey said, and he flew away.

He flew along until he came to where they were dancing, and there he glided down to the place and perched on the top crotch piece of the ladder, and then he sang,
"Kyana tok tok Kyana tok tok."
The one who was dancing heard him.

He flew back to the place where they were penned, and the girl ran all the way back. When she got to the place where they were penned, they sang again, they sang and flew away. . . .

When she came near they all went away and she couldn't catch up to them.

Long ago, this was lived. . . .

From *Finding the Center: Narrative Poetry of the Zuni Indians.* 2nd edition translated by Denis Tedlock by permission of The University of Nebraska Press. © 1999 by Denis Tedlock.

This narrative, "The Girl Who Took Care of the Turkeys," is told by the Zuni, a Native American people who live in what is now New Mexico. The Zuni traditionally supported themselves by farming. Their main crops were corn, beans, and squash. They also kept domesticated turkeys, whose feathers they used to make ceremonial gear. In the story, the young girl uses kin terms when addressing the turkeys in order to indicate her close bonds with them. The Zuni used these forms of address when talking to members of their community as a sign of respect and affection.

Many readers may have noticed similarities between the Zuni story and the European story of Cinderella. In both, the central character is a young woman who wants to go to a dance but is at first dissuaded or, in Cinderella's case, prevented from doing so. Eventually, she does attend, but is warned that she must be sure to return home early. In both stories, the girl stays past the appointed time because she is enjoying herself. Beyond a general outline, however, the Zuni and European stories differ in both outcomes and details.

A comparison of the European Cinderella story with its Zuni counterpart reveals many differences. These differences fit into a constellation of features—the languages they speak, how they feed and shelter themselves, what they wear, the material goods they value, how they make those goods and distribute them among themselves, how they form families, households, and alliances, how they worship the deities they believe in—that define Zuni and European culture. This concept—culture—is central to the discipline of anthropology in general and to cultural anthropology, the subject of this book, in particular.

THE STUDY OF HUMANITY

anthropology
The study of humanity, from its evolutionary origins millions of years ago to its current worldwide diversity.

societies
Populations of people living in organized groups with social institutions and expectations of behaviour.

Anthropology, broadly defined, is the study of humanity, from its evolutionary origins millions of years ago to its present worldwide distribution and diversity. Many other disciplines, of course, share with anthropology a focus on one aspect of humanity or another. Like sociology, economics, political science, psychology, and other behavioural and social sciences, anthropology is concerned with the way people organize their lives and relate to one another in interacting, interconnected groups—**societies**—that share basic beliefs and practices. Like economists, anthropologists are interested in society's material foundations—how people produce and distribute food and other goods and services. Like sociologists, they are interested in the way people structure their relations in society—in families, at work, and in other contexts. Like political scientists, they are interested in power and authority—who has them and how they are

Culture Change

SELECTIVE BORROWING AMONG THE ZUNI

The similarities and differences between the Zuni story of "The Girl Who Took Care of the Turkeys" and the European story of Cinderella are no coincidence. The Zuni first learned the Cinderella story from Americans in the 1880s and transformed the tale to make it consistent with their circumstances, values, and way of life. This is an example of selective borrowing that takes place when members of different cultures meet, share experiences, and learn from each other. Global influences have been instrumental in accelerating processes of borrowing over the last five centuries. Instead of a nameless European kingdom, the Zuni situate the tale in their own territory with references to specific villages, such as Wind Place and Middle Place. The aristocratic ball that Cinderella yearns to attend becomes the Yaaya Dance, an important Zuni festival. Consistent with the prominence of the number 3 in European tradition, Cinderella's ball takes place over three days, but the Yaaya festival, consistent with the Zuni belief that 4 is a sacred number, takes place over four days.

The Zuni also reverse the ethical standing of the story's characters. Cinderella is virtuous and long-suffering, her family wicked. Her stepmother and

How did the Zuni change the Cinderella story to fit their cultural folkways?

stepsisters oppress her, forcing her to serve them and depriving her of her deserved place at the ball. The girl in the Zuni story likewise serves as caretaker for her family, the flock of turkeys (whom she significantly addresses as "father" and "child"), but she is not a figure of virtue. On the contrary, to go to the dance she has to neglect her duties, threatening the turkeys' well-being.

And what happens? Cinderella emerges triumphant. She marries the handsome prince and lives happily ever after. No such good fortune befalls the Zuni girl. The disaster that ends her story occurs because she thinks of her own pleasure before her responsibility to those under her care. The European story of individual virtue and fortitude rewarded has become a Zuni story of moral failing and the consequences of irresponsibility to one's relatives and dependents. As the turkey tells the girl, "You must think of us."

used. And, like psychologists, anthropologists are interested in personality development and how society affects the individual.

Also, anthropologists share with those in the biological sciences an interest in human evolution and human anatomy. They share with historians an interest in humanity's past and in the history of particular peoples and communities. As the discussion of the story that opens this chapter suggests, they investigate literature, art, and music, philosophical systems, ethical systems, religion, and other subjects that fall within the humanities.

Although anthropology shares many interests with other disciplines, several key features distinguish it as a separate area of study:

- A focus on the concept of culture
- A comparative perspective
- A holistic perspective

These features are the source of anthropology's important insights into both our common humanity and the great diversity in which that humanity finds expression.

THE FOUR SUBFIELDS OF ANTHROPOLOGY

The breadth of anthropological interest in the human experience has led to the development of four separate subfields, which nevertheless remain interconnected: cultural anthropology, linguistic anthropology, archaeology, and biological (or physical) anthropology. Each includes further branches or interest areas. Table 1.1 lists the subfields and identifies some of the many kinds of work that anthropologists perform.

Cultural Anthropology

Cultural anthropology is, as the term implies, the study of culture, which is the main system that people employ to adapt to their varied environments and organize their social interactions. Cultural anthropologists use the **comparative perspective** to identify

Table 1.1 CAREER OPPORTUNITIES IN THE FOUR SUBFIELDS OF ANTHROPOLOGY

Field	Definition	Examples
Cultural Anthropology	The study of human culture.	Museum curator University or college professor International business consultant Development consultant Impact assessment analyst Urban planner Expert witness in Aboriginal rights cases Immigration services advisor Foreign Service officer Multiculturalism educator Cross-cultural researcher
Linguistic Anthropology	The study of language.	International business consultant Diplomatic communications worker Domestic communications worker University or college professor
Archaeology	The study of past cultures.	Cultural resource management worker Museum curator University or college professor Provincial archaeologist Historical archaeologist Zoo archaeologist Environmental consultant
Biological (Physical) Anthropology	The study of human origins and biological diversity.	Primatologist Geneticist University or college professor Medical researcher Genetic counsellor Forensic specialist Human rights investigator

cultural anthropology
The study of cultural behaviour, especially the comparative study of living and recent human cultures.

comparative perspective
An approach in anthropology that uses data about the behaviour and beliefs in many societies to document both cultural universals and cultural diversity.

similarities and differences in contemporary cultures. Their work centres on **ethnology**, building theories to explain cultural variation and cultural processes. The method of gathering these data is called **ethnography**, a study of groups through observation, interview, and participation from a **holistic perspective**.

To conduct ethnographic research, anthropologists live among the people they are studying to compile a full record of their activities. They learn about people's behaviours, beliefs, and attitudes. They study the ways in which they make their living, the way families and communities are organized, how people form clubs or associations, how they discuss matters of common interest, and how they resolve disputes. They investigate the relationship of local communities to the larger social institutions—the nations they are part of and their place in the local, regional, and global economies.

Collecting ethnographic information is a significant part of the preservation of **indigenous cultures**: it contributes to the fund of comparative data that cultural anthropologists use to address questions about human cultural diversity. These questions—such as how people acquire culture, or how culture affects personality, or how family structures and gender roles vary, or why people believe in the supernatural, how global economic forces affect local cultures—are the subjects of the chapters of this textbook.

Linguistic Anthropology

Language is a key concern of anthropology. Not only is it a defining feature of all cultures, language is also the primary means by which we express culture and transmit it from one generation to the next.

Linguistic anthropology, discussed in more detail in Chapter 3, is concerned with the nature of language itself but with an added focus on the interconnections among language, culture, and society. Linguistic anthropologists might investigate the ways people use language in different social contexts to gain insight into the social categories that are important to them. Do people use a formal style of speech in one situation and an informal style in another? Do they vary the words, pronunciation, and grammar they use in different social contexts? Do they speak differently to relatives and nonrelatives, friends and strangers, males and females, children and adults?

Some linguistic anthropologists study the languages of indigenous peoples to document their grammars and vocabularies. This is critical work, especially now in the face of increasing globalization. The advancement of English and other internationally prominent languages has been a prime factor in the extinction of native languages. Native peoples are losing their traditions and languages in their attempts to keep pace with the new world order.

For example, because of assimilation to Anglo-Canadian society, only 25 percent of the Aboriginal population can speak an Aboriginal language well enough to engage in a conversation. Only a few languages, most prominently Cree, have a chance of long-term survival. However, most Aboriginal Canadians feel that the retention and restitution of these languages is important for the preservation of their identity and culture, and numerous language educational programs have been established to achieve these goals (Norris 2007). Endangered languages include European languages as well, such as Irish, Catalan (spoken in Spain), and Yiddish.

ethnology
Building theories about cultural behaviours and forms.

ethnography
Observing and documenting peoples' ways of life.

holistic perspective
The way in which anthropologists view culture as an integrated whole, no part of which can be completely understood without considering the whole.

indigenous cultures
Comparatively homogeneous peoples or small-scale societies who share the same culture and are "native" to their territory or have occupied it for a long time.

linguistic anthropology
The study of language and communication and the relationship between language and other aspects of culture and society.

? *Do you use words among friends that you would never use in a job interview, in class, or with children? What does your use of language reveal about your relationships to the people you address?*

In 2003, these Somali Bantu refugees in Kenya were awaiting relocation to the United States. Their refugee status stems from their former lives as slaves in war-torn Sudan. The U.S. government transported 12 000 Somali Bantus to cities in Arizona, Texas, and other states. Their adaptations to American life, as well as the adaptations of American communities to the refugees, are topics of interest to cultural anthropologists.

With the spread of English and other languages of business, globalization has endangered native languages as well as the ways of life those languages express.

historical linguistics
The study of changes in language and communication over time and between peoples in contact.

archaeology
The study of past cultures, both historic cultures with written records and prehistoric cultures that predate the invention of writing.

These 3.6-million-year-old tracks of hominids walking through an ash fall from a distant volcanic eruption in Tanzania are the evidence of fully bipedal locomotion among our earliest ancestors.

Other linguistic anthropologists specialize in **historical linguistics**. Their work is based on the premise that people speaking related languages are culturally and historically related, descended from a common ancestral people. By looking at the relationships among languages in a large area, historical linguists can help determine how people have migrated over time to arrive in the territories they now occupy. For example, the Apaches in New Mexico, the Navajos in Arizona, and the Hupas of northern California all speak related languages, and these languages are, in turn, related to a family of languages known as Athabascan. Most of the people who speak Athabascan languages, of whom the largest group are the Dene of the Northwest Territories, occupy a large area of western Canada and Alaska, where the ancestors of the American groups must have originated. By studying how people have borrowed words and grammatical patterns from other languages, historical linguists can also gain insight into how groups have interacted over time. Combined with archaeological evidence, these kinds of analyses can produce a rich picture of the historical relationship among peoples who otherwise left no written records, contributing to our understanding of the processes of culture change.

Archaeology

Archaeology is the study of material culture. Its methods apply to both historic cultures, which have written records, and prehistoric nonliterate cultures. Archaeologists have also applied their methods to living societies, a subfield called ethnoarchaeology, with sometimes surprising results.

Unlike cultural anthropologists who can observe and talk to living people, archaeologists rely mostly on evidence from material culture and the sites where people lived. Such evidence includes the tools that they made and used, the clothing and ornaments they wore, the buildings they lived and worked in, the remains of the plants and animals they relied on, and the way they buried their dead. It can reveal how people lived in the past. The remains of small, temporary encampments might indicate that the people who used them lived by foraging for their food. If the encampment had a concentration of stone debris, it was likely used as a workshop for making stone tools. A settlement with permanent dwellings near arable land and irrigation canals would have been a village of agriculturalists.

Judging from the density of settlements and household refuse like fragments of pots, archaeologists can estimate the population of a region at a particular time. The size and distribution of dwellings in a settlement or region can reveal aspects of a society's social structure. If a few of the houses in a settlement are much larger than the majority and contain luxury items that are absent from other dwellings, we can conclude that some people were wealthier than others. In contrast, if all of the houses are more or less the same size and contain similar possessions, we can infer that all of the people lived in the same fashion and were of equal status.

Skeletal remains can provide similar clues to social structure. Archaeologists working at a site in Peru called Chavín de Huántar, which flourished from around 800 BCE to 200 BCE, found evidence from skeletons that the people living close to the site's centre ate better than those who lived on its margins. This evidence, combined with similar findings from other sites, suggests that society in the region was becoming more stratified (Burger 1992a, 1992b).

Archaeologists can also tell us about people's relationships with members of other communities. In much of the world, indigenous trading networks supplied people with goods and products not found in their own territories. Archaeologists can reconstruct these trading networks by studying the distribution of trade goods in relation to their place of origin. Similar evidence also can be used to trace migrations and warfare.

Written historical records add to our understanding of the past, but they do not replace the need for archaeology. Archaeology provides a richer understanding of how people lived and worked than documents alone do. People write about and keep records on what is important to them. Because only the elite members of a society are usually literate, the historical record is more likely to reflect their interests and point of view than those of the poor. Archaeology can help correct those biases.

Archaeological methods applied to living societies can help address important issues of public concern. In the 1970s, the archaeologist William Rathje founded the Arizona Garbage Project to study what Americans throw away and what happens to this refuse. Rathje defined archaeology as the discipline that learns from garbage (Rathje and Murphy 1992). Among the surprising findings of the project was that, contrary to popular and expert opinion, fast-food packaging actually makes up less than 1 percent of the volume of American landfills. Compacted paper takes up the most space.

Archaeology's great chronological depth—from humanity's origins millions of years ago to twenty-first-century landfills—makes it particularly suited to the study of culture change. Not surprisingly, then, theories of culture change are one of the discipline's main concerns. As one example, many archaeologists are interested in the processes that led to the appearance of the first cities thousands of years ago and with them the appearance of the first states—societies with centralized governments, administrative bureaucracies, and inequalities of wealth and power.

Biological Anthropology

Biological or **physical anthropology** is the study of human origins and contemporary biological diversity. In the popular imagination, the study of human origins, or **paleoanthropology**, is probably its most visible face. Paleoanthropologists seek to decipher the fossil record—the usually fragmentary remains of human forebears and related animals—to understand the process of human evolution. Paleoanthropologists have also turned to the science of genetics and the study of our relatives within the primate order, such as monkeys and apes, for clues to human origins. The combined evidence indicates that our ancestors diverged from chimpanzees in Africa between five million and eight million years ago.

Working from fossil evidence, paleoanthropologists are reconstructing the complex course of human evolution. They study changes in Earth's prehistoric environment to understand the adaptive benefits of the physical changes our ancestors underwent. They study the size and structure of teeth to learn about palaeolithic diets. And they study the distribution of fossils worldwide to learn how and when our ancestors migrated out of Africa and populated almost all the lands of Earth.

With culture, humans no longer depended exclusively on their physical characteristics for survival. They could create clothes, shelters, and tools appropriate for many environments, from the Arctic to the tropics. With language and more complex social organization, they could enhance group survival. Thus, paleoanthropologists are particularly interested in clues to the emergence of human culture. Here their interests and methods overlap with those of archaeologists as they excavate sites looking for evidence of early toolmaking in association with fossils.

Some physical anthropologists study nonhuman primates to gain insight into the nature of our own species. Jane Goodall, for example, spent years observing the behaviour of chimpanzees in the wild, and her discoveries about their social behaviour have a bearing on the origins of our own.

In addition to human origins and primate social behaviour, physical anthropologists also study the interaction of biology, culture, and environment to understand humanity's current biological diversity. For example, the Inuit, have developed ways to clothe and shelter themselves to survive in their harsh environment, but they also appear to have a greater rate of blood flow to the extremities in response to cold than other people do (Itoh 1980; McElroy and Townsend 1989:26–29). Indigenous inhabitants of the Andes in South America have a greater than average lung capacity, which

? *What might an analysis of refuse reveal about life in a dormitory?*

GLOBALIZATION

The global spread of humans was made possible by the evolution of the capacity for culture and the development and spread of the first tool traditions.

biological or **physical anthropology**
The study of human origins and biological diversity.

paleoanthropology
The study of the fossil record, especially skeletal remains, to understand the process and products of human evolution.

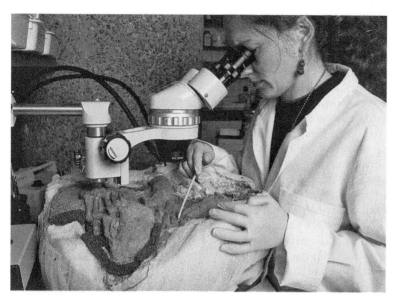

Paleoanthropologists analyze fossil skeletal material or otherwise preserved human remains to learn about ancient populations and their ways of life.

is an adaptation to the low oxygen of their high-altitude environment. And herding peoples are genetically adapted to digest milk easily. It is well known that skin colour is also in part an adaptation to climatic conditions and exposure to sun, since darker skin has a higher content of melanin, a substance that protects against over-absorption of the sun's harmful ultraviolet rays (Rensberger 2001:83). The social significance and interpretation of skin colour are discussed further in Chapter 10.

Some physical anthropologists focus their research on health and disease issues. They investigate the susceptibilities or resistances of certain populations to specific diseases. They also trace the spread of diseases within a population and from one population to another. Before the arrival of the first Europeans and Africans in North and South America in the sixteenth century, for example, smallpox, measles, and other infectious diseases were unknown. As a result, First Nations and Inuit peoples had no natural immunity to the diseases. The result of the influx of the new settlers was catastrophic—millions of Aboriginal people died. In contrast to the vulnerabilities of indigenous peoples of the Americas, some populations have advantageous resistances to diseases endemic in their area. One reason why Africa was a prominent source of slaves in the Americas was because its populations had evolved resistance to diseases carried by Europeans and to diseases endemic in the tropical regions of both hemispheres, such as malaria.

REVIEW

Anthropology has four subfields: cultural anthropology (also known as ethnology), linguistic anthropology, archaeology, and biological (or physical) anthropology. The work of linguistic anthropologists and archaeologists sheds light on culture change. All are concerned with the importance of the culture concept for understanding human behaviour.

APPLIED ANTHROPOLOGY

applied anthropology
An area of anthropology that applies the techniques and theories of the field to problem solving outside of traditional academic settings.

forensic anthropologists
Biological anthropologists who analyze human remains in the service of criminal justice and families of disaster victims.

cultural resource management (CRM)
The application of archaeology to preserve and protect historic structures and prehistoric sites.

Applied anthropology intersects with and draws from the four major subfields. Indeed, many anthropologists regard applied anthropology as a fifth subfield. Applied anthropologists employ anthropological understandings and perspectives to work outside academic settings. For example, some biological anthropologists work as **forensic anthropologists**, applying their knowledge of human anatomy to help solve crimes. Working for law enforcement agencies, forensic anthropologists can help determine the cause of death by examining the victim's remains and physical evidence found at a crime scene. Also, their knowledge of skeletal anatomy, blood types, and biochemical markers in the blood help identify the victim and the cause of death as well as provide leads to possible suspects. Forensic anthropologists have been called upon to study human remains for evidence of human rights abuses in the wake of wars and civil conflicts. They have been involved in collecting evidence on the serial murder site on the Picton pig farm in British Columbia and have helped to identify remains of victims of the terrorist attacks on the World Trade Center.

Applied archaeology has grown as a result of legislation protecting archaeological resources, which has led to the field of **cultural resource management (CRM)**. In addition, archaeological surveys must be conducted in advance of many large construction projects. The need for site impact assessments has led to the employment of archaeologists within large corporations, and to **contract archaeology**, in which archaeologists, working privately, contract themselves out for this kind of research.

In addition, archaeologists' findings about the past can sometimes be used to solve present-day problems. Archaeologists working in the region of Lake Titicaca in the Andes of South America, for example, discovered an ancient and productive method of cultivation that had fallen into disuse. They helped reintroduce the method to local farmers, who found that it substantially increased their yields.

Some linguistic anthropologists apply their skills to the preservation of indigenous languages. They may work with native speakers to prepare dictionaries, grammars, and other instructional aids for use in community language classes and schools. Their work helps indigenous communities counter the rapid decline in the number of people who speak local languages. Collecting data from speakers of endangered languages is a fieldwork priority for linguistic anthropologists.

Cultural anthropologists apply their training and knowledge in government agencies, nongovernmental organizations, charitable foundations, and private companies. Some help shape the policies of city, provincial, and federal agencies that deliver services to local communities, advising, for example, on the best ways to contact different populations in a community to deliver services related to health care, legal aid, or preschool and other educational opportunities for children. Cultural anthropologists work in research firms and think tanks to propose solutions to social problems. They also help communities, companies, and organizations in dispute management and conflict resolution. They help resolve labour and workplace issues and also work for courts developing and implementing programs of alternative sentencing for some offenders. Ethnographic research, performed by nongovernmental, anthropology-based advocacy groups, centres on protecting and preserving the native cultures of small-scale societies from the impacts of development and globalization and has contributed important evidence in First Nations land claim settlements.

Ethnographic research has also contributed to the preservation of traditional medical practices and pharmaceuticals and has encouraged practitioners of both traditional and Western medicine to understand the physical and psychological benefits of both medical models. Specialists in medical anthropology develop treatment procedures that combine indigenous medical beliefs and practices with those of standard Western medicine.

Anthropologists who work for industries and corporations analyze workplace interactions to suggest ways of improving the working environment and worker productivity. Businesspeople planning to travel overseas to meet with their foreign counterparts may receive sensitivity training from anthropologists. Anthropologists even study consumer habits to aid companies in increasing sales or developing new products and services. For example, Canon employed a team of anthropologists to go into people's homes to study the kinds of pictures and notes that families create and affix to their walls and refrigerators. Based on the findings, the company increased printer sales through the development of Canon Creative software, which allows families to make their own greeting cards, posters, and T-shirts (Hafner 1999).

The culture of these Sami includes everything there is to know about reindeer, living in the Arctic, and coping with citizenship in the modern state society of Norway.

? *What is so important about language that people feel the need to preserve it?*

? *How might Western pharmaceutical companies employ the services of anthropologists?*

contract archaeology
The application of archaeology to assess the potential impact of construction on archaeological sites and to salvage archaeological evidence.

REVIEW

Applied anthropology is the practical use of anthropology outside the realm of academia and is part of all four subfields of anthropology. Workers in applied anthropology include forensic anthropologists, workers in cultural resource management, and contract archaeologists, as well as linguistic and cultural anthropologists.

THE CONCEPT OF CULTURE

culture
The values, beliefs, technological knowledge, and rules of conduct acquired by learning and shared to some extent by the members of a society that govern their interaction with their environment, their ties with one another, and their thinking about themselves and the world.

symbolic culture
The ideas and knowledge people have about themselves, others, and the world, and the ways that people express these ideas.

social culture
The rules and practices that regulate membership and participation in social groups and networks.

material culture
The tools people make and use, the clothing and ornaments they wear, the buildings they live in, and the household utensils they use.

? *To what extent is culture shared? Do all Canadian have a common identity and agree on a single set of core values? If so what are they?*

In spite of the vast range of interests that the four subfields of anthropology cover, they all interconnect and look at the significance of the factors that each specialization investigates. Aside from this holistic perspective, they share a common view of the importance of culture in the shaping of human nature and behaviour.

Although defining what culture is may sound like a simple task, anthropologists have struggled with the concept since the late nineteenth century when anthropology was established as a discipline. The British anthropologist Edward Tylor was the first to attempt a formal definition:

> Culture is that complex whole which includes knowledge, belief, art, morals, law, custom, and any other capabilities and habits acquired by man as a member of society (Tylor 1871).

Tylor's classic statement captures several significant features that have been preserved in most definitions of culture today. It focuses on the holistic quality of culture ("that complex whole") and embraces all the activities, attitudes, and beliefs of human beings. Significantly, these are traits "acquired" by people. That is, people's attitudes, beliefs, and ways of acting are learned rather than inherited, instinctual, or automatic. Finally, Tylor stressed the social context of cultural transmission. As members of society, people learn skills and attitudes from other people and in turn transmit their knowledge and beliefs to others and to future generations.

For the purposes of this text, we briefly define **culture** as the values, beliefs, technological knowledge, and rules of conduct acquired by learning and shared to some extent by the members of a society that govern their interaction with their environment, their ties with one another, and their thinking about themselves and the world. Culture can be broadly divided into **symbolic culture**, people's ideas and means of communicating those ideas, **social culture**, their rules and practices of interaction among people, and **material culture**, the tools, utensils, clothing, housing, and other objects that people make or use.

A cultural anthropologist seeks to explain people's thoughts and behaviours in terms of their culture, or way of life. Culture is viewed as a complex whole made up of interdependent parts, so that a change in one element of culture affects other elements. Cultural anthropologists compare elements of culture at different times within a society and also among different societies at one time.

CHARACTERISTICS OF CULTURE

Although each culture is unique, some organizational and functional characteristics are universal. To begin with, any culture is a product of a group of people who share and transmit some basic attitudes and assumptions about the world. In addition, aspects of culture tend to interrelate and function together with some consistency to form a coherent system of behaviours and beliefs. Through their cultures, people adapt to their life situations and to changes in their social and physical environments. What do we mean when we say that culture is shared, learned, adaptive, and integrated?

These Mayan women from San Juan Atitlan in Western Guatemala dress in exactly the same outfit on every occasion. The dress code specifies that each village has a uniquely identifying uniform.

Culture Is Shared

Humans are social creatures. We necessarily depend on other people within families, communities, and larger societies. The way we behave, our attitudes about right and wrong, our ideas about the world we live in—all are formed through our interactions with others. To say that culture is shared is not to say that all members of a particular society have exactly the same attitudes and do exactly the same things in the same way. Canadians have a great range of choices in clothing styles and may deliberately seek out unique items to emphasize their individuality. However, they dress according to some general rules, such as selecting clothes appropriate to gender and occasion. Moreover, our very attempts to "express our individuality" conform to a cultural value. People who intentionally dressed exactly the same, unless they were wearing uniforms, would be considered odd. If they did so by accident, they would be embarrassed. In different societies, for example, the contemporary Mayan villages of Central America, dressing identically may be expected or even mandatory.

Societies can function as groups to minimize conflicts, because their members agree about the basic parameters of living. If this were not so, people would not be able to coordinate their activities or agree on what to do next. And even though they might speak the same language, they would not be able to accurately interpret each other's meanings and intentions if they did not share basic cultural assumptions about the world. These shared assumptions form a background ideology in terms of which behaviour becomes relatively coherent and consistent.

Despite shared assumptions, disagreements and conflicts occur within any community. In all communities, some people are more fully committed to general societal norms than others. Societal **norms** are sets of commonly held expectations and attitudes that people have about appropriate behaviour. And although these norms are generally held to be valid within each culture, not everyone acts in accordance with them.

Departure from expected and appropriate behaviour occurs in every community. Some alternative lifestyles are tolerated while others are not. And, in fact, behaviour that may be considered deviant within a community as a whole may be a marker of identity for a particular group. For example, body piercing or tattooing might violate adult conceptions of beauty, but teenagers may engage in these

norms
Sets of expectations and attitudes that people have about appropriate behaviour.

This young woman in Western dress was photographed with her aunt in a traditional East Indian outfit. The attitudes and values that lead young people to adopt new ways of expression might be sources of conflict in their families and community.

In the diverse society of Bolivia, this peasant woman of the Andes does not fully share the same culture as her counterpart in La Paz, the capital.

subculture
A group whose members and others think of their way of life as in some significant way different from that of other people in the larger society.

enculturation
Process of learning one's culture through informal observation and formal instruction.

The Chinese form a subculture represented in almost every part of Canada. Approximately one million Canadians speak a Chinese language and continue to uphold their cultural traditions. While currently a prosperous and vibrant community, they have had to overcome many obstacles. In 1885 Federal legislation imposed a head tax equivalent to two years wages on all Chinese immigrants. The provisions of the Chinese Exclusion Act of 1923 cut off almost all immigration from China until it was repealed in 1947.

physical alterations in order to conform to youthful standards. Violent behaviour such as assault and murder are deviant acts that are not tolerated in most societies. Other kinds of violence that occur within the family, such as spousal abuse, may be tolerated even if not condoned.

People occupying different social roles and statuses may hold opposing views about the existing social order and prevailing cultural norms. For example, age may be a factor in the way people organize their lives and in the kinds of attitudes that they hold. Cultural differences between elders and youth may be relatively stable, since, as people age, they adopt the lifestyles and norms of their elders. Generational differences may alternatively signal ongoing social and culture change. Gender is another common source of variation in people's activities and attitudes. In most societies, women and men usually have certain specific tasks for which they are responsible and may occupy defined roles and statuses that influence the ways they experience their lives. For example, depending on who are the dominant decision makers and authorities in their households, men and women are likely to have different ideas about their rights and responsibilities. Women who have the major share of the household and child-rearing responsibilities and tasks to perform may feel burdened and restricted, or they may feel challenged and fulfilled. In societies that sanction violence against women, women's experience of family life contrasts sharply with men's.

Like differences in age and gender, other status differences in society result in incomplete sharing of culture. Such differences also may be a source of social tension and cultural disagreement. Societies may be divided by class, race, ethnicity, occupation, or religion, creating distinctions in how people view their world and organize their lives.

In addition to differences in social roles and statuses, some societies contain groups that participate in identifiable subcultures. A **subculture** is a group of people who think of themselves, and are thought of by others, as different in some significant way from the majority. Their members interact more frequently among themselves than with "outsiders" and share attitudes and practices that distinguish them from other groups.

All of these sources of difference modify our understanding of culture as a constellation of shared behaviours and beliefs. Still, when people interact within the same society, they must share some basic premises about social order and social values. If they did not, community cohesion would disintegrate and the groups within the society would separate.

Culture Is Learned

Culture is transmitted from generation to generation and is learned mainly in childhood and during maturation. The ability to acquire culture in this way makes humans highly adaptable to different cultural environments. Humans are born with a potential to learn whatever values, knowledge, and skills are current within their communities. They do this through the process of **enculturation**—learning one's culture through informal observation and formal instruction,

Case study

Growing Up Mohawk

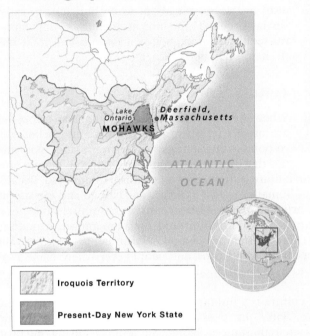

An interesting historical example of enculturation is the case of the abduction of a child from colonial New England and her integration into a First Nation's community in Quebec. In 1703, Eunice Williams was a seven-year-old English girl living in Deerfield, Massachusetts, the daughter of a Protestant minister, John Williams. John, his five children, and dozens of other people of the town were abducted during a raid carried out by a combined force of French soldiers and native warriors. Some of the captives were released, including Eunice's father, others escaped, and the rest were eventually taken to villages in the territory of the Mohawks, an indigenous people who inhabited a large region in what is now Ontario and western Quebec, eastern New York State, Vermont, and Massachusetts. Eunice was among those taken to Kahnawake, a mission village in Quebec established by French Jesuit priests and inhabited by Mohawks who had converted to Catholicism. Mohawk warfare was conducted in part to acquire children to replace members of their families who had died. Accordingly, Eunice was adopted and raised within a local household. She married a Mohawk man and settled into her life there. Despite her father's efforts to persuade her to leave, she remained with the Mohawks and adopted their culture. She learned their language, converted to Catholicism, and raised her own daughter according to Mohawk tradition. In 1743, Eunice agreed to meet with her father and brother, but refused to leave the people whose culture and language she had taken as her own (Demos 1994; Namias 1995). She died at Kahnawake at the age of 89, never returning to Massachusetts and never again speaking the English language.

The story of Eunice Williams demonstrates the power of a basic premise of anthropology, that *culture is learned* through social interaction in social contexts, and that in childhood this learning is especially powerful.

---

beginning in earliest childhood. Children learn the culture that they are exposed to, as the Case Study above illustrates. We all can acquire any culture if we are raised in it, just as any normal person can learn any language. It is through these processes that people acquire their culture and transmit it to others. Chapter 4 further explores the topic of enculturation.

While most human cultural behaviour is the result of learning, this behaviour is also influenced by biological needs. People need to eat, drink, sleep, eliminate body wastes, and engage in sexual activity. And, like other primates, people also need to interact with one another for getting food and for protection. Culture intervenes and influences the ways in which people satisfy these needs.

For example, each culture includes beliefs about what kinds of foods are edible and suitable for human consumption. People do not eat everything that is edible; they select some foods and reject others, expressing these choices as preferences and prohibitions, or **taboos**. In North America, most people consider eating insects distasteful, but many peoples of Australia, Asia, and Africa think of insects as a delicacy. Maasai drink the blood of their cattle. Koreans farm puppies for meat. Religion-based food taboos of Muslims, Hindus, and Jews further illustrate the mediation of survival needs through culture. Culture also imposes norms about how many meals to have, when to eat them, and which foods to eat at each meal.

? *Based on this case study, what effect would children's ability to acquire culture rapidly have on immigrant families?*

taboos
Norms specifying behaviours that are prohibited in a culture.

Anyone can acquire any culture if he or she is raised in it, just as any normal person can learn any language.

? *How many meals do you eat in a day and at what times? What kinds of foods do you eat at each meal? If you ate eggs at different mealtimes, how might you prepare them differently for each meal and why? What do your answers to these questions reveal about your cultural norms and values?*

The use of chemical fertilizers and pesticides increases yields per acre of land but may contaminate food with unhealthful toxins and deplete land productivity in the long term. Consequently, this crop duster's payload is carefully regulated today.

Although people need to sleep, they normally do so at a culturally prescribed time and place. No matter how tired you are at work, it would be inappropriate to lie down on the desk and go to sleep. People follow culturally prescribed rules about where and when to eliminate body wastes. Cultures also impose norms about when and how to satisfy sexual urges. These norms include strong taboos on sexual relations between parents and their children and between siblings.

Culture Is Adaptive

When anthropologists say that culture is adaptive, they are usually referring to behaviours and beliefs that respond to environmental constraints and opportunities that ensure a community's survival. People must adapt to their environment, and culture is their chief mechanism of doing so. Because of their capacity for adaptation, humans can live in nearly any habitat and can modify their environments and create artificial ones to enhance survival. Cultural strategies of adaptation often involve technological innovation and the elaboration of material culture. For example, people living in island or coastal environments construct rafts, canoes, and boats to cross rivers, bays, and oceans, and people everywhere make a vast array of tools and equipment to help them obtain food and perform other kinds of subsistence tasks.

While adaptation through culture is a fundamental and universal process, not all cultural practices are adaptive. Some practices may be maladaptive or have unintended negative consequences as circumstances change. Sometimes, solving one problem may lead to new, unforeseen ones.

The archaeological record gives us some clues about the decline of several large and prosperous ancient cultures in both the Eastern and Western Hemispheres because of agricultural techniques that turned out to have unforeseen negative consequences. The ancient Mesopotamian society of Sumer, located in what is now southern Iraq, developed into large-scale city-states by 3000 BCE. Their economies were based on intensive irrigated farming, which produced high crop yields that have not been matched since that time. However, harvests eventually declined and the empire that was built on them collapsed (Sasson 1995).

One reason for these developments was that intensive irrigation led to rapid evaporation of water from the soil, causing an increase in the salt content of the land and a decline of crop yields. As a result, Sumer was no longer able to support large populations without a decline in living standards. Families that controlled the land began to compete for political and economic supremacy and encouraged overproduction (Peregrine 2003).

As another example, the unintended negative consequences of the Industrial Revolution for people and their environments are well known. The ability to supply many millions of people with an ever-increasing amount and variety of products has led to problems of pollution, contamination, and overexploitation of natural resources. Many techniques and technologies commonly used in agriculture are maladaptive in the long run, although they may provide short-term benefits of increased productivity.

The idea that culture is adaptive therefore needs to be considered in context; a particular practice may be adaptive in one situation but not in another. For instance, farming techniques used in temperate climates to increase crop yields may be counterproductive in the Amazon rain forest because of the relative infertility of the soil. This is exactly what is happening in parts of the Amazon today, where environmentally inappropriate farming techniques are harming the long-term viability of agriculture (Schmink and Wood 1992).

MALADAPTIVE ADAPTATIONS: KURU AND MAD COW

By 1910, a new disease had appeared among the South Fore (pronounced *For'ray*), a farming people of New Guinea. The disease, called *kuru* (meaning "trembling" or "fear" in the Fore language), affects the central nervous system. It is a progressive disease that slowly leads to complete physical incapacitation and death. During the course of the illness, victims gradually become unable to control muscular movements. They cannot sit or walk unaided, focus their eyes, speak clearly, or even swallow. Death usually occurs in six to twelve months from the onset of symptoms, although some people may survive as long as two years.

Investigation of the spread of kuru during the 1950s led to suspicion that it correlated with particular ritual practices engaged in by Fore women. In Fore society, as elsewhere in New Guinea, women are the primary farmers, growing sweet potatoes, yams, and other vegetables. They also care for the domesticated pigs kept by each household. Men clear the fields but then do little of the farm labour. Men and women live separately most of the time. Men reside communally in a "men's house," eating and sleeping away from their families. Fore culture emphasizes concepts of pollution and danger, against which rituals serve as antidotes. This includes the belief that women pose a threat to male strength and vitality. Women live in separate small huts with their children and pigs. Men and

women participate in different social and ceremonial activities as well.

In the early 1900s, South Fore women began practising cannibalism as part of their mourning ceremonies when a female relative died. This ritual involved eating the brains and body parts of the deceased kin. According to anthropologist Shirley Lindenbaum (1979), this practice had some adaptive value in the context of protein scarcity, particularly for women. As populations increased and more land came under cultivation, sources of animal protein declined. In addition, men had access to more high-quality protein because they claimed greater rights to the pigs. They believed that other sources of protein, such as insects, frogs, and small mammals, were not only unfit for men but might threaten a man's health and vigour. In this context, according to Lindenbaum, women may have turned to cannibalism as a way of securing more protein.

When a South Fore woman died, her body was dismembered and eaten by her female relatives. Some of the meat was given to children of either sex, but it was rarely eaten by adult men because of the belief that contact with women (and, logically, eating their flesh) was dangerous and polluting. The Fore did not associate cannibalism with kuru, but they were alarmed by the high incidence of the disease, particularly among women. The people attributed kuru to sorcery, a common cause of illness and death in their medical belief system. When someone died of kuru, kinspeople tried to identify the evildoer, usually accusing someone who might have had reason to wish the victim harm.

According to Lindenbaum, between 1957 and 1968, when the disease was at its height, there were about 1000 deaths in the South Fore population of 8000. The fact that nearly all the deaths were of adult women added to the social and economic burden, because women produced the crops, tended the pigs, and gave birth. In some villages, nearly half of the adult female deaths and nearly all of the deaths of children between 5 and 16 years of age were due to kuru (Foster and Anderson 1978).

The riddle of kuru was not solved until the late 1960s. Following on the work of anthropologists Robert Glasse and Shirley Lindenbaum, the anthropologist-virologist Carlton

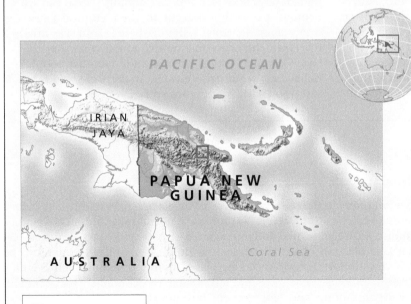

South Fore People

Gajdusek discovered the mode of transmission of the disease. Gajdusek (who was awarded the Nobel Prize for his discovery in 1976) identified the disease agent as a prion, the same kind of agent responsible for mad cow disease (or bovine spongiform encephalopathy). Prions remain dormant for many years after they are ingested, but eventually cause progressive damage to the brain. Thus, when South Fore women and children ate the brains of their female relatives, they unknowingly ingested the cause of their own deaths (Goldfarb, Cervenakova and Gajdusek 2004).

The incidence of kuru began to decline after the Australian colonial administration sent patrols into the Fore region of New Guinea and persuaded the people to discontinue ritual cannibalism and associated warfare. Kuru continued long after cannibalism stopped, however, because of the disease's long incubation period.

The Fore had adopted a maladaptive practice. Similarly, the spread of mad cow disease in Great Britain in the 1980s and 1990s resulted from a procedure that seemed financially beneficial in the short term but ultimately proved disastrous. Cattle feed companies began to use bonemeal derived from sheep brains as a cheap source of protein filler. However, some of the bonemeal was infected with a disease called *scrapie*, caused by agents of the family of prions similar to the agents that caused kuru. When living cattle ate the infected bonemeal, they became sick with symptoms similar to those manifested by the Fore. Humans who ate the diseased cattle also became ill.

Once the disease became known and its source identified, more than 140 000 cows in Great Britain had to be slaughtered to prevent it from spreading. In 1996, some people in Great Britain who died of a prion-caused disease called Creutzfeldt-Jakob disease were thought to have gotten sick after eating beef infected with mad cow disease. As a consequence, more British cattle were slaughtered to stem a potential epidemic. The European Union banned the export of British beef from 1996 to 1999, and nearly half of the country's 11 million cattle were destroyed (*Seattle Times* 1996). Mad cow disease has been a substantial problem in Canada as well. The appearance of a case in an Alberta herd in 2003 led to a ban on Canadian beef in the United States and Japan. Several cases have been reported since then. The loss of cattle markets and the ensuing price decline has cost the industry billions of dollars (Poulin and Boame 2003). The procedure of using cheap sheep brains to fatten cattle for market led to losses of income and lives that far outweighed whatever savings it provided.

Mad cow disease, like kuru among the Fore, demonstrates that people sometimes engage in practices that seem to make sense when first introduced but in the long term have consequences that are maladaptive and even life-threatening. These two syndromes are vastly different in their cultural causes, one stemming from religious beliefs and the other driven by the economic motive to cut costs. But they share a similar process, namely, the fact that people's behaviour, seemingly sensible at the time, often has unforeseen and dangerous consequences.

Culture Is Integrated

? *What are some other examples of "maladaptive" adaptations in today's world?*

cultural integration
The tendency for people's practices and beliefs to form a relatively coherent and consistent system.

Cultural integration refers to the observation that people's practices and beliefs form a relatively coherent and consistent system. Cultures are not simply random collections of activities but instead are patterned and interrelated in systematic ways. For example, behaviours that take place in one domain, such as political organization, tend to be compatible with and support behaviours taking place in other domains, such as family organization. Anthropologists recognize that terms such as "economy," "social organization," "family organization," and "government" are not discrete, separable units of activity but are closely intertwined. For example, economic activities usually affect and are affected by other kinds of activities. The work of obtaining food and other goods and services is often performed by people who occupy particular social roles and statuses.

Gender roles may assign men and women different kinds of work in contributing to their household economies. Also, social norms or, in complex societies, laws enacted by legislators and policies formulated by political agencies tend to be consistent with particular economic institutions and to reinforce particular economic goals.

The shared ways that people organize their lives are major integrating factors. In many societies, religious beliefs permeate and guide all aspects of daily life. Religion then becomes an overarching, integrative system of beliefs and practices often based on a premise that human and spiritual realms are not separable, but that spiritual forces are omnipresent and continually affect people's lives. Believers may perform daily rituals to bless and safeguard themselves and their families, they may recite prayers when hunting or planting crops to ensure success, and they may ask for spirit protection when engaging in any dangerous activity.

Not all aspects of cultural behaviour and belief are internally consistent or integrated with all others. Humans and their experiences are not so neat and tidy. Nevertheless, cultural systems as wholes tend toward consistency. A consequence of this consistency and integration is that change in one societal domain causes change in others. For example, the growth of the service sector in industrialized economies after World War II brought many women into the labour force. The freedom and income that this new resource provided has fostered changes in marriage and divorce patterns, child raising practices, civic participation, and many other areas in Canada and elsewhere.

Culture Is Based on Symbols

People's behaviours and understandings of the world are based on meanings expressed through symbols. A **symbol** is a sound or object that represents or stands for an idea, event, meaning, or sentiment. Language is a pervasive and powerful symbol system. Words in any language are just sequences of sounds but symbolize something other than the sounds themselves. The collection of sounds in each word in this sentence, for instance, stands for some arbitrarily assigned meaning.

Distinctions between words involve complex symbolization that forms and references broader meaning systems. The terms "uncle" and "father" in English put several different people into one category and emphasize the uniqueness of a nuclear family member. In another language, a father and father's brother may be lumped together, while mother's brother may constitute a unique term. The difference reflects different principles of family organization.

Linguistic symbolization may also be used to challenge basic assumptions encoded in ordinary speech. For example, a Caribbean dialect in Great Britain, called Afro-Lingua, focuses on the ways that standard English transmits common cultural assumptions that associate *white* with "good" and *black* with "bad." In common English expressions, "a black day" means a day when things go drastically wrong and "a black sheep" means an outcast family member (Bones 1986:46). Afro-Lingua speakers might refer to "a white day" and "a white sheep" in equivalent contexts. (Wong 1986:119).

Symbols permeate human culture in ways other than language. Objects, art, and artistic performances may represent powerful cultural ideas and attitudes. The colours and designs of national flags, for instance, come to be associated with complex levels of meaning. People can understand those meanings by examining the contexts of flag use, the way people talk about their national colours, and the way people react to them. Flags are used to symbolically represent a country, a territorial and cultural unit differentiated from all other similarly organized territorial and cultural units. Flags take on additional associations,

symbol
A word, image, or object that stands for cultural ideas or sentiments.

Until 1965 the Red Ensign was Canada's semi-official flag. What did the various symbols on the flag stand for? Why did the debate to replace it with the current maple leaf flag tie up Parliament for six months?

? *What emotional reactions can be stirred by images of national flags? What would be the significance of the burning of a Canadian flag in Quebec or of a Quebec flag in Ontario?*

demonstrated by the emotional reactions they can trigger in observers. Also, people may use their country's flag in ways that show their attitudes and political beliefs.

Religion, too, is a domain filled with symbolic meanings. Believers assign importance to tremendous importance to objects considered to have religious significance. Ordinary objects and substances used in rituals take on sacred properties. Books, cups, images, pieces of cloth or wood, or foodstuffs can be symbols of beliefs and can evoke powerful emotions and dramatize sacred actions. Symbolic culture thus includes both sacred and secular meanings and all the ways in which those meanings are communicated.

Culture Organizes the Way People Think about the World

naturalized concepts
Ideas and behaviours so deeply embedded in a culture that they are regarded as universally normal or natural.

ethnocentrism
A set of misunderstandings and prejudices based on the idea that one's own belief system provides the only accurate and moral view of the world.

cultural hegemony
The use of cultural beliefs to justify and support social hierarchy and political domination.

Through exposure to cultural symbols and through the acquisition of shared cultural concepts, people develop ways of thinking about themselves, their lives, other people, and the world. These underlying shared concepts become so ingrained that they are taken for granted, assumed to be true. People understand them as "natural" and "common sense." These are **naturalized concepts**, ideas thought to be essential and to exist in nature.

All societies have a core of naturalized ideas based on societal norms. For example, in most capitalist societies, it is taken for granted that people want to own property and obtain wealth. It is assumed that people are naturally competitive and want to continually acquire more property, own larger and more expensive houses, and have unlimited access to possessions. Yet people in these societies generally may not understand that their attitudes and values about property and wealth stem from the kind of economic system they live in. Those who lack an anthropological perspective think that their attitudes and values are natural and universal rather than products of their culture. Thus, naturalized concepts orient people's thinking about themselves and the world. They form a background ideology that organizes and gives meaning to people's behaviours and attitudes. And to the extent that they shape the way we view other cultures, they are also a source **ethnocentrism**, a set of misunderstandings and prejudices based on the idea that one's own belief system provides the only accurate and moral view of the world.

Interest groups can sometimes manipulate the internalization of naturalized concepts and values for their own benefit. In industrial societies, the themes of democracy and social mobility are often invoked to gain acceptance of class differences on the premise that anyone can achieve great wealth and high status. In reality, Canada and other Western societies have experienced a widening gap between rich and poor and increasing barriers to mobility over the last generation (see Chapter 10). The process of invoking cultural beliefs to justify and support social hierarchy and political domination is known as **cultural hegemony**. Apartheid in South Africa provides another

In these photographs, Chinese and American children are forming group identities through symbolic culture. What aspects of symbolic culture are evident in the pictures? What is being communicated to the children through these symbols? What is the role of children's exposure to symbols in these settings in the process of their enculturation?

In Their Own Voices

Aboriginal Children in Canadian Residential Schools

In the name of "civilization" the Canadian government removed thousands of First Nations children from their families and communities and placed them in Church-run residential schools in order to assimilate them into Canadian culture and society. The author comments on the affects of this system on his family and his cultural heritage.

The defining moment of [my father's] life came when he entered St. Mary's Residential School. Until then, he had been raised as a boy of respectable birth and reliable prospects, in both the Sto:lo community and the non-native world. St. Mary's, founded in 1863, was the pride of the Catholic Oblate order that had established a "mission" to the Indians in the Fraser Valley. From their dormitory windows, Sto:lo children like my father would grieve for parents and home, pining for the life on the river they had left behind.

The school was such a powerfully negative experience for my father that as a parent he used it as a kind of threat

to discipline us. If I didn't behave, he told me, I would be sent to a school where children had to rise at 5:00 a.m., say prayers on their knees for hours, and eat thin gruel three times a day. Porridge, porridge, and more porridge was his abiding memory of the school's fare, particularly galling to Sto:lo who thrived on the Fraser River's rich salmon and sturgeon resources.

My father was a fluent Halq'emeylem speaker, and he remembered having his knuckles rapped with a wooden stick or getting whipped for speaking either his language or the Chinook or N'laka'pamuz languages, both of which he spoke well as a child.

St. Mary's, like other Indian residential schools, was designed to strip aboriginal peoples of our culture. My father was at the school to grow up to be a little White man to enter the White world. . . . Some of the priest's words, enforced by the rod, must have stayed with my father. He refused to pass on his rich heritage in aboriginal languages to his children. He told us it was important to learn to read and write in English to get by in the world.

My father had been raised in a loving, nurturing Sto:lo family where he knew first-hand the benefits of traditional parenting, and he was under no illusions when he came out of residential school that the treatment he and others had received was the way to raise children, to be good parents. But like most school survivors, my father did not survive the direct assault on his self-esteem. . . . As a fisherman, trapper, and hunter, my father was proud to pass on to us these integral aspect of Sto:lo life. But the teachings he might have passed on about the heart and soul of Sto:lo life was withheld, as though his tongue was frozen.

From Ernie Cray, "Four Generations in My Sto:lo Family" In Fournier, Suzanne *Stolen from our embrace : the abduction of First Nations children and the restoration of aboriginal communities*. Vancouver : Douglas & McIntyre (1997). Reprinted by permission of the publisher.

example of this process. The legally mandated segregation between Whites and Blacks in such areas as employment, housing, education, and recreation, and denial of access to wealth and power to anyone of African descent was justified on the premise of innate racial differences.

On the other hand, dominant principles may be challenged by alternative and opposed cultural models. Participants in **countercultures** may advocate an alternative value system and lifestyle. For example, members of the Goth culture reject the mores of Western society and tend to dress and act in ways that are intended to be disturbing to the larger societies in which they live.

counterculture
An alternative cultural model within a society that expresses different views about the way that society should be organized.

worldview
Culture-based, often ethnocentric, way that people see the world and other peoples.

Challenges to widely recognized assumptions often come from members of groups that are marginalized or oppressed, who hold different **worldviews** than those of the dominant groups or elites. For example, apartheid in South Africa was the creation of a White settler minority which maintained exclusive control of wealth and power through policies of racial segregation and domination. The system was challenged by the majority of Black South Africans, who eventually rebelled against the government that oppressed them. Black South Africans asserted not only their political rights but also their right to replace the cultural model of White supremacy with one of racial equality. Thus, many political movements seek more than a reordering of social and political forces. They also seek the institutionalization of new cultural models as organizing principles in the society.

Similarly, through symbolic culture, some segment of a society might resist the official culture or offer an alternative cultural model. In the Middle East and North Africa, women's challenges to the ideology of male dominance often take the form of poetry and song, a low-risk context for expressing discontent. Bedouin women, for example, recite poetry and compose songs expressing their longings for love and respect. Song lyrics express passion and joy in attentions they receive from clandestine lovers (Abu-Lughod 1986, 1990). Artistic genres thus permit women to verbalize private feelings that run contrary to accepted norms of female deference and modesty.

The power of culture has important political implications. It may be manipulated to justify social inequalities and domination or be invoked to challenge and overturn them. Table 1.2 summarizes the characteristics of culture as defined in this chapter.

Table 1.2 CHARACTERISTICS OF CULTURE

Culture Is Shared	Behaviour, attitudes, and ideas are formed through interaction with others.
	Norms: Sets of expectations and attitudes that people have about appropriate behaviour.
	Subculture: A group whose members interact more frequently among themselves and share attitudes and practices that are distinct from others.
Culture Is Learned	Culture is acquired rather than inherited.
	Enculturation: The learning of one's cultural behaviours, attitudes, and values.
Culture Is Adaptive	Aspects of behaviour and belief are responses to environmental constraints and the need to ensure a community's survival.
Culture Is Integrated	Practices and beliefs that form a relatively coherent and consistent system.
	Cultural model: Comprehensive shared ideas about the ideal culture.
Culture Is Based on Symbols	People's behaviour and understanding of the world are based on meanings expressed through language, art, and symbolic objects.
	Symbols: Words, images, or objects that stand for cultural ideas or sentiments.
Culture Organizes the Way People Think about the World	**Naturalized concepts:** Ideas and behaviours so deeply embedded in a culture that they are regarded as universally normal or natural.
	Worldview: The culture-based, often ethnocentric, way that people see the world and other peoples.
	Cultural Hegemony: The use of cultural beliefs to justify and support social hierarchy and political domination.
	Counterculture: Alternative cultural model within a society that expresses opposition to dominant social and political views.

 *Anthropology Applied*

The Somali Affair and Military Culture

In 1993, the Canadian public was shocked by the actions of Canadian Airborne troops serving in a "peace enforcement" mission in Somalia. Two soldiers had captured a Somali teenager trespassing on their base and tortured him to death. In the wake of a public uproar, a commission of inquiry was formed to investigate the incident and to recommend changes within the army to rectify any problems that were identified. Many possible influences were cited including problems in the chain of command, poor training and discipline, malarial drug trials, "a few bad apples", and the "dark side of human nature." Among the researchers involved in this project, Donna Winslow (1997), an anthropologist from the University of Ottawa, considered the importance of culture in the formation of attitudes and practices that may have led to this act of violence. Her research indicated that the Canadian soldiers were enculturated formally and informally to adhere to strict standards of group loyalty within a distinctive regimental system. Regiments were organized as semi-autonomous units distinguished by region and collective symbols adopted by each group. Basic training procedures, complemented by hazing rituals, created a strong sense of collective identity and loyalty that cast the group as a single family. This orientation served an important function; it maintained military morale in combat settings. Soldiers were more likely to sacrifice their lives for their "brothers" than for more abstract ideals such as patriotism. In times of peace, however, intense bonding introduces a distinct problem. Both troops and commanders will cover for each other and refuse to report any problems up the chain of command out of loyalty to one another and concern that the unit as a whole bears responsibility for the actions of any of its members. As such, the offenders in the Somali affair proceeded to torture their victim under an assurance that if anyone became aware of their crimes they would look the other way and remain silent. In light of her findings, Winslow recommended that training and organization should focus less on maintaining strongly isolated units within the larger force.

REVIEW

Characteristics of culture include the fact that it is shared. Individuals who belong to a culture share assumptions about the world and develop cultural models and societal norms and taboos that define how one should and should not behave. Members of different subcultures in a society share culture differently. Culture also is learned through enculturation through interactions with other members of society. Culture is adaptive in that people depend on their culture to interact with their environment and change it when new opportunities or challenges are encountered. Culture is integrated—all aspects of culture are interconnected and mutually reinforcing. Thus, cultural integration means that change in one aspect of culture leads to changes in others. Culture is based on symbols, and language is the most important symbol system people use. Culture influences the way people organize their experience and their worldview. They use naturalized concepts to apply their cultural assumptions to other people's ways of life.

CULTURE CHANGE

Cultures are dynamic systems that respond to societal and historical changes from numerous sources. Some sources of culture change are internal, emerging from new practices and attitudes, technological innovations, or adaptations to the consequences of earlier practices. Other sources of culture change are external, emerging as people borrow ideas or artifacts from their neighbours or from people with whom they interact through migration, trade, or other contacts. Some borrowings take place in friendly interactions during **culture contact**, but others are forced on people through conquest or foreign intervention.

Internal changes are due to inventions of new technology and other material culture and to innovations in social practices and beliefs. They may be adopted to benefit

culture contact
Direct interaction between peoples of different cultures through migration, trade, invasion, or conquest.

cultural evolution
Theory which maintains that societies develop through a series of stages based on their technological development and according to which they can be grouped into categories. (see Chapter 5).

Marxist theory
Theory that analyzes society and culture in terms of class divisions and class conflicts.

diffusion
Spread of ideas, material objects, and cultural practices from one society to another through direct and indirect culture contact.

assimilation
Wholesale acceptance of the entire value and meaning system and abandonment of one's own beliefs and values. Often occurs under pressure from the domination of a more powerful group over a subjugated one.

acculturation
Process by which a group adjusts to the influence of a dominant culture, while at the same time maintaining its original cultural identity.

all the members of a society or just a select group. Cultures are always changing in this way, often in response to new challenges and opportunities. To the extent that individual societies come up with different solutions to these problems, their cultures diverge. Much of Canada and the United States once constituted a single unit, British North America. After the American Revolution they developed separate institutions and values. However, many cultures change in similar ways because they come up with the same discoveries. For example plant domestication was independently developed in the Middle East, China, West Africa, Ethiopia, Mexico, and Peru, with no evidence of contact between these regions. Canada and the United States both developed as confederations, granting some legislative and administrative powers to provincial and state governments.

Because of the forces of cultural integration, many inventions occur together as interconnected complexes. Pottery, permanent dwellings, and storage facilities occurred along with agriculture. The emergence of centralized states in the Middle East and in Mexico was associated with agricultural intensification, social stratification, occupational specialization, and the invention of writing. In consideration of these similar developments, anthropologists have formulated a theory of culture change know as **cultural evolution**, which maintains that societies go through a series of stages based on their technological development by which they can be grouped into categories, such as horticultural societies or industrialized societies.

Other approaches to internal changes take exception to the evolutionary perspective. Cultural ecology focuses on how societies change according to pressures within local environments that give each culture a unique character. **Marxist theory** stresses the impact of changes that result from resolving conflicts and contradictions that are due to social stratification and exploitation.

While all change is ultimately due to innovation, borrowing (technically termed **diffusion**) is a major source of new technologies, ideas, and values within particular cultures. Diffusion occurs through culture contact as people migrate, trade, invade, intermarry, or interact in other ways. These connections may involve direct interactions between societies or indirect flows of innovation passed on through intermediary groups. Diffusion may be localized or it may occur, as with the current trend towards globalization, on a worldwide scale. The changes involved are sometimes willingly adopted but can also be imposed by force. The extent and depth of the adoption of elements of another culture sometimes involves wholesale acceptance of the entire value and meaning system and abandonment of traditional culture, a process known as **assimilation**. Alternatively, people may borrow a limited range of innovations that allow them to retain their own core beliefs and values through **acculturation**.

Assimilation usually occurs as forced culture change when a dominant group imposes its control and culture on a subject population through conquest and colonization. Until recently, it was the main strategy for the incorporation of First Nations communities into Canadian society. The main mechanism was the residential school system, in which children were taken from their parents and placed in Church-run boarding schools. School curricula and discipline policies excluded and tried to erase Native culture by such measures as forbidding the children to use Native languages even outside of the classroom (Fournier 1997). Outside the schools,

The Hutterites are a Christian group who have settled on the Prairies on communal farms. They own all farm assets in common and closely adhere to the moral dictates of their faith, eschewing the adoption of secular Canadian values and practices. The scale of their operations has allowed them to survive changes in the Canadian agricultural economy at a time when single family farms have declined. (See Chapter 5 for more detail).

the government encouraged Natives to convert to Christianity and made their ceremonial activities illegal.

Acculturation occurs when the contact situation allows groups to control some of the conditions of cultural change. They have some leeway to be selective about the features they adopt and will reject or redefine innovations that threaten their core beliefs, values, and meanings. For example, Hutterite colonies are closely linked to the Canadian economy and enthusiastically accept new farming technologies. However, they reject popular media that conflict with their religion and dedication to communal life.

Acculturation can have more profound consequences since the adoption of a limited change in one area can have implications for others. The imposition of British colonial rule on the Luo of Kenya in the nineteenth century, for example, led to many interrelated changes in the economic, social, and political systems of that tribal society. The Luo had a mixed economy based on farming and herding. Women were responsible for the agricultural chores and men tended to the cattle. Land was owned communally by groups of relatives headed by men, but women actually controlled the production and distribution of crops resulting from their labour. In the colonial and postcolonial periods, however, women's rights to the land and their economic independence were undermined by British land reforms.

In 1899, the British colonial government imposed policies aimed at consolidating individual holdings that were intentionally scattered in different locations. Traditional Luo patterns of landholding gave individuals use rights in scattered parcels so that they could plant different crops in different ecological zones. British authorities did not understand this custom. In their view the traditional system was inefficient. In keeping with European ideals, the British combined landholdings into single parcels, which were registered in the names of male heads of households.

In addition, British colonial authorities imposed hut taxes that had to be paid in cash. To obtain cash for taxes, Luo men as heads of households often had to find wage work away from their local communities or introduce cash crops into the farming system over which they assumed greater control. Participating in the cash economy gave them access to valuable manufactured goods, and their official status as individual landowners gave them greater power and authority while the status of women declined. The Kenyan government continued these land policies after independence in 1960.

Colonized or conquered peoples can respond to external sources of culture change in ways other than assimilation and acculturation. In **reactive adaptation**, people respond to loss, deprivation, and oppression through passive resistance or violence. A **revitalization movement** is a type of reactive adaptation in which people try to resurrect their cultural heroes and restore their traditional way of life. A classic example of this is the Ghost Dance movement of the North American Plains Indians, discussed in the Case Study on page 26 (Wallace 1956; Mooney 1965). Traditional religious leaders and beliefs may play a role in social movements aimed at restoring or revitalizing the traditional culture.

Acculturation, assimilation, and revitalization can occur within the same societies at different times or among different sectors. Early in the history of contact with Anglo-Canadian society, Pacific Coast First Nations actively accepted European education offered by Christian missionaries. This service was provided with the intention of assimilating indigenous societies. However, the recipients of this benefit utilized the power of literacy in other ways than to read the Bible. Their main use of this new tool was to maintain records of donations that were made during potlatches, integrative ceremonies of critical economic, political, and religious importance. As such, it was an extension of a traditional method of record keeping, the totem pole (Codere 1961). In the course of time, the Canadian government shifted to a more aggressive assimilationist policy and directly forced the suppression of indigenous culture by making potlatches illegal and banning or discouraging other traditional practices. Native communities resisted this pressure through direct noncompliance and through various forms of revitalization, which included illegal potlatching, participating in the Ghost Dance movement (see the Case Study: The Ghost Dance Movement of the Plains Indians), and converting to Christianity while molding Church rituals and practices to conform to Native ideas of spirituality (Furniss 1995).

reactive adaptation
Coping response of captive, conquered, or oppressed peoples to loss and deprivation.

revitalization movement
Type of nonviolent reactive adaptation in which people try to resurrect their cultural heroes and restore their traditional way of life.

The Ghost Dance Movement of the Plains Indians

The Great Plains

Paiute Territories

The **Ghost Dance movement** of nineteenth-century North American Plains Indians was a nativistic revitalization movement that arose at a time when all of the native peoples had been forcibly confined to reservations after brutal military campaigns. Most of their land had been taken from them and their traditional economic systems were obliterated, as the buffalo on which they had depended were slaughtered by the millions. Epidemic diseases such as measles and small-pox decimated the populations, wiping out whole families and in some cases nearly whole communities. Reduced to poverty and dependent on rations mea-gerly handed out by the government, the people experienced a spiritual reawakening.

Although the movement advocated a message of peace and a return to traditional values and ways of living, it was completely misunderstood and distorted by agents of the U.S. government, with tragic results (Mooney 1965). Begun in 1889 by a northern Paiute prophet named Wovoka, the Ghost Dance movement predicted an imminent end to the world during a cat-aclysmic earthquake, to be followed by the reappear-ance of Indians who had died, the return of the buffalo, and the disappearance of White people.

Although Wovoka taught the necessity of establish-ing peace, harmony, and good moral principles, his mes-sage was distorted by frightened settlers and government officials who feared an armed uprising of impoverished and beleaguered native people who were forced to give up their lands, their economies, and their ways of living. Performances of the Ghost Dance were banned, and participants were threatened with imprisonment.

Finally, in 1890, after outlawing the dances and harassing followers, government superintendents in charge of the Lakota reservations in South Dakota had the influential leader Sitting Bull arrested and mur-dered and continued to harass Ghost Dance partici-pants. Army units were sent to arrest other Ghost Dance adherents, leading to the entrapment of more than 300 Lakotas and their massacre at Wounded Knee Creek on December 29, 1890. This final tragedy put an end to Ghost Dance performances.

Since then, the message of the Ghost Dance has changed from foretelling the end of American control to focusing on personal improvement and spirituality (Kehoe 1989). Nevertheless, Wounded Knee contin-ues as a potent symbol to Native Americans of govern-ment policies that crushed indigenous peoples and their cultures.

Arapaho Ghost Dancers, 1890. Specific elements of the Ghost Dance varied from group to group, but the main message was that Native Americans would achieve deliverance from White domination by supernatural means. The ritual dance with spirit possession would restore the balance of nature, and the Whites would disappear. In some groups, all the dead Indians would return to life, along with their horses and the buffalo. Whole again, the people would rebuild their societies and live as they had before contact.

REVIEW

Culture change can result from either internal or external forces, which usually are mutually reinforcing. Internal culture changes can come about from technological inventions or innovation within a society or introduced through culture contact and spread through borrowing, or diffusion. Outcomes of culture contact include, among others, assimilation and acculturation. Reactive adaptation is an outcome based on unrelieved stresses, often expressed through either violence or spiritual revitalization movements.

GLOBAL CULTURE

It is commonplace to hear people say that cultures throughout the world are becoming more similar, that a kind of **global culture** is spreading to all corners of the earth. Today's globalization stems from economic and political processes that have expanded from their original centres in Europe and the United States to many other countries. These processes have affected national governments, urban centres, and the cultures of traditional and indigenous peoples everywhere. Some observers claim that globalization is creating a homogenized world culture dominated by Western values and practices, while others see the development of ever greater variety and vitality through tbe cross fertilization of different cultures. These views emphasize contrasting themes in global change. The first stresses the dominance of Euro-American economic and political forces and associated cultural values, beliefs, and artifacts, while the second focuses on the exchange of products, peoples, and arts from every region of the world.

Globalization is the process in which the exchange of products, investment, and people across national boundaries is increased. It emerged after World War II in the wake of interrelated changes based on the replacement of nation-based and colonial

Ghost Dance movement
Nineteenth-century revitalization movement of the Plains Indians of North America.

global culture
A constellation of technologies, practices, attitudes, values, and symbols that spread internationally from one broad cultural origin, most prominently from the Anglo-European-American cultural complex.

globalization
The process in which the exchange of products, investment, and people across national and regional boundaries increases.

As governments, corporations, and the media spread their economic, political, and cultural influences, the traditional ways of life of the world's indigenous peoples are increasingly threatened. According to one estimate, about half of the world's 6000 languages will no longer be spoken by the end of the twenty-first century (Krauss, 1992). Urban settlers, displaced farmers, prospectors, miners, loggers, and a host of national and international interests put pressure on indigenous peoples, such as this Tarahumara woman's group and its territory. They, like other indigenous peoples today, are mobilizing to protect and preserve their environments, languages, and cultures.

Controversies

Should Canada Be Part of a North American Union?

For the last several years, the idea of a North America Union modelled on the European Union has been increasingly considered in academic and political circles. At the end of 2004, this interest was made more prominent by the formation of the Independent Task Force on North America under the chairmanship of John Manley, a former cabinet minister in the Chretien government with representation from the United States, Mexico, and Canada. The final report of the task force recommended the closer integration of the three economies through the relaxation of customs and immigration controls to allow the free movement of goods and people across the continent (Council on Foreign Relations 2005). Some people have also been considering the adoption of a common currency, the Amero, and even of political integration.

The North American Union proposal is built upon a history of close contacts and exchanges between the United States and Mexico and the United States and Canada. From the Canadian perspective, the flows of capital, goods, and ideas have been one-sided. Since the two regions of British North America went their separate ways after the American Revolution, the political and economic power of the larger and wealthier country has been dominant. Cultural and social influences have followed suit. American branch plants and American ownership in Canadian companies are a major force in our business community and business culture. Some industries such as oil and movie distribution are almost entirely American owned. American products line our shelves in malls and big box stores within sprawling suburbs designed for the convenience of the automobile. We are bombarded with American movies and television shows, and the Canadian book and magazine market requires government protection for its survival.

In spite of such forces, or perhaps because of them, Canada's political culture has stressed an independent course of development. Our government assumes a major role in regulating the economy, providing services for its population, and equalizing discrepancies between social classes and regions, while the United States stresses a more individualistic, laissez-faire approach. Canada has allowed more powers and responsibilities to devolve to its provinces than the United States has allowed to its states. While the United States has favoured the "melting pot" approach, Canada has implemented a pluralistic, multi-cultural policy for the integration of immigrants into its society. Levels of societal violence are lower in Canada (Gagnon 2001), and its military policy stresses peacekeeping. On another level, hockey is closely associated with Canadian identity, while the United States identifies baseball as its "national pastime."

However, a closer degree of continental integration threatens these cherished institutions. The *North American Free Trade Agreement* and the retreat of Canadian government involvement in the economy through the reversal of measures such as the *Foreign Investment Review Act*, government ownership of national transport carriers, and transport subsidies to farmers have led to changes in the Canadian economy, society, and culture. The Canadian Wheat Board monopoly, a pillar of our agricultural policy and important force for stability in rural society, is now under threat and may be history by the time this book goes to press. (See Chapter 5 for a discussion of the effect of some of these changes in the fabric of Manitoba's rural communities).

Concerns and fears for Canadian economic stability, its political autonomy, and the integrity of our society and culture have caused the formation of groups opposed to the current attempts to develop closer ties to the United States. Among other opponents, the Council of Canadians questions participation in American efforts to increase security and advocates the reversal of trends towards encouraging freer trade at the expense of weakening the public sector (www.canadians.org). Opposition, at least on a rhetorical level, is even evident within our political establishment. In successive elections, the Liberals have adopted a platform of supporting "Canadian values," in spite their own history of instituting liberalization policies. Nevertheless, strong pressures within the international financial community urge the continuation of current trends. The outcome of these conflicting forces will affect the long-term character of Canadian identity and culture.

CRITICAL THINKING QUESTIONS

How distinctive is Canadian culture? What are its main features and how do they contrast to those of American culture?

Are culture differences between Canadian and American differences greater than those within each country?

How would a North American Union foster economic growth within Canada? How might it affect it adversely?

How might closer ties with the United States affect Canadian culture?

Would you agree to an economic union with the United States? Would you agree to a political union?

economies by private multinational companies and international agencies, such as the International Monetary Fund (IMF) and the World Trade Organization (WTO). It involved the implementation of **liberalization policies** that attempted to eliminate state controls on investment, imports and exports, currency rates, and many other practices that were considered to constrain trade. As a consequence, national borders have become more open to investment, goods and services, immigration, values, ideas, and images from other countries.

This movement promises widespread economic prosperity and offers exciting possibilities of cooperation among peoples in an atmosphere of cooperation and tolerance. Alternatively, globalization may contribute to the growth and power of a few privileged nations and lead to economic crises and culture loss in the world's poorer regions. Chapter 14 further explores the efforts of small-scale societies to participate in a globalized modern economy without sacrificing their cultural traditions, natural resources, economic interests, and social welfare.

liberalization policies
Policies that attempt to eliminate national government controls on investment, imports and exports, currency rates, and many other practices that were considered to constrain trade.

? *What impact is globalization having on Canada? Is it desirable or not? Should our policies favour or discourage continuing this process?*

REVIEW

The world economy has become increasingly more open and integrated under the influence of multinational corporations, based predominantly in the United States. Economic and political forces and a global culture disseminated by the mass media threaten the loss of traditional ways of life of small-scale societies and cultural diversity among the world's peoples.

Chapter Summary

The Study of Humanity

- Anthropology is the study of humanity from its evolutionary origins millions of years ago to today's worldwide diversity of peoples and cultures.
- Anthropology is distinguished from other social sciences by three prominent features: a focus on the concept of culture, a comparative perspective, and a holistic perspective.
- Culture is the constellation of learned values, beliefs, and rules of conduct shared by members of a society. Culture change and globalization are two features of cultures that are important subjects of anthropological research.

The Four Subfields of Anthropology

- The academic discipline of anthropology encompasses four subfields, each with its own focus, methodologies, and theories.
- Cultural anthropology is the comparative study of living and recent cultures. Cultural anthropologists use ethnographic fieldwork and the perspective of cultural relativism.
- Linguistic anthropology is the study of language in its cultural and historical context. It includes the study of languages of indigenous peoples, language change, and the relationships between language and other aspects of culture, thought, and belief.
- Archaeology is the study of past cultures. Archaeologists study historic cultures with written records and prehistoric cultures whose lives can be inferred from

the collection of material artifacts, settlement patterns, and remains of foods and tools.
- Biological anthropology is the study of human origins, basing theories on the fossil record in order to understand the process of human evolution. Some biological anthropologists study present-day biological diversity of human populations.

Applied Anthropology

- Applied anthropology intersects with and draws from all of the major subfields. Some physical anthropologists work in forensics, applying their knowledge of human anatomy to help solve crimes. Some archaeologists survey and document archaeological resources prior to new construction. Some linguistic anthropologists apply their skills to the preservation of indigenous languages, helping to create dictionaries, grammars, and other instructional aids. And many cultural anthropologists work in nonacademic settings in public and government agencies, foundations, and private companies.
- Applied anthropologists can provide advice that helps shape government policies for delivering services to local communities. Others work with indigenous peoples to help them improve their economic conditions and secure their political rights.

What Is Culture?

- *Culture* refers to the customs, attitudes, values, and beliefs of members of a society. People acquire these elements of culture through their interactions with others.

As members of families, social groups, and communities, they learn the kinds of behaviours considered appropriate and encouraged. They also learn what kinds of behaviour are inappropriate and therefore disvalued and avoided.

Characteristics of Culture

- Culture consists of behaviours and beliefs that are "shared" by members of the group. However, disagreements and conflicts sometimes occur among members, often as a result of contrasting views and opinions held by people occupying different social statuses within the community. These distinctions may create differences in the ways in which people's lives are organized and in the attitudes and values held by members.

- Culture is "learned." That is, people's behaviour is the result of learning, not instinct. Even when human beings must fulfill critical physical and survival needs, their cultures intervene and influence the ways that their needs are satisfied. The fact that many of our attitudes and actions seem "natural" is testimony to the strength and the effectiveness of our enculturation.

- Culture is "adaptive." That is, people adapt to their environments through cultural means. Human beings can survive in nearly any climate and environment because of the inventions and cultural practices that they develop, keeping them sheltered, clothed, and fed. However, some practices that start out as adaptive may become maladaptive over time. Solving one problem may lead to the creation of new and unforeseen problems. Furthermore, a particular cultural practice may be adaptive in one context but not in another.

- Culture is "integrated," forming a relatively coherent and consistent system. Cultures are not random collections of activities but instead are patterned and systematic. Change in one aspect of culture usually affects and leads to changes in other aspects as well. And when cultural traits are borrowed from other peoples, they usually are altered and adapted to fit more closely with the borrower's norms and expectations.

- Culture is "symbolic." People's behaviour and understanding of the world are based on meanings expressed through symbols. Language is the most obvious and powerful of our symbolic systems, but human beings also use objects and rituals to represent deeply held cultural ideas and attitudes.

- Culture organizes the way people think about the world. Through learning and interacting with others, members of a society absorb an array of underlying, taken-for-granted assumptions about the world that help to integrate their activities and beliefs. These concepts become naturalized, so they feel innate and a matter of common sense rather than acquired. Not everyone, however, accepts the dominant cultural models of his or her society. In fact, these underlying assumptions can be the source of struggle and contention, which may, in turn, be sources of change.

Culture Change

- Cultures are dynamic systems that respond to change from internal and external sources. Internal development in particular practices and attitudes may take place over time through invention and innovation, leading to new adaptive strategies, new customs, new technologies, and new ideas about the world. Culture change also occurs through culture contact. People may borrow traits (both material and ideological) from other groups whom they meet in trade, travel, or social activities. Culture changes also may be imposed on members of one society by members of another through invasion and conquest.

- When a cultural group is in close contact with a dominant culture, the people may become assimilated or acculturated. Conquered and oppressed peoples may undergo reactive adaptation in an effort to cope with deprivation and loss. Revitalization movements are examples of nonviolent reactive adaptation.

Global Culture

- A global culture, originating in Europe and the United States, is spreading to all parts of the world. This global culture is characterized by consumer spending and is fuelled by advertising on behalf of multinational corporations. While globalization has helped to integrate many different peoples in a global economy, it may also lead to economic disparities and a loss of cultural and linguistic diversity and independence.

Key Terms

anthropology 4
societies 4
cultural anthropology 6
comparative perspective 6
ethnology 7
ethnography 7
holistic perspective 7
indigenous cultures 7

linguistic anthropology 7
historical linguistics 8
archaeology 8
biological or physical anthropology 9
paleoanthropology 9
applied anthropology 10
forensic anthropologists 10

cultural resource management (CRM) 10
contract archaeology 11
culture 12
symbolic culture 12
social culture 12
material culture 12
norms 13
subculture 14

enculturation 14
taboos 15
cultural integration 18
symbol 19
naturalized concepts 20
ethnocentrism 20
cultural hegemony 20
counterculture 21
worldview 22

Review Questions

1. What features distinguish anthropology from other social and behavioural sciences? What roles do the concepts of culture and culture change play in the field of anthropology?
2. Why is globalization a major concern in anthropology today? How does culture change relate to globalization?
3. How does each of the four subfields of anthropology seek to fulfill anthropology's mission?
4. How do cultural anthropologists conduct research, and to what end?
5. Why is cultural relativism important in studying other cultures? How does cultural relativism differ from ethical relativism?
6. What can linguistic anthropologists and archaeologists learn about symbolic and material culture?
7. How can research in each of the subfields of anthropology be applied to problem solving and policymaking in the world today?
8. In what sense is culture shared? How is it not shared?
9. How does the story of Eunice Williams illustrate that culture is learned?
10. What are internal and external culture changes? What are some examples of internal and external changes in your culture?
11. Why do you think the loss of a language is of concern to anthropologists? In what other ways is culture symbolic?
12. In what ways can culture be both adaptive and maladaptive? What is an example of reactive adaptation to culture change?
13. What are the characteristics and implications of the emergence of a global culture?
14. How has globalization affected life in Canada? Do you think that further expansion of global institutions and adoption of global culture are desirable or not?

CHAPTER 2

Preview

1. **How did anthropology begin as a discipline? What important figures shaped the development of anthropology?**

2. **What theoretical perspectives do anthropologists bring to their study of cultures?**

3. **What is ethnographic fieldwork? How is it done, and why is it important in anthropology?**

4. **What are some controversies about the validity of anthropological research and the impacts anthropologists have on the people they study?**

*A*nd the sons of Noah, that went forth of the ark, were Shem, and Ham, and Japheth: and Ham is the father of Canaan. *These are the three sons of Noah: and of them was the whole earth overspread. And Noah began to be an husbandman, and he planted a vineyard: And he drank of the wine, and was drunken; and he was uncovered within his tent. And Ham, the father of Canaan, saw the nakedness of his father, and told his two brethren without. And Shem and Japheth took a garment, and laid it upon both their shoulders, and went backward, and covered the nakedness of their father; and their faces were backward, and they saw not their father's nakedness. And Noah awoke from his wine, and knew what his younger son had done unto him. And he said, Cursed be Canaan; a servant of servants shall he be unto his brethren. And he said, Blessed be the LORD God of Shem; and Canaan shall be his servant. God shall enlarge Japheth, and he shall dwell in the tents of Shem; and Canaan shall be his servant. . . . Now these are the generations of the sons of Noah, Shem, Ham, and Japheth: and unto them were sons born after the flood. The sons of Japheth; Gomer, and Magog, and Madai, and Javan, and Tubal, and Meshech, and Tiras. And the sons of Gomer; Ashkenaz, and Riphath, and Togarmah. And the sons of Javan; Elishah, and Tarshish, Kittim, and Dodanim. By these were the isles of the Gentiles divided in their lands; every one after his tongue, after their families, in their nations.*

Genesis 9:18–27, 10:1–5 King James Version.

The account of Noah's life from the Hebrew Bible is one of the world's best known stories. It is multilayered tale that reflects many things, including a description of cultural diversity in the ancient world and an attempt to account for it. As such it constitutes a folk ethnography. Like other bodies of folk knowledge, the Biblical construction can provide clues to objective realities. A catastrophic flood may have once inundated the region, and some of the migrations and cultural connections recounted in the genealogies may have occurred. Nevertheless, any truth to the tale is conditioned by the character of ancient Hebrew culture and society. The model of origins and migrations of peoples as a sequence of genealogical branching reflects the kinship and territorial organization of ancient Israel. The key event, Ham's violation of his father and the resulting curse, justifies the slave status of Ham's purported descendants, the Canaanites, within Hebrew society. As such the story reflects the way in which cultural and social principles mold perceptions and representations of reality.

The story of Ham has been recast several times in Western history to account for and justify the domination of one people over another. One version has had a direct application to anthropological theory. The Hamitic hypothesis, proposed by the early twentieth-century anthropologist Charles Seligman (Seligman 1930), maintains that some of Ham's descendents, constituting a White race of Middle Eastern origin, migrated into Africa. There, they intermingled with the indigenous Black populations and introduced "advanced" cultural traits such as kingship and iron working. Two important assumptions about African biological and cultural diversity were central to this speculation: that biological race determined a people's culture and that cultural and racial

evolutionism
View that cultural variation can be accounted for by different degrees of intellectual progress, leading to different levels of cultural achievement.

diffusionism
View that similarities in culture could be explained by borrowing from a common source.

differences could be graded on a scale of superiority according to the degree of Hamitic "admixture." The tale again carried a political message—Seligman's hypothesis suggested that European colonial rule was needed to bring civilization to a people deemed to be innately inferior.

ANTHROPOLOGY AND THE EXPLANATION OF CULTURAL DIVERSITY

Like the ancient Hebrews, people everywhere have noted and speculated on cultural differences between themselves and others. Anthropology, as a systematic study of cultural diversity, has its roots in a heightened awareness of vastly different peoples that occurred during the global exploration and expansion that originated in Europe in the fifteenth century. Explorers, traders, and missionaries in the course of their distant journeys often wrote about the differences they observed in the ways of life of the peoples they encountered in Africa, Asia, the Pacific, and North and South America. Although many writers were biased and ethnocentric, they often left detailed observations of cultures at the time of contact. For example, Jesuit missionaries documented their experiences in North America in the seventeenth century. Although critical of many of the practices they described, they were often astute observers and recorders. They sometimes judged native customs and attitudes, such as rules for hospitality, generosity, and communal cooperation, to be superior to European practices. In some ways, these missionaries were like anthropologists, both observers and participants in other cultures.

Traveller's tales attracted the interest of social philosophers who were critically reevaluating the moral order of European society. Theorists such as Hobbes, Locke, and Rousseau sought comparative information to chart the growth of human institutions and help to design their future on the basis of evidence and secular reasoning rather than religious authority. By the end of the nineteenth century, a "science" of anthropology had emerged with a body of data and theory. Ethnography was devoted to compiling a record of human cultural diversity. Ethnology attempted to explain differences among peoples who were becoming increasingly interdependent in a system of Western-dominated world trade and European colonial expansion.

Ethnological Theory

Early Anthropologists. The nineteenth century gave rise to the first systematic collection of data from different cultures and a focused attempt to understand them from a scientific perspective. These activities became institutionalized within university departments and scholarly societies where opposing schools engaged in controversies over the theories of **evolutionism** and **diffusionism**. Both paradigms viewed cultural differences in somewhat the same light—as a result of varying degrees of progressive development among peoples that were rooted in their biology. They ranked cultural traits and social institutions as well the moral and intellectual abilities of the people that created them along a scale that ran from primitive to advanced. The theories differed over the explanation of similarities. The evolutionists believed in the parallel development of similar traits because of the action of the "psychic unity" of humanity. People in different places would find the same solutions to the same problems. The diffusionists believed that similarities were invariably the result of borrowing from a small number of centres of innovation, most notably ancient Egypt.

The principle of psychic unity may seem to be at odds with the evaluation of peoples as biologically superior or inferior. However, these two notions are consistent with the treatment of change within evolutionary theory. Evolutionists believed that culture and race evolved together so that improvements in one area instilled progressive changes in the other. "Primitive" people were thought to be in a lower mental and moral state but would eventually evolve through the same stages and towards the same end as more advanced Europeans.

Another early colonial observer in the Western Hemisphere was the Dominican missionary Bartolomé de las Casas, a sixteenth-century scholar, historian, and human rights advocate who observed Native Americans living in traditional and colonial conditions. His history of the Spanish conquest of Mexico and descriptions of the effects of colonial life on Native Americans led to humanitarian social reforms.

One evolutionist, Lewis Henry Morgan, made a particularly interesting use of kinship studies. He asserted that cultural development could be understood in terms of the extent of incest prohibition within society (1877). Morgan reasoned as follows. In the least advanced cultures, within the stage of "savagery", even the closest relatives could mate and produce children. This practice resulted in a physically and mentally degenerate race. At some point, people figured out a restrictive rule in which a group of men and a group of women married. This discovery resulted in mental improvements which led to the development of more advanced technologies and social control systems. The next stage introduced even more restrictive incest rules and further physical, mental, and cultural progress. The change in marriage rules meshed neatly with a now discredited theory that kinship universally progressed from matrilineal to patrilineal to bilateral forms. The nineteenth century evolutionist considered matrilineality the most "primitive" form of culture because it occurred at the stage of universal promiscuity in which they presumed nobody knew who his or her father was.

The adventures and misadventures of anthropologists living alone in "primitive" conditions with "uncivilized" peoples gave the new discipline romantic overtones that persist to this day. The public was astonished by Margaret Mead's reports about growing up in Samoa and living among the Manus of New Guinea. Other students of Franz Boas—Alfred Kroeber among the Zuni, Julian Steward among the Shoshoni, Robert Lowie among the Crow, and others—told the stories of the native peoples of California and the Great Plains.

Rethinking Culture and Society.   At the beginning of the twentieth century, a radical departure from the prevailing racial theories of cultural diversity emerged. It introduced a new formulation of the nature of culture and its relationship to mental and moral capacity that saw individuals as the products rather than the producers of their socio-cultural environment. It also sought for a new level of ethnographic documentation through the institution of direct field observations of exotic cultures. Emile Durkheim in France and Franz Boas in the United States, both born in 1858, were the central proponents of this new orientation, and each established a major school of followers who advanced his research program.

Durkheim.   Emile Durkheim (1858–1917) was a French sociologist, whose general theory of society and culture and use of non-Western examples had a deep impact on anthropology in both France and England. He developed the concept of society as a force that stands outside of the individual and determines his or her behaviour. As such, individual consciousness and action cannot be understood in terms of absolute notions of rationality but as a product of a social environment. Each society is composed of a consistent set of groupings, beliefs, and conventions that ultimately serve to maintain its social order.

Durkheim's theory focused on the central importance of **social structure**, which is the summation of the families, communities, and other groups which make up the larger society. The social structures he defined differed according to population scale, the number of groups into which people were placed, the number of levels into which they were organized, and the degree of group specialization. At the extremes, a structure of "mechanical solidarity" united people who did the same tasks and adopted a collective identity focused on common origin, while "organic solidarity" brought people together because of a need to exchange specialized products. Each social structure led to the development of social institutions and cultural values that functioned to enhance its integrity and ensure its reproduction as new generations became socialized according to group traditions.

Durkheim's work has had a significant impact in many fields, including sociology and anthropology in the United States and Canada. The main focus in anthropological research has been within the British **structural-functionalist** school, founded by A. R. Radcliffe-Brown. Radcliffe-Brown refined Durkheim's theories and supported

social structure
The integrated assemblage of formal groups and social roles that make up a society.

structural functionalism
The theory that social structure determines people's thought and behaviour and that culture functions primarily to uphold the unity and continuity of society.

Controversies

What Are the Limits of Cultural Relativism?

A controversial practice prevalent in twenty-eight African countries and found in other regions as well illustrates the conflict between cultural relativism and concern for human rights. Female genital mutilation (FMG), or female circumcision, involves the removal of part or all of the genitals of prepubescent girls. The procedure usually entails the removal of the clitoris. In some areas, it also includes infibulation, the removal of all external genitalia and stitching of the vaginal opening, leaving only a tiny space for the passage of urine and menstrual blood. An estimated 80 million women have undergone some form of the procedure (Armstrong 1991:42). Although it is now sometimes performed in hospitals, FMG is usually done by local midwives working with crude tools and without anesthesia on girls who are typically between 5 and 11 years old.

The two most common names by which the practice is known—female genital mutilation and female circumcision—reflect opposing attitudes toward it. Calling the practice *female circumcision* equates it with male circumcision, which is also debated but more widely accepted. The term *female genital mutilation,* on the other hand, was introduced by the United Nations Inter-African Committee (IAC) on Traditional Practices Affecting the Health of Women and Children, a group established to help end the practice. This term reflects "the cruel and radical operation so many young girls are forced to undergo" involving "the removal of healthy organs" (Armstrong, 1991:42).

FGM is a well-entrenched feature of the cultures in which it is found. It predates both Christianity and Islam and occurs among peoples of both faiths as well as among followers of traditional African religions. Whatever its relationship to religion, FGM is certainly associated with strongly patriarchal cultures—that is, cultures that stress the subordination of women to male authority.

Because the practice is often shrouded in secrecy, little systematic information has been collected about the medical consequences of FGM. Risks for girls undergoing the procedure reportedly include pain, shock, loss of bladder and bowel control, and potentially fatal infections and hemorrhaging (Gruenbaum 1993). Defenders of the procedure, however, claim that there is no reliable evidence of its increasing a girl's risk of death or of excessive rates of medical complication. Opponents claim that FGM reduces a woman's capacity for sexual pleasure and infibulation can make sexual intercourse and childbirth painful.

FGM is defended among the people who practise it—women as well as men—on cultural grounds. Some justifications involve beliefs about the dangers of female sexuality and the need to ensure virginity as a condition of marriage. Infibulation is said to help ensure a woman's premarital chastity and her sexual fidelity to her husband. Some prominent African women, such as Fuambai.

---

them though his own fieldwork and especially through the work of his many students. He focused on the importance of social groupings, social roles, and the norms attached to them in determining individual perceptions and behaviour. He also reaffirmed the position that all social and cultural institutions, particularly religion, functioned primarily to ensure social unity.

Franz Boas. Boas (1858–1942) began his career in Germany as a geographer and later became interested in indigenous peoples and their cultures. He spent a year living with the Inuit on Baffin Island, based on his conviction that only by living with other people can one truly understand their culture, producing one of the earliest intensive field studies. In 1886, he traveled to British Columbia to investigate Bella Coola (Nuxalk) culture. Two years later he immigrated to the United States, where he became the driving force in the development of American anthropology. Boas trained many of the most prominent anthropologists of both his generation and the one that followed, including Alfred Krober, Ruth Benedict and Margaret Mead, sending them into the field to collect data about many different cultures.

Ahmadu, an anthropologist from Sierra Leone, defend the practice. On the basis of her research, Ahmadu views it as a positive validation of womanhood (2000:304–305). Interviews with circumcised African women indicated that the practice did not diminish their sexual drive, inhibit sexual activity, prevent sexual satisfaction, or affect their health or birthing. The women supported the practice and looked forward to carrying on the tradition in initiating their younger female relatives into the pride of womanhood. Other native observers, such as Olayinka Koso-Thomas (1992), a physician and also from Sierra Leone, oppose the practice for its brutality, its dangerous consequences, and its role in perpetuating the subordination of women.

University of Toronto anthropologist, Janice Boddy, has attempted to understand infibulation in terms of how it fits into the wider culture of a Sudanese village (Boddy 1982). She maintains that the practice is predominantly encouraged by the women on the premise that it enhances fertility and stresses a woman's role as a producer of children rather than a sexual partner. As such it advances women's prestige, which is mainly based on their ability to bear sons. It also fits into to a complex symbolic and value system which stresses enclosed space and smoothness, the form of an infibulated vagina, as a representation of beauty, harmony, and close family ties. Boddy's work stresses cultural relativism and the ideal of objectivity. While not supporting the practice, Boddy indicates that changes must be introduced carefully with due consideration of the importance of infibulation for a woman's self image and social position and its role in the articulation of cultural values and ideals.

Many anthropologists, together with health workers, women's rights advocates, and human rights organizations, oppose FGM and are actively working to end it. They have had some success. In 1993, the Canadian Immigration Review Board granted refugee status to Khadra Hassan Farah and her daughter Hodan, who feared returning to their native Somalia where Hodan would be forced to be circumcised. The United States and many other countries have followed suit. In 1995, a United Nations-sponsored Conference on the Status of Women declared FGM to be a violation of human rights.

In response to campaigns against female genital mutilation by the World Health Organization (WHO) and UNICEF (United Nations Children's Fund), a few African governments have outlawed FGM, and others have taken steps to limit its severity and improve the conditions under which it is performed (Armstrong 1991:45–46). These initiatives, inadequately funded and only half-heartedly enforced, have done little so far to eradicate what many see as a dangerous and degrading practice. However, recent reports indicate that some women who specialize in the procedure have decided not to continue their work. For example, a grass-roots organization called Womankind Kenya has persuaded some influential practitioners to join their cause. Among the arguments they use are teachings from the Koran that some imams interpret as opposing FGM (Lacey 2004). When women with status and influence in their communities begin to oppose the practice, their opinions carry weight.

CRITICAL THINKING QUESTIONS

What do you think? Are there universal human rights? Who defines those rights? What might be some benefits and risks of intervening in other people's ways of life?

Boas' legacy also had a significant impact on Canadian anthropology. His focus on Inuit, Northwest Pacific Coast, and other North American indigenous cultures has been important in the development of Canadian ethnography. Boas' student Edward Sapir, one of the major figures in language and culture studies, established the anthropology division at the National Museum of Canada in Ottawa and trained many researchers to carry out his program to document disappearing First Nations traditions. The hiring of many American-trained anthropologists during the university expansion of the 1960s built on these influences.

Boas criticized the work of his nineteenth-century predecessors for being based on speculation rather than on hard evidence, asserting that their schemes were therefore invalid. He stressed careful methods of documenting culture through the collection of objective information and participant fieldwork. As such, he advocated an inductive approach in which data came first and theory later. However, his work was guided by an implicit theory of his own that firmly rejected the ethnocentrism and racism of the time. The evolutionists maintained that culture is the product of individual rationality and differs according to the unequal mental abilities of different peoples. Boas countered that it is a socially constructed meaning system that determines how people see,

cultural relativism
An approach that stresses the importance of analyzing cultures in their own terms rather than in terms of the culture of the anthropologist.

historical particularism
The theory that each way of life is a unique result of its particular historical conditions.

interpretive anthropology
View that cultural differences can be understood as complex webs of meaning.

think about, and act on their world. It is a closed system, whose assumptions are so internalized that people accept them unconsciously and without question. He drew two conclusions from his theorizing: cultures are built on arbitrary principles which cannot be ranked on a scale of superiority, the principle of cultural relativism; they also reflect unique patterns of organization that defy attempts at cross-cultural generalization, the assertion of historical particularism.

Cultural relativism has two implications, a cognitive one and a moral one. On a cognitive level, it maintains that the meaning of things, events, practices, artifacts, and concepts is not based on their intrinsic character but on the how they fit into the worldview that the culture imposes. For example, fatherhood may be based on biology in one culture or on the act of giving food, paying a bride price, or appearing in a vision in others. Accordingly, a trait that appears common to different cultures is only superficially so and cannot be employed to mark a progressive stage. On a moral level, it maintains that, the principle maintains that no culture has better reasoned or more acceptable ethical standards. Therefore, we must understand and evaluate ideas and behaviour from the perspective of the members of the society that upholds them and not from that of our own culture. **Historial particularism** is a closely related position and maintains that each way of life is a unique adaptation to particular historical conditions.

Although many aspects of Boas' work have been criticized and superseded, a focus on culture as a meaning system is still current and forms the basis of contemporary approaches within the fields of ethnosemantics and indigenous knowledge studies that we will consider in the next section. His advocacy of cultural relativism continues to hold a central and sometimes debated position in anthropological thought from both an analytical and a moral perspective. The question of whether Western anthropologists can set aside the meanings and values of their own culture has become an important issue within postmodernist anthropology, which contests claims to scientific objectivity in ethnographic research. The argument is that anthropologists are inevitably biased by their own cultural orientation in their recording, interpretation, and explanation of other people's behaviour. A second controversy centres on whether anthropologists, particularly within applied contexts, should condone or oppose practices that they would condemn in their own culture. (See the Controversies feature on pages 36–37).

Modern Theoretical Perspectives: An Overview

Although they differed in many ways, British and American anthropology in the early twentieth century shared a basic approach. Both maintained that individual thought and action were heavily conditioned by society and culture and focused on standardized, collective aspects of behaviour. They emphasized the homogeneity and consistency of cultural meanings and values and the continuity of tradition. Their ethnographic texts attempted to reconstruct uniform and unchanging traditional cultures, situated within a timeless "ethnographic present," among peoples who often were experiencing dramatic changes under pressures of colonization.

The period after World War II involved a second rethinking of theoretical positions. The classical British, French, and American approaches were challenged from a variety of perspectives that led to a fragmentation of ethnological thinking into many different schools. While some schools retained a focus on culture as meaning and an emphasis on thought systems, new materialist approaches looked to the uninvestigated areas of technology, environment, and economy as the main forces behind cultural and social institutions. Processual theories reinvestigated the relationship between the individual and society and the homogeneity and consistency of culture. Marxist models of class differences and conflicts influenced anthropology in many different ways. More broadly, anthropologists from many different perspectives became interested in understanding culture change and applying their methods to assist indigenous peoples in exercising some control over the process. (An overview of the varieties of contemporary anthropological theory is provided in Table 2.1.)

Many anthropologists have retained the Boasian understanding of culture as an integrated meaning system and have developed refinements in modes of analysis. Two approaches are current: the more general field of **interpretive anthropology**, and formal linguistic analysis within ethnosemantics.

Table 2.1 VARIETIES OF ANTHROPOLOGICAL THEORY

School of Anthropology	Founder	Central approach	Other well known anthropologists of that school
Historical particularism	Franz Boas	Views each culture as a result of its unique historical conditions. Culture traits must be understood in terms of their articulation to an integrated meaning system.	Alfred Krober Edward Sapir
Structural Functionalism	Emile Durkheim	Views people's values and behaviour as determined by their role in society.	Marcel Mauss A. R. Radcliffe-Brown E. E. Evans-Pritchard
Interpretive Anthropology	Clifford Geertz	Views culture as a unique system of symbols with multiple layers of meaning. Through their behaviour, people act out those meanings and communicate them to one another.	
Ethnosemantics	Floyd Lounsberry	Analyzes culture as a meaning system reflected in the way in which language classifies experience into categories.	Charles Frake Harold Conklin
Cultural Evolution	Leslie White	Classifies and explains culture according to standard technologies of food acquisition and production.	V. Gordon Child Marshall Sahlins
Cultural Ecology	Julian Steward	Analyzes culture as a system of adaptation to a local environment.	Marvin Harris Roy Rappaport
Processual Approaches	Raymond Firth	Views culture from the perspective of individual agency—how people react to the dictates of culture and society and modify and manipulate them to achieve personal goals.	Fredrich Barth Victor Turner
Marxism	Claude Meillasoux	Views culture as an aspect of a mode of production, particularly in the way it upholds and sometimes challenges class differences based on the ownership of productive resources.	Maurice Godelier Eric Wolf

American anthropologist Clifford Geertz (1973) has been an important proponent of interpretive approaches that focus on cognitive processes in the development and transmission of culture. His analysis stresses the multilayered symbolic meanings of people's actions. From this perspective, cultural behaviour is the acting out of those meanings. According to Geertz, "Man is an animal suspended in webs of significance

ethnosemantics
An approach that uses linguistic methods to reveal a culture's meaning system by analyzing the words it uses to name and classify items in the real and imagined worlds.

cultural evolution
Theory which classifies and explains culture according to standard technologies of food acquisition and production.

cultural ecology
A theory which analyzes culture as the means by which people adapt to their local environment.

etic
Objective, based on outsiders' views, as in explanations of people's behaviour by anthropologists or other observers.

emic
Subjective, based on insiders' views, as in explanations people have for their own cultural behaviour.

he himself has spun; I take culture to be those webs, and the analysis of it to be therefore not an experimental science in search of law but an interpretative one in search of meaning" (1973:4–5). Geertz has called culture an "acted document" that is essentially public and therefore observable and analyzable. Doing ethnography, then, is like trying to read a manuscript. To understand culture, interpretive anthropologists pay close attention to people's expressions of values, attitudes, meanings, intentions, and the felt importance of their actions (1973:9–10).

Ethnosemantics uses linguistic methods to reveal a culture's meaning systems. Cultures mold experience in different ways through the terms that they use to classify items in their real and imagined worlds. For example, the words of one language often create different categories of plants, animals, people, or gods than those of another. The degree of attention paid to any one area and the critical distinctions that separate one word from another provides an insight to the structured meaning system to which people refer when interpreting their experience. Ethnosemantic methods have been extensively used within the field of indigenous knowledge studies, where fields such as ethnobotany provide insight into how societies classify, understand, and utilize elements of their local environments. Further discussion and some examples of ethnosemantics will be presented in Chapter 3.

Materialist Approaches

Materialist perspectives challenge the emphasis on culture as a system of thought and stress its role as the mechanism by which societies survive in their environments, mainly through the use of technology to extract and produce food and other essential resources. Two approaches have been especially influential in directing research and theorization: cultural evolution, which focuses on technology, and cultural ecology, which assigns greater importance to environmental pressures on group survival.

The theory of **cultural evolution** attempts to place cultures into general stages based on the nature of their technologies of food acquisition and production. The main way in which people manage their local environment and the amount of energy that they can acquire will have a deep impact on their daily activities and affect other aspects of their culture, such as settlement, family organization, and even their political order and belief system. For instance, foraging, a primary subsistence strategy based on hunting and gathering wild foods, usually supports only a small local population and requires that family groups frequently relocate on the landscape. Group composition is flexible; property ownership and material accumulation are seldom possible. (See Chapter 4 for further consideration of subsistence and culture).

Cultural ecology is closely related to cultural evolution but looks at culture more fully as an adaptation to a specific environment. As such, technology is important, but its impact on people's lives and various aspects of their culture must be understood in terms of how it is applied in a particular local setting. For example, both the Ju/'hoansi of the Kalahari desert and the First Nations of the Northwest Pacific Coast traditionally lived by hunting and gathering. However, as we will see in Chapter 5, their environmental circumstances had very different implications for settlement and social organization.

Materialist approaches are often distinguished from interpretive and semantic approaches as providing *objective* explanations for cultural behaviour that are given by anthropologists or other observers (**etic** views) as opposed to *subjective* understandings that are offered by the people engaged in that behaviour (**emic** views).

In his popular book *Cows, Pigs, Wars and Witches: The Riddles of Culture* (1974), Marvin Harris contrasted

From the perspective of cultural ecology, cattle are not slaughtered for food in India because they are too important for agriculture as practised within the local environment. Cattle are used as draft animals to pull ploughs. In addition, their dung is used for fuel in cooking and heating houses in a setting where wood is scarce.

emic and etic explanations of why Hindus in India do not eat or even kill cows. According to an emic analysis, Hindus do not kill cows because they are sacred animals. In an etic analysis, however, the meaning of the sacredness of cows has to be analyzed in the context of the economic needs of farmers in India. Harris concluded that cattle are "sacred" in order to protect them from slaughter, because they are vital to the continuation of Indian farming practices.

Processual Approaches

While semantic and materialist approaches developed primarily within American anthropology in reference to the Boasian tradition, processual approaches emerged in Britain as a counter to structural functionalism. Post–World War II ethnological thinking reassessed the impact of society on behaviour and introduced a concern for **agency**, the way in which an individual reacts to and acts upon his or her culture and society. To correspond with this orientation, culture was no longer viewed as a homogenous and consistent system, but as a field that allowed for differences of interpretation, conflict, and manipulation. Analysis of cultural process is based on how people make decisions to enhance their economic well-being and political power as we will consider in Chapters 6 and 11.

Marxism

The theories of Karl Marx have been among the most influential of the modern world and have had an impact on anthropology in different ways and at different times of its development. Marx's general approach sees the **mode of production** as the key to understanding various aspects of society and culture. While the concept is partially based on productive technologies, it stresses the importance of social and economic class divisions based on ownership of critical resources. For example, contemporary industrial society can be understood according to the prevailing influence of a capitalist class, which owns its productive and financial infrastructure.

Several anthropological versions of Marxist theory have been important. Dependency or world systems theory has attempted to understand contemporary social and cultural process within societies of the developing world as a product of the expansion of international capitalism and the division of the world into powerful core nations and those on the periphery (Wolf 1982). Anthropologists concerned with internal patterns of stratification in indigenous societies have identified new categories, such as the African mode of production where divisions of wealth and power are based on who controls marriage rights (Meillassoux 1972). Recent approaches to culture have focused on how it reinforces hegemony by advocating ideals, symbols, and values that justify and enhance the privileges of dominant classes.

Anthropologist Eleanor Leacock's (1981) pioneering work on the Montagnais and Naskapi in eastern Quebec and Labrador pointed to the role of colonial government agents in undermining indigenous culture. These agents exerted both direct and indirect pressure on native peoples to change their practices and attitudes, including gender roles and patterns of leadership.

agency
The way in which an individual reacts to and acts upon his or her culture and society.

Marxism
Theory that views culture as an aspect of a mode of production, particularly in the way it upholds and sometimes challenges class differences based on the ownership of productive resources.

mode of production
Social type that is defined by the way in which society is divided into classes based on ownership of the "means of production."

REVIEW

Anthropology is a relatively new discipline; however, some missionaries, explorers, and colonists observing other cultures made accurate accounts of them. Observers also have recorded narratives and oral traditions of other peoples. Evolutionism influenced nineteenth-century works by thinkers such as Lewis Henry Morgan. Two important figures in early twentieth-century anthropology are Franz Boas, who called for an anthropology based on cultural relativism and empiricism, and Emile Durkheim, who explained cultural traits from the perspective of how they function to ensure social unity and continuity. Anthropologists use several other perspectives to describe and explain cultural differences, depending on their intellectual preferences. They may use a materialist perspective (either cultural ecology or cultural evolution), symbolic analyses of culture as meaning, processual perspectives that focus on individual agency, or Marxist perspectives involving the analysis of culture, wealth, and power.

fieldwork
In anthropology, living and interacting with the people or group under study.

ETHNOGRAPHY AND FIELDWORK

Ethnographic Fieldwork

Much of the work of anthropology consists of doing ethnography, collecting and analyzing information about culture—that is, people's activities, beliefs, and attitudes. Since cultural anthropology is concerned with the study of living cultures, anthropologists need to collect firsthand information obtained by living in the societies that they study over a lengthy period of time. Such **fieldwork** is usually a part of an anthropologist's training, a rite of passage that most graduate students go through as they complete their training and establish themselves in the discipline. Anthropologists' initial fieldwork experiences often set the framework in which their research interests develop and continue throughout their careers. Anthropologists traditionally chose research problems and sites in foreign countries. This is still a common approach, but today many anthropologists work in their own countries, even in their own communities.

GLOBALIZATION

Imagine that your e-mails or blogs are among the records on which an ethnohistory of internet culture is based. What kinds of information would your records provide? How could your records be interpreted to explain changes in internet culture? How could your records help to document the changes we call globalization?

Doing Fieldwork

Fieldwork involves a complex process of observing and participating in another culture. Participant observation is at the core of the fieldwork experience. Anthropologists both observe the activities taking place in the community and participate in them as much as possible and as appropriate. Anthropologists usually live in the community that they are studying, sometimes renting a house or a room in someone else's dwelling. Fieldwork, then, is an ongoing, multifaceted research experience.

Choosing a Problem and Site. Anthropologists begin by choosing a research problem and where to conduct their study. Most anthropologists do their first research project when they are graduate students. Their interest in a particular subject may develop from an especially exciting course or stimulating teacher. Some anthropologists have long-standing interests in a particular country or community. Others choose a research site that best suits their theoretical or topical interests.

Obtaining Funding. Fieldwork is often costly, especially if it involves travel to another country and residence far from home for an extended period of time. Most graduate students embarking on their first field trip are advised to plan to be on site for about one year. This allows observations during a full annual cycle of economic, social, and ritual activities. Longer field stays are always beneficial but may not be possible for lack

Today, much anthropological fieldwork takes place in large-scale societies, often focused on a village or subcultural group within the larger nation. Anthropologists realize that the older view, which saw small, indigenous communities as isolated and timeless, was a distortion and failed to appreciate the complexity of people's lives and their ties to other peoples. Here Elisha Renne (right) confers with University of Ibadan (Nigeria) professors Dr. Babatunde Agbaje-Williams and Dr. Aderonke Adesanya.

of funding. Public and private agencies and research institutions are potential grantors of funds for field studies. In Canada, the federal government, through the Social Science and Humanities Research Council, is the major source of funding for anthropological research.

Doing Preliminary Research.   Before embarking on the fieldwork trip, researchers gather as much information about their subject of study as they can in order to situate their own project within the discipline. They read what other anthropologists have written about the topic, attempting to understand the data and the theoretical approaches that others have used in analyzing the problem. They also gather information about their chosen place of study. To prepare themselves for entering a foreign country or community, they will want to know as much as they can about the culture, history, conditions, and significant current events of that region, as well as the rules for entering and residing in the country. Anthropologists also study the language of the country so that they can communicate directly with the residents. Before setting out for the site, anthropologists often make contact with local people to make sure that their presence in the community will be acceptable. In some situations, such as research in First Nation's reserves, formal approval from the community must be obtained before any interviewing can begin.

Arrival and Culture Shock.   After arriving at the field site, anthropologists often experience **culture shock**—the feeling of being out of place and disoriented in unfamiliar surroundings. In the field, researchers must immediately learn new customs, new faces, new foods and ways of living, and a new language and ways of communicating. This learning is intense, because anthropologists are immersing themselves in a new way of life in which they will participate. Often, it is the unstated rules of decorum and etiquette that are most easily, and unknowingly, violated. An anthropologist needs to be keenly observant, not only of other people's activities but also their reactions and the attitudes, values, and norms behind them. Their experiences also afford them new insights into their own culture, their own behaviour, and their own beliefs. Nevertheless, doing fieldwork has emotional ups and downs. At the beginning an anthropologist may have feelings of uncertainty or fear and loneliness as he or she seeks acceptance and cooperation.

Choosing a Place to Live.   Once on site, an anthropologist obtains a place of residence, arranging to live in a household or renting a dwelling. Living in a household has the advantage of proximity to people through family networks and routine participation in household and community events. Of course, the anthropologist needs to find someone willing to be a host, sometimes a difficult task. A disadvantage to staying with a family, however, is that members of a household may try to ally themselves with the anthropologist against the interests of others in the community or may try to involve the anthropologist on their side in local social and political networks. In many field locations, anthropologists may have high status among the people they study. In poor and marginalized communities, they may be perceived as rich and powerful. A challenge of fieldwork, then, is to establish good relations without allowing people to use a relationship to gain benefits or advantages over others in the community. Thus, while friendships may develop between an anthropologist and the people in the community, the researcher needs to remain nonpartisan in village conflicts, disputes, and controversies.

Working in an Unfamiliar Language.   As fieldwork begins, the anthropologist usually hires an interpreter unless he or she is fluent in the local language. Learning the field language is clearly desirable, and even necessary, if the anthropologist truly wants to learn what kinds of meanings people ascribe to their own behaviour. Working through translation is very different from speaking directly to the people. Many nuances of meaning and attitudes that are conveyed in language are lost in translation regardless of the interpreter's skill.

culture shock
The feeling an anthropologist may have at the start of fieldwork of being out of place in unfamiliar surroundings.

? *Have you ever experienced culture shock? What was the situation? How did you respond to it?*

Gathering Data. Once they are established, anthropologists often survey their village or community or other field site. They may draw a map, situating the site within its local environment and the houses, other structures, farm fields, open spaces, or other areas where people congregate and socialize. A social survey may include information about household composition and the relationships among members of nearby houses. From these data, the anthropologist learns about family ties and neighbourhood networks. Anthropologists sometimes hire assistants to help with these tasks. If the assistant comes from the village, she or he can provide a personal connection to other people and help broaden the anthropologist's social network.

The communities in which anthropologists conduct fieldwork are linked to other communities, the nation, and other nations through local, regional, national, and transnational systems of exchange and the global market economy. A farm family in India, for example, might sell produce and handicrafts in regional markets that link ultimately to international export and import markets. Anthropologists must trace these kinds of connections and understand their impacts on people's daily lives.

Gathering data includes interviewing members of the community. Formal interviews are usually lengthy and may take several sessions and many hours to complete. Accordingly, sample sizes tend to be small. This situation sometimes introduces problems of ensuring that the sample is representative of the community as a whole. One solution is to set up a **judgment sample** of **key informants** who the anthropologist considers to be representative, reliable, and well versed in local cultural traditions.

Traditional anthropological methodology includes collecting data concerning kinship, that is, how people trace relationships and descent from generation to generation and among members of the same generation. Combining genealogical information with residence histories that record how long people have lived in which houses allows the anthropologist to learn about systems of relationships, people's geographic mobility, and intercommunity relations. It is also traditional to gather data about the ways that people obtain their food, earn a living, and provide themselves and others with goods and services. Economic and social networks may link groups and societies through trade, intermarriage, and friendships.

The researcher also gathers data by attending meetings, informal gatherings, religious activities, and other community events. Anthropologists try to participate as much as possible to the extent that their presence is acceptable to members of the community. They need to be sensitive to villagers' attitudes about an outsider's participation in local life. Outsiders may be welcome in some settings but not in others, particularly in sacred or secret activities or in meetings where controversial issues are discussed. Female anthropologists might find their access to certain men's activities limited, and male anthropologists might likewise find their access to certain women's activities restricted. Anthropologists usually want to interview community political officials, religious functionaries, teachers, and doctors for certain kinds of information. It is important, however, not to become overreliant on local authorities in order to avoid interpretation of village life from the perspective of the local elite. Despite increasing involvement with villagers, researchers usually remain outsiders, except on occasion for those who are themselves indigenous or native to the group they are studying.

After living in the field for an extended period of time and becoming comfortable in a different culture, anthropologists often go through a period of culture shock after they leave the field, not unlike the culture shock they felt when they first entered the site. When they return to their own neighbourhoods, they may see the behaviour of their friends and relatives in a new light. For awhile they are the outside observers now observing their own culture, once so familiar and taken for granted. Of course, within a short time they are readily integrated into their own daily lives. But the experience of living with other people in another society has profound and lasting meaning. And for many, it gives them new insights into their own behaviour and their own beliefs.

Interpreting and Reporting Data. During and after fieldwork, anthropologists reflect on their interactions and the data they have collected. New research questions may arise, new opportunities for observation and participation may present themselves, and new understandings of what has happened may be revealed. Field notes are rewritten

judgment sample
A sample of research informants selected according to how well they represent the larger population rather than on a random basis.

key informants
Research subjects who are well versed in local cultural knowledge and representative of the larger community.

as ethnographic accounts and papers, which are published as books and journal articlesand presented at professional meetings. Sharing the results of research is important in a community of scholars and often leads to new research questions to investigate.

Anthropological reports are framed within the analytic and theoretical perspectives of the researcher. Other anthropologists may undertake reanalyses of data, focusing on additional questions and employing different theoretical frameworks. And although fieldwork is a fundamental experience and research method in anthropology, some anthropologists choose instead to focus on cross-cultural comparisons drawn from ethnographic data bases, such as the Human Relations Area Files, or on ethnohistory drawn from archival and historical materials as well as from oral histories. All of these various scholarly activities combine to enrich the discipline.

Anthropological Research in Large-Scale Societies

When anthropologists conduct research in large-scale societies, they use many of the same data-collection techniques that they use in smaller settings. Rarely, however, do they study a whole community. Instead, they investigate a specific topic within a defined subculture or group. For example, some researchers specialize in urban anthropology, a field that focuses on studying the lives of people living in cities or urban neighbourhoods. Urban anthropologists may analyze a neighbourhood association, a particular occupational group, a school setting, a religious network, a healthcare delivery system, or a senior citizen centre. The people in these groups may or may not reside near each other, but they interact frequently in particular areas of their lives.

In conducting this kind of research, anthropologists supplement their usual data-gathering techniques with those borrowed from sociologists and other researchers, including survey research. **Survey research** involves the use of formal questionnaires administered to a random sample of subjects to elicit background data such as occupation, income, level of education, marital status, participation in clubs and associations, political and religious affiliations, size of household, number of computers in the home, and so on. Questionnaires also elicit information about people's attitudes, values, and practices, which are then analyzed in terms of the background data. Surveys provide information about conditions and trends in the community under study, including socioeconomic conditions, social participation, social norms, people's attitudes and opinions, and cultural practices. In these studies data analysis can emphasize statistical correlations to answer a particular research question or summary descriptions to understand the life of the community as a whole.

The study of large-scale societies does not necessarily involve work in single locations. Increasing mobility is creating groups of people whose activities and networks are dispersed among many places or who may not even permanently reside within a fixed locality. Canadian anthropologists Dorothea and David Counts have carried out a pioneering study among one such migratory community, the RVers of North America (Counts 1996).

The Counts' interest in RVers stemmed from their work on cultural attitudes and practices involving aging in a New Guinea society. After several field trips to the Pacific over the course of a generation, they decided to make a comparable study in North America among retirees. They focused on one particular group, people who had devoted their leisure years to travelling across the continent in RVs. They discovered a particularly interesting and well-identified subculture within this group, the "full-timers," who lived permanently in their motor homes and maintained a nomadic existence travelling from one RV park to the next.

Fieldwork within the RV population posed some unique problems. The Counts took up the challenge of participant observation by purchasing an RV and hitting the North American highways. They chose to travel rather than to stay in a single site because the experience would give them a deeper insight into the problems and satisfactions of the way of life they were investigating. Participation took the form of setting up for several weeks in an RV park and engaging in informal interactions and get-togethers

survey research
Use of formal questionnaires administered to a random sample of subjects, eliciting social data that can be analyzed statistically.

? *How could you apply each of the steps described in this section in a fieldwork situation close to home?*

and attending formal occasions such as entertainments and celebrations in park clubhouses. The researchers also joined an RV association that maintained several parks and donated their time to voluntary activities, such as communal maintenance chores.

The study was based on information from a variety of sources. The Counts personally interviewed many of the full timers that they met on their journeys. Approximately 100 Canadians and Americans provided in-depth information about their backgrounds, motivations, and experiences. Informants were selected haphazardly, usually on the basis of casual contact made across open eating areas beside each rig or while walking dogs or sitting in the laundromat. The Counts also got letters, sometimes with detailed information, solicited in trade journals and from an interview they gave on an Ontario TV program. Another major database was compiled from a formal precoded survey questionnaire of 100 items that was deposited at RV parks and filled out by over 300 respondents. Further information was gleaned from newsletters of various RV associations.

The Counts were cautious in the interpretation of their results because of the problem of representative sampling. Because the population they studied was completely mobile and unidentifiable as a group, its size and characteristics could not be determined. As such their results likely would have been different if the study were done in other times and places. They also found discrepancies between the personal interviews and written questionnaire responses. For example, the survey results indicated that half of all American respondents carried guns in their rigs, while face-to-face discussions indicated that the figure was 80 percent. In general the researchers considered the personal interviews to be more accurate, especially in the context of the cultural emphases on reciprocity within the RV community. Formally administered questionnaires were viewed as imposing a power relationship between interviewer and respondent, while more open-ended interviews were seen as a give-and-take conversation.

The RV study yielded many interesting and unexpected insights into a little known way of life that may involve over a million North Americans. The Counts concluded that full timers constituted a distinct subculture with "their own system of values, their own social networks, their own symbols . . . to explain who they are to themselves and others. They have ways of identifying each other and ideas about how they should behave towards one another. They even have their own jargon—words and phrases exclusive to RVers" (Counts 1996: xiii). Their motivations included an obvious desire for travel and also an attempt to find friendship and community among fellow RVers. Paradoxically, a community formed among people who continually moved away from physical locations and the relationships established within them. It was rooted in a clearly articulated set of values and involved mutually accepted roles, norms, and obligations among people who were often strangers to one other. In spite of many problems faced by participants in this way of life, including the loss of a fixed abode (and consequently for Canadians the loss of provincial healthcare coverage) and the need to minimize personal possessions, this way of life provided a satisfying and engaging experience that had many advantages over life in a retirement community.

REVIEW

Fieldwork provides the basic ethnographic data from which comparisons and theories of culture are constructed. This information is usually recorded in descriptive accounts called ethnographies. Conducting fieldwork involves many steps before even entering the field, at which time most first-time anthropologists experience some degree of culture shock. Fieldwork can focus on entire small-scale societies or on subcultures or subgroups within a large-scale society. Anthropologists also study groups, communities, and institutions within their own societies. Using methods such as interviews and survey research as well as participant observation, researchers in urban anthropology focus on segments of larger societies and their connections with other societies and the world.

Case study

Canadian Anthropology

Unlike the countries where the core theories and approaches in anthropology first emerged, Canada has not produced an identifiable national tradition or school comparable to Boasian historicism in the United States, the Durkheimian approach in France, or structural-functionalism in England. Nevertheless, many Canadian anthropologists have attained international reputations. Richard Lee is one of the world's foremost authorities on foraging societies, and Richard Salisbury and Michael Asch pioneered the application of anthropology to represent indigenous rights. Moreover, some historians of the discipline have suggested that Canadian anthropology has come to assume unique emphases that are informed by distinctive trends and patterns in the wider society.

One of the reasons for the absence of an easily identified national tradition is the lateness at which Canadian anthropological institutions developed. While several Canadian anthropologists, such as Horatio Hale, carried out personally sponsored research or worked in association with specific projects, such as the British-funded study of First Nations of the Canadian Northwest (Nock 2006), an official anthropological institution was not set up until 1910, when Edward Sapir, an American trained in the Boasian tradition, founded the Anthropology Division of the Geological of Canada, later to become housed in the National Museum of Canada (Hancock 2006). This endeavour was mainly oriented towards salvage ethnography, the collection of information from Canadian Aboriginal cultures, in an attempt to record their traditions before they disappeared. It did little to establish an active scholarly community, as museums did not train cohorts of students, who could in turn transfer knowledge and theories to subsequent generations. The first anthropology courses were not taught in Canada until Thomas McIlwraith was hired at the University of Toronto in 1925. Toronto went on to establish the first anthropology department in 1936, but full development of a national network of university departments with graduate programs did not occur until the 1960s (Harrison and Darnell 2006). At that time a massive expansion occurred, drawing most of its personnel from American institutions, either Americans or American-trained Canadians. Thus by as late as 2000, only 25 percent of anthropologists teaching in Ph.D.-granting Canadian university departments held Canadian degrees (Howes 2006).

The trends in Canadian anthropology reflect a clear American influence stemming not only from the direct presence of Americans and Canadians with American training but also from a common focus on the study of First Nations and Inuit peoples. Accordingly, Regna Darnell (1997) has placed the Canadian discipline within the "Americanist tradition" typified by a Boasian emphasis on culture and the development of four field departments clearly distinct from British and French approaches that are more closely allied to sociology. She has argued however that it has developed a unique focus that reflects the Canadian context of a greater emphasis on First Nations' ethnography and of government policies that place a higher value on linguistic and cultural diversity and social justice than those of the United States.

David Howes has developed Darnell's themes further to suggest that Canadian anthropology differs from the American discipline insofar as it follows a "bicentric" as opposed to a "concentric" model of producing knowledge (Howes 2006). Because American society emphasizes unity around a single national culture, its anthropologists tend to formulate unitary, integrating models to understand social and cultural variation. Their Canadian counterparts live and study in a context of a bilingual country, a substantial degree of delegation of authority to the provinces, and a recognition of collective as well as individual rights. Howes documents this thesis by contrasting Canadian and American treatment of globalization in terms of "[highlighting] the diversity of the unity in the phenomenon [vs] the unity in diversity (Howes 2006: 206)." Unfortunately, he cites no specific works to illustrate his point.

Several historians of Canadian anthropology have advanced an opposite thesis: that it is not significantly different from the American discipline. Thomas Dunk (Dunk 2000) maintains that anthropology in Canada has followed a wider trend of American dominance of Canadian culture and society and that any singularities result from its position as a marginal producer of "staples" (raw materials) for the American industrial establishment. This status is perpetuated by a tendency of Canadians to devalue their own institutions. As such, American degree holders will continue to receive preferential treatment and give continuity to the American presence because Canadian academia rates them more highly than its own graduates.

The debate over the uniqueness of Canadian anthropology is not easily resolved. Both differences and broad areas of overlap, communication, and cooperation are present. One point is observable: American anthropologists are less concerned than their Canadian counterparts over the issue of national distinctiveness.

reflexive anthropology
The anthropology of anthropology, which focuses on the cultural and political bias in ethnographic research, the impacts of anthropologists on the people they study, and professional ethics.

polyphony
The many voices of people from all the different segments and groups that make up a society; a quality of ethnographic writing today that presents multiple views of a culture.

THE ANTHROPOLOGY OF ANTHROPOLOGY

The study of anthropology by anthropologists is called **reflexive anthropology**. It has been developed and championed by anthropologists in the tradition of postmodernism. The goal of such studies is to understand the influence of the observer's culture and society on the nature of the ethnographic data that he or she collects and writes about (Clifford and Marcus, 1986).

The critical theory approach in anthropology has often focused on the political orientations of anthropological research, especially in the context of colonized societies and communities with little power in the global arena. Early anthropologists were supportive of European imperialism of the nineteenth century, and theories such as evolutionism and the related approach of Social Darwinism provided a justification of Western dominance in terms of racial and cultural superiority.

Anthropology's role in contributing to colonial hegemony was tempered by the influences of Durkheim and Boas, who actively campaigned against racism and racial discrimination. Nevertheless structural functionalist and historical particularist theorist have been accused of supporting imperial designs on a more indirect level (Asad 1973). Viewpoints that stressed the presence and importance of order within society and culture may have given implicit justification to colonial and class hierarchies as the only alternatives to social chaos. Their emphasis on homogeneity, continuity, and stasis with the societies they studied may also have supported imperial endeavors, both ideologically and practically, insofar as colonial governments used and sometimes contracted ethnographic data to facilitate the implementation of their policies. For example, E. E. Evans-Pritchard's famous study of the Nuer was funded by the colonial administration of the Sudan in order to inform them about conflict within a group that had not yielded graciously to British rule (Evans-Pritchard 1940). At best, accounts based in a timeless ethnographic present avoided confronting audiences with issues of equity and justice within overseas dependencies, Aboriginal reserves, or urban ghettos.

More contemporary theoretical approaches have tried with varying success to correct cultural, social, and political biases in the interpretation of ethnographic data and formulation of new theories and methodologies. Anthropologists recognize that many voices cooperate and compete in the production of meaning, creating **polyphony**—the many voices of people in all segments or groups in a society. In this context, some anthropologists question the choice of voice in the texts that they produce and their own role in the process of presentation.

Since the 1960s, anthropologists have questioned their role as agents of change as they intentionally or unwittingly facilitate worldwide economic and political processes (Gough 1968). In addition, some anthropologists side with the people they study against oppressive government policies that destroy the people's land and resources or pressure the people to abandon their way of life.

Anthropologists interested in the impacts of North American and European ideologies on other peoples look at the ways groups represent themselves and others and structure people's ideas about these groups. As persons involved in the processes of "writing culture," Western anthropologists influence the representation of non-Western peoples. How do anthropologists write about and present another culture? Often, it is through the construction of the "other" as alien, unusual, different, and exotic. To counteract this tendency, some anthropologists present their findings as a dialogue between themselves and members of the society among whom they have lived. The production of any text, including an ethnography, can be seen as a "dialogic" process with multiple voices and multiple meanings (Bakhtin 1981). In the past, ethnographies tended to present a unified voice in their description of a people's way of life rather than taking a polyphonic voice. Very likely they contributed to cultural stereotypes and depicted greater conformity, uniformity of opinion, and idealized behaviour than were actually present. Deeply contested issues were often glossed over. Because ethnographies focused on a view of culture from the perspective of people with greater prestige and privilege, the voices of marginalized members of communities were muted or unheard.

In addition, because in the past most anthropologists were male and because they worked primarily with male consultants, ethnographies tended to be told from a male perspective. Women's concerns, women's lives, and women's voices were relatively unknown and unheard. Examples of gender bias in ethnological interpretation are common in the writings of some anthropologists. Writing about the Nuer of southern Sudan, for example, the British social anthropologist E. E. Evans-Pritchard concluded that Nuer family life was "remarkably harmonious on the surface" (1955:133). Yet his research, based entirely on the testimony of men, disclosed culturally sanctioned wife abuse and the wishes of both husbands and wives (reported by the husbands) for their spouse's death—not a very harmonious picture, even on the surface! From another perspective, Eleanor Leacock's work on the Innu of Quebec indicates that male anthropologists have misrepresented the importance of women's roles and status in hunting and gathering societies (1981). Today, anthropologists pay more attention to looking past their own subjectivity to more fully represent others.

Because of these problems with the ethnographer's voice, some anthropologists are producing "polyphonous" ethnographies with a multitude of voices. Rather than relying on a single, dominant perspective, they give multiple interpretations of activities and opinions from the points of view of people with different types of roles in the community. The voices of men and women, of the elites and the marginal, contribute to a diversity of representations. By focusing on dialogue and polyphony, anthropologists locate culture not only in behaviour but also in conversation about behaviour, ideas, attitudes, and emotions. Ethnographers also analyze their own issues of power, their relations with communities in their own societies, and their relations with those that they study.

Controversies within the discipline about the role of the anthropologist and the focus of ethnography do not weaken the field but invigorate it with debate, bringing out important issues for thought and dialogue. Anthropology plays a vital role in today's world. The discipline has the tools with which to understand and analyze complex issues of power that structure and confront our world. The theories and methods that anthropologists use provide the knowledge and techniques for understanding people's behaviour and the ways in which they organize, transmit, evaluate, and express their experiences. Anthropologists can contribute meaningfully not only to the collection of knowledge as an academic pursuit but also to debates about public policy in national and international arenas. They can help inform people about the value of all cultures.

? *How do you think your roles and status as a member of your society might affect your observations of other people? How might they colour what you say to an anthropologist interviewing you about your people's way of life?*

Ethical Issues in Anthropology

Other issues concerning anthropology relate to the ethics of conducting research involving human subjects. Cultural anthropologists make their living and build their careers by studying other people. They live among them, learn from them, and write about them. As a result, the most important ethical issues they face involve their relationships with and obligations to those people.

In Canada all anthropological research that involves living people is governed by the provisions of *Tri-Council Policy Statement: Ethical Conduct for Research Involving Humans*. Ethical obligations include respect for human decency, the acquisition of free informed consent, respect for privacy and confidentiality, and minimization of harm and maximization of benefits for the people and communities being studied. These policies are administered within each university by an ethical review board which accepts or rejects ethical statements attached to research proposals. The American Anthropological Association, to which many Canadians belong, has a similar set of guidelines and raises issues about specific cases of ethical dilemma or breaches.

Anthropologists do not agree on their proper roles in relation to the people they study. Perhaps their basic obligation can be phrased as "First, do no harm." For some anthropologists, research is an end in itself. People in the community extend their hospitality voluntarily. And while anthropologists should certainly avoid doing anything that they feel may be harmful (in the short or long term) to the community, some believe that they have no continuing obligation to the people. Other anthropologists believe that they have ongoing responsibilities to the community and lend their help. Anthropologists may be able to collect and analyze documents or testify in court proceedings regarding native territories and indigenous land claims cases

In Their Own Voices

The Delgamuukw Claim

In 1988 a group of Gitksan and Wit'suwit'en chiefs brought a case to the British Columbia court to acquire title to the lands that they occupied. The following text is taken from Chief Delgamuukw's presentation to the court (see the Anthropology Applied feature for further details on the Delgmuukw case).

My name is Delgamuukw. I am a Gitksan Chief and a plaintiff in this case. My House owns territories in the Upper Kispiox Valley and the Upper Nass Valley. Each Gitksan and Wit'suwit'en plaintiff's House owns similar territories. Together, the Gitksan and Wit'suwit'en Chiefs own and govern the 22,000 square miles of Gitksan and Wit'suwit'en territory.

For us, the ownership of territory is a marriage of the Chief and the land. Each Chief has an ancestor who encountered and acknowledged the life of the land. From such encounters come power. The land, the plants, the animals, and the people all have spirit—they all must be shown respect. That is the basis our law.

The Chief is responsible for ensuring that all the people in his House respect the spirit in the land and in all living things. When a Chief directs his House properly and the laws are followed, then that original power can be recreated. That is the source of the Chief's authority. The authority is what gives the fifty-four plaintiff Chiefs the right to bring this action on behalf of their House members—all Gitksan and Wit'suwit'en people. That authority is what makes the Chiefs the real experts in this case.

My power is carried in my House's histories, songs, dances, and crests. It is recreated at the Feast when the histories are told, the songs and dances performed, and the crests displayed. With the wealth that comes from respectful use of the territory, the House feeds the name of the Chief in the Feast Hall. In this way, the law, the Chief, the territory, and the Feast become one. The unity of the Chief's authority and his House's ownership of its territory are witnessed and thus affirmed by the other Chiefs at the Feast.

By following the law, the power flows from the land to the people through the Chief; by using the wealth of the territory, the House feasts its Chief so he can properly fulfill the law. The cycle has been repeated on my land for thousands of years. The histories of my House are always being added to. My presence in this courtroom today will add to my House's power, as it adds to the power of the other Gitksan and Wit'suwit'en Chiefs who will appear here or who will witness the proceedings. All of our roles, including yours, will be remembered in the histories that will by told by my grandchildren. Through the witnessing of all the histories, century after century, we have exercised our jurisdiction.

From Wa, Gisday. 1989. *The spirit in the land: the opening statement of the Gitksan and Wet'suwet'en hereditary chiefs in the Supreme Court of British Columbia.* Gabriola, B.C: Reflections. Used with permission of the Gixsan Chiefs' Office.

CRITICAL THINKING QUESTIONS

On what basis is the author claiming to be the "real expert" in this case? How does his testimony compare to the way in which an anthropologist might represent Gitksan culture? How might a judge evaluate the truth and relevance of his claims to territorial title?

(See the Anthropology Applied feature on page 51). Others can use their training and knowledge to represent native interests in dealings with local and national governments. At the least, anthropologists can present information about the needs of indigenous communities to the public in their writings and in classes. As experts, they can talk to the media, countering negative stereotypes about poor and marginalized peoples.

Anthropology Applied

Expert Witnesses in Aboriginal Rights and Title Cases

In 1982, the Canadian constitution introduced an important clause that recognized "aboriginal and treaty rights of aboriginal people," at least in principle. Subsequently, First Nations communities initiated legal claims to have territorial and resource rights recognized for groups that had not signed treaties with the Canadian government and to review existing treaty provisions. A number of landmark cases came before the courts, most notably the British Columbia Delgamuukw case, which will be considered at length below, and the Marshall decision, which gave rights to Maritime First Nations to engage in commercial fishing without licenses. In many of these cases, anthropologists served as expert witnesses and consultants to provide evidence of Aboriginal occupation and use of territories and interpretations of indigenous cultural understandings of land tenure and resource ownership. Their findings have been important for fair and informed judicial decisions since Aboriginal land use, especially in hunting and gathering societies, differs from that of settled Anglo-Canadian communities, and indigenous provisions for enforcing and adjudicating rights and title claims differ from Western legal conventions.

Several specializations within anthropology have contributed to the settlement of First Nations cases. Archaeologists have provided evidence of the length and intensity of settlement within specific areas. Cultural ecologists and indigenous knowledge specialists have produced land use maps that chart migrations and resource uses of nomadic communities. Economic and political anthropologists have documented important indigenous activities and institutions such as trading systems and leadership, ownership, and conflict resolution practices. Interpretive and symbolic anthropologists have outlined the critical principles of meaning and value that define how traditional communities understood their relationships and responsibilities to the land and each other. Ethnohistorians and folklorists have recounted oral traditions and explained how they encode information about past events and practices.

The contributions of anthropologists have generally been accepted and acted upon. However, some problems of ethnographic evidence have emerged that relate to issues in anthropological theory and research that we have considered in this chapter. Anthropologists have sometimes expressed opposed positions, appearing for both sides of the aboriginal rights issue. For example, in the Van der Peet case over Sto:lo rights to sell fish, the government expert witness, an archaeologist, argued that the group was organized on a band level (see Chapter 11) and therefore could not have had a tradition of commercial resource exploitation. The ethnographer appearing for the Sto:lo maintained that they had a tribal form and engaged in extensive trade consistent with this type of organization (Thom 2003). In other instances the anthropological evidence has been rejected as biased in favour of First Nations, lacking in scientific rigour, and irrelevant to the establishment of legally acceptable facts. In general, arguments based on "hard evidence" such as archaeological sites or land use maps have been accepted, while presentations of oral traditions and interpretations of meaning systems have been rejected.

The issue of the validity of ethnography in court cases was critical to the hearing of the Delgamuukw case in which the Gitksan and Wit'suwit'en First Nations attempted to establish title over the lands in northern British Columbia. Their case was first rejected by the provincial court, mainly because the judge questioned the truth of oral traditions presented in evidence. The case was appealed to the Supreme Court of Canada, which ruled that the trial judge had erred in his decision and that oral evidence should have been considered. The Court did not make an actual disposition but sent the case back to the provincial court which has not as yet acted. In the original trial, four anthropologists gave evidence, three for the plaintiffs and one for the government. Two of the witnesses for the First Nations communities, Antonia Mills and Richard Daly, submitted book length reports which have since been published as ethnographies with additional reflections on the case (Mills 1994, Daly 2005).

The anthropological evidence in Delgamuukw covered a variety of points but focused on the institution of the potlatch (see Chapter 6 for a description of this institution). This ceremony was usually held on occasions when hereditary chiefs claimed their positions of office. The new incumbents and their "houses" gave a major feast for the community, during which tales, songs, and dances acclaimed their status and importance and asserted their rights and responsibilities over territories and people. These claims form a body of oral tradition know as the *adaawak* (Gitksan) and *kungax* (Wit'suwit'en), which constitute evidence of aboriginal title (Daly 2005:35). Other claims to territorial rights were based on reincarnation beliefs, which were "relevant to their deep identity with their land" (Mills 1994:23). In addition, a tale of a great flood was correlated with an actual natural disaster that occurred several thousand years ago to document the antiquity of Aboriginal occupation of the area.

The detailed and complex ethnographic information presented at the trial fell on deaf ears. The judge rejected the oral evidence and dismissed the anthropological witnesses as biased in favour of the plaintiffs, specifically the Gitksan and Wit'suwit'en chiefs, and assessed their evidence as lacking in scientific objectivity and rigour. He then went on to make his own ruling against Aboriginal title because First Nations were "so low in the scale of social organization that their usages and conceptions of rights are not to be reconciled with the institutions or legal ideas of civilized society" (quoted in Mills 1995:15). Ironically, he reaffirmed the discredited anthropology of the nineteenth century while rejecting the findings of contemporary approaches.

CRITICAL THINKING QUESTIONS

While the British Columbia judgement was unacceptably ethnocentric and unjust, it raises issues of objectivity, bias, and representativeness in ethnographic methods and their applications that we have discussed elsewhere in this chapter. Consider the following questions:

1. What problems of objectivity are encountered in anthropological research? How do factors such as small samples, complexity of behaviour, and the effect of the observer's culture and its relationship to the culture under study affect the validity of the data collected? Is anthropology a science that provides provable evidence or a humanity which provides interpretations? What implications does your answer have for the admissibility of ethnographic evidence in judicial proceedings?

2. Does research inevitably involve a biased view of the groups under study, which has shifted from an expression of imperialist and patronizing attitudes to unduly partisan advocacy of indigenous claimants?

3. One of the British Columbia trial judge's objections was that the anthropologists gathered their information exclusively from the chiefs and, by implication, not from other sectors of First Nations communities. How might have contacts with traditional power holders have distorted the portrayal of Aboriginal culture? Could the anthropologists have been engaged in giving voice to the interest of a select group? What implications might granting them greater control of local resources have for different components of Aboriginal communities?

REVIEW

Reflexive anthropology focuses on anthropology itself, the language it uses to describe people, and its impacts on both knowledge and people. Today, many ethnographies are written to reflect polyphony—the many voices of people from all the different segments and groups that make up a society. Concern with the impacts of anthropologists on study populations has led to the establishment of professional codes of ethics for research.

Chapter Summary

Anthropology and the Explanation of Cultural Diversity

- Although the field of anthropology as an academic discipline is only slightly more than a century old, its intellectual roots in Europe go back much farther. It has its origins in the colonial expansion of Europe that began in the fifteenth and sixteenth centuries. Explorers, traders, and missionaries visited and commented on the peoples and cultures they encountered in their worldwide search for land, wealth, and religious converts. During the eighteenth century, European social philosophers consulted the journals and writings of earlier observers. Their evolutionism—proposals about the progress of humankind from one cultural stage to the next—established a basis for later anthropological theories.

- The anthropology that emerged in the late nineteenth and early twentieth centuries in the United States and Europe focused on classifying and comparing peoples and cultures throughout the world, attempting to determine their evolutionary relationships to one another. Two important figures were Franz Boas, who championed attention to historical details, empiricism, cultural relativism, and the predominance of meaning, and Emile Durkheim, who contributed the perspective of structural functionalism.

- Anthropologists have developed a number of conceptual frameworks to explain human cultures. Materialist perspectives (cultural ecology and cultural evolution) emphasize the centrality of environmental adaptation, technology, and methods of acquiring or producing food in the development of culture. Cultural ecology focuses on how the physical environment directly influences the satisfaction of basic human needs and how people's adaptive behaviours interact with other aspects of culture. Cultural evolution focuses on technology. Both perspectives distinguish between emic explanations of behaviour based on the reasons people themselves offer to account for what they do and etic explanations based on the analysts' observations of people's behaviour and other objective criteria. Processual perspectives have given special attention to the problem of agency and investigated how individuals react to their cultural and social settings and form strategies of acquiring wealth and power through the manipulation of values and meaning systems. Marxist approaches focus on issues of class divisions and class conflict in the structure and dynamics of society.

Ethnography and Fieldwork

- The central tool of anthropological research is field-work, especially participant observation. Anthropologists live among the people they are studying for an extended period of time to gain an understanding of their culture from the people's point of view. As participant observers, anthropologists observe and record the communities' activities and participate in them as much as possible and appropriate. Earlier anthropologists focused on foreign cultures, usually small, seemingly isolated indigenous societies. But today many anthropologists work in large-scale societies, including their own, focusing on specific subcultures or communities.

Fieldwork involves multiple tasks, including choosing a research problem and a site for study, finding a place to live, working in and learning an unfamiliar language, and overcoming culture shock.

- In addition to fieldwork, some anthropologists use the techniques of ethnohistory, researching in libraries and archives to learn about past conditions and events relevant to understanding the present lives of the people they are studying. Anthropologists also employ the comparative method in understanding cross-cultural similarities and differences in human cultures.

The Anthropology of Anthropology

- Cultural anthropologists have been concerned with sources of bias in the data-gathering efforts, especially with how their views of other culture are molded by their own meaning and value systems and their political ideologies. They are also concerned with ethical issues involving their relationships with the people they study. They think about what kinds of obligations they may have in return for the opportunity and privilege of living with, learning from, and writing about other people. Some anthropologists feel that they have legitimate roles as advocates for the communities that they have studied, while others see their obligations as scholars to disseminate information that counters negative stereotypes about poor and marginalized peoples.

Key Terms

evolutionism 34	historical particularism 38	etic 40	culture shock 43
diffusionism 34	interpretive	emic 40	judgment sample 44
social structure 35	anthropology 38	agency 41	key informants 44
structural	ethnosemantics 40	Marxism 41	survey research 45
functionalism 35	cultural evolution 40	mode of production 41	reflexive anthropology 48
cultural relativism 38	cultural ecology 40	fieldwork 42	polyphony 48

Review Questions

1. How did anthropology become an academic discipline? What were the principal goals of early anthropologists?

2. What influences did Boas and Durkheim have on the development of anthropology?

3. What main theoretical perspectives do anthropologists use to describe and explain cultural differences and changes?

4. What are the differences between an emic and etic perspective?

5. How might a cultural event, such as a pig feast, be analyzed differently by a cultural ecologist and an interpretivist?

6. What steps do anthropologists take to prepare for fieldwork? What are the key benchmarks in conducting fieldwork?

7. What are some pitfalls of living and participating in family and community life while doing fieldwork?

8. What are the sources of bias in ethnography? How can researchers correct for them?

9. What is the anthropology of anthropology? What are some issues concerning the roles of anthropologists and the writing of ethnographies?

10. What is polyphony? If you were writing an ethnography of your community, which "voices" would be important to include? What different points of view would they reflect? How would they balance your own account of your culture?

11. Is anthropology a science?

Language and Culture

Brueghel, Jan the Elder. *Tower of Babel*. Pinacoteca Nazionale, Sienna, Italy. Copyright Scala/Art Resource, NY.

CHAPTER 3

Preview

1. **What three features distinguish human language from animal communication?**

2. **How are languages described? What are phonemes and morphemes?**

3. **What were Edward Sapir's and Benjamin Whorf's contributions to linguistic anthropology?**

4. **What is a dialect? A jargon? How does language relate to gender, class, and race?**

5. **What might be included in an ethnosemantic study of communication?**

6. **What are some internal and external processes of language change?**

7. **How can the study of languages help reconstruct their histories and the history of human migrations and contacts?**

Now the whole earth had one language and the same words. And as they migrated from the east, they came upon a plain in the land of Shinar and settled there. And they said to one another, "Come, let us make bricks, and burn them thoroughly." Then they said, "Come, let us build ourselves a city, and a tower with its top in the heavens, and let us make a name for ourselves; otherwise we shall be scattered abroad upon the face of the whole earth." The Lord came down to see the city and the tower, which mortals had built. And the Lord said, "Look, they are one people, and they have all one language; and this is only the beginning of what they will do; nothing that they propose to do will now be impossible for them. Come, let us go down, and confuse their language there, so that they will not understand one another's speech." So the Lord scattered them abroad from there over the face of all the earth, and they left off building the city. Therefore it was called Babel, because there the Lord confused the language of all the earth; and from there the Lord scattered them abroad over the face of all the earth.

A Biblical narrative accounting for the diversity of languages (Genesis 11:9).

Creator and Changer first made the world in the East. Then he slowly came westward, creating as he came. With him he brought many languages, and he gave a different one to each group of people he made.

When he reached Puget Sound, he liked it so well that he decided to go no further. But he had many languages left, so he scattered them all around Puget Sound and to the north. That's why there are so many different Indian languages spoken there.

These people could not talk together, but it happened that none of them were pleased with the way the Creator had made the world. The sky was so low that the tall people bumped their heads against it. Finally the wise men of all the different tribes had a meeting to see what they could do about lifting the sky. They agreed that the people should get together and try to push it up higher. "We can do it," a wise man said, "if we all push at the same time. We will need all the people and all the animals and all the birds when we push." "How will we know when to push?" asked another. "Some of us live in this part of the world, some in another. We don't all talk the same language. How can we get everyone to push at the same time?"

At last one of them suggested that they use a signal. "When the time comes for us to push, when we have everything ready, let someone shout "Ya-hoh" that means 'Lift together!' in all our languages." The day for the sky lifting came. All the people raised their poles and touched the sky with them. Then the wise men shouted

"Ya-hoh." Every body pushed, and the sky moved up a little. They kept on shouting "Ya-hoh" and pushing until the sky was in the place where it is now. Since then, no one has bumped his head against it.

A Snohomish narrative accounting for the diversity of languages.

The Snohomish are an indigenous people of Washington State. Their story explains the extraordinary diversity of languages spoken in the Pacific Northwest of North America. It also tells how, despite their differences, the people of the region found a way to cooperate to make the world more to their liking. Like the Snohomish story, the Biblical story of the tower of Babel also explains the origin of linguistic diversity, but it has a very different outcome. In the Biblical story, the creation of different languages stops people from working together, confusing and separating them. In contrast, the Snohomish story depicts a world in which people join together to achieve common goals despite their linguistic (and cultural) differences.

Today, about 6200 languages are spoken in the world, some by millions of people and some by only several hundred. While 6200 is a steep decline from the number of languages spoken several centuries ago, it still reflects a rich array of linguistic and cultural diversity. Languages are repositories of cultural knowledge and history, and as such, they are integral to personal and group identity.

Language is a fundamental part of human behaviour. It is our primary medium for communicating and interacting with one another. We use it to convey our thoughts, feelings, intentions, and desires to others. We learn about people through what they say and how they say it; we learn about ourselves through the ways other people react to what we say; and we learn about our relationships with others through the give-and-take of conversation. Language also forms part of our cognitive system and is used to organize our perceptions and thoughts. In this chapter, you will learn something about the structure of human languages as well as the ways in which anthropologists study the relationship between language and culture.

WHAT IS LANGUAGE?

All animals communicate in some manner, but **language**, is unique (or almost so) to humans. Language has four key features that together distinguish it from other forms of animal communication (Table 3.1). First, language is symbolic. That is, it is based on symbols—the arbitrary association of sounds with meanings. The sounds in the word *cat* have no particular association with the animal the word represents. It is just that, in English, this sound has come to "mean" a particular animal. Even words that speakers think imitate noises (such as the words for the noises animals make) are only stylized approximations. Cats don't really say *meow;* dogs don't really say *bowwow.*

Another feature of language is **displacement**, the ability to communicate about something that is not happening at the moment. Indeed, we use language far more to

Table 3.1 FOUR KEY FEATURES OF LANGUAGE

Symbolism	Based on the arbitrary association of sounds with meanings.
Displacement	The ability to communicate about something that is not happening at the moment.
Productivity	The ability to add words and join them in different combinations.
Duality of Patterning	The independent ordering of speech at two levels: sound and meaning.

language
Any form of communication that involves symbols, displacement, and productivity.

displacement
The ability to communicate about something that is not happening at the moment.

communicate about things that have already happened in the past or will happen in the future than about what is happening right now. Displacement also permits us to talk about imagined events, to tell stories, as well as to deceive or lie.

Duality of patterning refers to independent ordering of speech at two levels: sound and meaning. Language is composed of discrete sounds that have no meaning on their own but are combined to make meaningful words, which are then strung together in sentences. Each aspect of this process involves rules that organize how we speak. For example, the word "blog" and "glob" mean different things. They have the same sounds but combine them in a different order. The word "golb" doesn't mean anything but conforms to the sound rules of English and could be used as a new word. The word "gbol" is not only meaningless but it also violates the rules. However, in a language with a different sound structure, it could be meaningful word. The construction of meaningful sentences from these individual sound units also has rules of its own that form the grammar and syntax of a language. For example I can add a suffix to the word "blog" to identify a "blogger," but the word "globber" would make no sense.

Productivity refers to the fact that words, in turn, can be combined in an infinite number of phrases and sentences. Every language contains many thousands of words and can easily add new ones to reflect the introduction of new items or concepts. They can be combined and recombined to form an infinite number of sentences. In a sense, nearly every sentence spoken or written is a new sentence because it is a new combination of words.

Many nonhuman animals communicate with **call systems**. Unlike human language, these systems consist of a relatively small number of sounds or vocalizations that express moods and sensations, like fear, delight, contentment, anger, or pain. They can be used as warnings, threats, alarms, or requests for attention and affection. Also, research suggests that the calls of some nonhuman primates indicate the direction and location of food sources (Jolly 1985). If so, this ability demonstrates a limited kind of displacement because the animals are signalling information that is not present at the time. But as far as we know, even such intelligent animals as chimpanzees and gorillas, our closest relatives, do not, in the wild at least, talk about their plans for the future or reminisce about the past.

For decades, researchers have been trying to determine whether or not chimpanzees and gorillas can learn language. While these animals are physically incapable of articulating words, they can make intricate hand gestures and can manipulate physical objects. Later studies sought to take advantage of these abilities. In some, chimpanzees and gorillas were taught American Sign Language (ASL), the gestural language of the deaf. In other studies, animals were taught to press keys on computers or to manipulate cutout symbols on boards. Many of the animals learned to recognize and use hundreds of words for objects, actions, and feelings. Some even appeared to make up new words by combining words into compounds.

The difference between the natural call systems of nonhuman primates and their abilities in the laboratory may provide some insights into the fascinating but difficult question of the origin of human language. Chimpanzees and gorillas apparently have a rudimentary capacity for understanding and manipulating symbols but seem not to use it in the wild. Presumably, our prehuman ancestors had the same capacity long before they began using language. If this is so, we can look for the origin of human language in conditions that would have made the complex communication it permits advantageous for survival. Displacement, one of the features of language that distinguishes it from call systems, makes it possible to communicate about the past and future. Perhaps language emerged because of our ancestors' need to apply memories of past experiences to present and future plans in order to coordinate group activities—to relocate their camps,

duality of patterning
The independent ordering of speech at two levels: sound and meaning.

productivity
The ability to join sounds and words in theoretically infinite meaningful combinations.

call systems (signal systems)
Animal communication systems that consist of a relatively small number of sounds to express moods and sensations, like fear, delight, contentment, anger, or pain.

? *How is human communication different from the call and signal systems of nonhuman primates?*

Since the late 1970s, researchers have taught chimpanzees and gorillas American Sign Language in order to study their ability to communicate. Most primate studies reveal, however, that apes do not understand the importance of putting words in order, patterns called syntax.

phonology
Study of sound systems in language, including phonetics and phonemics.

phonetics
Study of the articulation and production of human speech sounds.

phonemics
Analysis of the use of sounds to differentiate the meanings of words.

phoneme
A minimal unit of sound that differentiates meaning in a particular language.

for example, or to plan food-gathering expeditions. Language is also a primary vehicle for the transmission of individual and cultural knowledge. Although we learn from observing other people, we gain most of our knowledge and skills through language, through hearing other people's advice and instruction based on their stored memories and experiences.

Nonhuman primates, as already noted, are physically incapable of speech. The emergence of spoken language thus required changes in the anatomy of the mouth and throat. We cannot know exactly when these changes began to occur or when our ancestors first started to use spoken language. Some researchers suggest it may have been about 100 000 to 150 000 years ago. Almost all agree that the people who, some 40 000 years ago, created the earliest known examples of another characteristically human form of symbolic communication—art—were also speaking to one another.

> **REVIEW**
>
> Four principles that characterize human language are arbitrary symbols (association of sounds to specific meanings, with the sounds symbolizing the item being described); displacement (the ability of people to talk about events, people, and objects that are not present); productivity (the ability to add words and put words together to form sentences); and duality of patterning (the independent organization of language at two levels: sound and meaning). To understand the relationship between human language and animal call systems, researchers began to teach chimpanzees and gorillas American Sign Language and other methods of communicating.

THE COMPONENTS OF LANGUAGE

Languages consist of sounds, structures, and meanings. When we use language, we produce and understand these elements together as a whole. However, we can learn much about how language works by studying each element separately.

Phonology: The System of Sounds

Phonology is the study of sound systems in language. It includes **phonetics**, the study of human speech sounds, and **phonemics**, the analysis of the use of those sounds to differentiate words. The vocal apparatus with which we produce the sounds, or "phones," of language consists of lungs, pharynx, larynx, glottis, vocal cords, nose, mouth, tongue, teeth, and lips (Figure 3.1). As sound is produced, air passes from the lungs through the throat, into the mouth, and then is expelled either through the mouth or nose.

We produce specific sounds by manipulating various parts of the vocal apparatus—for example, by positioning the tongue on the teeth or palate; by closing, opening, or rounding the lips; or by constricting or opening the throat. In addition, sounds are either oral or nasal, voiced or voiceless. Oral sounds are produced when air is expelled only through the mouth; nasal sounds are produced when air passes through the nose. The consonants /m/ and /n/, for example, are nasal. (Linguists use slashes to set off specific sounds.)

Sounds are voiced if they are produced with the vocal cords close together and vibrating; otherwise, sounds are voiceless. The only difference between the English consonants /p/, as in "pit," and /b/, as in "bit," for example, is that /p/ is voiceless and /b/ is voiced.

No language uses the full range of sounds that the human vocal system can produce, but every language organizes the sounds it does use—its phonetic inventory—into a system of phonemes. A **phoneme** is a minimal unit of sound that has no

Figure 3.1
The Vocal Apparatus (adapted from Wardhaugh 1977:33)

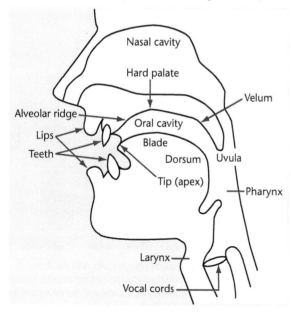

Nasal cavity
Hard palate
Velum
Alveolar ridge
Oral cavity
Lips
Blade
Teeth
Dorsum
Uvula
Tip (apex)
Pharynx
Larynx
Vocal cords

Table 3.2 EXAMPLES OF THE EFFECT OF STRESS ON MEANING IN ENGLISH

Noun	Verb
pre<u>s</u>ent	pre<u>sent</u>
<u>obj</u>ect	obj<u>ect</u>
<u>con</u>struct	con<u>struct</u>
<u>im</u>plant	im<u>plant</u>

meaning by itself but functions to distinguish one word from another. The contrast between the sounds /p/ and /b/, for example, distinguishes the English word "pit" from the word "bit." In English, then, /p/ and /b/ are separate phonemes. Not all sound differences are contrastive within a language. For example, trilling the /r/ in the English word "trill" will not change the meaning of the word. In Spanish, whether or not an /r/ is trilled can distinguish meanings as in *pero* (but) and *perro* (dog).

You learn to apply the rules for differentiating phonemes unconsciously as you acquire your native language in childhood. These rules are not universal but operate within each language according to its own patterns. People who speak a second language with a foreign accent are simply applying the pronunciation rules of their native language to the new one.

In addition to consonants and vowels, several other features of vocal sound can distinguish one word from another. These include stress, pitch, and length. **Stress** refers to the degree of emphasis placed on the accented syllables of words. In some languages, the placement of stress is unvarying. For example, the last syllable is always accented in French, while the next to last syllable is always stressed in Swahili. In other languages, such as English the placement of stress varies and can carry meaning (see Table 3.2).

Many languages also use the vocal **pitch** at which syllables are spoken to distinguish words from one another. Pitch is important in Asian languages such as Chinese and Thai; African languages such as Yoruba, Zulu, and Luganda; Native American languages such as Navajo and Sarcee; and the European language Latvian. For example, in Chinese, the sequence /ma/ can be pronounced with four different pitches or tones, giving each word a completely different meaning:

high level pitch	ma-	mother
high rising pitch	má	hemp
low falling/rising	mă	horse
falling	mà	scold

Pitch is also a feature of sentences. In English, for example, the tonal patterns of statements and questions contrast, with level or falling pitch at the ends of statements and rising pitch at the ends of questions.

Morphology: The Structure of Words

Morphology is the analysis of word structure. Words are composed of units of sound and meaning called **morphemes**. Morphemes may be words or sounds that are not words but carry special meanings when attached to words. In English, for example "-s" is a morpheme that attaches to the end of nouns to indicate plural, as in "cats." Thus, a word may contain combinations of morphemes. "Inactivity," for example, consists of the units of meaning, "in-" (meaning "not"), "act" (a verb meaning "to do"), "-ive" (making the verb into an adjective), and "-ity" (making the adjective into a noun).

Morphologies differ from language to language. For example, Old English had dual personal pronouns in addition to singular and plural ones. Thus in addition to

stress
Phonemic use of accented sounds or syllables.

pitch
Phonemic use of rising and falling speech cadences.

morphology
The study of the internal structure of words and the combination of meaningful units within the words.

morpheme
A unit of sound and meaning, either a separate word or a meaningful part of a word.

syntax
The rules that generate the combination of words to form phrases and sentences.

universal grammar
Abstract rules that underlie the structure of phrases and sentences in all languages, generally thought to be an innate capacity of human thought.

semantics
Study of systems of meaning in language.

"*we*," which has passed into modern English, the form "*wit*" referred to pairs, i.e. you and I only. Many languages, such as French, have morphological gender rules that demand the specification of nouns as male or female.

Syntax: The Structure of Sentences

Most talk consists of phrases and sentences rather than single words spoken in isolation. Every language has rules of **syntax** that govern the ordering of words to show their relationship. In English, for example, the subject of a sentence precedes the verb and the direct object follows it. All the words in the English sentences "The dog chased the cat" and "The cat chased the dog" are the same, but the meanings are different because of the difference in word order.

Each of the world's languages has its own rules of syntax, and these rules vary greatly. Yet all languages share certain features. In all, for example, sentences are composed of subject, object, and verb, and in most languages the subject comes before the object. What varies is the position of the verb. Thus, in English, a basic sentence is ordered Subject + Verb + Object (SVO); in other languages, the basic order is Verb + Subject + Object (VSO) or Subject + Object + Verb (SOV). In only a few languages does the basic word order place objects before subjects.

Since subjects precede objects in the vast majority of languages, this pattern probably reflects human cognition. People perceive subjects as more important than objects because subjects are more active and in control. That is, subjects initiate, control, direct, or affect actions and events. Objects, on the other hand, are not "doers" but "receivers" of actions and therefore are less significant.

According to the linguist Noam Chomsky, a number of abstract rules of word order and sentence construction appear to underlie all languages. These common structural features of language reflect a **universal grammar**, part of an innate capacity for language in the human brain. According to this view, the syntax of any particular language derives from the basic generic structures of universal grammar. The existence of an innate structure may account for the ease with which children quickly learn to understand and speak their native language (Chomsky 1968).

Semantics: The Study of Meaning

The function of language is to express meaning. We hear language linearly, one word at a time, but we grasp meaning as a unified whole. **Semantics**, or the study of meaning, is complicated because a host of factors contribute to that whole. To begin with, words often carry connotations beyond their specific meaning. For example, military officials who talk about "collateral damage" attempt to sanitize the killing of civilians by providing a technical sounding term.

Words or phrases and sentences also convey interactional meaning that varies with the relationship people have with one another as well as the context in which they are speaking. A husband and wife might call each other "sweetheart" at home, but as doctors in the same hospital, they are likely to address each other as "Doctor" at work. Finally, utterances can have affective meaning, indicating attitudes of speakers. For example, "John told me about his accomplishments" is a neutral statement of fact, whereas "John boasted about his accomplishments" is implicitly critical of John. The meanings of words and their use in context are powerful signals of people's intentions and reflect social relationships and cultural norms.

Despite these complexities, linguists have tried to develop tools for identifying some basic rules of semantics. One approach is to analyze words in terms of overlapping and contrasting components of meaning. Linguists have abstracted some components that they claim are universal, developing a kind of universal semantics on the model of the universal grammar of Chomsky and others. Among these meaning components relevant to nouns are "animate" (contrasted with "inanimate") and "human" (contrasted with "nonhuman"). Others include gender ("male" vs "female") and age ("adult" vs "nonadult"). For example, the word "woman" means "animate," "female," "human," and "adult." A change of one component—"female"—to "male" defines the closely related word "man." Similarly, replacing "adult" with "nonadult" gives us "girl" or "boy."

REVIEW

Humans are genetically predisposed to learn language. Phonology is the study of sound systems in language. Different sounds are made through manipulation of the vocal apparatus, whether the sound is oral or nasal, and whether the sound is voiced or voiceless. Phonology includes phonetics, the study of human speech sounds, and phonemics, the analysis of the use of those sounds to differentiate words. Phonemes are minimal units of sounds that differentiate meanings in words. Stress, pitch, and length cause differences in meaning. Morphemes are units of sound and meaning that make up words. Syntax is the word order in phrases and sentences. Universal grammar consists of abstract rules of word order and sentence construction that appear to underlie all languages. Semantics is the study of meaning.

NONVERBAL COMMUNICATION

Human communication is hardly limited to language. We also convey information nonverbally, through gestures, facial expressions, body posture, use of space, and touch. Some forms of **nonverbal communication** may be universal in that they mean the same thing to everybody, regardless of culture. Some research suggests that we share with other primates certain innate or biologically based signals of enjoyment, distress, threat, and submissiveness (Jolly 1985).

In general, the meanings of gestures, expressions, and body postures do not flow from the actions themselves any more than the meanings of words flow from the particular sounds with which they are made. The same gesture may mean one thing in one culture and something entirely different in another. In every culture, some nonverbal actions have the status of **emblems**—gestures often substituted for spoken words that are understood to have a specific meaning. Emblems in European and North American cultures include nodding the head to signal assent, or shrugging the shoulders to convey uncertainty.

Cultural differences in the interpretation of nonverbal behaviours, including **body language**, can lead to cross-cultural misunderstandings. A person from one culture simply may not recognize an emblem or signal used by someone from another culture, in which case no meaning is conveyed. More serious problems can arise when a particular behaviour is meaningful to both parties in an encounter, but the meaning is different for each. Confronted with an act you understand one way but which the other person intends to mean something else, you may respond inappropriately. For example, hand gestures that North Americans routinely make to convey positive support can be offensive in other countries. The familiar "thumbs up," meaning "good job" or "good luck" or "I'm okay," is interpreted in Bangladesh, Australia, and many Islamic countries as the equivalent of the raised middle finger. The "A-O.K." sign, made with the thumb and index finger joined in a circle, means "zero" or "worthless" in France.

A study conducted in Israel suggests how common misunderstandings are in nonverbal as well as verbal

In all primates, certain facial muscles are involved in the expression of fear or anxiety. Recently, however, anthropologists studying nonverbal communication have questioned the universality of even basic kinds of expressions and gestures. Culture, they argue, colours our understanding of any gesture or expression, whatever its origins (Farnell 1995).

nonverbal communication
Communication through gestures, facial expressions, body posture, use of space, and touch.

emblems
Nonverbal actions with specific meanings that substitute for spoken words.

body language
The meanings people communicate through their posture, stance, movements, expressions, gestures, and proximity to other communicants.

What roles will gestures and other body language play in the intercultural communication suggested in this photograph? What meanings will the participants' emblematic behaviours express?

GLOBALIZATION

Some gestures have achieved nearly universal meaning through the process of globalization as different peoples incorporate foreign gestures into their cultural repertoires. One example of this is the peace sign, which is made by extending the index and middle fingers, palm-out, to form a "V." The sign originated in wartime Europe as a sign for "Victory!" which implied a coming time of peace. The original meaning has been extended to mean nonviolence, to signal any hard-won success, and to make a gestural "bunny ears" joke at a peer's expense, commonly seen in snapshots. Many cultures around the world have adopted the peace sign along with one or more of its meanings.

intercultural communication
The communication of meanings between people of different languages and cultures.

intercultural communication. A group of students from fourteen different cultural backgrounds viewed videotaped gestures made by recent immigrants to Israel from Ethiopia. The students recognized 85 percent of the gestures as meaningful. However, of the gestures they recognized, they interpreted only 23 percent correctly to mean what the people who made them intended. They were approximately correct about another 7 percent and misinterpreted entirely the remaining 70 percent of the gestures (Schneller 1988:158). Some gestures, such as the peace sign, have achieved nearly universal meaning through the process of globalization.

In any society, nonverbal behaviours can signal differences in status, just as nonverbal behaviours reveal dominance and subordination among other primate groups. In human societies, determination of who has higher status and who has lower status depends on cultural attitudes. Dominant individuals tend to use broad gestures; look or even stare at others; maintain serious, unsmiling faces; and take up large areas of personal space. In encounters between nonequals, subordinates tend to use restricted, small gestures; avert their eyes when looked at; smile frequently; and allow the higher-status person to encroach on their personal space and even to touch them. High-status individuals try to make themselves appear large; low-status individuals try to make themselves small by lowering their heads and keeping their limbs close to their bodies.

Gender inequalities in North America, for example, are reflected in submissive and dominant nonverbal behaviours that women and men learn as members of their culture. Studies have shown that men are more likely than women to assume a dominant posture, and women are more likely than men to assume a deferential posture. Women typically smile, avert their eyes when looked at, condense their bodies and gestures, avoid encroaching on others' space, and allow intrusions into their own space (Henley 1977; Hall 1984). In studies of mixed-sex interactions, men touched women twice as often as women touched men; men initiated eye contact twice as often with women as women did with men; and women returned smiles of men nearly all the time whereas men returned only two-thirds of the smiles of women (Henley, 1977:115, 164, 176).

REVIEW

Nonverbal communication includes distance between speakers, facial expressions, body postures (body language), gestures, and touching. Nonverbal communication has a basis in primate evolution, but in human cultures few actions have universal meaning. Every culture has a repertoire of nonverbal communication called emblems. Cultural differences in nonverbal (and verbal) communication can lead to misunderstandings in intercultural communication. Common gestures, for example, can have completely different, and sometimes impolite or insulting, meanings in another culture. In human societies, culturally defined status differences, such as gender inequality, can be inferred from nonverbal communication that expresses dominance and subordination.

LINGUISTIC ANTHROPOLOGY

Linguistic anthropology investigates connections between language, culture, and worldview. Researchers study the vocabulary and grammar of particular languages to determine how language reflects and is reflected in culture. Linguistic anthropologists are interested in drawing connections between a people's language and their worldview, defined in Chapter 1 as people's perceptions of their environment, their relations with other people and other creatures, and their concepts of time and space. Linguistic

How would you describe the nonverbal interaction between these individuals?

anthropology also is concerned with understanding the social dimensions of language use, investigating the ways that social categories such as gender, class, and race influence the use and interpretation of distinctive speech styles. These concerns overlap with the field of **sociolinguistics**, the study of the interplay of social variables, such as class, gender, and race, on language use.

The Sapir-Whorf Hypothesis

The two most influential figures in the early development of linguistic anthropology were Edward Sapir (1884–1939) and his student Benjamin Whorf (1897–1941). Both men studied the languages and cultures of several Native North American peoples. And both are associated with the concept—known as the **Sapir-Whorf hypothesis**—that the language people speak influences the way they think.

According to Sapir, language affects all human experience to some extent. Vocabulary in particular reflects what is culturally important to a people and influences what they pay attention to. Speakers give names (words) to important entities and events in their physical and social worlds, and, once named, those entities and events become culturally and individually noticed and experienced. In other words, the relationship between vocabulary and cultural value is bidirectional. Over time, this interdependent process creates and reinforces a unique mental model for each culture. As Sapir noted, "The worlds in which different societies live are distinct worlds, not merely the same world with different labels attached" (1949:162).

As evidence for this conclusion, Sapir examined the vocabulary of the Paiute people living in semi-desert areas of Arizona, Utah, and Nevada. The Paiute, he noted, distinguish fine details of their environment with separate words. Among them are words for (as translated by Sapir) "divide, ledge, sand flat, semicircular valley, circular valley or hollow, spot of level ground in mountains surrounded by ridges, plain valley surrounded by mountains, plain, desert, knoll, plateau, canyon without water, canyon with creek, wash or gutter, gulch, slope of mountain or canyon wall receiving sunlight, shaded slope of mountain or canyon wall, rolling country intersected by several small hill-ridges" (1949:91).

As Sapir's translation indicates, English can be used to describe each of these features, but the Paiute language labels each feature with a separate word and thereby gives it distinctive value. This classification suggests how culturally important these

sociolinguistics
Study of the impacts of socioeconomic and cultural factors, such as gender and class, on language and communication within a society.

Sapir-Whorf hypothesis
The assertion that the form and content of language influence speakers' behaviours, thought processes, and worldview.

In Their Own Voices

Honouring Native Languages

The Spring 2000 issue of Tribal College Journal *focused on efforts by Native North American educators and elders to maintain and increase knowledge of indigenous languages by members of their communities. Contributors to the journal not only voiced their opinions about the types of language revival and maintenance programs suited to their localities but also made explicit connections between language and cultural heritage.*

Knowing diverse languages is important to the country, to the tribes, and to the individuals. Without the language, ceremonies cannot continue; children cannot communicate with their grandparents; and adults cannot voice their prayers. Some attribute their tribes' social disintegration to the loss of their language and culture. "Our moral imperatives are in the language," said Alan Caldwell, director of the College of the Menominee Nation Culture Institute in Wisconsin. On the Blackfeet Reservation in Montana, teachers at the Head Start have noticed that children with behavioural problems have been transformed by their experiences in [language] immersion school. By connecting them with their language, the Head Start instructors link the children with their traditional values. The Winnebago Tribal Diabetes Project Director believes that language classes help improve physical and mental health.

Native languages differ from English not just in the words used but also in the concepts conveyed. The common Navajo greeting, *Ya'at'eeh,* is much more than "Hello, how are you?" To the Diné people, it means, "Everything is good between us," according to Frank Morgan of Diné College. Many common expressions have spiritual connotations, according to Blackfeet Community College language instructor Marvin Weatherwax. In groundbreaking research, Blackfoot language scholars at Red Crow Community College in Alberta are using words and phrases to reconstruct their culture. In the process, they are healing themselves, according to Duane Mistaken Chief. For example, by studying the word *Ainna'kowa* (to show respect), they learned *Ainna'kohsit*—to respect themselves.

The Learning Lodge Institute [a project developed by seven tribal colleges in Montana] has the goal of "using education for the teaching of language and culture," said project director Lanny Real Bird. This dual mission is key. All this helps tribal communities reach a larger goal, said Real Bird. It is part of each college's mission to "empower the cultures so they can empower themselves," he said. This means directing "their own education, their own health, their own government. To utilize their own

kinds of environmental features are to Paiute speakers but not to English speakers. This contrast is consistent with the differences in the two peoples' ways of living. The Paiute depended on hunting and gathering to obtain their food. Therefore, detailed knowledge of their natural environment was crucial to their survival. Similar studies of specialized vocabularies in different languages can provide insights into the cultural attitudes and priorities of the people who speak them and the bodies of knowledge that they have accumulated.

Like Sapir, Benjamin Whorf was interested in the influence of vocabulary on culture, thought, and behaviour. Whorf went beyond vocabulary to consider the influence a language's grammatical structures might have on speakers' thoughts and behaviours. Comparing English to the language of the Hopi of Arizona, Whorf noted that whereas English tenses divide time into three distinct units—past, present, and future—Hopi verbs do not indicate the time of an event. Rather, they focus on the manner or duration of an event. He concluded that because of these differences, Hopi speakers have different concepts of time, number, and duration than English speakers do. In turn, because of these differences, Hopi speakers and English speakers perceive the world in fundamentally different ways. As Whorf put it, "Concepts of 'time' and 'matter' are not given in substantially the same form by experience to all [people] but depend upon the nature of the language or languages through the use of which they have been developed" (1956:158).

resources." Language instruction is therefore not an exercise in sentimentality but part of a strategy for self-determination.

A Culture Leadership Program is giving a select group of students a more intensive, culturally based approach to language instruction. In this innovative program, a small group of tribal members spend a year working with Salish elder Johnny Arlee. Language instruction is only one part of the program. Students also learn the traditional activities of the Salish people throughout the four seasons, learning about hunting, preparing game, gathering roots, and other wild foods. Arlee also presents the songs and spiritual aspects of seasonal activities. As a result, language is learned informally but also more naturally, crossing an artificial boundary between language and culture.

Learning Lodge participants believe language is essential for the survival of tribal cultures. Lanny Real Bird summarized it this way: "Without a language to speak, there is no culture because there are words and expressions unique to particular tribes. They are holy and supernatural. To be translated and used in the context of interpretation of another language would not be possible." Marvin Weatherwax gave an example from everyday experience. "I can tell somebody something in English, and it will sound so plain. Maybe I would say, 'Would you give me a glass of water?' But in Blackfeet the same request translates this way: 'Would you please take me to the water?' It has such a different feeling when you say it this way. Each word and phrase has spiritual connotations." So the loss of language is more than the loss of words. Instead, "it would be the loss of culture as it is. I cannot teach you culture. Culture is something you have to live. Through the language we can give a part of the culture that can be lived."

Elders involved in the Anishnabe or Ojibwe language program at the Bay Mills Community College in Michigan said that those who cannot speak their own language are only people whose ancestors were Anishnabe; they are no longer Anishnabe themselves. "It's harsh, but I kind of agree with that view," said Tom Peters, who graduated from the Institute this year. Peters views the Anishnabe language as a sacred gift. "Language is the first step to recovering culture. It's authentic culture because the Native perspective is not taken out of it." His fellow graduate, Sidney Martin, agrees. "The language means everything. It is the powwow, the culture, the basket making, the values," she said. "It is everything." And according to Doris Boissoneau, a language curriculum developer, "If we are going to call ourselves a Nation with sovereignty rights and inherited rights, we need a language and a culture. The fires have never gone out amongst the Anishnabeg. They have dimmed. The adults and Elders are rekindling the fires, and they will burn even brighter and rekindle the hopes of all Anishnabe."

From "Honoring Native Languages, Defeating the Shame," *Tribal College Journal* (Spring 2000). Essays by Marjane Ambler, Paul Boyer, and Jennifer Dale. Reprinted with permission from Tribal College Journal of American Indian Higher Education, **www. tribalcollegejournal.org.** Copyright © 2000.

The concepts underlying the Sapir-Whorf hypothesis focus on differences in the ways that language expresses and influences speakers' knowledge and attitudes. However, these differences do not imply that any language is superior to any other, only that people adapt their language to fit their environment and culture; that is, a language with a more elaborate set of words in any one category expressing certain concepts is not superior overall to any other language. And, although language may have a role in affecting the way people view the world, it is not strongly deterministic but consists of indirect links; that is, the words and structures of a language may set guideposts but do not ultimately constrain people's thoughts. Finally, since languages and cultures change all the time, there is no exact fit between a particular element of language and a particular element of culture.

Language, Culture, and Society

Most linguistic anthropologists today understand that language influences thought, and at the same time, thought influences language. The idea that language is an intimate part of culture and shapes people's worldview has influenced efforts to maintain or revive indigenous languages in Hawaii, New Zealand, Australia, North America, and other places. In regions where most native peoples no longer speak the language of their ancestors, community members have developed projects aimed at preventing

Ann Henshaw's work in Baffin Island indicates that the Inuit language, Inuktitut, contains eleven distinct words to designate cloud formations. This terminology provides useful information for predicting the weather that is critical for how people move on the land. Climate change has led to unfamiliar cloud patterns and more erratic weather that is testing the accuracy of such indigenous knowledge systems.

language loss. Many of these projects are based on the importance of the role of language as an integral part of cultural identity and cultural vitality.

In Canada, First Nations and Inuit language loss has proceeded at a dramatic pace. Only 25 percent of people claiming an Aboriginal identity speak an Aboriginal language as a mother tongue and less than 20 percent use an Aboriginal language in the home. Of fifty aboriginal languages currently spoken, only three—Inuktitut, Cree, and Ojibwe—have more than 10 000 speakers and have any assurance of survival. Most of the others are in danger of disappearing. For example, only 350 people speak Mohawk as a mother tongue and only 35 regularly use it at home (Norris 1998). Efforts are being made to retain and restore language knowledge and use in many Aboriginal communities. In the territory of Nunavut, which has an Inuit majority of over 80 percent, Inuktitut holds the status of an official language along with English and French. Legislation guarantees its use as a language of instruction and on all pubic signage. Many other aboriginal communities are also making efforts at revitalization through special school and community-based programs (see the In Their Own Voices feature on pages 64–65). However, these efforts have encountered some problems. The development of standardized forms of language can at times privilege some communities over others and create a gap between what is formally taught and actual vernacular use. Students are sometimes resistant or hesitant to use language forms which are imposed on them in a classroom setting (Patrick 2005). Generally, less than 25 percent of people who learn an Aboriginal language at school are fair to excellent speakers as opposed to 75 percent of those who learn it at home (Norris 1998).

The Study of Language Speakers

Linguistic anthropologists also study the demographics of specific languages—that is, the frequency, distribution, and range of languages and their variants within a nation, region, or geographic area. This is a concern that overlaps the work of sociolinguists. In Canada, language is a critical political issue that has in part defined our national identity. As the Case Study on page 67 demonstrates, the official policy of bilingualism has had different implications for majority and minority speakers in different provinces. Moreover, the majority of the population is of neither English nor French background, and 18 percent of Canadians have a mother tongue other than French or English. As immigration continues to serve as the main source of population growth, multilingualism will become increasingly significant for future generations.

Language, Politics, and Society in Canada

Language issues have played a prominent role in the formation of Canadian society and have had wide and complex influences on personal identity, political process, and access to opportunities. The most important element of Canada's language policy is the *Official Languages Act* of 1969, which established French and English as the country's official languages and mandated the use of both in all activities within the jurisdiction of the Federal Government. Additional provisions were included in the *Consumer Packaging and Labelling Act* in 1974 and *Canadian Constitution* in 1982. Constitutional provisions include a guarantee of primary and secondary education in either language to "linguistic minorities" throughout Canada, i.e. anglophones in Quebec and francophones in the rest of the country. Less specific recognition is extended to Aboriginal languages and those of immigrant groups "in a manner consistent with the preservation and enhancement of the multicultural heritage of Canadians" (Government of Canada 1982).

The government explicitly developed its bilingual policy in order to meet francophone concerns that their rights and statuses were not accorded due recognition within confederation and that their numbers, influence, and identity were declining due to the dominance of anglophone Canadians, who outnumber their francophone counterparts by a ratio of almost three to one (59 percent to 23 percent of the population). This imbalance has been strengthened by the large influx of immigrants, 90 percent of whom speak or learn English, and by the spread and influence of English as the main language of global communication. Recognition of francophone concerns

has been expressed in terms of a need "to adapt to the new realities, notably the 'Quiet Revolution' in [a growingly militant] Quebec" and "to establish a working relationship between two linguistic communities" (Canadian Heritage website). Similar provisions have been extended within areas of provincial responsibility in all of the provinces, both within the mandated area of education and for other public services. However, New Brunswick is the only officially bilingual province. Alberta and Saskatchewan have passed legislation proclaiming English as their official language, while French is the sole official language of Quebec (Hudon 2007).

Quebec's official language policy has adopted the most notable provisions within the country because of its concern with the preservation of French and the maintenance of francophone identity both within Quebec and the wider Canadian framework. In addition to exclusive recognition of French, laws have been passed to ensure that French is more prominently displayed than English or any other language on all signage. French is also the official language of instruction, and minority rights to public education in English are extended only to children of Canadian citizens who were educated in English within Canada and children of non-Canadians who received education in English in Quebec. As such, most immigrant groups, even those whose mother tongue is English, must attend French schools. These language regulations and other measures to enhance "francization" are placed under the jurisdiction of an imposing bureaucracy, the *Office Québécois de la Langue Française*.

Canada's bilingual policy and Quebec's attempt to preserve its language and heritage have met with mixed results that have forestalled rather than reversed the decline of French. Over the 40-year period that language policies and programs have been implemented, the percentage of Canadians that are proficient in both official languages has grown from 12 percent to 18 percent of the population, an impressive 50 percent increase. However, the distribution of bilingualism among different communities shows a marked divergence by language group and region. Nationally, less than 10 percent of anglophones can speak French, while the proportion of bilingual francophones is almost five times as high. In both cases, official language minorities contribute more heavily to bilingualism than do majorities. Sixty-seven percent of anglophones living in Quebec can speak French, as opposed to 7 percent elsewhere in Canada) (See Figure 3.2). Similarly, 85 percent of francophones outside of Quebec can speak English compared to 36 percent within Quebec (Marmen and Corbeil 2004).

Figure 3.2
Speakers of Official Languages by Linguistic Community and Region

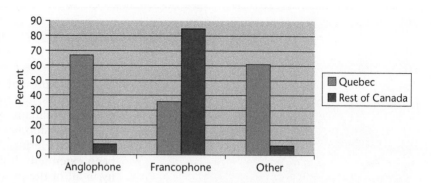

Other problems with minority language representation and preservation are evident in basic statistical trends. Since 1950, the relative size of the francophone community in Canada has declined by 25 percent. Outside of Quebec it has declined by almost 50 percent (see Figure 3.3). Losses are partially attributed to the increasing numbers of immigrants, who usually speak languages other than English or French. However, direct language loss among francophones due to assimilation and intermarriage has also been important. A corresponding 50 percent reduction of the English-speaking community in Quebec has occurred over the same period, although for different reasons. Anglophones have moved out of the province in large numbers in response to militant language policies and the separatist movement within the province.

The trends in bilingualism and in language learning and language learning and retention indicate that policies and efforts at federal and provincial levels to foster French and accommodate differences between English-speaking

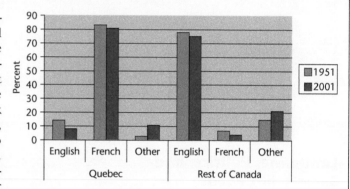

Figure 3.3
Changes in Mother Tongue.

and French-speaking communities have been less than effective. The patterns that are emerging indicate a decline of French, especially outside of Quebec, and increasing polarization between Quebec and the rest of the country.

Language and Dialects

All language communities contain regional or other variations in the ways that people speak. People in one group may pronounce sounds differently than those in another, or use different words for objects or actions, or structure sentences in a distinctive way. Taken together, these differences are called **dialects**. Even in small-scale societies, dialects vary from village to village. In modern nations with large territories and diverse populations, regional distinctions abound, especially in pronunciation or *accent*.

Among English speakers in North America, a Canadian accent differs from an American accent, with regional variants prevalent within each country. Similarly, accents differ among English speakers around the world, from Britain to Australia and India. You immediately notice a speaker's accent and can often guess where he or she comes from. Dialects also have distinctive vocabularies. Canadians use the term *eaves-troughs* for what Americans call *rain gutters*. Canadians turn on a *tap* while Americans turn on a *faucet*. Other differences include *chocolate bar* vs *candy bar*, *cutlery* vs *silver-ware*, *washroom* vs *restroom*, and *zed* vs *zee* (that is, the letter /z/). Canadian usage has shown some adoption of American forms. What once was a *chesterfield* is now a *couch* (Chambers 1995). *Zee* has an interesting dynamic. It has replaced *zed* among school age children, who switch to *zed* as they get older.

Canadian English dialect variation occurs over six major regions: the West, Ontario, Montreal, New Brunswick and Nova Scotia, Prince Edward Island, and Newfoundland. Because of its late entry into Confederation and a high incidence of West Country English, Irish, and Scottish immigration, Newfoundland English is the

dialect
A variety of a language spoken by a particular group of people, based on regional differences or social differences such as gender, class, race, or ethnicity.

most distinctive and is the only Canadian variant for which a separate dictionary has been produced (Story 1990). It has unique features of pronunciation, grammar, and vocabulary as the following sentence demonstrates: "I thinks this is unlawful, and as others informs me is onproper and onpossible, and this the liviers [settlers] here, all could tell ye." English speakers in Montreal have distinctive usages that reflect direct or indirect borrowing from French. Thus a convenience store is a *depanneur* and an ATM machine is a *guichet*. When they order a pizza with everything on it they use the term "all dressed," a direct translation of *toute-garnie*. Although less distinctive, other regional difference can be observed. Maritimers go to the *cabin* over the summer, while Westerners go to the *cottage* and Montrealers go to the *chalet*.

Language variants are also apparent among francophone Canadians. The two main dialects, Quebec French and Acadian French, differ substantially from Parisian French, which is generally considered to be the standard form for use in formal contexts, such as government or instruction. Both vernacular forms involve distinct pronunciations and word use which reflect the retention of words and forms no longer used in the standard language as well as Canadianisms and English **loanwords**.

loanwords
Words borrowed from one language into another.

Language and Gender, Class, and Race

In addition to region, languages may vary based on social categories such as gender, class, and race or ethnicity. The study of such differences is central to the field of sociolinguistics and forms an important part of inquiry in linguistic anthropology. Sociolinguists tend to focus on the social dimensions of language use in large urban societies, whereas linguistic anthropologists investigate these issues among peoples and languages of indigenous communities.

Since gender is a powerful feature of personal and social identity, it is often reflected in language use. Women and men may differ in the frequency with which they use certain pronunciations or words. In both North America and England, for example, women and girls are more likely to pronounce words ending in "ing"—*running, talking*—according to standard usage, whereas men and boys are more likely to employ colloquial usage, clipping the "ng" sound, as in *runnin'* and *talkin'* (Trudgill 1972). Men also are more likely than women to use profanity and obscenity. Gender differences can be great. In some societies women speak an entirely different language dialect among themselves than that used by men.

Accent and usage differ with class as well. Middle-class speakers studied in North America, England, France, and Belgium, for example, tend to use longer sentences and more complex grammatical constructions than working-class speakers (Labov 1972b; Trudgill 1974; Lindenfeld 1969; van de Broeck 1977). Differences in pronunciation, word choice, and grammar often become part of what defines ethnic and racial identities.

In most contemporary countries, one dialect is selected as "standard." There is nothing inherently "better" about this dialect than any other; rather, its dominance is the result of social, economic, and political factors. Usually, the dialect of a society's elite—the educated, the prosperous, and those in power—becomes the standard. In England, for example, the dialect of English spoken within the geographic triangle linking the cities of London, Cambridge, and Oxford emerged as standard sometime in the fourteenth century. This area was and continues to be Britain's economic and political centre. In North America, upper-class pronunciations often retain the sounds of standard British English which, in turn, is based on the dialect of upper-class British. Similarly, the French-Canadian elite speak standardized Metropolitan French, while members of the working class and rural dwellers tend to use Québécois or Acadian vernaculars.

? *What are the characteristics of your dialect, and what does that say about who you are?*

Language Standardization

As we have seen, languages tend to diverge into different dialects according to region and social category. Differences usually increase over time, and eventually the variants

Standard English
The dialect of English chosen as normative, a reflection of the social, economic, and political standing of its speakers.

code-switching
Changing from one dialect or language to another according to the context in which one is speaking.

become separate languages. In some contexts, primarily within large and powerful states, standardization policies have been introduced to counteract this process. For example, prior to 1861, the inhabitants of what is now Italy spoke at least three different languages and over a dozen dialects. With unification, the new nation adopted a standard form which most Italians had to learn as a second language. Such a policy was obviously warranted. It fostered communication between fellow citizens and acted as a symbol and force for national unity. However, it also created difficulties for those regions and classes which continued to use vernacular dialects and became stigmatized and marginalized the more they deviated from the norm. Standard pronunciation and usage are considered "correct" and other versions are considered "wrong" or "debased." Speakers of the standard dialect gain prestige and respect, whereas speakers of nonstandard dialects are looked down upon. Speakers of nonstandard dialects may look down on themselves as well, thinking that their speech reflects their educational and even moral shortcomings (Bourdieu 1991). For example, standard Italian is based on the Tuscan dialect and privileges northern Italians over southerners.

In the United States, language use identifies people by race and ethnicity. Many, but by no means all, African Americans in the United States speak a dialect known as African-American English. Some speakers use this dialect all the time, whereas others use it only within certain contexts—with family and friends, for example—and speak **Standard English** in other situations—as in school or at work. Individuals also switch from one dialect to the other, depending on the topic under discussion and the attitude and identity of the people they are speaking with, a process know as **code-switching**.

African-American English, also known as Ebonics, has patterned rules of phonology, syntax, and semantics equivalent to those of any other language or dialect. Most of them are identical to those of Standard English, except for a few regularly occurring exceptions. The current consensus among linguists is that some features of the dialect derive from the speech of rural white southerners—itself derived from the Scots-Irish dialect of the region's early white settlers—and that other features, particularly several grammatical rules in the verb system, have their origins in African languages. In consideration of the effectiveness of the language form, some educators in the United States have attempted to change the educational policy of discouraging vernacular use to adopting it as an aid to establishing literacy and a more positive attitude towards education within disadvantaged communities.

Some research supports the effectiveness of this approach (Rickford 1997; McWhorter,1997). In one study, children in kindergarten and first and second grades took a standard reading test that had been translated into African-American English. They scored significantly higher than children who took an untranslated version (Williams 1997:212). A more extensive undertaking, the Bridge Program pursues a strategy of conducting early years education in the vernacular and then gradually introducing Standard English to provide a smooth transition from variant to standard language use. After four months in the program, students' reading ability substantially exceeded the national norm (Rickford 1997:179). While this evidence suggests that the dual-language approach is the best answer, others believe that immersion in Standard English is preferable. Black scholars and public figures writing in special issues of *The Black Scholar* (1997) and the *Journal of Black Psychology* (1997) devoted to the Ebonics controversy argued both points of view.

To gain perspective on this controversy, consider the social context in which African-American English-speaking children may resist learning Standard English. When people elevate a particular language or dialect over another, they convey a message of superiority. Children in countries such as Switzerland, Germany, and Scotland who grow up speaking a regional dialect learn a standard dialect of their language easily when they enter school (McWhorter 1997:12–13). Unlike these European children, however, African-American children may confront a legacy of racial and regional prejudice and social attitudes demeaning to them as well as to the way they speak. As one commentary concludes:

> Many of our students resort to not learning as a means of resistance. . . . We need to help them move beyond the resistance that keeps them stifled and saddled in the same place. We are advocating that educators provide Black youths with the history of Black and

Culture Change

NONSTANDARD FORMS OF FRENCH IN CANADA

Standardization and adherence to a central set of linguistic norms has perhaps been even more salient for French than for English. France was the first country to institutionalize its language through the activities of the officially established *Academie Française,* which have focused on the elimination of regional variants and defended the language against the incorporation of English loanwords. The Academy's activities are paralleled in Canada by the *Office Québécois de la Langue Française,* which has balked at establishing a Canadian standard and continues to promote the use of Metropolitan French based on the Parisian dialect. However, its rulings sometimes differ from those of its French counterpart. The *Academie* mandates that the masculine form, *le minister,* be used to refer to a woman who holds the position, while the *Office* supports the use of a feminine alternative, *la ministre,* perhaps in recognition of a more gender-sensitive society.

The use of standard French has been an important issue in Canada because of the prevalence of dialect variants in Quebec and the Maritimes. These forms are widely used within working and rural classes and by a wider segment of the population in informal contexts. French-Canadian elites generally disparage these forms as indicative of poor education and language ability and as corruptions of the language because of the large body of English loanwords within their vocabularies. The official language authorities have generally ruled against these vernaculars, and the education system promotes the use of Standard French. Paul Laurendeau (1992) argues that the campaign against "*joual*" in Quebec intensified in the 1960s as a rallying point for the emerging elite within a changing economic and political order.

Because of the status implications of using the vernacular, speakers of these dialects often find themselves in a quandary over whether to use a mother tongue that provides them with comfort and identity or to adopt a form that carries higher prestige. Dilemmas are often solved by code switching according to the circumstances of communication. However, some situations may influence more permanent changes in usage. A comparative study on the impact of globalization on French use in Canada indicates that new forces are simultaneously weakening and strengthening distinct Canadian language forms.

Sylvie Roy (2004) has carried out a study of francophones in Ontario and Alberta who are employed in industries that require French speakers for their clientele. The Ontario case involves a call centre in a small town providing services to credit card holders, mostly in Quebec. The community has enthusiastically supported this enterprise as a force for counteracting the local decline of French. However, the company's policy has had an effect on which form of French is supported. It hires only people who can demonstrate good knowledge and use of Standard French and demands that the standard form be used in all services, even though clients would understand the vernacular. Roy argues that this policy extends from the call company's emphasis on Standard French as indicative of efficient business practice and as a way of exercising control over its workers; consequently, the loss of the Canadian dialect has been accelerated. Roy maintains that the Alberta case of the tourism industry has had a reverse effect. Local francophones are needed to provide services for francophone tourists from around the world. Employees are hired on the criteria of their identity rather than language use; consequently, vernacular forms are tolerated. A similar study of francophone tourism in Nova Scotia (Boudreau and White 2004) found that the use of Acadian French became a positive asset in meeting the tourists' desire to experience a distinctively local culture. However, the employees had mixed reactions to interactions with their visitors. Some were embarrassed by the local vernacular and switched to Standard French or Quebec French. Others used and sometimes exaggerated local forms out of a sense of pride in their community.

Standard English and encourage them to critically examine these two linguistic forms and the social and political situations that created them. Merging this knowledge with the pride and confidence that comes from a healthy sense of self and peoplehood, Black youths can move forward knowing the differences between languages and the value of language and culture, never having to surrender one language (Black English) for another (Standard English). (Smitherman and Cunningham 1997:230–231)

? *What do you think is the best approach to the education of African-American English-speaking children, and why? Would you encourage the introduction of similar programs into educational systems of vernacular-speaking communities in Newfoundland or Quebec?*

Issues in nonstandard language use are also prevalent in Canada, both within anglophone and francophone communities. Newfoundland English represents a distinctive regional dialect with unique features of pronunciation, vocabulary, and grammar. Its peculiarities are employed to comic effect on national radio and television but are also disparaged both nationally and among the more educated and urbanized elite of the province. Consequently, its use is declining at the expense of regional colour and some of the indigenous knowledge that is incorporated into its content. Similarly, Quebec and Acadian French have been under assault within the francophone community as the Culture Change feature on page 71 shows.

REVIEW

The field of linguistic anthropology examines the interrelationships between language and culture, for example, how language both influences and reflects a culture's worldview. The Sapir-Whorf hypothesis argues that language predisposes people to selectively perceive and think about things in certain ways and that those ways affect their behaviour and attitudes. Dialects, regional and group distinctions of a language, can include differences in pronunciation and vocabulary. They can vary by gender, race, ethnicity, and social class or socioeconomic background. Sociolinguistics is the study of the impacts of socioeconomic and cultural factors on language and communication within a society. Standard dialects, such as Standard English, usually are derived from the versions spoken by social elites. Speakers of alternative vernacular forms are often disadvantaged and beset with the dilemma of adopting standard norms or maintaining their regional, cultural, and social distinctiveness.

ETHNOSEMANTICS

? *What jargons do you use? How do you use them?*

ethnosemantics
Study of culture through people's use of language to categorize and classify people, objects, activities, and experiences.

jargons
Specialized or technical words and expressions spoken by people who share a particular occupation or interest.

Indigenous knowledge system
Body of classification, folklore, observation, and practice that local people have developed to adapt to their local environment.

Building on the pioneering foundations of the first half of the twentieth century, linguistic anthropologists have broadened their exploration of the relationship between language and culture. Some continue to study what vocabulary can reveal about the structure of human thought. Others investigate how cultural values and symbols are encoded in words or expressions and are then used by speakers to transmit emotional, attitudinal, and symbolic meanings. Researchers also examine the systems or ways in which words categorize people, objects, or forces in their physical and social environments, a field called **ethnosemantics**.

Studies of vocabulary usually focus on the comparative analysis of how words form categories within the systems of classification, such as words for animals, words for parts of the body, words for colours, words for phenomena such as weather, or kinship terms. Linguistic anthropologists also study occupational **jargons**, the specialized vocabularies used by people who share specific communication needs relating to their work or some other activity. Philosophy professors, baseball announcers, web hosts, and thieves are examples of groups that use jargons to communicate.

The ways in which vocabularies stress meaning distinctions and define categories are often based on specific knowledge that people have about their societies and environments. Accordingly, ethnosemantic analysis has become a critical element of the construction of **indigenous knowledge systems** that often contain useful information that has been incorporated into Western scientific literature and applied to local development projects. For example, ethnobotany, the study of indigenous plant classification and use, has led to the discovery of new drugs and helped communities plan and manage changes within their environments. Analysis of folk classification in other domains, such as weather, has yielded similar benefits (see the Anthropology Applied feature on page 77).

Table 3.3 COMPONENTIAL ANALYSIS OF TERMS FOR HORSES

Age	Gender		
	Male	**Female**	**Neuter**
Baby	*Foal*		
Juvenile	*Colt*	*Filly*	
Adult	*Stallion*	*Mare*	*Gelding*

Componential Analysis

By analyzing similarities and contrasts among the words in a category, you can learn something about what is culturally important to the speakers of a language and how they experience their world. This comparative approach, called **componential analysis**, involves isolating components of meaning within the words in a category. The goal is to understand the ethnosemantics, or indigenous systems of meaning, of a culture or group and its members.

Take, for example, words for animals in English. For some animals, English has many more words than it does for others, and these differences reflect differences in cultural interest. For horses, English has separate words that specify gender and age (see Table 3.3) The distinctions incorporated into this terminology, male-female-neuter, and baby-junvenile-adult constitute the components and reflect the principles of classification applied. English has a similarly extensive vocabulary to differentiate age and sex among cattle and other domestic food and draft animals, which have played a crucial role in the subsistence and economy of English-speaking peoples. In addition, many words are used to distinguish different breeds of these animals. In contrast, other species—chipmunk, otter, and moose, for example—are treated in a more generalized way, with only one term for all members of the class of animals.

Ethnosematics also reveals differences of meaning that are applied to the classification of humans. For example, Brazilians differ from North Americans in the way that they categorize people into physical types. They use over 40 terms to mark differences in physical appearance, while North Americans use only four or five. This semantic richness marks a different degree of concern with "race" in the two cultures. However, the systems vary not only in the number of terms but in the way in which they distinguish among them. In Brazil, race is determined mainly by skin colour, while in the United States and Canada, the "one drop rule" applies. A person is considered to be Black if he or she has a single Black ancestor in his or her genealogy (Harris 1964).

Ethnography of Communication

Linguistic anthropologists analyze speech behaviour and nonverbal communication in their widest cultural and social contexts. Dell Hymes (1974) introduced the term **ethnography of communication** to describe the study of all explicit and implicit norms for communication—verbal and nonverbal—in a particular setting. Included in such a study would be a description of the setting in which the communication occurred, the participants involved, the language they used, the way they communicated (speaking, writing, nonverbal signals), the genre or form of the communication (conversation, folktale, chant, debate), the topic or subject of the communication, and the attitudes and goals of the participants (1974:10).

An ethnographic description of communication in a courtroom, for example, might run like this: The setting, a courtroom, is structured to provide separate seating areas for various categories of participants and to regulate contact between participants. Among the participants are judges, lawyers, defendants, plaintiffs, witnesses, jurors, spectators, and court officials. Participants behave according to their role in the proceedings. The judge, seated on a raised platform at the front of the room and

componential analysis
A technique of analyzing the similarities and contrasts among words in a particular category, such as kinship terms or animal names.

ethnography of communication
Study of communication as it occurs within a particular cultural context, considering such features as settings, participants, and participants' attitudes and goals.

As a cultural anthropologist, what might you say about the ethnography of communication in a setting like the one in this photograph? Who are the participants, what language do they use, how do they communicate and in what forms, what are the topics of communication, and what are the participants' attitudes and goals?

distinguished by special attire, physically dominates the room. From this dominant position, the judge controls the communication of the other participants, each of whom has certain obligations to speak or not to speak. Failure to obey the judge may be considered "contempt of court," a legally punishable offense. Only judges, lawyers, and witnesses may speak publicly. Other participants (jurors, spectators, officers) must remain silent. Each type of participant communicates in expected ways. Lawyers may make introductory and concluding statements or ask questions. Witnesses answer questions. Judges make statements, ask questions, and issue commands and rulings.

Topics of discussion in a courtroom are rigidly defined. A trial is intended to resolve a specific issue, and all communication must be relevant to that issue. The goals of participants vary according to their roles in the proceedings. Speakers choose their words, tone of voice, facial expressions, and gestures to accomplish their goals. The judge seeks to appear impartial, lawyers speak and act persuasively or aggressively, defendants may portray themselves as innocent, witnesses appear honest and reliable, and jurors remain silent but convey interest in the speech and behaviour of others.

> ### REVIEW
>
> Ethnosemantics, or indigenous systems of meaning, can lead to a better understanding of what is important in a culture. Systems of meaning include jargons, which are specific to certain occupations or activities. Examples of word comparisons using componential analysis include kinship terms and terms for animals. The shared knowledge and assumptions that speakers use are cultural presuppositions. The ethnography of communication involves examining all aspects of communication (setting, participants, topics, and goals) to understand language as cultural expression.

PROCESSES OF LANGUAGE CHANGE

Languages change over time. Change sometimes results from processes internal to a language. For instance, a language may gradually eliminate grammatical distinctions, meanings of words may be altered, or the order of words within sentences may change. Evidence of such patterns can be found in the history of English. Old English (the language spoken in the British Isles until about 1066, the year of the Norman invasion from France), had noun endings that indicated whether the noun was a subject or object in a sentence. Modern English nouns lack these markers. However, English retains distinctions between subject and object for pronouns: "I, he, she, we, they" are subjects, whereas "me, him, her, us, them" are objects. "You" can be either subject or object. Modern English is currently undergoing a further loss of the subject-object distinction in the relative pronouns "who" and "whom." While the object form "whom" is still used in writing and formal speech, most speakers no longer use it in colloquial and informal contexts. We are therefore witnesses to ongoing language change.

Changes in the meanings of words also are commonplace. When modern English speakers read the works of William Shakespeare, for example, they often have difficulty understanding them because some words that Shakespeare used have different meanings today and others have gone out of the language entirely. Many nations try to "freeze" their official national language in time through such institutions as the *Academie Française*.

Language change is constant and natural as new words and expressions are invented and others discarded and as vocabularies are elaborated to reflect cultural priorities. Thus, people who are concerned about the "purity" of their language are chasing a phantom. Also, cultures often change more rapidly than languages. As a result of this "linguistic lag," a specialized vocabulary may not reflect a society's current cultural interests. In time, as linguistic change catches up with cultural change, the specialized words are likely to change meaning or to disappear.

Lingua Francas

Languages also change in response to the influence of other languages For example, English has a vast number of French words that were introduced in the language by the Norman invasion. It has borrowed words from other languages as well, such as whiskey from Gaelic, patio from Spanish, kibitz from Yiddish, orange from Arabic, and tomato from Nahuatl (Aztec). This kind of change is universal because no language is completely isolated from others. External change occurs when peoples with different languages and cultures come into contact, with three possible general results: The languages will remain distinct; one language will become dominant; or the languages will meld into a new language.

One important process of language change involves the creation and adoption of lingua francas. **Lingua francas** are languages that are used among numerous peoples who come into contact regularly but who speak distinct languages. For example, Swahili is a language spoken as a mother tongue in a small zone on the East African coast. However, it was widely adopted as a trade language throughout most of East Africa because of the prominence of Swahili merchants in the region. In West Africa a modified form of English known as pidgin English has become a lingua franca due to the British influence in the trade in the area. Although it is a second language for most West Africans, it has become a mother tongue, known as Krio, for Sierra Leonian communities founded by repatriated slaves from English possessions, including Nova Scotia. When a derived language becomes a mother tongue, such as Krio, it is known as a **creole**.

Through today's dynamics of globalization, English is now spoken by more than a billion people throughout the world, rivalled only by Chinese. English has become global in three ways: countries such as Australia and South Africa are dominated by English-speaking inhabitants; countries with few native English speakers nevertheless have English as an official language; and many other countries give priority to English in foreign-language learning.

Historical Linguistics

Among groups of people who speak variants of a language, differences between dialects can accumulate to the extent that people no longer understand one another. Thus, mutual intelligibility is a definition of language as shared by its speakers. When

? *In your experience, what are some examples of new vocabularies that reflect changing cultural priorities?*

GLOBALIZATION

Through todays dynamics of globalization, English is now spoken by more than a billion people throughout the world, rivaled only by Chinese. English has become global in three ways: countries such as Australia and South Africa are dominated by English-speaking inhabitants; countries with few native English speakers nevertheless have English as an official language; and many other countries give priority to English in foreign-language learning.

lingua francas
Languages used in particular areas by speakers of many different languages in order to communicate with each other.

creole
A language that has historic roots as an amalgamation of vocabulary and grammar derived from two or more independent languages.

Of the many different languages spoken in India, Hindustani remains the lingua franca of the western and northern regions. It is often used as the language of choice in popular culture. The Indian film industry produces movies in Hindustani. This industry is called Bollywood, a conflation of Bombay (a city today called Mumbai) and the American Hollywood.

language family
A group of languages that are historically related, descendants of a common ancestral form.

cognates
Words in different languages that are derived from the same word in their parent language.

? *Relationships between languages are determined by finding regularities in sound shifts between cognates. What regular sound shifts can you identify in the following Indo-European cognates for "father"?*

Examples of Indo-European Cognates

father (Modern English)
fader (Middle English)
faeder (Old English)
fader (Swedish, Norwegian, Danish)
vader (Dutch)
vater (German)
pater (Latin)
padre (Spanish, Italian)
père (French)
pai (Portuguese)
pate-r (Greek)
pitar (Sanskrit)
pita- (Hindi)

people no longer understand one another, new separate languages emerge. Tracing changes in languages over time and relationships between languages in the past is the goal of historical linguistics.

Over time, from centuries to millennia, as the descendants of people who spoke a single language separated from one another and migrated into different regions, their speech changed into distinct dialects and ultimately, when speakers could no longer understand one another, into separate languages. Mutual intelligibility is often taken as a test of whether two forms of speech are dialects of the same language or two different languages. By comparing the sounds, vocabularies, and syntax of today's languages, historical linguists can reconstruct the processes that led to change, grouping languages into families descended from a common ancestral form. A **language family**, then, is a group of languages spoken by people who are historically related.

One method for determining the relationships among languages, estimating when they separated, and even reconstructing features of the parent language is to study a core vocabulary of up to 500 words. This core vocabulary consists of words for objects or ideas that every language can be expected to have words for, including pronouns, some numerals, some colours, words for body parts, and common adjectives (such as large, small) and verbs (such as to eat, to sleep). Words with related meanings that are found to share a common heritage are referred to as **cognates**. The English speech and the German *sprach* are cognates, for example. English and German are related historically, and both are members of the larger language family called Germanic, which also includes Dutch, Danish, and many others. The Germanic languages originated in an even older language which gave rise to such diverse IndoEuropean languages as French, Hindi, Farsi, and Ukrainian.

Language families provide insight into the historical relationships between neighbouring and even distant peoples. For instance, if neighbouring groups speak unrelated languages, they probably did not always live near one another. They may both have migrated to their current locations from elsewhere, or perhaps one had long residence in the region and the other was a more recent immigrant. And if the language spoken by one group of people is related to a language spoken hundreds or even thousands of miles away, both groups have a common ancestor that spoke their one ancestral language.

Anthropology Applied

Inuit Indigenous Knowledge

TRADITIONAL ECOLOGICAL KNOWLEDGE

The Canadian Arctic is a beautiful and fragile landscape in which the Inuit have survived for millennia through their knowledge of the land and water and of the sea ice that forms a shifting boundary between them. Currently the environment, the people, and a unique nomadic way of life (see Chapter 5) are under threat because of government policies, development projects, pollution, and environmental change. Global warming, which is still a remote threat in most of the world, has already made deep inroads into the expanse of ice fields so important for Inuit winter migrations and has modified the abundance and distribution of natural species on which they depend.

Concerns for the future of the region have resulted in research and planning to mitigate environmental and social problems at international, federal, territorial/ provincial, and community levels. While physical scientists, such as climatologists and biologists, have played a critical role in these activities, an interest in local Aboriginal accounts of previous conditions and ongoing changes has developed. Accordingly, anthropologists, linguists, and indigenous communities are adding valuable insights on environment in terms of local perceptions, understandings, and adaptation through the field of traditional environment knowledge. Utilizing linguistic and anthropological data collection and analysis techniques, traditional knowledge specialists have provided important information on local ecologies that Western-trained "hard" scientists often overlook because of unfamiliarity with unique local conditions. The Government of Nunavut's *Memorandum of Understanding* with the Federal Government includes a clause endorsing "cooperation to advance knowledge of climate change impacts and adaptation strategies in Nunavut through Inuit *Qaujimajatuqangit* (traditional knowledge) and research" (quoted in Henshaw 2006a). NGOs, such as the Canadian Circumpolar Institute and Inuit Taparrit Kanatami, include indigenous knowledge in their development plans. Arcticnet, an academic consortium of 57 universities based in the Université de Laval, includes anthropology and indigenous knowledge studies within its interdisciplinary research agenda.

Anne Henshaw's work among the Sikusilarmiut (Cape Dorset Inuit) on Baffin Island, Nunavut (2006a, 2006b) provides a good example of how indigenous knowledge studies are carried out and applied to understanding current environmental change. Among other areas of inquiry she has found linguistic analysis within the domains of weather terms and place names particularly useful.

The Sikuslarmiut have a detailed classification of atmospheric conditions and utilize this knowledge to predict weather patterns and plan their movements over the landscape within their nomadic cycles. For example, they have eleven categories of cloud formations which help them to forecast temperature, precipitation, wind, and ice conditions. Climate change has been documented by the appearance of rare or unaccustomed cloud forms and unusually variable and unpredictable weather.

The naming of geographical locations, or toponymy, provides an equal wealth of detail about environmental conditions and changes. Inuit place naming encodes several components based on references to land form, ecological features, climate, harvesting activities, and settlement and migration route patterns. These factors provide a unique description and analysis of the local ecology, providing cues for eliciting additional ecological knowledge through memory, story, and myth. They also provide information about change, since place names sometimes designate features that have undergone modification after they were named. For example, two out of three places that are designated as seasonal snow house settlements are now located outside of land-fast ice, suggesting that warmer conditions have been prevalent. The implications of such environment knowledge and experience are important for other regions for which the Arctic may serve as a testing ground for how we deal with global warming and other environmental problems in the future.

CRITICAL THINKING QUESTIONS

How might differences in outlook, land use, and group interest oppose the views of government, industry, conservation groups, and indigenous communities on environmental action? How might these economic and political interests colour the construction of environmental knowledge?

Plotting the distribution of related languages helps to trace the history of migrations, contacts, and conquests among the world's peoples. Although no one knows when or how the first language was spoken or who spoke it, some historical-comparative linguists believe that they might one day be able to reconstruct "proto-human," the first language spoken by the first modern humans.

REVIEW

All languages change through time. Sounds shift, words change meanings, words are borrowed (loanwords), new words are invented, and languages become extinct. Language change can be both internal and external. Processes of language change that result from culture contact include the creation of pidgins and creoles. Historical linguistics is the comparative study of changes in languages over time and relationships between languages and language families in the past. Divergence of languages is measured by comparing changes in core vocabularies to find cognates, words from different languages with shared sound shifts and similar meanings. Historical linguistics can provide insights into the history of human migration and contact and relationships between contemporary cultures.

Chapter Summary

What Is Language?

- All languages are based on arbitrary symbols for relationships between the sounds of a word and the object, activity, quality, or idea that the word is used to name. Languages are characterized by displacement—that is, the ability to talk about events of the past and the future, not just events that are ongoing at the moment of speech. And languages are productive, in that sounds, words, and sentence constructions can be joined in infinite novel combinations.

The Components of Language

- Linguists have developed numerous descriptive and explanatory tools to analyze the structure of language. Talk is achieved through the interdependent components of sounds, words, sentences, and meanings. Although every language is unique, there are some universals, including the human range of phonetic inventories, recurring types of morphological and syntactic constructions, and underlying semantic relationships.

Nonverbal Communication

- Nonverbal communication also consists of both unique and common behaviours. Although some actions may occur in many societies, they are always given culturally specific interpretations.

Linguistic Anthropology

- Linguistic anthropologists investigate associations between language and cultural meaning. Some study the degrees of specialization and principles of classification within semantic domains that indicate cultural interest. Others examine the "presuppositions" inherent in words and expressions that transmit and reinforce complex social and cultural messages.

- African-American Vernacular English is a variety of speech employed by some (but not all) people of African ancestry in the United States that diverges from Standard English. It has some unique features, although it shares most linguistic rules with the standard variety. Attitudes toward vernacular speech are complex, both on the part of the speakers themselves and in the rest of society. Controversies focus primarily on proposals to incorporate vernacular speech in schools.

- Canada is a complex, bilingual and multilingual nation. English and French are official languages and a large proportion of the population speak other languages. These include languages of indigenous peoples as well as languages spoken by immigrants from every corner of the globe.

Ethnosemantics

- An "ethnography of communication" attempts to uncover all of the rules that connect language to social behaviour. Components of any speech interaction include the participants, the code used, the physical and social settings, the topic of conversation, and the goals of the speakers.

Processes of Language Change

- All languages are in constant processes of change. Some change derives from internal linguistic processes while others derive from contact with other languages. New sounds may be introduced and/or grammatical constructions may be altered. In addition, all languages borrow words from foreign sources to name introduced items, activities, or ideas.

- When varieties of the same language diverge to the point where people speaking different dialects can no longer understand each other, new languages come into being. A language family consists of languages that are related historically and are the common descendants of an ancestral code. Using methods of historical and comparative linguistics, researchers establish relationships among languages by discovering regular correspondences between their sound systems.

Key Terms

language 56
displacement 56
duality of patterning 57
productivity 57
call systems
  (signal systems) 57
phonology 58
phonetics 58
phonemics 58
phoneme 58

stress 59
pitch 59
morphology 59
morpheme 59
syntax 60
universal grammar 60
semantics 60
nonverbal
  communication 61
emblems 61

body language 61
intercultural
  communication 62
sociolinguistics 63
Sapir-Whorf hypothesis 63
dialect 68
loanwords 69
Standard English 70
code-switching 70
ethnosemantics 72

jargons 72
indigenous knowledge
  system 72
componential analysis 73
ethnography of
  communication 73
lingua francas 75
creole 75
language family 76
cognates 76

Review Questions

1. What are the connections between language and culture?
2. Why are chimpanzees and other apes unable to communicate verbally? How do they communicate symbolically? What are some differences in primate communication under laboratory conditions and natural settings?
3. What characteristics distinguish phonemes? What is the difference between a phoneme and a morpheme?
4. What are some applications of the Sapir-Whorf hypothesis? How are language and thought connected?
5. What is sociolinguistics and how does language relate to social issues in Canada?
6. Why have some societies attempted to enshrine standard language forms that their members must use? What effect do standardization policies have on different groups and classes?
7. What are some internal processes of language change that occur in all languages?
8. What are some processes of language change that occur as a result of cultural contact and forces of globalization?
9. What are the goals and methods of historical-comparative linguistics? How are all human languages ultimately related in space and time?

Learning One's Culture

CHAPTER 4

Preview

1. **What is enculturation?**
2. **How do people incorporate children into their society?**
3. **What are the social, cultural, and psychological effects of rites of passage?**
4. **What are some formal and informal means by which individuals learn their culture?**
5. **What social and cultural factors influence an individual's age- and gender-related behaviour?**
6. **How do culture, personality, and human psychology intersect?**
7. **In what ways is mental illness both culture-specific and universal?**

There once lived a widow, Ballingokan, and her son, Agkon. Every morning the rooster would wake up Agkon by crowing: "Kook-ko-ko-oook! Agkon, come and trap me." Agkon would answer, "Wait, I'll first look for some fibers to make up my snare." The next day, the rooster again jumped on Agkon's window and crowed: "Oo-oo-oo-o! Agkon, come and snare me." And Agkon said, "Wait, I'll get some strings for my snare." On the third day, the rooster flap his wings loudly and cried out: "O-oo-ook! Agkon, when will you come?"

Agkon ran out, laid his snare with care, and after a few moments it caught a wild fat rooster, which he proudly showed to his mother. "What a nice fat rooster. Now we shall have some nice food," his mother said happily when she saw the rooster.

Agkon burned the feathers of the rooster, cut it into pieces, and began to cook it. When it was almost cooked he dropped the ladle. "Mother," Agkon cried, "I dropped the ladle." "Never mind," his mother said as she quickly went out of the house, "I'll pick it up."

As soon as his mother was down, Agkon quickly drew up the ladder. Then he asked for the ladle and after telling his mother that he would eat first and call her later, he proceeded to do so. After a while the mother said, "Agkon, please leave the wings for me." "But the wings are delicious, mother," Agkon said and started to eat them. "Leave me the claws, my son," the mother pleaded. "They are just what I want, mother," he said. "Surely, you will leave me the neck, Agkon." "It is just what I am eating, mother," Agkon said.

Only the head was now left. "Agkon, my son, will you not give the head to your mother?" "But, mother," Agkon answered, "you know very well that I need to eat the brains."

When nothing was left of the rooster, Agkon put back the ladder and the mother wearily went up the steps. She looked at the pot and found a little soup left, which she took, and mashing some rice in it, ate in tears. She decided to revenge herself on her son.

The mother went upstream and after walking for a long time she heard loud weeping and found a family mourning over a man who had been dead [for a long time]. Ballingokan offered to buy the dead man, but the relatives were already happy to have someone take care of the dead so they gladly gave it to her free. She told the Ladag [Dead Man], "I will carry you on my back." The dead man climbed on her back and she brought him to her granary where she covered him with rice. Then going to the house she called her son and said, "There are some ripe bananas in the granary."

Agkon went down and peeped inside the granary where the Ladag caught him and proceeded to eat him. He shouted to his mother, "Mother," he cried, "the Ladag is eating my feet." "That is for the claws of the chicken that you would not share with your mother," the mother answered. "Mother, the Ladag is eating my arms." "But you did not give me the wings either, my child," his mother said. "Now he is eating my breast, mother." "Neither did you share the breast of the rooster with me, my son." "He's beginning to feed on my neck, mother." "Well, you ate the neck of the rooster, Agkon." "Go ahead, Ladag," said the mother, "eat his head."

That night, Balligokan felt lonely; there was no one to talk with. The following day, there was no one to carry fuel, no one to help her. Her loneliness was worse, and feeling sad, she went to the granary to look for any remains of her son. She found a little blood on the floor, which she took, and going to the river began to perform some ritual. She took some water and began to bathe the blood and said, "May I bathe Agkon! May I bathe his hands!" At once his hands were formed.

And as she said, "legs, feet, arms," all were formed into a man.

Then the mother and son were reconciled and both resolved to love each other truly. And Agkon said, "Mother, from now on, we shall always eat together!"

Excerpts from *Folktales Told around the World*, by Richard Dorson. pp. 257–259. Copyright 1975. Reprinted by permission of The University of Chicago Press.

This tale relates in vivid images the consequences of wrong behaviour. Agkon violates cultural rules of how one ought to treat other people, especially relatives and especially one's own mother. As punishment, he is eaten by the Ladag, as his mother wished. But in the end, she relents and brings him back to life because she recognizes that she needs him too. The narrative therefore teaches children proper behaviour and highlights the economic and social reciprocity that characterizes relationships among kin.

Culture is fundamentally a symbolic system. All humans have the capacity to learn any culture, but the specific culture they learn is the one in which they are born and raised. The process by which children acquire their culture is called **enculturation**, and it is similar to the process of learning social norms, called **socialization**. This chapter examines how enculturation works, then looks at a related issue, the relationship between culture and individual personality.

THE PROCESS OF ENCULTURATION

Humans are born helpless, too weak and uncoordinated to move on their own. Without speech, they are unable to communicate their thoughts, needs, and wants to others. Infants, as a result, are completely dependent on adults to be carried, cared for, and fed. Even after they can walk and talk, children remain dependent on adults. Indeed, humans have the longest period of juvenile dependency of any animal species. We don't reach sexual maturity until around the age of thirteen or fourteen, and don't reach full adult maturity until a few years after that.

Many evolutionary pressures account for these characteristics. Infant helplessness probably resulted from a combination of the increasingly large brains of our ancestors and their shift to an upright, or bipedal, posture. Structural changes in the skeleton that made bipedalism possible also favoured immature births, before infant head size grew very large. The lengthy period of childhood dependency reflects the human characteristic that a large brain made possible—culture. Where other animals depend mostly on their physical adaptations for survival, humans rely on culture. But culture is learned, and learning it—enculturation—takes a long time.

All societies have beliefs and practices surrounding childbirth and maternal and infant care. Ju/'hoansi mothers in Namibia and Botswana are attended by healers when they are in difficult labour. The healers go into a trance (called *kia*) in order to confront the spirits causing harm to mother and child (Katz 1982). The healer lays his or her hands on the mother's abdomen, transferring healing energy and substance (called *num*) in the hopes of protecting the mother and baby.

After the birth, mother and child often remain in their separate dwelling or room for a prescribed length of time. During that period, the mother may follow similar food, activity, and contact restrictions as she had before the birth. After a set number of days, weeks, or even months, the woman and her child are reincorporated into family and community life. That final transition and re-incorporation may be marked by ritualized blessings on both mother and child.

In all societies, the process of enculturation begins as soon as a baby is born and continues into maturity. Infants may be helpless, but they are immediately responsive to the world around them. Gradually, they learn how to communicate through gesture and sound, and they learn how to understand the myriad messages sent their way. Children not only learn to control their muscles, make purposeful actions, and acquire the

enculturation
The process by which children acquire their culture.

socialization
A similar process to enculturation that emphasizes social rather than cultural factors in learning one's culture.

language and communication practices of their society but also, most crucially, they learn to behave in ways that their culture deems appropriate.

Enculturation is so extraordinarily effective because it takes place primarily through informal, nonexplicit means. Because we learn most of our cultural rules unconsciously, we come to feel that our behaviour is natural, a result of our nature rather than our culture. And since we feel that our behaviour, attitudes, and values come from our nature, we generally don't question their appropriateness. Instead, we "naturalize" our culture, viewing these behaviours and attitudes as part innate rather than recognizing their cultural origins. Naturalization of attitudes and behaviours results in unquestioning acceptance of cultural norms. The practices that we engage in and the values that we hold become so much a part of our thoughts and feelings that we do not see them as distinct from ourselves. Rather, we see them as forming our very essence as people. We seem to absorb cultural messages without conscious effort, beginning with the great dependency of infancy and continuing through childhood's protracted period of physical, psychological, and social maturation.

While enculturation is a process begun in earliest childhood, learning one's culture does not end upon reaching adulthood. Rather, people learn throughout their lives, continually acquiring new skills but also continually reshaping and reinforcing attitudes and values. Life's experiences teach new lessons that may encourage people to question old ways of interpreting behaviour, or they may strengthen their convictions. Just as maintaining traditions reinforces cultural stability, discoveries and innovations enrich individuals and societies.

Becoming a Human Being

When does human life begin? This question may be familiar because of the heated debate over abortion, but there is more cultural variability in the answer than the two positions heard frequently in that debate: conception or birth. In many cultures, newborns are not considered human until a few days or even weeks after birth. They are thought instead to occupy some liminal (in-between), transitional, and not fully human state. Not until the end of this period are infants thought of and treated as members of their family and community. This transition to personhood, or **social birth**, is often marked by ritual.

Among the Lohorung Rai of eastern Nepal, babies are introduced to the ancestors when they are five (girls) or six (boys) days old (Hardman 2000). Until the rite is performed, infants (and their mothers) are thought to be both in danger and dangerous. As yet unprotected by the ancestors, they are vulnerable to harm from evil spirits. This vulnerability and lack of protection make them dangerous to other people, who avoid contact with them. The rite raises the child's ancestral soul and introduces it to the house ancestors, placing it firmly within its family and wider kinship group. Failure to perform the ceremony or to perform it well jeopardizes the child's future health and chances for success.

The Zuni of the American Southwest consider newborns to be unripe or soft "as are germinating seeds or unfinished clay vessels" (Cushing 1979:205). For eight days after birth, babies and their mothers are isolated indoors, away from the sun, until they are sufficiently hardened for safe exposure to "the world of sunlight." At the end of the period of seclusion, the baby's umbilical cord is buried nearby and the burial site becomes the child's "midmost shrine," connecting it to Earth Mother and the underworld from which the ancestors emerged in primordial times. At sunrise on the eighth day after birth, the baby's paternal grandmother washes the baby's head, puts it in its cradle, places cornmeal in its hands, and takes it out into the dawn air, facing east toward the rising sun. While other female relatives of both parents sprinkle offerings of cornmeal to Sun in the east, the paternal grandmother recites a blessing prayer (Bunzel 1932).

Practices of delayed social birth are generally found in societies that have (or had) high rates of infant mortality. High rates of infant mortality may discourage parental emotional attachment to their child. An infant is most vulnerable right after birth, and the belief that it is not yet fully human can temper parents' grief should it die during this period. For similar reasons, in many cultures deaths of infants or young children are not marked ritually in any significant way. The body is instead disposed of quickly

social birth
Social recognition of the transition to personhood.

and without ceremony. In contrast, in societies with comparatively low infant mortality rates, social birth may even precede actual birth—for example, in customs such as sending fetal sonograms and holding baby showers.

Beliefs about the humanity of infants also reflect a psychological accommodation to the political and economic circumstances that foster high infant mortality. According to a belief prevalent among impoverished communities in northeastern Brazil, for example, infants who are sickly, weak, and passive are thought to be uninterested in living (Scheper-Hughes 1989, 1992). In contrast to robust, emotionally engaged infants, sickly infants are thought to *want* to die. They are consequently often ignored, inadequately fed, and little cared for. Those who die are not mourned. A mother's tears are thought to weigh down the infant's angel wings and hinder its ascent to heaven. These beliefs may provide comfort to the child's mother, but they also divert attention from the crushing poverty responsible for the region's high infant mortality rate. Rather than a victim of its circumstances, the child becomes an agent in its own demise.

? *How were you named, and why? Does your name have any special meaning or carry any special expectations?*

Naming. An important process linked to the recognition of a baby as a social person is naming. In North American societies, a child is usually named at birth or before. Children may be named after a relative or friend of the parents, or they may be given a name from a large stock of familiar names or one that is made up. Some people name their son after the father or, more rarely, a daughter after the mother. Others, such as members of the Jewish faith, never name a child for someone who is living but prefer to name a child after a deceased relative.

In some First Nations societies, people often receive new names at various times in their lives, sometimes in hopes of obtaining spiritual powers or protection. For instance, a nineteenth-century Hidatsa woman from North Dakota recounted the reasons for her name change from "Good Way" to "Buffalo-Bird Woman":

> I was a rather sickly child and my father wished after a time to give me a new name. We Indians thought that sickness was from the gods. A child's name was given as a kind of prayer. A new name often moved the gods to help a sick or weakly child. So my father gave me another name, Waheenee-wea, or Buffalo-Bird Woman. My father's gods were birds; and these, we thought, had much holy power. Perhaps the buffalo-birds had spoken to him in a dream. I am still called by the name my father gave me; and, as I have lived to be a very old woman, I think it has brought me good luck from the gods (Wilson 1981:8).

On the Northwest Pacific Coast, families held title to names that were attached to chiefly offices. When a person was installed as a new chief he would be required to give a potlatch to validate his right to take on the new name and status.

Baptism for Christians marks a kind of social birth and functions as an introduction to a social and religious community. In many denominations, baptism ideally takes place as soon as possible after birth, because of the belief that if a baptized baby were to die, it would go to heaven. Other theological explanations for infant baptism also exist. Among Baptists and some other groups, however, people are not baptized until they are old enough to understand the significance of the ritual and to make the decision for themselves.

In many societies the choice of a name is never casual and always carries cultural implications. For example, the Ju/'hoansi of the Kalahari Desert in Botswana and Namibia have an extremely complex naming system. The Ju/'hoansi, who until recently were hunting-and-gathering nomads, have only sixty-seven names, thirty-five for males and thirty-two for females (Lee 2003). A name is assigned systematically to each newborn: a first son is named after his father's father, a second son after his mother's father; a first daughter is named after her father's mother, a second daughter after her mother's mother. Subsequent children are named after their father's and mother's siblings. In contrast to European and North American practice, children can never be named after their own parents, nor can they marry someone with the same name as a parent or sibling. Because of this convention, people with the same name are considered to be related regardless of their actual biological connection. People who share a name treat each other as relatives. Being treated like a relative means having rights to live near and share resources with one another. It sets up a network of reciprocal obligations, rights, and responsibilities. The effect of this system is to create a web of relationships throughout Ju/'hoansi society that individuals can call on for access to the Kalahari's scarce resources.

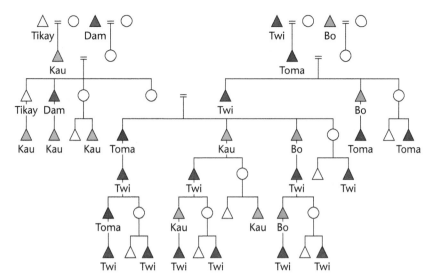

Figure 4.1
This diagram demonstrates an important feature of the Ju/'hoansi naming system—that cousins, many of whom are named after the same grandfather, have the same name. In fact the kin term for cousin, grandparent, and grandchild is the same and actually means "namesake."

Child Rearing

In the process of enculturation, once children are named and thought likely to survive, cultural practices begin to teach them the kinds of behaviours deemed appropriate and mold their personalities. **Child-rearing practices** vary greatly across cultures and across times. There is enormous cultural diversity in attitudes toward infants and children and in beliefs about what they are capable of. There are also cultural differences in practices aimed at teaching children and molding them into the kinds of people acceptable in their society.

Attitudes toward children and child-rearing practices are generally consistent with core values prevalent in a society. In societies where competition for economic resources and for social prestige and power is the norm, children are taught to be competitive and to develop a sense of individuality and uniqueness. In societies where adults need to cooperate economically and to feel part of a network of reciprocal rights and obligations, children are taught to play and work communally. Of course, no society has only one set of values and needs. No matter how competitive an economic and political system may be, people have to cooperate with others in some endeavours. And no matter how cooperative work and social networks may be, people sometimes compete with each other. However, while children in all cultures need to learn both cooperative and competitive strategies, one type is more dominant than another. Although child-rearing attitudes vary within a society, most parents accept the norms prevalent in their communities because these norms are consistent with environmental constraints or social goals.

Child rearing includes both implicit and explicit messages. Children learn by observing other people, seeing the ways in which they interact, and listening to what people have to say about other people's behaviour. Children are also directly instructed about their own behaviour. They may be given explicit directions about how to behave in particular circumstances. They may be praised and rewarded for some actions and criticized, punished, or ignored for others. And in all cultures, children are taught lessons about behaviour and values through storytelling. Sacred narratives and folktales impart fundamental cultural attitudes that children absorb by listening to stories told and retold by respected relatives and elders.

Feeding and Weaning.   In many traditional societies, infants are nursed by their mothers for several years, sometimes for as long as three or four years or until another child is born. They are fed on demand—allowed to nurse whenever they want.

child-rearing practices
Methods used to take care of infants and young children, including ways of feeding, playing with, carrying, and sleeping arrangements.

In other societies, even young infants are put on feeding schedules that conform more to the mother's needs than to the child's. In a classic study, according to data reported for fifty-one cultures around the world and analyzed by John Whiting and Irvin Child (1953), about half of the sample was clustered high on a constructed scale of nursing indulgence. Only a few societies had marked restrictions on infant feeding. The lowest rating was given to inhabitants of the Marquesas, an island group in the South Pacific.

The Marquesans believe that frequent nursing makes a child difficult to raise, too willful, and disobedient. No other groups were as restrictive as the Marquesans, but an American middle-class sample received a rating only two points higher than the Marquesans. Whiting and Child point out that some of the worldwide variation can be explained on the basis of allocation of mothers' time: that is, in societies where mothers can rely on other family members to perform household tasks, more time can be spent providing for and catering to a baby's needs. In societies where mothers have numerous other duties, either within their own households or outside the domestic sphere, they, by necessity, have to restrict their child's access to them.

Both the age at which children are weaned and the weaning process itself vary cross-culturally. In general, in societies where a child can nurse on demand, weaning tends to take place late and gradually, whereas in societies where nursing or feeding is scheduled, weaning tends to take place early and abruptly. Weaning also takes place later in rural or poor communities as mother's milk normally is a reliably available source of food. The interrelationships among these practices form an integrated cultural pattern varying from indulgence to restriction that is consistent with mothers' overall economic duties.

? *Did you sleep in the same bed or room with your parents or other family members as a child? Why or why not? At what age were you expected to sleep alone? To drink from a cup? To feed yourself?*

Sleeping.   Cultural differences are found in sleeping arrangements for infants, young children, and adults. A review of research by psychologists investigating relationships between American sleeping arrangements and children's independence reported that only about one-third of American infants slept in the same room as their parents (co-sleeping) and very few slept in their parents' bed (Morelli et al. 1992). Some studies indicate that more than half of infants as young as two months of age sleep in rooms separate from their parents, and by six months of age, 98 percent of American infants sleep alone. This pattern contrasts sharply with that of "most communities around the world," where infants usually sleep in the same bed with their mothers or, if not in her bed, at least in her room.

Data from the United States indicate variation in different cultural and regional groups. African-American parents are more likely to allow their children to sleep in their bed or room than are Caucasian parents. And all families in rural communities are more likely to sleep in the same room. American middle-class sleeping arrangements are consistent with child-rearing goals that emphasize independence. In contrast, co-sleeping may help develop interpersonal relationships (see the Case Study on page 87).

Physical and Social Stimulation.   The ways children are held and the degree of contact that they have with caregivers and with other children significantly influence their physical and emotional development. In many cultures, children are in nearly constant contact and involvement with other people, either older siblings or adult caregivers. In many societies, babies and young children are carried in slings on the backs or hips of their caregivers. Because of this constant body contact, they move about just as their caregivers do. The physicality of movement, of walking, bending, straightening, and turning, is a constant part of their daily stimuli. In contrast, in some native cultures of North America, babies were placed in cradleboards and carried around on the mother's back. If the caregiver were indoors or working or resting outside, she might prop up the cradleboard against a wall or tree, giving the baby a front-facing perspective and enabling the child to be part of the family group and always in visual contact with others. Other societies require babies to spend a good deal of their waking and sleeping hours separated from other people. In cribs, highchairs, and playpens, children may be essentially isolated from the rest of the family group for significant amounts of time.

Case study

Sleeping Arrangements in Two Cultures

Sleeping arrangements of American middle-class urban families have been contrasted with those of Maya Indians in rural Guatemala (Morelli et al. 1992). While all fourteen Maya mothers in the study slept in the same bed with their infants well into the child's second year of life, none of the eighteen American mothers slept in the same bed with their infants regularly, although fifteen had newborns sleeping in a crib near the parents. As early as three months of age, more than half the American babies were sleeping in a separate room, and by the sixth month 80 percent were sleeping alone. The remaining three American families never shared rooms with their newborns. American parents' comments about their practices revealed their concerns with dependency: "I think that he would be more dependent . . . if he was constantly with us like that" and "It was time to give him his own space, his own territory" (p. 607). These attitudes reveal a focus on individuality and self-reliance.

The researchers also found consistencies between sleeping arrangements and nighttime feedings of infants. Maya mothers allow their babies to nurse on demand during the night as well as during the day. Most of the mothers reported that they did not have to wake up to feed their babies but merely had to turn toward the child to make the breast accessible. American mothers, in contrast, reported staying awake during nighttime feedings even when they nursed their child. Few of them nursed the babies in the parental bed but sat in a chair in their own or the infant's room. These contrasting patterns are consistent with differences in attitudes toward on-demand and scheduled feeding. That is, since American mothers do not sleep in the same bed as their child, they need to interrupt their own sleep to feed their infants and thus strive to keep the baby on a regular schedule. Maya mothers are not disturbed when sleeping, so they are willing to allow the baby to nurse on demand.

Finally, Morelli and coworkers drew a connection between sleeping arrangements and bedtime routines. They noted the elaborate bedtime activities such as dressing for bed and storytelling typical of American families and the need to "coax the baby to sleep," in contrast with Maya patterns, where the transition to sleeping was made easily and without formality. The researchers suggest that American families often experience bedtime struggles because of the stress that infants may have about going to sleep without assistance or companionship. This stress results in the child's fear of falling asleep and being alone.

The contrasts between American and Maya practices reflect differences in each society's attitudes and values. While American parents stress the value of a child's independence and avoid encouraging dependent relationships, Maya parents stress the importance of interdependence between their children and themselves. Maya mothers believe that their children learn social rules more quickly, obey their elders' admonitions, and can be trusted not to touch dangerous objects because of the strong bond between mother and child. One Maya mother commented: "In our community the babies are always with the mother, but with North Americans, you keep the babies apart. Maybe that's why the children here understand their mothers more; they feel close. Maybe U.S. children feel the distance more. . . . If children do not feel close, it will be harder for them to learn and understand the ways of the people around them" (Morelli et al. 1992:610). In the United States, parents are concerned with fostering independence and self-reliance, in keeping with the society's dominant notions of the importance of individuality. Practices of American parents are also consistent with attitudes about privacy, stressing each person's needs for and rights to his or her own private space and own private concerns.

Efe infants and toddlers are always around adults, whom they see and hear performing numerous activities, learning through observation and interaction. They are almost never alone. Through nearly constant interaction with others, Efe children learn how to relate to male and female adults and children. This training leads to a high degree of sensitivity toward others and a "broad array of social skills" (Tronick et al. 1992:575). Given an economy of hunting and gathering, which necessitates initiative and risk, Efe child-rearing practices can be understood as adaptive strategies for survival.

GLOBALIZATION

While fully industrialized nations have tended to make child labour illegal, globalization has contributed to the exploitation of child labour in developing countries. Many organizations are working to help countries solve the problems of poverty and child labour in the face of forces of globalization. Education and improvements in living conditions are critical parts of the solution.

Research carried out among the Efe, a hunting and gathering society of Zaire, increases our understanding of the interrelationships between child-rearing strategies and personality values (Tronick et al. 1992). Observation of Efe children's activities revealed a high degree of interactions with parents, older siblings, community members, and peers. From the very beginning of life, Efe infants (from birth to four months of age) spent more than half their time with people other than their mothers, interacting with five or more different people per hour. And although they were frequently nursed by their mothers, other women nursed them as well. By the age of three, they were having social contact with people not their mothers for about 70 percent of the day. Tronick and coworkers believe that Efe child-rearing practices are enmeshed in economic and social systems that require adults' attention to multiple activities throughout the day. But they also reflect the people's value of "sharing and cooperation" and help to enculturate Efe children in this "intensely social society" (1992:569).

Like every other aspect of culture, child-rearing practices and attitudes toward children are not static. They may change when people introduce and develop new technologies and new ways of living. The possibility of children's contribution to household economies may influence attitudes toward them. In hunting and gathering and in farming societies, children's dependence on adults may be of much shorter duration than in modern industrial societies. This difference is because, in the former, children can begin to work gathering or producing food when they are fairly young. In contrast, children in modern industrial nations are in schools and in training for their future roles until well into their teens. If they go on to post-secondary education, their financial dependence on their parents may be lengthened.

Canada has experienced many changes in the circumstances and patterns of childrearing related to economic and social transformations over the last fifty years. In the 1950s, stay-at-home mothers spent much of the day tending to pre-school children. As women have moved into the workforce in massive numbers, infants and young children are increasingly placed in daycare facilities which have assumed some of their parents' enculturation responsibilities. In addition, changes in family roles and patterns have occurred. Reductions in family size have resulted in children with fewer siblings and very often none at all. Almost 50 percent have experienced a divorce among their parents and 33 percent live in either one-parent families or stepfamilies (see Chapter 8). Many debates have emerged over how these changes have affected personality and behaviour. Some researchers have argued that daycare promotes better cognitive and social development than home care does. Others decry the weakening of close one-on-one bonding with parents. One critical cultural implication of these trends has been suggested. The reduced parental presence may have resulted in a shift of identification and attachment from family to peer group. This change has been marked by the formation of distinctive youth cultures that emphasize and intensify the generation gap (Mate 2005).

Paradoxically, the reduction of parental presence in early childhood has been accompanied by an increase in the age at which children leave home and become independent. Fifty years ago, young adults usually "launched" after turning 21 and married in their mid twenties. Currently, 40 percent of 22-to-29-year-olds still live with their parents, and the average marriage age is over 30. While a number of causes have been observed, the main problem seems to be the greater difficulty that young people are experiencing in finding stable and well paid employment (Beaupré, Turcotte and Milan 2006).

In farming economies, children start work at a young age. Such tasks as scattering seeds, weeding, and manual harvesting can easily be done by children. Children as young as five or six can participate productively in farm labour and are taught to do so by accompanying adults and observing them at work. The Bangladeshi children in this photograph live in an industrializing nation. How do you think attitudes toward child labour will change as Bangladesh industrializes?

? What implications do the changes in conditions and patterns of childrearing have for personality and behaviour in areas such as self-awareness, identity, competitiveness, cooperation, and aggression? How have some of the trends considered affected you and people you know?

REVIEW

Enculturation is the process all humans go through to learn their culture. Enculturation begins with social birth and naming. In all societies, child-rearing practices meet children's dependency needs and include feeding, weaning, sleeping arrangements, toilet training, and physical and social stimulation. Attitudes and values about children and child rearing are adaptive and therefore vary culturally as well as with changing contexts throughout the history of a society.

INFORMAL AND FORMAL LEARNING

Children acquire their culture through both formal and informal means. They learn their future economic and social roles by observing older siblings and the adults in their family. Typically, children play with toys that represent or imitate these roles. In societies with economies based on hunting and gathering, boys play with bows and arrows or other hunting gear, while girls play with digging sticks, carrying devices, and dolls. Among herding peoples, children may begin to accompany adults to take animals to pasture. They observe adults working with animals and assist with minor tasks. In some herding societies, such as the Diné (or Navajo) of the American Southwest, boys and girls accompany adult herders as early as the age of five or six, preparing for the herding roles of both men and women. In other cultures, herding activities are restricted to men. For example, among African cattle herders such as the Nuer of southern Sudan, only men and boys who have been initiated are permitted to tend and herd cattle, although women and children usually milk the animals. Therefore, part of a boy's training consists of observing the work of older boys and adult men in anticipation of maturing and assuming adult roles.

In industrial societies, child labour can be efficient in certain settings, but laws regarding children's work vary from country to country. Children are physically capable of doing hand manufacture and working with light and simple machinery before the age of ten. However, many countries outlaw such practices because of ethical stances held by a majority of citizens or by the world community. In countries where child labour is permitted (whether overtly or covertly), children may be apprenticed to their future employers, acquiring manufacturing skills in home and work settings. In post-industrial societies, children would be in competition with their parents for jobs, a factor that delays the legal age of paid employment.

Learning Skills and Values

In much of the world, children are trained for their future roles in schools, where they learn to read and write, a prerequisite for most of the jobs that they will attain as adults. Education in formal settings so familiar to North Americans also instills competition and conformity even though these two values may seem contradictory. Children learn to compete with each other for the attention of the teacher when they raise their hands to answer questions. They compare their grades on tests and in classes with other pupils. They learn the value of individual achievement, feeling pride in their success or shame in their failure. But children also learn to conform to the rigours of obedience to authority, following explicit rules without questioning them as they are taught to respect the culture of institutions.

Cultural values are powerful influences on people's thinking and behaviour. Values include norms of behaviour, attitudes, and ethics. We manifest our values in how we act toward other people, in what we think about our own and other people's behaviour, and in our notions of right and wrong. These values are taught to children in numerous ways. Children observe how people act, and they hear what people say in the course of daily activities. They may listen to discussions of other people's behaviour, absorbing the attitudes expressed when someone is either praised or criticized.

Values are also transmitted in more formal settings. Children may be given direct instruction, told what to do and what not to do. They may be told why certain behaviour is acceptable and why other behaviour is unacceptable. Some actions or thoughts may even be seen as evil, loading negative attributes about people who commit them. Because children (like adults) want to be perceived as appropriate members of their culture, they learn to act in ways viewed positively and avoid negatively viewed behaviour.

In some societies, proverbs have a significant role in both private and public discourse. Among the Yoruba of Nigeria, for example, proverbs are used in child rearing, in ordinary conversations between adults, and in public and ceremonial settings. Yoruba proverbs teach proper behaviour and transmit cultural wisdom. Examples include "Children are the clothes of men" (that is, a man's most valuable possessions); "A hungry man does not hear sermons"; "Words are like eggs; when they drop, they scatter"; and "You are making love to your thigh" (that is, you are deceiving yourself) (Lindfors and Owomoyela 1973).

Sacred and secular traditional narratives, or **folklore**, convey important lessons about a people's philosophical and ethical principles. The power of the stories comes partly from frequent repetition and social validation. Their power also lies in the artistic and aesthetic appeal of dramatic episodes and heroic characters. The lives of ordinary people can be told and retold, making them larger than life and giving extraordinary meaning to ordinary events. The Philippine narrative that opened this chapter, for example, teaches lessons about the negative consequences of greediness.

Narratives also can be used to criticize someone's behaviour by repeating stories whose moral lessons are known by everyone in the community. For example, Western Apaches use the telling of "historical tales" about former events that had negative consequences to "alarm and criticize social delinquents . . . , thereby impressing such individuals with the undesirability of improper behaviour and alerting them to the punitive consequences of further misconduct" (Basso 1990:115). The tales are aimed at particular hearers in the group who come to understand that the message in the story is directed at them. They are thus encouraged to think about their behaviour and hopefully to profit from the lesson by changing their ways.

Learning Behavioural Expectations

In addition to training for their social acceptance and future occupations, children need to learn how to behave when interacting with other people. Children acquire

? *What are some traditional sayings in your culture that teach moral lessons of industriousness, courage in the face of adversity, and other valued personality traits?*

folklore
Texts that relate traditional stories, the exploits of cultural heroes and characters handed down from generation to generation.

appropriate social expectations and behaviour by observing their elders in the household and community. Because language is a key feature of human interactions, children need to know when to speak and when not to speak and what to speak about. They learn rules of authority and deference. They see how decisions are made, whose voices are heard and whose are silenced, who may exert authority over whom, and who must defer to whom. Children learn the ways in which differences of age, gender, and social standing influence the behaviour of others and mold their actions and speech. Through trial and error, they understand what behaviours are appropriate because they are corrected, reprimanded, or punished for transgressing social rules. Children also learn important lessons about social privilege because they see that certain people are occasionally permitted to violate social norms while others are not. These are powerful lessons children learn informally through which they construct themselves as social individuals with specific social identities (see the Case Study on page 92).

Age and Gender Socialization

Children learn through their socialization that people's rights and obligations differ depending on their status and the kinds of roles they perform. The term **status** refers to one's place in a hierarchical social order. The factors that determine status vary in different societies, though age and gender are common in most social systems. Older people usually are granted more respect and deference, and children generally have little social standing. In some societies, women and men have relatively equal status, while in others, one gender has higher standing than the other. Other factors that may contribute to social status in a particular culture include class, race, ethnicity, and religion.

Rules of politeness, deference, and status are often inculcated in children through language, through the ways in which people speak to them and the ways in which they are encouraged to speak. Children are encouraged to be cooperative or competitive through language interactions. In some societies, children learn to express their own opinions and judgments directly and forcefully, believing that speech is an aspect of one's individuality. In other societies, children learn to express themselves indirectly, to defer to others rather than to assert themselves. They become attuned to other people's needs and wishes. But since other people also express themselves indirectly, children learn to develop the skills of observation and inference.

Social status is a factor within families as well. In familial interactions, children first become aware of different categories of people based on such characteristics as age and gender. In a society stratified by age, gender, and other factors such as class, race, and ethnicity, a child eventually learns that social rights are unequally distributed, that certain types of people have more rights or powers than others. Unequal status within families, then, is a reflection of and reinforces inequality in the larger society. People must learn as children how to order themselves hierarchically as adults. As onlookers and participants, children observe the varied interactions among family members. They formulate conceptions of themselves and of their place in the world according to cultural models that are enacted daily in their households.

Age.   On the basis of age, children have restricted rights and limited ability to control others or even to protect themselves from other people's control. Children's lack of power is shown in several ways. First, they rarely contribute to group discussions related to community activities. In families, there is variation from culture to culture and from family to family. In some societies, it would be unthinkable for children to have a say in family decisions, while in others they might contribute significantly, especially if the discussion relates to an activity that affects them. Older children are more likely to have their opinions heard than younger children.

Second, children's behaviour is more directly constrained than is that of adults. As part of the socialization process, children may be verbally reprimanded or physically punished when they violate rules of cultural appropriateness. This process teaches them that some people have the right to comment on and control the behaviour of others. The rights of some to control others is one of the earliest lessons children learn.

status
The position or rank that one occupies in a group or society that carries certain role expectations.

Case study

Language and Interaction in Japan

A study of child-rearing and language-socialization practices in Japan reveals how children learn culturally appropriate patterns of interaction. Research concerned with Japanese social ideals uncovers the importance of *omoiyari*, or empathy with others (Clancy 1986). People are socialized to be sensitive to each other's feelings, attitudes, and needs. They learn to express their own opinions indirectly and ambiguously so as to avoid conflict and to interpret other people's intentions and opinions from surface clues.

Japanese caregivers teach communication skills to children by example and direct admonition to instill the virtues of politeness and attentiveness toward others. Adults often use explicit classifications of behaviours as acceptable or deviant. They correct children's behaviour by emphasizing the wishes of other people, especially elders, relatives, or people of higher social status.

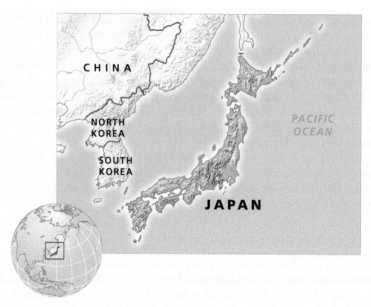

In the following exchange, documented in Patricia Clancy's study (1986) of Japanese families, a mother chastises her child for not responding to another adult's questions:

> [Child, age two years and one month, is pretending to eat food from a toy dish.]
>
> ADULT: "Are you eating something? What is in there?"
>
> CHILD: [No response]
>
> MOTHER: "I wonder what could be in there. Older sister is asking what is in there?"
>
> CHILD: "Pudding."

Repeating the question, the mother names a third participant, the researcher Patricia Clancy, whom the mother refers to as "older sister" to emphasize the child's kin-like obligation to answer the question. Aware of her place in a network of social responsibilities, the child responds.

Since Japanese culture highly values the expression of accommodation and agreement and the avoidance of overt conflict, children are taught to comply with the wishes of others regardless of their personal inclinations. One mother responded to her child's (age two years) refusal to lend a toy to a younger child by admonishing him:

> "Do you say 'No!'? You must lend one to Hirochan, saying, 'Help yourself.' The baby is cute/lovable, isn't he?"

Not only is the mother teaching her child to give in to the wishes of another, but she is instructing him to make an outright offer of the desired object. Whatever her child's inner feelings, she asks him to agree with her praise of the baby. In this way the mother teaches her child that complying with another person's wishes is more important than expressing one's own feelings.

As in all cultures, certain behaviours are considered appropriate while deviations from them trigger negative reactions. Japanese mothers often give exaggerated responses to a child's nonconformity:

> [Child, two years and one month, was playing hostess and suddenly began pretending to eat one of the toy dishes.]
>
> MOTHER: "Isn't it strange to do that kind of thing, if you eat a plate? No one eats plates, do they? Who eats plates?"
>
> CHILD: "Maho [the child's name] (eats) this."
>
> MOTHER: "You're eating it? Like a beast. It's scary. I don't like it. It's scary, like a monster. I hate monsters."

Here, the mother is essentially saying that if the child does something that violates social norms, the child is "scary." Furthermore, she is telling the child that people who behave in such ways are hated. This is an important lesson, powerfully transmitted, because it threatens a child's sense of security.

Societies function on the basis of implied principles of consensus and the restraint of conflict. People need to agree implicitly that the open display of too much conflict may prove to be socially disruptive and would impair the cohesion necessary for the viability of groups. This is perhaps most true within families but it is fundamental to any community.

Third, children have fewer and more restricted conversational rights than adults. For instance, children may be unsuccessful in getting the attention of adults, particularly when the adults are engaged in conversation and interaction with other adults. In a study of middle-class American families, Susan Ervin-Tripp et al. (1984) found that when children age two to four-and-a-half years tried to get the attention of someone already involved in conversation, they were unsuccessful 94 percent of the time. Older children, age four-and-a-half to seven years, fared somewhat better but still met with a failure rate of 79 percent. Adults also often interrupt children. Although our cultural stereotypes portray children as talkative and interruptive, laboratory and natural observations of familial interactions demonstrate just the opposite (Gleason 1987). Gender of adult and child is a significant factor in interruption. Research showed that fathers interrupted children more than did mothers, and both parents interrupted daughters more often than sons. Children replicate this gender-differentiated pattern quite early. In a study by Anita Esposito (1979) of children (from three-and-a-half to four-and-a-half years of age) who were observed in male-female encounters, boys interrupted girls twice as frequently as the reverse.

Conversational power is also displayed in the context of giving and receiving commands or instructions. Giving commands is indicative of social rights to control others, and the way in which commands are stated also can signal relative social standing. Imperatives ("Sit down!" or "Close the window!") assert power overtly, whereas indirect expressions, questions, and statements of rationales soften the speaker's control and acknowledge the other person's feelings ("Why don't you sit down?" or "Would you please close the window?"). Studies of parent-child interactions indicate that adults consistently issue more commands to children than they receive. Gender difference is manifested in the type of command. Gleason (1987) found, for example, that in a study of middle-class urban families, fathers gave imperatives twice as often as did mothers. A total of 38 percent of all fathers' utterances were overt commands. In contrast, mothers tended to make requests with polite constructions and questions.

In addition, some fathers socialize sons into competitive behaviour by adding threats or insults to direct imperatives. Commands such as "Don't go in there again or I'll break your head" and references such as "wise guy" or "nutcake" were sometimes addressed to sons. These encounters no doubt serve as training grounds for boys when they interact with other boys in competitive displays and challenges. Later, when they become parents, they may reproduce the same hierarchical status system with their children.

Gender.   Gender is a basic aspect of a person's individual and social identity. A child is socialized into his or her **gender identity** from the earliest age, beginning immediately after birth. Girls and boys may be treated differently, handled differently, and spoken to differently from the very beginning of life. Studies in child development indicate that North American parents and other caregivers interact with boys and girls differently .

Some cross-cultural research indicates similarities in patterns of gender socialization. For example, parents are more physical with boy babies than with girls. Boys are held, touched, and stimulated more, a pattern that helps them develop stronger muscles and motor behaviour. Boys also are handled more roughly than girls. In addition, when boys fuss, parents pay more attention to them than they do to girls. Through these modes of interaction, boys learn to seek attention, while girls learn to satisfy their own needs (Ember 1981). Fathers in particular tend to handle their sons more roughly than their daughters. And boys tend to be physically punished more than girls, especially by their fathers.

Studies also show that girls spend more time playing at home than do boys. They are therefore under more adult supervision and are more likely to take on household chores, including helping to care for younger siblings. Boys, in contrast, interact more with peers. These patterns also may affect aggression. A child is likely to defer to adults and nurture younger children. Girls are more likely to develop these personality and behaviour characteristics, therefore, because of their patterns of interaction at home, whereas boys develop more aggressive behaviour because of their patterns of interaction both at home and with peers.

gender identity
The way that people think about themselves in terms of their sex, how they present themselves as men or women.

Broad similarities among cultures are counteracted by culture specific gender roles and attributes that are related to differences in the way boys and girls are socialized. As we shall see in Chapter 9, societies vary in the roles and statuses they attached to gender and raise their children according to different values. Thus, although boys are almost universally more aggressive than girls within any given society, internal variation is much less than cross-cultural variation. In other words, girls in some societies are more aggressive than those in another (Rohner 1976). Similarly, patterns in gender socialization may change over time. For example, American and Canadian societies are increasingly attempting to remodel gender roles to conform to egalitarian values. Girls are being encouraged to prepare for a full-time profession, particularly in fields that were once male preserves, rather than for life as a homemaker. This pattern has led to noticeable changes in many areas of society. For example, fifty years ago women accounted for only 30 percent of university graduates; today they account for 60 percent.

? How are clothing styles, hairstyles, and jewellery used to challenge gender stereotypes in North America and Europe today?

Gender Identification.   Gender identity is marked in many ways, among them dress and body decoration. A common example is dressing baby boys in blue and baby girls in pink. Clothing styles, hairstyles, and the wearing of jewellery are other visual markers of gender. External modifications of the body are powerful, repetitive indications of one's gender identity and gender differentiation in one's society. Changes in cultural notions of gender may be reflected in changing habits of dress and body ornamentation.

Naming conventions are nearly universal means of distinguishing males and females. Many cultures bestow different names for boys and girls. In English, only a handful of names are ambiguous for gender, such as Leslie and Dana. English names for girls may refer to flowers (Rose, Iris, Lily), months of the year (April, May, June), and moral virtues (Prudence, Hope). Boys, in contrast, are rarely named for objects or abstractions. Certain sounds in the names also differentiate the genders: English girls' names often end in vowels, whereas boys' names rarely do. Finally, girls' names may be derived from boys' names by addition of "feminine" endings such as -a, -ine, -ette, for example, Paula, Pauline, Paulette. In addition, boys are more likely to be named for their fathers (John Jr., for example) than girls are to be named for their mothers. This pattern symbolizes and transmits the acknowledgment of kin ties through the male line.

In traditional communities in China and Taiwan, names given to boys and girls are strongly differentiated. Chinese names function as meaningful symbolic markers of men's social distinctiveness and the social nonbeing of women. In a study of naming practices in Hong Kong and Taiwan, Ruby Watson (1986) found that both girls and boys are given personal names based on literary sources, events occurring near the time of the child's birth, or a wish for the child's future. However, boys' names have positive or prestige implications, while girls' names more often have negative meanings. For example, an eldest boy might be called "Eldest Luck," but a second or third girl might be named "Too Many" or "Little Mistake." Names with these meanings are not given to all girls, but the fact that the pattern exists indicates negative cultural attitudes toward females. In addition to differences in first names, acquisition of subsequent names also distinguishes males and females. Throughout his life, a man acquires new names that indicate social standing in his household and community and that confer prestige to him, such as a school name given by a teacher, a marriage name selected when he marries, a "courtesy" name that marks economic or social success, and a posthumous name given to honour his life.

Women, in sharp contrast, have only their personal name. Even this name is dropped when a woman marries; but rather than acquiring a new marriage name, as men do, a woman becomes known thereafter by kin terms in reference to her husband and children, for example as "Eldest Luck's wife" or "Too Many's mother." In old age, a woman is simply called "old woman" by everyone except her closest relatives. And, finally, a woman's nonbeing is forever memorialized on her tombstone where instead of personal, courtesy, and posthumous names, as are engraved for men, a woman's existence is subsumed under her father's surname and she is listed eternally as "Family of [father's surname]."

Chinese naming patterns are consistent with traditional strong preferences for sons. These preferences go back to ancient times and the establishment of Confucian philosophy, which reinforced the Chinese kinship system. The preference for sons reflects a strongly patrilineal kinship system with inheritance rules in which wealth and property are passed from father to son. In societies where men and women are thought of as equally valuable, parental preferences for girls and boys may be personal but are not generally imbalanced in the society as a whole. In some cultures where people trace their descent and inheritance through women, girls may be preferred. For example, among the Mohawk and other Iroquois nations, parents preferred girls in order to maintain the family line that in Iroquois culture descended through women. However, children of either sex were equally welcomed and nurtured. The Mohawk pattern of preference was not, therefore, the mirror image of many societies' desires for sons. Although there are numerous cultures in which girls are routinely neglected and abused, even killed, because of intense preferences for boys, there are no reported cases of cultures where boys are neglected and abused because of preferences for girls.

Boys and girls learn their future identities as men and women by observing their parents and other household members. They see how men and women treat each other, what they say about each other, and how they respond to each other. They come to understand whether men and women contribute equally to group discussions and decision making. And they see the kinds of work that women and men perform. Through these observations, children absorb attitudes about themselves, about their own worthiness, as they prepare for their rights and responsibilities as adults.

One of the ways that children acquire models of gender and social relations is through participation in family interactions. Research conducted by Elinor Ochs and Caroline Taylor (1995) focused on 100 dinnertime conversations among family members. Ochs and Taylor analyzed the content of the conversations, looking especially at which family members introduced the stories, whose activities were discussed, and who commented on the actions described. They found that a majority of the stories were characterized by what they called a "Father knows best" family dynamic in which "father is set up to be primary audience, judge and critic of family members' actions, thoughts and feelings" (p. 99). A majority or 60 percent of the stories focused on the activities of the children, while mothers were central in 23 percent of the stories and fathers featured in 19 percent. Because children's activities made up most of the narratives, they became the focus of comments and evaluations by parents. Thus, children's actions and thoughts were most open to others' scrutiny, while fathers were talked about the least, making them the least vulnerable to evaluation. Children rarely selected the topic of conversation. They introduced only about one-third of the stories about themselves. Instead, parents (especially mothers) focused the narrative on the child's actions, which could be seen as reinforcing children's lack of privacy and control over information about themselves and the scrutiny of others. Stories were told about children for the fathers' hearing, thereby setting up the father as the "family judge" with the right to evaluate others.

Rites of Passage

In many societies, children undergo critical **rites of passage** as they move from the social role and status of child to those of adult. Other rites of passage occur at other life transitions, such as birth, marriage, and death, which are discussed further in Chapter 12. In the process of preparing for and undergoing rituals marking the transition to adulthood, children may be taught practical arts associated with their future roles.

rites of passage
Rituals that mark culturally significant transitions throughout the life cycle, including birth, puberty, marriage, and death.

The narrative dynamics of this conversation subtly teach these children their gender roles and status through a complex play of family and interactional power and control. Mother has introduced stories about the children's activities for the father to hear. Father takes family power to act as a judge of others' actions and thoughts. Children are socialized into the ideology of unequal gender relations, both because they are witnesses to their parents' behaviour and because they are chosen as central characters motivating the drama.

Culture Change

CHANGING MALE AND FEMALE SOCIALIZATION AMONG THE INUIT

Richard Condon has carried out several studies of Inuit methods of enculturation and has recorded changes in the ways in which boys and girls are socialized and the implications for their identity, attitudes, and behaviours (1990). Traditionally, social organization was based on isolated and nomadic family units. Parents assumed exclusive responsibility for training and socialization, mainly by including their children in daily tasks. Boys learned male roles by hunting with their fathers; girls learned female roles by remaining in the camp with their mothers and maintaining the household. This task specialization was not related to status differences. Female domestic activities, such as making clothing, were considered to be essential for survival and were respected. Moreover, women had a high degree of independence and participated in public decision making.

With integration into Canadian society after the 1950s, ways of life changed dramatically. Mobile populations were relocated into permanent settlements, and wage labour and government programs became the main income source for the community. Women normally sought out paid employment and became the primary wage earners, while men often continued to go out on the land on periodic hunting and trapping expeditions. This new division of labour affected boys and girls differently. Both genders attended the local schools for at least the primary grades, but high school completion was not common for either group. Boys spent some time accompanying their fathers on hunting and trapping trips, but only occasionally and at their own discretion. They spent most of their adolescence in all-male peer groups and devoted their time to leisure activities, such as playing hockey or other sports or just "hanging out." This pattern was partially based on the adoption of the youth culture prevalent in southern Canada. It represented a clear departure from traditional socialization and sociability, where few people of the same age cohort were in regular daily contact and much of the day was spent with adults in subsistence activities. Girls, on the other hand, tended to be raised according to a more traditional model. Daughters would stay home and take care of the house and their younger siblings while their mothers were at work. They would also sew items for sale or engage in wage employment to earn incomes to support their families. They generally did not perceive their greater responsibility as onerous or unfair. The different levels of responsibility assigned to boys and girls sometimes created hostility between them which deviated from the traditional patterns of mutual respect. Girls took pride in their roles and were critical about the boys' idleness. Boys were ambivalent about how well their own activities might prepare them for adulthood.

Traditional methods of Inuit task learning and gender socialization were based on observation and participation within family life. Incorporation into North American society involved major changes in the contexts and content of enculturation.

They also may be instructed in knowledge necessary for their roles as parents and spouses, learning their responsibilities, obligations, and rights.

Certain types of rituals and teachings have particular effects on molding the personalities and identities of children approaching adulthood. For example, in many African societies as well as in Aboriginal Australia, boys undergo intense, prolonged, and frightening **initiation rites** as they approach manhood. The rites are held once in several years (the number of years varies from culture to culture) for groups of boys of the appropriate age. The boys are taken out of their settlements and are subjected to weeks, months, or even years of instruction and preparation for their roles as men. (See the In Their Own Voices feature on page 98).

Among the Kpelle of Liberia, boys are initiated by groups into a men's secret society called *Poro*. Initiations occur sporadically, perhaps once every ten or fifteen years. Boys are brought from their communities to an isolated bush area for four years. During this time, they are instructed in the knowledge and skills—farming techniques, methods of house building, and craft specialties—needed to function productively in Kpelle society. They also learn various dances, songs, and traditional histories. Finally, they learn how to behave appropriately and how to act with elders and chiefs (Gibbs 1965). Social messages are reinforced by beatings and verbal harassment.

A number of physical changes are imposed on boys during their initiation, including circumcision and scarification. Scars formed from cuts made on a boy's back and chest are permanent, visible signs of adult status. Such scars are said to be the teeth marks of a "Great Masked Figure" who embodies a mythic spirit believed to eat the boy at the beginning of the initiation process. According to Kpelle beliefs, a boy dies when he enters the initiation camp and is reborn when the Great Masked Figure disgorges him. He then receives a new name signifying his new status. A boy's childhood name is never used thereafter. Boys who go through their initiation collectively form strong emotional and social bonds with one another. They learn to identify and empathize with the actions and needs of men in their own age cohorts with whom they have been associated in their periods of seclusion and transition. As well, they develop strong bonds of mutual assistance, interdependence, and loyalty that last throughout their lifetimes.

In contrast, some Native American people of the North American Midwest and Plains sent young boys (and sometimes girls) on individual quests for visions when they neared adulthood. The overt purpose of the vision quest was the acquisition of a personal spirit guardian who would come to the seeker after periods (typically four days) of isolation in the woods or on the plains. During the quest, the seeker abstained from food and sleep. Guardian spirits thus acquired formed a lifelong relationship with the seeker, coming to his or her aid in visions and dreams and imparting knowledge and comfort.

In addition to the spiritual lessons learned, children also learned the important lessons of endurance, self-control, self-reliance, and courage necessary to survive in harsh conditions. Through their experiences, children learned that they can endure the deprivation of food, water, and sleep. They also learned emotional resilience through the knowledge that they were able to survive loneliness and fear. These physical and psychological strengths are necessary for survival in nomadic societies where resources are occasionally scarce and difficult to obtain and where weather may be life-threatening.

In many societies, children's initiation ceremonies include instruction in secret ritual and lore. In the Amazon, Australia, and some cultures of central and southern Africa, boys are taught sacred songs that they are told never to reveal to anyone, especially to women and uninitiated children. These rites symbolize the segregation of the genders, fundamental to their society's economic and social roles. The selective transmission of knowledge defines and reinforces gender identity.

Schooling

In many societies, enculturation takes place in formal school settings where children are taught explicit lessons to acquire practical and intellectual knowledge. In

initiation rites
Rituals that mark a person's transition from childhood to adulthood.

? *What are some examples of initiation rites and other rites of passage in Canada?*

In Their Own Voices

A Malinke Initiation Rite

In this excerpt from his autobiography, The Dark Child, *Camara Laye vividly describes a Malinke initation rite. As in Kpelle culture, all the boys in this West African society collectively endure a series of rituals to mark their transition to manhood. The ceremony described is the first of many, which culminate in a circumcision rite.*

I was growing up. The time had come for me to join the society of the uninitiated. This rather mysterious society contained all the young boys, all the uncircumcised of twelve, thirteen or fourteen years of age, and it was run by our elders, whom we called the big Kondens.

As soon as the sun had gone down, the tom-tom had begun to beat. Even though it was being played in a remote part of the concessions, its notes had roused me at once, had struck my breast, had struck right at my heart.

The screaming crowd that surrounded Kodoke and his tom-tom was getting nearer. It would stop for a moment in each concession where there was a boy of an age to join the society, and it would take the boy away. That is why it was so slow in coming, yet as sure [and] as ineluctable as the fate that awaited me. What fate: My meeting with "Konden Diara."

Now I was not unaware who Konden Diara was; often my mother had talked of him only too much, had threatened me only too often with that "lion that eats up little boys." And here was Konden Diara, leaving the dim world of hearsay, taking on flesh and blood, yes, and was prowling, roused by Kodoke's tom-tom, around the dark town. This night was to be the night of Konden Diara.

Towards the middle of the night, the collection of uncircumcised boys was finished. We left the town behind and entered the bush by a path which leads to a sacred place where each year the initiation takes place. Just before we reached the hollow, we saw flames leap up from a huge wood fire that the bushes had hidden from us until then.

Our elders suddenly shouted, "Kneel!"

We at once fell to our knees.

Excerpts from *The Dark Child by Camara Laye,* translated by James Kirkup, Ernest Jones, and Elaine Gottlieb. Copyright © 1954, renewed 1982 by Camara Laye. Reprinted by permission of Hill and Wang, a division of Farrar, Straus and Giroux, LLC.

early societies, children of the elites (especially boys) were sent to schools to learn the responsibilities and practical applications of their future administrative or political roles. In early literate societies, elite children were taught to read and write and do mathematics.

Examples of educational systems that focused on the elite include ancient Egypt, Greece, Rome, and China but were present in other literate societies including those of the New World. For example, Aztec society was based on substantial social class differences and occupational specialization. People were socialized into their various roles from early childhood. Formal education was one of the means the state used to mold individuals to accept their place in the social order and to fulfill their responsibilities. At around the age of three or four, boys from "commoner" families were trained in their future economic roles by their fathers. Boys began to carry wood from the forests and water from the lakes to their households. They accompanied their fathers to the marketplace. Girls helped their mothers with domestic tasks, doing simple cooking and cleaning

"Heads down!"

We lowered our heads.

"Now hide your eyes."

We shut our eyes tight and press our hands over them. For would we not die of fright and horror if we should so much as catch a glimpse of Konden Diara?

Now that we are on our knees with our foreheads to the ground and our hands pressed over our eyes, Konden Diara's roaring suddenly bursts out.

We were expecting to hear this hoarse roar, we were not expecting any other sound, but it takes us by surprise, and shatters us, freezes our hearts with its unexpectedness. And it is not only Konden Diara roaring; there are ten, twenty, perhaps thirty lions that take their lead from him, uttering their terrible roars separated from us by a few yards only. No, not one of us would dream of venturing to open an eye, not one! Not one of us would dare to lift his head from the ground.

How I wish I was far away from this clearing, back in the warm security of the hut! Will this roaring never end? Oh! Those roars, I feel as if I can bear them no longer.

Whereupon, suddenly, they stop! And then the voice of one of the older boys rings out:

"Get up!"

A new command rang out, and we sat down in front of the fire. Now our elders begin our initiation; all night long they will teach us the songs of the uncircumcised; and we must remain quite still, repeating the words after them, singing the melody after them, very attentive and very obedient.

It is only after having taken part several times in the lion ceremony that we begin vaguely to understand what goes on, but we still keep it a secret, and even so the real secret is not revealed to us until the day of our final initiation into manhood.

Later I got to know who Konden Diara was, and I learnt also that the dangers were nonexistent. But I only learnt

these things when the time had come for me to learn them. As long as we are not circumcised, as long as we have not attained that second life that is our true existence, we are told nothing, and we can find out nothing.

When I finally got back to my concession [after the final rite of circumcision], the whole family was waiting for me. My parents held me tightly in their arms, particularly my mother, as if she was wanting secretly to proclaim that my second birth did nothing to alter the fact that I was still her son. My father watched us for a moment, then he said to me, almost regretfully:

"From now on, this is your hut, my son."

The hut stood opposite my mother's.

"Yes," said my mother, "you will sleep there now. But as you can see, I am still within earshot."

I opened the door of the hut; my clothes were laid out on the bed. They were men's clothes. I was a man!

"Are you pleased with your new clothes?" asked my mother.

Pleased? Yes, I was pleased. At least I think I was pleased. They were fine clothes, they were . . . I turned towards my mother: she was smiling sadly at me . . .

From Camara Laye. *The Dark Child*. Translated from the French by James Kirkup, Copyright © 1955. Used by permission of Collins. London.

CRITICAL THINKING QUESTION

The final episode described in the passage reflects a particular domestic arrangement in Malinke society. Men are often polygynous and place each wife in a separate hut, while keeping another hut for themselves. Children sleep in their mother's hut until they reach maturity. Can you see any connection between this sleeping arrangement, gender socialization, and the cultural emphasis on lengthy and dramatic initiation rites for boys?

---

chores. When children were between seven and thirteen years of age, they learned more difficult tasks. Boys were taught to fish and to steer and maneuver boats; girls helped their mothers spin cotton, weave cloth, and grind maize into meal to be prepared as the Aztecs' staple food (Soustelle, 1961).

Children began formal education between ages twelve and fifteen. The Aztec educational system included two tracks, one suited for children who were destined for membership in the bureaucratic and elite classes of Aztec society, the other geared for children of the commoner social stratum. Schools called *calmecacs* trained the sons and daughters of the elite ruling class of Aztec society, although children of the merchant class might also attend. These schools were run by priests who themselves had attended such an institution. Education in the *calmecac* prepared children for futures in the priesthood or in other high-ranking positions in the state bureaucracy, political organization, and military. Physical training and hard work were instilled in them as daily routines. They learned to use the weapons of war and had practical experience on the battlefield, under the protection of experienced warriors. Children were taught the values of self-control and respect for others. They were taught "to speak well, to make proper salutations, and to bow." Finally, children at the *calmecac* were given religious instruction, learning to sing sacred songs and to interpret dreams. Their intellectual learning included knowing how to read Aztecan pictographs and methods of reckoning time. They read and recited poetry and oratory.

Girls who attended the *calmecac* were treated more leniently than the boys. Their training was not as rigorous nor were they punished as severely. At the *calmecac*, girls were under the supervision of elderly priestesses who taught them the graces of native etiquette. They were taught to value obedience and purity of mind and body. They participated in making ritual offerings of incense to the gods each night. Their practical learning consisted mainly of becoming skilled weavers of cloth and artisans of embroidery. Girls, too, learned songs and stories that told the history and accomplishments of the Aztec people. Through these oral traditions, people acquired their identity as Aztec and took pride in their culture and their history.

A second type of institution, called *telpochcalli*, provided a different kind of experience. Most of the children at the *telpochcalli* came from the commoner stratum of Aztec society, although some of these might attend the *calmecac*. Children at the *telpochcalli* performed physical labour, including sweeping the schoolhouse, cutting wood for the school, repairing ditches and canals, and cultivating lands belonging to the school. These tasks prepared boys for their future economic roles and for their future public service in maintaining communal irrigation and water delivery systems. Boys in the *telpochcalli* were also trained in the skills of war. In fact, military training was central to the school program. Punishments for misbehaviour were sure and harsh.

The two kinds of educational institutions and the learning that took place in them exemplified the two contradictory and yet complementary strands of Aztec philosophy. One strand consisted of the ethics of self-control, sacrifice, and dedication to the public good; the other strand emphasized physical prowess and the glorification of war in the service of state defense and expansion. Children who were destined by family background and inclination to become the future leaders of Aztec society were steeped in the cultural traditions of learning, literature, and the arts. They were taught social graces and the burdens and responsibilities of leadership. Punishment for misbehaviour by nobles was harsher than that meted out to commoners on the assumption that with privilege went responsibility.

Unlike the Aztec and other ancient systems, most modern nations have universal education where all children are required to attend school. This principle is consistent with democratic ideals that all people can aspire to productive, rewarding lives in their societies. However, in practice, children have varying access to schooling in many nations. In many countries in Latin America, Africa, and the Middle East, rates of boys' attendance at school far exceed those of girls. Boys' greater access to education is reflected in statistics compiled in 2000 by the United Nations on enrollment in schools, especially at higher levels. Unequal opportunities for education result in much lower levels of literacy for women than for men. Even in the developed world, where nearly all of the adult population is literate, girls are somewhat more likely to be illiterate than boys, except in Malta, the United States, and Canada, where rates of illiteracy for males exceed those for females. Gender discrepancies in illiteracy widen in many Asian, Middle Eastern, and African nations, where women's rates exceed those of men by 20 or 30 percent (United Nations 2004).

The Western model of education is based strongly on the authority of the teacher-adult, question-answer interaction, and individual achievement. Many First Nations children are socialized to learn differently and have problems within formal Canadian institutions because of cultural differences between Aboriginal students and White teachers. In a study of a Western Canadian inner-city school, with a 60 percent Aboriginal component, Natalie Piquemal and Bret Nickels (2005) found that White teachers regularly misinterpreted responses from their Aboriginal students. Teachers often directed classroom participation by the standard technique of asking questions and expecting students to raise their hands to answer. This strategy was based on a Western value of competition and the desire of students to distinguish themselves from their peers. However, the authors found that Aboriginal values stressed cooperation and discouraged students from raising their hands to mark themselves as more knowledgeable. They suggest that classroom participation would have been achieved more effectively by focusing on group discussions in which the participants cooperated rather than competed. Another problem encountered was the reluctance of students to make eye contact with their teachers. The teachers interpreted this behaviour as hostile or disinterested, while the students meant it as a sign of respect. Piquemal and Nickels concluded from their research that Aboriginal education could be enhanced by cultivating a sensitivity to cultural differences and formulating new teaching strategies to accommodate them. However, the teachers to whom they communicated their findings were reluctant to make any changes, arguing that one of the important roles of the school was to instill Western values and practices in their students.

Studies of working-class African-American children in the United States and Afro-Caribbean children in the United Kingdom reveal that the school environment presents difficulties not experienced by middle-class children. Reacting to the demands for conformity to school authorities (teachers and principals) and to middle-class styles of learning and interaction, children from working-class or racially marginalized groups often behave defiantly, insisting on their own norms of action and speech. Sociolinguistic studies in the United States and Britain indicate that such children may reject middle-class standard speech in favour of nonstandard varieties that are distinguished on the basis of both class and race. In such communities, pressure from the peer group often supports nonconformity, noncompliance, and nonachievement. Children who excel in the school setting are sometimes teased, ostracized, or shunned by the social groups of their peers (Labov 1972b; Cheshire 1982; Richmond 1986).

> **REVIEW**
>
> Enculturation takes place both informally and formally—for example, through observation, folklore, family interaction, rites of passage (such as initiation rites at puberty), and schooling. Children learn skills, values, behavioural expectations, interactional norms, and role and status based on age and gender. Through enculturation, children develop a gender identity, which strongly affects the way they are perceived and treated in their society.

PSYCHOLOGICAL ANTHROPOLOGY

The field of **psychological anthropology** focuses on cultural factors in the development of **personality**, the consistent patterns present in the ways individuals think, feel, and behave, and on cultural influences on perception and cognition. Although every person has a unique character and personality, culture influences and constrains the ways that each person's underlying nature is expressed; that is, people are products of both their internal nature and their external experiences as a member of a society and culture. Genetic factors that contribute to a person's dispositions and feelings are modified and channelled by their culture, by the ideas that parents and other caregivers have about them as children, by their interactions with older and younger family members, and by relations with peers. Thus, personality is to a great extent culturally and socially constructed.

Culture and Personality Traits

Cross-cultural research in personality development suggests that culture and personality form an integrated, patterned, and adaptive system, suited to the social, economic, and political needs of societies. Put another way, people are molded (and mold themselves) to fit into the cultural contexts in which they live. Different cultures encourage and reward certain personality traits while discouraging and punishing others. Not everyone conforms to the expectations of their society, but most people seek to act in culturally appropriate ways most of the time. Internalized cultural values that

psychological anthropology
A subfield of cultural anthropology that studies the psychological motivations of behaviour and the personality types prevalent in a society.

personality
A constellation of behavioural traits and dispositions. Some features of personality emerge at birth while others are acquired in the process of enculturation and psychological and cognitive growth.

affect personality may include, for example, an orientation toward cooperation or competition, and a focus on a public or a private self.

Cooperation and Competition.   All cultures encourage the development of both cooperation and competition in particular situations among particular individuals. However, societies vary in the relative emphasis placed on one form of behaviour or the other and the degree to which individuals cooperate or compete in various settings. North Americans view competition as a critical motivational force behind the way our economy works and as an incentive to achieve excellence. In other societies cooperation may be more important in how people solve a problem or reach a goal. Studies based on experimental testing of children from several countries and from urban and rural areas revealed marked differences in children's willingness to compete or cooperate in achieving tasks (Munroe and Munroe 1975). Children in the United States were the least willing to cooperate and continued to compete with each other even when competition led to failure and cooperation would have led to success This pattern contrasts with that of urban Mexican children who initially competed but then quickly caught on that cooperation would aid them all and thus changed their strategy. Differences were noted within countries as well. That is, competitiveness was more typical of urban Mexicans than rural Mexicans, urban Israelis than kibbutz children, and urban Canadians than rural Canadians.

Studies of traditional or pre-industrial cultures from the anthropological record indicate a common focus on cooperation. Rather than stressing individualistic and competitive goals, these cultures emphasized the interrelationships between a person and the groups to which they belong. Strongest links were established with one's kin and a group focus reinforced through child-rearing practices. Children interacted with and learned how to get along with many different people on a daily basis. They were cared for by older siblings and adults besides their parents. They saw people engaged in group activities and they learned the value of cooperation. Personality traits that were encouraged were those of communal responsibility, generosity, and even temper. According to Ruth Bunzel, writing about the Zuni,

> In all social relations whether within the family group or outside, the most honoured personality traits are a pleasing address, a yielding disposition, and a generous heart. The person who thirsts for power, who wishes to be as they scornfully phrase it, "a leader of the people" receives nothing but criticism. (1932:480)

Public Self and Private Self.   Cultures vary in their focus on "private self" and "public self" (Triandis 1989). People have notions that focus on both their private and public selves, each coming into focus in particular contexts. **Private self** is the feelings and thoughts that involve characteristics and behaviours of the person, whereas **public self** is a person's feelings and thoughts that involve characteristics and behaviours of a "generalized others' view of the self" or of the "collective self" (p. 507).

Cultural notions of the private self emphasize self-actualization; cultural notions of the public self emphasize the norms and values of the group. According to Triandis, these divergent emphases on self correlate with societal scale and economic systems. The private self is the focus in large-scale, comparatively affluent societies, where individualism and personal achievement are stressed in the context of social and economic competition. The public self is the focus in smaller, more egalitarian societies, where collectivism and group well-being are stressed. Child rearing in individualistic societies emphasizes personal achievement and the value of standing out, being distinct and different. In contrast, child rearing in collectivist societies emphasizes conformity and fitting in with group norms, especially in public settings.

Culture and Self-Concept

Research suggests that people in different cultures have different ideas of themselves, or **self-concepts**. In an influential review of research, Hazel Markus and Shinobu Kitayama (1991) point to a basic distinction between cultures that have an "independent" view of the self and those with an "interdependent" view of the self. Markus and Kitayama characterize the **independent self** view as a primarily Western

private self
One's inner feelings and concepts of oneself.

public self
The self that one projects in public, in interactions with others.

self-concepts
Attitudes that people hold about themselves.

independent self
Concepts of individuals as self-contained, independent agents with a focus on their own thoughts, feelings, and achievements.

notion of a person with unique "dispositional attributes"... "detached from context" (p. 225). The **interdependent self** view, in contrast, sees the self as embedded in surrounding context, or "self-in-relation-to-other." These researchers believe that the only universal aspect of self, beyond an awareness of one's physical body, is awareness of internal activity, such as dreams, thoughts, and feelings, which cannot be known directly by anyone else. An inner private self results from this awareness of "unshared experience."

An independent view of the self is individualistic, egocentric, and self-contained, whereas an interdependent sense of self is based on feelings of "connectedness" to others. In cultures where independent views of the self dominate, people are most concerned with their own thoughts and feelings and with their own achievements. In cultures where interdependent views of the self dominate, one's inner feelings, opinions, and attitudes are secondary to the needs of the groups to which one belongs. Group and community consensus and expression of solidarity are valued.

Interdependent views of the self are more prominent in some cultures than others. Related values include the importance of respecting other people's feelings and adjusting one's behaviour to the needs of the group. Community goals become personal goals as well. People ideally observe other people's behaviour for the purpose of deducing their motives and feelings. People in societies with interdependent views of the self express strong needs for affiliation with others.

A person's identity emphasizes one's relationships and one's membership in groups of various kinds, including family and community. In-group and out-group distinctions are likely to be well marked in collectivist societies. People feel great loyalty to their own group, however defined. Self-discipline and emotional restraint may be valued in collectivist societies, whereas self-esteem and personal expression are valued in individualistic societies (Heine et al. 1999). In all cultures, though, people who conform to the expectations of their society, whether for individual accomplishments or for group cooperation, can have feelings of self-regard because they are acting according to cultural models of authenticity and appropriateness. Anthropological studies popular in the 1940s, 1950s, and 1960s focused on these cultural models as examples of **national character**.

interdependent self
Concepts of individuals as connected to others, related to other people, with a focus on group needs rather than individual inner feelings, opinions, and attitudes.

national character
A constellation of behaviours and attitudes thought to be characteristic of a modal personality type prevalent in a particular country.

?How would you describe your personality? What cultural factors influenced the development of your self-concept as a person?

The people in this Cinco de Mayo parade are expressing social solidarity as well as cultural identity through a public event. In personality characteristics, compared to people from some other cultures, they likely would score higher on psychological measures of emphasis on cooperation versus competition, interdependence versus independence, and public selfhood versus private selfhood.

Culture and Cognition

Cross-cultural psychological research raises some important questions about cultural impacts on styles of thinking. While it is impossible to isolate any one feature as causal, these questions can be approached from a holistic perspective, viewing cultures as integrated systems of practices, attitudes, and values. Studies with Inuit subjects from Arctic Canada and Alaska and with Kpelle subjects from Liberia illustrate cultural differences in the characteristic ways that people think.

The Inuit have a highly developed ability to make spatial judgments. In tests, subjects were required to sort out the components of their environment, separate an element from its context, and locate themselves accurately in relation to environmental features (Munroe and Munroe 1975:82). The Inuit also demonstrate a remarkable memory for territorial features. Their success at spatial tasks is consistent with the needs of their economic and settlement patterns. In Arctic terrain, where colour and shape are relatively uniform, it takes sophisticated knowledge and judgment to discern and recall significant environmental features. Such knowledge is critical to survival for people who depend on migratory animals for their food sources and who relocate their settlement sites with some frequency (See the Anthropology Applied feature in Chapter 3).

Inuit child-rearing practices encourage the development of complex spatial abilities. Children have freedom of movement and activity, but the rules that prohibit risky, life-threatening behaviour are made clear and are applied consistently. The Inuit language has a rich array of terms that describe location, relations of objects to backgrounds, and relations connecting the speaker to directions, distances, and objects in the environment (Denny 1982). Correlations between hunting and gathering economies and spatial acuity are supported by data from Australian Aborigines, who also score high on spatial judgment tests (Segall 1979).

Recall from Chapter 3 that people classify objects and experiences according to different principles. In one study, members of the Kpelle tribe of Liberia were asked to sort twenty objects into categories. The objects included five members of four categories: food, clothing, tools, and utensils (Segall 1979). Rather than sorting into these categories, however, Kpelle subjects sorted into functional groupings. For example, a knife was sorted with an orange, a hoe with a potato. When questioned about their choices, some commented that "was the way a wise man would do things." In response to an experimenter's question, "How would a fool do it?" the subject sorted the objects into "four neat piles with food in one, tools in another, and so on" (Glick 1975:636).

Additional studies with Kpelle focused on the contextual nature of memory. Kpelle subjects had difficulty remembering objects out of context, but when they were able to classify them into functional and experiential categories, their recall ability improved. Recall also increased when items were embedded in folktales (Munroe and Munroe 1975:87). In addition, Kpelle subjects had a superior ability to estimate quantities of some items but not of others. For example, they were accurate in estimating quantities of rice, their staple food, but not of other substances. Munroe and Munroe suggest that context-bound thought is adaptive in small-scale pre-industrial societies where "categories and processes of thought operate with what is immediately relevant—as culturally defined—and this is seldom knowledge for its own sake" (p. 89).

In contrast, cognitive processes that children learn in the United States stress intellectual functioning leading to "more and more flexible and general schemata." This type of thinking is also adaptive. It is adapted to situations of rapid change where people are confronted with numerous types of problems requiring both multitasking and specialized knowledge. Studies indicate that in all cultures, increased formal schooling correlates with increased success in memory tasks involving abstract concepts and out-of-context items. Intelligence and cognitive styles, too, prove to be adaptive.

Formal education favours decontextualized thinking, which may present difficulties to Kpelle and other children adjusting to the demands of school settings (Rogoff and Morelli 1989). They may find it odd to be expected to answer questions out of context without any perceived need or functional goal. They also may find it odd to provide information to an adult who clearly already has the information being requested.

Controversies

Is There Such a Thing as National Character?

Research on national character attempted to elucidate personality types prevalent in different cultures. Ruth Benedict's pioneering work, *Patterns of Culture* (1934), characterized a society by what Benedict proposed was an overriding personality type. Working with Native American and Melanesian materials, Benedict attempted to describe contrasting cultures in terms of general, overriding thematic constructs. She suggested that every culture develops a particular configuration of behaviours and beliefs that becomes associated with specific personality types. As illustration, Benedict labeled the Kwakwaka'wakw (or Kwakiutl) of the North Pacific coast of British Columbia as "Dionysian" because of their competitive economic and ritual cycles of feasting (potlatching) and their competitive and boastful personality styles. The Zuni of the American Southwest she referred to as "Apollian" because of their nonaggressive, consensus building and conformist social ethics. And the Dobu Islanders of Melanesia were "paranoid" because of their intense concern with witchcraft and fears of being the target of malevolent witches.

During World War II, Benedict and others attempted to characterize Japanese society, personality, and mentality through handy catchphrases, summed up by the title of Benedict's book on the subject called *The Chrysanthemum and the Sword* (1946). Some of these efforts were related to the war effort, in attempting to understand Japanese culture and specifically their motivations and actions during the war. Studies of Japanese personality focused on the contrast, as perceived by Western observers, between their peaceful, harmonious family life, serene artistic aesthetic, and violent militarism. Benedict's work was later criticized for seeming to reduce culture and personality to stereotypes.

Although it is certainly true that specific personality types may be more or less favoured in different cultures or more or less adaptive in cultural context and, therefore, more or less nurtured in the development of children into adults, national character studies overgeneralized personality types and value orientations while overlooking actual differences that are attested. The concept of national character also risks constructing an "other" that masks the similarities among people.

These studies have lost favour in the anthropological discipline. Nevertheless, the tendency to overgeneralize and stereotype particular groups may re-emerge in public discourse and social policy. For example, the profiling of racial or ethnic groups in criminal investigations and, most recently, in cases of suspected terrorism has become a widely known and greatly contested issue.

CRITICAL THINKING QUESTIONS

How might concepts and attributes of national character be used or misused by governments and power elites? What might be some examples from recent history?

REVIEW

Personality development, self-concepts, and cognitive skills are affected by culture and the individual's internalization, or naturalization, of cultural norms. These are all topics in the field of psychological anthropology. People's personalities and cognitive skills, though highly variable, tend to be fitted or adapted to the culture in which they live. Examples of differences in personality traits include cooperative or competitive tendencies, individualistic or collectivist tendencies, and a focus on the private self or public self. This is not to say, however, that societies have a national character characterized by an overarching specific personality type.

DEVIANCE AND ABNORMAL BEHAVIOUR IN CROSS-CULTURAL PERSPECTIVE

Societies differ in what is considered normal or abnormal behaviour. They also differ in the ways in which abnormal behaviour is interpreted and treated. Cultures teach people how to act appropriately in different situations. People learn the behaviour expected of them, attuned to the contexts, the people they are interacting with, and the

deviance
Behaviours that violate cultural norms and expectations.

? *Do you know anyone who has been diagnosed with a mental illness? What type of treatment has been prescribed for him or her?*

GLOBALIZATION

Using Western medical models, a study conducted by the World Health Organization in 2001–2003 focused on incidences of psychological disorders in fourteen countries: Belgium, China, Colombia, France, Germany, Italy, Japan, Lebanon, Mexico, the Netherlands, Nigeria, Spain, Ukraine, and the United States. In the findings, untreated panic attacks, phobias, and posttraumatic shock syndrome topped the list everywhere, except in the United States and Ukraine, where untreated mood disorders and depression were most prevalent. The researchers noted that culture-specific disorders, such as attention deficit hyperactivity disorder (ADHD), were not included in the study.

goals that they wish to accomplish. Most people try to act in accordance with the expectations that their cultures teach them, and most people do act appropriately most of the time.

Rules vary from culture to culture, so that what might be considered appropriate behaviour when interacting with relatives, acquaintances, officials, or strangers in one society might be considered rude, unusual, or even "crazy" in another society. In addition, cultures differ in how underlying psychological fears, tensions, and conflicts are manifested. And they contrast in their ways of interpreting people's actions and speech as normal or abnormal and in responding to or treating that behaviour. What is considered **deviance** in one culture might be considered powerful in another.

Responses to "Mental Illness"

In Western societies, medical interpretations of psychological disorders have gained great currency among experts whose opinions influence the general population. These interpretations lead to treatments that are medical and pharmacological. People with "problems" are advised to take drugs to alleviate their symptoms. Drugs are developed by scientific researchers and prescribed by doctors with increasing frequency. Although these treatments may relieve symptoms, they may not cure underlying problems. Whatever we may think of these modalities, however, they are an improvement over the treatment common in Europe and North America several centuries ago, when people suffering from anxiety, depression, and hallucinations were isolated in asylums where they were verbally and physically abused (Foucault 1976).

Other cultures have viewed seemingly disturbed behaviour in a different light. Consider this alternative response to Black Elk, a nineteenth-century spiritual leader of the Oglalas (Neihardt 1961). Beginning when he was a child of nine years, Black Elk experienced periods of intense anxiety and fear, followed by his receiving of visual and auditory messages from the spirit realm. These messages were not exclusively for Black Elk but for his community. A modern physician-psychiatrist might diagnose Black Elk as prone to anxiety attacks or panic disorder and hallucinations, but the Oglalas interpreted his experiences as powerful episodes of contact with the spirit world. Rather than ostracizing, punishing, or medicating him, the Oglalas respected Black Elk as a visionary who could receive messages from the spirit world. Oglala culture gave Black Elk a respected central role in the life of the community.

Research comparing the ways that unusual or deviant behaviour is treated in diverse societies uncovers both similarities and differences in specific actions and reactions and underlying attitudes. For example, the Inuit recognize a condition they deem aberrant, called *nuthkavihak*, a word translated as "crazy." It refers to a condition where "something inside the person—the soul, the spirit, the mind—is out of order" (Murphy 1981:813). Manifestations of this ailment include talking to oneself, screaming at somebody who doesn't exist, believing that a child or husband was murdered by witchcraft when nobody else believes it, believing oneself to be an animal, refusing to eat for fear one will die of it, refusing to talk, running away, getting lost, hiding in strange places, making strange grimaces, drinking urine, becoming strong and violent, killing dogs, and threatening people. While you may recognize some of these behaviours as deviant or "crazy" in your community, others are highly specific to the Inuit culture and environment.

According to the Yoruba, some people are *were*, a word translated as "insane." Manifestations include hearing voices and trying to get other people to see their source when the other people cannot, laughing when there is nothing to laugh at, talking all the time or not talking at all, asking oneself questions and answering them, picking up sticks and leaves for no purpose except to put them in a pile, throwing away food because it is thought to contain *juju* (sorcery), tearing off one's clothes, setting fires, defecating in public and then touching the feces, taking up a weapon and suddenly hitting someone, breaking things while in a state of being stronger than normal, and believing that an odour is continuously being emitted from one's body. Again, some of these behaviours have analogues in descriptions of psychosis in Western medicine.

Inuit and Yoruba reactions to people with these conditions, which are thought to be incurable, vary with the severity of the symptoms and the danger of the behaviour to the sufferer and to others. Such people may be avoided, restrained, or assaulted as the situation warrants. Both the Inuit and the Yoruba also recognize certain emotional and behavioural conditions that disturb the individual and others in the community but are not "insane." According to Jane Murphy (1981), Westerners would describe many of these conditions as instances of anxiety and depression. Inuit and Yoruba treatment theories consider these types of ailments as curable, especially by ritual practitioners, who perform curing ceremonies that alleviate both the symptoms and their cause. However, they also recognize that some people cannot be cured and may suffer lifelong emotional stress.

Finally, the Yoruba and Inuit are aware of people who simply deviate from social norms. Each group focuses on particular aspects of inappropriate behaviour that violate their cultural rules of propriety. The Yoruba call such people *arankan*, which means a "person who always goes her or his own way regardless of others, who is uncooperative, full of malice, and bullheaded" (Murphy 1981:821). The Inuit word describing such people, *kunlangeta*, means "the mind knows what to do but the person does not do." In both societies, the negative labels are not applied to people who occasionally act in inappropriate ways, recognizing that all people violate social norms from time to time. Instead, they are used to refer to people who repeatedly offend and violate cultural norms, seemingly without remorse. In both societies, people who behave in these ways are subject to informal means of social control such as gossip, teasing, and reprimands. If their behaviour continues, they may be physically punished or even killed. And in both societies, such people are considered social incorrigibles rather than illness sufferers. As a result, rituals or other treatments are not offered to them.

Culture-Specific Psychological Disorders

Researchers have noted specific psychological disorders that occur with some frequency in certain cultures but are rare or absent in others. Such **culture-specific psychological disorders** are named and recognized as aberrant behaviour by members of the culture (Yap 1969). Specific reactions to or treatments of such syndromes also may be culture-specific.

culture-specific psychological disorders Psychological disorders that seem to occur with some frequency in certain cultures but are rare or absent in others.

In American society, eating disorders such as anorexia and bulimia have relatively high rates of incidence, particularly among young women, although men and women of any age are susceptible. The behaviours are associated with an exaggerated concern with weight and distorted body image. Sufferers who might be very thin see themselves as overweight. The syndromes arise in the context of cultural obsessions with appearance, especially for women, and an obsessive fear of gaining weight which are linked to emphasis on youth and fear of aging. Most Americans do not become anorexic or bulimic in avoiding weight gain but are sympathetic with those who do, because of shared cultural images. Some researchers argue that the majority of women in North America has some form of eating disorder, even though they may not be anorexic (Bordo 2004). In other societies, these preoccupations might appear to be bizarre in the extreme.

In some Southeast Asian, North African, and Siberian cultures, people may become victims of a syndrome called *latah*. *Latah* is manifested as a startle reaction, involving trembling, involuntary sudden movements, and overreacting to the behaviour of others. People who experience *latah* episodes have difficulty coping with sudden sounds or movements. They become disoriented and extremely anxious. They may have phobic reactions toward common objects and may especially fear worms and certain animals. *Latah* sufferers are particularly vulnerable to repeated episodes after an initial traumatic experience. People in the grip of *latah* usually are not violent, but they may occasionally exhibit aggressive, even homicidal, impulses.

In the Pacific islands and in Indonesia, some people exhibit a syndrome referred to as *amok* (the origin of the English expression "to run amok"). *Amok* is manifested by intense outbursts of rage triggered by relatively simple frustrations of daily life and interactions with others. *Amok* sufferers often have amnesia following an episode, not remembering anything that they said or did during the incident. Extreme cases are rare but might include generalized blind rage. In such instances, sufferers may be forcibly restrained.

Case study

Serial Killing as a Culture-Specific Disorder

Elliot Leyton of Memorial University is renowned for his work on multiple murderers in industrialized societies. His major book *Hunting Humans* (2005), which has gone through several editions since its first appearance in 1984, attempts to provide an anthropological insight into the motivations and behaviours of serial killers, who commit their crimes over an extended period of time, and to a lesser extent mass murderers, who kill many people in a single event. Leyton affirms that, contrary to the received wisdom, these criminals are not aberrant psychopaths or schizophrenics but are the products of specific social influences and cultural values prevalent in modern industrial nations, especially the United States. Serial killing is therefore a culture-specific disorder in the same sense as the *windigo* syndrome or Arctic hysteria. Like these conditions, it is influenced by a specific set of sociocultural conditions and worked out in terms of culturally standardized behaviours.

Based on general statistics and his analysis of the detailed records and personal narratives available for six American serial killers, Leyton concludes that multiple murders are clearly distinct from more pervasive forms of homicide. Aside from those who kill for material gain, murderers usually act out of rage, kill people whom they know, and seldom repeat such a crime. In Western societies, the perpetrators of such crimes of passion are usually from the poorest and most deprived segments of the population whose basic conditions of life involve a heavy degree of deprivation and frustration. Multiple murderers are much less common in the population and never come from the very bottom of the socioeconomic ladder. They plan out their crimes carefully in advance and kill complete strangers who are chosen because they represent a particular social class or category.

Leyton suggests that, while nonrepetitive homicides are present in all cultures, multiple ones have only occurred recently within Western societies, particularly since the industrial revolution, and are a product of cultural trends that have emerged since the nineteenth century. The most important force is a competitive and individualistic ethos and a striving for social mobility that is affirmed as a cultural ideal but is often unattainable. Within this sociocultural context, serial killers and mass murderers usually originate within the upper working class with a strong desire to pursue the "American dream" and rise in the social hierarchy to enter the middle class. They all experience a failure in their attempts. Their frustration leads them to a campaign of retribution against members of the class to which they aspire and whom they perceive as having excluded them. Their actions are further reinforced, especially within the United States, by a culture that tolerates and glorifies violence. For serial killers, the cultural emphasis on violence provides an additional source of gratification as they are given abundant publicity and often receive fan mail and even marriage proposals after their capture.

Among Algonquin peoples of northeastern Canada, people may be afflicted by a syndrome called *windigo*. According to Algonquin beliefs, this disorder is the result of possession by a supernatural being, called *windigo*, a cannibal spirit. Victims of *windigo* manifest depression and anxiety prior to an episode of spirit possession. Algonquins believe that if not properly treated, *windigo* can lead to murder and cannibalism because the victim is in the clutches of the cannibal *windigo* spirit. In traditional communities, shamans treated cases of *windigo*, but if the sufferers became homicidal or cannibalistic, they were more often put to death. Fear of possible starvation during prolonged, intensely cold winters may be an ecological trigger to the development of *windigo*, given its emphasis on eating a forbidden source (another human).

In the Arctic, Inuit may experience a syndrome called *pibloktoq* (or "arctic hysteria") that is manifested by convulsive fits, sobbing, and running around in the cold outdoors without adequate clothing. Women more than men may be prone to episodes of *pibloktoq*, especially after the death of a close relative. Incidents of *pibloktoq* sometimes occur epidemically, one victim setting off the disorder in others.

Some researchers suggest a seasonal and physiological trigger for *pibloktoq* (Wallace 1961; Foulks 1972). Incidents tend to be concentrated toward the end of winter when sunlight is scarce or absent and people are unable to synthesize vitamin D, a necessary factor in the absorption of calcium. Calcium deficiency may therefore be a factor leading to the syndrome and may also result from low amounts of calcium in the Inuit diet. Another possible reason is the disturbance of circadian or daily

Anthropology Applied

The Ethnobotany of Psychotropic Substances

Since prehistory, people around the world have used medicinal and psychotropic substances found in plants. Preserving and passing down botanical knowledge is one of the earliest specializations in human social organization, usually performed by shamans or other spiritual leaders or healers. And it is not surprising that humans would have embraced the use of mind-altering substances to enhance religious or spiritual experiences or healing effects. The study of these and other interactions of plants and people is called *ethnobotany*. Researchers interested in this subject also include medical anthropologists. Increasingly, as shamans' and their peoples' ways of life disappear, preserving and passing down ancient botanical knowledge and the species and varieties of medicinal and psychotropic plants fall to ethnobotanists and medical anthropologists.

Psychotropic (or psychogenic) substances, called *entheogens*, may be intoxicating, narcotic, depressant, or hallucinogenic. They may be absorbed through the skin, ingested, or inhaled. In South America, traditional religious sacraments, healing ceremonies, and divination involve the use of liquid or solid tryptamines derived from native plants with high concentrations of alkaloids. Tryptamines include LSD, psilocybin, and other powerful hallucinogens. Administered by shamans,

a drink—*ayahuasca*—causes hallucinations in which people, while sweating and convulsing, may see jaguars, snakes, and vivid colours (Hill 2002). Depending on the culture, *ayahuasca* may be used by everyone in the community, by males only, or by shamans only.

Tryptamines also may be administered as solids, such as ground seeds. The Otomac use a snuff called *yopo*, inhaled nasally through the hollow leg bones of birds. The Waika boil resin from the inner bark of certain trees, which is then dried and ground for use as snuff (Balick and Cox 1996).

Transnational pharmaceutical companies and others compete for access to these and other psychotropic and medicinal plants indigenous to tropical rain forests. Also, biopiracy, stealing native plants for profit, has become a growing concern of developing countries. At the same time, governments have moved to criminalize the use of tryptamine-based entheogens, even in religious contexts. Together, these developments threaten native plants. Fearing the loss of wild plant genomes and heirloom varieties, many ethnobotanists work with other specialists in efforts to preserve the living species on which modern synthetic drugs are based.

CRITICAL THINKING QUESTIONS

Why do most modern states treat tryptamines as controlled substances? Why might it be important to preserve ancient species and varieties of plants?

---

rhythms that influence many physiological functions, including blood pressure, body temperature, blood sugars, and hemoglobin levels. The rhythms are adjusted to light-dark cycles and are disrupted by the lack of sunlight in the Arctic winters. Lack of synchrony in physiological functioning can disturb the central nervous system, leading to irritability and anxiety. In addition, such factors as isolation, intense cold, and legitimate fears of starvation may contribute to anxiety and depression that are expressed in *pibloktoq*.

In China and Southeast Asia, some men are gripped by *koro*, an intense and depersonalized fear of the retraction or shrinking of the penis. A man believes that his penis will retract into his abdomen, leading to death. *Koro* panics, which tend to occur as epidemics, may be associated with guilt over real or imagined illicit sexual encounters or over autoerotic thoughts or actions. They can also be triggered by generalized anxiety or by cold. Significant historical and cultural contexts for *koro* include the demands or

Inuit men are more likely than women to experience "kayak fright." They report feelings of dizziness and paralysis and are afraid to go out in their boats to hunt on the open seas. Victims of kayak fright also report a fear of being abandoned. As a culture-specific psychological disorder, such fears of the dangers of open-sea hunting may be both well founded and culturally adaptive. What might be some examples of culture-specific psychological disorders in North American society?

perceived demands of sex in polygynous households. Husbands may be uncertain about their sexual adequacy or performance in a culture that places high value on the fathering of children to ensure continuation through the male line.

REVIEW

All societies have informal and formal ways of dealing with deviant behaviour. For example, people commonly apply informal social sanctions to alert individuals that their violations of social norms are not acceptable. People also define behaviour regarded as mentally ill. While there are behaviours that people everywhere identify as "insane," there also are culture-specific psychological disorders. Many of these disorders have physiological causes, but each society explains them differently based on its system of beliefs and values.

Chapter Summary

The Process of Enculturation

- Human beings are born helpless and completely dependent on adults. Although infants may be helpless, they are immediately responsive to the world around them and begin to learn their culture as soon as they are born. Gradually, they acquire the language of their society and they learn to behave in culturally appropriate ways. This process, called enculturation or socialization, takes place primarily through informal means over a period of many years.

- Child rearing differs considerably from place to place and over time. In general, a society's child-rearing practices are consistent with its core values. Child rearing includes implicit messages absorbed by children as they observe and interact with members of their family and community. It includes methods and techniques used to feed and care for children, sleeping arrangements for children, and ways in which children are held and carried.

- Attitudes toward children and child care change over time. In North America, for example, advice given to parents and other caregivers by medical doctors, psychologists, and sociologists has varied considerably, even in the twentieth century. The advice about how to raise one's child is generally consistent with the economic needs of the nation and with the social values about family, individuality, and gender roles that are shared by members of the culture.

Formal and Informal Learning

- Children absorb cultural values, including norms of behaviour, attitudes, and ethics, by observing how people act and hearing what they say in the course of their daily activities. The repetition of sayings and proverbs and storytelling are powerful symbolic means of transmitting core cultural values. Children also need to learn how to properly interact with others by observing their elders and interacting with peers, family members, and people of different social roles in their communities. In addition, children learn their place and their social role in their family and community. They learn that factors such as age, gender, and status influence the rights that people have and the ways in which they behave.

- Children are also socialized in formal settings such as schools. The ways in which schools are organized and instruction is given vary cross-culturally. Although today most nations support universal education, in practice children in many nations don't have equal access to schooling. School attendance and literacy rates may vary according to gender. In many countries, rates of school attendance for boys are higher than for girls, resulting in lower rates of literacy among women than among men. Class, ethnic, and racial differences may also affect rates of attendance in school as well as a child's success in school. These differences have long-term effects on an individual's adult role in society and on his or her economic potential and security.

Psychological Anthropology

- Although we tend to think of personality as an innate part of our identity, our personalities are largely shaped by environmental factors, including our culture. Personality emerges from the interaction of nature and nurture. And the anthropological study of personality demonstrates that cultural differences in underlying core values lead to differences in the kinds of personality developed in each society. Although all cultures contain and approve of some elements of competitiveness and cooperativeness, cultures do differ markedly in the emphasis that is placed on one or the other. Many post-industrial societies emphasize individuality and competitiveness, whereas many non-industrial societies favour the group over the individual and value cooperation more than competition.

- Differences in personality are also reflected in differing cultural concepts of the "self." Cultures contrast in their emphasis on individualistic approaches to the self and collectivist approaches to the self. The former emphasize individual traits, experiences, and accomplishments. The latter emphasize a person's relationships with others and membership in groups of various kinds, including families and communities.

Deviance and Abnormal Behaviour in Cross-Cultural Perspective

• Societies differ in what is considered normal or abnormal behaviour. They also differ in the ways in which abnormal behaviour is interpreted and treated. In addition, cultures differ in how underlying psychological fears, tensions, and conflicts are manifested. What might be considered deviant behaviour in one culture might be considered a sign of spiritual power in another. Anthropologists have isolated a number of culture-specific psychological disorders that seem to occur with some frequency in certain cultures but are rare or absent in others.

 ## Key Terms

enculturation 82	gender identity 93	private self 102	deviance 106
socialization 82	rites of passage 95	public self 102	culture-specific
social birth 83	initiation rites 97	self-concepts 102	psychological
child-rearing practices 85	psychological	independent self 102	disorders 107
folklore 90	anthropology 101	interdependent self 103	
status 91	personality 101	national character 103	

 ## Review Questions

1. What kinds of beliefs and practices do societies have for managing the physical and social birth of new members? What is the relationship between infant mortality rates and definitions of social birth?

2. What child-rearing tasks must all societies address? How do child-rearing strategies commonly vary?

3. What are some examples of formal and informal modes of enculturation?

4. How does status and inequality within a family reflect status and inequality within a society as a whole?

5. How are age and gender socialization reflected in naming practices?

6. What are some examples of rites of passage? What social and psychological functions do rites of passage serve?

7. How do individuals acquire personality traits in the context of enculturation? What are some examples of cross-cultural differences in personal identity and self-concept?

8. What is national character, and why was it controversial as a concept?

9. What are some examples of the diverse ways in which societies deal with deviant and abnormal behaviour?

CHAPTER 5

Preview

1. In what basic ways do humans satisfy their need for food?
2. To what factors affecting food supply and availability must people adapt?
3. How does subsistence influence the size of populations and people's habitation patterns?
4. How does subsistence shape people's work, social organization, and social relationships?
5. What are some characteristics of foraging and examples of foragers?
6. What are some characteristics and examples of pastoralists and horticulturalists?
7. How does peasant society differ from that of tribal horiticulturalists?
8. How have patterns of food production changed in the course of industrialization and globalization?

*A*t first there was no earth, only sky above and water below. In the Sky-World lived a woman who was pregnant. One day, while searching near roots of a large tree for medicines for her husband, she fell through a hole in the sky and descended toward the waters below. Animals in the sea saw her falling and decided to make a soft place for her to land. They dove beneath the water and took up some mud which they placed on a turtle's back. The woman landed unharmed and the turtle's back, covered with mud, gradually expanded to become the earth.

The woman soon gave birth to a daughter. This daughter later became pregnant and gave birth to twin sons. One son was born in the normal manner but the second was born through his mother's armpit, killing her in the process. The woman's mother buried her and out of her body grew the plants on which people depend for their sustenance: Corn grew from her breast, out of her abdomen grew Squash, and from her fingers grew Beans. These plants are called "The Three Sisters" and "Our Life Supporters."

From Mohawk narrative relating the origin of food crops (compiled from narrative accounts, Bonvillain, n.d.).

The Mohawk lived in the woodlands of what is now eastern New York, western Vermont, and southwestern Quebec, before European settlers began to displace them in the seventeenth century. Today, many of their descendants live on reserves (or reservations) in Quebec, Ontario, and New York state. Although they supplemented their diet with game and wild plants, they obtained the bulk of their food from farming. Their principal crops—like those of all First Nations farmers in North America at that time—were corn, beans, and squash.

In this narrative, a traditional story told today as well as in ancient times, the Mohawk account for the origin of these crops and acknowledge their dependence on them. All three emerge from different parts of the buried body of the daughter of the earth. Corn, the daily staple, springs from her chest, squash from her belly, and beans from her fingers. The symbolism in the story connects the growth of plants from the woman's body with the continuing fertility of the earth. Through her death, she gives us life because she gives us the foods that we eat to survive. The narrative also expresses the Mohawk understanding of the fundamental connection between women and food production. In Mohawk society, women were the farmers. They controlled the use of land, planted the fields, and harvested the crops. Although men provided their families with fish and meat, women sustained their families with the crops that they grew.

In Vietnam, rice paddies are owned by individual families, and land is subdivided and passed on to sons or male relatives through inheritance. At the same time, in the transition to a market economy, rice farming has become women's work, as men leave the paddies in search of wage work. Rice farming—for both subsistence and export and often combined with duck raising—is highly labour intensive. Women and children manage most of the burdens of this labour along with household tasks.

ecological anthropology
Specialization within anthropology that focuses on subsistence strategies and how people exploit and adapt to their environments.

subsistence patterns
Methods of obtaining food using available land and resources, available labour and energy, and technology.

foragers
Peoples whose subsistence pattern is hunting and gathering.

food producers
Users of a subsistence strategy that transforms and manages the environment in order to obtain food.

ECOLOGICAL ANTHROPOLOGY

This chapter looks at the many strategies, farming among them, that humans have developed to meet their basic need for food. It examines the cultural implications of each of these strategies—their influence on everything from population size to social structure. Chapter 6 continues this discussion by examining people's economic systems and systems of exchange.

Ecological anthropology is the subdiscipline of anthropology that focuses on subsistence strategies—how people meet their survival needs and make their living. Meeting survival needs requires resources and the labour and technology necessary to obtain those resources and transform them into usable foods and goods. People therefore need to develop practices that allow for efficient adaptations to their environments, adjusting their settlement patterns and their populations to the available resources. Specific subsistence strategies are generally associated with particular types of social and political organization and influence the ways that other cultural practices develop in order to meet physical and social needs.

> **REVIEW**
>
> Ecological anthropology is the study of subsistence strategies—how people meet their basic survival needs—and how those strategies shape their society and culture. Basic subsistence underlies the economic system of a society and strongly influences every other social system in that society as well as people's daily decisions about living their lives.

UNDERSTANDING HUMAN SUBSISTENCE PATTERNS

All cultural groups must feed themselves. The way they do so—the way their people make a living—influences and constrains many other cultural traits. Anthropologists use the term **subsistence patterns** to refer to basic methods of obtaining food within a society. Subsistence patterns differ across cultures, according different systems of using land and resources, labour, and technology within specific environments. Other aspects of culture tend to co-occur with particular subsistence strategies. These include the size and permanence of settlements that people establish, the kinds of households that they live in, their ideas about property and ownership, and even the ways that they think of themselves and other people.

Two basic modes of subsistence involve finding food (foraging, or hunting and gathering) and growing food (food production).

Foraging versus Food Production

Our early ancestors were **foragers**, or hunter-gatherers. They hunted, fished, and collected wild plants, nuts, fruits, and insects. Foraging was humanity's only subsistence strategy for countless millennia until about 10 000 years ago when people living in the Middle East began to herd animals and grow their own crops. Foragers are food collectors. They make use of the resources growing wild in their environment.

People who grow crops or manage herds are **food producers**. They transform and manage their environment in order to obtain their food. The three major types of food production are pastoralism, horticulture, and agriculture. **Pastoralism** involves raising and caring for large herds of domesticated animals as primary subsistence. Horticulture and agriculture are types of farming. Although some people still live by foraging and pastoralism, the forces of globalization are making these ways of life increasingly peripheral. Many people have multiple subsistence strategies based on mixed economies, combining farming, herding, and other methods of food production.

The earliest farming techniques were of the type referred to as **horticulture**, which refers to small-scale farming using a relatively simple technology. Later, intensive farming techniques, or **agriculture**, were developed. Today, agriculture is often combined with industrial processes that eliminate much of the need for human labour. These modes of food production are ideal types and often are combined or practised in relation to trading with other peoples. We discuss how these subsistence strategies work in the following sections.

Ecosystem, Adaptation, and Carrying Capacity

Subsistence techniques vary considerably, in part depending on available resources, climate, and topography. They are developed in order to satisfy people's needs for food, clothing, and shelter. They must also be adapted to available resources, water, land, and labour supply. Some areas of the world are rich in natural resources while others are meager, each presenting an array of possibilities and challenges for human populations.

The **carrying capacity** of any region or environment is the number of people who can be sustained by its resources. Carrying capacity, however, is not a fixed number; rather, it varies with such factors as subsistence techniques, labour expenditure, and technology. Some subsistence strategies and technologies are able to extract more resources from the land than others. This means that people can change a region's carrying capacity by changing their way of life. For example, the same region can support a bigger population of farmers than of foragers. As farmers work harder to cultivate more land, or develop technologies like irrigation to make their land more productive, they can increase yields and the size of the population that the land can sustain. At some point, however, new limits may eventually be reached beyond which the productivity of the land can no longer be increased and may, in fact, begin to decline. The resulting problems are something that every society must consider in their subsistence strategies.

Another factor influencing carrying capacity is the resources within an ecosystem that people choose to exploit. People in all cultures make distinctions between the foods that they consider to be edible and those they consider inedible, whether or not they are actually capable of consuming them. For example, different peoples regard different kinds of animals, insects, fish, or plants and seaweeds as inedible or edible because of cultural attitudes.

Communities need to keep their population size within the limits of the carrying capacity of their territory. Their adjustments to their land and resources should be attuned to productivity in good times in order to be able to sustain their numbers when conditions are not optimal. Different subsistence modes entail different kinds of strategies for adjusting population size to resources and land.

Many aspects of society and culture, including population density, the way people reckon kinship, and the way they organize their communities, may influence and be influenced by the way they feed and shelter themselves. Thus, subsistence is related to settlement patterns, population factors, division of labour, and other elements of culture. We must keep in mind that people engage in a variety of subsistence

pastoralism
A subsistence strategy focusing on raising and caring for large herds of domesticated animals.

horticulture
A subsistence strategy that focuses on small-scale farming using a relatively simple technology.

agriculture
A subsistence strategy focusing on intensive farming, investing a great deal of time, energy, and technology.

carrying capacity
The number of people who can be sustained by the resources and environment in which they live.

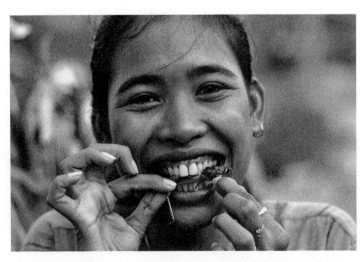

Culture as much as biology dictates the foods we choose to eat. Many foods that most North Americans would consider unfit to eat—such as insects, grubs, or snakes—may be considered tasty or even delicacies elsewhere in the world.

GLOBALIZATION

Currently food production and consumption patterns are being shaped by a vast and increasingly complex global economy. In *Tasting Food; Tasting Freedom: Excursions into Eating, Culture, and the Past* (1996), for example, Sidney Mintz explores the globalization of sugar, tea, chocolate, and the ubiquitous Coca-Cola.

modes of production, often shifting over time and interacting with people who practise other modes of subsistence. No subsistence system functions in isolation or in a timeless way unaffected by the forces of culture change.

Subsistence and Settlement Pattern

Subsistence strategies tend to be related to particular types of settlement patterns. The term **settlement pattern** refers to the way people distribute themselves in their environment: where they locate their dwellings, how they group dwellings into settlements, and how permanent or transitory those settlements are. Foragers are usually mobile. They do not have fixed, permanent settlements but move from camp to camp to secure resources in different places at different times of the year. Pastoralists also tend to relocate their settlements throughout the year, although their movements may be more predictable than those of foragers. They often alternate between two or three locations during the year, making use of familiar available grazing lands for their animals. The size of pastoral settlements varies significantly. Some are quite small, numbering less than 100 people, while others may be in the hundreds or even thousands. In contrast to foragers and pastoralists, farmers often establish relatively permanent settlements. Horticulturalists might move among their gardens and groves or relocate to more fertile fields. Many farmers live in small, scattered villages and may change location every generation or so when their farmland becomes depleted of nutrients. Agriculturalists often live in large, permanent towns or cities.

Subsistence and Population

The number of people living in a community depends on the resources available and the strategies used to extract them. Foraging communities tend to have relatively few people. Some may number no more than a few dozen, whereas others may number into the hundreds. In most foraging societies, community size fluctuates throughout the year, depending on the availability of resources. Food producers tend to have larger populations than foragers. The security afforded by producing one's own food, along with the possibility of storing crops, enables larger populations to concentrate in one settlement.

Subsistence, Work, and Division of Labour

Different subsistence strategies involve different kinds of work, allocated to different people. In foraging societies, most work is assigned according to gender. In general, men do the hunting and fishing and women gather food from plants. However, these patterns are rarely rigid. In practice, men's and women's roles overlap so that men may participate in gathering and women may assist in hunting and fishing. In farming societies, the heavy work of clearing fields is usually assigned to men. Thereafter, there are no hard-and-fast rules cross-culturally. In some cultures, women are the principal farmers; in others, men are. Age is also a factor in allocating work. In foraging societies, young children may contribute by gathering wild plants, and in farming societies, by helping to plant and weed fields and harvest crops.

Among the Dani of New Guinea, the men do the heavy work such as preparing the fields and maintaining the irrigation ditches. Women do the daily labour of cultivating crops.

Subsistence and Social Relations

Modes of subsistence are related to people's interpersonal and intergroup relationships. Subsistence strategies influence and are affected by the way that resources are allocated among different groups and the patterns of social equality and hierarchy. Societies also differ in their emphasis on cooperation or competition in producing and consuming resources and place greater or lesser value on **reciprocity** or mutual gift giving. And societies differ in having more or less effective systems for **redistribution**—the gathering together and reallocation of food and resources to ensure everyone's survival and to lessen the concentration of wealth.

reciprocity
Principles of mutual gift giving.

redistribution
The gathering together and reallocation of food and resources to ensure everyone's survival.

nomads
People who do not have permanent homes but travel to sources of food as the food becomes seasonably available.

REVIEW

Subsistence strategies include the way that people extract resources from their environment, allocate their land, and utilize labour and technology in order to obtain food and other goods necessary for their survival.

Subsistence patterns are broadly divided into foragers (hunting and gathering) and food producers (growing food). Pastoralism (herding), horticulture (keeping gardens and groves), and agriculture (growing field crops on a large scale) are three forms of food production. People's subsistence strategies depend in part on the carrying capacity of the environment they occupy, which in turn affects their settlement pattern, population size, and movements within a territory. The greater the carrying capacity, the more people can be supported. Subsistence strategies also shape and are expressed in people's social relationships and systems of exchange, such as reciprocity and redistribution.

FORAGING

Foragers depend on nature to supply them with resources, although they need to develop technologies and techniques to exploit them. Foraging societies once existed in all parts of the world, but today very few people, if any, remain dependent exclusively on a food-collecting subsistence strategy. Over many centuries, foraging societies have been transformed into food producers, either because they adopted new subsistence techniques on their own in response to environmental or internal social change or because they were absorbed by expanding agricultural or industrial societies.

Foraging survived longest in environments that have proved inhospitable to other subsistence strategies. The indigenous foraging peoples of the Arctic, for example, until recently lived off the scarce resources of a region that is extremely cold for most of the year. At another extreme, the indigenous foragers of the Kalahari Desert depended on the resources of a hot and dry environment. Now, however, the indigenous people even of these regions have become enmeshed in the national economies of the countries within whose borders they live, and they no longer rely exclusively on foraging.

? *What foraging have you done? How might your practices differ if your foraging was for subsistence rather than recreation?*

Ecological Factors

Because they depended on widely dispersed and relatively scarce resources, most foragers were **nomads**. They had to travel to particular sources of food as the food became seasonally available. In some cases, seasonal migration meant frequent relocations; in others, only a few relocations were necessary, depending on the abundance and distribution of food. Nomadism does not entail random wandering over the landscape. Foragers have a good knowledge of their environment and tend to return to fixed locations where they know that specific resources are available. In some rare cases such

Table 5.1 AN ESTIMATED JU/'HOANSI WORKWEEK

	Subsistence Work	Tool Making/ Fixing	Housework	Total Workweek
Men	21.6	7.5	15.4	44.5
Women	12.6	5.1	22.4	40.1
Average both sexes	17.1	6.3	18.9	42.3

as in the Pacific Northwest of North America, resource concentration and abundance, complemented by food storage technologies, allowed people to live in permanent settlements for part of the year. The need of most foragers to exploit a wide variety of plants and animals added interest and novelty to their diets and supplied a well-balanced assortment of nutrients. Exceptions to this foraging diet included the diet of people like the Inuit, which consisted almost exclusively of meat and fish because of the scarcity of vegetation in the Arctic.

To exploit the resources available to them successfully, foragers needed an intimate knowledge of their environment. They had to be familiar with the life cycles and properties of the plants and animals they depended on and adjust their own migrations to coincide with their seasonal availability. In arid environments, they also had to know where and when they could find fresh water. This crucial knowledge was gathered from experience and, along with critical skills such as fire making, transmitted from generation to generation.

A common misconception is that foraging requires constant labour in the pursuit of food. Observations of the Ju/'hoansi of the Kalahari, however, suggest that they spent considerably less time in subsistence activities than do people living in farming or industrial societies (Lee 2003:56). As Table 5.1 indicates, the Ju/'hoansi workweek—including foraging for food, making and repairing tools, and food preparation and other household maintenance—averaged only 42.3 hours.

Although men spent more time and energy in subsistence work than did women, women provided the bulk of the calories (56 percent) in the Ju/'hoansi diet (Lee 1982:40). Women were more productive than men because success in hunting is appreciably lower than success in food collecting. On average, men killed one animal for every four days of hunting, while women gathered enough plants, fruits, insects, and nuts in a few hours' work several times a week to feed everyone in a camp each night.

Population Factors

Most foraging societies had to keep their numbers low to avoid literally eating themselves out of their territories and seldom exceeded a size of one person per square kilometre. Family sizes were kept small according to the limited resource availability and the problems of carrying too many infants and small children when families migrated from one location to another. Foragers adopted a variety of strategies to curb population growth. These included ritually prescribed periods of sexual abstinence. In addition, women in many foraging societies (as in many other types of indigenous societies) often nursed their children for many years. Women are less fertile when they are nursing than when they are not. Reinforcing this contraceptive effect, many foraging societies (like many societies generally) had taboos or restrictions on the sexual activity of nursing mothers. Some indigenous peoples knew of plants and other natural substances that may have some contraceptive or abortive effects. Finally, when all else failed, many societies permitted infanticide as a response to the need to limit population growth. Taken together, these strategies could not control fertility completely, but they helped to stabilize population growth over time.

Social and Cultural Factors

Foraging societies generally followed the pattern of a band level of organization, which involves small scale and flexible communities (see Chapter 11). The size of settlements—the number of people living together—was small but usually varied over the course of the year. Richard Lee has observed that foragers regularly congregate into relatively large groups, sometimes as large as several hundred people, during some seasons and disperse into smaller family units in others (Lee 1972). For example, the Ju/'hoansi gathered in large groups at the site of permanent waterholes in the dry season but dispersed when the rains came. The peoples of the Pacific Northwest Coast congregated within their permanent villages during the winter but divided into smaller groups and migrated inland to hunt during the rest of the year. The Inuit also congregated in winter in snow house settlements on the sea ice and dispersed when it melted. Interpretations of this phenomenon have focused on resource scarcity or abundance, but Lee advances a different explanation. He argues that people need to congregate not because of their subsistence strategies but for social, political, and economic purposes. The most important of these is to arrange and celebrate marriages, which cannot be contracted within smaller family units because of the incest taboo, a cultural universal. However, living in a large settlement has a cost. People have to travel further from their encampments to find food than they would if they were more dispersed. After a time this cost becomes too onerous and the group subdivides into smaller units that can subsist within smaller areas.

Foraging peoples tended not to accumulate much property. For nomadic peoples, having many possessions is a burden because they have to carry them whenever they move. Foraging peoples were rarely interested in claiming land as property. Since they could not control the resources on which they relied, ownership of land would be futile and counterproductive because it would tie people to a particular location. Instead, subsistence based on foraging required territorial flexibility. Ownership of land contradicts that principle of flexibility and might potentially stifle the freedom of movement foragers needed to survive.

Social etiquette in foraging societies was often based on the principle of communal sharing. Sharing the meat of large animals was a critical way of distributing resources and making sure that everyone in the community had the same chances of surviving. People in foraging societies depended on one another in times of need, and sharing food is a way of symbolizing community interdependence just as it ensures everyone's well-being. In such societies, people understood the needs of others to be just as important as their own needs. What is good for all is good for each one. They also understood that the people whom they help feed one day might help feed them the next. Thus, while physical storage of food was normally not feasible, "social storage" was widely practised.

Most foraging societies were characterized by social equality. Foragers generally believed that all people have equal rights to resources, equal rights to social respect and prestige, and equal rights to a decent standard of living. In foraging societies, there was usually little differentiation among families in terms of possessions, wealth, housing, and equipment. Similarly, there was usually little differentiation among people in terms of social standing except as a reflection of individual differences in intelligence, skill, and personality. Only a few foraging societies had significant distinctions of wealth and social standing.

Finally, in many foraging societies, people had religions that included the belief that animals, plants, and some objects had souls similar to the souls of human beings. Animals were understood to be capable of thought and speech. Foraging peoples also performed rituals aimed at securing successful hunting.

Complex Foragers

Not all foragers conform to the model of a small-scale, nomadic, and egalitarian band society. For example, the peoples of the Pacific Northwest lived in large

? *What are the implications of foraging for the accumulation of material culture? What kinds of social relations would foraging tend to foster?*

complex foragers
Foraging societies that have developed permanent settlements, territorial exclusiveness, property accumulation, and social stratification on the basis of food storage technologies.

Case study

Foraging Societies in the Arctic and the Kalahari

A close look at nomadic foraging societies provides insight into the cultural characteristics common to many such societies. For example, although the Inuit of Arctic Canada and Alaska and the Ju/'hoansi of the Kalahari Desert in Botswana and Namibia live in starkly different environments, they share a dependence on dispersed and seasonally variable resources.

THE INUIT AND INUPIAT OF THE ARCTIC

The Arctic regions present inhabitants with enormous difficulties. Resources are scarce, and weather conditions often make subsistence activities hazardous. The Inuit, indigenous peoples of Arctic Canada, and the Inupiat, closely related peoples of Arctic Alaska, live along the coast and until recently depended primarily on sea mammals, fish, and birds for their sustenance. Because of the nearly total lack of edible plants in the Arctic, the Inuit diet consisted almost entirely of meat and fish. Their only plant sources were the berries and mosses that grow briefly in the summertime and the plant contents of the stomachs of seals, walrus, whales, and caribou that the people hunted.

Because large animals found in the sea and inland regions are migratory, their availability is subject to seasonal changes. Breeding patterns and disease can have an unpredictable effect on both the caribou and sea mammal populations from year to year. Fluctuations in the supply of meat made Inuit life precarious. Learning to endure periods of deprivation and harsh weather was an essential aspect of life. To survive, they developed sophisticated technology for hunting and making clothing. But even with the best equipment, the ablest hunter could fail and families starve.

Environmental and resource constraints kept Arctic settlements small. Along the coast, settlements were largest in winter when people hunted seals, but these winter camps typically had no more than forty or fifty inhabitants. Inland groups tended to congregate for collective caribou drives in late autumn, when the animals were most numerous. Fall was also the time for making and repairing clothing, so essential to survival in Arctic winters. As spring approached, people began to disperse, setting up smaller camps usually consisting of two to several small families. Inuit families could reside with either the husband's or wife's kin, but usually preferred the husband's. Men had to cooperate with one another to hunt large animals.

Inuit families hoped for at least one son and one daughter who could fulfill the complementary subsistence tasks associated with each gender (see the Culture Change feature in Chapter 4). In Alaska, families sometimes adopted children in order to balance the size and gender composition of their households (Bodenhorn 1988). Alternatively, parents with only boys or only girls might train one child to do both

In the wake of the loss of the traditional way of life for the Inuit, soapstone carving has become an important source of income in some communities.

men's and women's tasks (D'Anglure 1984). Because of their knowledge of the full range of Inuit subsistence skills, these individuals were valued as spouses.

In Alaska, whale hunting often involved a crew of men working under the direction of a leader, called *umialik,* who owned a boat and hunting equipment and recruited the crew. The men in a whaling crew were a cohesive social group, forming relationships with one another that were second in closeness only to those with their families (Spencer 1984).

Distribution of meat from large animals was a ritualized process that underscored people's social and economic interdependence. It ensured that everyone received adequate portions of food, and it ensured that over time people would receive different sections of the meat based on the role that they played in any particular hunting expedition. Distribution was managed by the "acquirer" of the meat (D'Anglure 1984). If the kill resulted from individual hunting, the acquirer was the man who killed the animal. In collective seal or walrus hunting, the acquirer was the man who first harpooned the animal.

Whales, walruses, and seals were butchered into specific sections and allotted according to traditional rules. Men in the hunting party received certain sections, women received others, and the whole community shared in a broth made from the remaining parts. In Alaska, the *umialik* directed the butchering and allocation of whale meat. The hunter who killed the animal received the hide. He and other members of the crew and any man or woman who contributed labour or equipment to the hunt were entitled to meat. The captain generally received extra shares but later distributed them at public gatherings and ceremonials rather than keeping them for his own household. Once the meat for formal distribution had been cut from the whale, any woman in the community could carve what she wanted from the carcass (Bodenhorn 1988). Such redistribution ensured that no one in the community went hungry when food was available.

Inuit ways of life changed substantially after the middle of the twentieth century. Most people in the region have been moved to settled communities and have curtailed their traditional subsistence activities. Like other people in the United States and Canada, they now make their living through wage work. Fur trapping provides additional opportunities as does craft production, such as the Cape Dorset soapstone carving and print making industries. Still, some families continue to supplement the foods they buy in stores with meat and fish caught in the wild, aided by new technologies such as snowmobiles.

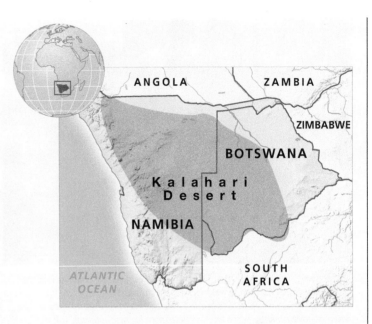

THE DOBE JU/'HOANSI OF THE KALAHARI DESERT

The Ju/'hoansi live in the hot, dry Kalahari Desert in Namibia and Botswana. The Dobe are a group of Ju/'hoansi who, in the 1960s and 1970s, numbered about 400 and lived by foraging in 3000 square miles of semidesert terrain. Water is the most critical scarce resource in the Kalahari, and its availability determined settlement size and location (Lee 1982, 2003; Shostak 1983). The Dobe area had ten permanent water holes, each "owned" by a resident group, which, however, did not have exclusive rights to the water hole. They regularly shared it with anyone who could claim kinship by birth or by marriage to any member of the resident group.

The Ju/'hoansi settled around permanent water holes during the dry season and dispersed during the rainy season when water was more widely available. Dry-season camps generally consisted of eight to fifteen huts, housing twenty to fifty people, although at times several camps joined together form a super settlement. Rainy season settlements, located near seasonal and secondary water sources, varied in size from three to twenty huts (Lee 2003:32).

Each camp had a core group of residents, usually siblings, with other residents related by blood or marriage to members of the core group. Camp composition was kept balanced. If a persistent imbalance emerged between numbers of males and females, some families would shift residence to another camp. Similarly, families would move if the camp's population placed too much pressure on local resources. In general, women's main subsistence activity was to gather wild foods. The Dobe region has more than 100 edible varieties of plants, roots, fruits, and nuts. In all, gathered foods accounted for approximately

This photo of a Dobe family suggests the effects of modern influences on the Ju/'hoansi way of life. Today, very few people sustain themselves by hunting and gathering. Most Ju/'hoansi live in small settlements, many established by the national governments. Some work as herdsmen for neighbouring tribal peoples; others have jobs either in their own communities or in the cities of southern Africa.

70 percent of the diet. Although men also gathered wild foods, their primary subsistence task was hunting (Lee 1982:40). Men individually tracked and hunted small animals, but larger animals, especially antelope and giraffe, were usually hunted by groups of men.

The Ju/'hoansi valued meat highly. First, meat provided a more concentrated source of protein and calories than plant food, making it important to people who expended a great deal of energy in their daily activities. Second, given the relatively low rate of success in hunting, meat was a scarce resource, and scarcity contributed to its desirability. Third, and perhaps most important, meat had great social value. Whereas gathered foods were usually consumed within the gatherer's household, meat was distributed throughout an entire camp. Meat from an especially large animal might be given to residents of other camps as well. A successful hunt provided the opportunity for feasting and the display of proper etiquette in distributing portions to kin and neighbours. As among the Inuit, the distribution of meat had great social significance. As Richard Lee observes:

> Distribution is done with great care, according to a set of rules, arranging and rearranging the pieces for up to an hour so that each recipient will get the right proportion. Successful distributions are remembered with pleasure for weeks afterwards, while improper meat distributions can be the cause of bitter wrangling among close relatives. (2003, p. 48)

The Ju/'hoansi had several customs to prevent successful hunters from gaining disproportionate wealth, status, and authority over others. For example, "ownership" of a kill went not to the hunter who shot it but to the owner of the fatal arrow. Arrows were given to hunters through reciprocity—gift exchanges called *hxaro*. An individual could give a present to anyone and thereby establish a relationship based on future reciprocity. When a man went hunting, he might use arrows that he made himself as well as arrows given to him by one or more of his *hxaro* partners. Prestige accrued to the arrow owner, who supervised the distribution of meat. A similar practice involved "insulting the meat." A successful hunter did not immediately bring his kill into camp. Instead, he left it a distance outside and returned alone. He would then announce his deed and gradually persuade other men to come and see. When the group arrived at the kill site, they made derogatory comments about the animal and voiced annoyance at the hunter for bothering them with such an insignificant kill. The hunter was expected to join in insulting the meat and ridiculing himself. The Ju/'hoansi were well aware of the "leveling" purpose of these social rituals. An elder hunter explained:

> When a young man kills much meat, he comes to think of himself as a chief or a big man, and he thinks of the rest of us as his servants or inferiors. We can't accept this. We refuse one who boasts, for someday his pride will make him kill somebody. So we always speak of his meat as worthless. In this way we cool his heart and make him gentle. (2003, p. 52)

settled communities under the rule of hereditary chiefs who assumed exclusive title to territories and resources, such as salmon runs, on behalf of their family groups. Land rights were reinforced through warfare in the course of which captives were seized and kept as slaves. Status differences were incorporated into the possession and redistribution of stored food and wealth items and the commissioning of artworks of monumental proportions, such as furniture, house fronts, and totem poles.

The development of such large and complex societies in the region has been attributed to the prevalence of storage. Subsistence was primarily based on the salmon harvest, which was normally abundant and further enhanced by intensive fishing technologies, such as traps and weirs. The catch was smoked and dried and then stored in pits to support settlement within villages over the course of the winter. Stored food and

This massive carving from the Pacific Northwest Coast is a throne that depicts a chief's mother carried by several slaves. How does it reflect aspects of settlement, social stratification, and complexity among indigenous foragers of the region?

the accumulation of wealth and prestige items were redistributed in large feasts that supported the unity of the community, the status claims of its leaders, and the linking of communities within a regional network of exchange and alliance.

This example and others have led theorists of foraging societies to suggest two social types: "immediate-return societies," which consume food within a short period after it is acquired, and "delayed-return societies," which have long-term storage arrangements (Daly 2005:29–31). Unlike small-scale egalitarian bands, delayed-return systems exhibit lesser degrees of nomadism, firmer insistence on territorial boundaries, larger accumulations of wealth, and greater social stratification. The literature suggests that these more complex forms occur when resources are more abundant, concentrated, or amenable to storage. However, a reverse argument is possible. Societies that become more complex may adopt accumulation and storage practices that support concentrations of people, wealth, and power.

REVIEW

Foragers such as the Inuit of the Arctic and the Ju/'hoansi of the Kalahari share hunting and gathering as a subsistence strategy. They are nomadic, moving seasonally to different resources as they become available. Foragers live in small groups, typically have egalitarian relationships, cooperate in food getting, share food across kin groups, and do not have individual ownership of land or resources. Complex foragers are able to store food and live in settled communities for at least part of the year. Status distinctions based on wealth and power differences among individuals and families are often present.

PASTORALISM

Pastoralism is a way of life that centres on the herding and care of domesticated animals. A very broad term, it applies to people dependent on diverse animals in diverse environmental and social contexts who exploit their animals for various products—rarely just for their meat and in some cases not even for food. Pastoralism differs from simple animal husbandry, which is the keeping of domesticated animals. It is a way of life in which a people's economy, settlement patterns, and social systems are adapted to large-scale herding. For example, North American farm families in rural communities are not pastoralists by virtue of keeping a small number of chickens, cows, and horses. In contrast, pastoral families in Africa, the Middle East, and Asia may own hundreds of cows or sheep and goats or horses or camels whose needs for grazing land and water determine people's daily routines and seasonal movements.

Like farming, pastoralism allows people some control over their food sources. Perhaps by about 9000 years ago, people in the Middle East were keeping domesticated sheep and goats. Pigs were domesticated in southeastern China at about the

In Their Own Voices

An Inupiaq Whaler's Wife

Sadie Brower Neakok was an Inupiaq woman living in Barrow, Alaska. She died on June 18, 2004, and was praised in the U.S. Senate for her work as the first woman to serve as a magistrate in the state of Alaska. Daughter of a native mother and an Anglo father, she was raised in both traditional and non-traditional ways. From her mother, who was a skilled hunter, Sadie learned to hunt and fish. And from her father, a whaler, she learned the importance of education in the "outside" world. Sadie grew up to be a social worker and magistrate in Barrow. She married an Inupiaq man, and she accompanied him on many hunting trips. In this excerpt from her life history, Sadie Brower Neakok: An Inupiaq Woman, *Sadie describes women's contributions to whale hunting.*

Inuit whalers.

Being a whaler's wife is just as much work as preparing to go out with a crew. You have to see that they all have warm clothing. So your husband buys all the fur. In the olden days, it was caribou hides, ruffs, fur socks, fur pants. We didn't have down clothing, so everything was made out of caribou hide or reindeer hide and sealskin for waterproof boots. New clothing is made every year because it's tradition.

If you want a good skin on your husband's boat, you have to hire several women to sew together six or seven ugruk hides with waterproof seams and stretch them over

same time. And African peoples domesticated cattle as early as 9500 years ago. Andean peoples in Peru began to domesticate animals about 7000 years ago, keeping alpaca and llamas for their meat and wool. European Sami domesticated reindeer to develop pastoral ways of life in Norway, Finland, and Russia.

Combined Subsistence Strategies

Rarely has pastoralism been a self-contained subsistence strategy. Some pastoralists combined herding with foraging, others with small-scale farming, and still others traded for food with their settled farming neighbours. Like foraging, pastoralism is disappearing as a way of life in today's world. Most pastoralists have adopted farming or wage work or trade as their primary mode of making a living. It has become increasingly difficult for pastoralists to keep control of a large enough territory in which to graze their animals, as the pressure on land has increased with population growth and national economic policies.

Pastoralists may raise herds based on one or more of several domesticated animals. The Nuer of southern Sudan combined cattle herding with farming. They consumed milk from their animals and used dung for fuel but ate meat only on ritual occasions or when an animal died of natural causes. Middle Eastern sheep and goat herders like the Basseri of Iran drank milk from their animals and processed it into butter, cheese, and yoghurt. They also traded milk, wool, and other animal products for grains and other crops from their farming neighbours. The sheepherding Diné (Navajo) kept their animals mostly for their wool, used for weaving into blankets and clothing for household consumption and for sale. In the past, the Diné obtained food primarily through farming, hunting, and gathering plant foods. Horse pastoralists, such as Mongols, not only used their animals for milk but for transport and warfare. Mongolian mobility a frame. . . . The sewers also have to know how to make the thread; it's braided from caribou leg sinew, and then the part where you put the needle [i.e., eye of the needle] is made from the back sinew.

Nate [Sadie's husband] has been a whaling captain for quite a while. And in his time, I guess he has gotten about five whales. The last one was in 1984. And you could see him cutting it up, measuring it for the various parts that go to certain people.

The fluke area is for the whaling captain, and then there's a belt of about eighteen to twenty inches wide, which is for the captain's pleasure. It's up to the captain whether he wants to sell it; he talks with his crew whether they want a share of it for their own consumption or to sell it. And the captain's part is set aside by itself, to give to people at the whale catch celebration—Nalukataq time—and Thanksgiving and at Christmastime. We cut it up in thirds for all the people. That's a lot of work, cutting it up. You have to feed the whole town; that's the custom.

Everybody enjoyed our whale. There are so many people in town now—even our whites have acquired the taste of fresh maktak and meat, and they mingle in with our people—and feeding some three and four thousand in one day out of that whale, by 10:00 p.m. we were all in.

Then you do it all over again at Nalukataq time. You have to cut up meat and maktak and put it into containers to age. You cook the heart, and the kidney, and the intestines at Nalukataq time. Oh, it's a lot of excitement when it happens. Then there's the blanket toss and the dances, but it's not like the old days anymore. People didn't work in those days when I was young. Now we have to wait till everybody gets off work to serve our big portions of whale. It starts at five.

As far back as I can remember, in the old tradition, women were out there on the ice with the men. They could go out and hunt with the menfolk; they would cook for them, or sew, or tend to their men's needs out there. But we are shying off from that today. There's not very many women who would go out and stay out there, but Nate gives our girls a chance to be out there.

When you're a whaling captain's wife, your part is just as important as the men's because you're entrusted with keeping your husband's crewmen out there comfortable and fed. You're in charge of all their care, preparing their food. . . . When the boats start chasing a whale, all you do is just listen to see who is catching it. It gets so exciting, like you are inside of the boat yourself. It's an exciting event when your crew gets a whale, a lot of work, but when all the women's work of feeding the whole town is done, then you feel like you have shared in the whale catch.

From *Sadie Brower Neakok: An Inupiaq Woman*, pp. 209–216, by Margaret Blackman. Copyright 1989. Reprinted by permission of the University of Washington Press.

Pastoral nomads of Mongolia have a mixed economy, combining subsistence bases tied to the modern Mongolian state, which achieved independence from China in 1921. Yet their way of life is similar to that of other horse-herding peoples in different cultures in other parts of the world. These similarities reflect the power of basic modes of subsistence such as pastoralism to shape peoples' ways of life as well as their daily activities.

allowed the group to conquer large territories and build one of the world's largest empires in China. The Tuareg utilized their camels to organize caravans transporting salt and gold across the Sahara.

Land and Labour in Pastoralist Societies

? *What different patterns might you predict for relationships between pastoralists of the ranges and farming peoples of the valleys?*

Pastoralists' strategies for organizing and controlling land and resources differ significantly from those of foragers because, in pastoralist societies, land and resources such as domesticated animals are controlled, even owned, by individuals or groups. Pastoralist societies closely regulate and manage rights to use land to ensure that there is enough forage for the animals. Sometimes, herds may put excessive strain on lands and resources because of overgrazing. To prevent overgrazing, pastoralists take their herds to different grazing areas throughout the year in a pattern known as **transhumance**. Pastoralists make total use of their animals and allocate these crucial resources according to rules of ownership and control. For example, Nuer cattle herders in southern Sudan own livestock individually. Each animal is the personal property of a man or teenage boy who has completed initiation rituals at puberty. These people are the primary caretakers of the cattle, although a family's herd is taken to pasture collectively. Individuals or kinship groups also own pastureland. Among the Basseri of Iran, the animals are individually owned, but different groups may use the same pastureland at different times of the year according to customary cycles of use. Among the Diné, livestock is tended as a family herd on family land. In pastoralist societies, as a consequence of individual ownership, domesticated animals become objective measures of wealth, and inequalities of wealth and competitive status seeking can arise based on the size of herds.

The division of labour by gender varies in pastoralist societies but is generally not as egalitarian as in foraging societies. Men and boys generally tend to the animals while women and children do related tasks, such as milking, dressing skins, and watching over animals. Among some pastoralists, people of any age and either gender may assist with herding animals to and from grazing lands.

Pastoralists may accumulate some animals beyond their immediate subsistence needs. Families usually try to add stock to strengthen herd size and increase the products derived from animals (hides, furs, bone) that can be used for many purposes, including the manufacture of clothing, tools, and utensils. The animals and the products crafted from them become important items in trading networks, enabling families to obtain other foods, goods, and services. Excess animals may also be loaned out to poorer herders, who will benefit their patrons by taking care of their stock and extending other services and forms of support.

Nomadic Pastoralism

Most pastoralists shared a common self-concept as pastoralists, constructing their social and personal identities around herding. Certain cultural features are commonly associated with pastoralism; for example, because pastoralists needed access to land for grazing and seasonal control over access to specific areas, they tended to define and defend their territories more vigorously than foragers. Some pastoralists, such as the Nuer of Africa and the native peoples of the North American Plains, used the strategies of raiding and warfare to defend their territories and to expand into the grazing lands occupied by others. Nomadic pastoralists might be satisfied with customary rights to graze their animals on some defined but not necessarily exclusive territory. They might be content to share their grazing lands with other people, negotiating occasional or seasonal usage. The Yoruk of Turkey rent pasture from their agricultural neighbours, while the Fulani of West Africa graze their animals on farmer's fields after the harvest, extending a benefit of free fertilizer.

Population density varied in pastoral societies, depending on the size and quality of grazing lands and herds. Unlike foraging societies, measuring and accumulating wealth and property, especially in the form of animals, has been a major feature of pastoralism. Because animals are easily countable and their numbers increased by breeding, pastoral peoples generally measured wealth by the size of a family's or individual's herds or

transhumance
The practice among pastoralists of moving to new pastureland on a seasonal basis.

Case study

Pastoral Societies of Iran and Sudan

The following case study compares two pastoral societies, revealing some of the common features of this type of subsistence strategy as well as the differences that reflect the specific environment of each group and the kinds of animals that they herd.

THE BASSERI OF IRAN: NOMADIC PASTORALISTS

Pastoralists in the Middle East, such as the Basseri of Iran, herded sheep and goats and traded animal products for grains with nearby settled farmers (Barth 1964). The Basseri, numbering about 16 000, were until recently nomadic pastoralists living in southern Iran. Today most Basseri have given up their traditional lifestyle, principally because of the pressure exerted on them by the central Iranian government. Like national governments elsewhere, Iranian authorities actively discouraged indigenous pastoralists from pursuing their economic strategies because nomadic peoples are difficult to identify and control. In addition, central governments and economic planners often view pastoralism as an outmoded way of life that retards economic development. This attitude is one more of ideology than of fact; the Basseri's traditional way of life was an efficient use of sparse resources and territories. Their territory—about 300 miles long and 50 miles wide—is varied in terrain, with mountains, deserts, and plains. Rainfall is light, occurring mainly in the winter. Precipitation, often in the form of snow, is heaviest in the mountains, which, as a result, have the regions richest in vegetation. The rest of Basseri territory is extremely dry and covered with only sparse grasses.

The Basseri did not have exclusive rights to their territory but instead shared it with other pastoral peoples. Each group had its own migration route and schedule, however, so that two or more groups were never at the same pastureland at the same time of year. Each route and schedule—called the *il-rah,* or "tribal road"—was the collective property of the group that followed it. Groups, not individuals, thus controlled access rights to pastureland.

The Basseri moved frequently—on average once every three days—among the pasturelands on their route. Their winter pastures were in the low-altitude southern part of their region, where snowfall is relatively light. As spring approached, they moved to middle-altitude pastures, and in summer to high-altitude pastures that are snow-covered at other times of the year. Each day's trek took about three hours, with some people on foot and others on donkey or horseback. The sheep and goats were led from camp first, under the care of a man or a child. Usually about thirty or forty families travelled and camped together. In the winter, large groups dispersed into smaller camps to avoid overburdening pastureland.

A Basseri family usually consisted of a couple and their children. Each family had its own tent and flock. A family required a herd of about 100 sheep and goats to sustain itself. Boys and men herded the animals to their daily grazing areas, sheep and goats together. Although girls sometimes led the animals on migratory treks, they generally did not herd when their families stayed in the same location for several days. Families with many animals and few able-bodied sons might hire boys to work for them. One shepherd could usually handle about 300 or 400 sheep and goats. People kept donkeys as pack animals and as mounts for women and children. Men rode horses. The Basseri also owned some camels, which they used for heavy loads.

Milk from their animals and milk products, such as butter, buttermilk, sour milk, and cheese, were the basis of the Basseri diet. Milking was done by men and women, usually in a group. The animals were milked at least once a day and sometimes more often. Preparing foods derived from the milk was women's work. The Basseri rarely slaughtered adult sheep and goats to eat, but they did eat excess lambs and kids to keep their herds from growing unsustainably large. They used wool and hides for clothing, tent coverings, and carrying bags. They also traded hides, wool, and finished goods made from animal products to people in settled farming communities.

The Basseri had complex relations with their neighbours in settled farming communities along their migration route. They traded for grains, fruits, vegetables, and cash. During lean years, some Basseri occasionally took seasonal jobs in towns along their routes to earn money for farm goods, clothing, tools, household utensils, and other manufactured goods. Some Basseri amassed enough wealth to buy land, which they leased to farm families, receiving money or produce as rent.

THE NUER OF SOUTHERN SUDAN:
FARMING PASTORALISTS

The Nuer are a pastoral people in eastern Africa who combined cattle herding with the cultivation of grains and other crops. The Nuer lived in semi-permanent villages along the Nile River and its tributaries and followed a seasonal round between villages and cattle camps. With a total population of more than 300 000 in the 1940s, the Nuer were organized into at least ten separate tribes. They felt a strong allegiance to their tribes but otherwise had no sense of themselves as a unified people (Evans-Pritchard 1940, 1955).

Today, the lives of the Nuer have drastically changed. Caught up as victims of civil wars in the Sudan that raged in the 1990s, most of the Nuer are refugees. Tens of thousands, possibly nearly 200 000, Nuer became refugees in camps in Ethiopia (Holtzman 2000). Then, when fighting broke out between government and revolutionary forces in Ethiopia, many Nuer moved into Kenya, where they

These Nuer focus on the challenges of living as immigrants in the United States, where a pastoral way of life is not possible.

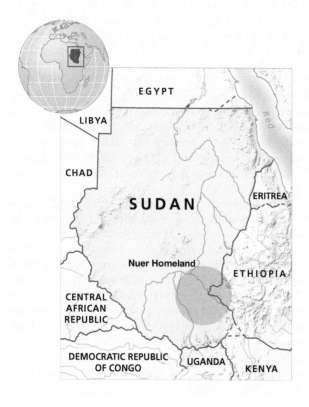

established their homes. Finally, about 4000 Nuer were permitted to emigrate to the United States in the mid-1990s. According to Jon Holtzman, most of these immigrants now reside in Minnesota, where they have maintained a strong sense of community and Nuer identity, focusing on kinship and on affiliation with Christian churches.

Although traditional Nuer subsistence combined herding and farming, their ideology centred around their relationship to their herds. Significantly, boys took a personal name derived from an attribute or name of their favourite animal. Although the Nuer seldom slaughtered animals for meat, they made total use of the animals. Their diet was primarily based on milk, but they also consumed blood—bled in small amounts from shallow incisions in their cattle, which they drank fresh or mixed with other foods. For instance, a favourite Nuer food is cow's blood mixed with warm milk and a dash of cow's urine. The people worked the animals' hides and bones into various utensils, and they used dung as fuel for fires and as plaster for the walls and floors of their dwellings.

The Nuer rigidly distinguished men's from women's work. Men (including boys of about 15 years or older who had been ritually initiated into manhood) were responsible for herding cattle. In addition, men's productive roles included fishing in the many streams and rivers in the region. Fish constituted an important year-round food source. Men also did some hunting, although game added little to the Nuer diet. Women, girls, and young boys, although not permitted to herd cattle, were responsible for milking the animals twice a day, once in the morning before the cattle were led to pasture and again in the evening when they returned to the corrals. Women also tended gardens, principally growing millet and maize.

Nuer settlements varied seasonally. During the heavy flooding of the rainy season, they inhabited higher ground in settled villages in which they grew millet and other agricultural crops. Cattle were led out to pasture each morning and returned to the settlement at night. When the dry season arrived, they moved their herds to cattle camps on the sites of permanent water sources Villages were usually organized around relatives tracing descent through men. They were composed of extended family homesteads consisting of a cattle byre and several huts. The byre, in which the cattle sleep during the rains, is the central building of the compound and is used as a meeting place for household members and guests. Each

hut was occupied by an adult woman, usually one of the wives of the household head and her children. Men would sleep in their wive's huts in rotation, while unmarried men would often sleep in the byres with the animals. This pattern reflects the importance of gender and age divisions in Nuer society and the strong bond between men and cattle in Nuer ideology.

In the Nuer view of the world, cattle are the focus of life. A family's animals are said to be owned by the male head of household, but a man's wives and sons have rights to them as well. When a man marries, he receives some of the cattle owned by his father. Brothers are, therefore, potential co-owners of cattle and are bound together both by their own blood relationship and by their ties to their family herd. When a woman marries, her family receives cattle from her new husband's kin that are then divided among her male relatives, especially her brothers. Cattle, therefore, are essential to economic and social life, as they are used to establish and solidify social relationships.

flocks. In addition, because animals or products derived from them (meat, hides, wool) can be traded for other goods, herds represent both present and future wealth. In some pastoral societies, wealth in animals became the basis for social stratification. People with larger herds had higher social standing, prestige, and influence than others. And because in most nomadic pastoralist societies men are usually the owners of most, if not all, of the animals in the herds, systems of descent and inheritance typically follow in the male line.

Despite a focus on ownership and competition, pastoralists maintained values of reciprocity, especially sharing with relatives and the expression of generosity and hospitality. Social norms calling for generosity acted as a levelling mechanism, ensuring that richer families shared some of their wealth with poorer families.

? *Why did pastoralism as a subsistence mode favour competition over cooperation?*

REVIEW

Pastoralists such as the Basseri of Iran and the Nuer of southern Sudan traditionally depended on the animals they herded for all their subsistence needs. Animals also became the basis of wealth. Some pastoralists practise transhumance, moving herds to different pasturelands as they become seasonally available for grazing. Control of grazing land and rights in a herd are major concerns in pastoralist societies.

HORTICULTURE

Horticulture and agriculture are two types of farming that are not always easily distinguished. The term *horticulture* refers to farming on a small scale with a relatively simple technology consisting of digging sticks, hoes, and other handheld tools. The term *agriculture* refers to large-scale farming and the use of more complex technology, which can include, for example, draft animals or irrigation. Intensive agriculture involves substantial modification of the natural environment and large labour inputs. Horticulture, by contrast, does not try to reshape the land or add to its fertility beyond clearing the vegetation on plots meant for cultivation. After a crop is harvested, the land is allowed to lie fallow and revert to its natural state. Some farming peoples may be horticulturalists and others agriculturalists.

sedentism
A settlement pattern involving long-term, permanent settlements.

slash-and-burn (swidden) cultivation
A farming technique for preparing new fields by cutting down trees and bushes and then burning them in order to clear the land and enrich the soil with nutrients.

Impacts of Sedentism

The cultivation of crops in a confined area allows horticulturalists to maintain a degree of sedentism or permanent settlement and to support larger population densities than foragers or pastoralists. They tend to live in relatively small settlements of from one hundred to several thousand people at a density of up to 100 people per square kilometre. **Sedentism**, unlike nomadism, allows for the construction of substantial permanent dwellings, the accumulation of property, and the storage of food items, which is necessary to maintain the community between harvests. The general social order conforms to a tribal pattern of kinship-based settlement and land tenure, egalitarian status systems, and a limited degree of formalization of political organization and leadership (see Chapter 11).

Slash-and-Burn Horticulture

The tasks involved in farming include preparing fields or gardens for cultivation, planting, weeding, and harvesting. The most strenuous of these is preparing new fields for cultivation. Many horticulturists, especially those who live in tropical forest areas, use **slash-and-burn**, or **swidden**, **cultivation** to accomplish this task. Once an area of land is selected for planting, men cut down trees and bushes and then burn them, which both clears the land and enriches the soil with nutrients. Swidden plots are usually farmed for only two or three years, after which the soil is usually exhausted. The land is then fallowed for a much longer period to allow the forest to regenerate. The lengthy fallow period does not usually require communities to move their locations but some horticulturalists do so. For example, the Yanomamo of the Amazon forest abandon their farms and settlements every ten years, usually on the occasion of outbreaks of warfare with their immediate neighbours.

Swidden farmers in Borneo transform forests on marginal mountain slopes into palm groves for producing rattan, used in caning and weaving. They cut and burn the forest vegetation and plant palm canes in the ashes. In other mountainous areas of Indonesia, reclaimed forestland is cut into terraces for rice farming. Terraces depleted of nutrients are left fallow as others are farmed. Without organic or chemical fertilizers, however, depleted soils ultimately must be abandoned and more forests cut down to create new cropland.

Gender Allocation of Work

In horticulture societies, gender allocation of work typically calls for men to do the heavy work of clearing forests and woodlands to make new fields. In some societies, men continue as the primary workers, while in others, women are the farmers. In other societies, both men and women do farm work, growing the same or different crops.

Among the Pueblo of the American Southwest such as the Zuni, both men and women grow crops, although they employ different methods and work in different types of farmland. Zuni men plant, weed, and harvest crops in the fields surrounding their villages. Traditionally, some work was carried out by individuals, while other tasks were done collectively, usually by a group of relatives consisting of fathers, their unmarried sons, and their resident sons-in-law. Before marriage, men worked the land controlled by their mother; after marriage, they worked on land under the direction of their wife's mother.

Because of the difficulty of farming in an arid environment, the people developed a system of floodwater irrigation that made best use of available water from rainfall and from the small Zuni River and a few nearby springs. When a man cleared new land for planting, he built small dams and canals with mud walls to direct water from rainfall and from overflowing streams. The walls were constructed by packing mud over a row of stakes made of branches, rocks, sticks, and earth. In contrast to men's work, women grew some produce in "waffle gardens" along the banks of the Zuni River. Waffle gardens were divided into small square or rectangular cells surrounded by low mud walls that helped conserve water and protect the plants from wind. Women watered their plants by hand, using ladles to distribute water brought from the river or from nearby wells in water jars.

Farming families are able to utilize the labour of their children at early ages. Young children can plant seeds, weed gardens, and pick fruits and vegetables. Some people may become part-time specialists, making pottery, baskets, canoes, houses, and other items. By bartering or selling their products, artisans and other part-time specialists may free themselves from some subsistence work. Horticultural societies produce enough to store crops as a buffer against hunger and starvation in years of low yield. People prevent the over-burdening of land and its fertility by fallowing their land for several years or relocating every generation or so. Social norms calling for hospitality and generosity contribute to the redistribution of food and resources so that no one goes hungry.

Among the Yanomamo of the Amazon, men are the principal farmers. They clear and prepare fields and plant and harvest crops. Principal crops include plantain, manioc, and sweet potatoes. Men grow tobacco, used for chewing, and cotton, used to make yarn for weaving hammocks. Men also hunt and fish. In effect, men provide all the food for the family. Women's work, which includes food preparation and child care, is entirely domestic. Their work is considered secondary to men's work, and they have a correspondingly low status in Yanomamo society (Chagnon 1997).

In contrast, among the Jivaro (HE-va-ro) of Peru, women were responsible for planting, tending and harvesting crops, notably manioc, sweet potatoes, and squash. These crops, supplemented by fish and game provided by men, supplied the bulk of the Jivaro diet (Meggers 1971). Women were also responsible for performing the garden rituals that ensure a good crop. The Jivaro valued these tasks, and Jivaro women still have a higher status in their society than Yanomamo women do in theirs.

In some West African societies, horticultural work is performed by both men and women but the crops that they plant differ. Among the Igbo of Nigeria, for example, tasks are strongly demarcated according to gender. Men traditionally plant yams, considered to be the staple crop. Women plant and harvest all other crops, including manioc, cocoyams, maize, beans, and okra. Women also weed their husbands' yam gardens. Even when work has a collective focus, tasks are demarcated according to gender. For example, men harvest yams, but women and children carry the yams to the household yam barn (Ottenberg 1965; Ottenberg and Ottenberg 1962). Other subsistence and household activities are likewise allocated according to gender as are the rewards. The income from the sale of palm oil, a major cash crop, is controlled by men, but women are entitled to the kernels that are left intact after oil is extracted from the palm fruit. They extract an edible oil from the kernels and are entitled to sell it and keep the income for their own purposes (Uchendu 1965:26).

Horticulturists may keep domesticated animals for meat. For example, indigenous peoples of the Melanesian Islands of the western Pacific cultivate yams and other food crops and also keep pigs. Pigs, however, are not grazing animals like cattle, sheep, or goats. They eat the same foods as humans. Melanesian horticulturalists usually allow the pigs to furrow on harvested fields and eat crops that are not fit for human consumption. The Tsembaga, however, grow additional crops to feed their pigs. As the pig population grows, the effort to feed them becomes increasingly burdensome. Eventually, the pig population grows so large that it triggers a round of ceremonials accompanied by pig sacrifices and feasts. The pig population plummets and the cycle begins anew (Rappaport 2000).

Land Ownership

Because of the lengthy fallow periods involved in horticultural production, most of the land is held in fallow, and plots that are used in one season may not be farmed again for up to a generation. This arrangement does not encourage private ownership since households are always in the process of utilizing new plots. In general a pattern of corporate ownership in which a group holds land in reserve for its members is prevalent.

GLOBALIZATION

The expansion of slash-and-burn farming into tropical rain forests in Indonesia and the Amazon region contributes to global deforestation but on a smaller scale than commercial lumbering. Deforestation alters climate and weather patterns and contributes to global warming.

Case study

Mohawks: Farmers of the Eastern Woodlands

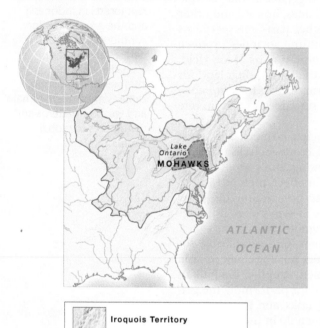

Iroquois Territory

Present-Day New York State

The economy of the Mohawks combined horticulture and foraging. Settlements were relatively stable, although people moved to new locations every generation or so when their farmland became less productive and they had exhausted the supply of readily available firewood. Village size ranged from about 50 to 1000 people and averaged several hundred. Settlements were composed of longhouses in which several families related through women resided. Each longhouse group owned the farmland and allocated it among its members. Women and men performed different but complementary tasks. Men cleared new fields with slash-and-burn techniques. Then women took over as the principal farmers, planting varieties of corn, beans, and squash, the three staple crops of Native North America. Using wooden hoes, women dug holes in small mounds of earth and planted seeds in them. Before planting, seeds were soaked in herbal solutions for several days to keep crows away from the crops.

Corn was central to the Mohawk diet. They ate it in soups and stews, often mixed with berries, meat, or fish. Corn kernels were preserved by drying them in the sun and later were baked into breads. In addition to farming, women gathered wild plants, fruits, berries, and nuts. In the early spring, women extracted sap from maple trees that they used to sweeten corn dishes and teas. Women controlled distribution of the food they produced and the resources and goods contributed by their husbands and sons. They also collected and distributed supplies for public feasts and ceremonial occasions (Lafitau 1974). Consistent with this control over resources, Mohawk women had high status within their households and communities (Brown 1975; Bonvillain 1980).

Men's subsistence roles included hunting and fishing to supplement the plant diet. They hunted deer, elk, moose, bear, beaver, partridges, and wild turkeys. Bows and arrows were the basic hunting gear. Hunters also used wooden traps to capture deer, and spears and nets to catch birds and fish. Men and women occasionally organized communal deer-hunts in which they might kill as many as 100 animals. They walked through the woods in a long V-shaped formation shaking rattles and making other noises. The frightened deer were driven into the ever-narrowing arms of the V and killed. Men were also responsible for trading with other peoples.

The units involved are most usually groups of kin who are descended from a common ancestor in whom the land is vested. For example, among the Ashanti of West Africa, the members of the matrilineage, a group of people who trace descent through their mothers to a common ancestress, ask the lineage elders for access to the plots that they need. The elders exercise control over the land as stewards for the ancestors, the acknowledged land owners. The members of a matrilineage live together in a section of villages that contains several such groups. When crops are harvested, the ancestors must be rewarded with sacrifices of the first fruits. Such forms of communal ownership discourage the development of differences in wealth based upon ownership of productive resources. Consequently, horticultural societies maintain traditions of egalitarianism in which status differences are dependent on age and moveable forms of wealth rather than ownership of land or other fixed assets.

REVIEW

In horticultural societies such as the Mohawk and Yanomamo, people plant gardens with staple crops and may keep small animals. Sedentism—living in one place—is possible for small populations. Work is allocated by gender and age. Slash-and-burn (swidden) horticulture involves a constant round of abandoning depleted land and allowing it to return to natural vegetation through fallowing. Land ownership is present in the form of corporate kin-group control.

AGRICULTURE

Agriculture differs from horticultural in its strategy of land and labour use. Horticulturalists are able to maintain their communities by utilizing large amounts of land, most of which is held in fallow. Agricultural cultivators are more concerned with increasing yields on plots that are farmed every year. To do so, they must modify their environment to facilitate cultivation and make the soil more fertile. While many ways of accomplishing these tasks have been recorded, the most common preindustrial forms have been irrigation and animal-drawn plowing. The oldest irrigation systems known are those of the ancient Near East in the Tigris-Euphrates valley, which developed five thousand years ago and supported the emergence of the first urban-based, literate societies organized into centralized states. Similar complexes have emerged in other parts of the world, such as China and Mexico.

Intensive agriculture has many implications for society and culture. Increased crop yields can support a denser population and a higher concentration of people in urban centres than can horticulture. They also encourage private ownership of land since people use their plots permanently and make investments to increase their productivity. Private ownership in turn leads to inequalities in land ownership as more successful farmers acquire acreages from less successful ones. In many agricultural societies, this process has led to a division between a small landowning elite and a large group of landless or land-poor **peasants** whose subsistence depends upon working for the landlords. The elite often become established in cities which provide them with special amenities and a centralized administrative system which protects their property and privileges. The urban system also supports the emergence of specialized craft workers, organized religion, and the development of a literate tradition.

The rural peasantry usually comprises the largest component of agricultural societies. Peasants are distinguished from other types of farmers, such as tribal horticulturalists. While they produce primarily for their own subsistence, they also provide a "fund of rent" which is used to support a regional economic and administrative infrastructure based in cities and controlled by an urbanized elite. Rent may take one of several forms. Individual peasant families may receive allotments from their landlords and pay back a portion of the harvest, an arrangement known as sharecropping. They may be subject to the payment of taxes, usually a fixed share of the harvest, to government officials. Alternatively, they may be required to perform unpaid labour service on state-owned or private estates and to contribute labour to public works projects, such as road or building construction. Similar socio-economic patterns have appeared in colonial societies, in which the peasantry contributes to the support of a foreign elite and their systems of commerce and administration (Wolf 1966).

In general, its participation within the larger system gives the peasantry few economic or political returns. In the more exploitative systems, peasants develop forms of defense and resistance to counteract the outflows of wealth and power from their communities. They often adopt an inward focus and strong bonds of local identity and mutual support to ensure the survival of the group. Peasant villages often stress in-marriage and otherwise discourage out-migration. Local cultures assume distinctive features to reinforce identity and exclusiveness. Villages may have their own ceremonial traditions, such as the worship of a patron saint. They may even adopt identifying clothing, a pattern that is common in Guatemala and Mexico. The achievement of local solidarity often entails limitations on wealth differences within the community by demanding that richer peasants fund lavish public ceremonies.

peasants
Rural agriculturalists who are partly enmeshed in a larger social and economic system. Part of their production is devoted to supporting the larger system and its dominant elite.

Anthropology Applied

Foraging Diets

We often believe that technological changes, such as those related to the introduction of agriculture, result in improvements to living standards and overall well-being. However, the benefits of new ways of doing things are sometimes not as clear as they seem. The introduction of new technologies often supports social stratification and demands greater exactions of labour from those at the bottom of the ladder. Dietary changes often lead to poorer health. Early farmers were much more likely to suffer from malnutrition, nutritional diseases, and tooth decay than their foraging predecessors (Diamond 1995). Contemporary diets in industrialized societies, based on highly processed foods, indicate an even greater nutritional crisis. Currently, 33 percent of Canadian adults are overweight, and 5 percent have diabetes, conditions that are directly related to the quantity and types of food eaten. Other diseases resulting from poor diets, such as heart conditions and cancer are endemic. Moreover, this deplorable state comes at a high cost. A kilogram of breakfast cereal, which contains 3600 calories, requires 15 675 calories for its production and transportation (Bartlett 1989). This expenditure draws on scarce soil and energy resources at an unsustainable rate.

Studies of subsistence, diet, and traditional knowledge of foragers and other indigenous people can contribute to the mitigation of some of the dietary problems that we are now facing. For example, studies of Inuit populations that depended on traditional subsistence resources have shown a low incidence of nutritional diseases, despite their heavy dependence on animal foods that contain a high ratio of fat in contravention to Canadian standards that emphasize balanced, low fat diets. They obtained a full range of vitamins by eating organ meats such as liver and did not need concentrated calories contained in carbohydrates, since the body converts proteins and fats into glucose in the absence sugars and starches. Moreover, the fats that the Inuit ate were generally healthful. Unlike domesticated animal meat, game and fish tend to be low in saturates and high in beneficial monounsaturates and omega-3 fatty acids (Gadsby 2004). These findings are significant, since Inuit diets may be similar to those on which our ancestors depended for all but 10 000 years of human evolution. Accordingly, our biology may be better attuned to the consumption of wild animals and other lean meats than to our usual carbohydrate-rich fare (Cordain 2006).

CRITICAL THINKING QUESTION

If the introduction of domesticated foods has created so many problems, why did people bother to go through the trouble of developing and cultivating them?

REVIEW

Agriculture constitutes an intensive form of farming based on modifying the landscape and incorporating complex technologies, such as irrigation, to enhance yields. It allows for greater density and concentration of population than horticulture does. Cultivation entails the permanent use of land and favours private ownership. The social correlates of agricultural development include social stratification, urbanization, occupational specialization, and the rise of the state. Food production is based on the activities of rural peasants, who support urban infrastructures and class division through the export of their crops, usually on unfavourable terms. They develop inwardly focused institutions to limit and mitigate external exploitation.

INDUSTRIALIZATION AND GLOBALIZATION

Over the course of the nineteenth century a new technological and economic regime began to spread its powerful influence from European centres of origin to every corner of the globe. The changes in society and culture that resulted from this industrial transformation have been comprehensive, numerous, complex, and controversial. Recording and understanding their impact on the various world regions constitutes a major research agenda of contemporary anthropology, both within industrial heartlands and in developing countries on the margins of the industrial order.

Case study

A Farming Community in Saskatchewan

Cattle ranchers reinforce a strong sense of community during roundup, when neighbours help each other brand their animals. Implements of the cowboy way of life provide additional symbolic support to group identity.

The Canadian prairie has been the location of widespread and intensive mechanized agricultural and farm family settlement. Its grain, oil-seed, and livestock output not only feeds Canada's cities but also supplies a vast international market. The economic and social character of the early phases of this expansion has been documented in an anthropological study carried out in Saskatchewan in the 1960s (Bennett 1976). The details cover the basic social order of rural Canada at the time, some interesting complexities and variations within its local communities, and forces that have since led to dramatic changes in economic and social patterns. The research site covered the area around a small service town of 2500 people. The total regional population was 7500, made up primarily of farmers. Four distinct groups, which differed according to economic activity and culture, populated the rural sector: a Plains Cree reserve, a ranching community, a farming community, and several Hutterite colonies.

Regional settlement involved the expropriation of Aboriginal land by the federal government and the railways and the resettlement of the Cree on a reserve with few economic opportunities. Land was virtually given away to settlers from Eastern Canada, the United States, and Europe in anticipation of the development of a commercial agricultural economy that could support the government, railways, and trading companies through taxation, freight, and commerce. The cattlemen were the earliest of the settlers, arriving at the end of the nineteenth century. A generation later, the farmers followed. The Hutterites began to settle in the 1950s.

The ranchers originally grazed their cattle on open rangeland but were eventually forced to restrict their pastures to government-owned leaseholds. Although they technically owned little land, they held permanent leases that they could pass on to their children or sell for the market value of the land. However, transfers had to be approved by the government land department, which stipulated that holdings could not be subdivided and that new leasees demonstrate their potential to be successful ranchers. Cattle production depended mostly on natural forage, although some fodder crops were grown. Families lived on scattered homesteads two or more kilometres apart. The ranchers tended to be wealthier than the farmers and also claimed superior status as original settlers who still represented a valued pioneer way of life. As such, cowboy cultural traits, such as Western dress, horse owning, rodeos, and rugged individualism, were stressed. This pattern produced the dominant regional cultural symbols which the farming community also adopted, especially within its socially mobile substratum. The special status of being a rancher was maintained by the development of closely knit social networks within the community. Exclusiveness was consolidated through a high incidence of in-marriage.

THE RANCHERS

The social organization of the rancher community presents something of a paradox. On one hand, their basic economy was dependent on the market for their income and all their consumption needs. They preferred to sell their cattle to private buyers on a one-to-one basis rather than through a marketing pool or public auction. They also emphasized individualism and self-reliance as esteemed personality traits and were not involved in the co-operative and populist movements which were mobilizing much of rural Saskatchewan at the time. They were active in local politics, which they dominated, but did not take an interest in provincial or national affairs. On the other hand, they maintained a high level of co-operation within the community. Mutual support was reflected in communal cattle round-ups, in which all the ranchers in a locality came together to help each other brand their cattle. Ranchers also organized voluntary associations, including roping and riding clubs and the Oldtimers Association. Informal systems of aid were articulated through kinship, marriage, and neighbourliness. Peer groups united ranchers at similar stages of their life and business cycles.

Cooperation revolved around exchange rings and dyadic partnerships involving reciprocity among and between friends. The rings incorporated ranchers, whose operations were of the same size and involved the lending of tools and equipment and the pooling of labour for major tasks, such as fencing. Dyadic relationships involved pairs of individuals, who ran different-sized ranches. The wealthier partner loaned goods and equipment to the poorer one, who reciprocated by offering labour services. As with nomadic pastoralists, cattle loans allowed marginal producers to remain in the system. In doing so, this patronage arrangement decreased opportunities for the larger operations to buy up leases vacated by smaller ones, maintaining community stability at the expense of further growth of the more successful operations.

The economy of the individual ranch was based on the family as an integral unit of production. It supplied most of the labour, except for the largest operations, which were able to acquire help through the dyadic exchange system or to employ ranch hands. Bennett does not discuss women's activities to any extent, but indicates that there was a marked ranch wife role and identity. The son's role, however, is discussed at length. A boy began serious work in his mid-teens and continued to work for his father into his mid-twenties, when he would marry and take over management of the family holdings. The son's family moved into the main house and his parents were given a smaller outbuilding from which they continued to participate in ranch operations. Any additional sons had to buy farms of their own, work as ranch hands, or migrate to the city.

THE FARMERS

The farming population was larger than that of the ranchers. Its members formed a distinct and relatively homogeneous group. Although the community was ethnically diverse, cultural differences were generally submerged within a uniform farming way of life that was common to all sectors of the community. The basic operation involved an equal emphasis on grain cultivation and cattle rearing. Farmers differed from ranchers mainly in the smaller scale and more diversified patterns of their operations and in their more intensive use of cultivated fodders. They did, however, depend upon natural pastures as well and competed with the ranchers for grazing leases. More importantly, they were considered to be a distinct group, located further down the economic and social ladder than ranchers.

Like the ranchers, farm families lived on dispersed homesteads. Each farmer owned his own land but supplemented his acreage with the use of free communal pasture and grazing leases. The economy was market based. The bulk of all grain and cattle were sold, except for crops that were fed to the animals. Most of the family's food and all of its other goods were purchased.

The social organization of farming was similar to that of ranching insofar as it reflected a balance of co-operative and competitive patterns. However, each group was in a somewhat different situation. Farmers had to be more businesslike than the ranchers. Their operations were smaller but required heavy investments in farm machinery that usually involved borrowing and paying interest. They had to pay strict attention to profit margins and, accordingly, had to place individual viability above mutual support. However, they were more dependent upon government policies and the practices of private marketing companies. Collective action emerged as an important mechanism for effectively dealing with these external forces. Small groups of farmers often formed grazing cooperatives to purchase government leases for their members. The community joined the Saskatchewan Wheat Pool, which emerged as a farmer-owned buying agent that jointly marketed their members' wheat. This arrangement allowed farmers to receive higher prices than they did from the private buyers who dealt with them on a one-on-one basis and often extracted large profits. It also set up an income stabilization fund that helped to balance year-to-year price fluctuations. Farmers became active in the populist CCF (Co-operative Commonwealth Federation), and its successor, the NDP (New Democratic Party), which formed the provincial government and represented the interests of the smaller agricultural producers. Aside from participation in province-wide institutions, the farmers also were active in formal and informal group activities at the local level. They participated in many agricultural and general community organizations. On an informal level, they set up reciprocal aid rings, similar to those of the ranchers.

In spite of the high level of collective action and support, the farm community also reflected a significant degree of individualism and competition. Farmers were less likely than ranchers to help smaller, less viable operations and were more interested in acquiring land that may have been put on the market by liquidations. They regularly bid against each other for land in attempting to expand their uneconomically sized holdings. They competed and often argued over the utilization of communal pastures. More importantly, they were involved in controversies over water rights, which were needed for irrigated fodder crops, sometimes monopolizing streams that ran through their properties or stealing water from private or public sources.

Aside from competitive relations, three other forces exerted pressure on community identity and cohesiveness: the external orientation of the farm family, emigration of the younger generation, and the turnover of farm ownership. Farmers were generally more open than ranchers to products, ideas, and other innovations that diffused from provincial and national centres. They were also more likely to participate in provincial and national politics. This openness to outside influences was reflected in migration patterns. Farmers were less likely to inherit the family holdings and a large majority left for work in the cities, usually in unskilled jobs. Thus the permanent outmigration rate of farm boys, 50 percent, was almost twice as high as the rate for ranchers' sons. Girls of both communities left in even larger numbers because of the absence of opportunities. Consequently, the farm community had less continuity of personnel and was continually absorbing newcomers.

THE HUTTERITES

The Hutterites are a Christian group who espouse a communal way of life,. They form communities of approximately 100 people who live in small mixed-farming settlements and jointly own and work the land and share in its output. They also have larger operations than most family farms in terms of land, machinery, and output.

The Hutterite colonies formed a distinct social and economic phenomenon both because of their unique community organization and because of their profitability and success. Their social order was based on communal ownership of the farmland and equipment. All members were expected to work on the farm or in various service capacities without direct remuneration. They jointly shared in the produce and income received from crop and livestock production. They were organized under an elected council of elders, who were drawn from the senior men of the community. These leaders were responsible for organizing the religious, social, and economic activities

and for distributing and investing the returns from the operation. They adopted a curious combined ideology of aggressive capitalism and intense communalism. Hutterites adjusted very well to the external market environment and continually expanded their output, efficiency, and profitability by investing in the most up-to-date machinery and purchasing more land. However, internally economic and social relations were governed by firm restrictions. Adherence to Christian and communal morality and to the norms and decisions of the group was strictly enforced. Consumption patterns reflected an emphasis on practical items. Some creature comforts were supported, but purchases of goods that reflected the ideas and trends of North American mass culture, such as TVs, were forbidden.

These three agrarian communities provide an interesting range of adaptations to the local environment and regional economy in the context of commercial farming in an industrial society. The ranchers represented, in some sense, a preindustrial community that remained culturally distinct, socially cohesive, and locally focused. They were able to maintain their mode of subsistence as a unique way of life because cattle production was a land-intensive activity that did not require continual innovation and capital improvements to maintain an adequate living standard. They were, of course, dependent on the market for income but did not need to manipulate the economic or political system to sustain their families and community. The farmers were more typical of an industrial agrarian order. They developed a more open economic and social orientation. They continually adopted new machinery, inputs and techniques from the outside. They also participated in the wider political system more fully and were more likely to be affected by external economic, social, and cultural influences. Their communities were more open and flexible and involved a high rate of out-migration. In general, they placed individual interests ahead of those of the group and maintained a balance between commitment to the locality and their personal and class interests. Paradoxically, their adaptation to the natural and economic environment was the most precarious. Many farmers did not have large enough holdings or produce enough to cover their expenses, and liquidations were common. The Hutterites reflect a dual pattern. On the colony level, they were very much like a pre-industrial agricultural community. They were internally cohesive, had a strong sharing ideology, and actively fended off external cultural and social influences. However, they had developed holdings on an economically viable scale and had made a businesslike, effective, and dynamic adaptation to the external economy.

Some features of rural Saskatchewan in the 1960s foreshadowed the developments that have since become dominant. At the time, the family farming system was experiencing significant economic stress. Farm size was often too small to yield enough income to maintain the payments and investments that expensive inputs and equipment required. A trend towards the development of a smaller number of larger farms was apparent. In 1956, there were 100 000 Saskatchewan farm families with an average size of 600 acres (Offert ND). In 2006 the number of farms had dropped to 45 000, and average size had increased to 1450 acres (Statistics Canada 2007a).

The changes evident in the Saskatchewan case are related to an emerging structural transformation of Canadian farming. Larger-scale operations are moving into the agricultural sector with a different rationality and socio-economic organization than traditional rural residents. Giant corporate-owned agribusiness has become a major force on the rural landscape of Saskatchewan and the other Prairie Provinces (see the Culture Change feature: Pig Farming in Manitoba). Government policy changes and the privatization of agricultural cooperatives have withdrawn support for the family farm and the traditional rural way of life. The Saskatchewan Wheat Pool, formerly owned by local farmers, is now a private company traded on the Toronto Stock Exchange. At the time of writing, it had just been successful in a hostile takeover bid to acquire Agricore, itself a privatized amalgamation of the Manitoba and Alberta wheat pools, and became the largest grain buyer in Canada with annual sales of four billion dollars.

The Industrial Revolution began in the British textile industry, which developed on the basis of fuel-powered machinery and factory-based mass production. These innovations and the expansion of markets that they fostered spread to the manufacturing of many other products, and, consequently, industry replaced agriculture as the dominant sector of the British economy. Investment and employment were transferred from the rural countryside to growing industrial centres. The mass of the population moved out of their rural villages to join the ranks of the urban working classes. A new and wealthy capitalist class emerged to dominate national and international economies. Similar developments occurred in Europe and the Americas as these regions struggled to match and compete with British industry.

The industrial economy introduced a new economic and social order. Commercialization expanded to organize the distribution of a wide array of goods and services and penetrated into completely new areas. Many items that were previously produced for subsistence and gift exchange were transformed into saleable commodities to be traded in national and international markets. Land and labour, which had previously been regulated by social principles, became valued, allocated, and transferred according to the "laws" of supply and demand. This wholesale commercialization of the economy was in part due to the dynamics of industrialization and capitalist competition, which encouraged continual growth of production and profit and consumed an increasing amount and variety of resources. It was also influenced by a redefinition of the economic role of state, which, according to thinkers of the time, should limit its control over the economy and allow the market, competition, and private interests to operate freely. In accordance with these forces, nineteenth-century Europe and North America became the locus for the appearance of a new social system. The market principle entailed the development of individualistic values, which dictated that people compete against each other for resources, profit, and wealth. Private decisions to realize these objectives created a social order based on the expression of individual interests rather than the application of social rules. This regime encouraged the development of a more open society allowing for a wider range of choices in the construction of social identities, roles, statuses, and relationships. The market model was extended to governmental forms that became organized according to democratic principles that reflected and still reflect the utilitarian ethos of the era.

Industrial development has affected the rural sector as much as the urban one in which the manufacturing infrastructure was located. Mass migrations to cities led a reduction of the rural sector from a large majority to a small minority of the population in most industrial countries. The relative and absolute decline of the rural population

Culture Change

PIG FARMING IN MANITOBA

Since the end of World War II, older patterns in industrial society have been changing. The emerging era, which some social theorists have labeled post-industrial society, has involved a rapid growth of service economies and of information processing and distribution, the expansion of international investment and trade, and the withdrawal of government economic controls and social supports. A description of recent developments in the Manitoba farm sector illustrates the impact of some of these forces within rural Canada.

While we usually associate its landscape with endless fields of wheat, Manitoba's main agricultural product is not grain but pork. In 2005, hog production in the province reached a value of $955 million, substantially more than either of its most important crops, canola ($357 million) and wheat ($267 million) combined (Province of Manitoba 2006). This prominence is the result of a six-fold increase in hog production since 1981. It is a consequence of two related forces: the globalization of the Canadian farm economy and the liberalization of government agricultural policies.

The expansion of the pig industry has been fostered by the increasing export orientation of the Canadian economy in general. Over 80 percent of Manitoba's $3 billion farm economy is devoted to international sales. Hog production has been particularly stimulated by the rising American demand for meat, with an additional impetus from Japan. Globalization of Manitoba agriculture is also evident in investment patterns, as foreign capital is making inroads into the rural economy.

Trade liberalization and the related decline of government support for agriculture have also had a marked influence on agricultural ways of life. Two major changes introduced in Manitoba during the 1990s have been critical: the cancellation of the Crow rate and the elimination of the Manitoba Pork Marketing Co-operative. The Crow rate was a federally subsidized arrangement that maintained low, fixed prices for the shipment of prairie grain. When this was abolished, it became more profitable to use the grain as feed and to ship the animals. The marketing co-operative was organized among Manitoba hog producers, who were all required to join and to sell their animals through its facilities. This provincially mandated arrangement helped the small producers by maintaining stable pork prices and providing services. When the pork market became privatized, wider opportunities were opened for the larger producers who heavily invested in expansion. Because of their greater scale, they could not only provide their own services but also sell them to smaller farms. They could make a profit when prices were low and better withstand the risks of price fluctuations.

Under the pressure of new global forces and the withdrawal of government and co-operative support, hog raising has not only expanded but has also engendered a new structure in the Manitoba farm economy and modified the social order of rural communities. The main effect has been the increased expansion of the corporate farms and of larger-scale operations in general. Thus, in spite of the phenomenal expansion of the industry, the actual number of hog farms has declined from over 3000 in 1990 to less than 1200 in 2006. In the process, the size of the average operation has increased by a factor of five from 434 to 2500 pigs (Statistics Canada 2007b). More significantly, the industry has become dominated by a small number of large operations. Over 50 percent of production is now under the control of fewer than a hundred farms, with an average stock of almost 10 000 hogs per operation (Novek 2003).

Two interesting patterns are apparent in an examination of large-scale operations in Manitoba's pork industry. The first is the significance of Hutterite colonies, which are responsible for a third of provincial production (Deveson 1995). This group has been favoured by the economies of scale that communal life has allowed. The second is the presence of a few huge corporate farms that are setting the major directions for the industry as a whole. The two largest producers, Elite Swine, a subsidiary of a transnational company, and Hytek, a local family operation, exemplify two different patterns of expansion.

Elite Swine is a subsidiary of a Maple Leaf Foods, a Toronto-based transnational corporation with sales of over $5 billion annually. Its major share-holders are the McCain Capital Corporation and the Ontario Teachers Pension Plan. It has a diversified agribusiness through which it attempts to control every aspect of the food market from "farm-to-fork." In the Manitoba hog industry, this policy involves the ownership of Landmark Feeds; Elite Swine's hog production, research, and management facilities; meat packing plants in Winnipeg and Brandon; and Rothsay Rendering. Elite Swine maintains a herd of 116 000 hogs, with an annual turnover capacity of two million animals, almost 25 percent of Manitoba production. It is the largest hog producer in Canada and the eighth largest in North America (Freese 2006). The company maintains its own mega-barns but also markets pigs for smaller producers, to whom it also sells equipment and supplies and technical services.

Hytek began as a small family-run operation that has expanded to become Canada's second largest hog producer. It plays a sizable role in Manitoba's pork industry. It maintains a herd of 54 000 pigs and produces approximately a million animals per year. It also cultivates grain for the production of animal feed for its own use and for sale, and runs genetic, nutritional, and veterinary research and service operations. It employs 250 workers locally and has a significant impact on the small community in which it is based. It has established hog farms and agribusiness services in the United States and China and is planning to build a meat-packing plant in Winnipeg (Hytek 2007).

As in other parts of Canada and the rest of the world, corporate agribusiness is increasingly dominating Manitoba agriculture through direct ownership of resources and vertical control of all aspects of the industry. In the process, agriculture, which once supported local community organization, values, and continuity, is becoming reorganized according to formal business principles with an international scope and expansionary dynamic. In the wake of this trend, the family farm and the Canadian prairie way of life are in decline as large operations buy out and displace the smaller farmers. Of course, the new farms create jobs and opportunities in the rural environment. As such, some municipalities look to the hog industry as a means of reversing the decline that has resulted from farm closures and out-migration. However, much of the work that the large barns provide is unskilled and low-paid. The people who become employed in these positions will very likely form a new type of rural stratum, very different from the self-employed farmer.

Some problems of the change that is occurring are evident in controversies over the establishment of new barns. The province has the power to curtail expansion under environmental impact legislation and in fact imposed a moratorium on all new facilities in 2006 because of ecological concerns. Until then, it had delegated responsibility for assessment and approval to the rural municipalities. As a result, many communities have gone through divisive debates over approving new hog operations and the costs of water and air pollution and benefits of new jobs and investment. Older farming interests, sometimes allied with urban cottage owners, have voiced opposition. The local commercial elite, along with a new class of managers and technical workers, has advocated acceptance in the name of economic growth. A trend towards polarization of occupational and class interest is apparent (Novek 2003).

had important consequences. Farmers had to feed a much larger number of people than they had in the pre-industrial setting and adopted mechanized agricultural equipment to increase the productivity of their land and labour. Tractors, combines, fertilizers, genetically modified seed, and pesticides are now ubiquitous in farm operations in the developed world. They allow less than 5 percent of the population to feed not only the much larger urban majority but to supply an export market as well. This new productive technology has introduced many changes into the operations, form, and orientation of the farm enterprise. The most significant has been the intensive commercialization of production and the emergence of the farm as a business operation. Except for some experiments in collectivization, agricultural production in industrial societies is based on a capitalist enterprise. Farmers are solely dependent upon the market for their livelihood and for the food and other items that they consume. They organize their resources and activities in terms of a desire to make a profit. Their long-term strategy is geared towards investing their returns to increase output and profits.

Investment focuses on the purchase of more land and on further technological improvements.

The development of commercialized farming involved two different kinds of enterprise: the large corporate farm and the small-to-medium family farm. These two alternatives represent not only a size variation but also different organizational forms and to some extend different cultural values. The corporate farm operates in the same way as an industrial corporation. It is run through a management hierarchy, usually centred in an urban office complex, organized through several administrative levels at the bottom of which are paid field workers. The family farm operator works on his or her own holdings within a local community of similar farmers with common interests and problems and depends on the help of unpaid family labour. However, the family farm is still dependent upon the market and must organize its operations to maintain profitability. Until recently, family farms have been more prevalent than corporate enterprises in the core regions of industrialization, such as Europe and North America. This pattern has occurred because small-scale operations have lower costs due to the use of family labour. In addition, government farm policies have tended to support the small farmer in an attempt to capture rural votes.

Social and cultural features of farming communities in industrial societies are different from those of peasants or horticulturalists. This pattern has been partly due to the greater openness of the wider society and the significant degree of rural representation in national governments. It has also been influenced by a similar openness in the other direction. Farmers are dependent on the city for their markets and consumption goods as well as other resources such as financing and education. In the process, they also incorporate urban cultural values. However, the most important determinant of rural social organization is the commercialization and capitalization of agriculture and the market orientation of the rural economy. As such, farm families must temper cooperative relationships and participation in their communities according to the values of self-interest inherent in a commercialized society. In the process, collective forms are weakened, and an individualistic and competitive social order becomes prevalent.

REVIEW

The development of manufacturing in the Western world has introduced an economic, social, and cultural transformation. Production and employment has shifted from rural agriculture to manufacturing and subsidiary services based in cities. The market has created an ever-expanding array of goods and services and has extended its reach to the organization of land and labour. Society has become more individualistic and competitive. Populations have been redistributed from countryside to city, and communities have become more open and flexible in their membership and values.

 Chapter Summary

Ecological Anthropology

- Ecological anthropology is a specialization within anthropology that focuses on subsistence systems—how people meet their survival needs and make their living within their environments.

Understanding Human Subsistence Patterns

- Subsistence strategies include methods that people use to obtain food. People need to develop techniques to adapt to their environment, exploit available resources,

or produce their own food. Subsistence strategies affect and are affected by environmental conditions such as topography, climate, and available plants and animals. The techniques that people use have an impact on population size, settlement patterns, and household composition.

Foraging

- Foraging is a subsistence strategy that depends directly on plants and animals available in the environment.

Foragers collect wild plants, fruits, nuts, and seeds and hunt animals and fish in the waterways of their territory. Because foragers depend on naturally available resources, they require a large territory for subsistence. Most foragers are nomadic, changing their settlement sites frequently. They usually live in relatively small communities in order to not overly burden their environment.

Pastoralism

- Pastoralism is a subsistence strategy that centres on the herding and care of large numbers of domesticated animals. Settlement patterns among pastoralists vary. Some are nomadic, moving frequently as they take their animals to new pasturelands. Others retain a home base and make daily excursions as they take their animals out to graze. Settlement size also varies, although most pastoralists live in communities numbering no more than several hundred people. In most pastoralist societies, animals are owned by individuals, although they may be cared for in a collective herd.

Horticulture

- Horticulture is a subsistence strategy based on growing crops. Horticulture is small-scale farming, using hand-held tools and a relatively simple technology. Farmers need to remain near their fields during the planting season. Some horticulturalists live in permanent villages while others shift their locations in different seasons. Their settlements usually number from several hundred to at most several thousand people. Horticulturalists generally store enough of their harvest to last a year or two beyond their minimum requirements.

Agriculture

- Agriculture is a form of food production based on permanent settlement; large-scale farming using complex technology; and the storage, distribution, and trade of agricultural production. Agriculture developed independently in different parts of the world based on different kinds of domesticated plants and animals. Increases in population and food supply were offset by problems of poor nutrition increasing social inequality and economic exploitation.

Industrialization

- The Industrial Revolution introduced new economic forces that shifted the locus of production from rural agrarian society to urban manufacturing centres. The market became the main institution for the organization of the economy. Society has become more individualistic and competitive. Recent changes have focused on the globalization of trade and investment and the dominance of transnational corporations with the manufacturing, service, and agricultural sectors.

Key Terms

ecological anthropology 114	pastoralism 115	reciprocity 117	sedentism 130
subsistence patterns 114	horticulture 115	redistibution 117	slash-and-burn (swidden) cultivation 130
foragers 114	agriculture 115	nomads 117	
food producers 114	carrying capacity 115	complex foragers 119	peasants 133
	settlement pattern 116	transhumance 126	

Review Questions

1. What do economic anthropologists study?
2. What are the essential differences between foraging and food production? Which is more costly in terms of time, effort, and calories? Which is more costly in terms of short-term survival?
3. What is carrying capacity, and how do people adapt to this subsistence constraint?
4. How are settlement patterns influenced by modes of subsistence? How is nomadism an example of settlement pattern adaptation?
5. How do subsistence modes influence population size, density, composition, and distribution?
6. How do subsistence modes influence a society's division of labour by age, gender, skill, and social status?
7. How do peoples' systems of roles and status both reflect and reinforce their subsistence?
8. What ecological, demographic, and sociocultural factors characterize foraging?
9. What is complex foraging? How is it illustrated in Northwest Coastal society?

10. What ecological, demographic, and sociocultural factors characterize pastoralism?
11. Why do many pastoralist societies avoid using their animals for meat?
12. What are the impacts of greater sedentism and storage capacity among pastoralists and horticulturalists?
13. How does swidden farming work as a subsistence strategy? What are its advantages? Its disadvantages?

14. What are the chief characteristics of agriculture as a subsistence strategy?
15. How has a market orientation changed agricultural ways of life in the Canadian countryside?
16. How do subsistence patterns change over time? How can changes in subsistence cause other changes in a people's way of life?

Economic Systems

CHAPTER 6

Preview

1. **What is an economic system? How is it integrated into a culture?**
2. **How are land and labour allocated in different cultures?**
3. **What are the different types of economic exchange and how are they different from each other?**
4. **What are the characteristics of an economy based on capitalism?**
5. **What effects has industrialization had on economies and cultures?**
6. **What is colonialism? How and why did it develop? What effects has it had on indigenous cultures and societies around the world?**
7. **What are some characteristics of post-industrial societies and today's global economy?**

Three men went into the forest: one was the Cultivator, the other the Trapper, the third the Gatherer-of-Honey. Arriving in the forest, they asked themselves: "How shall we build our houses?" They said: "You, the Cultivator, build your house in the middle of the three hills." The Trapper built his house on a hill, the Gatherer-of-Honey built his on a hill. No sooner had they finished building their houses than the Cultivator had already finished growing plants behind his house. The Trapper asked the Gatherer-of-Honey to make a blood pact with him, stating that they should not make such a pact with the Cultivator. Having finished making friendship, and having killed game, the Trapper went with the meat to his friend. They did not show it to the Cultivator. The following day, the Gatherer-of-Honey passed with a jar of honey to bring to his friend the Trapper. They did not give anything to the Cultivator. And so it was every day; they made things pass at the entrance of the village of this one, the Cultivator. He said to himself that his children alone would die of hunger.

This Harvester, this Cultivator, went to sow discord between the two friends. He called in a loud voice, "You man of the rodents Mikii, you the Trapper, it is you will kill my children, never again bring rodent Mikii here at my house." The Cultivator also set out to the village of the Gatherer-of-Honey calling, "You Gatherer-of-Honey, it is the flies that you bring here that cause my children to be sick; also it is my rodents Mikii, which you eat, that makes you factor." On his side, the Trapper reflected much, stating that so then his friend had just insulted

him; on his side the Gatherer-of-Honey also thought that his friend had just insulted him. Having heard that, the Trapper and the Gatherer-of-Honey, one left from his house, the other left from his house, they met in the valley at the Cultivator's. Arriving there, they questioned each other.

One said, "You yelled to me that it was my rodents Mikii who are the reason why your children have caught the kwashiorkor, yes my rodents Mikii!" And the other said, "You yelled that because of me your children have their throat obstructed by larvas of bee." The one denied and the other denied, both at the same time. At this time, the Cultivator was dancing, while his wife beat the drum for him. This instigator, the Cultivator, took to dancing and singing:

I, the instigator Cultivator.
I just finished placing in discord those who are two.

The two friends understood, having heard the manner in which this Cultivator had placed them in discord, one against the other. Having considered that, they made a pact of friendship with the Cultivator. As such, the three became friends among each other; and they began to give meat, honey, and agricultural products, all of them giving to one another mutually.

That is why a man should never refuse the mark of friendship because the mark of friendship is a thing capable of saving the family group.

Excerpts from *Folktales Told around the World* by Richard Dorson, pp. 384–385. Copyright 1975. Reprinted by permission of The University of Chicago Press.

In this narrative, the Nyanga of Zaire dramatize the three significant elements in their economic system: hunting, gathering, and farming. They express the mutual interdependence of these subsistence strategies, and they relate the importance of exchange and reciprocity in binding a community together.

ANALYZING ECONOMIC SYSTEMS

Societies organize their subsistence strategies in ways that utilize their land and resources efficiently. Available land must be made accessible to members of the community. People need to agree about methods of allocating their resources so that everyone has at least a minimal share in order to survive. People also need to know how to assign tasks and organize their work, taking account of differences in age and gender and skill, as well as whatever other social variables are considered significant (such as class, race, or ethnicity). Societies must have methods of distributing food, goods, and services within and among their communities. Rarely do people consume all and only what they produce individually. Instead, they share with others or exchange their products or services for other products or services. These basic processes of allocating resources, and producing, distributing, and consuming the goods and services that are created from them constitute an **economic system**.

Economic anthropologists study economic systems and behaviour cross-culturally. In trying to understand how people solve the problems of allocation, production, distribution, and consumption in different societies, they adopt a holistic perspective: that is, they try to situate features of land and resource use and labour organization in the context of people's adaptation to their environment. They also try to delineate the ways that the control of economic resources and the distribution of products are interrelated with other features of culture, including social and political systems. For example, Canadian society organizes most of its economic processes through the institution of the market in which most resources and products are bought and sold among anonymous, self-interested individuals. If we want land or labour, we must pay for them according to uniform prices that are in theory established by bidding against competing buyers. In another society these resources may be available as rights that a person obtains as a member of a community or a kinship group or through gift giving. If prices are exacted, they may be fixed according to a customary understanding or may vary according to the social identities of the parties involved in the exchange.

economic system
Methods of allocating resources, and the production, distribution, consumption, and exchange of goods and services.

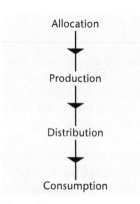

Figure 6.1
Economic Processes

Allocating Land and Resources

Land and other natural resources are critical for producing goods in all economic systems but the ways in which they are managed differ from culture to culture. Ideas and rules about rights to these resources and their valuation, allocation, and use depend in part upon basic subsistence modes. In industrial and post-industrial societies, land and natural resources are considered commodities and are given to the highest bidder, who gains exclusive ownership rights protected by the legal system of the state. Capitalist values stress the exploitation of these resources to create an ever-increasing supply of consumer goods and wealth. By contrast, foragers usually have relatively open access to the lands in their territories. This strategy is especially useful for nomadic peoples who rely on their ability to exploit available resources seasonally. Their occupation of specific sites places little pressure on the land because of low population densities and limited storage and accumulation. Pastoral peoples may also extend rights to exploit all available land in their territory to graze their herds. However, some pastoral societies limit access to land to particular groups on either a seasonal or permanent basis. Farming peoples need to make claims to specific parcels of land that they cultivate. Among agriculturalists, farm fields are often permanently owned by individuals and may be unequally distributed within the community. For horticulturalists, land is often owned communally and reallocated among members of a community or kinship group to provide for a balance of cultivated and fallowed fields and to meet the needs of households of different sizes.

Political, religious, and other cultural considerations may affect land tenure patterns as well. The peoples of the Pacific Northwest Coast imposed more restrictive land rights in their territories than other foragers. The land was owned corporately by family-based "houses" and administered on the group's behalf by hereditary house chiefs. Territories were clearly bounded, and exclusive use was imposed and defended. All house members were allowed to fish, hunt, and gather in the group's territories, although the chief had the power to decide on location and timing of harvests and to collect a portion for his or her own use. He or she would usually accumulate large stores for later distribution in communal feasts to which the chiefs of other houses were invited (see the Case Study on page 149). Harvesting rights were also regularly granted to other people, such as in-laws, who had to contribute to the chief's larder in return (Daly 2005). Land was vested in the ancestors of the group but could change hands on occasion. In this matrilineal society, a chief's father's kin provided the necessary resources to hold his burial. In return, his heir, usually his sister's son, had to repay the donors. If he could not do so, he was bound to give them his territory and become their dependent.

The horticultural Akan of Ghana had a similar but more complex system of communal land tenure. Rights in land were divided between local kinship groups and larger and more inclusive chiefdoms. Family elders allocated temporary cultivation rights to their kin for a few seasons. Recipients could harvest all of the crops they produced without obligations to the elders or the state. However, as in the Pacific Northwest, they were required to hand over a portion of any naturally occurring product they acquired. Hunters had to hand over a portion of any animals they might kill. More importantly, anyone mining or panning for gold had to give a portion of any gold found on their land to the chief. Royal accumulation of gold was important for decorating royal regalia and for exchange for European and Asian imports within an intercontinental trading system.

While some societies focus on communal land holding, private ownership is also widespread and is similarly subject to different rules in different cultural contexts. In many rigidly hierarchical societies, land is monopolized by a small elite. The majority of the members of society have little or no access to land, and certain groups, such as foreigners, serfs, or slaves, may be prohibited from ownership entirely. Some practices, such as primogeniture—exclusive inheritance by an eldest son—may be established to avoid the division of large estates. Land is often allocated according to social status and patronage. For example, in Medieval Europe, large landowners, including the high nobility and the church, distributed parcels to lower ranks in return for obligations of loyalty and service. Allocations provided for access both to the land and to the labour of the serfs who lived on it.

Organizing Labour

Societies allocate the labour of their members to productive according to the social statuses and backgrounds of their members. Work roles are assigned minimally on the basis of age and gender. In addition, certain individuals may specialize in full-time or part-time craft production or other arts and skills. Men and women are often assigned different but complementary tasks. Elderly people usually retire from direct productive work depending on the ability of the family or society to support them, although their advice may be sought because of their knowledge and experience. Young children are assigned household and subsistence tasks consistent with their physical and cognitive maturation as well as the type of economy. Whereas farm families depend on children's labour, in industrial societies children typically are legally prevented from work for their protection and in the interest of their education. Nevertheless, children are widely exploited as sources of labour in some parts of the world today.

As with land, labour in industrial and post-industrial societies has become commoditized. For example, most Canadians earn their living by selling their labour within the "job market." Other forms of allocation have been prominent in different economic systems. Labour services are most often acquired within the household and devoted to domestic forms of production such as family farming. Spouses and children

? What do you own, and how did you come to own it? What rights, obligations, and limitations does ownership involve?

In Their Own Voices

"Free to Do as You Like"

In this excerpt from his autobiographical novel, Fragments of Memory: A Story of a Syrian Family, *Hanna Mina describes the plight of sharecroppers, bound to and dependent on landlords who extract most of the profits from the farmers.*

Ever since February, Mother had been gathering the hen eggs with great care. We were living and working as day laborers in a field belonging to the village *mukhtar*. It was a small field, empty except for mulberry trees. Our only duty was raising silkworms during the silk season. It was a raw deal that Father had contracted with the *mukhtar*.... He didn't succeed here either but he was forced into it ... He had to find shelter somewhere, so he agreed to take the abandoned field. The *mukhtar* opened a page for us in his debt ledger. The first thing he put down in it, against the account of the silk harvest, was five kilos of mixed sorghum and barley, a few meters of unbleached cotton and a few articles like salt, oil, kerosene and soap. He also advised Father to be a faithful share cropper who knows his obligations and pays his debts. Father raised his hand to his forehead and then placing it over his heart said, "At your service, Mr. Elias!"

Our house was a rectangle built of unbaked clay bricks, divided into two parts by a wall. One part was for animals, the other for living in. Since we possessed no animals, that part remained empty. Hens that relatives had generously bestowed upon Mother ran around and pecked there. In one corner we piled up firewood and dung, and in another near a small window high in the wall was a hearth made of stones and clay.

Father began, with the help of the family, the cultivation of the land and the care of the mulberry trees by borrowing a neighbor's animal. Before the work was finished, a messenger arrived from the *mukhtar* asking for Father. So he went only to be told that he must work in his fields first and that Mother must work in the *mukhtar's* house. Father raised his hand to his forehead, lowered it and placing it over his heart said, "At your service, Mr. Elias!"

Although the parents worked hard as sharecroppers, their precarious situation worsened because synthetic silk made in India undersold natural silk. The landlord shut down silkworm production, forcing sharecroppers to leave.

So we bundled up the belongings we had left, and our parents went to inform the *mukhtar* that we were leaving.

We could have left covertly at night or in the early morning without our departure arousing anyone's attention or interest. The surrounding houses were empty, the mulberry groves were being cut down and burned or their trunks gathered for wood. The paths were filled with columns of travelers on the backs of animals or in carts drawn by donkeys or cows. The fathers who lacked these means carried their things on their backs, dragging their children along, fleeing from hunger, fear, and thieves, traveling together to be safe from highway robbers who lay in wait for them in the valleys and the foothills of the mountains.

It was possible for us, in this state of collective emigration, this mutual dissolution of contracts to forsake our mud hut and the mulberry grove, empty except for the whistling wind, and flee the whole village without letting anyone know and without anyone asking about us. But our oldest sister was with the *mukhtar*. Considering her to be payment for the debt, he had tightened his watch over her since learning that Father had returned and that we were on the point of leaving since it had become impossible for us to stay on.

Father's lengthy beseeching diatribe, Mother's tearful entreaties, and requests from those who were acquainted with our circumstances and sympathized with us, were of no avail. The *mukhtar* spurned them all. He would not give us anything to eat and could not cope with us remaining hungry. We were of no use to him as *fellahin*. So he made it known that we were free to leave, but as far as our sister was concerned, he would keep her until we paid our debt.

"You're free to do as you like!" said the *mukhtar*. The landowners had said that before him, and he said it to other *fellahin* beside us. The sweet word "freedom" had become frightening, meaning no money, no food and no concern for the unpredictable destiny of the families who had lived on raising silkworms. The arrival of artificial silk was finishing off them and the silkworms together.

Therefore the word "free" became an odious term to the *fellahin*, who came from their fields seeking aid from the owners of the fields. As a consequence, they rejected this term, bringing up the matter of their servitude being in exchange for certain conditions, among which was the stipulation that they should be sustained until winter was over and the growing season arrived.

From *Fragments of Memory: A Story of a Syrian Family* by Hanna Mina, pp. 19–20, 88–89. Copyright 1993. Reprinted by permission of the Center for Middle Eastern Studies. The University of Texas at Austin.

CRITICAL THINKING QUESTIONS

Why were Hanna and his family not really free to do as they wanted? What patterns in agricultural societies lead to social inequality?

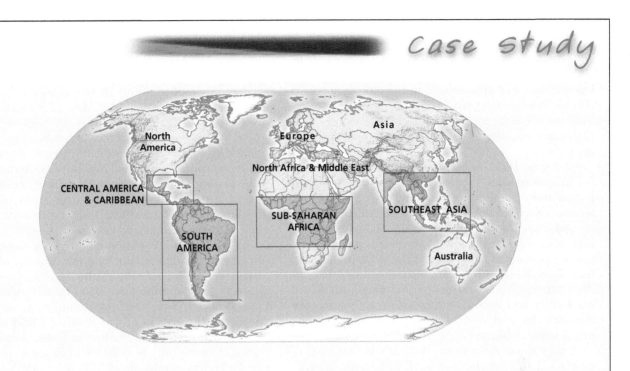

Child Labourers Today

The exploitation of child labour is an international concern today. According to a 2002 report by the International Labour Organization (ILO) in Geneva, Switzerland, children who work are divided into four categories: "children at work in economic activity," "child labourers," "children in hazardous work," and "children in unconditional worst forms of child labour." "Children at work in economic activity" is a broad category that encompasses most productive activities performed by children, including all market production (paid work) and some types of non-market production (unpaid work), such as producing goods for one's own use. Work may be in the formal sector (especially factory work) or the informal sector (street vendors, construction) and may encompass legal or illegal activities.

"Children at work in economic activity" includes children who work in a market-oriented establishment operated by a relative in the same household. It also includes children who are domestic workers in someone else's household, but it excludes children who do the same chores in their own households without pay. The ILO estimates that some 352 million children between the ages of five and seventeen "work in economic activity." Of these, about 211 million are under the age of fourteen, and 73 million are younger than ten.

Boys and girls are equally likely to be engaged in economic activities. For children younger than fourteen, no significant gender differences are found, but for older children, ages fifteen through seventeen, the number of boys is greater. This disproportion may

reflect the fact that, by the age of fifteen, many girls in developing countries are married or otherwise performing unpaid productive work in their own households (a class of economic activity excluded from the ILO conventions).

The ILO study discovered world regional differences in the incidence of children engaged in economic activity. The largest numbers are found in the Asia-Pacific region (127.3 million), followed by sub-Saharan Africa (48 million), and Latin America and the Caribbean (17.4 million). In terms of the ratio of working to non-working children, sub-Saharan Africa has the highest ratio of child workers. There, about 29 percent of children younger than fifteen are engaged in economic activities. In contrast, in developed countries, only about 2 percent of children below the age of fifteen are economically active.

The second ILO category, "child labourers," refers to child workers under the internationally agreed minimum age for specific kinds of work. For example, "child labourers" are children under the age of eighteen (or sixteen years under certain strict conditions) who perform "hazardous work." Any working child who is younger than twelve or thirteen is considered to be a "child labourer," but children between the ages of twelve and fourteen may also be classified as "child labourers" if they do light work for more than fourteen hours per week. The ILO defines "light work" as work not harmful to a child's physical development and health and which does not interfere with his or her attendance at school or a vocational training program. By this definition, it is estimated that there are about 186 million child labourers under age fifteen.

The ILO found that boys are more likely than girls to be child labourers. However, among children in the age group five to fourteen, girls and boys participate in child labour at about the same rates. The gender difference becomes pronounced in the older age group (fifteen to seventeen), where boys are more prominent. That is, of children classified as child labourers ages fifteen to seventeen, 57 percent are boys and 43 percent are girls.

The third ILO category is that of children engaged in "hazardous work," defined as "any activity or occupation that, by its nature or type has, or leads to, adverse effects on the child's safety, health (physical or mental), and moral development." Hazardous work may also refer to excessive workloads or long or intense periods of work, even if the work itself is not hazardous. Some examples of hazardous work for children are mining, construction, working with heavy machinery, and exposure to pesticides. The category also includes work underwater, at dangerous heights, or in confined spaces.

Using these definitions, the ILO estimates that nearly 171 million children work in hazardous situations. This figure accounts for about half the total number of economically active children (48.5 percent) and more than two-thirds of the world's child labourers (69.5 percent). For all groups, 52 percent of boys and 44.6 percent of girls were working in hazardous conditions.

The final category, "children in unconditional worst forms of child labour," includes human trafficking, forced and bonded labour, armed conflict, prostitution and pornography, and criminal activities. The total number of children in this category stands at about 8.4 million worldwide. About 1.2 million children are trafficked to and from all regions of the world. While boys and girls are both subject to human trafficking, there are gender differences depending on the purposes for trafficking. Boys are more often trafficked for forced labour (especially in commercial farming), petty crimes, and the drug trade, whereas girls are likely to be trafficked for commercial sexual exploitation and domestic service.

An estimated 5.7 million children are engaged in forced and bonded labour. The vast majority of these (about 5.5 million) reside in the Asia-Pacific region, although large numbers are also found in Africa and Latin America. Some 300 000 children, mostly boys, are forced to serve in armed conflict. Child soldiers are most prevalent in Africa and the Asia-Pacific region. The majority of children engaged in prostitution and pornography are girls. In total, about 1.8 million children are affected, and all regions of the world participate in this exploitation, as both tourists and domestic clients sexually exploit child prostitutes. The ILO estimates that about 600 000 children are engaged in illicit activities, including petty crimes and especially the production and trafficking of drugs.

carry out much of the work. Such family labour can be considerable in situations where a man can include more than one wife within his household or maintain his adult sons and their wives and children within an extended family unit. Economic exchanges are often involved in establishing such families. For example, in many societies a man must pay a bride price to his in-laws before he can marry. This sum may in part be rationalized in terms of the labour that a family loses when their daughter leaves for her husband's household. Such compensation is sometimes explicitly spelled out. Among the Dani of New Guinea, a man must pay a bride price in two installments. The first gives him the right to have his wife work on his farm, but he may not have sexual relations with her until he makes the second payment a year or two afterwards (Heider 1996). An alternative means of acquiring a woman's labour is through bride service. A man is required to work for his father-in-law for a period of time, after which he can then bring his wife to his own household.

Even in household-based economies, labour may be exchanged among families. Extra labour for intensive tasks, such as harvesting, is sometimes acquired by inviting neighbours to assist. The host will usually compensate his workers by supplying food and drink and will return the favour by participating in any work parties that his guests may organize. The labour of others may also be acquired on less amicable terms. The institution of slavery has been prominent in several societies and has involved the allocation and exploitation of labour through direct force. Forced labour may also be invoked by state societies that require their subjects to work on special projects for at least part of the year without compensation. Similar labour obligations are present in other hierarchical contexts. In Medieval Europe, the serfs were bound by hereditary obligations to work for their lords. They did not have the right to leave the manor on which they were born to seek out employment or income elsewhere. According to the Hindu *jajmani* system, members of different castes have fixed hereditary obligations to provide their specialty products and services to each other. A carpenter may be obligated to supply farm tools and household furnishing to a farmer in return for which he will receive a portion of the harvest. Compensation is determined by agreements among caste councils, called *panchayats*, although the more powerful castes normally have a greater say in the prevailing rates. Partners in these arrangements inherit their obligations from their parents as they do their occupations.

Capital Goods and Social Capital

Capital constitutes the third category of productive resources. **Capital goods** are understood as items that are produced not for consumption but for the production of other goods. They can include tools and other technological inputs, such as irrigation works. In pastoral societies, herd animals can be considered to be capital, since they are seldom eaten and are usually utilized to produce such items as milk or wool as well as calves or lambs. Farmers may also keep animals as sources of capital and stores of wealth and often are reluctant to slaughter them for anything other than a highly public ceremonial occasion. In New Guinea, pig ownership is widely employed as a way of demonstrating wealth. However, a man must balance his desire to accumulate pigs against the need to a hold pig feast or acquire a wife. In doing so, he dispenses his physical capital but acquires **social capital** in the form of friendships and obligations within the community.

Distributing and Exchanging Products and Services

Once goods, whether foodstuffs or manufactures, are produced, they enter into patterns of distribution and consumption. Because societies are organized on principles of interdependence in cooperation and competition, individuals must always be connected to others in networks of distribution. Systems of exchange include reciprocity, defined in Chapter 5 as giving and taking "in kind" between individuals and families, as in simple spontaneous gift exchange. Reciprocity can be far from simple, however. In traditional societies, networks of reciprocal relations may be complex and of long standing and may organize a large proportion of the transactions within an economy. For example, commenting on the Trobriand Island economy of Melanesia, Bronislaw Malinowski observed local life as "a constant give and take . . . [in which] . . . every ceremony, every legal and customary act is done to the accompaniment of material gift and counter gift . . ."(1922: 167). Such events included the annual presentation of an entire yam crop to a brother-in-law and complicated patterns of inter-island trade that linked people through gifts of shell jewellery.

Types of Reciprocity.   Members of families and households may be intertwined in recurring series of exchanges, a type of distribution called generalized reciprocity. In **generalized reciprocity**, goods and services are exchanged, but the value of the products or services given and received is not exactly or objectively calculated. There may be an expectation that goods and services will be given and received frequently and will have approximately equivalent worth, but the frequency and the amount of value are not specified. Many exchanges between parents and children, for example, are examples of generalized reciprocity. Distribution of food in traditional societies likewise involves principles of generalized reciprocity, as in the exchanges of foraging peoples such as the Inuit and Ju/'hoansi. Through generalized reciprocity over time, all families become both givers and receivers of food.

In contrast to generalized reciprocity, some exchanges are characterized by **balanced reciprocity**, in which exchanges are more formalized and specify the nature and values of the objects that are given and received and the occasions on which an exchange will take place. It formally obligates the parties involved to both accept and give the gifts involved. Balanced reciprocity characterizes exchanges between people

capital goods
Items that are produced for the purpose of producing other goods rather than for production.

social capital
Bonds of reliable friendship and support that a person can call on to achieve a goal.

generalized reciprocity
The exchange of goods and services without keeping track of their exact value but often with the expectation that their value will balance out over time.

balanced reciprocity
Exchange of goods and services of a specified value.

Case study

The Potlatch as a System of Exchange

The potlatch was a critical institution among the peoples of the Pacific Northwest. It involved the staging of ostentatious public feasts to which a host would invite prominent leaders from neighbouring communities. Along with massive amounts of food, all the guests were given valuable gifts, including trade items. On some occasions, the host's wealth was further demonstrated through the actual destruction of valuable items.

Potlatches were held on occasions such as births and funerals, but the taking of a hereditary title of leadership, distinguished by a name and the right to display the crest associated with the office, was the most important. The massive gift giving and feasting not only validated the host's assumption of authority but also determined relative importance of the status relative to other leaders in the community and in neighbouring settlements. A large potlatch entitled the holder to the esteem of his peers and the right to take a highly ranked seat at their potlatches. A meager feast brought dishonour. The event served functions other than status acquisition and validation. It was an event in which rights to territory, symbols, and indigenous knowledge were recounted, and sometimes contested and affirmed, and at which important public announcements were made.

The potlatch was a complex event that involved both reciprocal and redistributive exchanges. The host was usually a chief, who gathered food and wealth items from the members of his house and from other relatives. Supplementary resources could be borrowed from other sources. He would then present the accumulation to fellow chiefs who regularly potlatched each other. The expectation would be to repay each guest with an amount at least equivalent to the sum that the host had received from him previously—in the spirit of balanced reciprocity. In some circumstances, however, the ante was increased to require the host to return something extra or in some instances a double amount, creating an inflationary force. This competitive potlatching, with its implications of negative reciprocity, has often been attributed to a destabilization of populations and status hierarchies due to contact with European traders. It did however have a redistributive effect within the economy. Since hosts in richer territories could give larger potlatches than their rivals, food was redistributed from surplus to deficit zones, thereby balancing the distribution of resources over a large region.

Although potlatching was a core feature that filled a logical place in the indigenous Pacific Coast economy, Europeans considered it to be irrational and wasteful. Consequently, the settler government that assumed authority over First Nations societies within British Columbia illegalized the practice, fining and sometimes imprisoning the celebrants. Potlatches were legalized in the 1950s and have been restored as central events among indigenous communities within the province. They are now funded by cash contributions rather than subsistence goods and can involve gifts of DVD players as well as more traditional blankets and ceremonial objects. Costs usually run in the thousands.

of equal social status who are not closely related. The Trobriand *kula* trade provides a classic example of this institution. It involves annual inter-island visits between trading partners who exchange highly valued shell ornaments in the form of necklaces and armbands. Each participant is linked to two partners: one to whom he gives a necklace in return for an armband of equivalent value, and the other to whom he makes the reverse exchange of an armband for a necklace. Although each individual is tied to only two partners, each contact has an additional connection along a distribution chain that forms a great circle linking more than a dozen islands over hundreds of miles of ocean. Paradoxically, although the principle of the system depends upon

In Sumatra today, horticulturalists still barter for manufactured goods, especially hunting tools, or even for tourists' personal objects. Is barter relevant in today's industrial economies?

maintaining a balance, such a state is never achieved. Each act balances the previous one, but creates a new debt that must be honoured. As such, the institution serves to permanently link trading partners and their localities into a regional alliance. By exchanging goods and services, people enact their mutual interdependence.

A third type of reciprocity, **negative reciprocity**, characterizes exchanges in which some parties take or try to take advantage of each other. Negative reciprocity is rarely found within families or among members of small communities but is typical of trade or market exchanges in which the goal is profit. Negative reciprocity is common between strangers or enemies. However, negative reciprocity may occur among people in the same community who operate on the principle of competition. Trade exchanges called barter may be based on negative reciprocity. In **barter**, people trade a product they have in excess in order to obtain an item they need but do not produce themselves.

Redistributive Networks

In **redistributive networks**, produce and other goods are collected by an organizer and then distributed to community members or guests at a large public gathering. The occasions for redistribution are many. Ceremonial events, especially those marking rites of passage (birth, marriage, death), may provide the context for redistribution by the host to the guests, as in the potlatch (see the Case Study on page 152). Political events, such as installations of chiefs in Melanesia and Polynesia, are occasions for redistribution as the new leaders or their relatives provide giveaways displaying their generosity and at the same time attracting loyal followers. And in some early states that had agriculture as an economic base, such as the Inca, central governments collected produce and other goods, stored them in granaries and warehouses, and distributed them to needy people in times of poor harvests or other catastrophes. In modern societies, state governments organize networks of redistribution. One of the state's functions is to collect taxes, now paid in money, from its citizens to fund and support public projects and programs. In theory, the value of these monies is returned to citizens in public services such as road construction, water supplies, educational institutions, justice systems, health care, and defence. In many countries, taxation and government expenditure redistribute resources and incomes from richer to poorer regions and from the

negative reciprocity
Exchange of goods and services in which each party seeks to benefit at the expense of the other, thus making a profit.

barter
An exchange of products in which one person gives one type of product in exchange for another type of product.

redistributive networks
Economic systems in which food and other goods are amassed by an organizer and then distributed to community members or guests at large public gatherings.

wealthiest to the poorest groups in the population. For example, in 2005 the poorest 20 percent of the Canadian population paid less than 4 percent of their income ($800 per person) on taxes while the richest 20 percent paid almost 30 percent ($40 000 per person) (Statistics Canada 2006:12). Nevertheless, economic disparities within Canada have not only remained a problem but have actually gotten worse over the last twenty years in spite of government attempts to reduce them (see Chapter 10).

Markets and Trade

Markets constitute another way of allocating resources and distributing goods and services within an economic system. Unlike reciprocity and redistribution, which are regulated by social or political relationships between the people involved in a transaction, market exchanges are immediate and impersonal. People barter goods or buy and sell them for money on a single occasion. As such, the transaction neither reflects nor creates any social ties or obligations between the parties involved. Market exchange very often occurs between strangers who lay aside concerns for each other's welfare and pursue their own self interest. In an attempt to make the best deal possible, market participants normally compete against each other according to supply and demand forces. In a buyer's market, sellers with an oversupply of their products will try to offer lower rates than other people producing the same goods, thereby pushing down the prices. A seller's market will push up prices because of competition among buyers vying for a scarce item.

While a market-based economy is typical of modern industrial settings, markets can be found in many other societies. The most basic and widespread institution is barter trade. This activity is usually carried out between separate societies located in different ecological zones. Participants will meet in neutral territory and offer the specialties of their homelands. Commodities are directly exchanged without the use of a monetary medium so that each trader is simultaneously a buyer and a seller. The rates for which the items exchange are haggled over until a price is agreed upon. For example, external trade was an important part of the indigenous economy of the Pacific Northwest. Inland groups traded meat, dried salmon, and berry cakes for coastal products, such as candle fish oil and sea otter pelts. Trading parties that met would engage in mutual feasting and gift giving of ceremonial items as a prelude to more utilitarian barter of their specialties (Daly 2005:214). These groups were further linked into a wider North American trading system that connected regions across the entire continent.

As in the Pacific Northwest, market institutions in most pre-industrial societies existed along side reciprocal and redistributive exchanges. As such, commercial transactions were usually confined to only a limited number of goods and services and seldom entailed transfers of land or labour, which remained bound by social obligations based on strongly held moral values. As such, the economic flows of resources and goods and services were bound within compartmental spheres that protected core social interests and cultural precepts.

General and Special Purpose Money

general purpose money
Money that can be used to acquire any of the resources, goods, and services within an economic system.

special purpose money
Money that can be used for only a limited range of transactions.

In many societies the conduct of exchange is facilitated by the use of money, a medium of exchange that can be used to acquire many different goods and services and held as a store of value for later use. Various money forms have included precious metals, shells, domesticated animals, and cigarettes. In Western societies, money has developed as a **general purpose** medium, which can be used in all transactions, including purchases of land, natural resources, and labour and thereby supports a unitary economic system in which any item can potentially be exchanged for any other. Money uses in other societies are often limited to only a few transactions within a compartmentalized sphere of the economy. Such **special purpose money**, can be illustrated by the bride price system in some southern African societies. Among the Zulu and related groups, a man is required to pay his father-in-law a fixed number of cattle, know as the *labola*. When a person receives such a payment, he will usually not consume, sell, or otherwise expend the animals but will use them to acquire wives for his own family. In some cases this use is directly mandated. For example, a man who receives cattle from his sister's marriage must later provide animals to her when her son becomes engaged. In this situation (Kuper 1982), cattle act as a medium of exchange, but only for one "item," namely wives.

In some societies several special purposed monies may coexist alongside of each other. In the pre-colonial African kingdom of Dahomey, both cowrie shells and gold ounces were used to exchange goods, but in different contexts. Cowries were used in the purchase and sale of items within a local marketing system, whereas the gold ounce was use to value imports and exports within the international Atlantic slave trade. Cowries were not acceptable for purchases of exotic goods and could not be exchanged for gold (Polanyi 1966).

> ## REVIEW
>
> An economic system can be understood in terms of interdependent systems of production, consumption, allocation of land and resources, organization and specialization of labour, and exchange. In systems of exchange-based generalized reciprocity, people exchange goods and services of unequal or unfixed value. In balanced reciprocity, equal exchanges are sought, whereas in negative reciprocity, people expect to get more than they give. Systems of exchange also include redistributive networks and market transactions. Exchange transactions may be facilitated by the use of a medium of exchange, which may take the form of general or special purposed money.

MARKET ECONOMIES AND CAPITALISM

While market exchanges have been widely observed in different societies, the development of market economies, in which market relationships govern all aspects of allocation and distribution, is a fairly recent occurrence. A **market economy** is a system of allocating resources and distributing goods and services according to prices determined by market forces, such as supply and demand. Pricing is dependent upon the use of a general purpose money which ties different economic flows and exchanges into a single, unitary system in which the price of one item, such as automobiles, affects the price of others, such as labour. Money is thus used to "commodify" (make into a saleable **commodity**) essentially noneconomic things, such as people, their talents, events in their lives, or even their DNA.

Capitalism is both an economic system based on money and markets and an ideology based on the private and corporate ownership of the means of production and distribution, especially the manufacturing and trading infrastructure and the capital needed to finance business operations. It first emerged in Europe after the Middle Ages as the feudal economy based on the control of productive resources through hereditary patronage gave way to the dominance of urban-based trade. In the course of this development, the market system expanded to control a wide range of resources and goods, including land and labour. This commodification freed up previously restricted resources to feed the quest for profit and accelerate economic growth. Merchant capitalists grew increasingly wealthy and eventually expanded their businesses by investing in industrial plants that yielded profits from a wider range of activities than simple trade.

The capitalist mode of production differs in many significant ways from modes of production in traditional indigenous societies. In contrast to economic relations in small-scale, kin, and community-based societies, capitalist economic relations are impersonal and institutionalized.

Capitalist production is characterized by three fundamental attributes (Plattner 1989):

1. Workers do not control the means of production; they cannot by themselves produce the goods they need for survival. In contrast to subsistence farmers and artisans, workers in modern production are dependent on the owners of factories or industries that organize and produce goods and services.

market economy
Economic system in which products are traded in impersonal exchanges between buyers and sellers using an all-purpose currency.

commodity
A product that can be sold or traded in return for money or other products.

capitalism
An economic mode of production in which the goal is to amass wealth in the form of money in order to gain control over the means of production and then use this control to accumulate even greater wealth.

Arab traders first brought cowrie shells to Africa from islands in the Indian Ocean in the thirteenth century. The use of the shells as currency gradually spread westward, and later the Dutch and English traded them at West African ports.

2. Workers can earn incomes only through working for wages. According to the classic Marxist paradigm, because of this relationship, capitalist societies are divided into two basic classes: owners of the means of production (capitalists) and workers (proletariat). While some discussions of capitalism describe workers as "free" in the sense that they can sell their labour independently of kinship or other constraints, they are not free in that their lack of capital forces them to work for someone else.

3. Workers produce value that is greater than the wage paid to them. This **surplus value** is retained by the owners of capital and contributes to their profit (above the costs of maintaining the means of production). In contrast to economic systems that strive for balance and stability in labour output and the benefits reaped, capitalist systems strive for continual increases in profits and rates of growth. Capitalists raise profits by increasing the scale of production, purchasing more machinery, increasing the efficiency of production, investing in new technology, finding inexpensive labour, and increasing labour output.

Cultural beliefs and values support the principles and practices by which economic systems operate. Ideological constructs that support capitalism include the idea that benefits accruing to owners are "natural" and legitimate. Owners deserve their wealth because they plan ahead, take risks, make sacrifices, and work hard. In contrast, people who are poor are seen as undeserving. Poverty, which actually results from fundamental social and economic inequalities, is presented as the consequence of an individual's personal failings—lack of intelligence, laziness, or even moral deficiencies. Through formal and informal enculturation and the reinforcement of political and religious beliefs, most members of capitalist societies learn to accept their "proper" roles without question. Members of elite classes expect to be

surplus value
The amount of value produced by workers in capitalist production that is greater than the wage paid to them.

What values, beliefs, and practices support the type of economic system in which Tokyo thrives?

privileged, to have wealth, and to exert social and political power; in turn, members of lower classes accept their comparative disadvantage. This philosophy also suggests that governments and communities must not impose restrictions on markets or business activities. It maintains that unregulated markets will result in ever-increasing economic opportunities and benefits for all sectors of society, not just the capitalist class. Social support programs to mitigate the exploitation and dislocation that the market imposes are viewed as counterproductive in the long run.

REVIEW

A market economy is based on supply and demand and the use of money and other capital as mediums of exchange. A good, service, idea, or even a place or a person is treated as a commodity to be bought and sold. Three characteristics of capitalism are that workers are dependent on owners to organize and produce goods and services; workers sell their labour for wages or salaries; and workers produce a surplus value that is retained by the owners as profit. Capitalism is based on private property and profits from the buying and selling of commodities in free markets. As in all types of economies, ideological beliefs and values justify the relationships in a capitalist society.

INDUSTRIAL ECONOMIES

Capitalism and the market system became particularly dominant in the course of the Industrial Revolution. Industrial production began in Great Britain as an outgrowth of cottage piecework in the making of textiles and quickly spread through North America and Europe. Women traditionally wove woolen cloth and made garments for their families in keeping with a gendered division of labour within the farm household. Gradually, they began to produce surplus cloth and garments for sale to merchants, who supplied them with raw materials and bought up the products for sale in regional, national, and international markets. Initially, women worked in their homes. Eventually, cottage piecework shifted to factories, whose owners hired workers and directed their labour on site, away from homes and household duties. In some cases, entire families were hired to work in the factories, but many married women dropped out of the labour force to fulfill domestic and child-care responsibilities. By 1820, manufacturing incorporated complex machinery and new sources of energy that enabled workers to create more products in the same amount of time. Increased production made higher levels of consumption possible, and consumption stimulated more demand which, in turn, fuelled more production. Industrial capitalism spread to continental Europe and North America and also opened supply and consumer markets on a worldwide scale.

In the wake of these industrial and capitalist forces, a dramatic shift has taken place in the types of work that people do. A century ago, the majority of people in the world worked in the agricultural sector. Today in many countries only a small fraction of the population does so, as Table 6.1 shows. Those areas where agriculture is dominant export their raw materials and tend to be poorer, while the richer regions are supported by higher employment in industry and services. The particular prominence of the service sector in North America is indicative of a recent trend within post-industrial society that has in part been supported by the rapid expansion of knowledge-based industries.

The technological and economic dynamics of industrialization have had many social implications. People have moved from the countryside to the city in massive numbers and frequently relocate as an ever-changing labour market shifts demand across industries and locations. Economic growth and changing opportunities have allowed greater possibilities for increasing incomes, standards of living, and personal social mobility. However, some sectors of society have received more of the benefits of industrial growth than others, and, in the long run, inequality has tended to increase in capitalist economies based on industrialism. (We will discuss this trend in more detail in Chapter 10).

The pattern of growth of production and consumption in capitalist societies raises several questions about the desirability of contemporary ways of life beyond the basic

**Table 6.1   PERCENT OF POPULATION INVOLVED IN FOUR
ECONOMIC SECTORS**

	Agriculture	Industry (total)	Industry (manufacturing)	Services
Africa	63.21	11.10	6.49	25.69
Asia	61.85	16.91	12.57	21.24
Southeast Asia	59.17	13.85	10.45	26.98
Eastern Asia	64.76	17.49	12.89	17.76
Europe	12.18	36.23	25.36	51.58
North America	2.89	25.92	17.51	71.19
South America	23.32	23.75	13.45	52.93
Latin America and the Caribbean	25.39	23.60	14.15	51.00
Oceania	19.62	22.34	13.73	58.03
Australia and New Zealand	6.30	26.09	16.31	67.61

Source: International Labor Organization, 2002.

issues of social and economic equality. Contrary to common belief, people in capitalist societies do pay a cost for a seemingly more affluent lifestyle than those in foraging or horticulture societies. For example, an anthropological study comparing middle-class French people and members of the Machiguenga society in Peru (Johnson 1978) points out that horticulturalists like the Machiguenga spend less time in subsistence work and have more leisure time than workers in modern industrial nations. In addition to devoting more hours to work, the French spent far more time in consumption,

This industrial employee in northern India is performing work that a pre-industrial counterpart would have done at home without the aid of machines. India began its painful transformation to a modern, independent, manufacturing state during Great Britain's colonial rule. In what other ways was Indian society and culture transformed through industrialism?

Anthropology Applied

Economic Anthropologists and Consumer Behaviour

Methods of cultural anthropology include ethnographic observation and interviews and recording qualitative (as well as quantitative) information about human behaviour. Anthropologists also are trained in cross-cultural research. For these reasons large corporations hire anthropologists to do consumer research, especially to reveal the underlying cultural and social patterns that shape consumer behaviour.

People's economic behaviour is shaped by their cultural identities, beliefs, and values, as well as by environmental influences. As researchers, anthropologists can take the role of the "other" and see through the other's eyes to yield insights that companies can use to make business decisions and offer new products to increase their sales. Anthropologists also might be called upon to analyze company and product brands, to conduct focus groups, and to write employee or customer ethnographies.

Economic anthropologists might help a company test a new product, enter a new market by appealing to an ethnic group or other demographic, decide on the right interface for selling products online, analyze a wedding registry for consumer preferences, observe shoppers in a new setting, gather information on customer satisfaction or loyalty, predict trends in technologies for the home, or identify the contexts for people's shopping decisions, such as deciding to buy organic produce (**www.ethno-insight.com**). Anthropologists also are involved in market research for pharmaceutical firms and professional sports teams, as well as companies such as Pizza Hut and Coca-Cola (**www. ethnographic-solutions.com**).

Anthropologists who work for corporations are concerned with the cultural, material, and health and safety impacts that products and services have on consumers and the company employees and their communities. In addition, they analyze the sustainability of economic growth and development in relation to people's physical, social, and cultural environments.

CRITICAL THINKING QUESTION

What problems might an applied anthropologist have to confront in balancing the goals of corporations with anthropological perspectives?

---

in fact, about three to five times as much. In contrast, the Machiguenga had much more leisure time.

The study also observed that people's ideas about their needs and satisfactions are subjective and culturally constructed. For example, although North Americans and Europeans consume more goods and services than any other group, they often feel a shortage of time. Consumption behaviour provides pleasure and excitement, but people sometimes do not enjoy consumption activities because they feel pressed for time, needing to keep busy schedules and cram in as much as possible in a day. Time itself is treated as a commodity. In English, metaphors for time as a commodity include "spending time," "saving time," "having time for [something]" (Lakoff and Johnson 1980).

The prevailing ethos of **consumerism** has introduced problems in its own right. The expansion of consumer credit enables people without cash on hand to accumulate possessions that represent a lifestyle above their means. The extent of consumer debt in Canada and elsewhere reveals the power of culturally constructed demand, including the desire to display the trappings of wealth and prestige. For example, in 2001 the average Canadian carried about $20 000 in debt, a 100 percent increase from twenty years previously (Chawla and Wannell 2005) Moreover, the proportion of people who spent more than they earned increased from 39 to 47 percent, almost half of the population. These "spenders" were concentrated in certain segments of the population, including people earning under $20 000 annually (66 percent of people in this income range), single mothers (55 percent), and people under forty-five years of age (50 percent). This over-expenditure has been fuelled by a dazzling array of new consumer products and services and by opportunities to buy them with credit cards, lines of credit, store credit, and payday loans. Such a trend has led to lower national savings rates and will inevitably mean lower spending power in the long run. A University of

consumerism
Culture of consumption of goods and services.

colonialism
Policies in which countries establish colonies in distant places in order to exploit their resources and labour and possibly to establish settlements of their own citizens abroad.

Global trends in consumerism are fuelled by the advertising industry which seeks to create and sustain demand for certain products and services. By creating a perception of need, these advertisements in Vietnam contribute to overspending and the accumulation of debt.

Waterloo study indicates that people need to regularly put aside 14 percent of their incomes to ensure a comfortable retirement but are currently saving only 3 percent. Consequently, two out of three Canadians will have to make do with a substantial cut in income when they retire. (Canada Press 2007).

Impacts of Colonial Expansion, Industrialism, and Globalization

The growth of European capitalism depended on continual increases in the exploitation of land, labour, natural resources, and raw materials. Beginning in the fifteenth century, European explorers, traders, soldiers, missionaries, and settlers travelled throughout the world in an effort to acquire new territories, resources, markets, and souls. Each colonial power had its specific goals but all of them attempted to expand their national wealth and power. In the process, they had to control and conquer other lands and peoples.

Through **colonialism**, conquered or dominated peoples were incorporated into European economic systems as suppliers of raw materials. In North America, for example, indigenous peoples became enmeshed in trading networks organized by Dutch, French, British, and Russian merchants, delivering animal furs in exchange for manufactured goods (see the Culture Change feature on page 161). In Mexico and Central and South America and the Caribbean, indigenous peoples were forced to work on plantations and in mines operated by Spanish and Portuguese owners. In Africa, people were extracted as resources to be bought and sold along with gold and ivory. Many millions of other people died from warfare, overwork, and disease as the direct and indirect casualties of European colonial expansion.

In Asia, European expeditions met powerful, centralized, and well-organized states that they were not able to defeat militarily. Instead, they developed trading networks that brought resources and products to Asia from colonies in other parts of the world. In exchange, they obtained Asian luxury items to sell in Europe. Some indigenous peoples in all parts of the world readily and even enthusiastically welcomed European traders, wanting to acquire manufactured goods and luxury items. They willingly supplied the merchants with the resources, products, and people so much sought after in European and world markets. The participation of many other indigenous peoples, however, was not voluntary.

GLOBALIZATION

The Europeans needed to develop markets to sell goods manufactured in Europe and to expand markets for materials extracted from their colonies. This dynamic produced the complex economic system that we refer to as globalization.

ECONOMIC TRANSFORMATION OF THE INNU AND THE TONGA

The Innu

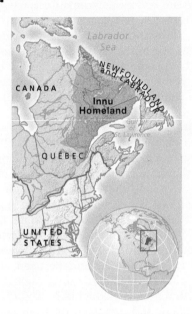

Changes in patterns of economic organization have had cultural consequences for all peoples throughout the world, especially foragers. The Innu (or Montagnais), for example, exploited the forests, lakes, and rivers of Labrador and northeastern Quebec. They hunted animals, fished, and gathered wild plants and fruits. The people relocated to follow the seasonal availability of food. Access to land and the products of the land traditionally were considered common to all members of a band—a flexibly defined social and economic group inhabiting a vaguely defined territory. The principle of sharing extended from natural resources to food, clothing, and other necessities for survival, which were shared among community residents and even were given to travellers in need.

The Innu's traditional practices were transformed as a result of contact and involvement with European traders. Because of their location on the edge of the continent, the Innu were among the first indigenous North Americans to meet European fishermen, traders, and missionaries. By the middle of the sixteenth century, the French had established a permanent post in Innu territory along the St. Lawrence River.

As the French presence grew in the region, the Innu's involvement in trade grew as well. They were especially interested in obtaining kettles and other metal tools and utensils. To obtain European products, they trapped beaver and other animals whose pelts were the medium of exchange. As reported by Paul LeJeune, a seventeenth-century Jesuit missionary, "The [Montagnais] say that the Beaver is the animal well-loved by the French, English, and Basques. I heard my host say one day, 'The Beaver does everything perfectly well, it makes kettles, hatchets, swords, knives, bread; in short, it makes everything'" (Thwaites 1901, 6:297).

The Innu's role in the fur trade expanded as they functioned as intermediaries between French merchants and native peoples living far from trading posts. Innu territory positioned the people to exert regional influence. Through trade, the Innu gradually became dependent on European goods. As their dependence on trade deepened, they wanted to control access to trade routes, which led to wars that pitted native nations against one another. As a result of their success in these wars, the Innu dominated eastern Canada.

Innu bands living closest to French trading centres came to rely on European goods as early as the middle of the seventeenth century. Because of their preference for metal, the Innu gave up making their own implements and eventually lost the skills to do so. Innu bands whose territories were more remote were more insulated from European influences. After the British gained possession of Quebec in 1762, following the French and Indian Wars, economic interest in the region waned. Nevertheless, native trappers continued to bring their furs to the European trading posts for sale.

As a result of concentrating on trapping, fundamental changes occurred in concepts of property, ownership, and cooperation within families and communities. In contrast to traditional patterns, where resources were consumed quickly, participation in the fur trade required people to keep animal skins on hand for many months during the trapping season until they could visit trading posts and exchange their catch for goods. Whereas in the past all resources and goods were shared among community residents, some possessions became the restricted property of individuals (or families) and were withdrawn from social and economic networks. Rather than sharing, people began to hoard some of their property. This change also had the consequence of creating differences in wealth among families.

The people expanded the concept of individual property from objects to territory. Innu territory was no longer open for exploitation by any member of a band.

Today the Innu are the most populous native people in Quebec. To supplement wages, some Innu hunt caribou, the most important food source for their ancestors.

Rather, families claimed some land as "hunting territories" for needs of trapping and trading (Leacock 1954). Families owned the beaver houses located within their territory, but if members of another group were starving, they could kill and eat the beaver, leaving the fur and tail for the proper owners. The system of group or family ownership initially operated only during the trapping season, but by the second half of the eighteenth century, family allotments were stable and passed on through inheritance from parents to children.

Innu bands also began to alter traditional nomadic patterns, settling near trading posts and leading to the formation of "trading post bands." During the summer, people remained near the posts, preparing and trading the furs they trapped during the fall and winter. Gradually, trappers' families were less likely to accompany the men on expeditions and remained at home camps for most of the year. The social composition of bands located near trading posts also tended to become more stable and to develop more structured leadership patterns than did the more remote groups. Traditionally egalitarian gender patterns became distorted as men's wealth based on trapping and trading increased.

In the 1950s, 1960s, and 1970s, the Canadian government forced the Innu to permanently settle in reserves encompassing only a fraction of their prior lands. Access to traditional hunting grounds was further eroded by settler encroachment, licensing laws, resource extraction, and the flooding of major tracts of land by the construction of a reservoir and dam. The notoriously poorly provisioned site at Davis Inlet in Labrador was further affected by the increase in the low-flying NATO Air Force runs in the 1980s. In 2002, the Labrador Innu were relocated to a better-provisioned site with modern amenities, but subsequent events have seen a reoccurrence of severe problems marked by substance abuse, violence, and suicide. Government spending on facilities and services has not been able to compensate for the loss of traditional lands and resources, high levels of unemployment, and the weakening of indigenous institutions.

The Tonga

In societies characterized by inequality, elite groups have greater control over land than do commoners; therefore, they have greater opportunity to exploit and amass resources, and they often control the labour of others. Such systems developed among many island peoples of Polynesia. People of the Tongan Islands, for example, developed a complex economic system based on horticulture and fishing. Tasks were divided between men and women and between chiefly and nonchiefly classes. Nonchiefly men carried out farming and fishing tasks. Nonchiefly women collected shellfish, fished, and extracted oil from coconuts. In addition to subsistence activities, men were responsible for cooking, an occupation that carried low prestige in Tongan society. Other household tasks, such as child care and house building, were not linked to gender but were performed by both women and men.

Production of crafts, utensils, and weapons was assigned according to gender and rank. Nonchiefly

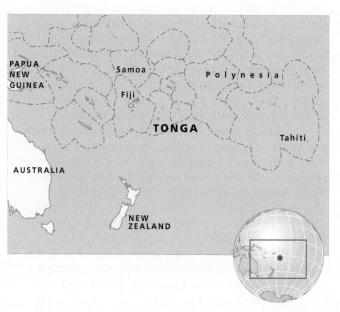

men made canoes and weapons. Nonchiefly women made mats, bark cloth (called *tapa*), bedding, and net bags. Chiefly people usually did not engage in food getting, but chiefly men made rope and decoration on weapons, and chiefly women made *tapa*. Craft production in Tonga was extensive, an example of the economic diversity and specialization found in most complex Polynesian societies (Sahlins 1970).

The Tongan populace was divided into two primary social strata: chiefs (*eiki*) and nonchiefs (*tu'a*) (Gailey 1987b). These two groups had different relationships to land as well as differences in their subsistence roles. Paramount chiefs controlled Tongan land, allocating portions to lower or district chiefs. Chiefs were perceived as guardians but not exclusive owners of land. Each chief gave the rights to use land under his jurisdiction to heads of kinship groups, usually men, who lived in the chief's district. In return for land use, families owed a part of their produce to the chiefs. This tribute helped support chiefs and their families. Chiefly people did not usually engage in subsistence activities but instead obtained food and goods from the productive work of commoner men and both chiefly and nonchiefly women. Chiefs also used surplus resources to sustain other dependents, such as attendants and warriors, who thus owed their well-being to the chief's largesse. In return, they were loyal followers. Tongan chiefs used their role as the centre of networks of redistribution in order to increase their own authority and prestige.

Tongan economy was based on a strict division of labour according to gender. Two kinds of goods were produced: women's products, called *koloa* or "valuables, wealth," and men's products, called *ngaue* or "work" (Gailey 1987b). *Koloa* items were considered more valuable than *ngaue* because they were made by women. Although the value of *koloa* reflected the social worth of women, both *koloa* and *ngaue* were necessary and fulfilled daily needs of household members.

Koloa products included bark cloth and mats made by both chiefly and nonchiefly women. The value of a particular item was determined by the status of the maker, the status of the person who ordered its production, the time involved in producing the item, and the age or history of the product.

Koloa, or women's wealth, had many uses (Gailey 1987b). *Koloa* products could be given as barter for other items and as payment for services rendered. They could also be given as gifts on ritual or other special occasions, such as weddings and funerals. People could exchange *koloa*, both parties giving and receiving valuables. *Ngaue*, or men's products, though, could not be given in return for *koloa*, because *ngaue* items were inherently of less value (Gailey 1980).

In Tongan society, one's father's sister held high social status within the family and wielded authority over her brother and his children. Rights of a sister, called *fahu* rights, included the ability to command labour and products from her brother and his wife and children. An older sister had even greater status and *fahu* rights. In addition to the *fahu* rights of a sister, a woman's children had *fahu* rights and could claim labour and products from their maternal uncles and cousins.

Transformations in Tongan economy, the organization of production, and social relations began to occur

In Tonga today, the processing of coconut into copra is the only significant industry.

as a result of European contact, especially in the mid-1800s, when European trade and whaling in the South Pacific became more frequent and sustained. Through trade, Tongans obtained metal goods (axes, nails, knives), beads, and cloth. In exchange, they gave fish, coconuts, yams, bark cloth, and other crafts. Women, especially unmarried nonchiefly women, offered sexual services in exchange for manufactured goods from traders and sailors. Chiefs were keenly interested in trade with the British, especially wanting to obtain firearms that could be used in conflicts with one another over goals to increase their territorial control.

Expansion of trade throughout the nineteenth century changed the traditional division of labour and the value of *koloa*. At first, coconut oil, processed by women, was an important trade item. It was employed by Europeans to light lamps and manufacture soap. As a result of its use as a trade commodity, women's production of coconut oil intensified, enhancing their status. Then, in the late 1800s, the world market for coconut oil declined. Instead, Europeans sought dried coconut, called *copra*. Because the collection and processing of coconuts was men's work, or *ngaue*, the shift to trade in copra began a realignment of traditional Tongan beliefs about the inherent value of women's and men's products. The prestige traditionally associated with the production of coconut oil (a woman's product) shifted to the production of copra (a man's product). The prestige value of products then shifted to the product itself rather than to the gender of the producer, thus undermining the very foundation of Tongan economic and social principles.

Influenced by British colonial administrators and missionaries, the Tongan legislature granted land-use rights to individual men as heads of households. The inheritance of land, formerly a sister's right to claim, became inheritance from father to son. Competing claims through fathers' sisters were dismissed by law, and the exercise of *fahu* rights by sisters was made illegal. A woman can no longer lay claims to her brothers and their families, thus altering the network of relationships that linked people to their kin.

This expansion was closely connected with nation building. Governments controlled much of the trade, directly or through state-supported merchant organizations, such as the Hudson's Bay Company, and pursued policies of political and military intervention to promote and protect their economic interests. These policies often led to military invasions and wars of conquest, followed by the establishment of direct colonial rule. Far-flung empires were established, with European powers competing to acquire the most colonial possessions. The French and British claimed much of North America, for example, and the British claimed India while the French seized Indo China. At the end of the nineteenth century they both became the central players in the "Scramble for Africa," in which military and commercial interests raced through the continent to acquire the last pieces of colonial real estate available. By the end of the era, the British could boast of an empire on which "the sun never set" and on which the dominance of British trade, industry, and capital depended.

As colonial control spread throughout the world, capitalism and market economies were introduced to peoples whose subsistence strategies were based on foraging, pastoralism, and horticulture. Transformation of their economic systems was promoted by involvement in trade, as illustrated in the Culture Change studies in this chapter covering the Innu and the Tonga. Because economic systems are integrated with other aspects of culture, the changes in work and landholding practices caused by colonialism and trade stimulated political, social, and ideological changes as well. However, colonized peoples have not necessarily been passive victims of exploitation and manipulation. They have often modified their acceptance of European practices and values to maintain the continuity of their indigenous social and cultural institutions and have in some instances organized outright resistance.

Colonialism and the Exploitation of Labour

Slavery was the most extreme form of colonial exploitation of labour of indigenous peoples. Slavery deprived the victims of all rights to determine their own labour, forced them to produce goods directed by their owners, and expropriated all their products to be distributed and consumed according to the wishes of their masters. In the Caribbean and the southern United States, slaves in the eighteenth and first half of the nineteenth centuries were the primary agricultural workers and produced most of the crops intended for external trade. They received nothing beyond their minimal substance needs in return. In other areas populations were left free but were subject to forced labour. In Mexico and Guatemala, Spanish landowners seized the territories of Aboriginal communities and were given rights to command their labour for parts of the year. In Africa, the French and British introduced communal labour requirements which demanded that local peoples work on major public projects, such as road building, without compensation. The French also promoted the expansion of their colonial export industries by demanding that local farmers produce a minimum amount of export crops. Those that did not meet their quota were fined or jailed.

Another means of controlling indigenous labour was the imposition of colonial taxes, for example, mandatory **poll taxes** or head taxes. Because taxes had to be paid in cash, people were compelled to seek wage employment in the European-controlled economic sectors in their countries—in European-owned mines, plantations, or service and construction jobs—or they grew crops for cash, removing land from subsistence farming. Their crops thus entered national and international markets under the control and distribution of colonial powers.

Ideologies that supported these practices focused on perceived benefits to the native peoples. In the words of a member of the British Parliament, speaking in 1926, "Under all circumstances the progress of natives toward civilization is only secured when they shall be convinced of the necessity and dignity of labour; and therefore I think that everything we reasonably do to encourage the natives to work is highly desirable" (Joseph Chamberlain, quoted in Wellington 1967:250). In 1934, another British official stated, "As the natives were often reluctant to leave their homes, a little gentle pressure was brought to bear upon them with the introduction of a poll tax. This measure quite effectively stimulated their desire for earning the white man's money" (Eiselen 1934:71). Comments such as these show how colonial powers were able to rationalize the economic exploitation of colonized peoples.

Post-Industrial Society

Since World War II, new trends have occurred within national and global economic systems, which have assumed a new order alternatively classified as late capitalism, **post-industrialism**, post-modernism, or the information age. These labels gloss several interrelated changes in patterns of production, business organization, national and global economic policies, international flows of capital, goods, and people, all of which have had an impact on cultures and societies around the world. The motivating force behind these developments has been a continued commitment to growth that has involved a push for new technologies, higher consumption levels, and larger profits.

Changes in production patterns have involved the expansion of the industrial goods sector, particularly with the emergence of widespread home and automobile ownership in the wake of the boom that emerged in the 1950s and with the later expansion of the electronics industry that has made televisions, computers, stereo systems, and cell phones ubiquitous within industrialized countries. Growth in the service sector has been even more dynamic and has involved increases in health and education facilities, research and development, financial and business services, and in the retail, restaurant, entertainment, transportation, and hospitality sectors. Accordingly, service employment now dominates the powerful North American economy and has increased the work force to incorporate a large majority of the female population, which had mostly remained out of the labour market in the earlier half of the twentieth century.

Changes in production and consumption have been closely integrated with important technological innovations. Both the pace and the quality of new technologies have been increased within the "hi-tech" sector that has become a catch phrase for the age. Businesses have focused on research and other forms of acquiring new knowledge and processing information to the extent that knowledge in itself has become both a crucial business resource and prime commodity. Even more dynamic changes have occurred within the transportation and communications sector. Improvements of road and air travel and telecommunications, and the rise of computers and the internet have drastically reduced the barriers of space and time and have reorganized land use and people's work, consumption, and leisure patterns. Innovations in these areas have been associated with changes in the nature of business organization and culture. In the classic industrial era, corporations were grounded within individual nations, which provided aid and protection in anticipation of higher investment, employment,

poll taxes
Taxes levied on households.

post-industrialism
An economic order based on the expansion of the service economy, especially within the knowledge sector, and on globally organized corporations and institutions.

and national wealth within their borders. International relations were marked by nationalist competition, the source of two world wars, and by colonial expansion and exploitation, the source of many smaller ones.

In the post-industrial period, a trend towards transnational corporate expansion and integration has emerged. This new business climate has encouraged the dissolution of colonies, tariffs, and other trade barriers. Countries once wary of foreign investors now declare themselves "open for business." Operations of the largest corporations are now internationalized with offices and branches in numerous locations around the world that can change from one year to the next, depending on shifts in consumer markets and the quest for lower costs and friendly political regimes. Direct investments are complemented by mergers, outsourcing, and business alliances.

The patterns of globalization inherent in the post-industrial economy are closely linked to changes in governmental roles and structures within nation states. In the interest of increasing external trade and private investment, the prevailing fiscal policy has stressed the liberalization of controls on the economy and privatization of state-owned industries and pubic services. These processes have involved many changes in industrial countries, as we have already seen in Canada, and the disappearance of socialist policies in Eastern Europe and China. In the developing world, the new order has meant independence from colonial rule but also new forms of pressure and exploitation because of weak economies based on raw material exports, conditions placed on vital aid from Western powers, and the dominant position of transnational companies in the control of trade.

The rise of the global post-industrial order is partly dependent upon several critical international agencies that have emerged to regulate international transactions and to set and enforce new standards of economic and political conduct. The most important have been the International Monetary Fund, the World Bank, and the World Trade Organization. Their objectives have been to introduce a globally integrated system of governance, stability, and growth through establishing uniform policies and constructing and enforcing economic agreements. In practice, the main force of their activities has been to advance the cause of liberalization and privatization, often to the benefit of the international business community.

Beyond the establishment of global organizations that focus on economic matters, the last fifty years have also seen major attempts to deal with more general economic, social, and political problems such as war, poverty, and injustice. Unfortunately, the United Nations' attempts to build a widely representative world governance framework have had mixed success. They have not attracted the same degree of agreement and cooperation as their international financial and trade counterparts, nor have they developed powerful sanctions to ensure adherence to their decisions. However, on a less formal level, some progress has been made. Nongovernmental organizations are becoming more numerous and prominent in providing aid and holding governments to account on a global scale. Improved transportation and communication facilities have aided the formation of global collations, such as the environmental, feminist, and indigenous peoples' movements, that can assemble economic resources and political support to advance the causes of justice and equality. Of course, terrorist and criminal organizations are also capitalizing on the opportunities of global networking.

The major features of the current global economy—the expansion of the service sector, the globalization of investment and trade, the importance of knowledge creation and information processing, the rise of powerful transnational business interests, and the reduced role of the nation state—have had a complex impact on the local societies and cultures in which anthropologists do most of their research. Each locality has been influenced by many different forces and has attempted to balance them against its own interests and values. Broad trends have been observed in the status of women as they become increasing integrated into the workforce and seek better representation within their communities, in the growing gap between rich and poor regions and among segments of the populations within them, and in dislocations and migrations of people as they seek out refuge from economic and political exploitation and opportunities within dynamically growing regions. We will revisit these issues in the chapters that follow.

Case study

Gambling in Newfoundland and Labrador

Over the past fifty years, Canada has experienced major changes in its economic order, such as those we have considered in the Prairie Provinces in the last chapter. Newfoundland and Labrador has also been subject to transformations that have been compounded by a major environmental crisis, the collapse of the cod fishing industry, which supported outport villages that had maintained a unique culture and close-knit society for generations. Reade Davis of Memorial University conducted a revealing study on how local people adopted VLT gambling as a strategy for reconstructing a threatened way of life (Davis 2006).

The cod industry has been an important element of the Newfoundland and Labrador economy. It supported fishing families located in coastal communities who harvested the inshore fishery with small boats and crews. Although they were market oriented, they were able to earn only modest incomes and were dedicated to fishing as a way of life rather than a means to become rich. Community values and support systems and ties to the land and sea were critical features of their culture. These institutions were supported on a provincial level through development and employment programs that focused on the community as a whole.

Although the Newfoundland and Labrador economy has traditionally been one of the weakest in Canada, the disappearance of cod stocks and the federal moratorium on cod fishing posed an unprecedented threat to the survival of coastal communities.

Some mitigation resulted from the harvesting of other fish, particularly shellfish, but the government granted only a limited number of licences for these stocks, and most fishers could not afford the more expensive boats and equipment that were required for the type of fishing involved. The federal government responded to the unemployment crisis by introducing a new form of aid that focused on retraining individuals and supporting migration to more prosperous provinces. This strategy was a departure from past practice and reflected a new governmental philosophy of individual incentive and responsibility that had come to replace the traditional values of communalism.

Davis' research on how local people and communities responded to the crisis and the government's way of meeting it indicates a marked resistance to the new policies. He observed that some recipients of government compensation payments and retraining opportunities were spending a good deal of their time and funds in local clubs drinking, socializing, and using the automated gambling machines. Not all of the patrons were heavily involved, but one component, known as the "gamblers," used the machines continuously and also managed their winnings in a characteristic manner. Upon hitting a jackpot, which was referred to as "ringing the bells" after an animation that would appear on jackpot screens, they would buy a round of drinks for all the patrons, even if the tab exceeded their winnings for the night. They would also share their winnings with fellow gamblers with whom they had formed close relationships and who would regularly use such proceeds to continue their betting. Accordingly, by the end of the evening, much of the money that the gamblers brought to the club would be expended on the machines and the bar.

Davis comments that the gambling behaviour he recorded was neither improvident nor a desperate and vain attempt to temporarily escape from a harsh reality. He interprets it as a means of resisting governmental strategies of solving local problems by moving people out of the locality. As such, in playing the VLT machines, the gamblers were both voicing resistance and constructing a means to establish coherent networks of sharing and aid. Nevertheless, he observes that these attempts were not totally effective. When the funding ran out after a five-year period, the poorer members of the gambling groups had to drop out, an act which their richer friends looked on as antisocial. The author concludes that gambling is a multifaceted activity with contradictory implications and we must "resist the temptation to uniformly glorify or condemn these practices in ways that fail to do justice to the ongoing struggles of those involved in them."

REVIEW

Native peoples across the world became enmeshed with European market economies beginning in the fifteenth century. Through colonialism and trade, the exploitation of native lands and resources and labour, and coercive practices such as poll taxes and the mission system, capitalist and industrial economies gradually came to dominate the growing present-day global economy. Foraging, horticulturalism, and pastoralism have been replaced by industrial agriculture and manufacturing in most regions of the world. Industrialism is a system of production that increases efficiency and productivity through the use of machines and automation. Increases in production lead to greater wealth, and increases in consumption and consumerism further stimulate economic growth. Over the past fifty years, service industries have replaced agriculture and industrial manufacturing as the dominant economic sector in wealthy post-industrial societies. Further capitalist growth has occurred in the rise of large transnational corporations, which has led to the globalization of the economy and encouraged enhanced cross-border trade and investment.

Chapter Summary

Analyzing Economic Systems

- Economic systems include strategies for allocating land, resources, and labour. People everywhere need to produce, distribute, and consume foods and other goods. They obtain their resources from their land through various modes of production. People in different cultures employ different methods to allocate land and resources.

- Societies need to allocate the labour of their members to productive tasks. Work roles are often assigned to people on the basis of age and gender. Children are usually given work to do that is compatible with their lack of strength and stamina. The way in which gender affects work roles varies considerably in different cultures: in some, men's and women's roles are rigidly separated; in others, women and men may perform many of the same tasks and work cooperatively.

- Economic exchanges occur among family members, friends, traders, and other members of communities. Exchanges between family members or other familiars are usually of the type called generalized reciprocity, where no immediate return is expected, while exchanges between other members of communities are called balanced reciprocity, where there is usually a mutual exchange of goods. Exchanges between strangers, especially in the marketplace, are characterized by negative reciprocity, where each party tries to receive more value than he or she gives.

- Systems of exchange also include redistributive networks, barter, trade, and market transactions.

Market Economies and Capitalism

- Market economies are based on the buying and selling of commodities of fixed value, depending on supply and demand and using standardized mediums of exchange. Markets also are where these transactions take place.

- Capitalist economic production is based on the desire by owners of the means of production to increase their profit. In capitalist production, workers do not control the means of production but instead must sell their labour to owners of factories or other institutions that organize and produce goods and services. Workers sell their labour to the owners for a wage. Workers produce "surplus value" or the value of the goods produced by their labour that is greater than the wage paid to them. This surplus value becomes profit for the owners. Capitalist economic systems are geared toward an ever-increasing rate of profit. Unlike traditional indigenous subsistence economies, capitalist production is inherently unstable.

Industrial Economies

- In the fifteenth century, European powers began a process of economic and colonial expansion aimed at expropriating resources and labour from indigenous lands and peoples. In this process of globalization, which is not confined to Europeans historically, resources and trade items were incorporated into a worldwide economic system that led to the growth and concentration of wealth in Europe. This wealth and desire for even greater profits motivated the development of industrialization.

- In complex agrarian and industrial societies, systems of distribution have developed to circulate foods and other goods from direct producers to those who do not produce food. Members of elite classes, in particular, benefit from the distribution of goods. Through kinship networks or through state organization, they are able to make claims on other people's labour. Whether this is called tribute, taxes, or slavery, some segments of society are not able to control at least some of the products of their labour.

- Post-industrial societies increasingly rely on consumerism and the provision of information and services to the global economy rather than goods.

Key Terms

economic system   146

capital goods   151

social capital   151

generalized
   reciprocity   151

balanced reciprocity   151

negative reciprocity   153

barter   153

redistributive
   networks   153

general purpose
   money   154

special purpose
   money   154

market economy   155

commodity   155

capitalism   155

surplus value   156

consumerism   159

colonialism   160

poll taxes   165

post-industrialism   165

Review Questions

1. What social behaviours are part of any society's economic system? How do anthropologists view economic systems?

2. What kinds of economic exchange are seen in societies? How do systems of exchange relate to modes of subsistence?

3. What are the different types of reciprocity? Why is balanced reciprocity seen in foraging groups? How is the potlatch an example of negative reciprocity?

4. How do allocations of land and labour differ among foragers, pastoralists, horticulturalists, and agriculturalists?

5. How are economic concepts, such as ownership, integrated with other cultural systems, such as kinship, social status, political power, and ideology?

6. What are the distinguishing features of a market economy? What are the impacts of capitalism on a society's systems of production, distribution, and consumption?

7. How does the rise of social inequality relate to changes in economic systems?

8. How were indigenous peoples brought into European economies? What impacts did colonialism have on those peoples and their economies?

9. Why do capitalist economies depend on ever-increasing consumerism?

10. What important economic trends are emerging in the world today and what kind of impact have they had on local societies and cultures?

Kinship and Descent

Top, left to right: James Richardson, Founder 1857; George A. Richardson, President 1892–1906; Senator Henry W. Richardson, President 1906–1916; James A. Richardson, President 1916–1939; Agnes M. Benidickson, Board of Directors/Director Emeritus 1941–2007; The Honourable James A, Richardson, Board of Directors 1946–1968 & 1980–1989, Chairman & CEO 1966–1968. Bottom, left to right: Muriel S. Richardson, 1939–1966; Carolyn. A (Richardson) Hursh, Board of Directors 1991–2000, Chairman of Board, 2000– ; Hartley T. Richardson, President & CEO 1993– ; Kathleen M. Richardson, Board of Directors/Director Emeritus 1954– ; George T. Richardson, President 1966–1993, Chairman, 1993–2000, Director Emeritus 2000–.

CHAPTER 7

Preview

1. **What is descent, and why is it significant in organizing human relationships?**
2. **What different types of descent are found in human cultures?**
3. **What kinds of kin groups do the various descent rules create?**
4. **How do different unilineal descent rules affect people's interrelationships?**
5. **How do kinship systems interrelate with other aspects of culture, such as economic and political systems?**
6. **How and why do kinship systems change?**
7. **What kinship terminologies do people use to classify their kin?**
8. **How do kin terms reveal the type of kinship system people have?**

Hartley Richardson will join nearly 3000 fellow employees in six cities tonight in raising a glass to honour the 150th anniversary of James Richardson & Sons, Limited. The 53-year-old is president and CEO of the longest-running, 100-percent family-owned business in Canada.

"The past is something we want to celebrate," Richardson said in an interview from the 30th-floor boardroom in the Richardson Building at Portage and Main. "It's the next 150 years that we want to end the evening focused on."

Richardson is the seventh family member and fifth generation to run the company, which was founded 10 years before Confederation and has been instrumental in the growth of the country's agricultural, aviation, financial services, and energy sectors.

He said the "real celebrities" of tonight's festivities are the members of his "other" family. In particular, there will be 38 people in attendance in the six cities who were at the company's centennial party in 1957, an event hosted by Richardson's grandmother, Muriel, who ran the company for 27 years

Richardson said he's confident the company's four core businesses—agriculture and food processing, financial services, energy, and real estate—are well positioned and will continue to grow, making the bicentennial celebration even bigger. It's an event he said he plans to attend.

According to the June issue of Financial Post Business magazine, JRSL is the 147th biggest company in the country by revenue, bringing in an estimated $2.2 billion in 2006, a 23 percent jump from the previous year.

JRSL has eleven shareholders, all of whom are direct descendants of the company's founder and first president, James Richardson.

Combined, the family ranked 20th on Canadian Business magazine's 2006 Rich 100 list, with $1.8 billion in net worth, a 20 percent rise from the previous year.

Richardson started out at JRSL as a summer student in 1978, where he learned about the business by working in grain elevators and terminals doing "every kind of nasty job they could find for me."

That included cleaning out the elevator "boots"— essentially the part where the conveyor belt takes the grain up into the elevator.

While the grain is being moved, its dust all falls into the boot. Cleaning it in those days required climbing in with a trouble light, a pail, and a shovel.

"Generally, when you're down there, you're not alone. There were other creatures that tended to be down there," Richardson laughed. "It was an interesting experience."

From there, he worked in the grain business as a district manager and divisional manager and head of the real estate operations before taking over as CEO in 1993.

Richardson said the family remains "very committed" to Winnipeg, which he said is an ideal base for conducting cross-Canada business.

"The reason is really quite simple. It's our home; it's where we have grown up. While we have family in other centres across the country, when we meet four times a

year, this is where we meet. This is the head office. This is where we believe, without any question, we can build a globally competitive company," he said.

Source: "City's first family celebrates 150th birthday bash for Richardsons' thriving empire," By Geoff Kirbyson, *Winnipeg Free Press.* June 16, 2007. Used with permission of Winnipeg Free Press.

? *Our vignette for this unit departs from our previous chapters in presenting a presumably factual rather than a fiction account. However, the lines between these two forms may be blurred. Folk tales can include elements of truth and newpapers can sometimes put a spin on reality. Can you observe any folk tale elements in this story from a major Canadian newspaper? What are the main themes and messages, and how do they reflect cultural themes myths, and realities of Canadian society?*

Although kinship is usually the most dominant feature of social organization in pre-industrial societies, many theorists have suggested that its role has declined in the course of modernization throughout the world. Anthropological studies, however, have shown that this institution has been more resilient and adaptive than expected. One particularly important force for family solidarity lies within the arena of corporate wealth and power where capital assets and inheritance patterns tie parents and children as well as siblings and cousins into close-knit groups that share ownership, management rights, and profits. This news item from the *Winnipeg Free Press* relates the history of one such dynasty, which, like other prominent Canadian business families such as the McCains, Irvings, Bronfmans, and Bombardiers, have been held together, at least for a time, by common interests and loyalties. The story underscores the importance of kinship, not only in its account of the growth and longevity of the Richardson Corporation, but also in the metaphorical use of "family" to evoke paternalistic ties between management and workers.

KINSHIP SYSTEMS

In all societies, people have ways of organizing their relationships with others, especially their primary relationships with kin. As children, our earliest and most influential interactions are with our parents, siblings, and other relatives. We rely on our families for all of our survival needs. They feed us, clothe us, and provide our shelter. They also help us adjust to the world around us and to learn the behaviour and attitudes that our culture expects. And families provide emotional support in both good times and bad.

Many of our relatives continue as important economic and emotional supports throughout our lives. Even as adults, we can turn to our kin in networks of reciprocity, asking for aid in times of need. In turn, we may be asked to respond to their requests when fortunes are reversed. We may align ourselves with our relatives when they are engaged in disputes with others. And we may expect loyalty from our kin when we are in conflict with neighbours or other community members. During personal or family crises, we may expect emotional support from our relatives. Together we celebrate happy occasions such as births and marriages, and we mourn the deaths of our kin. Kinship relations may even extend beyond the grave through contacts with ancestral spirits who are believed to retain an interest in the affairs of their living descendents.

In large-scale societies, friends, colleagues, co-members of clubs, and other non-relatives also function significantly to give us companionship and support. But in most societies, kinship relations permeate people's daily lives and mold their identity and their sense of themselves. In small-scale societies and in cohesive communities within pluralistic states, family members may be united in dense, complex networks. They may perform important functions in the absence of the formal institutions that regulate and organize economic, political, and religious life in large-scale societies. People identify themselves not just as individuals but as members of kinship groups.

A **kinship system** consists of connections between people by common descent, marriage, or adoption, and the beliefs and practices according to which people regard and treat each other as relatives. Kin may be genetically related (**consanguines**, "related by blood") or related by marriage (**affines**), or they may be related according to other ideas of closely shared substance or identity. Many kin groups include adopted kin and **fictive kin,** unrelated individuals who are regarded and treated as relatives. Thus, the notion of kinship is essentially a social and symbolic idea, not based on universal objective criteria.

The term "fictive" kin is perhaps an unfortunate usage since its suggestion that some kinship relationships are more "factual" than others reflects a Western bias. Biological reality is an elusive concept, especially within a cross-cultural perspective. For example,

kinship system
System of determining who one's relatives are and what one's relationship is to them.

consanguines
People related by blood.

affines
People related through marriage.

fictive kin
Unrelated individuals who are regarded and treated as relatives.

among the Ju/'hoansi, any two people that have the same name are considered to be kin even though no genealogical connection between them can be traced. However, the possession of a common name is understood as indicative of common origin, since all "namesake kin" are believed to have descended from a single ancestor of that name at the beginning of time. An example from Western tradition stretches the idea of physical relatedness even farther. Catholics have long adhered to the practice of godparenthood, in which a child receives a godmother and godfather in the course of its baptism. Traditionally this sacramental act was understood as establishing a bond of shared substance or "spiritual kinship" that was equivalent to common biological descent. Accordingly, at one time, godparents and godchildren were forbidden to marry, as were godchildren of the same baptismal sponsors on the grounds that sexual relations between them would be incestuous (See the Case Study on adoption in Quebec).

In some instances, bonds of kinship may regularly not be thought of in biological terms. In ancient Israel the practice of the levirate forced a woman to marry her husband's brother if her husband died. Any children of such a union were considered to be the descendants of the dead brother rather than the biological father. In a similar institution, the Igbo of West Africa require that a man pay a bride price to his wife's family before he can be considered to be the father of her children. If a woman gives birth before she marries, her father will assume the status of father to her child, a situation which can be advantageous if he has no sons to carry on his line. Moreover, a woman can pay the bride price for another woman and assume the status of father to any children to whom her wife gives birth.

Among foragers, pastoralists, and horticulturalists, kinship relations were the primary regulators of social and economic life. Through kin relations, people organized their households, allocated work roles, controlled land and other property in common, made decisions affecting the group, and carried out ritual functions. In agrarian societies, kinship relations generally continued to be paramount in organizing and integrating communities, but new patterns of interaction also emerged. Gradually, as state societies developed, many of the functions carried out by kinship groups were taken over by specialists and state institutions. The state regulated intergroup trade, established formal procedures for making decisions and settling disputes, and set up institutions to carry out some social functions, replacing the critical roles of kinship groups. In industrial and post-industrial societies people may live apart from their relatives, and many of the functions of kin groups can be fulfilled through public or private institutions. Thus, differences exist between those societies where people's lives centre around their kin and where kinship regulates many social, economic, and political functions and those societies where ties among kin are more flexible and less intense and where formal institutions provide for most of people's needs.

Kinship systems are organized around rules of marriage (the subject of Chapter 8) and **rules of descent,** which stipulate how identity, rights, and duties are passed down from one generation to another. Although the notion of kinship is subjective, people trace descent and organize kinship groups in two fundamental ways. In societies with **bilateral descent,** people think of themselves as related to both their mother's kin and their father's kin at the same time (*bilateral* means "two sides," from *bi* meaning "two" and *lateral* or "side"). In **unilineal descent** systems, people define themselves in relation to only one line of descent, either their mother's or their father's (from *uni* meaning "one" and *lineal* or "line").

Bilateral Descent

Bilateral descent creates a potentially limitless group of people to whom one may claim relationship. People usually do not interact with everyone in this large kinship group; they tend to know, socialize with, and depend on a smaller group of relatives within the wider network. This smaller group of bilateral relatives is called a *kindred* (see Figure 7.2).

rules of descent
Social rules that stipulate the nature of relationships from one generation to another.

bilateral descent
Principle of descent in which people think of themselves related to both their mother's kin and their father's kin at the same time.

unilineal descent
Principle of descent in which people define themselves in relation to only one line, either their mother's line traced back through a series of women or their father's line traced back though a series of men.

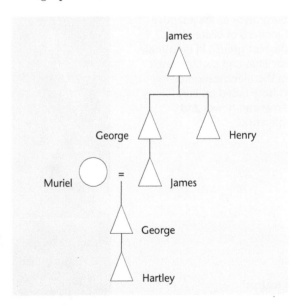

Figure 7.1
This diagram traces the succession to the position of CEO of the Richardson Corporation since its founding in 1857 by James Richardson. What rule of descent is being followed? (Note that all individuals depicted bear the Richardson surname.) How is the descent pattern related to the one usually in force in Canadian families?

Figure 7.2
A Kindred. A group of people, traced through bilateral descent, related to the brother and sister shown at the bottom row, centre. Circles represent females, triangles represent males, horizontal lines link siblings, vertical lines link parents and children, and equal signs link husband and wife.

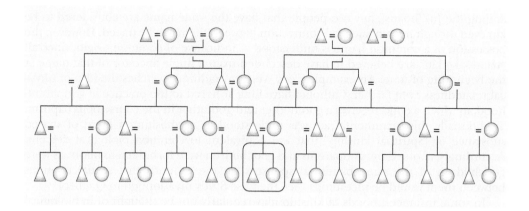

? *What are the names of the people you regard as members of your kindred? How are they related to you? What kind of relationships do you maintain with them?*

GLOBALIZATION

The increasing prevalence of bilateral descent in the world today is partly an outgrowth of the adaptive functions of bilateral descent groups in industrial societies and partly a result of the globalization of culture based on Euro-American power and influence.

Reckoning one's kin through bilateral descent is common in modern industrial societies, but it is also found in many small foraging societies. **Kindreds** are adaptive in both kinds of cultures, but for different reasons. In foraging societies, bilateral descent allows people to make claims on a wide group of people for economic assistance and emotional support. This strategy is adaptive, especially when resources are variable. In times of need, people may ask relatives for aid based on the principle of reciprocity. In better times they may be asked to return the favour. Bilateral descent is also adaptive for people in modern industrial countries, where it provides flexibility and openness within a situation in which people change locations and social roles and status. Thus, the same system of descent can have different outcomes and serve different purposes, depending on people's needs as they adapt to specific ecological, social, and economic conditions. While bilateral descent provides a large number of people with reciprocal obligations and responsibilities, it also creates a loosely organized kin group without definite social limits or boundaries. People can establish greater individual autonomy, freeing themselves from claims that others might make on them. Individuals and small family units can advance economically and accumulate more wealth if fewer people ask them for support. But although autonomy and independence can free people from

The San of the Kalahari reckon their kinship bilaterally, tracing relationships through both father and mother. They depend on their kin for aid and support in times of need. This reality reinforces traditional social ethics that stress generosity, hospitality, cooperation, and loyalty.

kindred
Kinship group consisting of known bilateral relatives with whom people interact and socialize, and on whom they rely for economic and emotional assistance.

obligations, they may also have the consequence of social isolation and may limit the number of people from whom a person might seek aid in times of need.

In historical context, bilateral kin groups in industrial societies reflected changing economic and social conditions favouring individual achievement and personal advancement. These conditions tended to weaken kin ties. Nevertheless, both the poor and the wealthy can benefit from membership in bilateral kin groups. Carol Stack's research in African-American urban families (1975) and Rhoda Halperin's study of rural Kentuckians (1990) demonstrate that low-income people and people living in rural areas tend to maintain large networks of kin, which diversifies and widens their possibilities of support in times of need. The very wealthy, as we have observed in the opening story of this chapter, may depend on kinship because of shared rights in the ownership and management of business assets. And they rely on each other for political support based on common interests, identities, and goals.

Unilineal Descent

Unilineal descent has two principal forms: matrilineal and patrilineal (see Figures 7.3 and 7.4). In both forms, kinship is traced through descendants in one line only, either through the mother or the father. In **matrilineal** societies, people reckon descent through their mothers and her female relatives; that is, a child belongs to the kinship group of his or her mother. In **patrilineal** societies, people reckon descent through their fathers and his male relatives, so that a child belongs to the kinship group of his or her father.

> ### REVIEW
>
> A kinship system consists of the beliefs and practices by which people regard and treat each other as relatives. The people may be genetically related (consanguines) or related by marriage (affines). As well, they may be unrelated, adopted, or fictive kin. Rules of descent stipulate the nature of kin relationships from one generation to another. Two ways that people trace their descent are bilateral descent (tracing relationships through both parents and both sets of their parents) and unilineal descent (tracing relationships through either the mother's kin or the father's kin). Bilateral descent groups are called kindreds.

MATRILINEAL AND PATRILINEAL SYSTEMS

Of known cultures whose kinship systems were organized on principles of unilineal descent, the great majority were patrilineal; possibly only about 15 percent were matrilineal (Aberle 1961:663). Matrilineal societies were concentrated among peoples whose economies were based on horticulture, especially those where women were responsible for the farmwork. Because women were the primary subsistence workers and helped one another with both child care and farmwork, they benefited from the existence of stable and co-operative units. Tracing descent through women in such societies stressed the communal and permanent bonds among women and between women and their children, especially their daughters. Most horticultural societies were patrilineal, however, even those that relied on women's labour.

The proportion of matrilineal societies was highest among horticulturalists of West and Central Africa, such as the Akan, and Native North America, such as the Pueblo and Mohawk (Aberle 1961:665). Patrilineal societies were most prevalent within agrarian societies and among pastoralists, who rely on men's cooperative labour. Although subsistence plays an important role in shaping patterns of kinship, it is not sufficient to explain these patterns. Exceptions show that other cultural variables are involved.

Patrilineal Descent

Patrilineal descent is the most common kinship form in the world. Currently, it is prevalent in many Asian societies, most notably China and Japan, and throughout most of Africa. Examples can be found in every other inhabited continent. While Western family

matrilineal
Descent system in which kinship group membership and inheritance pass through the female line.

patrilineal
Descent system in which kinship group membership and inheritance pass through the male line.

? *If your kinship system were matrilineal, who would be in your kin group? Who would be your closest relatives if your kinship system were patrilineal?*

Case study

Adoption in Quebec from 1900 to 1960

Adoption occurs in many cultures and provides solutions to problems of child rearing and family continuity when families cannot be reproduced through biological means. As with other aspects of culture, these institutions are understood, valued, and treated differently from society to society. Chantal Collard, of Concordia University, provides us with an account of adoption practices within one particular society, Quebec, during the first half of the twentieth century (Collard 1988). Her findings detail the treatment of unwed mothers and their children within the context of the uniquely French-Canadian Catholic values and institutions that dominated the moral and social life of the province until the Quiet Revolution of the 1960s.

In Quebec, the Church was responsible both for proclaiming the core values that informed kinship and marriage patterns and for providing almost all of the public services upon which family welfare depended. Procreation was considered the main reason for sexuality and marriage and a primary duty of a married couple, an ideal which perpetuated large families and Canada's highest birth rate, at eight children per married woman in 1901. On the other hand, sex and pregnancy outside of Church-ordained unions were viewed as cardinal sins. These moral premises were correspondingly affirmed within the community, where unwed mothers and illegitimate children were severely stigmatized. Such events were traditionally rare, since girls were married off at a very young age. The few births to unwed mothers that occurred were carefully hidden. Collard recounts that some mothers of

wayward teenagers would feign to be pregnant and then claim their daughter's babies as their own.

With the advent of the twentieth century, industrialization, urbanization, and the diffusion of new values led to both a later age of marriage and more liberal sexual mores. Consequently, teenage pregnancies and other threats to the Church's moral and temporal hegemony increased. In response, the Church set up homes for unwed mothers, know as *crèches* (nurseries), to assist in the birth of the children and their transfer to adoptive families. The Church had two reasons for establishing these institutions. It wanted to extend its control over family services and also ensure that children of Catholic parents would remain within the faith. In return it provided two essential services to the teenage mothers: refuge and anonymity. Girls afraid of showing signs of pregnancy could be housed within the *crèches* where they were secluded, given false names, and sometimes veiled. In the process they attended confession regularly and were "rehabilitated" and restored to virginal status so that they could be reintegrated into society with their reputations and marriage prospects intact. The details of their transformation were very like those of the nuns who ran the institutions. Along the same vein, the children to whom they gave birth were absolved of their "illegitimate" status by being considered as "children of God."

The children were reintegrated into society through the adoption process. A mother could adopt her own child but only if she married the biological father, who had to both agree to the marriage and affirm his paternity. Otherwise children would be given to other families or held until the age of three when they would be sent to orphanages, also under Church control. Families adopted for the obvious reason that they were unable to have children, but many were motivated by a desire to add a child of the opposite gender to an only-child or all-boy or all-girl household. As well, couples beyond childbearing years sometimes wanted to continue to have young children around for companionship. The desire to do a charitable act was also important. In general, girls were preferred over boys, since they were thought to be easier to raise and more devoted to family life. In contrast to the Québécois preference for large families, a couple would usually adopt only one or two children.

Collard concludes from her studies that the values and practices concerning adoption in the particular setting of early twentieth-century Quebec differed from what were understood as the normal patterns of kinship. Accordingly, this "marginal" form of family reproduction was guided by separate rules than those of the "dominant" form constituted by biology and the blessing of the Church. This pattern was generated by the power and value system of the Québécois Catholic establishment which, unlike European Catholicism, had not been influenced by Protestant notions or the liberal values of the nation state within industrialized societies.

Collard's study is reminiscent of Jack Goody's work on the influence of the Church on kinship in the early Middle Ages, when it exerted omnipotent control over society, in part through its influence on the kinship system (Goody 1983). His thesis maintains that the decline of the extent and power of kinship bonds in Western societies that is usually associated with industrialization was actually the result of the medieval Church's influence on marriage and family patterns. Goody argues that the Church attempted to weaken kinship ties as part of its program to become a dominant institution that would exclusively serve all of its adherents' temporal as well as spiritual needs. In the process, it needed to extract wealth, power, and personnel from the kinship groups and networks that formed the core institutions of a decentralized society. It introduced many marriage and family regulations to rechannel the reproduction of wealth and people through its offices. For example, Goody observes that the Church expanded existing incest rules to prohibit marriages between the most distant relatives and affines. This restriction put an end to the standard practice of cousin marriage, which supported the concentration of wealth and power within families. The weakening of these power blocks enabled

the Church to increase its own political presence and to absorb wealth through bequests that were increasingly influenced by personal projects rather than family interests.

Another important Church innovation was the institution of "spiritual kinship" through the incorporation of godparents within the baptismal ritual. Because godparents were expected to take in godchildren whose parents had died, this practice helped to redirect adoptions within the society from the family sphere, where it once concentrated, to an area that the Church had defined and in which it could exert some influence. The Church also acted as a direct source for the absorption of children, both through the establishment of orphanages and through the recruitment of young candidates for the clergy. As such, the Church needed to draw from the kinship sphere to reproduce itself, since its personnel were forbidden by vows of celibacy from reproducing on their own. In the process, it created its own kinship world—of fathers, mothers, brothers, sisters, and brides.

CRITICAL THINKING QUESTION

How are unwed mothers and their children treated differently in early twentieth century Quebec and traditional Igbo societies (discussed earlier)? How can you explain the difference in terms of more general patterns of kinship within these cultures?

patterns have been predominantly bilateral since the Germanic tribes spread over Europe, ancient societies such as Greece, Rome, and Israel were organized according to patrilineal principles. The twelve "tribes" of Israel were formed by tracing descent through men to male ancestors after whom the groups were named. Each occupied a defined territory and was represented as a group within the larger kingdom of Israel. Jews still follow patrinineal lines to assign men to Levite or Kohan status as descendants of Levi or Aaron respectively. People who belong to these groups perform special roles during religious ceremonies.

Patrilineal descent involves tracing kinship from a male ancestor to his sons and down through a series of male descendants to current generations of living relatives (see Figure 7.3). Although this arrangement focuses on men, it does not necessarily exclude women as important members of their families of origin. They may be included in their descent line but do not pass it on to their children, who will be linked to their father's lineage rather than their mother's. Nevertheless, women may at times serve to carry on a descent line if a family has no male children. For example, one Biblical text suggests that a man without sons should marry his daughter to a slave. Since a slave had no lineage status within ancient Hebrew society, his children would be incorporated into their non-slave mother's patrilineage by default.

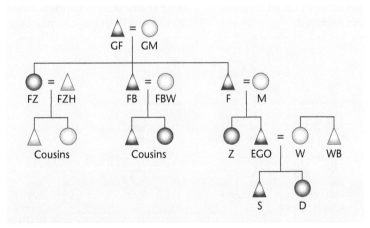

Figure 7.3

Patrilineal Descent. The relationships in the diagram are traced through a single central individual labelled as "Ego." Brown circles and triangles are in ego's kin group. Note that not all of Ego's relatives on his father's side fall within his patrilineage. His father's sister's children are excluded. Abbreviations used to designate kin in a kin diagram are M = mother, F = father, Z = sister, B = brother, D = daughter, S = son, H = husband, and W = wife. Using combinations of these symbols, anthropologists can describe all kin relations in any kinship system.

In parts of rural India that are strongly patriarchal, once a woman marries and moves to her husband's household, she cannot expect emotional or financial support from her birth family. Even if she becomes a victim of psychological or physical abuse by her husband or his relatives, her parents are unlikely to respond to her complaints. Parents also are unlikely to welcome a daughter who seeks divorce or tries to return home.

In general women do not assume the same importance in patrilineal groups as men do because they usually leave their natal groups and move in with their husband's family after marriage, thus losing daily contact with their parents, siblings, and other relatives. In some societies this separation may be formally acknowledged by switching a woman's membership to her husbands' line. For example, in some Chinese traditions a girl will be betrothed in childhood and become adopted into the household of her prospective husband and raised by his parents. On the other hand, many African cultures stress a continuation of patrilineal ties among women, even if they live away from their natal families. Among the Igbo of West Africa, a woman retains membership within her father's lineage. An eldest daughter owes special responsibilities to her younger siblings and performs an important role at her father's funeral. More generally, a woman will regularly visit her paternal village and will bring her children along to become acquainted with her relatives. This tradition forms an important bond between a boy and his maternal grandfather and uncles that entitles him to privileges that supplement rights that he holds in his own patrilineal group.

The variation in women's roles in patrilineal societies points to an important distinction between patrilineality and partiarchy. **Patriarchy** involves a social system in which men assume dominance over women in political, economic, and social spheres. Patrilineality simply refers to a rule of descent. Some patrilineal societies are strongly patriarchical, but others give women opportunities to act autonomously and gain some degree of wealth, power, and status.

In addition to defining a person's basic family membership, patrilineality entails the assignment of important rights and responsibilities, in particular the right to inherit property or succeed to hereditary positions held by deceased relatives. Inheritance in patrilineal societies usually involves the transfer of property from father to son, although in some societies a brother is considered to be the rightful heir. Moreover, the property may be divided among several sons or kept intact under the control of a brother or designated son, usually the eldest. In some patrilineal societies women may inherit and in others they are excluded. In patrilineal Islamic societies, a woman's share of her father's estate is given to her as a dowry upon marriage and will pass on to her children and thus out of her lineage. In ancient Hebrew society, daughters inherited only if a man had no sons. One Biblical passage suggests that in such a case the female heirs should marry men within their patrilineages to avoid the transfer of family property to other lineages.

patriarchy
Social system in which men occupy positions of social, economic, and political power from which women are excluded.

Matrilineal Descent

Matrilineal kinship involves the tracing of the descent line from a female ancestor through her daughters and subsequent female descendants to the current living generations (see Figure 7.4). As with patrilineal descent, members of the opposite gender are still included as members of the family but do not pass on their status to their children. Men's sons and daughters are included in their mother's line. Similarly, descent can on occasion pass through a man. For example, among the Akan of West Africa, woman with no daughters could

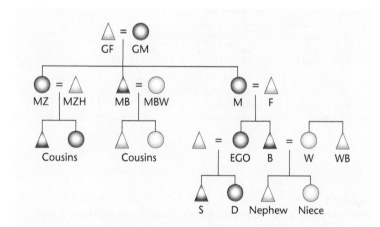

Figure 7.4
Matrilineal Descent. Brown triangles and circles are Ego's kin group. Note that not all relatives on Ego's mother's side of his family fall within a single matrilineage. The children of Ego's mother's brother in this diagram are excluded.

In Their Own Voices

Wedding Songs from North India

The poignancy of women's separation from their kin is vividly dramatized in North India at the moment of departure, when a newly married woman first leaves her natal home in the company of her husband and his male kin. Both men and women are apt to shed tears at the sight of the heavily veiled young woman being carried to a waiting vehicle. The women of the bride's village sing "departure songs" at the doorway. Many of these songs are commentaries on the fragile position of a woman in her husband's household and on her relationships with her blood relatives and her in-laws.

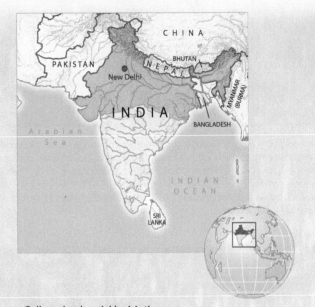

1. Refrain [bride's kin speaking]

    Dear girl, today you have left your father's house, today you have become "other."

    The streets in which you spent your childhood have today become "other."

[Bride speaking]

    My grandfather cries, my grandmother cries, the whole family cries.

    My younger brother cries, your sister born from the same mother has left and gone away.

[Verses are repeated with bride speaking, using different kin terms]

2. Two water pots are on my head

    A beautiful golden pendant is on my forehead.

    Call me back quickly, Mother.

    Beg with folded hands.

    My heart is not here in my husband's mother's house.

    My heart is not here with this foreign man.

    Call me back quickly, Mother.

    Beg with folded hands.

    My friends still played with dolls together.

    But I went off to my in-law's house.

    Call me back quickly, Mother.

    Beg with folded hands.

[The first verse is repeated a number of times, changed only by the substitution of the names of other ornaments worn by married women.]

From Gloria Goodwin Raheja and Ann Grodzins Gold, *Listen to the Heron's Words: Reimagining Gender and Kinship in North India.* Copyright © 1994 The Regents of the University of California. Reprinted by permission.

continue her line if her son married a slave, following the same logic as the ancient Hebrews.

Matrilineal descent is theoretically the mirror image of patrilineality, but tracing kinship through women rather than men introduces some complications. Males usually have greater access to wealth, power, and status in matrilineal societies than women do in patrilineal cases. Accordingly, no real cases of matriarchy have been recorded in the ethnographic record. However, matrilineality imposes a problem on men's ability to participate in his natal family's affairs. The main line of organization and inheritance in many matrilineal societies is from mother's brother to sister's son, the closest lineal male relatives other than a brother. The formation of a marital household, however, may not easily bring the two together. The most frequent domestic arrangement in a matrilineal society is to have a man move in with his wife's family. This rule allows a core group of women within a matrilineage to stay together,

Although Japan is a patrilineal society, mothers encourage the development of strong, enduring emotional bonds, called amae, *with their children, especially their sons (Sofue 1984). The son benefits from the emotional involvement and protection offered by his mother, and the mother benefits from the loyalty of her son. Each can call on the emotional support of the other when in conflict with an authoritarian father.*

These Trobriand Islanders are sorting yams from a garden. In this matrilineal society a brother is responsible for supplying his sister and her husband with yams. In doing so, he benefits his sister's children who are his primary dependents and heirs.

an arrangement that is often essential for the allocation of land and other assets which women control. However, husbands will be separated from their matrilineal relatives. Communication and interaction will necessitate frequent visits to each other's residences. For this reason, matrilineal groups often live in highly nucleated settlements, such as the apartment complexes of the Pueblo societies of the southwestern United States. In an alternative arrangement, a woman may move in with her husband's family but any boys, usually after puberty, will move in with their mother's brothers. As such, all the men of a matrilineal family live together with their wives and children, but the women of the lineage will live separately.

Some analysts have suggested that matrilineal systems impose a quandary for fathers who might want to exercise authority over and provide for their sons but are not allowed to do so because mother's brothers are assigned these primary rights and responsibilities. However, the absence of such a jural relationship can eliminate sources of tension that occur across the generations in patrilineal or bilateral societies, and fathers may more likely develop relaxed and friendly relationships with their sons. Accommodations can also be made to strengthen this bond. Among matrilineal groups of the Pacific Northwest, a son lived with his father until he came of age, after which he would be expected to join his mother's brother's household where he held rights to territorial resources. However, he had the option of staying with his father to fish and hunt on his land. In return, a son had to give his father a portion of the harvest and make additional payments. Often, only the men who were to take names within their lineages would make a permanent move to their uncles' households. The relative abundance of resources in the areas of each group influenced the final residential decision. The Akan of West Africa made a different accommodation to paternal ties. Any property that a man inherited from a member of his matrilineal family had to be passed on to his brother or his sister's son. However, he could dispose of personally acquired wealth by giving it to a son during his lifetime or bequeathing it to him. Such flexibility within both matrilineal and patrilineal systems allows kinship patterns to adjust to changing ecological, demographic, economic, and political conditions. See the Culture Change feature on page 190.

See the Culture Change feature on page 190.

REVIEW

Unilineal descent rules include matrilineal (reckoned through one's mother's line), patrilineal (reckoned through one's father's line), ambilineal (reckoned through either parent's line) and double descent (reckoned through both one's mother's line and one's father's line). For instance, in societies within patrilineal descent, men hold wealth and when they die pass it to their sons. In matrilineal societies, women pass property on to their daughters, and male property and status is often passed on to a man's sister's sons.

UNILINEAL DESCENT GROUPS

Unilineal descent systems usually organize people into a more clearly defined kinship order than bilateral descent rules can because they can more easily assign people to exclusive and discrete units. Four kinds of unilineal descent groups are lineages, clans, phratries, and moieties. Some cultures have all four types; others have only one or two. All have in common a focus on lineal descent, following either the mother's or the father's line, so that the specific descent group may be a matrilineage or patrilineage, or a matriclan or patriclan, respectively. Lineages are formed among people who can trace their relationships through known genealogical links that may go back many generations. In clans, people are merely assigned to their mother's or father's group without any detailed tracing of ancestry. Phratries are groups of clans. A moiety system divides a society into two halves (*moiety* comes from the French word meaning "half"), each of which may be a lineage, clan, or phratry. (Phratries and moieties will be discussed in more detail later in the chapter.) In some cultures, lineages and clans have become localized and occupy a single settlement site. They have corporate functions such as owning or controlling land and resources in common. Lineages and clans have continuity independent of their specific membership at any one time. Their structures and functions are perpetual, and their membership is continually replenished with the births of new members. Lineages and clans also usually regulate marriage, favouring some unions or forbidding others between members of the same or related groups. Other social functions of unilineal kin groups vary from culture to culture, such as making communal decisions, settling disputes, selecting leaders, and performing ritual obligations.

Lineages

The smallest kinship unit is a **lineage**, or a set of relatives tracing descent from a known common ancestor. In a matrilineal system, a matrilineage may consist of a female ancestor, her sons and daughters, her daughters' children, and her daughters' daughters' children. A patrilineage may consist of a male ancestor, his sons and daughters, his sons' children, and his sons' sons' children. The depth of lineages varies in different cultures. In some societies, people know the names of their lineage ancestors over only a few generations, whereas in other societies lineages may have a known depth of nine or more generations. In some West African societies, the names and deeds of lineage members are memorized and passed on by word of mouth from generation to generation, in some cases covering 200 years or more. Among the Malinke, oral historians know as *griots* can trace family genealogies back to the Mali Empire which flourished over 500 years ago. Written records create greater time depth. The Old Testament of the Bible, for example, contains a chronology of ancient patrilineages through over twenty generations.

Among the Akan of West Africa, matrilineages known as *mbusua* (singular *abusua*) are named groupings that occupy a residential ward within a town and jointly own land for agricultural use. They settle many of their own affairs internally, but also select representatives to sit on the town council, which regulates public functions in cooperation with a hereditary chief. The lineage also forms a religious community, worshipping its ancestors who are enshrined within carved wood stools that they owned in their lifetime. The stools are placed within a family stool house and are taken out every six weeks for sacrificial rituals. The ancestors bless and punish their living descendents and are thought to become continually reincarnated within the same lineages into which they were originally born. The lineage is thus composed of the living, the dead, and the yet-to-be-born.

Siblings belong to the same patrilineage or matrilineage, depending on the descent rule in effect. New lineages are formed after the death of the senior parent. At that time, surviving sons in patrilineal systems and surviving daughters in matrilineal systems establish themselves as the heads of new groups. In societies where seniority contributes to one's social standing and prestige, sibling order determines the relative status of each new lineage; that is, an individual who is a member of the lineage of an elder son has higher status than an individual who is a member of the lineage of a younger son.

lineage
A set of relatives tracing descent from a known common ancestor.

The stools of the ancestors of the chief of Elmina in procession during a royal ceremony.

Exogamy and Endogamy

As mentioned previously, in some societies lineages have corporate functions. That is, they hold land in common, apportioning land and resources to member households. They may have formal procedures for selecting leaders and settling disputes among members or with members of other lineages. And they regulate marriage, forbidding unions between certain members. Most unilineal kin groups practice **exogamy**, or marrying out. In exogamy, people cannot marry members of their own lineage or clan but must forge alliances with members of other groups. Lineages and clans are usually exogamous.

A less common marriage rule is **endogamy**, or marrying in, as, for example, in parallel cousin marriage. A **parallel cousin** is one's mother's sister's child or one's father's brother's child. In parallel-cousin marriage, one of these sets of children would be one's preferred marriage partners—the mother's sister's children in a matrilineage and the father's brother's children in a patrilineage. Parallel-cousin marriage is prevalent among Middle Eastern Arab societies with patrilineal descent. In patrilineal systems, brothers belong to the same patrilineage or patriclan, and descent is traced through men. Marriages between their children conserve wealth within the patriclan. Thus, land, wealth, and resources stay within the kinship group rather than being dissipated or fragmented through inheritance among a wider group of claimants. Endogamous marriage patterns also solidify and strengthen bonds between brothers and avert conflicts over inheritance.

The opposite of a parallel cousin is a **cross-cousin**: one's mother's brother's child or one's father's sister's child. In cross-cousin marriage, these children would be preferred as one's marriage partners. Unlike parallel-cousin unions, cross-cousin marriage creates a flow of alliances and exchanges between unilineal groups as we will see in Chapter 8. Figure 7.5 shows the types of cousins. Notice that cross-cousins are related through opposite-sex siblings (father's sister, mother's brother), whereas parallel cousins are related through same-sex siblings (father's brother, mother's sister).

Clans

Many cultures with unilineal descent organize their members into clans. **Clans** are named groups of people who believe that they are relatives, although they may not be able to trace all the actual relationships with clan members. Clans differ from lineages in this feature; members of lineages can trace their exact relationship to all other

exogamy
Marriage principle in which people cannot marry members of their own lineage or clan but instead must forge alliances with members of other groups.

endogamy
Marriage principle in which people marry members of their own group.

parallel cousin
A child of one's mother's sister or of one's father's brother.

cross-cousin
A child of one's mother's brother or of one's father's sister.

clans
Named groups of people who believe that they are relatives even though they may not be able to trace their actual relationships with all members of their group.

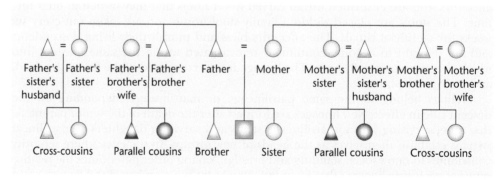

Figure 7.5
Distinctions between Parallel Cousins and Cross-Cousins.

members of the same lineage, but members of clans, which are much larger kin groups, can trace relationships only to close relatives.

Clans recruit new members through the birth of children. **Matriclans** obtain new members from women of their group (a child belongs to the clan of its mother), whereas **patriclans** recruit new members from men of their group (a child belongs to the clan of its father). Depending on the size of a society, clan size may range from several hundred members to many thousands. Although clan members cannot know all their relatives, they can always determine if a stranger is related to them by asking the person to identify his or her clan by name.

The conventions for naming clans vary cross-culturally. In some societies, clans are named after animals or plants; in others, they are named for locations. Where clans are named after animals, people often have beliefs about some mythic connection between the originators of the clan and the animal for which they are named. The origin myth might describe how the clan animal saved the human ancestors from some calamity or mated with the human ancestor to found the clan.

In some societies, clans are totemic. A **totem** is an animal or plant with a special spiritual connection to the members of its clan. Ritual prohibitions, or taboos, mark the relationship between clan animals and members of the kinship group. For example, people may not hunt or eat the animal that is their totem. By observing taboos, people express their respect for their ancestors. Totems also identify people in terms of their eligibility for marriage. In societies with clan exogamy, for example, two people with the same totem would not be allowed to marry.

Thus, clans, like lineages, not only establish and organize relatives but also regulate social relations, especially marriage. Clans usually are exogamous, that is, a person cannot marry someone belonging to his or her own clan. Such a marriage would be considered incestuous. Marriage rules may also preclude people from marrying into the clan of either parent. For example, according to marriage restrictions among the matrilineal Diné, a person cannot marry someone of his or her own clan or father's clan, even though by rules of matrilineal descent people are not members of their fathers' groups. An even wider proscription bars people from marrying anyone whose father is a member of one's own father's clan.

In addition to social features, clans often have corporate functions. In some societies these functions may be similar to those of lineages, whereas in others they may be more highly structured and formalized. Clan members may hold land in common, apportioning fields or resource sites to their members individually or by household. Clan-held territory can be periodically reapportioned to adjust to changes in resources as well as to changes in the size of households.

matriclans
Clans formed through descent and inheritance from women of their group.

patriclans
Clans formed through descent and inheritance from men of their group.

totem
An animal or plant believed by a group of people to have been their primordial ancestor or protector.

Australian Aborigines believe that in mythic times, called "the Dreaming" or "Dreamtime," human ancestors rose out of the earth and had encounters with ancestral animals who protected them and endowed them with spiritual knowledge (Hume 2000). As the people procreated and survived, they honoured these relationships by naming themselves after their animal protectors.

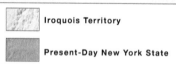

A Matrilineal Society: The Mohawks

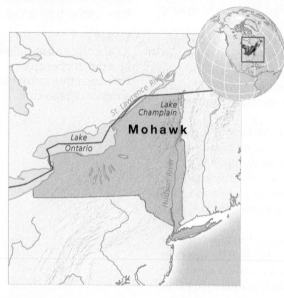

Iroquois Territory

Present-Day New York State

that people could not marry members of their own clan. These rules created marriage alliances between the clans. Today, restrictions on marriage choices have largely been abandoned, but Mohawks who want their weddings performed in the indigenous Iroquois religion, now know as the Longhouse Religion, must belong to different clans.

Mohawk clans controlled and distributed farmland to their members. Land was said to be owned by the leading woman of the matrilineage, who was bound to distribute to the women of her household for cultivation. Clans also owned the large communal longhouses in which their members lived.

Due to the influence of Canadian and American culture, much of the traditional family structure has been replaced by independent nuclear families of parents and children who live alone and own property privately and pursue individual economic pursuits. Mohawk clans continue to have leaders, both women and men. Leading clan women, now referred to as clan mothers, are chosen informally through public recognition of their intelligence, sound advice, and personal charisma. They lead by example and play a central role in protecting Mohawk lands, culture, and language. Clan mothers select the men who serve as

The Mohawks were, and are, one of the member nations of the Iroquois Confederacy. Organized on kinship principles of lineage, clan, and moiety (Bonvillain 2001:69–70). Mohawk descent is reckoned matrilineally so that children belong to the lineage, clan, and moiety of their mother. In former times (until about 200 years ago), residence was based on the ideal that members of a matrilineage lived together. Therefore, a household typically consisted of an elder woman, her husband, their daughters and daughters' husbands, and any boys or unmarried men. Each subgroup of parents and children had its own quarters within a large longhouse separated by bark partitions. Matrilineages had a depth of three or four generations, depending on the age of the eldest female member. If a woman survived to be elderly, she might become to be the head of a lineage of four generations with dozens of members. In other cases a lineage might span only two or three generations. The deeper the lineage, the more respected was the leading woman, who would also be distinguished by her age.

Individual Mohawk lineages made up larger matrilineal clan groupings which were three in number: Bear, Wolf, and Turtle. In former times, clans regulated marriage through rules of exogamy, stipulating

Clan mothers nominated men of their clan to function as chiefs. The chiefs attended councils to discuss and make decisions about issues of importance to their communities. Clan mothers continued to give advice to the chiefs and could depose chiefs who lost public support. Clan mothers are influential members of their communities today.

clan chiefs. They make their choices based on a man's intelligence, good judgment, even temper, and charisma. Clan chiefs represent their groups in community meetings and at meetings with representatives from other Iroquois nations.

The Mohawk nation is divided into two moieties. The Wolf and Turtle clans form one moiety; the Bear clan is the other. Like clans, moieties were formerly exogamous. Today, as in the past, moieties have mainly ceremonial functions, the most important of which is to prepare and conduct funerals for members of the opposite group. This custom reflects the Mohawk belief that people from the deceased's clan or moiety are too overcome by grief to be able to conduct a proper rite. Viewed as a feature of social structure, the reciprocal exchange of funerary duties symbolizes and enacts the mutual interdependence and unity of all members of the Mohawk nation.

Clans usually have structured means of decision making and problem solving. They have recognized leaders who may be informally selected by public opinion and consensus or formally chosen by representatives of households or lineages. Such leaders have various functions in different societies. In some, they may serve as spokespersons for their clan when interacting with similarly structured groups. They may meet with leaders of other clans to make decisions that affect the whole community, to resolve inter-clan disputes, and to act as a unified body when dealing with outsiders. Clan leaders may also adopt strategies to help foster community cohesion and co-operation by exhorting members to behave properly and to help one another.

Among the matrilineal Iroquois nations of Quebec, Ontario, and New York State (the Mohawks, Oneidas, Onondagas, Cayugas, Senecas, and Tuscaroras), chiefs were chosen to represent their clans on the basis of their intelligence, generosity, even temper, and other desirable personality traits. The men were selected by leading women of matrilineages within the clans. The chiefs represented their clans in village councils that debated issues of common interest. They made decisions, or at least recommendations, that affected their members. They helped settle disputes between their members and members of different clans. Clan chiefs also represented their groups in intertribal meetings, calling together all of the nations in the Iroquois Confederacy. In that body, issues of trade, intertribal relations, and war and peace were discussed and decided.

In some societies, clans and lineages are organized in a complex hierarchical structure in which different levels of the hierarchy have different social or political functions. Several peoples in Sudan, for instance, were organized into clans composed of **segmentary lineages** hierarchically ranked according to the number of generations they encompassed. The Nuer, for example, were organized into about twenty patrilineal clans (Evans-Pritchard 1955; Sahlins 1961). Each clan was subdivided into four levels of lineage segments. The first subdivision was into large units, called maximal lineages. Each maximal lineage was segmented into smaller groups, called major lineages, and these were divided into still smaller groups, called minor lineages. Finally, the smallest segment, referred to as a minimal lineage, consisted of a group of relatives descended from a common great-grandfather or great-great-grandfather. In other words, a minimal lineage had a depth of four or five generations. Members of these smallest segments interacted frequently, lived near one another, and shared resources in times of need. Seniority in a lineage conferred influence and prestige. Lineage segments could temporarily become allies in times of conflict, but there was no established leadership beyond the smallest lineage and no permanent structure that united them. However, when disputes arose, the parties concerned could appeal for support to members of structurally similar units in wider and wider networks. Therefore, the segmentary system was a flexible solution to the problem of resolving disputes within and between the twenty clans.

Phratries and Moieties

Clans may combine to form larger organized kinship units, such as phratries and moieties. **Phratries** are groups of linked clans that usually are exogamous: in a phratry, a person cannot marry someone belonging to a clan associated with his or her own clan.

segmentary lineages
Lineages organized in a hierarchical structure, ranked according to the number of generations they encompass.

phratries
Groups of linked clans that are usually exogamous.

Case study

A Patrilineal Society: The Ganda of Uganda

The Ganda are a horticultural people who live in small villages in Uganda. Each village has between thirty and eighty homesteads. Homesteads contain several huts and the yards in between huts are used for socializing and tending domesticated animals, especially chickens and goats. Most households consist of husband and wife, although some men have more than one wife. Co-wives usually reside in the same household, each having her own bedroom, but women sometimes have separate huts within the homesteads. Some men establish residences for their several wives in separate villages. In any case, women leave their natal village when they marry to live with their husband. The marital bond tends to be somewhat unstable today, although in the past, men had greater authority and control over their wives (Southwold 1965:105).

The people's principal subsistence crop is bananas or plaintains. Sweet potatoes, yams, peanuts, and a variety of leafy vegetables, roots, and fruits are also grown. Men clear the fields for planting when needed, but women do most of the subsistence farmwork. In the past, men hunted and fished to supplement the diet, but today men grow cash crops, especially cotton and coffee.

Ganda society is organized around membership in clans and lineages. Descent is patrilineal, so children belong to the lineage and clan of their father. Clans are exogamous, husband and wife belonging to different kinship groups. There currently are forty-eight named clans, derived from an original six clans of

mythic times (Southwold 1965:95). Each clan is composed of several lineages, organized in a hierarchy of segments, or "segmentary lineages." Among the Ganda, there are four levels of segmentary organization: a clan, a segment of a clan called a *ssiga*, a segment of a *ssiga* called *mutuba*, and the smallest segment, a segment of a *mutuba*, called *lunyiriri*.

In daily life, one's patrilineal kin are prominent in social interactions and share economic and personal responsibilities toward one another. People secure rights to use land and plant their gardens on the basis of membership in patrilineal clans. Men obtain these rights through descent from their fathers. Women obtain rights to gardens through marriage; that is, a woman plants her crops on her husband's land. After marriage, a man chooses his place of residence from among the villages in which he has rights through patrilineal affiliation, selecting acreage in clan-controlled territory.

Men prefer to marry women from villages other than their own in order to expand their network of relatives and allies. They also prefer not to live in either their father's village or in their wife's father's village but to make a new homestead near more distant kin (Southwold 1965:96). Ganda men wish to establish their independence from their fathers and also to avoid conflict with their brothers. Ties to other male relatives provide men with the aid and allegiance they expect from kin. Families may move to new villages periodically as their needs or inclinations change.

Ganda clans have a number of corporate functions. Each clan and lineage has a leader who is responsible for administering his group. He is assisted by a council made up of the heads of subordinate lineage segments. They settle disputes after hearing testimony from both sides. Decisions made by councils can be appealed to the council of the next higher segment in the lineage and clan hierarchy. In the past, final appeals could be made to the highest authority or king, called *kabaka*.

The corporate nature of clans is demonstrated in formal obligations that each clan owes to the *kabaka*, or hereditary king. For example, clan members supply bark cloth to the *kabaka* and herd his cattle. They also perform services for the *kabaka*'s mother, a person of great authority and prestige in her own right. Each clan provides boys to serve in the king's household.

Clan councils and clan members are responsible for supervising the activities of their group. If anyone commits an offense, it is up to the clan to settle disputes and punish their members if judged to be in the wrong. In the past, a clan could also suffer collective punishment if one of their chiefs committed an offense against the *kabaka*. In such cases, the *kabaka* might order the execution of all clan members.

In addition to their administrative role, clans and lineage segments own land in common. Each clan has an allotted territory in which its members have a right to live. Prominent members also have a right to be buried in clan territory. Residence on clan land is complicated by the fact that each clan owns territory in several areas. People therefore may make diverse claims to residential land, adjusting their needs to available acreage. People also base their decisions on the qualifications of political leaders who control each territory, choosing to affiliate where they might seek an advantage. Personal and political allegiance, then, contributes to settlement patterns as much as kinship connections do (Southwold 1965:102).

In earlier times, clans controlled the distribution and inheritance of movable property from a deceased male clansman to his successor. The successor was formally chosen and ceremonially installed, taking the place of the deceased in kinship networks. He adopted the deceased's name and was called by kin terms appropriate to the deceased, and he received most of the dead man's property. Succession was inherited through kinship, but a man's eldest son was not eligible. In fact, there was a preference to bypass a man's sons altogether and instead choose a more distant patrilineal relative. This preferential pattern had the effect of dispersing kinship ties and creating linkages with more distant relatives, broadening one's alliances. The traditional rules of succession were changed in the late nineteenth century so that a man's son could succeed him. Today, father-to-son inheritance is preferred. Clan power has been reduced by the practice of making wills setting out one's wishes for the inheritance of one's property. Still, clan leaders influence the process through their high prestige.

Collective principles underlying clan organization include the obligation to be hospitable to all members of one's clan. Men who move to new villages can expect to receive banana shoots from their resident clansmen in order to start their gardens. People are expected to be helpful to clansmen in economic difficulty or to help pay a fine for some offense that a clansman commits. Similarly, clansmen have the obligation of avenging an injured or murdered member of their group. Thus, despite many changes in the postcolonial era, clan membership remains fundamental in defining one's identity, organizing social relations, restricting marriage choices, and promoting ethics of hospitality and collective responsibility.

The phratry may or may not be named. Unlike clans, phratries rarely have corporate functions. In a phratry system, there are always three or more linked groups.

Like phratries, **moieties** are groups of linked clans, but they differ in that there are only two of them. A moiety system divides a society into two halves (*moiety* comes from a French word meaning "half"). Thus, in such a system, all clans are apportioned into two groups. Like clans and phratries, moieties are usually exogamous, although in some cultures people can marry within their moiety even though they cannot marry within their clan. Moieties generally are named groups. They may or may not have corporate functions such as owning land, resource sites, and other property communally. In some societies, moieties may have ceremonial functions.

REVIEW

Four levels of descent organization are lineages (relatives who trace descent from a known common ancestor), clans (groups of people who believe but do not know that they are relatives), phratries (groups of linked exogamous clans), and moieties (two groups of linked clans that divide the society). Depending on the unilineal descent rule in effect, a lineage may be a matrilineage or a patrilineage, and a clan may be a matriclan or a patriclan. Lineages often form localized groups with corporate functions, such as land owning, political representation, and ancestral rituals. Segmentary lineages are subdivisions of lineages that place people in a set of increasingly inclusive groups.

moieties
Groups of linked clans that divide a society into two halves, usually exogamous.

double descent
Kinship principle in which people belong to kinship groups of both their mother and father.

Complex Forms of Descent

While most societies with unilineal descent trace kinship through either matrilineal or patrilineal principles, some societies reckon descent according to both. In this system, called **double descent**, people belong to kinship groups of both mother and father. Some kinds of property might be inherited along matrilineal lines and other kinds along patrilineal lines. For example, the Yako of eastern Nigeria have a double descent

ambilineal descent
Principle of descent in which individuals may choose to affiliate with either their mother's or their father's kinship group.

avoidance relationships
Patterns of behaviour between certain sets of kin that demonstrate respect and social distance.

GLOBALIZATION

Within the past century, the economies of pre-industrial peoples worldwide changed from subsistence activities to wage work and the production of food and goods for cash and export to national and international markets. How have these changes transformed people's kinship behaviour and relationships?

system in which property is divided into patrilineal and matrilineal ownership (Fox 1984:135). Patrilineal descent groups own farmland and grazing pastures while matrilineal descent groups own cattle and other livestock. People inherit these two different kinds of resources, one permanent and inalienable and the other consumable, from each of their parents.

Finally, some peoples have systems of **ambilineal descent**, in which individuals may choose to affiliate with either their mother's kinship group or with their father's group. Each person makes this decision based on a strategic consideration of the territory, wealth, and social prestige of each group he or she is eligible to join. In societies of the South Pacific where such systems operate, a person can affiliate only with one group during his or her lifetime, but the person's offspring may choose a different affiliation. In societies with ambilineal descent, such as the Kwakwaka'wakw (or Kwakiutl) of British Columbia, a person could make claims to be a member of multiple descent groups. For example, he or she could inherit material and ceremonial wealth, as well as access to food resource sites, through claims to multiple kin groups. Ambilineal forms are similar to bilateral ones since either parent can form the basis of group membership, but like unilineal descent, they allow clearly bounded groups to be formed.

PATTERNS OF RELATIONSHIPS

In addition to establishing structured groupings of relatives, kinship systems also define and enforce expected behaviours among kin. Members of every society share ideas about appropriate attitudes and actions between any set of individuals, especially relatives. For example, we may be taught to be respectful of our elders and gentle with younger siblings. We learn how to behave with our relatives, what to say to them, and what not to say to them. We learn our rights with respect to them, and we learn what obligations we owe them. We learn that toward some relatives we must behave with respect, deference, and obedience, whereas we can exert influence and authority over others. With some relatives, we must comply with their wishes and acknowledge their dominance in other ways. With others, we may joke, tease, and act informally. As with other social rules, or norms, the types of behaviours prescribed between relatives vary cross-culturally and among different groups within a single culture. Factors of gender, age, and class may have an effect on people's attitudes and actions.

Two common patterns that anthropologists observe in many cultures are avoidance relationships and joking relationships. Some societies focus on relationships of avoidance or respect. In some societies, **avoidance relationships** characterize the relationship between parents-in-law and their sons-in-law or daughters-in-law. For example, among the Diné, a man does not speak directly to his mother-in-law and avoids being alone with her. If he needs to make a request of her, he asks his wife to intercede on his behalf. He defers to his mother-in-law, complies with her wishes and requests, and makes himself helpful and cooperative.

This kind of behaviour is fairly common between men and their mothers-in-law in matrilineal societies. In such societies, men usually leave their natal homes when they marry and take up residence with or near their wife's kin. Circumspect, deferential, and "bashful" behaviour helps minimize potential conflict that may exist between a man and his mother-in-law in matrilocal households. A new husband does nothing that could be interpreted as a challenge to her authority or of anyone else in the household. After many years of a stable marriage, a husband's behaviour may be modified and he may begin to assert himself more with his wife's relatives. Eventually, he may take on leadership roles in the household.

Avoidance and respectful behaviour on the part of a daughter-in-law toward her father-in-law is especially expected in patrilineal societies, where the married couple lives with the husband's kin. In this situation, a daughter-in-law lives in a household dominated by her father-in-law. Here, too, avoidance behaviour mitigates any potential conflict. Rarely would a daughter-in-law have authority in such a household; rather, the potential conflict might concern the emotional allegiance of her husband, their son.

To avoid forcing the husband to choose sides between his parents and his wife, the wife acts with deference and respect. In strongly patriarchal societies, daughters-in-law are expected to be acutely aware of their subordinate status and act with extreme deference and obedience to their husbands' parents.

The pattern of **joking relationships** between certain relatives involves reciprocal joking, teasing, and playfulness. Joking may take the form of flirtation, sexual innuendo, and even explicit sexual remarks. This type of behaviour is found most commonly between certain kinds of cousins, as between cross-cousins in societies in which cross-cousin marriage is preferred. Joking behaviour also may be common between an individual and his or her spouse's same-sex sibling. For example, a woman may joke with her husband's brother, and a man may joke with his wife's sister. In many cultures, these in-laws are potential spouses. They may be preferred marriage partners in the event of the death of one's own husband or wife, so joking relationships between some types of relatives (cross-cousins, spouse's siblings) acknowledge the potential sexual or marital relationship that might be established between the individuals. In some patrilineal societies the mother's brother/sister's son relationship is marked by joking behaviour and stands out in contrast to more formal father/son patterns.

? *Do you have avoidance relationships and joking relationships among your kin?*

> **REVIEW**
>
> All societies identify specific behaviours as appropriate for specific sets of relatives. Two common patterns of relationship are avoidance relationships and joking relationships. In patrilineal societies, bashful behaviour and avoidance are common for daughters-in-law toward their fathers-in-law, whereas in matrilineal societies, these are seen with sons-in-law toward their mothers-in-law. In some cultures, avoidance may also be prescribed for siblings. In some societies joking relationships are common among cross-cousins or spouse's siblings or others who may be potential sexual or marital partners.

PATTERNS OF CHANGE

One would think that the way we reckon our kin would be a permanent feature of our culture. As you have read, however, even kinship systems respond to changes in the way people make their living or adapt to their environment. One pattern of change, for example, involves shifts from matrilineal descent to other rules of descent based on changes in men's and women's subsistence roles. Forces of cultural contact and change, such as the introduction of Christianity or Islam, the commercialization of the economy or the privatization of land ownership, also bring about changes in the way people reckon their kin, identify their kin group, and interact with relatives (see the Culture Change feature on page 190).

When studying changes in kinship systems, we can see how sensitive these systems are as indicators of cultural transformation. Principles of kinship reckoning are consistent with other cultural practices. When behaviour changes, kinship systems respond by altering the way that kin groups are organized. Changes may come from internal dynamics within a society as adjustments are made to environments and new ways of living are developed and transmitted. They also may come from external sources when societies come into contact with others, either learning and adopting new systems voluntarily or being forced to adapt to more powerful peoples.

joking relationships
Patterns of behaviour between certain kin that involve reciprocal joking, teasing, and playfulness, sometimes taking the form of flirtation and sexual innuendo.

> **REVIEW**
>
> Patterns of change in kinship systems are based on the functions of kin groups in relation to environmental adaptations. Foragers tend to develop bilateral descent rules, for example. Kinship also changes in response to cultural adaptations. For example, people may adopt the kinship system of another people with whom they come into contact.

Culture Change

MATRILINEAL KINSHIP AMONG THE AKAN OF GHANA

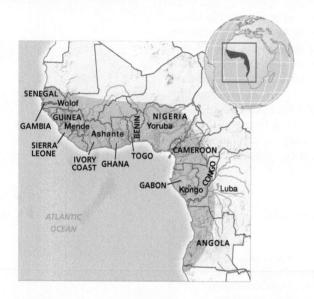

The understanding of change in kinship institutions must acknowledge the resiliency, flexibility, and adaptability of culture. For example, although it has been subject to many pressures, matrilineal kinship is still relevant to social and family patterns in many societies. For example, the Akan of have been exposed to many changes, including British overrule, Christianity, Western education, economic commercialization, and urban migration. However, matrilineal forms of family organization and inheritance are still in force and in some ways have been consistent with the various forces of change we have cited.

The introduction of cocoa farming for export was one of the major forces behind the rapid implementation of change among the Akan. At the turn of the twentieth century, relatively early in the colonization process, Akan farmers integrated cocoa into their horticultural plots to earn cash incomes that were becoming essential in the new society. Production grew so rapidly that the Gold Coast Colony (now the Republic of Ghana) in which the Akan were located became the world's largest cocoa producer. Cocoa farming involved the commercialization of agricultural production and led to purchase of land, which was traditionally subject to ownership by localized matrilineages. These processes created substantial amounts of personally acquired wealth, which could be transferred from father to son rather than according to the traditional mother's-brother-to-nephew rule. However, Akan farmers made several accommodations to balance the interests of their wives and children and of the demands of their matrilineages. One solution was to expand into new lands in order to provide cocoa farms to both groups. This process was enabled by the economies of cocoa production which initially created boom conditions in the regions in which it was introduced.

A less direct force for matrilineal continuity has also been at play. Some observers have maintained that increased father-to-son inheritance among the Akan has engendered a patrilineal system (Hill 1963). This observation may be true in a narrow sense but overlooks the dynamic nature of matrilineal kinship. When a son inherits his father's self-acquired property, it retains its status as an individual, rather than a group, asset. As such, the management of the property remains an individual concern and a patrilineal group as such is not formed. However, if any of a man's personal holdings are inherited by a matrilineal relative, they are transformed into group property. Over the course of time, therefore, collective matrilineal ownership continually consolidates wealth creation and retains the importance of matrilineal ties and groupings.

KINSHIP TERMINOLOGY SYSTEMS

Kin terms constitute a culture's kinship vocabulary, a catalogue of the words that are assigned to relatives, such as "mother," "uncle," or "cousin." Different societies use different labels to designate their kin; "uncle" is "*oncle*" in French, from which it is borrowed, and "*tío*" in Spanish. However, cultures frequently go beyond mere labelling differences to group relatives into completely different categories. For example, the Akan term that corresponds to "uncle" is "*wofa*." This category includes a person's mother's brother but not his or her father's brother, who is called "*agya*," the same term that is used for "father" (see Figure 7.6). Often the particular system of categorization gives clues to a culture's principles of social organization and construction of social roles. For example, the Akan distinction between *wofa* and *agya* reflects a division between kin on the mother's and father's side of the family within a unilineal kinship system.

kin terms
The set of names that people use to designate and address their relatives.

Table 7.1 ENGLISH AND AKAN KIN CATEGORIES

English Term	Specific Relationship	Akan Term
Father	F	Agya
Uncle	FB	
	MB	Wofa

Anthropological analysis of kin terms is based on an understanding that they are categories that group more than one relationship together as indicated in the above table.

Different cultures can potentially group their relatives in an indefinite number of ways, but comparative studies have shown that almost every culture uses one of six widely occurring systems. These are customarily designated as follows according to the culture in which they were first observed:

Hawaiian
Eskimo
Sudanese
Iroquois
Omaha
Crow

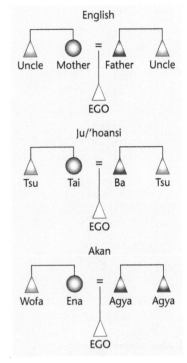

Figure 7.6
Ju/'hoansi and English systems use different words for the same categories. Akan terminology differs from English both in the words used and the categories they mark.

Hawaiian, Eskimo, and Sudanese Systems

The **Hawaiian system** is the simplest and uses the fewest categories. It makes distinctions on the basis of sex and generation only. Thus a single term is used for father, father's brother, and mother's brother and another for mother, mother's sister, and father's sister. Similarly, there are no distinctions between siblings and cousins or between sons and nephews or daughters and nieces. Hawaiian systems are usually found in the Pacific region and conform to a social pattern of ambilineal descent in which people can choose between joining either their father's or mother's kinship groups.

English kin terms (see Figure 7.7) and those of most other European cultures are based on an **Eskimo system**. Eskimo terms reflect a bilateral emphasis—no distinction is made between patrilineal and matrilineal relatives—and by a recognition of differences in kinship distance—close relatives are distinguished from more distant ones. Another feature of Eskimo terminology is that nuclear family members are assigned unique labels that are not extended to any other relatives, whereas more distant relatives are grouped together. Because of predominant marking of immediate family members, Eskimo terms usually occur in societies which place a strong emphasis on the nuclear family in comparison to extended relatives.

English terms didn't always conform to an Eskimo system, as might be expected from their history of borrowing terms for extended relatives from French. Before the Norman Conquest, English patterns were based on a **Sudanese system**, in which every

Hawaiian system
Kin terms making distinctions only of generation and gender.

Eskimo system
Kin tems making distinctions between the nuclear family and all other types of relatives and on gender.

Sudanese system
Kin tems that give separate terms for all kin relationships.

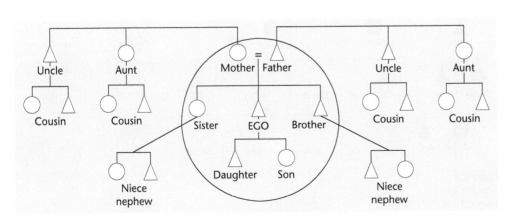

Figure 7.7
English Kin Terms.

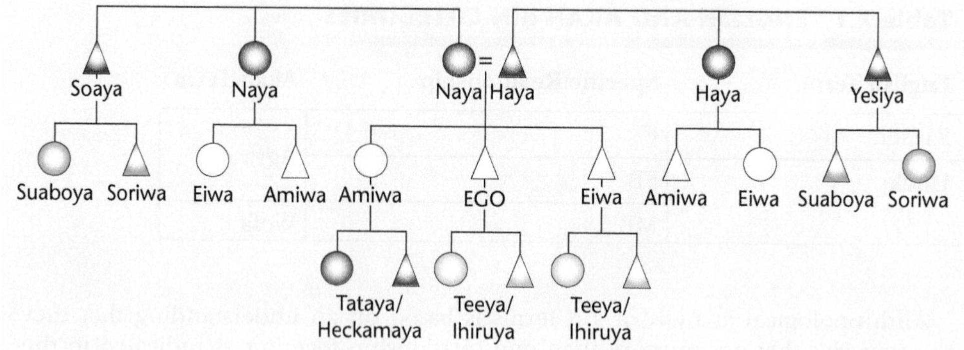

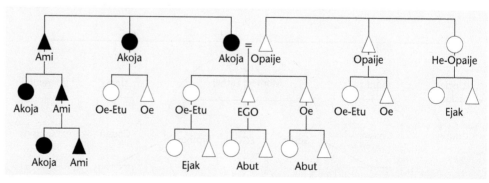

Figure 7.8
Yanomamo Kin Terms.
Source: Heider 1996

different relationship was assigned its own term. Thus, aside from the terms for mother and father (*modor* and *faeder*), a mother's sister was called *modriga* and father's sister *faedera*. Mother's brothers were called *eam* and father's brothers were called *fathu*.

Iroquois, Omaha, and Crow Systems

? *What reasons might have been responsible for changes in English kin terms?*

Iroquois, Omaha, and Crow terms all reflect the patterns of unilineal descent. The **Iroquois system** is the most generic. In all three systems, the same term is used for a father and his brother and a mother and her sister, while mother's brother and father's sister receive a separate term. Similarly, parallel cousins are given the same terms as siblings, while cross-cousins are distinguished. The basic logic of the system can be understood with an example from Yanomamo kin terms (see Figure 7.8).

The features of Iroquois terminology are consistent with Yanomamo patrilineal kinship practice. Fathers and their brothers (*haya*) fall within Ego's patrilineage, while his mother's brother (*soaya*) is a member of a separate lineage which is related by marriage. The affinal tie between the groups is usually continued from generation to generation as the groups are expected to intermarry. Thus, the distinction between *amiwa* (sister) and *suaboya* (cross-cousin) divides women whom Ego cannot marry from those he is expected to marry. In fact, the term *suaboya* also means wife.

Omaha and **Crow systems** retain the distinctions between father's and mother's sides of the family and mark cross-cousins, while grouping parallel cousins and siblings together. However, each system treats cross-cousins in a slightly different way. In the Omaha system, as illustrated in Dani kinship terminology (see Figure 7.9), a mother's brother's son received the same term as his father (*ami*) while a mother's brother's daughter is classed together with mother (*akoja*). On the other hand, a father's sister's children are grouped together with nephews and nieces (*ejak*).

Iroquois system
Kin terms that emphasize the difference between one's parents' same-sex siblings and parents' opposite-sex siblings, classifying parallel cousins with one's own siblings.

Omaha system
Kin terms used by some patrilineal peoples that extend the term for mother and mother's brother to include cross-cousins on the maternal side.

Crow system
Kin terms used by some matrilineal peoples that extend the term for father and father's sister to include cross-cousins on the paternal side.

Figure 7.9
Dani Kin Terms.
Source: Lizot 1971

Anthropology Applied

LINKAGES Genealogy Projects

When doing ethnography in the field on any subject, cultural anthropologists gather kinship data for the people they are among. Then they link these data into a local genealogy. Anthropologists use this information to know who people are and how they relate to one another. As you have seen from reading this chapter, understanding a society's kinship system is also a key to understanding the way people organize their communities, subsistence activities, and leadership. Kin relations are the building blocks of human social organization. But what can ethnographic and historical genealogies of particular people tell us about what it takes to build self-sustaining human communities?

LINKAGES is an international network of researchers concerned with the long-term assessment of populations in relation to the impacts of economic development and culture change on those populations. These researchers create database sets of recorded kinship data and track long-term changes in those data. By doing so, the researchers hope to show how knowledge of kinship must be taken into account when planning social policy and economic change. In addition, the knowledge gained from large-scale, long-term comparisons of kin networks may help local communities to participate more effectively in changes that affect their lives and the sustainability of their cultural ecologies.

The data sets that LINKAGES maintains are diverse; among them are Alyawarra kin networks in Australia; kinship in the village of Tlaxcala, Mexico; genealogies of American presidents; Muslim elites in an Indonesian village; Old Testament patriarchs; Mbuti Pygmies of the Ituri rain forest of Africa; genealogical censuses for many band societies; and many others such as !Kung of Africa, Chechu of India, Ainu of Japan, Vedda and Semang of Indonesia, and Inuit of North America. Affiliates of LINKAGES around the world have established long-term field sites for tracking changes in kinship. Data are displayed in maps and graphs generated by special software, such as Large Network Analysis and Genealogical Information Manager. Studies on such a large scale have been made possible only though recent advances in computer technology and the Internet (**http://eclectic.ss.uci.edu/linkages**).

CRITICAL THINKING QUESTIONS

What do you know about your families' genealogies? How far back do they go? How might information about long-term changes in your networks of kin contribute to LINKAGES' goals?

The key to understanding Dani and other Omaha terminologies is that they reflect inter-relationships between patrilineal descent lines. Thus all the men in Ego's mother's patrilineage are called *ami* and all the women, *akoja*. This pattern is indicative of a special relationship between a man and his or her mother's family and conversely with the children of any women of his patrilineage, whom he calls *ejak* and for whom he assumes an *ami* relationship. In fact, this tie is especially important in Dani society and defines certain obligations, including a series of ritual exchanges. The Crow system is similar to the Omaha terminology except that it marks members of a person's father's matrilineage and is accordingly found in matrilineal societies.

? *What term would a Dani woman use to refer to her son? Her nephew? How did you arrive at your solution?*

REVIEW

Kinship terms determine how relatives are classified. They identify specific kinds of relationships and the rights and obligations that they entail. In the Eskimo system, which generally uses bilateral descent, the nuclear family is distinguished from other relatives. The Hawaiian system makes distinctions with gender and generation and is often associated with ambilineal descent. The Iroquois system distinguishes between one's parent's same-sex and opposite-sex siblings and also between parallel and cross-cousins. The Omaha and Crow systems are variants of the Iroquois pattern found in patrilineal and matrilineal societies respectively. The Sudanese system is unique in that every individual has a distinct term. Differences in kin terms reflect differences in people's social systems.

Chapter Summary

Kinship Systems

- In every society, people have systems for tracing descent and organizing kinship groups to which they belong.

Bilateral Descent

- In many cultures, people consider themselves related to both their mother's and their father's families. In such systems of bilateral descent, the most significant kin group is that of the kindred, a loosely defined network of relatives who interact on a regular basis and acknowledge mutual rights and obligations to one another. Systems of bilateral descent are commonly found in many foraging societies as well as in modern industrial nations. Bilateral descent is adaptive in societies where mobility is a premium. In small-scale foraging societies, people are able to make claims in a wide network of kin in times of scarcity and need, whereas in modern industrial countries, people can loosen their kin ties in order to promote their economic independence.

Matrilineal and Patrilineal Descent

- The second major kinship system is one of unilineal descent. In this system, people acknowledge relationships on either their mother's (matrilineal) or their father's (patrilineal) side. Through unilineal descent, people form kin groups that restrict membership to particular people who can trace relationships through only either their mother or father. Unilineal descent is commonly found in farming and pastoral societies. Of the groups that can trace relationships through unilineal principles, about 15 percent are matrilineal and the remainder are patrilineal.

- A few societies have (or had) systems of double descent, in which people could belong to kinship groups of both their mother and father. Some had systems of parallel descent, in which men were considered descended from their fathers and women from their mothers. Finally, some peoples have systems of ambilineal descent, allowing them to affiliate with either their mother's or their father's kin group.

Unilineal Descent Groups

- Unilineal descent systems usually organize people into structured groupings of related people. The smallest such unit is a lineage, a specific set of relatives that trace descent from a known common ancestor. A matrilineage consists of a female ancestor, her children, her daughters' children, her daughters' daughters' children, and so on. A patrilineage consists of a male ancestor, his children, his son's children, his son's son's children, and so on.

- Many cultures with the unilineal descent organize their members into clans, named groups of people who believe they are relatives but cannot trace the actual relationship that they have with all members of their clan. Whereas members of lineages can prove their common descent from a specific ancestor, members of clans stipulate or claim relationship. In addition to establishing relationships, clans often regulate marriage by forbidding marital or sexual unions between their own members. Clans also often have some corporate functions: holding land in common and apportioning fields or resource sites to their members. They may have recognized chosen leaders who speak for their group. And they may have acknowledged methods of making decisions and settling disputes.

- In some societies, clans join together to form larger groups of related people. Phratries are groupings of linked clans that may or may not be named but serve primarily to regulate marriage by forbidding unions between members. Moieties are even larger groupings, dividing the society as a whole into two groups or halves. Typically, people cannot marry members of their own moiety. Moieties are usually named groups that may or may not have corporate functions, but some do control land, resource sites, and other property. Some have ceremonial functions as well.

Patterns of Relationships

- Kinship groups sometimes have preferences for the kind of marriage that their members may make. Clans are often exogamous, their members marrying people of other groups. Endogamy, in contrast, is a pattern of preference for marriage with a member of one's own group. In some societies, there are preferences for marrying particular types of cousins, either cross-cousins or parallel cousins. Marriage patterns tend to be consistent with other rules that organize social groups.

- Members of every society share ideas about attitudes and actions that are deemed appropriate between any set of relatives. In some societies, there are highly structured behaviours appropriate between certain relatives. At one end of the behavioural spectrum, some people are in a "joking" relationship, allowing them to tease each other and make critical or sexual remarks, while at the other end, people may be in an "avoidance" relationship, barring them from teasing or criticizing but instead encouraging them to be "bashful," avoiding eye contact, and refraining from speaking directly to or even being alone with a dominant person.

Patterns of Change

- Kinship changes as a result of changes in the environment affecting people's economic systems. Contact between people and the forces of globalization also cause people to change the way they reckon their descent and their rules for inheritance and kin relations.

Kinship Terminology Systems

- Kinship terminologies are words that people use to refer to and address their relatives. Worldwide, there are a small number of such sets of terminologies.

Anthropologists are keenly interested in kinship terms because they are more than just words. Rather, they are labels that symbolize relationships, including the rights and obligations that relatives have for one another. The kinds of systems used reveal the kinds of distinctions that people make, identifying some relatives as similar in status and relationship while distinguishing others.

Key Terms

kinship system 172	patrilineal 175	patriclans 183	joking relationships 189
consanguines 172	patriarchy 178	totem 183	kin terms 190
affines 172	lineage 181	segmentary lineages 185	Hawaiian system 191
fictive kin 172	exogamy 182	phratries 185	Eskimo system 191
rules of descent 173	endogamy 182	moieties 187	Sudanese system 191
bilateral descent 173	parallel cousin 182	double descent 187	Iroquois system 192
unilineal descent 173	cross-cousin 182	ambilineal descent 188	Omaha system 192
kindred 174	clans 182	avoidance	Crow system 192
matrilineal 175	matriclans 183	relationships 188	

Review Questions

1. What is bilateral descent? What are some cultural correlates of this descent rule in societies that practise it?

2. What are the two types of unilineal descent? With what kinds of societies is unilineal descent associated?

3. How would you compare and contrast the descent groups that are created by the application of descent rules? How are kindreds different from lineages?

4. What are the distinctions among lineages, clans, phratries, and moieties?

5. What patterns of relationships among kin group members do anthropologists observe?

6. How, and why, do kinship systems change?

7. What are the six methods of classifying relatives? What are the distinguishing characteristics of each?

8. How are kinship systems and rules of descent functionally interrelated with other social systems, such as the economic and political systems?

Marriage and the Family

CHAPTER 8

Preview

1. **How do anthropologists define marriage and family?**
2. **What are the characteristics of nuclear families and extended families?**
3. **How do residency patterns relate to other aspects of a culture?**
4. **How do marriage rules extend kinship while observing incest taboos?**
5. **What are some theories about the origins of the incest taboo?**
6. **In what ways is marriage a rite of passage?**
7. **What are some social functions of marriage?**
8. **What forms of marriage are known to exist?**
9. **How is marriage a form of political alliance and economic exchange?**

A woman had an only son who became grown up and had not been married yet. She wanted to find him a bride, but he always told her, "Later, not now," and things like that. One day his mother said to him, "Listen, my son, I've grown old and become tired of household work. You must get married before I die."

He said to her, "Well! Find me a good girl from a good house."

She looked until she found him a girl from one of the most notable houses in their town and he married her.

When the wedding [party] was over and after seven days or so, he went back to his shop to work, while his mother stayed with his wife. "Listen, in this house [you] don't open what is closed or close what is opened, nor uncover what is covered or cover what is uncovered, nor unwrap what is wrapped or wrap what is unwrapped, nor unfold what is folded or fold what is unfolded. Do you understand?"

The girl, his wife, said, "Yes."

Days passed with things like that. His mother is everything in the house; his wife works all day while his mother orders her around. When the man returns home, his mother would set the dinner for him and if he would say "[Let us] call [his wife] to eat with me," his mother would answer him, "This can't be. She is still new in the house. She would get bold with us. Wait for a few more days."

After a few more days her son would say, "Let her come and eat with me."

His mother would say, "She hasn't been broken to our house yet. She does not need to eat for she has been eating all day."

He would say to his mother, "May God extend his grace upon us. Let her eat as much as she wants," And [he] used to eat only until he was half-full and leave some of the best food to his wife. His mother would hide it and would give her only hard bread and water.

The girl grew sicker and weaker by the day. Whenever her husband asked her, "What is the matter with you?" she would answer, "Nothing."

One day he said to one of his friends at the store, "By God, my wife is becoming sick. Every day she is getting thinner and paler. I am afraid she doesn't want me. Ever since she set foot in my house, she doesn't speak to me, and she is always sad."

His friend said to him, "I'll tell you what to do to see whether she wants you and wants to stay in your house, or whether she hates you and would like to return to her father's house. After dinner swear by God that she joins you and your mother for the coffee, then break wind. If she laughs at you, she doesn't care for you and you should send her back to her father's home. If she doesn't, then she is ill."

That same day after the man ate his supper and thanked his God, he said to his mother, "Call [his wife] to have coffee with us." He swore by God, and his mother went to call her. As they were drinking their coffee, he broke wind. His mother laughed, but his wife didn't and kept on drinking until she finished her cup. . . .

The following day he told his friend about what had happened. His friend said to him, "Your wife is hungry. Your mother is starving your wife."

He built a new house for his wife and moved out of the old one and got his mother a servant.

Excerpts from *Folktales Told around the World* by Richard Dorson, pp. 166–168. Copyright 1975. Reprinted by permission of the University of Chicago Press.

household
A group of people occupying a common dwelling.

family
A married couple or other group of adult kinfolk who co-operate economically and in the upbringing of children, all or most of whom share a common dwelling.

This narrative from Iraq tells of the conflict and tensions between a new bride and her mother-in-law who live together in a household. In the story, the young husband is beset with divided loyalties. His respect for his mother is tempered by his concern for his wife. The wife, knowing her place, is obedient and deferential to the older woman. The narrative raises issues of power for women in patrilineal and patriarchal households. The mother tries to exert power over her daughter-in-law, but in the end she has less authority than her son because he is the man, the recognized head of the family. And in this story, the son chooses to protect his wife's interests and allies himself with her.

This Iraqi family unit was formed not only through rules of descent but also through marriage rules. The family unit at the household level consisted of a man, his widowed mother, his wife, any children borne by his wife, and the man's unmarried siblings. This chapter explores marriage and the family and how they interrelate with other elements of culture in a society.

Kinship systems and family arrangements are basic elements in all societies. They are among the topics of central concern in anthropology because they help structure people's daily lives and lay the foundations for the ways that individuals are integrated into their communities. But societies differ greatly in how families are formed, who constitutes a family, and what the rights and obligations of family members are toward one another. As we shall see, variations in family organization are not random but are consistent with economic and social needs. Thus, different types of families are preferred in different types of societies.

DEFINING MARRIAGE AND FAMILY

People are social beings. We live together in groups, work with others, and form emotional bonds with each other. Although in every society some individuals may live alone at any given time, most people live with others during all or most of their lives. Most people who live together are members of families. In everyday speech, we use the word *family* casually to refer to our relatives without specifying how we are related to these people. Even anthropologists do not agree on a single or concise definition of family.

Anthropologists tend to make a distinction between family and household, although people often use the two words interchangeably. A **household** refers to a group of people occupying a common dwelling. The Iraqi man, his wife, and his mother are members of a household. The term *homestead* refers to multiple dwellings occupied by related and interacting people.

As you read in Chapter 7, members of families are related either through descent (consanguines) or marriage (affines). For example, one's grandparents, parents, aunts and uncles, siblings, children, and cousins are all consanguinal relatives, whereas one's spouse and all the people called in-laws are affinal relatives. North Americans differ in the ways they apply the word *family* to many of these relatives. Some people use the word to encompass all their relations, but others restrict the term to refer to close relatives with whom they interact regularly.

A useful starting definition of **family** is one given by anthropologist Kathleen Gough (1975:52). She

These roommates share a household. Unlike family households, roommates typically do not share all economic resources and have no expectations of mutual obligation or of an enduring relationship.

defines the family as a "married couple or other group of adult kinfolk who co-operate economically and in the upbringing of children, all or most of whom share a common dwelling." In this definition, a family is more than just a couple. Gough's definition includes several important features of family, stressing the co-operative links among members who share social and economic responsibilities. On this basis, the Iraqi man, his wife, and his mother constitute a family.

There are other definitions of family, however, and family members need not occupy the same household. Some members of polygynous families may occupy different households within an area. In addition, although marriage is the most common bond that creates families, marriage itself is not a required component of family. Single-parent households constitute families as do common-law partners, which taken together account for over 30 percent of Canadian households. So do gay and lesbian couples, among whom full marital status is currently recognized by an act of Parliament.

Although issues of family composition, family life, and "family values" are controversial in the current climate of North American social and political discourse, the American Anthropological Association has taken a strong position supporting the legitimacy and viability of all family types. In its statement, issued in 2003, the association said,

> More than a century of anthropological research on households, kinship relationships, and families, across cultures and through time, provides no support for the view that either civilization or viable social orders depend upon marriage as an exclusively heterosexual institution. Rather, a vast array of family types can contribute to stable and humane societies.

The family is a basic unit of economic cooperation and stability. Members of families usually perform at least somewhat different economic tasks, a pattern that highlights the interdependent relationships among family members. And they pool all or at least some of their resources for the survival of the group.

The family serves social needs as well, providing members with companionship, emotional support, and assistance, and families function in the propagation and survival of society. They provide the context for biological reproduction and for the training and enculturation of children. Families function universally as vehicles for socialization of children into expected roles and goals. Children learn what is appropriate by observation of adults and by overt instruction and practice of skills for roles they will assume as adult women and men. In the context of their families, children learn their gender identity and their role in households and communities. Through observation of social relations between their parents or among all adults in their households, they learn whether men and women have equal rights to contribute to discussions and decision making. They deduce social rights through the ways that conflicts are resolved. Girls and boys also learn whether they can expect emotional and economic support from their natal kin groups once they reach adulthood and form their own families.

In addition, families are decision-making groups. Members of families consult with each other, make decisions together, and may function as political units with others in their communities to establish and provide leadership. In some societies, positions of leadership are inherited within families. Everywhere, inheritance of property and the transmission of cultural knowledge take place within family units.

All societies contain units recognized as families, but there are differences in the ways in which they are formed. Throughout the world, most families are formed through marriage. *Marriage* is another word that we use casually with reference to a union between a man and a woman, but anthropologists have not settled on an uncontested definition of marriage. There is even some debate in the field about whether marriage and the family are universal constructs. Still, even if we accept that marriage is a recognized social status in most, if not all, cultures, there are differences in the ways that marriages are contracted and in the relationships between the spouses.

Marriage is generally understood as a socially recognized, enduring, stable bond between two people who each have certain rights and obligations toward one another. These rights and obligations vary from culture to culture but are likely to include some common features. For example, married partners have the right to expect to have a sexual relationship with each other, although the number of partners

marriage
A socially recognized, stable, and enduring union between two adults that publicly acknowledges their rights and obligations and forms a new alliance between kin groups.

? *Based on your experience in your family, what are some specific expressions of the functions of the family as a social institution?*

? *What do you think might be some sources of disagreements about the definitions of marriage and family?*

These Mexican families are celebrating the Day of the Dead. In many cultures, households and families perform religious functions. Ceremonies celebrating family members at birth, puberty, marriage, and death may be organized and enacted on the basis of household units, with or without the participation of larger community groups.

may vary. In plural marriages, for example, a person may have more than one spouse. In most societies, husbands and wives have obligations to assist one another in the rearing of children and the provisioning of their household. They share economic resources and provide shelter, clothing, and household equipment. And marriage establishes bonds between groups of kin (the wife's relatives and the husband's relatives), who also have rights and obligations toward each other.

It is through marriage that men and their kinship groups may claim rights to children. For this reason, there is a fundamental difference in the emphasis on marriage in patrilineal groups, where descent and inheritance are traced through men, and matrilineal groups, where they are traced through women. In matrilineal societies, kinship groups obtain new members when the women of the group give birth to children. A mother's child automatically becomes a member of her own kin group, whether she is married or not. In contrast, patrilineal kinship units cannot obtain children from their own women, because a child does not belong to its mother's kin group but to its father's. In this case marriage serves the purpose of securing a stable relationship between men and women from outside their kin group. Marriage also provides for the establishment of what Kathleen Gough calls "social fatherhood." **Social fatherhood** may or may not be the same as biological paternity. One's social father is the person who assumes paternal rights and responsibilities; examples would include adoptive fathers and stepfathers. In some African traditions, a woman can contract a marriage with another woman and assume the status of father for any children that are born to her wife.

> **REVIEW**
>
> A family is a group of people related by blood (consanguines) or by marriage (affines) who live together, raise children, and share economic and other social responsibilities. A household consists of relatives and, often, nonrelatives who live together and share economic responsibilities. In all societies, enculturation of children and the inheritance of property and status take place within families. In most societies, families are formed through marriage, a public acknowledgment of a couple's commitment and a new alliance between kin groups. Marriage enables men in patrilineal societies to add children to their kin group, whereas in matrilineal societies, children are automatically in their mother's group. Marriage also allows for social fatherhood.

FAMILIES AND IDEAL TYPES

Anthropologists differentiate between one's family of orientation (the family one grows up in) and one's family of procreation (the family one founds as an adult). In addition, anthropologists have long used a classification of ideal family types that is generally descriptive of different family structures. Many real families diverge from these types in some way or to some degree. Nevertheless, the types are useful because they broadly correlate with other aspects of culture. The nuclear family, extended family, joint family, and single-parent family are some of these types.

Nuclear Families

Among nomadic foragers and members of industrial societies, most families are of the type that anthropologists call "nuclear." A **nuclear family** consists of one or more

social fatherhood
The status of a man who fulfills the responsibilities of parenting, a role that may or may not be the same as biological paternity.

nuclear family
Family consisting of parents and their children.

parents and their children, although another relative, such as a grandparent or an unmarried sibling of one of the parents, may reside in the same household temporarily. The nuclear family is the characteristic family form of societies with bilateral descent, which, as discussed in Chapter 7, are typically either foraging or modern industrial societies.

A nuclear family structure provides certain benefits. For instance, it has the advantage of mobility. The relatively small number of people in a nuclear family unit can easily separate themselves from the larger community in which they live. In foraging societies, nuclear families aid in survival in conditions of scarcity; if there are insufficient resources to support a large group, nuclear families can go their own way, dispersing into a larger territory. In industrial societies, nuclear families allow for economic independence and promote the weakening of wider kinship bonds. This pattern is advantageous for societies where competition and individual advancement are goals.

Comparatively small families are an advantage for people in both foraging and industrial societies. Family size is limited among foragers in order not to exceed the carrying capacity of the environment. In addition, infants and young children need to be carried when travelling, which favours the spacing of births. Because foragers lack grains and animal milk as foods for babies, mothers nurse their children for as many as three or four years. Therefore, closely spaced children have a low chance of survival. As well, frequent pregnancies and deliveries have a negative impact on the health and long-term survival of mothers. In industrial societies, small nuclear families have the mobility necessary for leaving larger kin groups and moving from job to job and region to region. Distant relatives are unlikely to make claims for assistance, and if they do, families can easily avoid contact with them or deny their requests for aid. Small families are an advantage because dependent children are economic liabilities in modern industrial economies where work requires strength, stamina, and skilled training and where laws forbid or restrict child labourers. However, nuclear family life may contribute to social isolation.

Some **single-parent families** in industrial societies are formed as the result of divorce or the death of a spouse and parent. Others develop when the parents do not marry or live together or when women do not wish to marry but still want children. In Canada, single parent families account for 25 percent of all households with children. Eighty percent of these are headed by a single mother. Single-parent households, especially those headed by women, are more likely to have incomes near or below the poverty line. Their economic difficulties stem from a common problem of nuclear families: Economic independence is fine for people with resources and jobs, but for those with meagre incomes, the isolation of single-parent families increases the difficulty of obtaining support from kin. In contrast, in extended family systems, people who lose or lack a spouse can rely on a large network of relatives for assistance.

Extended and Joint Families

Family systems based on an extended family principle are more common worldwide. Extended family arrangements are especially prevalent in farming and pastoral economies. An **extended family** consists of three or more generations of people. Typically, it is composed of an elder parent or couple, their unmarried children, some of the married children, and the children's spouses and children. As you read in Chapter 7, rules of descent determine which adult married children remain with the

This Japanese nuclear family is enjoying a day out like other nuclear families around the world.

single-parent family
Family consisting of one parent (either mother or father) and her or his children.

extended family
Family formed with three or more generations, for example, parents, children, and grandparents.

This four-generation extended Polish family, grouped around their 96-year-old matriarch, is characterized by vertical ties between generations.

Culture Change

THE CHANGING CANADIAN FAMILY

Fifty years ago, most Canadian families conformed to a standard pattern: a working husband, a stay-at-home wife, and three or four children. Today, married-with-children households account for only 31 percent of all domestic units, and in two-thirds of these cases wives have entered the labour force. Divorce rates have increased tenfold, creating a sizeable number of single-parent families in the process (16 percent of all families and 25 percent of those with children). Common-law partnerships are regularly formed and in fact are the most common first union for women in their 20s (Milan 2000). Same-sex marriages have been legalized and some consideration has even been given to permitting polygamous unions. Similar trends can be observed in the United States and in many other countries around the world.

While many Canadians view these changes with alarm and disapproval, anthropological approaches to family structures indicate that they reflect understandable adaptations to new economic and technological circumstances as have diverse and dynamic domestic arrangements in other parts of the world. Our society is in the process of transition from an industrial order based on manufacturing consumer goods to a post-industrial, knowledge-based economy. Greater demand for educated workers, the entry of women into the expanding service sector, higher rates of migration and mobility in a globalizing economy, and new cultural values have created stresses and opportunities that have made family patterns more flexible and varied.

Since the 1950s, post-secondary education has become a more important requirement for entry into the work force and for personal development. Once the preserve of a small elite, advanced study at a university or college level is now undertaken by 75 percent of Canadian high school graduates (Shaienks et al. 2006:13). This trend has resulted in an increase in the marriage age from approximately 25 in 1960 to 30 in 2000. As a consequence, young adults are more frequently living with their parents or forming an increasing number of single-person households that now account for 27 percent of all domestic units. When people eventually marry, they are having fewer children. The birth rate for Canadian women has fallen from 3.5 to 1.5 children and family size has fallen from five to three. The shrinking birth rate has had a number of far-reaching effects (Milan 2000). Since 2000, immigration has been twice as important as natural increase in adding to Canada's population size and has significantly contributed to greater ethnic and racial diversity. New Canadians from other cultural backgrounds are introducing new family patterns and values, including a growing number of extended families.

Marriage patterns are changing in other ways than the age of marriage. The marriage rate has declined from the post war "baby boom" level of 11 per 1,000 to an all time low of 4.7. Many people are opting for common-law unions, which now account for 18 percent of all couple-households. While many of these are temporary "trial marriages," some involve long-term relationships; almost half of common-law families include children. The decline in marriage is particularly concentrated in the low-income sector of the population among young people with little education and unstable employment whose lifestyles are diverging from those of the middle class (Milan 2000).

While marriages are becoming less prevalent, those that are established are less stable than they were in the past. A variety of factors, such as women's economic independence, federal legislation, and related value changes have resulted in a high divorce rate and the likelihood that almost 40 percent of all first marriages will end before a couple's thirtieth anniversary (Clark and Crompton 2006). The process of marital breakdown has had many implications for Canadian family patterns, including a growing number of single-parent households, second marriages, and stepfamilies. The transformation from the uniform and idealized nuclear family of the early industrial age to the complex and flexible alternatives of post-industrial society has created many strains on the basic domestic processes such as childrearing and mutual economic and moral support. We must understand, however, that these trends are inevitable consequences of forces that are unlikely to be reversed. Although dislocating, they open up new possibilities for personal choice and social and cultural innovation.

Anthropology Applied

Anthropologists as Expert Witnesses

As we have discussed in Chapter 2, cultural anthropologists often are called to testify in court cases involving possible cultural misunderstandings on issues ranging from land ownership to family law and child custody. In her article "Infighting in San Francisco: Anthropology in Family Court, Or A Study in Cultural Misunderstanding," anthropologist Barbara Jones (1998) outlines a custody dispute in which she was an expert witness. The dispute was between a mother seeking custody and the father, with whom the child was living. The mother had married a fourth time, was pregnant, and planned to leave the country. The father was single but closely tied to an extended family network. A psychologist, who was hired by the court and assumed to be unbiased, examined both households and concluded that the mother should have sole custody of the child. Jones believed

that the psychologist's conclusion was based on a lack of understanding about the benefits that the father and his extended family could offer the child.

Jones was invited to explain these benefits to the court. She observed that the child had been interacting almost daily with loving grandparents, cousins, aunts, and uncles. In addition, the father had hired a full-time nanny to assist in daily care of his daughter while he worked. Contrary to the psychologist, then, Jones concluded that the extended family of the father provided greater benefits to the child than the mother's situation would allow.

CRITICAL THINKING QUESTION

What perspectives do anthropologists have that might make them valuable contributors to the adjudication process?

parents. That is, in patrilineal systems where descent and inheritance are traced through men, it is more often the sons who remain with their parents, whereas daughters leave home after marriage to reside with their husbands' families. In matrilineal societies a more complex set of alternatives is present. According to one arrangement, a newly married couple will move in with the wife's family. According to another, they will live with the husband's maternal uncle.

Extended family systems have the advantage of establishing a more or less stable group of people who can share resources, household tasks, and subsistence work and provide emotional support and material aid. However, because many people live together, conflicts may develop. Intergenerational tensions may arise because of the authority of the eldest couple over their adult children, or sibling rivalry may develop in a joint family compound. Conflicts over authority, inheritance, and loyalty are common. In addition, extended family systems may lead to social difficulties for in-marrying spouses. Women moving in with their husbands' kin, for example, may face demanding mothers-in-law. Because economic cooperation and interdependence is a prominent feature of extended families, people in industrial societies may form this type of family unit on a temporary or permanent basis when they are unemployed or otherwise lack resources.

? *Which ideal type best characterizes your family? What are some benefits and challenges of life in this type of family in relation to the larger culture?*

REVIEW

Ideal family types include nuclear, single-parent, extended, and joint families. A nuclear family consists of parents and their offspring and occasionally another relative. This type is commonly found in both foraging and industrial societies. Single-parent families have a mother or a father and children as a result of single status, divorce, or the death of a parent. The majority of single-parent families are headed by women. Extended families, found in many societies, consist of parents, their unmarried children, married children and their spouses, and their grandchildren. Extended families are most prevalent among agrarian and pastoralist societies.

Controversies

Explaining the Incest Taboo

The origins of the incest taboo are much debated. One theory proposes that the incest taboo arose out of an instinctive aversion toward sexual relations within the nuclear family. The problem with this theory is that incest is known to occur fairly widely in human societies, so avoiding it could not be an instinct. Another biological theory is based on the fact that inbreeding can increase the incidence of undesirable or harmful (as well as desirable and beneficial) genetic traits in a population. This theory suggests that the incest taboo is a learned, cultural response to the possible negative biological consequences of inbreeding. However, it assumes that ancestral human groups understood the relationship between mating and the variability of traits in their population. It also assumes that this cultural adaptation then spread to all human societies through diffusion or contact to become a universal element of culture or, alternatively, that human societies in different areas independently invented an incest taboo.

A theory championed by Sigmund Freud focused on the origin of the incest taboo as a response to the need to lessen sexual competition within the nuclear family unit. This theory might account in part for the ban on sexual relations between parents and their children, which would strain the marriage bond between husband and wife. However, this psychological theory does not account for the near-universal prohibition on marriage between siblings. Sibling marriage occurred among the emperors of ancient Peru, Egypt, and Hawaii but was not defined as incest. Marriage between a brother and sister at the highest level of the state functioned to consolidate power and minimize struggles over succession. However, sibling marriage was not permitted among ordinary citizens.

Many anthropologists favour understanding the incest taboo as a means of ensuring survival by forcing people to make alliances with others outside the nuclear family. This "marry out or die out" theory emphasizes that marriage within a small unit will lead, over time, to the isolation and genetic homogeneity of the group, which makes it more vulnerable to population loss or even extinction. Mating outside the nuclear family reduces this risk and also leads to the formation of social alliances and bonds of reciprocity with other people. Reciprocal social networks are critical in times of scarce resources and other dangers to survival.

We may never know why the incest taboo started, but the fact that it is universal indicates its importance. All these theories add interesting dimensions and clues to the debate.

CRITICAL THINKING QUESTION

Which theory or combination of theories about the origin of the incest taboo do you favour, and why?

ENDOGAMY, EXOGAMY, AND THE INCEST TABOO

Marriage serves as a means of consolidating kinship within a particular group (*endogamy*) or extending kinship to other groups (*exogamy*). All societies ban marriage—and condemn sexual relations—within the nuclear family, particularly between parents and children and also, with very few exceptions, between brothers and sisters. This ban is referred to as the **incest taboo**. The incest taboo is essentially a rule of nuclear family exogamy, forcing people to marry outside their families. The incest taboo is universal, but beyond the nuclear family the "forbidden" relatives are different in different societies. For example, in some societies cross-cousins are preferred for marriage, whereas parallel cousins are forbidden under the incest taboo.

Effects of Exogamy on Social Organization

incest taboo
A ban on sexual relations or marriage between parents and their children and between siblings.

The marriage rules of endogamy and exogamy are predicated on the incest taboo. Both exogamy and endogamy reflect and reinforce the structure and organization of a society. For example, village exogamy is the norm in societies in which people contract marriages with residents of other villages. Through inter-village marriages, people create alliances over a broader geographic area, thereby widening their networks of allies and supporters. In areas of frequent warfare, such marriages also give some protection against raids because people are less likely to attack villages where they have relatives.

In addition, some stratified societies practise exogamy, stipulating that members of identifiable social groups or strata need to marry outside their own group. For example, the Natchez of the south-central United States were divided into two major classes—nobles and commoners. These groups had different, unequal access to resources, services, and power. The nobility consisted of three graded ranks: Suns, Nobles, and Honoured Persons. Descent was matrilineal. The chief was the highest-ranked member of the highest ranked matrilineage, the Suns. The Suns were never able to consolidate their power and wealth, however, because the Natchez social system required that all members of the nobility practise class exogamy. That is, they had to marry commoners. The Sun matrilineage was perpetuated through children of Sun women who were Suns themselves, but children of Sun men, including children of the Great Sun, were not members of that chiefly lineage. The children and more distant relatives of Sun men became Nobles and Honoured Persons, whose male children were commoners through membership in their mothers' lineage. On the other hand, children of male commoners became members of the nobility if their fathers married noble women. (Bonvillain 2001:132–133).

Another form of exogamy, lineage exogamy, binds descent groups into larger systems of relationship through marriage alliances. Claude Lévi-Strauss (1949) based his **alliance theory** of marriage on the analysis of how a particular rule that required cross-cousins to marry links a number of unilineal descent groups into a systematic exchange system.

The cross-cousin rule works as follows. We may start with the marriage of brothers and sisters from three separate patrilineages (see Figure 8.1). A woman from lineage A marries a man from lineage B, a woman from lineage B marries a man from lineage C, and a woman from lineage C marries a man from lineage A. These marriages will link the three families together within the generation concerned. All three couples have children, conveniently a boy and girl each. A cross-cousin marriage rule is applied that requires each son to marry his mother's brother's daughter. The outcome of this union is that each man marries into the same lineage as his father did, thus linking the three groups into the same alliance pattern that was established in the first generation. The third generation of men follows the same marriage rule and reproduces the alliance between the lineages and so on. Lévi-Strauss noted an intriguing aspect of this particular cousin marriage rule: a lineage will give one of its women in marriage to another without directly receiving a wife from it in return. However, it will obtain a woman in marriage from another lineage within the marriage circle generated by the rule. He accordingly labelled the system as one of "indirect exchange."

Effects of Endogamy on Social Organization

Many stratified societies also practise endogamy, in which people marry within their class or rank in order to maintain social, economic, and political distinctions. Endogamous marriages solidify and preserve the privilege of elites by consolidating wealth and power.

A strong form of endogamy occurs in caste systems (described further in Chapter 10). **Caste** is an ascribed social category identifying a group by status or by occupation. At birth, a person automatically becomes a member of the caste of his or her parents and remains in that caste throughout life. In India, for example, people traditionally must marry other members of their own caste. Caste exogamy (marrying someone of another caste) is, in principle, forbidden, although it does occur.

alliance theory
Theory that maintains that the major function of marriage is to bind groups together into a larger social system.

caste
Social grouping whose membership is determined at birth and is generally inflexible.

? *What would happen if the cross-cousin rule stipulated that a man married his father's sister's daughter rather than his mother's brother's daughter?*

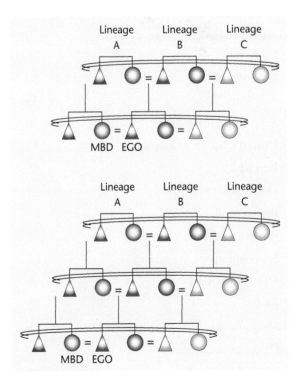

Figure 8.1
Cross-cousin marriage.

Brahmans, like the one in this photograph, traditionally were teachers and spiritual leaders. Brahmans are the highest of four main castes identified in ancient Hindu sacred writings. Castes are tied to specific ranked occupations. India's many tribal societies and ethnic minorities were not included in the caste system and thus became "outcasts."

Informal class endogamy is widespread in stratified societies, simply because people with similar backgrounds tend to associate with one another and marry within their group. Members of the same class tend to socialize together, attend the same schools, live in the same neighbourhoods, perform the same social activities, and so on. Therefore, even in the absence of a strong marriage rule, proximity and informal sanctions against marrying down tend to lead to class endogamy. Other marriage preferences that follow informal social norms include the tendency for people in pluralistic societies to marry within their own racial or ethnic group and to choose partners who speak the same language and observe the same religion.

Several studies document a clear pattern of in-group marriage within Canada. For example, there is a high propensity to marry within specific religious communities. Table 8.1 shows a general adherence to endogamous preferences, accounting for approximately 60 percent of marriage choices, as well as substantial differences among separate faith communities. Liberal Protestants are most likely to marry partners from other religions. More conservative groups as well as those with pronounced ethnic concentrations are less likely to do so. To some extent religious lines approximate those of class.

Race and ethnicity also condition marriage choices. A recent Statistics Canada study (Milan and Hamm 2004) indicates that 97 percent of marriages occur within perceived racial categories. Although miniscule, the intermarriage rate has increased between the 1991 and 2001 census and is slightly higher in Canada than in the United States.

While ethnic intermarriage is increasing, endogamy according to another social variable, education, is become more pronounced. Another Statistics Canada study has found that the rate at which people marry partners with an equivalent amount of education increased from 42 percent in 1971 to 55 percent in 2001, a 30 percent increase over a generation (Hou and Myles 2007). The pattern was particularly strong among the most highly educated. Almost 70 percent of men and 55 percent of women with university degrees married spouses who also had obtained degrees. (The gender difference was partially explained by the larger numbers of university-trained women.)

The increasing rate of in-marriage based on education reflects several changes within Canada's post-industrial social order, including an emphasis on education as a critical economic and social resource. It also demonstrates that, although we think of marriage as a consummate act of individual choice, this important decision is made within a social context that imposes clear pressures on us. Moreover, endogamy has implications for other aspects of our society. Since education is related to class and income, increased marriage within educational groups has an effect on social stratification and mobility. If husbands and wives have the same training and income levels, skills and wealth become more concentrated than they would if the choice of a spouse were more open. This factor contributes to broader trends in Canadian society towards greater and more rigid socio-economic divisions that we will revisit in Chapter 10.

Table 8.1 PERCENTAGES OF MARRIAGES WITHIN RELIGIOUS GROUPS IN CANADA

Lutheran	25
Presbyterian	36
Anglican	33
Salvation Army	36
United Church of Canada	41
Baptist	43
Orthodox	57
Pentecostal	61
Roman Catholic	61
No religion	65
Other Christian	70
Jewish	71
Mennonite	72
Other non-Christian	78
Jehovah's Witness	92

Source: Statistics Canada. *2001 Census.* CANSIM generated tables.

REVIEW

The incest taboo, universal in human societies, is a general ban against sexual relations between individuals within a nuclear family. Explanations for the origins of the incest taboo include biological and psychological explanations and hypotheses based on cultural adaptations to survival factors. Marriage rules affect the organization of a society. Village exogamy, for example, links villages in political and economic alliances. Examples of impacts of endogamy on social systems include the caste system of India, alliances created through cross-cousin marriage, and class systems with preferential marriage based on shared membership in a social, racial, or ethnic group.

GLOBALIZATION

Increases in rates of multiracial marriage and in numbers of mixed-race children in many parts of the world can be seen as an extension of the process of globalization.

FORMS OF MARRIAGE

Marriage rules define the forms that marriages can take, and these forms vary. For example, norms concerning the number of spouses that can constitute the marital unit differ among societies. In most societies, marriage is a union between two people—**monogamy**—but in some societies the marital unit may consist of three or more people—**polygamy**, or plural marriage. Monogamy is the most common form of union today, even in societies where plural marriages are possible. Societies that permit remarriage after the death of a spouse or divorce practise **serial monogamy**, meaning that a person can be married to only one person at a time, although individuals may have two or more spouses during their lifetime.

Polygyny and Polyandry

There are two forms of polygamy. **Polygyny** is marriage between a man and two or more women, and **polyandry** is marriage between a woman and two or more men. A common type of polygyny is a pattern in which a man marries two or more sisters, usually wedding one first and the other years later. This system is called **sororal polygyny**. Sororal polygyny has the advantage of minimizing potential conflicts between wives, because the women have close emotional and supportive bonds as sisters. When co-wives are not related, there may be tensions between them, each vying for favouritism from their common husband to benefit themselves and their children. Different societies favour different kinds of residence patterns for plural marriages. In some, the entire unit of husband and several wives lives together in one dwelling. In others, each wife of a polygynous homestead has a separate home for herself and her children.

Polyandrous marriages are less common than polygynous ones. They are particularly prominent in some communities in the Indian Himalayas and Chinese Tibet. Among the Nyinba and the Pahari, brothers may jointly contract for a wife. This fraternal polyandry permits all men to be married and also promotes economic cooperation among brothers for their mutual benefit. Rather than fragmenting a family's property through inheritance by numerous and possibly conflicting heirs, polyandrous unions solidify wealth, property, and social status and raise people's overall standard of living (Levine 1988), and where resources are scarce, it may limit population growth. Finally, in societies where men frequently travel for trade or military expeditions, polyandry ensures that households will likely have at least one man at home to accomplish male economic tasks. Although most of the relatively few societies that practice polyandry are in South Asia, it has been reported elsewhere, as among the Inuit of Arctic Canada and the Iroquois of New York State.

Explanations of Polygyny

Polygyny develops in different societies for different reasons. In communities where women greatly outnumber men, polygyny helps correct imbalances in the sex ratio. Among the Innu of eastern Canada, for example, polygyny, limited to two or three wives, ensured marriage for all women in a society with a scarcity of men. Male mortality rates were comparatively higher than female mortality rates because of the dangers

monogamy
Marriage rule that stipulates a union between two people.

polygamy
Marriage in which the marital unit consists of three or more people.

serial monogamy
Marriage pattern that stipulates that a person can be married to only one person at a time, although individuals may have two or more spouses during their lifetime. Subsequent marriages may be formed after the death of one spouse or after divorce.

polygyny
Marriage between a man and two or more women.

polyandry
Marriage between a woman and two or more men.

sororal polygyny
Marriage between a man and two or more women who are sisters.

In this West African family, each co-wife has her own hut, which she occupies with her children. To prevent jealousy and competition, the most senior wife is often given the highest status. In other cultures, co-wives are treated and supported equally. Economic changes in African societies put pressure on this form of marriage, however. Today only the wealthiest of men can afford many wives.

for men in hunting and warfare. As the seventeenth-century French Jesuit missionary Paul LeJeune observed, after lecturing the Innu about the evils of plural marriage: "Since I have been preaching among them that a man should not have more than one wife, I have not been well received by the women; for, since they are more numerous than the men, if a man can only marry one of them, the others will have to suffer. Therefore this doctrine is not to their liking" (Thwaites 1906, vol. 12:165). In the case of the Innu, polygyny prevented population decline by maintaining an effective rate of reproduction.

Polygyny also occurs in some strongly patriarchal societies in which women are viewed as property and a source of status. Men who can afford to support a greater number of wives and dependents are seen to have greater wealth, power, and prestige in their communities. Historically, hereditary high chiefs of polygynous Central African kingdoms boasted hundreds of wives and concubines. In pre-Communist imperial China, wealthy men measured their status and good fortune in the number of wives they accumulated. Daughters became mediums of exchange between men seeking to form alliances with each other.

Polygyny also develops as an adaptation to economic needs or goals because of the important economic roles women serve. For example, as the economy of the Plains Indians shifted to dependence on the buffalo by the middle of the nineteenth century, men wanted to obtain the economic services of more than one wife, because women were responsible for tanning the buffalo hides and thus turning a raw product into a marketable item. To advance themselves in trade networks that were supplied by the labour of women, men wanted several wives.

In some farming societies, polygyny also serves the purpose of supplying additional labour of women and their children. For example, among the Tswana and Herero, two cattle-herding and horticultural societies of southern Africa, men with more than one wife were able to accumulate greater farm surpluses because of women's key roles as subsistence farmers. Also, the more wives a man had, the more children he acquired. His children raised his social standing because they contributed to the growth of his patrilineage and patriclan. A man's sons helped care for his cattle, and his daughters brought cattle to the family as bride prices from their husbands' kin.

GLOBALIZATION

The shared practice of polygyny fostered the rapid spread of patriarchal Arab culture and Islam to African nations. It is well known that culture change occurs more rapidly and more completely when peoples in contact share basic cultural characteristics such as forms of marriage and family.

"Ghost Marriage" and Other Adaptive Forms

Cultures demonstrate a great variety in the ways that people think of sexual relations, marriage, and family. Marriage might even be entirely symbolic and not involve procreation. Yet, even in rare forms of marriage, descent and household composition and ways of establishing bonds with others form systems of relationships and meaning that integrate individuals into families and communities.

In some African societies with patrilineal descent, marriages can be contracted in ways that emphasize the importance of descent and the continuity of patrilineal kin groups. Among the Nuer, for example, if a married man died without sons, one of his younger brothers married his widow. The children of the new couple, though, were considered heirs of the deceased (Evans-Pritchard 1955). Nuer **ghost marriage** thus permitted an elder brother to maintain his patrilineage even after his death. In Nuer society, seniority in a lineage was an important criterion for determining relative social status, so allowing descent to follow from an elder sibling, dead or alive, was a strategic practice. In this way, children born to the younger brother but claimed by the dead older brother would have seniority over members of junior lineages.

ghost marriage
Marriage practice among the Nuer of Sudan in which a widow marries her dead husband's brother and in which the children ensuing from the second marriage are said to be the children of the dead husband.

Another Nuer marital option was allowed when a lineage failed to produce a male heir. In that event, a woman in the lineage could take the role of husband and be married to another woman. The woman who became a husband refrained from having sex, because husbands cannot conceive. The "wife" conceived by having sex with a chosen man from any lineage other than her own. The children borne to the "wife" belonged to the "husband's" lineage, thus supplying the line with heirs (Evans-Pritchard 1955:108).

In marriages between women, the woman who acted as husband was transformed into a legal man. As a "man," she could receive bridal payments given in marriages for her kinswomen, and she could inherit cattle from her father. She also could be compensated with cattle if her "wife" had an adulterous affair without her consent. Nuer practices of marriage between women and "ghost marriage" both create social fatherhood for the purpose of securing the continuation of patrilineages.

In another rare form, the matrilineal Kwakwaka'wakw (Kwakiutl) of British Columbia developed a marriage option that created daughters for men who had none. Such a strategy was necessary because status, wealth, and named titles were transmitted from men to men through women. In practice, men needed daughters because wealth and titles passed from a father to his daughter's children. To accommodate men who had no daughters, several types of marriage could be arranged. According to George Hunt, a Kwakiutl chief, a man "turned the left side of his son's body into a woman and gave ['her'] the name belonging to the oldest daughter of his line" (quoted in Boas 1966:55). Then another man proposed marriage to the first man's "daughter." After they were married, the first man was able to acquire the titles belonging to "her" lineage and could pass these on to children whom he had with a subsequent wife. If a man had no children at all, according to Hunt, "the father may call his foot or one side of his body his daughter for purposes of marriage and inheritance." This was called "taking hold of the foot" (Boas 1897:359). These marital options allowed for the transmission of wealth and status controlled by men but passed on through women.

The Nayar, a matrilineal people living in Kerala, South India, have concepts of marriage that differ from that of most peoples (Mencher 1965). Nayar kinship centres on matrilineal relatives, organized into matrilineal descent and residence groups called *taravad*. The *taravad* consists of sisters and brothers, the sisters' children, the sisters' daughters' children, and so on, all descended from a female ancestor. They hold land and other property in common, managed by the senior man, and they care collectively for children born to their female members. Shortly before a girl reaches puberty, she is married to a man chosen by her family. The man and woman have no social or economic responsibilities toward one another and do not live together. However, when the man dies, the woman honours him in mourning ceremonies.

The Nayar man and woman have a succession of lovers over the years. A lover acknowledges and legitimizes his sexual relationship with a particular woman by giving her gifts three times a year for as long as the liaison lasts. Children produced from these unions belong to the *taravad* of the mother, and her family takes responsibility for the economic care of children. Fathers have no economic obligations for their children, but establishment of paternity is critical to the social standing of mother and child. One of the lovers publicly declares himself the father of a child by giving a gift to the mother and to the midwife who assisted in the birth.

Same-Sex Marriage

Although most marriages in most cultures are unions between men and women, some societies allow marriage between individuals of the same sex. This is not the same as the same-sex marriages practised by the

Amazing Race contestants Lynn Warren and Alex Ali were able to marry legally in Ottawa in 2005 after being declined this right in California.

same-sex marriage
Marriage between two men or two women.

Nuer, in which a woman is legally defined as a man for purposes of marriage to another woman. In this case, the couple does not have sexual relations. Rather, the female wife has sex with a man in order to bear children for her female husband.

Same-sex marriage was an option in many Native American societies as late as the early decades of the twentieth century. Especially in cultures of the Great Plains, the Southwest, and California, two women or two men might marry, have sexual relations, and share household and family responsibilities. These people, now often referred to as "Two-Spirits," were publicly recognized as forming legitimate couples. Chapter 9 discusses in greater detail the Two-Spirits and their roles in their communities.

In North America today, growing numbers of lesbian and gay couples agitate for the right to marry in ceremonies that have legal standing. While American courts and legislatures have been ambivalent over the issue, Canadian courts and legislative bodies have been more open to granting legal marital status to same-sex unions. Beginning with an Ontario judicial decision in 2003, courts in eight provinces have ordered recognition of such marriages. In 2005, the Canadian Parliament, controlled by a Liberal minority, passed a bill granting full marriage rights to same-sex couples that was applicable throughout the country. The Conservative minority government that came to power in 2006 has made a commitment to reverse this legislation but has not as yet (summer 2007) initiated any action. Legislative endorsement has not meant general acceptance of homosexual marriage throughout the country. Debate over whether churches should perform same-sex weddings has been especially contentious within the majority Christian community. The more liberal denominations, such as the United Church of Canada, have endorsed them, while more conservative ones such as the Catholic Church have been opposed. In 2007, the Anglican Church of Canada narrowly rejected a motion to allow its parishes the choice of sanctifying homosexual unions.

The emergence of Canadian patterns of same-sex marriage offers an interesting area for anthropological research and the documentation of emerging social and cultural trends in our own society. So far this phenomenon is too new to provide many results. According to the 2006 Census of Canada, there were 45 000 same-sex couples in Canada, less than 1 percent of the number of couple-households. Only 7500 of them were legally married. This level does not seem to pose a real assault on the "sanctity" of marriage that many opponents of this practice envision. Studies have shown that same-sex couples fulfill all of the same obligations and responsibilities toward each other as do heterosexual couples. They share their resources, make joint decisions, and make commitments to exclusive sexual relationships. Many also raise children together. Moreover, the desire of gay and lesbian partners to make marital commitments and assume the added responsibilities that they entail can be viewed as a reaffirmation of this institution at a time when it is being discounted by an increasing proportion of the population (Ambert 2005).

> **REVIEW**
>
> Monogamy, which is most common, is the marriage of two people, either for life or for a given time (serial monogamy). Polygamy, or plural marriage, can be in two forms: polygyny or polyandry. Polygyny is marriage between one man and two or more women. Marriage between a man and two or more sisters is called sororal polygyny. Explanations for the development of polygyny relate to population sex ratios, the status of women, and economic adaptations. Polyandry, marriage between one woman and two or more men, often brothers, is rarer. Other rarer forms of marriage include ghost marriages and same-sex marriages.

MARRIAGE AS ALLIANCE AND ECONOMIC EXCHANGE

The relationship established through marriage is not only social but economic as well. Each spouse usually has certain obligations to the other and to their children to supply basic needs such as food, clothing, and shelter. The economic factor in

Some of these Botswana cattle may be destined to become bridewealth for sons from the owner's family to give to the parents of their prospective wives. The bridewealth is offered as symbolic compensation for the woman's loss to her own family and as material compensation for her family's loss of an important economic asset.

marriage may also be expressed through exchanges of goods and services prior to, during, or after marriage rites. In most Native American cultures, gifts were mutually exchanged before and during a marriage ceremony. Relatives of the bride and groom gave each other foods, clothing, and ornaments as a sign of their mutual respect and support.

Bridewealth and Brideservice

In some places, substantial gifts may be given, not mutually by both sides, but more often by one side to the other. In patrilineal societies, for example, **bridewealth** is given from the husband's group to that of the wife. Among the Nuer and most of the cattle-herding societies of eastern Africa, bridewealth was primarily in the form of cattle. In the plains of North America, people gave horses as bridewealth. The number of cattle or horses given was taken to be a reflection of the wealth and prestige of the husband's kin and an indication of the esteem in which they held the bride and her family. Offering too little, then, could be an insult.

In societies where a married couple lived with the husband's kin, the transfer of goods from the husband's group to that of the wife was symbolic compensation for the loss of a woman. Bridewealth was also recognition that, after the wedding, the husband's family benefited from the bride's labour while her own kin would be deprived of it. In addition, bridewealth was a means of legitimizing the couple's children and their membership in the husband's patrilineal group. Bridewealth typically was returned if a couple divorced, so the wife's kin often had a large stake in discouraging the dissolution of the marriage.

In another form of gift giving, called **brideservice**, men are obligated to perform services for their wife's parents. A period of brideservice may predate the marriage ceremony, or the period may extend for many years after marriage. During this period, the future or newly married husband contributes his labour to his parents-in-law. Depending on the subsistence strategies employed, he may give all or a portion of animals he has caught or help with planting and harvesting crops. In addition, the husband may help construct his parents-in-law's dwellings, fetch wood or water, and perform other domestic tasks.

bridewealth
Presents given by the husband's family to the wife's kin before, during, or after the wedding ceremony.

brideservice
A period of months or years before or after marriage during which the husband performs labour for his wife's parents.

Culture Change

DOWRY IN INDIA

Dowry was the traditional marital exchange in India. There, a woman's family had to amass wealth in jewellery, fine cloth, and money to present to the husband's family before the marriage took place. The amount of wealth given was an indication of both the bride's status and the esteem of the husband's kin. A great deal of property was given by wealthy parents, but even poor families made every effort to collect as many valuables as they could so as not to shame their daughter and themselves.

The economic burden of dowry contributed to a preference for sons over daughters, because girls were a financial liability while boys brought in dowry wealth when they married. The custom of dowry thus contributed to female infanticide and the neglect of the health of daughters in India and Bangladesh. However, dowry was not the only factor involved in preferences for sons and the consequences of such preferences. The constellation of behaviours and attitudes grew out of a context of kinship based on patrilineal descent and inheritance, of subsistence strategies emphasizing intensive agriculture with farmwork primarily the responsibility of men, and of male control over land. All of these practices place value on men and undermine the worth of women.

Today, asking for and giving dowry is illegal in India, but there are reports that the custom is still practised and may be gaining in popularity. Although outlawed by the *Dowry Prohibition Act* (1961, amended in 1984 and 1986), dowry often is demanded by a husband's family (Ghadially and Kumar 1988:175). Such demands specify amounts of cash or goods necessary to contract a marriage. Young men of high status, good education, and favourable employment prospects command large sums. In many cases, dowry demands are made after a marriage is contracted and even after a wedding.

Public controversy over dowry has arisen in India because of increasing incidences of deaths of young wives whose families have not satisfied the dowry demands of their in-laws. Rehana Ghadially and Pramod Kumar report a study indicating that, of a registered 179 "unnatural deaths" of young married women in Delhi in 1981–1982, 12 to 16 percent were dowry-related (Ghadially and Kumar 1988:167). In two-thirds of these cases, young women committed suicide; the remaining one-third were murdered by their in-laws. The families involved were of all social classes, educational levels, and occupations.

Ghadially and Kumar (1988) also report a study conducted in the Indian state of Maharashtra concluding that dowry deaths rose from 120 in 1984 to 211 in 1985, an increase of 64 percent. By the mid-1990s, dowry deaths, including bride burnings, had climbed to an estimated 5800 incidents a year. Many cases of "unnatural deaths" of women are classified as "kitchen/cooking accidents" and "stove-bursts," a common method of killing unprofitable daughters-in-law. Retaliation against wives whose families fail to meet dowry demands takes many forms, from verbal abuse to beatings, burns, hanging, poisoning, and strangulation.

A disturbing finding in studies of dowry abuse and death is the fact that the wife's parents are sometimes aware of the violence perpetrated against their daughter but do nothing to give her emotional or legal support. The abused daughter is told to endure her situation rather than stir social controversy that would negatively affect her family's reputation.

Dowry and the related mistreatment and deaths of women gave impetus to the birth of the feminist movement in India. Beginning in 1979, women's groups staged public protests to bring the issue of dowry harassment out in the open. As a result, many families of abused and murdered daughters came forward to give testimony and ask for redress. The Indian government responded in 1980 with passage of laws against dowry-related crimes, mandating police investigation of the death of any woman who had been married less than five years at the time of her death. Legislation passed in 1983 strengthened the first law, making "cruelty to a wife a cognizable, non-bailable offense" and stipulated that "cruelty" included both mental and physical

harassment (Kumar 1995:68). Cases reported as sui-
cides (frequently involving death by dousing and
burning) could be investigated as "abetment to suicide," shifting the burden of proof to the woman's
husband and his family. In addition, amendments
required autopsies of women who died within seven
years of marriage.

The latest studies, however, indicate increases in
dowry demands. For example, the All India Democratic Women's Association conducted a survey in 2002,
questioning 10 000 people in eighteen of India's
twenty-six states and found "an across-the-board

increase in dowry demands" (Brooke 2003). Government statistics report that, in 2001, nearly 7000 women
were killed by husbands or in-laws angry because of
small dowry payments. In 2003, a well-publicized case
brought the issue of dowry demands to national attention. A bride called police on her wedding day when
her in-laws demanded an additional $25 000 in cash.
The refusal of her father to pay caused a scuffle and
prompted the young woman to summon the authorities. The husband was eventually arrested and made to
serve fourteen days in jail for violating laws against
dowry (Brooke 2003).

Dowry

In some societies, goods of value are given by the bride's family rather than the
groom's family. These gifts are given to the newly married couple and/or to the husband's kin prior to or upon the marriage. This type of exchange is called **dowry**.
Dowries are prevalent in some patriarchal cultures that stress the prestige of men and
their families. In theory, dowries are a kind of insurance that protects the interests of a
wife in a patrilineal and patriarchal society. In practice, however, dowry wealth is often
appropriated by the husband and his family.

In Europe, from medieval times until well into the nineteenth century, well-to-do
families bestowed dowries on their daughters when they married. The ability to give
large amounts of money, property, and annual incomes was a sign of a family's wealth,
enhancing their prestige. In turn, fathers who could afford handsome dowries could
bargain for wealthy and powerful sons-in-law. Through marriage exchanges of dowries
for husbands with property and status, men acquired a host of affinal relatives as personal and political allies. The legacy of the European dowry system is preserved today
in the custom of collecting fine clothes and linens in a bridal hope chest.

Marriages are economic transactions, but they are also occasions for celebration.
What is celebrated is not simply the union of two people but the alliances formed
between two families, lineages, or clans. When marriage takes place between a man
and a woman who come from different villages, the wedding may symbolize extended
networks and alliances between two communities.

REVIEW

As well as creating alliances among families and larger social units, marriage has important
economic functions, and economic exchange is a common feature of marriage arrangements.
Gifts are exchanged in many societies to represent the new economic obligations the spouses now
have to each other and their in-laws. Bridewealth, found in patrilineal societies, consists of forms of
wealth or objects of value given to the bride's family by the groom's family. Brideservice consists
of work that the groom does for his in-laws. In the dowry system, the family of the bride pays or
promises to pay wealth to the family of the groom in exchange for the marriage of their daughter.

MARRIAGE AS A RITE OF PASSAGE

For individuals, families, kin groups, and communities, marriages are crucial rites of passage. Because of the importance of the alliances formed by marriage, in many societies,
marriages, especially first marriages, are arranged by one's parents or other relatives. A
proposal of marriage may be made from one side or the other, although it is more
common worldwide for the future husband's kin to approach the family of the intended
wife. This is true whether the people follow patrilineal or matrilineal rules of descent.

dowry
Gifts given by the wife's
family to the married couple
or to the husband's kin
before, during, or after
the wedding ceremony.

In Their Own Voices

"I Hear That I'm Going to Get Married!"

BRITISH
COLUMBIA

CANADA

Kwakwaka'wakw
(Kwakiutl) Homeland

Vancouver
Island

UNITED
STATES

Florence Edenshaw Davidson, a Haida woman from Vancouver Island, British Columbia, was born in 1895. She was 14 years old when her parents told her that she would be married to Robert Davidson. As was proper in this matrilineal society, the proposal was made by Robert's kin to Florence's parents. Her father deferred to his wife's brother (Florence's mother's brother), who was a senior member of Florence's matriclan. She went on to have thirteen children and became an accomplished artist known for her button and appliqué blankets. These are Florence's recollections about how she came to be married to her husband.

I was still going to school yet when several people came into my dad's house to propose for my husband-to-be. I was wondering what was going on when all these people came in. The women all belonged to C'al'lanas, my husband's tribe [lineage], and the men all belonged to my husband's dad's tribe, Stl'ang'lanas, except for my husband's brother. They were all streaming in and I didn't know what was going on . . .

"Don't say anything when I tell you something," my mother said to me. "Those who came in last week proposed to you." I didn't know what to say. Propose! Why? I thought. I was just a kid yet. I didn't know what to say and mother advised me not to say anything about the proposal because they were high-class [y'a Yet] people . . .

"They want you to marry Robert Davidson." "Did you say yes?" I asked her. "No, your dad sent them to your uncle [Florence's mother's brother]. Your dad says he's got nothing to do with it; it has to go through your uncle. You have more respect for your uncle than for us," she told me. "That's the only brother I have." "You're going to make me marry," I said. "Yes, you're going to marry him." "I'm not going to marry him," I said. "Don't say that, Florence, he's a real prince [y'a Yet]."

It bothered me so much. For a long time I couldn't sleep when I went to bed. Every day I bothered my mother. "I'm not going to marry that old man. I'm not. If you make me marry him, summertime I'll run away. You won't see me again." My mother didn't say anything, though every day I used to bother her. My dad didn't say a word to me about it. Finally, my mother said, "Don't say anything dear. Your uncle thinks it's best for you to marry him. He's a prince. He's going to respect you all your life and if you don't want to marry him you're going to feel bad all your life. He belongs to clever people; you're not going to be hard up for anything. We need a young man's help, too. You must remember that. We belong to chiefs too and you're not supposed to talk any old way. You have to respect yourself more than what you worry about." I don't want to say any more because my mother said I'd be sorry for the rest of my life if I didn't marry him. I made up my mind not to say anything much as I disliked it.

From *During My Time: Florence Edenshaw Davidson, A Haida Woman* by Margaret Blackman, pp. 95–96. Copyright © 1982. Reprinted by permission of the University of Washington Press.

arranged marriages
Marriages that are arranged by the parents or other relatives of the bride and groom.

Arranged marriages symbolically emphasize the fact that such unions are not simply relationships between a woman and a man but are more fundamentally alliances between families. Each side measures their own worthiness in relation to the social standing and resources of the other side. Their willingness to promote a marital union is an indication of their trust in their future affines.

Weddings are rites of passage in which the participants change their status from single to married. In societies without arranged marriages, preparation for marriage

And these are the recollections of James Sewid, a Kwak-waka'wakw man from Alert Bay, British Columbia. He, too, was married when he was nearly 14 years old to a girl he knew only by sight.

And that's when the big day came. It was late in the fall and I was going on fourteen. . . . I had been out late that night to a dance with my friends and when I came in I lay down on the couch. That was when I heard Jim and Mary Bell talking about me to Ed and Rachel Whanock and my mother and stepfather. One of them was saying, "You might as well go and see her parents because I think he should get married because we don't want him running around like this.". . . I lay there and pretended that I was sleeping and pretty soon my grandparents walked out. So as soon as they had gone I got up and said to my stepfather, "Let's go take a walk. It's pretty warm in here." I used to be very good friends with him and we were just like pals. "All right," he said, "we'll go for a walk." When we got outside and were walking along the road I asked him, "What was going on in there? I heard the people talking about me." "Well," he said, "you're going to get married." "Well," I said, "I can't get married! I'm too young!" "Oh that's all right," he said. "We'll look after you. I think it is the best way for you, to get married now, because if you're not going to get married now you might go haywire." "Well," I said, "who is this girl anyway?" And just then we happened to be passing by the house where Moses Alfred lived, and David said, "It is the girl that lives here." I didn't know what to say. I used to see her around the village but I didn't know her.

Well, it was the Indian custom for someone to go to the parents of the girl and ask their consent. That is where my grandparents had gone that night when they walked out of the house. So I just waited for the answer that this girl's parents would give to the old people who went to talk with them. I was careful after that not to listen anymore because I didn't like to butt in on what was going on. A few days after that I was alone with my mother, just the two of us, I said to her, "I hear that I'm going to get married. You know that I'm too young to get married." "Oh, no!" she said. "Don't talk like that. We want you to get married. You are going to marry Flora Alfred. It has already been arranged with her parents and it's all right. Now you have to go and see the minister so it can be announced in the church and published in the band." "Well," I said, "I don't think I should get married. It isn't that I don't want to get married, but what am I going to do if I have children?" "Well," my mother said, "we'll look after you some."

After that I went to see my old grandmother, Lucy. She had already heard about it. I went in and sat down and said, "Well, they say I'm going to get married." "Yes," she said, "I heard about that and I think it's a wonderful thing. I would really like to see it. I want to see you get married and have children before I die. There is nothing better that I wish to see than your children before I go." Well, that is what made me kind of give in. I didn't want to get married but of course I had no business to my own personal opinion. I had no business to try and argue or anything like that because I knew that the older people knew what was right for me; that's what I figured. I never did like to argue with anybody that was older than me but I always liked to respect what they said to me.

From *Guests Never Leave Hungry: The Autobiography of James Sewid, a Kwakiutl Indian* by James Spradley, pp. 66–67. Copyright © 1972. Reprinted by permission of Yale University Press.

Although both Florence and James voiced serious reservations about their arranged marriages, especially concerning their young age and fears about taking on adult responsibilities, they gave up their objections in the interests of their families. As James said, "I had no business to my own personal opinion." As it turned out, they both had successful marriages, long and loving relationships with their spouses.

CRITICAL THINKING QUESTIONS

Would you be willing to have your family arrange your marriage? Why, or why not? What might be some of the benefits and risks of doing so?

---

usually involves some form of **courtship**, in which a couple tests their attraction and compatibility as well as the acceptability of their union to others who are important in their lives. Mate selection is the common goal of courtship, and weddings mark the passage from courtship to marriage. The bases on which people choose their mates may include personal compatibility, desired personality traits, likelihood of reliability and economic contributions, and physical attraction. In most societies, the Western concept of romantic love is not a prerequisite for courtship or marriage, although

courtship
Period prior to marriage when a couple tests attraction to and compatibility with each other.

Case study

A Wedding in Nepal

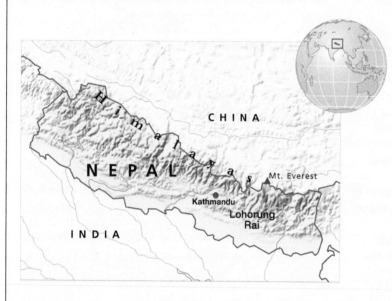

In societies of larger communities and settled populations, especially where lineages are important kinship, economic, and political units, marriages may be complex, lengthy procedures. Among the Lohorung Rai of eastern Nepal, marriage involves a ten-step process (Hardman 2000). The most complex aspect of the marriage is the negotiation that takes place between the families of the intended husband and wife. These negotiations underscore the social and economic as well as spiritual alliances created between two families, their clans, and their villages.

Most Lahorung Rai marriages are arranged when the boy and girl are young, beginning with an initial presentation of a gift of liquor brought to the girl's parents by the boy's kin. The boy's emissaries recount his good qualities and those of his family. It is not uncommon for the girl's family to refuse the initial request, returning the gift to the boy's relatives. Typically, a second visit is undertaken, and several trips may be needed before the girl's parents accept, drink the liquor offered, and tell the boy's relatives how much meat they will need to distribute to their kin.

Additional gifts subsequently are brought by the boy's kin to those of the girl. Eventually, the final gift of a live pig, some rice, and liquor are presented to the girl's kin. This final gift, referred to as a "ransom," marks the formal betrothal of the couple and commits the families

to the certainty of the marriage. The wedding, lasting all night, takes place at the bride's home. The groom proceeds there accompanied by his cousin (father's sister's son). The rite not only celebrates a marriage but also marks the transition of a male from boyhood to manhood.

After the wedding, the bride accompanies her husband to his parents' home, but the following day she returns to her own parents' home, bringing additional gifts from her husband's family. She returns to her husband's home sixteen days later but remains for only a few days, not finally taking up residence there for perhaps as long as a year. Several years later, usually after the birth of her first child, she returns to her parents' home for a final rite of separation, receiving gifts from her brothers.

The lengthy and complex Lohorung Rai marriage process not only solidifies an alliance between two families but also symbolizes and enacts the difficulty of a young woman's separation from her family in a society where post-marital residence is in the husband's locality and usually involves village exogamy. The woman's family demonstrates their reluctance to lose her by their hesitation in accepting the initial gifts offered, and she shows her difficulty in leaving by repeatedly returning to her parents' home.

At this Nepalese wedding, both sets of relatives express the difficulties that they had to overcome to achieve the desired marriage, praising each other. At the end, the bride's relatives accept gifts of gold, clothing, silver bangles, and necklaces that all symbolize the marriage.

these feelings may develop when people begin to live together, adjusting to one another and sharing their lives. The stories of Florence Davidson and James Sewid, given in the In Their Own Voices feature, illustrate that feelings of caring and love can follow, but do not necessarily precede, a successful marriage.

In small-scale societies, especially among foraging and horticultural peoples, a wedding ceremony is usually a simple affair. Among the Mohawk, a marriage traditionally was proposed by a young man's family to the family of the intended bride, or a couple announced their plans to marry. Before the wedding, the couple separately presented gifts to their future mothers-in-law. The future husband gave his bride's mother a gift of deer meat, and the future bride gave her husband's mother a gift of cornbread. These presents were symbolic of the economic roles of men as hunters and women as farmers, thus representing the interdependence of spouses and households.

A Mohawk wedding involved a feast sponsored by the bride's family for relatives, clan members, and villagers. The father of the bride made a formal announcement of the couple's marriage and bestowed the family's approval. Then followed speeches from a number of respected elder guests who exhorted the couple to behave properly, responsibly, and kindly to each other.

This couple married through mutual consent after declaring their love for one another, and their families were the last to know about their plans. The rite of passage in which this couple is participating is a variation on an ancient theme. Originally, a groom fed his bride to symbolize his ability to support her. Here the bride and groom feed each other.

> **REVIEW**
>
> Weddings are rites of passage that publicly confirm the changes in marital status and kinship status of the participants. Societies that place high value on kinship and community relations often have arranged marriages, and others have courtship practices in which individuals choose their own marriage partners. Weddings also extend the alliance and economic transaction functions of marriage.

PATTERNS OF RESIDENCE AFTER MARRIAGE

The elaborate Nepalese wedding process described in the Case Study is partly a result of post-marital residence patterns that call for a bride to separate herself from her relatives. In all societies, after people get married the new couple follows norms dictating where they should live. They may live with or near the husband's or the wife's family; they may alternate their residences between families; or they may establish a place of their own apart from any of their relatives. Their choice may depend on factors such as the amount of resources available or the composition of existing households. Societies vary in the patterns of post-marital residence that they encourage. Particular post-marital **residence rules** often are associated with different descent systems and specific economic strategies.

Matrilocal and Patrilocal Residence

Arrangements in which a married couple lives with or near the wife's family are termed **matrilocal residence**. Usually (but not always) matrilocal residence is associated with matrilineal descent; that is, societies that reckon descent matrilineally usually prefer that couples live with the wife's family. Because children resulting from marriage belong to the lineage of the mother, matrilocal residence ensures that women of the kin group remain together. Matrilocal households typically consist of an elder couple, their daughters, their daughters' husbands and children, and their unmarried sons. Married sons live with their wives' kin. This kind of residence pattern is also called **uxorilocal**—living with the wife's family.

residence rules
Rules that stipulate where a couple will reside after their marriage.

matrilocal residence
Pattern for residence after marriage in which the couple lives with or near the wife's family.

uxorilocal
Living with or near the wife's parents.

patrilocal residence
Pattern of residence after marriage in which the couple lives with or near the husband's relatives.

virilocal
Living with or near the husband's parents.

avunculocal residence
Patterns of residence after marriage in which the couple lives with or near the husband's mother's brother.

bilocal residence
Patterns of residence after marriage in which the couple alternates between living with the wife's kin and the husband's kin.

neolocal residence
Pattern of residence after marriage in which the couple establishes a new, independent household separate from their relatives.

Patrilocal residence refers to arrangements in which a married couple lives with or near the husband's family. Patrilocal residence usually occurs in societies that reckon descent patrilineally. Because children resulting from marriage belong to the father's lineage, patrilocal residence creates stable, interacting groups of patrilineally related men. Patrilocal households, therefore, consist of an elder couple, their sons, their sons' wives and children, and their unmarried daughters. Married daughters live with their husbands' relatives. This kind of residence pattern is also called **virilocal**—living with the husband's family.

Avunculocal Residence

In some societies with matrilineal descent and inheritance, an arrangement called **avunculocal residence** is preferred (from the Latin word *avunculus* meaning "mother's brother" and origin of the word *uncle*). In these cases, a married couple lives with the husband's mother's brother. Accordingly, the men rather than the women of the kin group live together. An especially important feature of this arrangement is that a man lives with the person who has authority over him and from whom he will inherit. Avunculocal residence is found in societies where inheritance follows matrilineal descent but wealth, property, and social status are held by men.

Bilocal and Neolocal Residence

In **bilocal residence**, married couples live alternately with the husband's and the wife's families. Bilocality has the advantage of flexibility, adapting residence to economic and resource conditions. When resources are scarce, couples can make adjustments by relocating from one household to another. Bilocal patterns also are adaptive in realigning living arrangements depending on the composition of households. That is, if households grow too large by the addition of in-marrying spouses and their children, then some people can leave and align themselves with their spouse's kin.

In societies with **neolocal residence**, a married couple establishes a new household independently of the residence of either the husband's or the wife's kin. Such systems typically are found in modern industrial and post-industrial societies where couples tend to form new households immediately after marriage or within a year or two. Neolocal residence has the feature of independence, another reflection of the loosening of kinship bonds advantageous in capitalist economies. Neolocal residence separates people from larger kinship groups, allowing them to ignore claims from relatives who might want to share their resources.

? *What residence rule is observed in your culture? Are there different historical patterns in residence that relate to people's cultures of origin?*

> **REVIEW**
>
> Residence rules tend to ensure that people belonging to the same kin group remain close to one another. Matrilocal patterns, in which the couple lives with or near the wife's parents, are common in matrilineal societies. Patrilocal patterns, in which the couple lives with or near the husband's parents, is common in patrilineal societies. In avunculocal residence the couple moves in with the husband's mother's brother. Bilocal residency allows for the couple to live with either the husband's or wife's family, depending on the resources available. Neolocal residency allows the couple to establish their own independent household.

WIDOWHOOD AND DIVORCE

All societies have strategies intended to preserve kin ties, marriage bonds, and household units. All cultures have patterns of beliefs and behaviours for dealing with widows and orphans, for example, and for regulating divorce and remarriage. These cultural patterns reveal the underlying principles of kinship, marriage, and family that are most important in a society. For example, the importance of family alliances is highlighted by marriage preference patterns that anthropologists refer to as "levirate" and "sororate."

Case study

Residence in Rural North India and among the Hopi

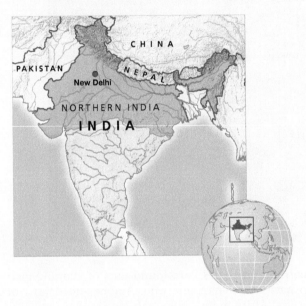

RURAL NORTH INDIA

Households in rural villages in North India were made up of large extended or joint families. Village economies centred on farming, although people living within a village had a variety of occupations. Descent followed patrilineal principles, that is, people belonged to the kinship group of their father. Marriages were arranged by parents. Men typically married when in their early twenties to young women in their teens. Girls may have been betrothed as young children. Post-marital residence was generally patrilocal. Residential groups, therefore, consisted of a couple, their sons and sons' families, and their unmarried daughters. Women moved to their husbands' homes upon marriage and subsequently had infrequent contact with their own kin. Because girls usually married shortly after puberty, they were often in their early teens when they left their parental homes. A wife who relocated at such a young age to her husband's household generally accepted her subordination, as it was based on age as well as on gender. She was thus easily dominated by her husband and especially by his mother. As many researchers of Indian culture have noted, wives often experienced their greatest difficulties at the hands of their mothers-in-law rather than of their husbands (Chitnis 1988).

Wives' domination by their mothers-in-law was due in part to the uncertain quality of relationships between spouses. Rarely were newlywed couples acquainted prior to marriage, and unions were arranged without consent from either the bride or the groom. Once married, couples actually had little interaction. The husband was himself a young man and lived under his father's authority. As a subordinate in his father's household, he took great care not to shift away from his first allegiance to his parents. Because wives were perceived as potentially destabilizing to established familial order, married sons refrained from showing too much affection or even concern for their wives, especially early in their married life. Couples rarely interacted publicly or had extended conversation when other family members were present. A wife thus spent most of her time in the company of other women in the household. These women, unmarried daughters and in-marrying wives, were all under the supervision of the elder woman. A new daughter-in-law was typically met with some degree of hostility by her husband's mother and sisters. As a result, authoritative statuses were immediately established and reinforced.

THE HOPI

The Hopi of the southwestern United States were organized into matrilineages with matrilocally focused households. Domestic groups were built upon a core line of women whose husbands regularly resided with them (Egan 1950:29). Women exercised a good deal of domestic authority, since they owned the houses, land, and the basic crops that support and feed their families. However, men were allowed to claim ownership of any livestock they raised. They also held important ritual and judicial offices within the settlement.

Matrilocality presented several quandaries for matrilineally related men. Several contexts required them to participate in the affairs of their families of origin. The disciplinary role in the household was allocated to mother's brothers rather than fathers, so frequent avuncular visits were required. Brothers regularly undertook joint economic projects. These necessary interactions among men in different households were enabled by the Hopi settlement pattern, which traditionally clustered the population into apartment-house-like "pueblos." These structures formed a continuous expanse of attached rooms, which could house up to a thousand inhabitants. Thus, although they may have lived in separate suites of rooms, the men of a single lineage were located close enough to each other to regularly meet on short notice to deal with common concerns.

The Hopi case raises a question of how matrilocality affects marriage possibilities. It quite clearly favours

village endogamy, since men cannot retain regular lineage contacts if they marry into different locality. It also discourages polygyny, as the possession of several wives would create a considerable problem of maintaining conjugal relations in several separate households. Accordingly, Hopi men were monogamous, although they did divorce and remarry quite frequently. Other matrilocal societies have found ways of allowing men to have more than one wife. Among the Bemba of central Africa, men reside matrilocally after their first marriage, but bring subsequent wives into their first partner's household. Among the Manangkabu of Indonesia, polygynous husbands, who are often itinerate traders, circulate among their wives' households.

The Levirate and Sororate

In the levirate and sororate marriage patterns, if a spouse dies, the deceased's family of origin supplies a younger sibling to marry the surviving spouse. So, for example, in the **levirate**, if a husband dies, his (usually younger) brother will marry the surviving widow. In the **sororate**, a man will marry his wife's sister, in some cases during his wife's lifetime and in others after her death. On some occasions a sororate marriage will be arranged if a man's wife cannot bear children. These kinds of marriages symbolically stress family alliances, because they say in effect that once two families are joined through marriage, it is in their interest to maintain the established alliance. Because the death of a husband or wife potentially disrupts the bond between families, a sibling of the deceased spouse perpetuates the alliance by marrying the survivor. The "ghost marriage" of the Nuer is a type of levirate, since a younger brother marries the widow of his elder brother. It differs from the more common pattern only in that children of the subsequent union are considered the offspring of the dead brother.

levirate
Marriage preference rule in which a widow marries her deceased husband's brother.

sororate
Marriage between a widower and his deceased wife's sister.

Divorce

Societies vary in their views about the dissolution of marriages. In some societies, divorce is a common outcome of an unhappy union, whereas in others, it rarely occurs because of social or religious restrictions. In some societies, either husband or wife may seek divorce; in others, only one of the parties (usually the husband) may initiate a breakup of the marriage. The ways in which marriages are dissolved also vary across cultures.

In general, matrilineal societies have more lenient attitudes toward divorce than do patrilineal societies because of the differences in principles of descent and the resulting claims that kinship groups have over children. It is nearly universal (although there are exceptions) that young children continue to live with their mothers after a divorce. Because children belong to the kin group of their mother in matrilineal societies, divorce does not cause a contradiction between location and kinship. In contrast, the dissolution of a marriage in patrilineal societies causes a problem, because it is through marriage that patrilineal descent groups are able to make claims over children produced by the wives of their male members. In addition, patrilineal societies generally exert more control over women's sexual behaviour than do matrilineal societies, because they need to establish paternity to ensure a child's legitimate place in the father's kinship group.

Small-scale foraging and horticultural societies most often have flexible attitudes toward divorce, regardless of the type of descent system in their culture. In Native North America, for example, with few exceptions, either husband or wife could initiate a breakup of their marriage. Divorce was fairly common, especially in the early years of a marriage and especially if the couple had no children. Acceptable grounds for divorce included adultery, failure to provide or fulfill domestic obligations, or simply personal incompatibility. Few societies had formal procedures for divorce. Rather, the couple would separate, each returning to his or her natal family, or the in-marrying spouse would leave. A divorce could be the result of a joint decision by husband and wife, or it could be initiated by one or the other.

In some Native North American societies, a person could signal his or her wish for a divorce in a publicly recognized way. For example, among both the Mohawk and the Diné, two matrilineal, matrilocal societies, if a woman wanted a divorce, she might remove her husband's personal belongings from the house when he was away and place them outside. When the husband returned, he would collect his belongings and go back to the home of his mother or sister. If the husband initiated the divorce, he would simply take his possessions and leave. No social stigma was attached to either husband or wife after a divorce.

In Saudi culture, children belong to the father, his patrilineage, and his patriclan. He automatically would retain custody of them in the event of divorce, which, until recently, was a prerogative only of men. Saudi society and certain sects of the religion of Islam reinforce the relative confinement of women and strict regulation of their sexual and social behaviour.

Among the Lakota and some other peoples of the Great Plains, a divorce could be jointly agreed upon by both parties. However, a man had a public way of signalling his wishes to end their marriage that was not available to a woman. He would beat a drum at a warrior society dance and proclaim that he wished to "throw away [his] wife" (Hassrick 1964:130). Through this strategy, a man not only ended his marriage but publicly humiliated his wife as well. Although men did not suffer social criticism if their marriages ended, divorced women were shamed.

There are economic deterrents to divorce. For example, exchanges of bridewealth tend to lessen rates of divorce. The husband's kinship group does not favour divorce because a couple's children, although belonging to the husband's kin group in patrilineal societies, usually stay with their mother and therefore leave the husband's household if divorce occurs. A wife's family may also be reluctant to sanction a divorce because when couples break up, the wife's kin must return the goods that they received as bridewealth. Therefore, they may pressure an unhappy wife to remain with her husband. Conflicts over bridewealth and its return in cases of divorce may result not only in the end of family alliances but lead to interfamilial tension and conflict.

In extreme patriarchal societies, such as in some villages in India, in pre-revolutionary China, and in many Middle Eastern nations, women rarely have the right to divorce, whereas men are free to break up their marriages, usually on grounds of their wives' disobedience, laziness, or adultery. In some societies, a woman's failure to produce sons might also be a cause for divorce. In such cases, great social criticism is heaped on a divorced woman and on her family as well, although little if any criticism is levelled at the husband.

Case study

Marriage and Divorce among the Kpelle of Liberia

Marriage patterns among the Kpelle, a farming society of Liberia, provide several options of payment and service that lead to differences in the strength of bonds between couples and the rights that a man exercises over children born of the union (Gibbs 1965). The ideal form of marriage involves transfer of bridewealth from a husband's kin group to that of his wife. This is the standard type of union. It permits a husband and his lineage to claim children produced by the marriage. A second form involves performance of brideservice rather than payment of bridewealth. In this type of marriage, a couple resides with the wife's family for a fixed period of time agreed upon by the parties concerned. During this period, the husband performs labour for his in-laws. Children born to the couple during the years of service belong to the wife's lineage rather than to the husband's. Once the period of brideservice is completed, the children become members of the father's patrilineage.

A third marital option is "male concubinage." In this option, the status of the couple is somewhat ambiguous. It involves an economic and sexual union between a poor man and one of the wives of a chief or wealthy man. Although the woman remains the legal wife of the patron, her relationship with the client is publicly recognized and sanctioned. Such a marriage provides benefits for two kinds of men. A poor man who would otherwise have few marital prospects can marry and ally himself with the wealthy person, and a wealthy man who is either already a chief or wishes to become one can gain a client in a dependent relationship. The client's dependence is turned into political support for the patron. Since the client and patron's wife farm land controlled by the patron, the latter obtains products of their labour that he can sell for cash income or can distribute to others and thereby gain their support as well. Finally, since the woman remains the legal wife of the patron, children born to the client couple belong to the patron's lineage rather than to that of their biological father.

Kpelle marriages, then, are basically differentiated in terms of the legal status of women and the rights that husbands and their lineages may claim over a woman's children. If a woman is a full legal wife, that is, in standard marriages with payment of bridewealth, her children belong to her husband's patrilineage. If a woman's legal status is in transition, as during the period of brideservice, her children belong to her patrilineage and cannot be claimed by her husband. And if the woman is the legal wife of a patron even though she lives with another man, her children belong to the patron.

Although marriage is the usual and preferred state for adults, rates of divorce are reported to be "moderately high" (Gibbs 1965). Divorces are granted by formal courts under the jurisdiction of local chiefs. Proceedings involve public hearings to determine the party at fault. Women usually initiate divorce, in part because fixing of blame is most often placed on the initiator and men are reluctant to be publicly criticized for ending their marriages. Even though women are characteristically blamed for failed marriages, their request for divorce is usually granted. A man who wishes a divorce may mistreat his wife so that she will seek a formal divorce in court. In this manipulative manner, he obtains his objective but is not publicly faulted.

Kpelle divorce benefits both wife and husband in an unhappy marriage. A wife who seeks to divorce is given her freedom and thus is personally satisfied. A husband, whether or not he wants to be divorced, retains two prerogatives: He receives the return of bridewealth that he had given to his wife's kin when he married, and he retains rights as father to his children. Such rights significantly include the privilege of receiving bridewealth for his daughters when they marry.

In some cultures, religious beliefs are used to strongly condemn and even outlaw divorce. Today, Roman Catholicism, Islam, and Orthodox Judaism place barriers to the breakup of marriages. In these belief systems, because a marriage was sanctified in the wedding ceremony, people have no right to dissolve the union. In strict Islamic and Orthodox Jewish communities, it is very difficult for women to initiate divorce, but men may seek divorce in religious councils if they cite acceptable grounds.

REVIEW

The levirate and the sororate marriage patterns maintain alliances between families after the death of a spouse. Marriage is not only a relationship but an economic obligation to the other party. Divorce is viewed, and occurs, differently across societies. Patrilineal societies generally have stricter rules concerning divorce than do matrilineal societies.

Chapter Summary

Defining Marriage and Family

- Families serve economic and social functions. Members of families usually reside together and provide for biological reproduction and for the training and enculturation of children. Families provide people with companionship, emotional support, and assistance, and are the basic unit of economic cooperation and interdependence. Families, particularly households, work together to complete the daily tasks necessary for survival. They are also decision-making groups. Members consult together and make decisions regarding joint actions. In many societies, families perform religious functions, planning and carrying out rituals that celebrate significant events in members' lives.

- Marriage is the most common way in which families are formed. Marriage is a socially recognized, enduring, stable bond between people who each have certain rights and obligations with respect to one another. Husbands and wives can expect to have an exclusive sexual relationship and assist one another in the raising of children and in the provisioning of their household. Through the marriage bond, men are able to claim "social fatherhood" by establishing themselves as the husband of the mother.

Families and Ideal Types

- Although the family is a universal cultural construct, the types of families found in different kinds of societies vary. Nuclear families consist of parents and their children, whereas extended families consist of a larger number of relatives, usually representing at least three generations. Nuclear families are often found in modern industrial societies, which stress economic independence and promote the loosening of wider kinship bonds. They are also found in many foraging societies because they are

adaptive to survival in conditions of resource scarcity. In the context of insufficient resources, nuclear families can splinter off and disperse into a large territory.

- Extended families are more common in farming and pastoral societies. They have the advantage of perpetuating the social unit, sharing resources and work, and providing emotional support and material aid. Members of extended families can rely on each other for help in their work, in childcare, and in support in times of crisis or conflict with other groups.

- Family types are responsive to changes in productive modes and general social values. In the United States and Canada, as well as in many countries throughout the world, the idealized model of husband, wife, and children has declined in frequency throughout the twentieth century. Many households consist of single parents and their children, others consist of unmarried couples, and still others consist of stable unions between same-sex partners. Numbers of children per household have declined throughout the century.

Endogamy, Exogamy, and the Incest Taboo

- The incest taboo universally forbids marriage between parents and their children and between siblings. In some societies, the incest taboo is extended to include other relatives as well. For example, marriage may be forbidden between cousins or between aunts/uncles and their nieces/nephews.

- Anthropologists and other researchers have offered various explanations about the origin of the incest taboo. Suggested theories include an instinctual revulsion and aversion toward sexual relations within the nuclear family, the biological consequences of inbreeding that may increase frequencies of undesirable physical and mental traits, a reduction in the fitness of a population through genetic homogeneity, a response to the need to diminish sexual competition within the nuclear family unit, and a means of forcing people to make alliances with others in order to survive.

Forms of Marriage

- Societies differ in the expected or permissible number of spouses that a person can have at any one time. Marriage between one man and one woman is called monogamy; marriage between more than two people is called polygamy. There are two kinds of polygamous marriages: Polygyny is the marriage between one man and two or more women, and polyandry is the marriage between one woman and two or more men.

Marriage as Alliance and Economic Exchange

- Marriage often involves an economic exchange either preceding, during, or following the wedding ceremony. The term *bridewealth* refers to a gift given by the husband or his family to that of his intended wife. Bridewealth is most often given in patrilineal, patrilocal societies as a symbolic compensation to the woman's family for the loss of her economic labour. Instead of or sometimes in addition to a gift, a husband may be required to perform services for his wife's parents, a custom called *brideservice*. He may hunt for them, construct their homes, fetch wood or water, or fulfill other household tasks. Finally, in some societies, economic goods or wealth are given by the bride's family to the new couple or to the husband's kin prior to or upon the marriage. Such gifts are called *dowry*.

Marriage as a Rite of Passage

- Marriages may be arranged by parents or by the couple themselves through courtship. The marriage ceremony publicly sanctions marriage and symbolizes the rights and duties of couples to each other and to their families after marriage.

Patterns of Residence after Marriage

- Societies tend to have preferences for where couples reside after they marry. In some societies, a couple resides with or near the husband's relatives (patrilocal residence) and in others, a couple resides with or near the wife's kin (matrilocal residence). Bilocal residence refers to living arrangements where married couples live alternately with the husband's and the wife's families. In some societies with matrilineal descent and inheritance, a couple may live with the husband's mother's brother (avunculocal residence). Finally, some societies prefer neolocal residence, in which couples establish a new household of their own, separate from either group of kin, and this is the most common pattern in Canadian society.

Widowhood and Divorce

- In some societies, the emphasis on marriage as an alliance between families is highlighted by marriage preference patterns called levirate and sororate. In these marriage patterns, if one spouse dies, the deceased's family of origin supplies a younger sibling to marry the surviving spouse. In the levirate, a deceased husband's brother (usually younger) marries the surviving widow; in the sororate, a younger sister of the deceased wife marries the surviving widower.

Key Terms

Review Questions

1. What definition of marriage would cover all the marriage types discussed in this chapter?
2. How is subsistence related to family forms? How can changes in marriage and family reflect adaptations to changes in subsistence?

3. How do endogamy and exogamy affect a society's social organization?
4. What are some hypotheses about the origins of the incest taboo?

5. What are the benefits of polygamous marriages? What are the drawbacks?

6. What are common forms of political and economic exchange in marriage, and what types of kinships are associated with those forms?

7. How are postmarital residence patterns related to kinship? How are residence rules related to women's and men's status in a society?

8. What are some reasons that marriages are arranged? Why is divorce discouraged in arranged marriages?

9. How are levirate and sororate different? Why do societies have these practices?

CHAPTER 9

Preview

1. **What is the difference between sex and gender?**
2. **How do gender roles and gender relations vary cross-culturally?**
3. **How does subsistence strategy relate to gender roles and relationships?**
4. **How do gender constraints relate to a culture's ideological system?**
5. **What are some outcomes of male dominance or of gender equality for a society?**
6. **What global factors affect women's participation in the work force?**
7. **How have ideologies affected gender constructs in the industrial and postindustrial eras?**

A man and a woman were once making a hard journey through the bush. The woman had her baby strapped upon her back as she walked along the rough path overgrown with vines and shrubbery. They had nothing to eat with them, and as they travelled on they became very hungry.

Suddenly, emerging from the heavily wooded forest into a grassy plain, they came upon a herd of bush cows grazing quietly.

The man said to the woman, "You have the power of transforming yourself into whatever you like; change now to a leopard and capture one of the bush cows, that I may have something to eat and not perish." The woman looked at the man significantly, and said, "Do you really mean what you ask, or are you joking?" "I mean it," said the man, for he was very hungry.

The woman untied the baby from her back, and put it upon the ground. Hair began growing upon her neck and body. She dropped her loincloth; a change came over her face. Her hands and feet turned into claws. And, in a few moments, a wild leopard was standing before the man, staring at him with fiery eyes. The poor man was frightened nearly to death and clambered up a tree for protection. When he was nearly to the top, he saw that the poor little baby was almost within the leopard's jaws, but he was so afraid, that he couldn't make himself come down to rescue it.

When the leopard saw that she already had the man good and frightened, and full of terror, she ran away to the flock of cattle to do for him as he had asked her to. Capturing a large young heifer, she dragged it back to the foot of the tree. The man, who was still as far up in its top as he could go, cried out, and piteously begged the leopard to transform herself back into a woman.

Slowly, the hair receded, and the claws disappeared, until finally, the woman stood before the man once more. But so frightened was he still, that he would not come down until he saw her take up her clothes and tie her baby to her back. Then she said to him, "Never ask a woman to do a man's work again."

From *African Folktales* by Roger D. Abrahams, pp. 148–149. Copyright © 1983 by Roger D. Abrahams. Used by permission of Pantheon Books, a division of Random House, Inc.

This narrative of the leopard woman from Liberia transmits attitudes about the proper work of women and men. Women perform the tasks of farming and fishing, and men are responsible for hunting. But the story also tells of the dangers of violating social norms about gender. These are powerful lessons, meant to instruct through example, drama, and humour. This chapter explores the cross-cultural study of gender and gender relations, about which every human society has something to say. People's norms for gender behaviour vary widely, yet common patterns exist. These patterns of thought and behaviour relate in part to the way people make their living and the ideologies that support those ways.

gender
The roles that people perform in their households and communities and the values and attitudes that people have regarding men and women.

sex
Biological differences between males and females.

gender construct (gender model)
The set of cultural assumptions about gender roles and values and the relations between the genders that people learn as members of their societies.

cultural constructs
Models of behaviour and attitudes that a particular culture transmits to its members.

SEX AND GENDER

As anthropologists use the word, **gender** refers to the roles that people perform in their households and communities and the values and attitudes that they have regarding men and women. Thus, gender is a cultural category. It is not the same as **sex**, which is a biological category. That is, females and males are born, but women and men are products of their culture's definitions of how females and males should act.

The term *gender identity* refers to how people internalize and enact those attitudes and expectations that are associated with their gender category. Gender identity is conveyed, for example, by the way people dress, walk, and speak, and it is shown by the kinds of activities that people engage in and the attitudes they have about themselves and others. The term **gender construct** (**gender model**) refers to the set of cultural assumptions about gender roles and values and the relations between the genders that people learn as members of their societies. Unlike sex, gender is in every way "culturally constructed."

People in every culture maintain and transmit ideas about the roles that are appropriate for women and men to fill, the rights they have in relation to each other, and the values associated with their activities. These gender constructs are based in part on biological differences between males and females, but they are culturally conditioned and vary widely across cultures. For example, in many societies, women's activities are constrained by the reproductive role that is exclusive to them. However, restrictions and taboos related to childbearing are often exaggerated and ignore the fact that periods of pregnancy and breast feeding are only temporary.

The Cultural Construction of Gender Identity

Gender as a social or cultural construct is a primary aspect of one's personal and social identity. It develops in earliest socialization through the ways that a baby is handled, treated, and spoken to. **Cultural constructs** are models of behaviour and attitudes that a particular culture transmits to its members. These constructs are shared beliefs and values that become taken for granted as guiding principles. Childhood learning teaches appropriate behaviour and molds personality to conform to cultural norms. Girls and boys learn skills and attitudes that make them functioning members of their community.

Ideological messages about women's and men's places in their families and communities and about their social value may be conveyed through religious beliefs and practices, language, and daily interactions between men and women in their families, communities, and wider social arenas. Rights to make decisions, to speak, and to participate in particular activities reflect cultural valuations and privileges allocated to people.

One universal expression of gender identity is the signalling of gender differences by bodily adornments and comportment. For example, men and women generally wear different kinds of clothing or jewellery. They may fashion their hair in different styles or use body decorations such as tattoos or makeup. In North America and Europe, pants were not considered appropriate attire for women until the middle of the twentieth century; even so, styles, colours, and designs used for women's clothing still differ from those commonly used for men. However, while it may be acceptable for women to wear garments styled like men's pants and shirts, it is not considered appropriate for men to wear dresses or skirts. Until 1995, cross-dressing to

Gender identity in conservative Islamic societies is both unambiguous and complex. This veiled figure is easily recognized as a woman in Saudi Arabia. According to many women, wearing the veil is a privilege of becoming a marriageable adult and represents a woman's responsibility to her family, whose identity and social standing depend upon the morally correct behaviour of all its members.

look and act like someone of the opposite gender was officially listed as a mental illness.

Other kinds of gender-differentiating behaviour are subtler and less conscious but just as powerful. Social presentation includes dynamics of walking, sitting, and general body posture. As we have discussed in Chapter 3, speech styles employed by women or men are also often distinct. Nonverbal communication, such as gestures, smiling, eye contact, and touch, may be differentially employed.

Gender and Sexuality

Although we commonly think of our sexual feelings and practices as part of our nature, they, too, are shaped by our culture. Our culture teaches us what kinds of sexual feelings and practices are "normal" or "natural" and what kinds are "deviant." We learn who are suitable sexual partners, when and where sexual relations are appropriate, and the proper ways to engage in sex. With few exceptions, these expectations are culturally constructed.

As discussed in Chapter 8, all societies institute some form of the incest taboo that bans sex between members of the nuclear family and between certain other relatives. Many societies also set an appropriate age to begin sexual relations. In Canada, for example, it is illegal for an adult to have sex with someone younger than fourteen, a crime called statutory rape. Our society also has gender-based attitudes about the relative ages of men and women engaging in consensual sex. In many "normal" couples, a man may be fifteen or twenty years older than the woman, but it is rare to hear of a couple in which a woman is significantly older than the man. One reason may have to do with reproductive potential; that is, an old man can still have children with a young woman, but a young man cannot have children with a much older woman. Nevertheless, negative attitudes about men who choose much older women reveal cultural values about both sexuality and gender.

Another cultural element in attitudes about sexuality is the accepted relationship between sex and marriage. In Canadian society, public discourse regards sex between unmarried people as inappropriate or less appropriate than sex between a husband and wife. Actual practice regularly contradicts moral ideals, but the fact that political and religious leaders are reluctant to condone sex outside of marriage indicates the strength of underlying cultural constructs.

In contrast, many other societies consider it normal and natural for unmarried people to engage in sex. In some societies, proving one's ability to conceive is a prerequisite for marriage. While no society encourages extramarital sexual activities, the punishment for adulterers varies widely and is not severe everywhere. In addition, patriarchal societies often have a double standard about these issues: Men are permitted and even encouraged to have premarital sexual experiences, while women are taught to remain chaste before marriage. In some patrilineal societies, a woman's virginity is a prerequisite for marriage, and a woman who has committed adultery will be more severely punished that a man will. In some Islamic countries, adultery is a capital offense for both partners. In others, only the woman is singled out for punishment. In 2003, for example, a divorced Nigerian woman, Amina Lawal, was condemned to death by stoning by an Islamic court for bearing a child out of wedlock; the man, who denied he was the father, received no punishment. However, an appeals court acquitted and released Lawal later that year, in large part because of international pressure.

The complementarity and interdependence of genders are represented in this ancient symbol of yin (femaleness) and yang (maleness). This symbol, based on astrological observations of the changing solstices, comes from the Han period (207 BCE–9 CE). The light area represents the greater sunlight of the summer solstice, which is associated with maleness; the dark area represents the greater moonlight of the winter solstice, associated with femaleness. The small circles within the arcs of colour show the mutual interdependence of yin and yang, as each is "born" within the other.

berdaches
Male Two-Spirits in some Native North American societies who adopted some of the economic and social roles of women.

Two-Spirits
In Native North American societies, males who adopted some of the social and economic roles of women, and females who adopted some of the social and economic roles of men.

? *Why do you think that third gender roles such as the* hijras *exist?*

Gender and Homosexuality

Attitudes about homosexuality are a further reflection of cultural learning. Judeo-Christian-Islamic teachings convey negative messages about homosexuality, considering it to be a violation of natural law. Many nations dominated politically by religious thinking have laws that criminalize homosexual conduct and institute policies that discriminate against homosexuals. In Canada, sexual relations between members of the same sex were illegal and punishable by imprisonment until 1969. Federal legislation since then has progressively removed other restrictions on gays and lesbians and granted them full marital rights in 2006. In the United States, homosexuality was not decriminalized until 2003 and most states still do not permit same sex-marriages. Massachusetts became the first state to legalize same-sex marriage in 2004.

Anti-homosexual attitudes are far from universal. In India, for example, Hindu belief regards homosexuality as one of the possible expressions of human desire. Hindu mystic stories portray both heterosexual and homosexual experience as natural and joyful. In addition, the pantheon of Hindu deities includes some who are sexually ambiguous, combining aspects of maleness and femaleness, or who transform themselves from one gender into the other. Finally, some Indian male homosexuals and transvestites adopt the role of *hijras*, people thought of as "neither man nor woman" (Nanda 1990). Although *hijras* are sometimes feared and ridiculed, they also are considered sacred, combining and mediating between female and male aspects believed to exist in all humans.

As another example, the Etoro and several other horticultural societies in New Guinea insist on male homosexual activity to ensure a man's physical growth as well as to enhance his physical and spiritual strength. According to Etoro beliefs, people have a kind of spirit essence called *hame* that is needed to develop and maintain one's energy and vitality. At birth, only a small amount of *hame* is placed in a child, not enough to protect it for a long, healthy life. So, as people mature, they must try to augment their store of *hame* or life force. They must also protect it from potential sources of depletion, and one of the major causes of depletion is heterosexual intercourse. Men protect themselves from depleting their *hame* by avoiding sexual intercourse with women during periods associated with farming and trading cycles, estimated by anthropologist Raymond Kelly (1976) to be between 205 and 260 days per year. Protection against depletion is not enough, however, because the Etoro also believe that boys lack semen, which contains *hame*. Youths can acquire *hame* only by receiving semen from adult men. Boys orally consume a man's semen after manipulating his penis to the point of ejaculation.

In contrast to men, women are thought (at least by men) to have a limited amount of *hame*, thus explaining their relative weakness compared to men. Women's beliefs about *hame* were not collected by Kelly, however, because "a male anthropologist cannot develop an informant relationship with a female" (p. 47). Although Etoro men claimed that "only the women know what the women do," they believe that women engage in some form of homosexual activity through which adult women may transmit menstrual blood to young girls to initiate their reproductive capacity.

REVIEW

Gender, cultural constructs that refer to the roles people perform in their households and communities, differs from sex, which is a biological category. Gender identity is expressed in clothing, makeup, personal names, speech, nonverbal communication, economic roles, and the way people are enculturated into appropriate behaviours for men and women. Attitudes and practices concerning homosexual and heterosexual sexual behaviour are also culturally constructed. Gender constructs also include third gender roles, such as Two-Spirits and berdaches, people who are biologically male or female but take on the cultural and economic roles of the opposite gender.

Case study

Two-Spirits: A Third Gender

Although the division of humans into two gender categories is the most common cultural pattern, other possibilities exist. For example, many native cultures in North America recognized a third gender category. The concept of a third gender was based on separating the social being (the gender category) from the biological body (the facts of sex). The third gender was a social concept that included biological males and females who assumed social roles other than (or sometimes in addition to) the roles usually associated with their sex. This third gender was a distinct gender category, different from woman and man. Western observers formerly misused the term **berdaches** to refer to third-gender individuals in a derogatory way.

According to documentary evidence reviewed by Charles Callender and Lee Kochems (1983), 113 Native North American societies provided a third gender status as a possibility for their members. Lack of mention of third genders, now often called **Two-Spirits**, in other cultures does not necessarily mean that they were absent. Rather, their existence may not have been noted by Euro-American observers. In any case, third genders were well established in most regions of North America, especially in the west, from the Great Lakes to California. Callender and Kochems find no correlation between types of social or economic systems and the use of third genders, except that Two-Spirits were least likely to be found in societies that relied heavily on hunting.

People became Two-Spirits as a result of personal inclination, spiritual calling, or parental selection. From an early age a young girl or boy might take an interest in the occupations and demeanors usually displayed by members of the other gender. Parents thereafter trained the child in the subsistence skills appropriate to his or her chosen role. Among some groups, parents who had no sons might choose one of their daughters to learn hunting skills so that she could contribute directly to household subsistence as a son would.

A second, more common mode of recruitment was to receive a spiritual calling through a vision or dream. Dreaming to assume the third gender gave both spiritual and social validation to a male's or female's gender transformation. Two-Spirits who came to their status through a spiritual calling were often thought to have extraordinary powers to heal and to foretell the future.

A Two-Spirit's social role was formally validated with rituals that publicly marked his or her special status. Among the Kaska of Yukon Territory, when a female Two-Spirit reached the age of five, her parents tied a bear's dried ovaries to her belt to protect her from becoming pregnant. At puberty, female Two-Spirits of the Cocopa had their noses pierced like men rather than tattoos on their chins like women. Among the Mohave, when a male Two-Spirit was about ten years old, he participated in a public ceremony in which he was led into a circle surrounded by an audience and a singer. When the singer sang initiation songs, the Two-Spirit danced as women did and was proclaimed an *aylha* (Two-Spirit) after the fourth dance. He/she was then ritually bathed, given a woman's skirt, and announced a new woman's name for him/herself.

Two-Spirits typically performed economic duties usually appropriate to the opposite gender, sometimes in addition to those associated with their own biological sex. Female Two-Spirits were hunters, trappers, and occasionally warriors as well. Male Two-Spirits contributed their labour as farmers (where economies included horticulture) and were trained in domestic skills, such as sewing, embroidery, and food preparation.

Where warfare was a significant activity, male Two-Spirits generally did not participate. However, in some societies, male Two-Spirits did join war parties, either as active fighters or as carriers of supplies. Among the Cheyenne, male Two-Spirits accompanied war expeditions, serving critical religious functions as healers of the wounded and guardians of scalps obtained in battle. They also had charge of the Scalp Dances that followed victorious raids. Although female Two-Spirits did not always participate as warriors, they were not

George Catlin made this drawing in the 1800s during an expedition among the Sac and Fox Indians. It shows warriors dancing to a male Two-Spirit. According to the observer, while the warriors are making fun of the Two-Spirit, who appears in women's attire, they are also competing to attract his/her attention, which is seen as a sign of good fortune. (Smithsonian American Art Museum, Washington, DC/Art Resource, NY).

barred from doing so, and some became famous for their military and tactical skills.

Two-Spirits are often described in the literature as unusually prosperous in comparison with other members of their community. They had economic advantages due to their ability to perform both women's and men's work. In some societies, Two-Spirits had sources of income not available to any other people because they performed ritual functions specifically assigned to them. For example, Lakota Two-Spirits bestowed secret, spiritually powerful names on children, receiving horses in payment for their services. In several California groups, Two-Spirits were responsible for burial and mourning rituals. And in societies such as the Diné, Cheyenne, and Omaha, they functioned as go-betweens between men and women by resolving conflicts between spouses or arranging liaisons and marriages, usually receiving payment for their services (Williams 1986:70–71).

One of the consistent features of third-gender tradition was that members wore clothing and hairstyles associated with their chosen social role rather than with their biological sex. The significance of this pattern is that it demonstrates that gender distinctions are given symbolic as well as practical value. In a literal as well as figurative sense, people wear the markings of the gender with which they are associated. In some cultures, Two-Spirits who performed both men's and women's occupations changed their clothing to reflect the gender identity of the work. For instance, Western Mono Two-Spirits wore men's clothing when hunting and women's dress when gathering, and male Osage and Miami Two-Spirits wore men's clothing when they joined war expeditions but dressed like women when

they returned home. Deceased male Zuni Two-Spirits were buried in women's dress and men's trousers (Williams 1986:454).

The social and sexual lives of Two-Spirits were consistent with their gender roles. Sexual activity and marriage usually involved relationships with members of the opposite social gender. That is, female Two-Spirits had sexual relations with and might marry women, and male Two-Spirits had sexual relations with and might marry men. Two-Spirits often were highly desired as mates because of their economic prosperity and productive skills and their spiritual knowledge and abilities. According to recorded accounts, they had little difficulty marrying and establishing successful households. The wives of female Two-Spirits sometimes had children fathered by men but claimed by the Two-Spirit husband in an expression of social fatherhood. In some societies, Two-Spirits might marry either men or women. Significantly, Two-Spirits never married other Two-Spirits, because two people with the same social gender could not marry.

Native North Americans did not view sexual relations between Two-Spirits and their mates as either homosexual or heterosexual because Two-Spirits were not men or women. They were a distinct third gender. Symbolic transformation made gender, not biological sex, the important factor. Two-Spirits' sexual activity, like all their behaviour, was seen as private and specific to them as members of a distinct third gender. In Aboriginal worldviews, this privacy was extended to all sexual activity, including homosexuality and heterosexuality.

Gender equality is a prerequisite for the respect and high status most often conferred on Two-Spirits, because it meant that neither males nor females gave up or acquired social prestige by abandoning roles usually associated with their sex and instead assuming other roles. Euro-American observers did not understand this underlying gender equality, however. They could not understand why males chose not to identify as men, interpreting this choice as a voluntary decline in status. In contrast to Euro-American values, in most Native North American societies males did not give up dominance by abandoning men's roles because men's roles did not include rights to dominate. Most examples of men's dominance over women occurred in Aboriginal societies that had already been transformed by contact with European and North American traders, officials, and missionaries.

By the late nineteenth and early twentieth centuries, the number of Two-Spirits had declined due to voluntary or forced adoption of Euro-American attitudes and practices. These insisted on only a two-category system of gender, denigrated males who dressed like women or assumed women's roles, and proclaimed homosexuality to be a violation of natural and divine laws. Agents of the Canadian and American governments who supervised native reserves with varying success tried to force male Two-Spirits to wear men's clothing and short hair. In the words of a Lakota religious leader speaking of events that occurred in the 1920s:

> When the people began to be influenced by the missions and the boarding schools, a lot of them forgot the traditional ways and the traditional medicine.

Then they began to look down on the winkte, Two-Spirits, and lose respect. Some changed their ways and put on men's clothing. But others, rather than change, went out and hanged themselves. (quoted in Williams, 1986:182)

Female Two-Spirits also were forced to abandon their social and sacred roles. Despite decades of concerted social and ideological pressures, however, Two-Spirits continue to exist in some Native American societies.

GENDER ROLES AND RELATIONS

In all societies, certain behaviours and activities are deemed appropriate for women and others for men, with some overlap for both genders. Constellations of behaviours that are culturally associated with each gender are referred to as **gender roles**. Gender roles include the kind of work typically assigned to men and women, the familial roles that people play, the positions of leadership at home or in the community, and the ritual practices in which they engage. In some societies, women's and men's roles may be quite distinct with little overlap, whereas in others, gender roles may be flexible.

Men and women carry out their gender roles in relation to one another, interacting in their households and their communities in nearly every aspect of life. Even in activities in which women and men are separated from each other, same-gender groups usually act in a way that is mindful of the other group. Coming-of-age rituals for girls and boys, for example, may be organized around gender differences.

Gender relations consist of interactions between men and women, which may reflect differences in the relative status, prestige, and power. In some societies, gender equality generally prevails. Women and men are thought of as equal, having the same rights to respect, autonomy, and independence. Although men and women may have different roles in their households and communities, their work and activities are equally valued and socially rewarded. In other societies, the genders are not considered equal, and some degree of male dominance prevails. Men are thought of as superior to women, as more capable, intelligent, or spiritually endowed. Men occupy more prestigious roles as leaders and decision makers. In their homes, men may have control over the activities of their wives. Extreme forms of male dominance may be reflected in physical abuse and rape. These behaviours tend to be more acceptable in strongly patriarchal societies, where men hold positions of authority and power to the exclusion of women. As mentioned in Chapter 7, there are no known examples of matriarchal societies in which women have exclusive power.

gender roles
Constellations of rights, duties, attitudes, and behaviours that are culturally associated with each gender.

gender relations
Norms of interaction between men and women, which may reflect differences in the relative status, prestige, and power of women and men.

Division of Labour by Gender

As you read in Chapters 5 and 6, in all societies some form of division of labour by gender influences the range of daily work that an individual carries out. Men's and women's work is often complementary, both contributing to the maintenance of their households by providing food, shelter, clothing, and necessary equipment. There is a great deal of cross-cultural variation in the allocation of work according to gender, but certain patterns tend to be found in most societies. Table 9.1 summarizes some of these frequent associations between tasks and gender.

Inferences about division of labour by gender can be made from data concerning nonhuman primate behaviour and traditional foraging societies whose cultural patterns are well documented. Such data led Lila Leibowitz to postulate that a division of labour was not necessary when human ancestors engaged in "unspecified and undifferentiated" production (1983:123). Our early hominid ancestors, like modern nonhuman primates (chimpanzees, gorillas), spent their days in the same pursuits. They moved from one resource site to another, gathered and ate fruits and plants, and socialized together. Male and female tasks were not differentiated except for childbearing,

Table 9.1 TASKS AND GENDER

Tasks Usually Performed by Women	Tasks Usually Performed by Men
Gathering plants, seeds, fruits, nuts	Hunting animals
Caring for children	Fishing as a primary responsibility
Caring for the sick and elderly	Herding large animals
Keeping up dwellings	Clearing fields for planting
Making clothing	Conducting warfare
	Conducting long-distance trade

Variable Gender Assignment or Cooperative Tasks

Hunting small animals	Making crafts: pottery, basketry, tools
Fishing as a secondary resource	House building
Herding small animals	Conducting local trade
Planting/harvesting crops	

nursing, and caring for the young, all obviously female responsibilities. However, at some point in our ancestral past, a division of labour developed when people began to engage in more specialized economic techniques, requiring more complex skills and learning. A division of labour was efficient because it allowed different people to learn different sets of skills, enabling them to specialize, refine, and deepen their knowledge and proficiency.

A division of labour based on gender helped coordinate a group's activities, since women were restricted in their mobility because of their reproductive roles. Unlike other mammals whose young are able to walk and feed themselves fairly soon after birth, human infants remain dependent on adults for a protracted period of many years. As a consequence, caregivers are limited in their own activities. Pregnancy, child-bearing, and nursing limit women's ability to travel during significant periods of their lives. Travel becomes more burdensome and also more dangerous to a mother's and child's survival. In almost all cultures, women are allotted the care of infants and young children. Presumably as an extension of these duties, women generally perform other caretaker activities, such as preparing family meals and caring for the sick or disabled or aged individuals within the household.

In contemporary or recent foraging societies, women gather wild plants, fruits, and nuts and may also hunt small animals. In contrast, men are allotted economic roles that include travel away from home settlements, requiring a man's absence all day or over a period of days or longer. Hunting and trading with other groups are typically the work of men. Anthropologists extrapolate from these data to make assumptions about the lives of prehistoric peoples.

In addition to considerations of energy and mobility, foraging societies may assign home-based activities to women and external hunting and travelling to men because of the need to protect women against possibilities of accidents and deaths that might occur away from local settlements (Friedl 1975:135). Because the survival and continuity of a community depend on the successful reproductive life of women, protecting them from unnecessary danger is adaptive. At the same time, co-operative labour may include both men and women within a community. For example, communal hunting and farming might involve adults and youths of both genders.

Gender roles change as economic and material factors change. Although task divisions may have arisen because women and men have different reproductive functions and different energy and mobility requirements, when productive work is historically transformed and can be performed equally well by women or men, the adaptive basis of earlier division of labour by gender is lost. However, more than economic and material factors are involved. For example, in modern industrial societies, most jobs can be accomplished equally well by women or men, but many jobs are held predominantly by one gender or the other. Men or women equally could be brain surgeons or typists, but most brain surgeons are men and most typists are women. Therefore, we need to explain gender roles in non-economic terms as well.

One explanation is the social organization of households. Economic cooperation within families helps sustain them, because members perform different kinds of work that complement each other's tasks, becoming interdependent in providing basic necessities. Households are established and maintain stability on this basis, so the gender division of labour remains a convenient method of organizing domestic production even when it is no longer an economic necessity. Another explanation is that attitudes about work and its association with gender are part of the background ideologies that members of a society take for granted. These beliefs and attitudes are naturalized and thought of as human nature rather than understood as endowments of one's culture. Ideological processes, then, contribute to the maintenance of a gender division of labour, regardless of economic or other considerations.

What socioeconomic and sociocultural changes in Canada permitted the changes in gender roles that this photograph represents? What are some economic, structural, and ideological sources of changes in the gender division of labour in Canadian society?

One aspect of these ideologies is the evaluation of some work roles as inherently more attractive or fitting for men and others as inherently more appropriate and appealing to women. For example, women are thought to make good nurses because they have an innate desire to be nurturing. They are thought to make good elementary school teachers because they like to work with children, an extension of their motherly roles. Men, in contrast, are thought to make good leaders and heads of corporations because they are innately assertive and like to be in control. Nurturance and dominance, however, are learned behaviours. Nevertheless, positive judgments become associated with the proper performance of one's gender roles. People who resist assuming their culturally prescribed gender identities are negatively viewed.

Gender and Status

Gender roles are complicated by the fact that work and other tasks assigned to men and women may not be considered equivalent or equally valuable. In theory, gender relations may be characterized on a continuum from approximate equality to the complete domination of members of one gender by members of the other. In practice, whenever there is gender inequality, men are dominant.

Gender equality refers to a constellation of behaviours, attitudes, and rights that support the autonomy of both women and men. In a gender equal society, women and men may have different economic, social, and political roles but the rewards given to them are roughly similar. For example, in Mohawk communities, women did most of the farmwork and household tasks while men hunted, fished, and traded. Although their activities were distinct, their work and contributions to their households were equally valued. Both men and women could hold positions of prestige and influence in their communities. Gender equality is more likely to exist in foraging and small horticultural societies, where all individuals make important contributions to subsistence and where hierarchical leadership is absent or minimal.

In contrast, **gender inequality** refers to denial of autonomy and equal rights to one group of people based on their gender. Gender inequality tends to be most marked in large-scale societies with strong economic specialization, where social and political stratification affects the allocation of rights and privileges among social categories, including class and gender. In patriarchal societies, for example, in India, Pakistan, and many Middle Eastern countries, women generally do not occupy positions of authority and are restricted in many of their daily activities. In these and other male-dominated societies, men contribute most of the productive labour that supports their families. They make most of the important decisions that affect their families, and they serve their communities as political or religious leaders.

Cultural values and social rewards mold people's attitudes about themselves and their relations to others. In societies where **male dominance** is pervasive, men learn to

gender equality
A constellation of behaviours, attitudes, and rights that support the autonomy of both women and men.

gender inequality
The denial of autonomy and equal rights to one group of people based on their gender.

male dominance
A constellation of behaviours and attitudes that grant men access to roles of prestige and reward and deny the same to women.

Controversies

Is Male Dominance Universal?

Anthropologists long maintained that, in all societies, the status of women was at least to some extent subordinate to that of men (Friedl 1975:7; Rosaldo 1974:17). In other words, although women's status varied from society to society, in no society were they fully equal to or superior to men. But an important question remains: Are there (or were there) genuinely egalitarian societies? From the data, it seems that the answer to this question is yes, but this is a complex issue, for several reasons. One is that there has been a long history of Western male bias in reporting behaviour and beliefs in non-Western cultures (Leacock 1981:17; Rohrlich-Leavitt et al. 1975:110–111). Explorers, missionaries, soldiers, and travellers in early periods of European colonization of the Americas, Africa, Asia, and the Pacific were almost exclusively men, who interpreted the cultures of native peoples through their own ethnocentric worldviews.

Later observers, including anthropologists, economists, and historians, also were predominantly men. Notwithstanding their supposed objectivity, they brought with them, as all people do, biases and frames of reference dominant in their own cultures. They usually asked for the opinions of men, partly because it was difficult for a foreign man to interact with women, but also partly because male investigators considered men's opinions to be more significant than the opinions of women. It is well to be reminded of the admonition made by Joseph Lafitau, a French observer of Native American cultures, who commented in 1724 that "authors who have written on the customs of the Native Americans concerning the rights and status of women have formed their conceptions, in this as in everything else, on European ideas and practices" (1974:344).

In addition to the inherent problem of obtaining a truly objective view of another culture, colonial contact often swiftly and dramatically altered traditional gender relations by transforming the indigenous cultures of colonized peoples (Leacock 1981; Etienne and Leacock 1980; Gailey 1987; Wolf 1982). Economic roles were radically changed in response to trade. Emphases on external trade rather than household production and consumption undermined women's contributions and enhanced male control over resources. As a result, the allocation of productive roles changed.

Changes in production often were accompanied by rapid realignments of indigenous political formations to meet colonizers' demands. Among the northeastern Iroquois, for example, British, French, and American officials bypassed the authority of women and ignored their opinions, dealing instead only with male chiefs. As described in Chapter 11, however, among the Iroquois, female heads of matrilineal clans were responsible for choosing men of their group as leaders and appointed spokespersons to voice their opinions in council meetings.

In Africa, too, the European colonizers introduced economic pressures and administrative policies that favoured men over women. Commercialization of agricultural production, privatization of land tenure, the introduction of Christianity and Western education, and waged-labour migration all created opportunities and restrictions that reduced women's participation and status within the society.

CRITICAL THINKING QUESTIONS

How could changes in gender relations caused by colonialism be interpreted as proof of the theory of universal male dominance? Why would that interpretation be wrong?

? *How does a religion with which you are familiar define the status and roles of women and men?*

devalue women and to assume rights to control women's activity. Women in these cultures learn to expect and accept male domination. These gender models often are conveyed unconsciously and go unquestioned.

In all societies, ideological constructs support and perpetuate existing ways of living. For example, as we will see in Chapter 12, religion often provides explanations and justifications for existing social relations. Religious beliefs sanction the status and roles of women and men, explaining divine origins for personal freedoms or restrictions, for differences in the prestige or power of men and women, and for the rights and obligations that they have. Myths of creation may give greater or lesser prominence to male or female deities, justifying the social value of human women and men (Sanday 1981). For example, religious practice affects gender by allowing or restricting the ability of men and women to perform rituals. Barring people from sacred roles limits their status and prestige.

Even in societies that restrict women's public participation, however, women nevertheless have some power and informally control much of what happens in their households. Women's lives are sometimes described as focused on the "domestic sphere" and men's lives taking place in the "public sphere." This distinction may be fitting for some societies, especially large-scale agrarian or industrial states where labour tasks are highly specialized and gender roles are rigidly defined. But the distinction loses its value when applied to small-scale foraging or horticultural societies (Lamphere 2001). In these societies, there is little differentiation between a public and private domain. Most activities take place communally, often out in the open or indoors in dwellings inhabited by multiple family groups. Much work requires the cooperative efforts of men and women. Although there are certainly gender distinctions in these societies as well, a demarcation of domains is generally less rigid.

Women are sometimes able to exert influence, even in the most rigidly segregated communities, through direct personal religious experiences. In Ethiopia, for example, women may be possessed by spirits known as *zars*, whose presence is manifested through ecstasy and out-of-body experiences. Women who are possessed by spirits must attend a communal ceremony in the company of other afflicted individuals. At these rituals, held about once every month, healers cure the women in an atmosphere of festivity and abandon (Boddy 2001). In addition to the ritual functions of *zar* beliefs, afflicted women have the opportunity to socialize together away from the control and supervision of their fathers or husbands. *Zar* spirits may possess any individual, but their most frequent targets are married women. In the context of a male-dominated society, *zar* beliefs and practices provide married women with an outlet for frustrations, a release from restrictions imposed upon them, and an escape from household responsibilities (Lewis 1989).

In societies with gender equality, men and women are equally able to occupy positions of prestige and authority in their communities. Both contribute to making decisions that affect them and their families, and their rights to act independently and autonomously are equally respected. Gender equality does not necessarily mean that women and men do the same kinds of work or have the same social roles and responsibilities but that their contributions are equally valued. In addition, attitudes about gender reflect positive evaluations. In family and personal life, women and men have the same opportunities and rights. Attitudes toward male and female sexuality are comparable. If premarital sex is permitted for men, it is permitted for women as well. If men can initiate divorce, women may also end their unhappy marriages.

While the status of men is generally secure in most societies, the status of women varies greatly across cultures. Anthropologists attempt to explain this variability by drawing attention to economic, structural, and ideological factors. A basic feature of society and influence on gender status is the productive contribution that women and men make to their household and community economies. Ownership or control over resources interrelates with participation in economic production. Risk taking in hunting and warfare further influences the relative status of men and women.

In general, women's status is higher in societies where their labour contributes the major share of food that their family consumes. For example, among foragers such as the Ju/'hoansi of Namibia and Botswana, the plants, roots, and nuts that women gather make up about 70 percent of the people's yearly caloric intake (Lee 2003). Significantly, women's social rights are respected and their independence is secure. In

These Orthodox Jewish men are praying at the Wailing Wall in Jerusalem. Judaism, Roman Catholicism, and Islam are male-dominated religions. These religions make women equal in the eyes of God, but women are not permitted to worship in mosques, and in Orthodox synagogues they may be seated together in a separate section. Controversies in Jewish and Christian denominations over the ordination of women bring to the surface underlying issues of gender and ideology.

GLOBALIZATION

Beginning in the fifteenth century, European explorers and colonizers directly and indirectly altered the gender roles, status, and relations of people in the societies with which they came into contact. Europeans imposed their own cultural beliefs and attitudes on those peoples, devaluing women and regarding men as dominant.

? *Would you say that gender equality exists in the Canada? How would you defend your answer?*

Anthropology Applied

Advocacy for Women

Anthropologists work in organizations that champion women's rights, economic independence, and quality of life. For example, anthropologists conduct and report research on the impacts of economic development on women as well as on their households and communities. It has been found that women play an important role in the economies of developing countries as both producers and consumers, even in strongly patriarchal societies that tend to ignore women's contributions outside the home.

International organizations involved in advocacy for women include the Women's Environment and Development Organization (WEDO), the International Centre for Research on Women, and the Women's Rights Project of EarthRights International. Through the efforts of organizations such as EarthRights International, rural Burmese women had an opportunity to address the United Nations about human rights abuses against women in their country. They reported on their dislocation, forced labour, abandonment, and abuse related to the construction of the Burma-Bangladesh-India natural gas pipeline. The International Fund for Agricultural Development (IFAD), another example, is concerned with ending poverty for rural people. IFAD attempts to strengthen the roles of women in their communities by ensuring that they serve as advisers in projects and as intermediaries between women's organizations and the government. IFAD also attempts to construct projects so that both women and men are involved in the outcomes, thus avoiding the tendency for development projects to favour men's interests.

A contention of IFAD is that gender inequality helps to perpetuate poverty. To break the cycle of poverty,

Female delegates from the Karenni ethnic minority look on during the opening of the Myanmar Constitutional Convention.

IFAD attempts to increase women's access to resources (including food, water, and education) and enable women to attain political positions. IFAD also seeks to involve men in the new roles of women, because women cannot become empowered to change their roles and status without the support of men. The idea is that, with equal access to resources, women and men in poverty will be able to help each other and their society together.

CRITICAL THINKING QUESTIONS

How does gender inequality perpetuate poverty? As a cultural anthropologist, how might you conduct research to determine if goals like those of IFAD are viable?

contrast, in foraging societies such as the Inuit of the Alaskan and Canadian Arctic, where the percentage of food obtained by women's direct labour is relatively low, women's status is correspondingly lower.

In farming societies, a generally consistent relationship can be seen between the amount of farmwork that women do and their social and political rights. For example, among the northeastern Iroquois, women's labour, planting and harvesting crops, supplied most of the food that people ate, supplemented by meat and fish brought in by the men. In addition to their direct labour, women controlled the allocation of land through the matrilineages that they headed, and they controlled the distribution of food to families within their kinship groups. All these responsibilities in production and distribution gave women a secure basis for their high social status. In contrast, among the farming and hunting peoples of the Amazon region in South America, women's relatively low status can be understood partly as consistent with their minor roles in obtaining food, as most of the planting, hunting, and fishing is done by men.

As you read in Chapter 6, historical evidence shows that when relations of production are transformed in a way that limits women's participation, then women's social and political rights become restricted and their social value declines. Recall from Chapter 8 that patterns of post-marital residence also play a role in women's security and independence. Matrilocal societies provide women with continued emotional support from their kin, whereas patrilocal residence patterns remove women from their kin groups and the support they can provide when conflicts arise. In addition, social and political complexity and the patterns of community leadership also affect gender status.

The degree and type of warfare in a region also influence gender constructs. Success in warfare usually confers social prestige on men. However, men's ability to translate their military achievements into control over women in their communities is in part related to the frequency of warfare and to characteristics of warfare. Where warfare is frequent and directed against distant enemies, warriors are absent from home for long periods of time and are less able to dominate the households they leave behind. Women in these societies have higher status. Warfare directed against nearby settlements, however, creates conditions in which warriors can extend their military dominance to other aspects of social life, including gender dominance. Furthermore, frequent internal warfare endangers noncombatants, affirming men's roles as defenders and protectors.

REVIEW

In some societies gender roles are strongly segregated, whereas in others common activities are performed by both men and women. Gender roles strongly affect gender relations. Societies exhibit either gender equality or gender inequality, which is almost always in the form of male dominance. All societies have some division of labour by gender, which allows people to specialize in a few skill areas rather than having to master all the survival skills of their culture. All societies also have co-operative labour. Gender division of labour reflects biological as well as economic and cultural realities. The status of women in a society is based in part on the importance of their roles in the production of goods or provision of food; on their importance as householders, depending on the type and frequency of warfare; and on their access to kin support based on postmarital residence patterns.

GENDER AND SUBSISTENCE

Modes of subsistence relate to gender roles, gender status, and gender relations. Foraging societies tend to have gender equality and egalitarian gender relations, except where men's economic or political roles are critical to the survival of the group, a situation that favours male dominance. Horticultural, pastoral, and agricultural societies tend to have greater gender inequality, depending on the control of subsistence resources and other factors, with the likelihood of some degree of male dominance. This pattern, however, varies considerably. Industrial societies tend to retain ideological male dominance while gradually enlarging economic opportunities for women and extending legal and institutional equalities to both genders.

Foragers and Gender

In many foraging bands, women's and men's interdependent contributions to their households were (and in some cases still are) reflected in equality of social relations and social status. The Ju/'hoansi of southern Africa provide an example.

Ju/'hoansi sociey was traditionally organized around bilateral kin groups. Economic roles were defined according to gender, but flexibility and overlap also were found. The productive labour of both women and men was essential for survival and was socially recognized and rewarded. Marriages were usually monogamous, although polygyny and polyandry occured infrequently. Since a man was expected to perform bride service to his in-laws, initial post-marital residence was matrilocal, providing a young wife with support from her kin until children were born and her marriage became stable. Divorce, though, was common, particularly in the early years of marriage, and could be initiated by either spouse. Fathers took an active role in child care and were affectionate and playful with their children. In general, attitudes toward premarital sexual activity were permissive for both girls and boys. Although adultery was not condoned, its only punishment was gossip and criticism. Formal political structures and formalized leadership were absent. Group decisions were made during public meetings in which both men and women could voice their opinions and influence outcomes.

The role of subsistence in gender constructs is also reflected in culture change. Economic and political changes experienced by the Ju/'hoansi, for example, have had significant impacts on gender roles, relationships between women and men, and cultural evaluation of the genders. Ju/'hoansi society has been affected by modern technology, involvement in wage work by large segments of the population, and incorporation into national states that first surrounded and then engulfed Ju/'hoansi territory. These changes occurred over a relatively short time. Beginning in the 1960s, the majority of Ju/'hoansi in Botswana and Namibia became involved in pastoral and farming activities, first as labourers for Herero and Tswana villagers and later as owners of their own herds and fields (Lee 2003:157–158). Most Ju/'hoansi today live in sedentary villages where subsistence is based on farming and herding. Men carry out these tasks, whereas women's work consists mainly of domestic tasks and occasional foraging for wild foods (Draper 1975:101–103).

Three factors have led to transformation of gender relations among the Ju/'hoansi. First, while men and women formerly contributed roughly equal amounts of labour and time to subsistence, in modern villages men's contributions are much greater, both in terms of the amount of labour expended and the quantity of food produced. Second, where once both women and men had individual control over the use and distribution of resources, now it is primarily men who own herds and fields. And third, the division of labour by gender has become rigid, so that working with livestock is a male domain along with the heavy labour involved in clearing fields for planting, erecting fences, and harvesting crops (Draper 1975:103). Perhaps because women's work has declined in visible social value, men are extremely reluctant to carry out any tasks identified as "women's work" (Draper 1975:96).

As a consequence of economic changes, settlement patterns and the flow of daily life have been altered in ways that also affect gender constructs. Villages now consist of permanent houses spaced at greater distances from each other rather than the casual shelters previously built in the bush. Women spend more time and energy on upkeep of these new larger and more permanent structures. Domestic responsibilities keep women indoors more and apart from other villagers. Women engage in foraging activities for shorter periods of time and remain closer to their settlements. In contrast to decreasing mobility for women, men have become more mobile, leaving their villages for substantial periods and engaging in herding, farming, and trading with other peoples. Greater social prestige accrues to men because of their involvement with other peoples and cultures. Ju/'hoansi men are frequently bilingual and often serve as intermediaries in bringing technological innovations into Ju/'hoansi communities. In addition, many Ju/'hoansi men are now employed for wages in nearby towns and even as far away as the gold mines in South Africa (Draper 1975:103; Lee 2003:159–160).

Notions of private ownership of property by individuals have become incorporated into Ju/'hoansi ethics. Goats and cattle in Ju/'hoansi herds are owned separately by men. Houses are also said to be "owned" by the male head of household. Particular men who have amassed greater material wealth than others are even said to be "owners" of a village (Lee 2003:98). Because property that constitutes wealth is identified men they are endowed with greater status.

Gender in Pastoral and Horticultural Societies

In pastoral and horticultural societies, control over the distribution of produce and goods influences gender status. In societies that are generally egalitarian, women exert

These Mbuti Pygmy women live in a foraging society in the Ituri rain forest of Zaire. Like the Ju/'hoansi of the Kalahari Desert, they enjoy greater gender equality than groups with more hostile environments. Gender division of labour gives men and women different economic and social roles. In Mbuti society, women are valued artists. They gather materials to make pigments and express in art the key themes of Mbuti culture. These themes centre on the rain forest as the parent, birthplace, provider, arbiter, resting place, and god of all. As their canvas, the women use barkcloth, their bodies, and the bodies of their children.

their rights to make decisions concerning economic activities. In Iroquoian economies, for example, women performed most of the farm work, including planting and tending crops and harvesting. In addition, women gathered a wide assortment of fruits, nuts, and roots and were responsible for domestic tasks and child care. Men's subsistence roles included hunting and fishing to supplement the basic plant diet. Trading with other native peoples for animal skins and utilitarian and luxury articles was also the work of men (Thwaites 1906:15:155). Both women's and men's work was highly valued, socially recognized, and rewarded.

Iroquois women not only were responsible for food production but also controlled distribution of both the food and the resources contributed by their husbands and sons. This control over resources was a crucial factor in Iroquoian women's high status in their households and communities (Brown 1975:236; Bonvillain 1980:50). In addition to allotting food for daily consumption, women collected and distributed supplies for public feasts and ceremonial occasions (Lafitau 1974:318). Their economic roles in household production and as resource distributors were thus extended into public domains.

Household organization centred around matrilineal clans that formed the basis of Iroquoian kinship. Matrilocality was the preferred residence pattern, so a house typically consisted of an elder woman, her husband, their daughters and daughters' families, and the couple's unmarried sons.

Iroquoian behaviours and attitudes related to sexuality and marriage reflected the independence and autonomy of women and men. People freely chose to engage in sexual relationships and to form marriages. Marriages were monogamous. Violence against women in the form of wife beating or rape was unheard of (Bonvillain 1980).

Iroquoian women's prestige was strengthened through many features of their roles within clans. Senior women of matrilineages composing each clan had responsibility for overseeing domestic tasks performed in their households and for allocating farmland to their kinswomen (Lafitau 1974:69). And clan mothers chose lineage and clan chiefs from among prominent men in their kin groups. Thus, both men and women made important, socially valued contributions to their society and had ultimate control over their own behaviour.

Among the Igbo of Nigeria, both men and women contribute to subsistence through their farm labour, but men control land and resources. Preferred post-marital residence is patrilocal, and, since villages are exogamous, women live away from their kin while men live in the same community as their fathers, sons, brothers and other patrilineal relatives. Men are exclusively represented as heads of patrilineal groups and as participants in village assemblies, which decide on important issues concerning the community. However, women assume some degree of autonomy, independence and control, although often within realms separate from those of men. Women are allowed to keep the rewards of their labour, including income from exclusively defined women's activities, such as extracting palm kernel oil. Most Igbo women engage in trade, as do the women in many cultures throughout West Africa. Few of them are full-time traders but engage in marketing as an extension of their roles in agricultural production. However, some women do engage in more complex and lucrative whole-saling activities. Through these various efforts, they function as catalysts for wide redistributive networks. Tradeswomen's husbands avoid interfering with their activities or making too many demands on their labour. Successful women have the income and prestige to manage on their own and, therefore, are able to leave an abusive or domineering husband. Wealthy women can even take wives of their own and establish themselves as household heads (Green 1964).

Igbo women's independence within the economic sphere has had an effect upon social status and power. Women maintain relations with their families of origin and frequently visit their natal villages as well a female kin living in other villages. They also form women's associations within the communities into which they have married. These groups can issue edicts that affect men's activities and sometimes enforce them through organized boycotts on domestic services for their husbands. The force of feminist power was vividly demonstrated within colonial Nigeria by the "women's war" in which a movement originating among Igbo women snowballed into a national protest against British rule. It was one of the earliest and most effective African resistance actions and led to reforms in colonial policy and practice. An observer documents the women's militancy as follows:

> . . . mobs of frenzied Amazons, sometimes numbering 10 000, with their heads decorated with palm-leaves and wild fern (a symbol of war). . . carrying cudgels . . ., marched from village to village assaulting the 'Warrant Chiefs' and compelling them to deliver up their caps of office . . . pulled to pieces or burnt down the Native Court buildings, destroyed bridges, looted European trading stores, released prisoners, and offered active opposition to armed bodies of Government police (Meek 1937).

Nigerian women conduct trade in the markets.

In contrast to the Iroquois and Igbo, Yanomamo women of Amazonia are excluded from direct productive work. This exclusion is then used as justification for their social subordination. Yanomamo culture sanctions men's dominance over women in every feature of ideology and practice (Chagnon 1973, 1997). Settlement patterns, social systems, subsistence activities, and village leadership are all dominated by men. These conditions of Yanomamo society have been strongly influenced by economic changes as a result of culture contact (Kellman 1982), a subject taken up further in Chapter 14.

Residence patterns among the Yanomamo are patrilocal, based on affiliation among patrilineal kin. Marriages are usually arranged by men, a father giving his daughter to be wed to a man with whom he wishes to forge an alliance. Young girls, often as young as eight or nine years old, are married to men in their twenties or thirties. Polygyny is common and desired by all men but not economically possible for everyone. A man may contract multiple marriages through establishing alliances with several men who have daughters. Men also obtain wives by capture when raiding other villages.

Prestige in Yanomamo culture is principally based on success in two roles held exclusively by men: warrior and shaman, a type of ritual practitioner who makes contact with the spirit world and performs ceremonies to heal the sick and protect warriors. Successful warriors also function as influential village leaders. Warfare is common and is characterized by raids against nearby villages with the aim of killing as many inhabitants as possible. Young women, however, are often captured and brought back to become wives.

Although men are more likely than women to die as the result of raiding, there is still a relative lack of women in most communities because of the practice of female infanticide, a dramatic reflection of the unworthiness of females. This artificially created scarcity of women is a motivation for warfare, giving men the opportunity to capture a wife from a neighbouring village (Harris 1974). Warfare creates a dangerous situation for noncombatants, enhancing men's status in their role as defenders. Thus, men's success is rewarded by both high social prestige and the subordination of women. Women's subordination is demonstrated by frequent violence in the form of beatings and rapes.

Finally, in an area of scarce resources, practices may develop in order to disperse populations (Siskin, 1973). The scarcity of women, created by female infanticide and polygyny, helps limit population growth and also generates conditions of warfare conducive to forcing people to relocate away from centres of conflict.

Gender in Agricultural States

Agrarian states are complex societies with centralized political systems that maintain some degree of control over local areas within the state. They are subject to rule of an elite which usually derives its wealth and status through land ownership. There is marked segmentation of the population into classes that occupy different positions in society, have different kinds of occupations, and different standards of living. Many such societies are (or were) characterized by male dominance in gender relations. As in other types of societies, however, the degree of male dominance varies widely, depending on economic, political, and historical factors, as well as on patterns of kinship, marriage, and family.

Industrialism and Gender

In Europe and North America in the late eighteenth century, innovations in productive modes began a process that transformed agricultural societies into industrial nations. Industrialization began in the manufacture of textiles, using mainly women's labour for the first several decades and then marginalizing women as manufacturing became fully established as the dominant productive mode. During the early nineteenth century, the independent self-sufficiency of farming families was gradually eroded by the need to purchase commodities. At the same time, transformations of production in manufacturing resulted in owners' need to hire workers for the burgeoning industrial sector. These two processes coalesced in the growth of industrial production.

Women were marginalized in the industrial sector through intersecting links between gender segregation in employment and unequal pay. Some occupations were considered appropriate for women and others for men. For example, industrial jobs requiring operation of large, heavy machinery were open to men, whereas women were employed in industries that

Mill life reproduced the patriarchal relations that existed in households. Men were owners and supervisors, controlling the organization of production, whereas young, unmarried women laboured as subordinate workers. On average, mill workers in the mid-nineteenth century worked for four-and-a-half years, most leaving to marry (Matthaei 1982:150).

Case study

Male Dominance in Traditional Chinese Culture

Traditional Chinese culture was intensely patriarchal. Patriarchal gender relations were developed through several millennia of Chinese history. Centralized imperial dynasties took hold in the eighth century, succeeding one another after wars among rivals. To stabilize and expand political and military power, ruling classes adopted philosophies that supported the legitimacy of state control. The thoughts of Confucius (551–479 BCE) and his disciples were especially influential. A cornerstone of Confucianism is the notion of "filial piety" that ordains obedience to one's social superiors. Thus, all Chinese owed obedience to the emperor, sons to their fathers, and women to their husbands.

Male dominance was manifested in numerous social, economic, political, and religious spheres. Households consisted of members of patrilineages, headed by the eldest male. His wife, unmarried children, married sons and their wives and children—all were under his authority. The rule of a head of household was potentially harsh, involving culturally sanctioned beatings of wives and children. Because post-marital residence was patrilocal, wives could rarely depend on their relatives for support in times of conflict with their in-laws (Wolf 1974:158). A wife experienced subordination within her husband's household, especially when young and not yet the mother of sons to carry on her husbands' lineage.

Mothers-in-law often acted as "surrogates for male authority" (Diamond 1975:376). They had little authority in relations with their own husbands and instead asserted authority over their sons' wives. Wives had few, if any, allies in their husbands' households. In keeping with notions of filial piety, a man's allegiance was first and foremost to his parents. His wife was secondary and could not depend on him for social support. Women began to receive deferential treatment after they reached middle or old age and had adult sons. Sons were a woman's main allies, and mothers could attempt to control their sons through strong emotional bonds (Wolf 1974:168). With stern authoritarian relationships with their fathers, sons gravitated toward their mothers' emotional warmth.

Patriarchal attitudes were reflected in a marked preference for sons. Sons were necessary for the social, material, and spiritual well-being of their parents. Through sons, patrilineages maintained their continuity, and the economic division of labour contributed further justification for preferring sons to daughters. According to gender-assigned tasks, men were primarily responsible for agricultural production. Women's work was usually confined to domestic household tasks. When additional labour was required for farmwork at harvest time, women, especially among poor families, helped in the fields.

Women living in prosperous households were restricted to domestic labour and often to the physical confines of the home. The Chinese word for wife, *neiran*, literally means "inside person" (Croll 1982:224). By keeping one's wife in the home, a man demonstrated his wealth and the fact that he did not need his wife working in the fields. Thus, women's social subordination was justified, in part by their economic dependence on men (Wong 1974:234).

Marriages were arranged by fathers of the prospective couple without consulting the bride or groom. Girls generally were married when in their late teens but were often betrothed as children. These betrothals solidified alliances between men. Girls' chastity before marriage was absolutely essential to maintain the honour of the girl and her family, but men were not constrained by premarital restrictions. Men frequented brothels to gain sexual experience before marriage (Wong 1974:236–237). This double standard about sexual activity was another instance of male privilege.

Traditional customs related to divorce further discriminated against women. Only husbands could initiate divorce, often because of a wife's disobedience or failure to produce a son (Wong 1974:234). Divorce carried no stigma for a husband, but a divorced woman was shamed.

With four sons, this traditional Chinese family has a strong future. Families depended on sons for labour and crucial religious functions.

Ideally, widows were not supposed to remarry, but poor men who were unable to find suitable women for marriage sometimes sought them (Wong 1974:236). Because widows had few alternatives, they often agreed to such unions to escape the social stigma and economic hardships of widowhood.

From an outsider's viewpoint, the practice of foot binding symbolized restrictions on girls and women in traditional Chinese society. The feet of young girls at the age of four or five were tightly bound with cloth so that their toes curled under their feet. As the girls grew to adulthood, their feet became more deformed and normal walking became impossible. Adult women took tiny, faltering steps on feet as small as three inches long (Wong 1974:232). Only among the very poor, where women's agricultural labour provided a necessary financial contribution to family survival, did daughters escape this practice.

In the early twentieth century, some customs began to change because of the influence of Chinese

intellectuals and administrators, as well as British and French colonial agents (who had defeated the Chinese military in the Opium Wars of 1839–1842). Although British and French societies were certainly dominated by men, colonial influences had a beneficial effect on women's status in China. For instance, foot binding was outlawed in 1902, although the ban was widely ignored until the 1950s, when the new Communist government undertook a vigorous campaign to eliminate the practice.

After coming to power in 1949, the Chinese Communist government enacted several laws that attempted to transform social and familial relationships between women and men. The Marriage Law of 1950 declared that the "New-Democratic marriage system is based on the free choice of partners, on monogamy, on equal rights for both sexes, and on the protection of the lawful interests of women and children" (quoted in Wong 1974:242). Additional laws banned child-marriage and dowry.

However, patriarchal attitudes continue in a preference for sons, even in the face of government reforms and programs for population control. To limit population growth, the Chinese government began a "One-Child Certificate Program" in 1979. A couple who pledge to have only one child receives substantial benefits in the form of cash bonuses, preferential housing, job assignments, and educational opportunities for their child. According to a study conducted by Fred Arnold and Liu Zhaoxiang (1986), 37 percent of Chinese couples with one child enrolled in the program, but a disparity exists between those with one son and those with one daughter. Of all holders of One-Child Certificates, 60 percent have sons, whereas only 40 percent have daughters (Arnold and Liu, 1986:227–228). Although the program has been a significant success in reducing population growth, a matter of critical importance in China, the gender disparity is significant for future opportunities of men and women.

relied on handwork and small machinery that produced such items as soap, hats, and cigars (Hartmann 1979). Even where both men and women worked in the same industry, they were differentiated according to specialization. In the manufacture of boots and shoes, for instance, men were employed as cutters and finishers and women were stitchers and sewers (Matthaei, 1982:189).

In addition, women generally received lower wages than did men, even when both performed the same jobs. This differential in pay, or **gender gap**, as it is now called, was—and is—often masked by the segregation of work and workplaces. Men's social dominance can then be justified by the fact that they earn more money than do women. And paying women lower wages was justified by an ideology that women were only interested in working until they married and would leave the labour force to become wives and mothers.

gender gap
The difference in wages and income earned by men and women for comparable work.

cult of domesticity
Constellation of beliefs popular in the late nineteenth and early twentieth centuries that women were, by nature and biology, suited to the domestic tasks of nurturing and caring for their husbands and children.

In the early and mid-nineteenth century, a cultural construct currently referred to as the **cult of domesticity** became popular and justified separation of the genders, relegating women to the domestic sphere. Its popularity grew throughout the nineteenth century and remains in one form or another as a gender construct in Western society. According to this cultural ideal, separate roles and domains are appropriate for women and men. Men provide material support for their families; women are suited to perform domestic tasks. Married women who joined the labour force as an economic necessity were told that by working outside the home they were neglecting their proper duties to nurture their husbands and children. Husbands of working women were similarly made to feel derelict in their duty. Since the ideal man was one who supported his wife and children, a man whose wife worked was less than a real man.

Labour leaders also used these attitudes to restrict women's involvement in wage work as competition between employed women and men intensified at the beginning of the twentieth century. Although ostensibly dedicated to bettering conditions for all workers, most unions in the nineteenth and early twentieth centuries discriminated against women, barring them from membership or relegating them and their interests to auxiliary status (Berch 1982). When men were faced with competition from women, who often were willing to work for lower wages, unions had two possible responses: They could advocate equality of pay for all workers, to remove the financial incentive for employers to hire women rather than men, or they could advocate restrictions on women's employment as a strategy for maintaining men's advantages. They chose the latter course.

In another response to competition from women workers, labour leaders and public figures advocated enactment of "protective legislation" to protect women from harmful conditions on the job. Hours for women were decreased, night work in some occupations was forbidden, and exposure to dangerous chemicals, materials, or machinery was banned, but the same protections were not extended to men. Although the rules protected women from dangers on the job, they carried hidden costs, rendering women less attractive as employees and therefore hurting their chances of being hired.

Despite strong pressures to keep women in the home, some women sought to obtain higher education and to participate in the work force, spurring social changes in gender roles and expectations. Their political activism also increased.

An organized women's movement in Canada began in earnest at the turn of the twentieth century. At the time, women were clearly viewed as second class citizens, relegated to the domestic sphere, denied rights to own and control property, and not considered to be legal "persons" under the *British North America Act*. One of the first formal organizations, the Political Equality League, was formed in Manitoba in 1912, including among it founders Nellie McClung, one of Canada's most famous suffragettes. The organization represented middle-class women of British ancestry who had gained some prominence as career women. Aside from demanding full employment, legal, and political rights for women, they also advocated reform and social justice in many other aspects of Canadian life. In spite of the scope of their social activism, they remained conservative in outlook in contrast to the militant stance of the British suffragette movement, which advocated a more comprehensive transformation of gender status. Their philosophy is sometimes termed "maternal feminism" in light of the stance that giving women a voice in the public forum would foster a more nurturing society. According to Nellie McClung, "a woman's place is in the home; and out of it whenever she is called to guard those she loves and to improve conditions for them."

The League successfully petitioned the Manitoba government to pass Canada's first bill to award women the right to vote and hold public office in 1916. In 1918, women's suffrage was granted for federal elections. The other provinces followed suit, but Quebec did not grant women the right to vote until 1940. A second critical set of rights was granted to women in 1929, when the British Privy Council overturned a Supreme Court judgment and ruled that women were to be acknowledged as "persons" under the law and entitled to the same rights as men.

Women, Work, and Family in the Post-Industrial Era

We have already noted that the movement of women into the work force has been one of the major social consequences of the dramatic economic changes that have occurred in industrialized societies in the aftermath of World War II. Expansion of the service sector, especially within the areas of health, education, sales, and clerical work and the intensification of consumerism created the demand, opportunities, and pressures for women to seek employment. For example, in 1951 less than 25 percent of Canadian women of working age were employed outside the home and accounted for only 22 percent of the total work force. The rate for men at the time was 84 percent. By 2001, a sizeable majority of women, 71 percent, were working and made up 46 percent of the work force. The rate for men had fallen slightly to 82 percent, an effect of a trend towards early retirement (Cooke-Reynolds and Zukewich 2004).

The transition from housewife to working wife and mother within a dual-income family has fostered many changes in gender patterns in Western societies. Women have reduced their dependence upon their husbands for material support and have acquired a better negotiating position within their marriages and the ability to leave an unsatisfactory relationship without a complete loss of income. New resources, ambitions, and public presence have led to an active feminist movement and the implementation of new laws, policies, and practices that have advanced women's status within the larger society. Accordingly, gender equality and the elimination of the gender gap have become incorporated as central values within many contemporary societies. However, as with other ideals, the realization of these goals is still incomplete. While advances have been made, women are still subject to discriminatory conditions that affect their incomes, job stability, and position in the public arena.

In Canada, women have entered a workforce in which jobs and incomes are still strongly influenced by gender. Clearly marked female jobs, such as nurse, teacher, clerk, or sales and service agent, employ 70 percent of women as opposed to 30 percent of their male counterparts. In general, salaries in these positions pay less than those that men with similar educational qualifications receive in such fields as engineering. In addition, although women have made gains in acquiring management and leadership positions, they are still not as well represented at the top of the corporate ladder. While women make up 75 percent of office workers, they account for only 25 percent of upper management positions (See Table 9.2). Accordingly, women's

Table 9.2   GENDER DIFFERENCES IN EMPLOYMENT

Occupation	Women	Men %	Women as % of total in occupation
Senior management	0.2	0.6	25.1
Other management	6.2	10.4	34.0
Professional	28.5	21.8	53.1
Clerical and administrative	24.1	6.9	75.0
Sales and service	32.2	19.7	58.6
Primary production	1.4	5.2	19.8
Trades	2.0	24.7	6.5
Manufacturing	5.2	10.7	29.6
Total	**100.0**	**100.0**	**46.4**

Source: Data adapted from the Statistics Canada CANSIM database http://cansim2.statcan.ca/, Table 282-0010.

incomes stand at 72 percent of those of men in spite of the fact that women's educational status is higher because of a higher rate of university enrollment. Women's economic status is also affected by their predominance in part-time work as a consequence of continued expectations that wives retain the primary responsibility for childrearing. Part-time hours not only pay less but provide fewer benefits.

Changes in gender patterns within employment have implications for other areas of society, most notably within the household. As women move into the male province of the workplace, men are expected to assist their wives with housework, so the domestic sphere has become another context where gender equality has become an ideal. Studies of Canadian household dynamics have shown that men are taking greater responsibility for housework and child care than they have in the past, but that the gender gap has not been completely closed. Older attitudes towards gender divisions within the family are still in force. A 2006 study indicates that men and women spend an equal amount of time each day, 8.8 hours, doing both housework and paid work but that the balance is different. As such, men spend 6.3 hours at work and 2.5 hours doing unpaid work, while the levels for women are at 4.4 and 4.4. Trends over the last twenty years indicate that, in all, the total hours of paid work have gone up for women as have the hours of housework and child care for men, but not to the same degree. As such, men are not fully taking up the slack, and chores in the home are either not getting done or are being covered in other ways, such as through take-out meals or paid domestic help. Changes in women's roles are leading to greater commercialization of domestic activities (Marshall 2006).

The increasing employment of domestic workers in the contemporary Canadian family shows some interesting patterns which intersect with other post-industrial developments, such as globalization. In general, 10 percent of households hire maids or nannies. As might be expected, the rate increases with income, so that 43 percent of

Swedish Prime Minister Goran Persson and Foreign Minister Laila Freivalds sign the European constitution for Sweden in 2004. The under-representation of women is universal in all national governments. Sweden and Norway have the highest percentage of women in elected parliaments (about 40 percent) (United Nations Division for the Advancement of Women, 2001). In only twenty-one other countries do women constitute 20 percent or more of elected representatives.

the richest families, those who earn over $160 000 per year, engage home help. Accordingly, the top stratum can claim to have achieved full gender equality, since husbands and wives in these families assume equal responsibilities for housework as responsibilities are transferred from wives to hired help. However, gender inequalities have not been totally eliminated but have been shifted from the household to the global marketplace, where domestic employment has drawn on the movement of poor women from less developed countries, primarily the Philippines, into low-paying jobs and often exploitative conditions (see the Culture Change feature on page 252).

In spite of widespread movement into the work force, some Canadian women still choose to become nonworking wives and mothers. Women who remain at home and fulfill the traditional ideal of domestic roles are involved in the important work of social reproduction. **Social reproduction** entails the care and sustenance of people who will be able to contribute productively to society. Necessary tasks include obtaining and preparing food, maintaining the physical premises of the home, purchasing clothing and other material goods, tending family members when they are ill, and planning and supervising the education of children. However, the worth of labour contributed by stay-at-home wives and mothers is socially devalued, reflected, for example, in the phrase "just a housewife," which women themselves often use as a self-definition. But the work of social reproduction performed by such women is vital to society and to the economic system. Although nonemployed wives are perceived as dependent on their husbands, husbands also depend on their wives. Just as men contribute their wages to support their families, women contribute their unpaid labour to family survival.

? Why is housework devalued? What role does household labour play in statistics about the productivity of the American economy?

social reproduction
The care and sustenance of people who will be able to contribute productively to society.

REVIEW

Relationships between subsistence and gender relations vary, depending on the allocation of power and control of resources and other factors. Foragers such as the Ju/'hoansi were egalitarian, whereas others, such as the Inuit, tended toward male dominance. Some horticultural societies, such as the Iroquois, had gender equality, whereas others, such as the Yanomamo, have male dominance in every facet of their culture. Agrarian societies, such as imperial China, were generally male-dominated. Industrialism in Europe and North America brought about changes in gender relations. Segregation and a gender gap (unequal pay) developed in factory wage work. A cult of domesticity called for women to stay at home, responsible for social reproduction. Post-industrial developments have supported a mass movement of women into the work force and a trend towards gender equality both within work and household contexts. The transfer of some domestic responsibilities to the marketplace has involved the exploitation of women from less advantaged groups.

GLOBALIZATION

Gender and Development

Agricultural and industrial development programs sponsored by national governments or international agencies aim to strengthen economies, raise living standards, and improve health in impoverished rural communities. Development theory emphasizes the importance of modernizing in technology, agricultural production for trade, and industrialization dependent on a mobile labour force. When measured by gross national product (GNP), median family or household income, and longer life expectancy, advances can be demonstrated, but researchers still question the impact of economic development on different sectors of the population.

When the differential effects of development on men and women were first systematically explored, evidence suggested that modernization contributed to a decline in women's status, especially in Africa and Asia. In Africa, landownership has passed from the collective control of kinship groups to individual control, increasingly concentrated in the hands of men. As land utilization has changed from an emphasis on subsistence to production for trade in national and global markets, women have seen their role in subsistence farming diminished, and as their centrality in

European colonization had a significant impact on gender roles and attitudes. European traders preferred to deal with men and thus ignored or subverted the economic contributions of women. Missionaries affected gender relations directly and indirectly by redefining marriage and family in terms of European principles. Colonizers also tended to legitimize men's political authority and diminish women's public political roles.

In Their Own Voices

Tsetsele Fantan on Women and AIDS in Botswana

In this address from a 2003 conference on Botswana's Strategy to Combat HIV/AIDS, Tsetsele Fantan, from the African Comprehensive HIV/AIDS Partnership, talks about the cultural constraints affecting HIV/AIDS prevention and treatment programs in Botswana. She talks about attitudes about sex, marriage, and women's roles that hamper the effectiveness of these programs, and she emphasizes the need to involve men and women working together to achieve change. Africa is the world region hardest hit by HIV/AIDS. In Botswana, 67 percent of HIV infected people ages 16 to 49 are women. In addition, women are the principal caretakers for AIDS sufferers in their households. Since farming is primarily the work of women (eight out of ten farmers are women), their illness and death from AIDS affect their entire communities.

Globally, women are exposed to HIV transmission because of four main vulnerabilities: the social/cultural context, economic subordination, sexual subordination, and the female biological makeup. As far as the social/cultural context in Botswana is concerned, boys and girls are socialized differently, predominantly along traditional norms that emphasize female subordination throughout the lifecycle. This is also emphasized when young women get married. We remind them that they need to honour and obey. This becomes extremely difficult when women are abused in marriage, because as they go to uncles and aunts for counsel, they are reminded of their marriage vows. This gender power differential is compounded by age differences.

As far as economic subordination is concerned, poverty does force some women to adopt economic strategies, survival strategies, such as transactional sex. As far as sexual subordination is concerned, women are expected to have one lifetime partner, while male deviation is condoned, generally expected, or even encouraged. Women are also vulnerable to coerced sex, including rape and other sexual abuse, both inside and outside of the family, including marital rape. Young women and girls are increasingly targeted by older men seeking safe and/or subservient sexual partners, or just sexual adventure.

In addition to all the education that is being given about HIV and AIDS, I would like to mention three areas where I believe work needs to be done. The first is a need to redefine traditional gender images. There is an urgent need to redefine images of masculinity and femininity through culturally relevant public education, and this is an area

where the media can play a very important role. We need to emphasize the role of men, not only as breadwinners, but as ensuring the protection of the health of themselves and their families. We need to clearly articulate the imperative for men to change attitudes and behaviours in a nonthreatening way. We need transformational programs that acknowledge that men are partners in the fight against HIV and AIDS. Secondly, we need to engage men in the empowerment of women. We need to recognize and come to terms with the realities of women in Botswana, and the realities of our social circumstances in Botswana, and recognize that women's empowerment cannot be realized without full involvement and engagement of the men. We therefore need to develop initiatives, innovative community-based programs that empower grassroots men to work with women. We need to develop programs that assist men and women to effectively negotiate for space, recognition, and acknowledgment of each other. To develop targeted programs for men that utilize informal, traditional structures, led by traditional and opinion leaders in the districts.

We need to develop gender and culturally sensitive programs and support services that address the vulnerability of women to HIV and AIDS. We need to develop women's entrepreneurial skills, as well as giving them or facilitating their access to credit, because acquiring skills without the capital to start a business which has a market will not change much.

Attitudes and practices that are deeply rooted in culture are unlikely to change in the short term. Programs to address this will require long-term commitment from development partners. Local traditional leaders must be empowered to advocate for and effect these changes at the community level. This should be done through proper dialogue. We need to identify and liberate the positive aspects of culture for gender sensitive prevention initiatives. Lastly, we need to make sure that the valuable elements in our culture must be preserved and passed on to the next generation.

From Center for Strategic and International Study HIV/AIDS Task Force, Botswana's Strategy to Combat HIV/AIDS, Empowering Women and People Living with HIV/AIDS, November 12, 2003. Reprinted by permission of the Centre for Strategic & International Studies, Washington D.C.

CRITICAL THINKING QUESTIONS

What aspects of traditional culture encourage the spread of HIV/AIDS among women in Botswana? What features of traditional culture can best address the challenge of preventing this spread?

family production shrinks, their status has also declined. In Asia, mechanization and technological advances in farming have tended to favour male farmworkers (Boserup 1970).

An additional element in weighing the changes in women's status is their role in social reproduction and the gender division of labour in the household. The domestic labour that women do helps support family members and makes their participation in agriculture or industry possible. This element is often ignored by policy planners and analysts of economic development (Beneria and Sen 1986). Furthermore, in societies where attitudes about gender limit women's ability to participate in work outside the home, their social status declines as societal value is placed on wage-earning activities.

Women's actual contributions to the world economy are often distorted and rendered invisible because of the inadequacy of research and statistics on labour force participation in the public sphere and because women's economic contributions in the home are ignored. Productive work or "active labour" is generally interpreted as participation in income-earning activities. Because much of women's work is in subsistence agriculture, home craft production, or the "informal" labour sector in urban environments (peddling, domestic service), their economic contributions are often seriously underestimated. In addition, census classifications of workers according to their "main" occupation tend to ignore women's economic contributions because they are classified as home workers without detailing their specific contributions to subsistence and also to extra household income such as making foods or crafts for sale. Finally, development programs often focus on the generation of work itself rather than on the reasons that women are not qualified, rooted in their lack of training and education because of discriminatory attitudes.

Women's Roles in Urban and Rural Economic Development

In some countries, industrial development favours women's employment in certain sectors. For example, in Malaysia, China, Singapore, and Taiwan, national and multinational corporations have established factories, especially in electronics and garment assembly, that employ mainly young women. According to some estimates, about 80 percent of workers in light manufacturing plants worldwide are women between the ages of 13 and 25 (Moore 1988:100). In Singapore, labour force participation rates for women have increased dramatically since the government embarked on rapid industrialization, providing tax incentives to foreign investment and curtailing labour union organizing (Wong 1986:208). By 1995, women's economic activity rate had risen to 51 percent (United Nations Division for the Advancement of Women 2000). Factories in Malaysia have also increased the wage-earning opportunities of young women (Ong 1983). There, and in other Asian and Latin American countries, rural women leave their homes to improve their skills and chances of economic advancement. Their needs are especially acute in the context of increasing poverty in the countryside and the resulting dislocation. In the decade of the 1970s alone, shortly after the government began its industrialization program, the number of Malay women factory workers increased dramatically, from about 1000 to more than 60 000 (Ong, 1983:429).

Young women benefit from their job opportunities by earning an income that gives them some economic independence and greater status in their families. They also escape the intense control traditionally exerted over them in their households, and they meet friends and socialize in the industrial centres. The wages they earn are higher than available in other jobs. However, the companies take advantage of the workers' poverty, lack of skills, and few alternative opportunities, paying them relatively low wages and offering few benefits.

Today, economic development increasingly affects small, relatively isolated communities. For example, the Pacific islands of Melanesia and Polynesia have become incorporated into national and global export networks. The production of copra (dried coconut) as a cash crop on the Melanesian island of Vanuatu (formally called New Hebrides) has gradually involved villagers in globalization while also maintaining a diversified subsistence and cash economy (Rodman 1993). The people of Vanuatu first

Culture Change

MIGRATION AND DOMESTIC SERVICE AMONG PHILIPPINE WOMEN IN CANADA

The movement of women into the workplace in post-industrial Canadian society has stimulated a demand for paid domestic workers, especially within the most prosperous sectors of society, where almost half of the families hire maids or nannies. This emerging market has been partially informed by gender and race and has engaged a considerable immigration stream of Philippine women that number in the hundreds of thousands. Pauline Barber of Dalhousie University has carried out a long-term study of the dynamics of this process, the impact of domestic service on the lives of Philippine immigrants, and the ways in which they have coped with often adverse conditions (Barber 2000).

According to the study, the Philippines has actively encouraged the outmigration of its citizens as a solution to its economic woes. Over four million Philippine nationals work overseas and support their families that stay behind with remittances that account for 4 percent of the country's GDP. Other revenues accrue from commissions paid for labour recruitment and fees required for travel documents. Traditionally the

migrants were male, but over the last generation the emphasis has shifted to women workers engaged primarily in domestic services. Much of this migration is directed towards Hong Kong and Taiwan and the Persian Gulf, but an increasing number has been recruited by Canadian families. The movement into Canada has been facilitated by the Canadian Government's Live-in Caregiver Program, according to which a worker receives a temporary visa to enter the country but can apply to become a permanent resident if he or she is continuously employed for 24 months within a three-year period. Applicants for this program must be approved, but the criteria for acceptance are lower than those for would-be immigrants in other categories on the grounds that few Canadians are interested in the jobs involved. The program attracts approximately 6000 immigrants per year, 75 percent of whom are from the Philippines. An equivalent number may be coming into the country illegally.

The migrants are from poor families and see migration to Canada as both a way of improving their economic prospects and helping their relatives. They are expected to send back some of their earnings as remittances, often to support their siblings' education and further contribute to the family's social mobility. Some of the contributions are also used to finance sisters who will also emigrate to become domestic workers, thus perpetuating the system. In Canada, Philippine nannies receive minimum wages, and are especially subject to abuse, since they are either illegal or dependent upon continuous employment in order to qualify for permanent status. In spite of the discriminatory and exploitative nature of their position, many of the domestic workers have been able to realize or at least feed some of their dreams for security and mobility for themselves and their families. One of Barber's informants was able to complete a nursing program and obtain employment in a health care facility, but was disappointed when she was unable to convince her son to live with her in Canada. In general, the hardships of domestic work in Canada are mitigated by the flow of information and support through family and ethnic networks that the transnational migration system helps to maintain.

became involved in coconut production in the 1930s, but by the early 1980s, world prices for copra declined and the local market collapsed. At that time, the Vanuatu government sponsored a fisheries development program to diversify sources of income and employment.

The shift from copra to fishing has had an impact on gender relations and contributions to household economies. Although most land under copra production was owned or controlled by men, both men and women worked cooperatively in the fields. The fisheries industries, however, tend to recruit men because deep-water fishing is an occupation reserved for them. Women continue some traditional roles by marketing the fish locally. In addition, although people have become involved in the global economy, they have also continued subsistence farming, fishing, and craft production. Melanesian women have thus been able to maintain much of their traditional status and equality.

In Polynesia, Tahitian women also have been able to retain or even enhance their status in the context of economic change because cultural values supporting gender equality have remained intact. Local governments initiated agricultural development projects oriented toward growing potatoes and green vegetables. These programs are largely successful, involving both men and women by granting financial support and technological training to all. By the early 1990s, approximately 43 percent of potato farmers were women (Lockwood 1997:511–512). Women's involvement in farming represented a break with the traditional division of labour that had limited women to performing domestic tasks, but they were able to use their customary access to communal land and their new access to government programs to produce crops for export. In addition, women's crafts, such as woven mats, hats, and quilts, have become major income-generating occupations, allowing women's economic contributions to be seen as central to the welfare of their families. Women's rights are protected by the traditional view that people control the products of their labour and the income received.

REVIEW

Development projects in the less-developed regions of the world often overlook or disadvantage women because they do not consider the importance of domestic tasks and subsistence agriculture for the generation of wealth and security within the community. Projects that have involved women, such as those involving light industry, have often led to exploitation through low wages and exploitative conditions. International migration of women into personal service sector jobs has had a similar effect. Projects that attempt to understand and preserve traditional gender roles in different societies have had more beneficial results.

Chapter Summary

Sex and Gender

- Gender is a cultural construct that assigns an identity and appropriate roles to people based partly on sexual differences and partly on cultural beliefs about sex and behaviour. Gender models make use of sexual differences between males and females, but cultures vary in the roles that women and men perform, the rights they have in relation to each other, and the values associated with their activities. People learn their gender identity from their earliest socialization in infancy through their childhood, learning appropriate behaviour and molding personality to conform to cultural norms. Females and males are born, but women and men are products of their culture.

- Most cultures organize their concepts of gender into a dual division of man and woman. However, some cultures provide a third possibility, a third gender. In

these societies, found in Native North America, India, Indonesia, and some other cultures, males and females could choose to identify as a third gender. The specific roles and behaviours appropriate to members of the third gender varied in different cultures. Two-Spirits in North America and *hijras* in India might perform the work usually associated with the opposite sex. Two-Spirits often had significant ritual roles that granted them prestige in their communities.

- Although we commonly think of our sexual feelings and practices as part of our nature, they are shaped by our culture. Our culture teaches us what kinds of sexual feelings and practices are "normal" and what kinds are "deviant." We learn who are appropriate sexual partners, when and where it is appropriate to have sexual relations, and the proper ways of engaging in sex. Another cultural element in attitudes about sexuality is the accepted relationship between sex and marriage. Attitudes about homosexuality are a further reflection of cultural learning. In some societies, homosexuality is viewed as unnatural or sinful or criminal, whereas in others, it may be regarded as one of the possible expressions of human desire.

Gender Roles and Gender Relations

- In all societies, some form of division of labour by gender influences the daily work of an individual. Women's work always includes caring for young children, performing household tasks, usually including cooking and cleaning, although in some South Pacific societies, men do the daily household cooking. Men's work always includes large animal hunting and warfare. Other economic activities, such as farming, small game hunting, and fishing, might be done by men, women, or both. As with other elements of culture, gender roles change as economic and material factors change.

- In some societies, men and women are considered equal, each having rights to autonomy and independence, each permitted and encouraged to participate in decision making, productive work, and prestigious roles in their societies. Gender equality is likely to exist in foraging societies where all individuals make important contributions to subsistence and where hierarchical leadership and control is absent or minimal. In other societies, male dominance may be reflected in men's control over access to resources, economic production and distribution, household and community decision making and leadership, and ritual activity. The most intense forms of male dominance tend to occur in agricultural states. However, in male-dominated societies, women may have some degree of independence and power in some spheres of life, as in the case of West African women who control local and regional trade.

- Some anthropologists suggest that some form of male dominance exists in all societies, whereas others point to the variation that occurs in known societies in which women and men have or had equal rights and privileges and their economic, social, and political roles were equally valued. Rapid culture change brought about by European colonization led to greater subordination of women, as Europeans favoured men as individuals and as a group, thereby enhancing their status and power to the exclusion of women.

Gender and Subsistence

- Egalitarian relationships develop among foragers and in industrial and post-industrial societies. In Europe and North America, women were central to the industrializing economy in the late eighteenth and early nineteenth centuries, as farmers' daughters went to work in textile mills. At first, young unmarried women worked for wages in many types of industries, but later married women and even those with young children joined the work force. These women were compelled by economic conditions to contribute their salaries to the growing needs of their families. However, although many women worked outside the home, they remain marginalized in the industrial sector by gender segregation in the workplace and by unequal pay. The "gender gap" in pay between men and women continues to this day.

- After World War II, the expansion of the service sector in post-industrial societies has led to massive increases in female employment with implications for many other areas of society. Trends have led towards gender equality but full parity has not yet been reached.

Globalization and Gender

- Globalization has affected men and women differently as national and international agencies have introduced agricultural and industrial development projects in rural and poor communities. Women often lose their central roles as subsistence farmers when land is taken out of household production and dedicated to growing crops for national and global trading networks. Multinational corporations build light manufacturing plants that employ predominantly young, unmarried women at low pay. These jobs offer advantages to the employees, who gain an income and some degree of independence, but they also have disadvantages.

Key Terms

gender 228	cultural constructs 228	gender relations 233	gender gap 245
sex 228	berdaches 230	gender equality 235	cult of domesticity 246
gender construct (gender model) 228	Two-Spirits 230	gender inequality 235	social reproduction 249
	gender roles 233	male dominance 235	

Review Questions

1. What are cultural constructs? How are they used to define gender in societies?

2. Cross-culturally, what are some economic roles typically undertaken by women, and how are those roles different from those undertaken by men?

3. What is a third gender identity? How do third gender concepts relate to sexuality? To homosexuality?

4. How do contributions to production, post-marital residence, and warfare patterns affect the status of women in a society?

5. How are gender roles and relations related to the subsistence strategy of a group?

6. Why would economic developers of business enterprises in Nigeria be wise to give Igbo women a key role in planning and implementation?

7. How did gender relations among the Ju/'hoansi, Inuit, Iroquois, and Chinese change in part as a result of both external contact and internal change?

8. Discuss gender roles and statuses in post-industrial society and how the movement of women into the work force has affected Canadian society.

Equality and Inequality

CHAPTER 10

Preview

1. **What is social stratification? How does inequality arise in human societies?**

2. **What are three basic types of social stratification? How do they work?**

3. **How do caste and class systems differ as two forms of stratified societies?**

4. **What are some determinants and indicators of social standing in stratified societies?**

5. **How are societies stratified by gender, race, and ethnicity?**

6. **Why is the concept of race controversial?**

7. **How and why do people create, accept, maintain, reject, and change their ethnic identities?**

8. **How do ideologies reinforce systems of stratification?**

9. **What can we learn from an anthropological perspective of class, ideology, ethnicity, and race in Canadian society?**

O*n a bright Sunday morning some peasants sat on the door-step, chatting about their affairs.*

The village shopkeeper went up to them and began to boast that he was this, that and the other, and had been in the lord's own chambers.

One of the peasants, the poorest of the lot, sat and scoffed.

"Pooh, that's nothing. I could dine with the lord if I wanted to."

"What—you? Dine with the lord? Never in all your life!" cried the rich shopkeeper.

"But I will, just to prove it."

"No, you won't."

They argued on until the poor man said:

"Let us lay a wager. If I dine with the lord, I win your black and your bay; if I do not, I shall work three years for you for nothing."

The shopkeeper was mighty pleased.

"Very well, I bet you my black and my bay with a calf thrown in for good measure. Let these good men stand witness."

And they shook hands on it before the witnesses. The poor man went to the lord.

"I should like to ask you in secret—what might be the price of a gold nugget the size of my cap?"

The lord said nothing. He just clapped his hands.

"Ho, there! A drink for this man and myself! Be quick about it. And serve us dinner, too. Sit down, sit down, my man, make yourself at home. Help yourself to all that is on the table!"

The lord treated the poor man as he would an honoured guest, and all the time he was agog with impatience. There was nothing he wanted so much as to lay hands on that gold nugget.

"Now, my man, go quickly and fetch the nugget. I will give you a sack of flour and a piece of silver for it."

"But I haven't got any nugget. I was just asking what a nugget the size of my cap would be worth."

The lord flew into a rage.

"Get out, you fool!"

"How can I be a fool when you yourself have treated me as such an honoured guest and the shopkeeper owes me two horses and a calf for this same dinner?"

And the peasant went home happy as a lark.

From Alex Alexander (1975), *Russian Folklore: An Anthology in English Translation*, pp. 216–218. Belmont, CA: Norland Publishing.

wealth
Economic resources, whether in land, goods, or money.

power
The ability to exert control over the actions of other people and to make decisions that affect them.

prestige
A social resource reflected in others' good opinions, respect, and willingness to be influenced.

In this tale from Russia, differences in people's wealth and status are at the centre of the narrative action and resolution. The story turns on the success of the lowly peasant who, by his cleverness, is able to outwit the wealthy lord. In doing so, he also succeeds where the rich shopkeeper has failed. The story acknowledges the system of class that existed in pre-revolutionary Russia, dividing people and granting privileges to some and disadvantages to others. The story sides with the peasants. Peasants are generally looked down upon because of their poverty, but it is the peasant who prevails by his wit. While the narrative acknowledges the system of class, it can also be read as a form of resistance to the dominant ideology of inequality. And although poor, the peasant shows his worthiness by outsmarting the rich shopkeeper and the wealthy landlord. This story, then, exposes the prevailing system of inequality but with a subversive message.

EQUALITY, INEQUALITY, AND SOCIAL STRATIFICATION

In previous chapters, we encountered societies in which everyone has equal access to resources, livelihood, and respect. We also encountered societies in which some individuals and groups enjoy greater access to these benefits than the rest of the society. The first type of system, based on principles of equality among members of communities, is called egalitarian. The second type, based on social, economic, and political inequality, is called stratified. In this chapter we are particularly concerned with systems of social and political inequality.

Before we begin, though, several important distinctions must be made clear. Although people in egalitarian societies have equal access to resources and to positions of prestige and respect, all people are not equal in ability. Individuals everywhere differ in that some have more talent, intelligence, skill, or valued personality traits than others. Those people with more desirable characteristics are more respected, appreciated, and liked than those people lacking such positive traits. Nonetheless, everyone may make use of the group's resources, secure subsistence, and live a decent life more or less comparable to other people in their community.

In contrast, some people in stratified societies achieve positions of respect, influence, and power that grant them privileges and opportunities denied to others. We will be examining the bases on which stratified societies make social distinctions and the differing rewards and benefits available to some.

Three categories of culturally valued resources are wealth, power, and prestige (Fried 1967). **Wealth** refers to economic resources, whether in land, goods, or money. **Power** refers to the ability to exert control over the actions of other people and to make decisions that affect them. **Prestige** is a social resource. It is reflected in other people's good opinion, in their respect, and in their willingness to solicit and to listen voluntarily to one's advice. According to Max Weber (1968, 1981), prestige, or honour, as he called it, is central to the establishment and maintenance of status. Weber related honour to the notion of personal charisma. People strive to be well thought of because they then can influence other people. In stratified societies, prestige is linked to wealth and power. Since social values emphasize the worthiness of accumulating wealth, wealthy people are considered successful and looked to as models to emulate. Prestige, then, built on wealth, can be used to obtain and exercise power.

Another set of terms relevant to our discussion of egalitarian and stratified societies has to do with

This African king shows his wealth in a grand festival. In any stratified society, wealth, power, and prestige confer privileges, along with opportunities to amass greater wealth, power, and prestige.

various statuses and roles. Some of these are achieved and some are ascribed. An **achieved status** is one that people attain on the basis of their own efforts and skills. An **ascribed status** is one that a person occupies simply by birth or through a culturally determined right. In our society, leadership is an achieved status; we elect our political officials, presumably because of their abilities. In monarchies, leadership is an ascribed status; a king occupies his position simply because he is the eldest son of the previous king.

Finally, the distinctions among societies are not absolute, discrete types but rather form a continuum from egalitarian to stratified. Many societies contain elements of both, combining principles of equality in certain contexts with principles of inequality in other contexts. Indeed, there is a type of society, called ranked, that exhibits characteristics of both. **Ranked societies** differentiate individuals or, more usually, kinship groups along a continuum from lowest to highest, based partly on achieved status and partly on ascribed status. The benefits of high rank are social rather than economic or political. People of high rank have prestige and respect but they do not have a living standard significantly better than that of people of lower rank.

Egalitarian Societies

Egalitarian societies are ones in which all people have equal access to valued resources. Everyone has available land and natural resources to supply the food that they need to survive. Everyone can achieve positions of respect and influence. And while people may seek the advice of respected individuals, no one is able to exert control or dominance over other people. Egalitarian social systems are usually found in cultures with economies based on producing for subsistence and use rather than to accumulate large surpluses and wealth. Small foraging and horticultural societies are also egalitarian. For example, among the Innu, an egalitarian society of northeastern Quebec, social ethics stressed generosity, hospitality, cooperation, and loyalty. People were expected to share resources and to aid each other in household and community work. Coupled with responsibilities to kin and community members, individual autonomy and the rights of all men and women to make decisions and act independently were valued. Coercion, either within households or in camps, was not tolerated and, given the strong negative reactions against such behaviour, it was rarely attempted. Group leadership was diffuse, flexible, and dependent on personal qualities and subsistence skills. People looked for advice to those who were intelligent and successful in the particular endeavour requiring assistance or consultation—for example, skilled hunters were consulted regarding hunting. However, a man's or a woman's influence was temporary, fitted to the given occasion. Advice, therefore, was sought among local "experts," but such people could not exert authority or control. Decisions were made jointly by all involved. No formal leadership existed.

In spite of the label, social relations and statuses in egalitarian societies involve some degree of inequality. Differences of intelligence, skill, and personality may render some people more respected and influential than others. There are also attribute inequalities, such as age and gender, that may affect one's position in the household and society. Older people may be consulted and asked for their opinions about personal or community matters because of their greater experience in life.

The importance of age may be reflected within the household as well. Some of the authority and influence of parents derives from their age as well as from their genealogical relationship to their children. In some societies, the importance of seniority among siblings may be reflected in kinship terms that distinguish older and younger siblings and in behaviour where younger siblings act deferentially toward their elders.

In addition, gender may be a factor in the respect and authority that people exert. If men and women are thought of as equal, both have influential roles in family and community decision making, conflict resolution, and group action. In male-dominated societies, however, men's opinions have paramount weight in these matters and women's voices are muted. Other kinds of inequalities derived from kinship relationships may exist as well. Heads of lineages or clans may have important, decisive roles,

? *What is an example of one of your achieved statuses? What is an example of one of your ascribed statuses?*

achieved status
A social position attained by a person's own efforts and skills.

ascribed status
A social position that a person attains by birth. A person is born into an ascribed status.

ranked societies
Societies in which people or, more usually, kinship groups are ordered on a continuum in relation to each other.

egalitarian societies
Societies in which all members have equal access to valued resources, including land, social prestige, wealth, and power.

big man
A status within egalitarian societies that places people in leadership positions based on personal wealth and influence over supporters.

levelling mechanism
A custom, such as a feast, in which individuals give away their wealth to obtain prestige.

certainly within their families and often in wider social contexts. In some societies, lineage or clan leaders may form village or district councils to discuss matters of community concern.

In some egalitarian societies, status differences lead to the recognition of especially influential individuals known as **big men**, a term that anthropologists have borrowed from Melanesian culture, according to the prominence of the institution in this region (Sahlins 1970). These important figures assume recognized statuses that place them in leadership roles. Their positions and power, however, are not dependent upon a formal office that they occupy but upon their personal abilities and the amount of influence they can exert over their personal body of supporters. Accordingly, the status is acquired in the course of an individual's lifetime and may be relinquished.

Big man status is attained and marked through the possession and exchange of special wealth items, such as pigs or cattle, which assume an important symbolic value and constitute a "fund of power." An aspiring big man may amass a sizeable accumulation through savings or often through the clever manipulation of the exchange system. He then uses his wealth in strategically hosting feasts and initiating exchange relations. As a consequence, the status seeker attains both public prestige and recognition and a group of followers and allies on whom he can depend for social and political support. He will also dissipate his wealth accumulation in the process. In this regard, status holders in egalitarian societies are distinguished from those in other systems of stratification in that they must disperse any resources that might go to a successor. Their sons do not inherit their wealth or status and must establish their positions through their own efforts. Moreover, characteristic patterns of polygyny in the societies that support big men will mean that the largest estates will have the greatest number of heirs wishing to subdivide them. As such, the system of display and exchange acts as a **levelling mechanism**, which reduces inequalities in productive resource ownership.

The Igbo of West Africa lived in an egalitarian society, which nevertheless allowed both men and women to attain prominent leadership status within their communities. Many aspects of Igbo status were determined by gender and age differences. However, wealth also constituted a major source for funding and claiming positions of prestige and influence and provided an avenue for young men and sometimes women to acquire exceptional status. Wealthy individuals in Igbo communities could distinguish themselves in several ways. The most usual status of distinction that individuals could achieve was that of "big compound head." To obtain this position, people invested their wealth in bride prices to acquire several wives and through them a large number of dependents. Wives and children formed a large labour pool and a significant political support base. Accordingly, big compound heads could exert greater influence in public meetings than people with smaller households (Uchendu 1965).

Beyond their immediate domestic achievements, Igbo status seekers could also invest their wealth in formal channels of title taking. Igbo titles conferred special status on their holders that gave them a high amount of general prestige as well as public influence that was normally afforded to a small number of elders. These positions were controlled by formally constituted title societies which were variously associated with general status attainment and with special prestige gaining activities, such as the cultivation of a large yam crop, funding of a father's funeral, or success in warfare. Separate societies were established for men and women, but a few women were also allowed to join men's societies. Title taking depended upon the accumulation and distribution of a substantial amount of wealth. Fixed entry fees were paid to the existing title holders, who shared the receipts within the group. In addition, the title taker funded public feasts and displays to validate the attainment of the status and to demonstrate his or her wealth and generosity. The occupants of the top grades assumed the highest statuses within their communities and sometimes constituted a formal ruling body. However, even where titles conferred real power, they still supported an egalitarian economic structure. Title taking dissipated accumulations of wealth and mitigated against the concentration of productive resources in a few hands. Moreover, in contrast to the titles assumed in a ranked society such as the Kwakwaka'wakw names (see the Case Study on page 262), Igbo titles could not be inherited.

Ranked Societies

In systems of rank, every person—or, more accurately, every lineage or kin group—has a different position in the social hierarchy. Each rank is ordered in relation to all others. People of higher ranks have more social prestige than people of lower ranks, but they do not have significantly greater wealth. Their rewards are social, manifested in the respect given to them and the influence allowed them. If people follow their advice and direction, it is only because they have earned respect by their intelligence, behaviour, and sound judgment. Ranked positions are established and maintained through a complex interplay of economic resources, political alliances, personal demeanour, and charisma, all leading to the formation of people's opinions of others.

Ranked systems are not static. Indeed, they are inherently extremely dynamic, even potentially volatile types of social organization. People can raise their status by their behaviour and achievement and by the support of their relatives, but status can also fall. In order to move up the metaphoric "ladder of success," people have to mobilize public opinion because it is public opinion that legitimates one's place in the system. People attempt to increase their economic wealth, forge alliances, and attract dependents or clients, and act in ways that convey self-respect and conform to social norms of personality and attractiveness. In order to be successful and achieve these results, people need the support of their kin. And because of the competitive nature of ranked systems, competition within the family might prove disruptive if members of the family itself vied with each other for access to rank. Therefore, many such systems include the rule of primogeniture, or inheritance by seniority, so that the eldest child has the privilege of representing the family by occupying a position of rank that it holds. (In some societies, only men may hold rank; in others, women or men might occupy status positions.) See the Case Study on page 262.

Stratified Societies

In **stratified societies**, people do not have equal access to productive resources. Some people accumulate the lion's share of land or capital and utilize their wealth to gain greater rewards than people in other sectors of society. Some people have more power than others, and they are able to exert control over the actions of other people by making decisions that affect them with or without their consent. As a consequence of having more wealth and power, they also have more social prestige. People respect them and regard them with envy. In stratified societies, some wealth, power, and prestige accrue to people because of their achievements, hard work, and personal characteristics, but some of their good fortune comes to them because of their birth. They are the children of wealthy and powerful people. Prestige, wealth, and power, therefore, are both ascribed and achieved.

Social stratification refers to a division of society into two or more groups, or strata, that are hierarchically ordered in relation to each other. Within each stratum, members are all of more or less equal social standing. While there are differences among individuals in stratified systems, people in the same stratum have equivalent opportunities, privileges, and standards of living, at least when compared to people in other strata.

One of the significant features of all systems of stratification is that the highest group is usually, if not always, a numerical minority. Why, then, is it that the majority of people are willing to accept a system that does not benefit them? There are many and complex explanations. One reason is that the elite group controls the means of forcing compliance with their wishes. Because the **elites** control social, economic, and political resources, they are in a position to use economic, political, and even military power against those who resist their control. But the use of force is costly, not just in economic terms. When force is used against people, especially if they constitute the majority of the population, they will likely rebel against a system that exploits them. Instead, social attitudes and beliefs are developed to induce conformity. People are taught to believe that the system they live in is just, and, if not entirely just, it is, at the least, legitimate.

? *Have you been a member of a ranked social organization? How would your experience compare with living in a ranked society?*

stratified societies
Societies in which people have differential access to valued resources, including land and property, social prestige, wealth, and political power.

social stratification
Divison of society into two or more groups, or strata, that are hierarchically ordered.

elites
Members of a social group in a stratified society who have privileges denied to the majority of the population.

Case study

The Kwakwaka'wakw as a Ranked Society

BRITISH COLUMBIA

CANADA

Kwakwaka'wakw (Kwakiutl) Homeland

Vancouver Island

UNITED STATES

The Kwakwaka'wakw are a Pacific Northwest Coastal society, whose institutions are similar to the other groups in the region that we have considered in previous chapters. Unlike many of their neighbours, they are not matrilineal but allow their members to belong to either their mother's or father's lineage and to inherit rights to land use and status positions through either parent.

The lineages collectively owned the houses in which their members lived, as well as access to fishing sites, berry patches, and other resource areas. They also held title to ritual property, such as songs, dances, and ceremonial gear, and more importantly names and crests. All Kwakwaka'wakw tribes and all of their constituent lineages were ranked in relation to all others. In addition, each lineage possessed a number of names that were also hierarchically arranged. Each name was held by a particular individual, although people could hold more than one name at a time. Names were inherited from parents or grandparents and could also be acquired through marriage. Inheritance of ranked positions followed rules of primogeniture to the first-born child, whether boy or girl. Although the rule of primogeniture was absolute, rivalries between siblings sometimes surfaced. When a woman was the chosen inheritor, she generally received a man's name and transmitted her social position to her own eldest son as soon as he was grown. It was common for holders of rank to choose their successors and pass on their names before their death, often beginning the process of transfer when the child was young.

Most marriages took place between people of different lineages. The higher one's social position, the more necessary it was to marry one's social equal or, even better, to marry someone of higher rank. However, since high-status people did not want to marry beneath them, it was unlikely that a person of low rank could achieve social advancement by marrying far up the social scale.

The Kwakwaka'wakw social system differentiated among three groups: nobles or chiefly people, commoners, and slaves. The first two groups were not discrete classes but gradations of relative rank. Slaves, in contrast, were socially distinct and could not achieve social mobility. The difference between slaves and the rest of society was a distinction of stratification, not rank.

Most slaves were acquired in warfare or were the descendants of slaves. They generally performed menial subsistence and productive tasks. Their major constraint was that they could not be part of the system of social rank and prestige that was fundamental to society. The contrast between commoners and nobles was much more complex. These were not fixed categories but were on a continuum from lowest to highest social standing. People of highest status constituted the leadership of kin groups and villages. Chiefs were recipients of portions of animal, fish, and plant products obtained by members of their group. They were usually exempt from most subsistence tasks. Chiefs were responsible for organizing cooperative productive activities such as house building. They acted as representatives of their lineages in the system of potlatching or feasting that was the occasion for ceremonial validation of one's social standing.

Potlatches functioned to redistribute wealth and to claim status. Wealth was related to status, but wealth was accumulated in order to give it away publicly. The potlatch system demonstrated levelling mechanisms that barred the concentration of extreme wealth in any individual or family. Potlatching also confirmed status and contributed to social solidarity. For instance, to be invited as a guest at a potlatch given by a high-ranking person was a public acknowledgment of one's own high social status. Chiefs needed others of comparable standing to raise their own social rank, and chiefs needed their own kin to amass the goods distributed at feasts. In these ways, potlatching served to unite families and lineages. One's own social status rose and fell with the social status of other members of one's family and larger kin groups.

This woman is one of many working poor who earn minimum wage in Canada. In some stratified societies, common people accept inequality because they believe that with hard work and diligence, they too can achieve success and social mobility.

Through this process of exercising cultural hegemony, attitudes and ideologies of dominance and subordination are transmitted in many ways. Religious teaching, for example, is an effective means of instilling obedience to the rulers. People may be taught that their leaders have been chosen by the deities or they may be pacified by the hope that divine beings will reward them in another life. In addition, social ideologies transmit the notion that elites are more capable, more intelligent, and in other ways superior to common people. Common people absorb these ideologies through their socialization and through exposure to public discourse that is controlled by the elites.

Explaining Social Stratification

Social stratification is a characteristic of complex state societies. Among other traits, states have economies based on unequal ownership of land or capital. Labour specialization develops so that some people may work as farmers, others as artisans, traders, soldiers, or government officials. States are also characterized by unequal access to resources. Some people accumulate more goods, land, and other property than others. Rather than distributing their wealth to community members in need, they use their property for themselves, raising their standard of living and living better than people with fewer resources. Over time, inequalities in standards of living become entrenched as children of wealthy parents are born with advantages and opportunities lacking to the children of poor people. (Characteristics of state societies are discussed further in Chapter 11.)

Several explanations are offered to explain the existence of stratification. Functional analyses focus on social and economic distinctions as necessary artifacts of the division of labour in state societies. Large, wealthy, and complex social systems are based upon occupational specialization, which emerges primarily because it contributes to higher economic output. Functionally distinct groups become integrated into a coherent social order through the mutually beneficial exchange of goods and services. Functionalists understand wealth concentrations that benefit some groups and not others as an inevitable result of the economic advances that have occurred because of specialization. They argue that the elite have a right to power and to the extraordinary privileges that they hold because they provide administrative coordination and legal protections to a complex system of exchange and integration.

A second explanation for social stratification emphasizes the conflicts between members of different strata or classes. These analyses, following Karl Marx, focus on the processes that create groups in opposition to each other. In this formulation, social and economic divisions are based on differences in the ownership of productive resources and the control of labour. In situations where a restricted group has achieved a monopoly over the possession of land, capital, or other essential resource, the elite can use its advantage to dominate subordinate classes and benefit from their labour. The specific social order depends upon the character of differential ownership, which is incorporated into the mode of production model. Different types, such as the slave mode, feudal mode, and capitalist mode are defined in terms of how and in what form the means of production are controlled. For example, the feudal mode is based on land ownership,

GLOBALIZATION

Systems of stratification based on the control of capital and the concept of social mobility have spread throughout the world as a consequence of globalization. Stratification based on class membership is rapidly replacing other forms of stratification, as well as ranked and egalitarian societies.

Karl Marx explained social stratification as an outgrowth of class conflict over the control of resources and wealth. Neo-Marxist approaches to the study of social stratification focus on conflicts between different groups in a society.

Case study

Class Consciousness among Fish Processing Plant Workers in Cape Breton

According to Marxist theory, class divisions and antagonisms tend to foster ideological divisions among different social strata. Upper classes will adopt values, beliefs, and theories that justify their hold on wealth and power, while lower classes will formulate alternative visions for society and use them to advocate and organize for change. Accordingly, working class consciousness has been especially important in capitalist societies. It has supported unionization, and has encouraged broader changes, such as labour-oriented political parties and at times revolutions. However, not all capitalist societies have fully reflected the emergence of class consciousness and mobilization. In general, labour militancy has been more important in Europe than in North America. Pauline Barber's study of labour organization within the Cape Breton fish processing industry details some of the forces that have discouraged and contributed to the formation of Canadian working class identity and organization (Barber 1990).

The economy of Cape Breton was traditionally based on mining, steel making, and fishing. The mining and steel sector was active during the early years of the twentieth century but had substantially declined at the time of Barber's study. Fish harvesting was organized on a small scale basis by individual fishers, while the processing was carried out in a large number of

small plants employing between 50 and 250 workers. Mine and steel plant workers, who were mainly men, were once at the forefront of one of the most militant labour movements in North America; by contrast, the fish processing industry was not unionized until 1987.

According to Barber's study, fish processing involved work divided among trimmers, cutters, and packers, along with a smaller number of jobs devoted to plant maintenance. Workers doing different tasks were located in proximity to each other and would socialize intensively. Management took on a paternalistic attitude and personalized their relationships with workers, often offering aid on occasions of economic difficulty. Local kinship and strong community ties were important for labour–management relations. Employees would regularly obtain jobs for relatives and friends on the assurance that the company would honour their requests. This process created an atmosphere of gratitude, which led to adherence to the company's needs for productivity and labour peace. Demands relating to pay and working conditions were dealt with informally. Workers would meet among themselves to formulate their requests and then meet with the management to negotiate for a final settlement.

In the 1980s technological and organizational changes occurred within the industry. To lower labour costs and achieve higher efficiency, one of the larger plants put in a new production line with more up-to-date equipment and also made changes to the work process and to management style. Workers became positioned along an assembly line and could no longer talk to one another. Personalized and paternalistic management styles gave way to formalized administration, often involving the replacement of supervisory personnel in order to discourage older forms of workplace organization. Recruitment also became impersonalized and focused on hiring better-educated workers. The workers resisted these changes in a variety of informal ways but finally adopted the strategy of unionization, which created a class-based rather than a personal response to labour relations. In forming the union, the workers utilized values and organization forms of kinship to recruit members to the union and to maintain loyalty and solidarity. Thus, local cultural values and practices affected labour relations in contrasting ways. In the traditional economy, they supported paternalistic management styles that emphasized the common identity and interests of employer and worker, and discouraged class consciousness. As the workplace became "rationalized," the same values facilitated the emergence of a working-class identity and mobilization.

whereas capitalism is based on investment in industrial technology. Thus, while functionalists interpret status differences as adding to social well-being and harmony, Marxists suggest that they create and exploit the lower classes and lead to social strife.

Members of different classes have different class interests. They develop a consciousness of their class and strive to protect and expand their interests. Members of elite classes try to influence economic and political policies that will benefit themselves. Members of lower classes are bound by the economic, political, and sometimes ideological hold that the upper classes have over them, but at times will organize resistance to the dominant institutions of society (see the Case Study on page 264).

These explanations focus on societies as dynamic systems. They emphasize the processes of struggle between members of opposing groups. It is through these struggles that societies can be transformed, and new types of group formation and new types of opposition and conflict lead to further series of changes and adaptations. Although complex societies are composed of groups with different, often conflicting, interests and goals, societies also attempt to build consensus and foster cooperation among groups. Therefore, functional and Marxist explanations for social stratification both offer insights that can be useful in analyzing societal structures and processes.

How might a functionalist explain homeless street youth in a stratified society such as Canada? What explanation based on conflict might a Marxist offer?

REVIEW

Societies become stratified through the unequal distribution of wealth, power, and prestige which attach to the different ascribed statuses (inherited) and achieved statuses (acquired) in a society. In ranked societies, different groups are ranked hierarchically on the basis of both ascribed and achieved statuses. Egalitarian societies provide equal access to resources, whereas in stratified societies some individuals and groups have more resources and others less. Structuralism, functionalism, Marxism, and other theoretical perspectives offer alternative explanations for social stratification.

CASTE AND CLASS

A caste is a social group whose membership is hereditary. Castes are endogamous. That is, people must marry within their caste, and their children are also members of the same group. Thus caste is an ascribed status with automatic, involuntary, and unchanging membership and identity. Separation on the basis of caste may be manifested by restrictions on living spaces, occupation, style of dress, and demeanour. In caste systems, each group is assigned a particular order of prestige relative to the others on a scale from lowest to highest. Unlike rank, caste order cannot change. Caste stratification is exemplified in the Hindu caste system (see the Culture Change on page 266) and in

Culture Change

CASTE IN INDIA

In India, there are hundreds of discrete castes (called *jati*), all ranked in relation to one another (Koller 1982). The caste system unifies constituent groups into four large groupings (called *varna*), each containing numerous castes that are perceived to be somewhat similar in their origin, function, and especially in their ritual purity. Members of the highest varna, called the Brahmins, were traditionally the priests and scholars. The second-highest category are the Kshatriyas, who were the warriors. The merchants and traders constitute the third varna, called Vaishyas, and the fourth varna are the Shudras, or artisans, carpenters, blacksmiths, barbers, farmers, and menial workers. Finally, there is a fifth group, ranked below all the others: the untouchables. Untouchables are people considered ritually impure, fit to do only the most menial work, such as cleaning toilets. According to Hindu religious and ethical beliefs, a member of one of the higher castes can become ritually polluted by touching or being touched by an untouchable.

Caste in India is an example of a comparatively closed system of stratification. Although in practice some social mobility is possible, people traditionally are born into a particular caste and remain in that caste for the rest of their lives. Rural villages often are divided into caste neighbourhoods, and occupations are determined by caste. In the most traditional contexts, there is little, if anything, one can do to change one's circumstances. Even if a person were to move to another community and not reveal his or her heredity, a person's way of talking and behaving would probably

be telltale signs of the person's ancestry and, by implication, his or her caste identity.

The behaviour of people in different castes functions as a barrier to social interactions, acting as boundary markers. People belonging to different castes should not eat together and certainly should not have sexual relations with each other. Members of higher castes may avoid taking food offered by members of lower castes. Higher caste people are more likely to be vegetarians and to refrain from drinking alcoholic beverages. Members of different castes may have somewhat different ways of speaking, including their pronunciation of sounds and in some cases their choice of words. The most stringent restrictions are placed on the behaviour of untouchables. In rural villages, untouchables must reside in their own section and cannot take drinking water from wells used by the higher castes.

The most prestigious group, the Brahmins, is thought of as ritually pure and needs to maintain their purity through social distance. While many Brahmins have respected occupations and earn high salaries, many do not; Brahmins are not necessarily wealthy. For example, Brahmins may work as cooks in restaurants because members of all castes may eat food touched by the highest group.

Although Indian castes are perceived to be primarily social and ritual categories, they also have economic functions. High caste people cannot perform important subsistence and productive functions for themselves because of the polluting nature of these activities, such as working with wood or making pottery. These goods and services are provided by lower caste people, who in return receive food, clothing, and money. A permanent and stable relationship between patron and client may become established over the years, providing for an exchange of goods and services between the two parties. The patron-client relationship may pass to the descendants of the originators, continuing important economic exchanges through the generations. In this way, both groups receive significant benefits.

Caste economic relationships serve both divisive and integrating functions. They are divisive because people are restricted to performing caste-specific economic roles, but at the same time they are integrating because they create necessary interdependence among people of different castes. However, despite the advantages of stability and security obtained by lower caste people from their patrons, it is still true that the system as a whole stigmatizes them and takes more from them than it gives. As in any system of social stratification, higher ranked people benefit most.

Finally, Indian castes were intimately associated and intertwined with political power. The structures of caste functioned in villages and regional territories to both segment and articulate various kinship groups and residential communities. They formed the basic structure of political alliances and political control. Much of the political significance of castes was ignored and obliterated by British colonial administrators beginning in the nineteenth century. By reinventing caste significance as primarily ritual, the British were able to pretend that India lacked "genuine politics," in effect providing a rationale for British control (Dirks 2001).

The system of caste in India is not as static as it is often described, however. Since India's independence in 1948, a number of laws have been enacted that affect restrictions on caste behaviour. People belonging to different castes can now legally marry and cannot be prosecuted for engaging in sexual relations. Family and community opinion, however, still often frowns on such unions. It is currently illegal to discriminate against untouchables. Indeed, the government specifies that certain jobs and a percentage of

openings in universities must be reserved for members of the lower castes. All people have the right to vote, a right that carries with it the potential, if exercised, to seek wider political changes to improve the economic and social position of the lower castes.

In modern India, especially in the cities, caste ranking is not immutable. Upward mobility for the caste as a group is possible if members have achieved a degree of wealth and prestige, but upward mobility pertains to the group; it is not a narrowly individual process. However, striving for upward mobility does not necessarily undermine the system of stratification, as it merely results in a change of the ordering of groups rather than in a challenge to the legitimacy of the existing social principles on which the system is based. It is still possible that, over time, fluidity in caste may lead to fundamental challenges to the system. Members of the untouchable caste are especially vocal opponents of the system, calling for laws that ban discrimination. Many thousands have converted from Hinduism to Buddhism as a protest against the injustices of caste hierarchies.

the rigid systems of racial discrimination that were once institutionalized in the United States, Canada, and apartheid South Africa.

Determinants of Class

Systems of class are also ways of grouping people in a hierarchical order. Whereas castes are differentiated according to the sole criterion of ancestry, class may be defined in various ways, such as economic factors, primarily income, wealth, education, and occupation. These factors tend to go together, so that people with the highest incomes usually have the most advanced education and the most prestigious occupations. However, cases can easily be cited that contradict this general tendency. For example, university professors must usually have Ph.D.s but earn lower incomes than some groups in the private sector with less education. In this economic meaning of class, the groups are not closed, discrete units but rather are categories differentiated along a continuum. There are no absolute boundary markers between them.

Unlike caste, class is an achieved status because the criteria for determining class membership are subject to achievement by individuals as well as to change. Also, unlike caste, where a person's identity is rigidly determined, the factors used to determine class membership are less easily and less consistently specified. Unlike the fixed and closed nature of caste, systems of class are open and allow for mobility from one group to another. Class **mobility** may be either upward or downward.

Another way of talking about class is to talk about relations of production. In this Marxian sense of class, there are two contrasting groups—the group

mobility
A principle that people can move from membership in one social group to another.

Hindus revere many deities, including the goddess Lakshmi, here being worshipped at the rice harvest.

These Saudi royals experience privilege in their living standards, their health, and the control they have over other people. They may influence ordinary citizens through the laws they enact, the policies they implement, and the media outlets (television, radio, and newspapers) they regulate.

that owns the means of economic production and controls the distribution of products and the group that does not own the means of production. These two groups, or classes, can be simplified as owners and workers. Owners control production and distribution and profit from the productive labour of others, and workers sell their labour to the owners for a wage. In modern corporate capitalism, the distinction between owners and workers is more complicated than was true in the late nineteenth century, when Karl Marx developed his insights about the European capitalist economic system.

In North American discourse on class, there are strong pressures against public discussion of class interests and underlying class conflicts. Rather, we are led to believe that anyone can grow up to be a corporate executive or a Prime Minister. Nevertheless, members of different classes, however defined, occupy different places in society and their life experiences are fundamentally different.

Slavery

? *How does your social class influence your life experiences? How does your culture reinforce the class system of which you are a part?*

Slavery, the most extreme form of stratification, is an ascribed status. People become slaves either by being born into slavery or by being captured in warfare or slaving raids. Slavery is thus forced upon a person, either through accident of birth or through the deliberate actions of others. The slave group, like castes and classes, is endogamous; slaves usually marry other slaves, not necessarily because of their preferences but because non-slaves are unwilling to marry them. Slavery generally entails the loss of a person's independence and autonomy. At the least, slaves work at the direction and the behest of their owners. They cannot control their own labour, and they do not benefit materially from the goods that they produce. In addition, slaves cannot leave and find homes and work elsewhere. With low social status, slaves cannot hope to achieve any position of prestige or influence in their society, except within the community of other slaves. Social attitudes attribute negative qualities to slaves. They are thought to be inferior and incapable of valued achievements.

slavery
An ascribed status forced on a person upon birth or through involuntary servitude.

The quality of a slave's life varies across cultures. We are familiar from the history of the United States with a form of slavery in which slaves had no rights of any kind. In other societies with slavery, the life of a slave was not necessarily much different from that of ordinary people. For example, among the Kwakwaka'wakw and other indigenous societies of the Pacific Northwest, slaves lived in the homes of their owners, ate the same kind of food, and wore the same kind of clothing. They usually performed menial tasks and suffered the indignity of low social status, but they could be ransomed by their relatives and returned to their own communities. In West Africa, domestic slaves could rise to a higher status and establish households and own slaves of their own.

A group of slaves gather under a tree as they wait for freedom in southern Sudan. On July 4, 2001, three African-American ministers and a Harvard student, with funds from Christian Solidarity International, bought the freedom of 2035 slaves in Sudan. The price they negotiated for each slave on this "redemption mission" was less than the cost of one healthy goat, about $40. Slavery and the slave trade were outlawed in the United Nations Universal Declaration of Human Rights in 1948, but today an estimated 27 million people in the world are enslaved.

Anthropology Applied

Working against Human Trafficking

In both government and non-government organizations, anthropologists are among those combating international human trafficking. Human trafficking includes buying and selling women and children into indentured servitude or slavery, illegally transporting migrants, and marketing body parts. The United Nations and various national governments publish reports on the effectiveness of nations' measures against human trafficking. In the summer of 2004, the U.S. State Department's report on human trafficking named ten countries—including Sudan, Myanmar, and North Korea—as among the world's most negligent in protecting human rights. A second tier of nations with inadequate measures against human trafficking included forty-two countries, Japan among them. Japan is a destination for Asian, Latin American, and East European women and children trafficked for forced labour and sexual exploitation by the *yakuza*, Japan's organized crime groups. Other countries on the second tier watch list include Russia, Thailand, Vietnam, the Philippines, Pakistan, India, Zimbabwe, Greece, Mexico, and Peru (Sakajiri 2004).

Anthropologists may work against human trafficking in different ways. For example, anthropologists working for HimRights (International Institute for Human Rights, Environment and Development), a watchdog organization, in Nepal conduct preventive educational campaigns and help monitor Himalayan border crossings to detect and report suspected trafficking and protect Bhutanese and Tibetan refugees. They may help rescue and repatriate trafficked persons. They also provide data for the region to the United Nations Commission on Human Rights (**www.inhured.org/download/HimRightsbrochure.pdf**).

In addition, human rights work often involves surveillance (or observation) and documentation, which are the skills of an ethnographer. The underworld trafficking of human organs for transplants was exposed largely through "undercover ethnography." This kind of work, which raises serious ethical issues for anthropologists as well as for the medical profession, led to the discovery of an extensive network of "outlaw surgeons, kidney hunters, and transplant tourists" engaged in trade for human body parts (Scheper-Hughes 2004).

CRITICAL THINKING QUESTIONS

Why might anthropologists disagree about becoming involved in human rights work? What might be arguments for and against undercover ethnography?

REVIEW

Societies may be stratified by caste—a hierarchy of hereditary, endogamous, closed system of social strata defined by occupation and concepts of religious purity. Societies also may be stratified by class—a hierarchy of social strata based mainly on achieved economic status, in which people may be upwardly or downwardly mobile but tend to marry within their own group. Class membership typically is identified by lifestyle factors and the use of language. Slavery is an extreme form of social stratification, based on ascribed status, in which people are defined and treated as commodities.

GLOBALIZATION

A dark side of globalization today is widespread trafficking of women and children for the sex trade and illicit trade in human body parts for transplants. These and other transborder crimes feed on a global service economy.

ETHNICITY

Identifying people according to their ethnic heritage gives us a way to categorize them and assign them to groups on the basis of their cultural traditions. Broadly speaking, **ethnicity** is a universal phenomenon, as all human behaviour is based on culture and reflects cultural differences among societies. However, anthropologists usually reserve the use of the term to depict a situation in which the units of analysis do not stand in isolation but form parts of a larger system. As such, ethnic groups are present in societies where they interact with one another, often in an unequal arrangement, and form part of a society's system of stratification. The members of an ethnic group are sometimes expected to fulfill special economic or occupational services according to an ethnically defined specialization of labour.

The understanding of ethnicity as an aspect of social hierarchy helps to explain several curious features about it, in particular the arbitrary and sometimes contested

ethnicity
Social category based on a complex mix of ancestry, culture, and self-identification in the context of a wider pluralistic and often stratified society.

definitions of ethnic categories and the presence of invented ethnic traditions (see the Case Study on page 271). In a multiethnic system, groups are identified according to broad characteristics that overlook their internal diversity. Few Canadians appreciate the cultural differences between northern and southern Italians, Jews from eastern and central Europe, highland and lowland Scots, or among East Indians from 35 different traditions. Such distinctions may become significant for internal divisions and relationships but don't necessarily pattern interaction within the ethnic system. For example Jewish history in Canada has been marked by much diversity. Early settlement involved migration from England and Germany of professionals and small business owners who easily adjusted to Canadian society and established synagogues based on a modernized Judaism. Later waves of immigration at the turn of the twentieth century introduced large numbers of working-class Jews from Eastern Europe, some of whom kept to Orthodox religious traditions and other aspects of old-country culture (Chouinard 1994). This group was further divided between immigrants from the northern and southern regions of Eastern Europe, by people originating from particular localities, and between political conservatives and radical socialists. However, mainly under pressure from the larger society, these disparate factions have tended to amalgamate into a single ethnic group. Established communities organized financial and social support to newcomers in an attempt to minimize their distinctiveness, which might have drawn unfavourable attention within the wider society. The system of rewards within the prevailing Canadian model of ethnic diversity encouraged further homogenization and unification. Ethnic leaders were able to both benefit their co-religionists and advance their own careers by participating in the "third element" project of the 1960s. This movement, which culminated in a formal policy of multiculturalism, introduced the issue of minority cultural rights that were balanced against Francophone claims for special status within confederation (Menkis 2002:20).

The character of ethnicity that has been revealed so far suggests that popular attempts to understand this paradoxical phenomenon in terms of the persistence of a primordial cultural past are oversimplified. It must be understood and analyzed according to how identities and groups form within a larger political, economic, and social context that promotes ethnic identification and mobilization in specific ways. As a consequence, ethnicity assumes different forms and meanings in different social settings and changes over time.

The development of different patterns of ethnicity within different social contexts can be illustrated by a comparative study of Sikh ethnicity in Singapore and Canada. The Sikhs form a distinct cultural and social group within the Indian state of Punjab. They share some general features of Indian culture but have followed their own religion with unique symbols and practices since the fifteenth century. Their minority status within India has led the more radical and militant members within the Sikh community to advocate for the creation of an independent Sikh homeland, Khalistan, within the Punjab. As other East Indians, the Sikhs have also attempted to deal with economic and political problems within their homeland by immigrating to other countries which offer new opportunities and higher standards of living. In some cases outmigration has not involved a withdrawal from political and social concerns over conditions in India. Some expatriate Sikhs have actively supported Punjabi independence and have at times engaged in terrorist acts, such as the 1985 Air India bombing. However, not all overseas communities have been involved in nationalist movements. Sikh ethnicity and militancy have assumed different patterns and degrees of intensity in different host societies as a comparison between Singapore and Canada will show (Dusenbery 1997).

Both Canada and Singapore are multicultural societies with official policies that support the expression of distinct ethnic traditions within their borders. However, Singapore has adopted a corporatist model of ethnic integration, in which ethnic groups are treated as basic units thorough which the provision of many basic services is channelled. Canada has a more complex system which mixes both corporatist and individualist approaches. Ethnic groups are treated as collective units for cultural matters, such as grants for ethnic programs and activities, but most services are distributed on an individual rather than a group basis. On a more idiosyncratic level, the two countries view Sikh ethnic status differently. The Singapore government treats them as distinct from other East Indians, recognizes their leaders, and supports the use of Punjabi as

Case study

The Invention of Carib Tradition in Trinidad

The arbitrary and fluid nature of ethnicity is best demonstrated in situations in which ethnic identities and cultures are constructed de novo or from a vaguely remembered past that has long ceased to be relevant. Such "inventions of tradition" are not uncommon and reflect the relationship of ethnicity to the wider structures of control and reward within society. Maximilian Forte of Concordia University has carried out a study on Carib ethnicity in Trinidad that provides a detailed example of this process (2006).

Trinidad's population is derived from immigration from Europe, Africa, and India. The Europeans expropriated and settled in the territory of the indigenous Caribs, whose numbers declined precipitously. The ranks of the rural work force were filled by slaves imported from Africa and indentured servants from India. Europeans and Africans interbred at a fairly high rate, producing a blended population of Creoles with a common heritage based upon English culture, but with a secondary division into three ambiguously bounded racial groups: White, mixed, and Black. Creoles are generally urban and fill most of the administrative, professional, and service positions. The East Indians are a distinct ethnic and racial group that forms a rural peasantry. East Indians and Creoles form a rural peasantry. Each group constitutes about half the population and tends to vote as a single block. The indigenous people form a very small minority and have never assumed a significant role in the political system or the economy. They have been heavily Creolized and retain no knowledge of their ancestral language or many of their pre-Columbian traditions.

While Carib identity and culture had long ceased to be a factor in Trinidadian society, a major cultural revival movement occurred in the 1980s. The project was organized by a self-styled shaman who attempted to reconstruct traditional Carib culture by visiting other Caribbean areas with Aboriginal populations as well as members of other indigenous peoples' movements. Salient traits adopted included smoke ceremonies and feathered headdresses from the Canadian Plains, Mexican maracas, and Australian bullroarers. The group also advocated a central defining value—a spiritual connection to the earth and a concern for environment stewardship—that conformed to models of indigenous culture that were current within international agencies. Material aid for the movement came from the Trinidadian government and international donors including UNESCO, which provided additional support through a certification of authenticity.

The successful "recreation" of Carib culture was due to a number of factors in the development of Trinidad's economic and political structure and the emergence of international development agencies and movements. It is paralleled by other local developments, such as an identification with a once-maligned African past within some sections of the Creole community. Invented indigenous traditions are also noticeable in other countries, including Canada, and reflect a strengthening of ethnic identity that seems to be on the rise throughout the world. Similar developments were also apparent in nineteenth-century ethnic nationalist movements in Europe. For example, Norway's independence from Sweden at the turn of the twentieth century was validated in part by the premise of a distinct and authentic Norwegian culture. This construction was crafted by a Danish-speaking urban elite and assembled from a selected range of local peasant customs with some Mediterranean and Central European borrowings and some completely new additions (Erikson 1993:101–104).

one of four ethnic languages that is taught along with English in the public schools system. The Canadian multicultural bureaucracy, at least on the federal level, has not recognized Sikhs as a separate group and has authorized the delivery support for cultural activities to all East Indians as a single group through the National Association of Canadians of Origins in India. Canadian Sikhs have been disinclined to accept these arrangements and have not participated in the organization through which they are supposed to be represented (Dusenbery 1997:742).

In Their Own Voices

Austin Clarke on the 1992 Toronto Riots

Austin Clarke is a Canadian novelist and recipient of the Giller prize, who has written extensively about the lives of West Indian immigrants in Canada. In this essay he describes his reaction to the Toronto riots in 1992. While renowned as a haven of racial tolerance and harmony, the city experienced a violent protest from black youths after the acquittal of the policemen who had brutally beaten Rodney King in Los Angeles earlier in the year. They had clearly responded to this event several thousand kilometres away in another country because of a shared experience of police harassment and brutality. Clarke reflects on this reaction, comparing it to that of an older generation of Black immigrants who had been more likely to suffer racism without protest.

The targets of racist policemen are black. It is an axiomatic statement. Are the police racist? Not every policeman can be racist. But in the same way as we are touched by the power applications of stereotype, so too, in this ironic way, are all the police assumed racist. In a very real sense, when you are on my side of this confrontation, it does not matter whether all police are racist, or whether only 10 percent are; the target cannot enjoy the luxury of liberal consideration. Unless there are no white youths robbing stores, stealing cars, and taking drugs, then the unjustified, excessive force upon black suspects is racist behaviour. It can't be anything else but this.

But we have still to look at the question of black youths and black culpability. Are they indulging in this behaviour, and expecting a silk-gloved treatment, because they are black, and can therefore raise the hackles of a black protest? And if this protest is bellowed and placarded only because the suspect is black, and the demonstration of anger taken up without examining the facts of the case, then these messianic "leaders" are doing those suspects a profound disservice; and, in a more serious way, they are pitting the black community against the police in a monolithic confrontation.

This was made crystal clear on the evening of Monday, May 4th, 1992, a date that will reoccur from now on in any serious dissertation of what is called, loosely and disadvantageously to blacks, "race relations." This term can only mean the confrontation born of the *presence africaine*; it certainly cannot mean or imply that there is a relationship between the races, since "relations" is a positive and reciprocal interaction. I am not speaking about private, individual intercourse. I am speaking,

---

The different multicultural policies have led to contrasting patterns of Sikh integration into the host societies and participation in nationalist movements within India. In Singapore, the community has coalesced around an accepted leadership through whom benefits and communications from the national government are channelled. Many Sikhs have become successful within Singaporean society and have shown little enthusiasm to support a sovereign ethnic homeland in India. Because of their adjustment to the host society, other ethnic groups and public officials in Singapore perceive the Sikhs positively, as a "model minority." In Canada, however, the lack of a clearly supported leadership has led to fragmentation in the community and the emergence of several competing Sikh organizations, some of whom have given strong support to nationalist and secession movements. Because of their fragmentation, the presence of a radical fringe, and "the absence of publicly recognized and politically well-connected spokesperson licensed to speak on their behalf" (Dusenbery 1997:744), Canadian Sikhs have become negatively viewed as radicals and terrorists. Some Sikhs have achieved success in leadership roles in Canada, but usually through support outside of the Sikh community rather than within it. As such, a paradox is evident. Singaporean Sikhs have achieved a more comfortable place in their host society but have remained insular. Canadian Sikh's have experienced more assimilation into Canadian society as individuals but have experienced more discrimination against them as a group.

rather, about the entire system, that institutional structure of unapproachable, unseen power.

The first reactions to the fourth of May, as reactions without the benefit of thought or reasonableness usually are, were offensive, crude, racist and, at the same time, naïve. The *Toronto Sun*, a newspaper that may not be accused of racial reasonableness, blurted out in characteristic sensationalism, "Ugly," with an action photograph of a black man to illustrate the metaphor. When looters terrorized downtown Toronto, the *Sun* regarded this black outburst, the extemporaneous explosion of years and years of pent-up fury and disillusionment at the unchastised, brutal behaviour of the police towards young black suspects, as, "Toronto loses its innocence." What innocence? In all the years I have lived in this city, I have never considered Toronto to be innocent. Not in its attitude towards black people. Not in its knowledge that this attitude was racist. Not in the "race relations" discussions and meetings. Not in the meetings we have been having with the politicians since the Sixties, when we marched with others to City Hall, to Queen's Park, to downtown Loblaws stores to protest the treatment of blacks in this city and this country. What does "innocence" mean? It has a connotation of purity, of blissful unawareness. It has a connotation of being vulnerable to evil, vile forces. It has the connotation of inciting undeserved abuse, manipulation.

The boil of contained animosity and anger on the fourth of May was therefore no surprise to me, whether intellectual or political. The historical use of unjustified police force against suspected black youths, culminating in the acquittal of the policemen accused in the Lawson murder, soon after four Los Angeles policemen were set free in that other case of police brutality. It does not take a sociologist, an expert in "race relations," or a Premier's Committee—a committee headed, ironically, by a former leader of the Provincial NDP, who in all those years made no statement, took no moral position, did nothing to demonstrate that anything more than the usual band-aid treatment of a boil that has been festering in Toronto since 1958, was needed—to inquire into the cause of this "loss of innocence." We say and have been saying until May 4th, that it cannot happen here. It! The innumerable blows delivered on the unprotected body of that black man in Los Angeles, caught in human motion and in slow motion, were felt by each and every black man and woman living in Toronto. In the same way, as we felt the remark made by Mr. Garfield Weston in South Africa, the bombing of those four black children in that church in Selma, or Montgomery, Atlanta, Mississippi—it doesn't matter in which town or city, in which state or country, the metaphor remains indelible, fixed, understood by use, and as stinging as if we ourselves had received those blows; as if our young, beautiful black bodies had been torn apart like a crushed watermelon.

From Clarke, Austin. 1992. *Public Enemies: police violence and black youth.* Toronto: HarperCollins. pp. 10–14. Reprinted by permission of the author.

REVIEW

Ethnicity involves the identification of a social group with a specific cultural tradition within a pluralistic society. Cultural attributes may be based on ancient traditions but may also be modified or invented within specific social, economic, and political contexts. Ethnic groups are often placed in different statuses within a social hierarchy and are sometimes associated with different occupational specializations.

? *Do you consider yourself a member of an ethnic group? What importance does this identity have for you? What value do you attach to the maintenance of ethnic languages and other customs?*

RACE

Like ethnicity, **race** is a social category that is closely tied to a society's system of social stratification. Although ostensibly constructed on biological premises, it has little to do with the actual genetics of human diversity. Human physical variation is too complex to allow us to group people into a fixed number of non-overlapping groups with an interrelated set of biological characteristics. In spite of the lack of evidence for clear racial dividing lines, however, some cultures have formulated folk classifications that arbitrarily sort people into distinct "races" with powerful economic, political, and social consequences.

In the process of constructing race as a cultural category, people are identified as belonging to different "races" based on supposed biological differences. Social ideologies are then developed to justify the system. The next step associates certain constellations

race
A cultural category that groups people according to so-called "racial" distinctions.

of behaviour with each group; for example, members of one race are said to be more intelligent, more honest, more capable than members of another. These associations and the social foundation on which they are based privilege some groups and disadvantage others. The group that controls the social, economic, and political structures of the society thinks of itself as superior and of others as inferior. Whether a majority or minority of the population, the group in power has the ability to control the ideological grounds on which the social order rests.

Race as Caste

Race is very much like caste. In both systems, particular groups are said to have separate ancestral origins, thus explaining their appearance, behavioural characteristics, and place in society. Both caste and race are ascribed statuses and both are closed systems. Like castes, racial groups tend to be endogamous. In some racialist societies, marriage between members of different races is legally forbidden, but even where there are no legal boundaries to intermarriage, people generally choose to marry members of their own group for a number of social and emotional reasons. Finally, race is like caste in the attribution of purity to superior groups and impurity to inferior groups who are often thought of as "unclean" in some ways. Contact between the races is thought to pollute those of higher status. For example, in some southern American states, African Americans were legally barred from drinking from the same public water fountains as whites, from using the same restrooms, and from sitting in the same sections on buses and trains. Although these laws were repealed in the 1950s and 1960s, their underlying symbolism has not been entirely eradicated.

Members of privileged groups benefit from a system that pits poor people against one other based on race, each group believing that its problems are caused by members of other racial groups rather than by members of other classes.

Although racial categorization springs from and is connected to issues of control and oppression, "race" identity can also be a means of mobilizing and countering oppression. In the words of Manning Marable:

> "Race" for the oppressed has come to mean an identity of survival, victimization, and opposition to those racial groups or elites which exercise power and privilege. What we are looking at here is not an ethnic identification or culture, but an awareness of shared experience, suffering and struggles against the barriers of racial division. These collective experiences, survival tales and grievances form the basis of an historical consciousness . . . this sense of racial identity is both imposed on the oppressed and yet represents a reconstructed critical memory of the character of the group's collective ordeals. Definitions of "race" and "racial identity" give character and substance to the movements for power and influence among people of colour. (1995:365)

Because they are cultural rather than objective biological constructs, racial systems of grouping people differ from society to society in the same way that ethnic distinctions do. As we observed in Chapter 3, North and South Americans have developed contrasting racial definitions. In terms of Black/White distinctions, Americans and Canadians recognize only two polar categories. Individuals are exclusively assigned to one or the other on the basis of the "one drop" rule. If someone has any traceable African ancestry, he or she is classified as Black. Only if all of his or her ancestors are of European origin is he or she considered to be White. In Brazil, a completely different system is in place. Numerous racial categories incorporate intermediate gradations, and people are classified into one or another on the basis of physical appearance without any consideration of ancestry. Accordingly, in Brazil, children of the same parents can belong to different races; in the United States or Canada, they cannot. Moreover, Brazilian racial identity can also be influenced by social factors, especially class. Richer or better educated people are generally thought to be whiter than their mere physical appearance might suggest.

Curiously, the logic that Americans and Canadians apply to the Black versus White dichotomy is not used to distinguish Aboriginals from Whites. In the United States, at least for official census purposes, people with one Aboriginal parent are classified according to the origins of the other parent as White, African-American, or Hispanic in most cases (Forbes 1990). In Canada, however, mixed-race people have traditionally been categorized as Métis to form a threefold classification. The indeterminacy and flexibility of assigning Canadian Aboriginal ancestry is reflected in fluctuations in identity over time. A Statistics Canada study indicated that between 1971 and 1996 the Aboriginal population of Canada rose more than threefold, from 300 000 to 1 100 000 while the national population increased by only 30 percent (Statistics Canada 1996). Only a small part of this dramatic increase could be attributed to a higher birth rate. Most of it was due to the fact that people who may have once denied their Aboriginal roots have been increasingly recognizing them and identifying themselves accordingly. Improvements in government benefits to Aboriginal groups and greater media focus on Aboriginal issues are the main forces behind this trend.

Arbitrary and inconsistent definitions of race are evident in other stratification systems as well. In Japan five percent of the population is considered to belong to racial minorities. The largest minority group socially defined as "not Japanese" are the Burakumin. Numbering about three million, they are descendants of an ancient group of outcasts. Their traditional occupations included work that was thought to be ritually polluting such as slaughtering animals, disposing of the dead, and making musical instruments containing leather and other animal products. Despite the absence of any clear physical distinctiveness, the majority of Japanese believe that racial factors set the Burakumin apart. Some members of the group accept their minority status and actively identify as Burakumin, but others attempt to "pass," principally by learning new occupations. Negative stereotypes about the Burakumin are widely held. They are thought to have personality traits that violate general social norms. They are considered impulsive, volatile, hostile, and aggressive. A similarly vague distinction is drawn between Tutsi and Hutu in Rwanda. Defined in part by Belgian colonial policy, members of these groups cannot be usually distinguished from one another unless they are extremely tall or short, since height is considered to be the salient racial marker. Accordingly, the Belgians had to issue racial identity cards to indicate who was who (see Chapter 11 for a fuller discussion).

REVIEW

Although people exhibit biological differences, race is a social and not a biological classification. Race and ethnic identity are culturally constructed and are stratified differently in different societies. Racial or ethnic minorities, such as the Burakumin in Japan and native Indians in Brazil, may be viewed negatively and experience discrimination.

CLASS, RACE, ETHNICITY, AND IDEOLOGY IN CANADIAN SOCIETY

According to its professed values, Canada is one of the world's most egalitarian nations. Our ideology stresses democratic rule, impartial legal institutions, government equalization programs, employment equity, open immigration, and the celebration of cultural diversity. While other nations also proclaim these causes, Canadians believe that they have come the closest to realizing them and often stress that they have done a better job of achieving justice and equality than their neighbours to the south. However, a closer investigation of Canadian society indicates significant patterns of stratification according to class, race, and ethnicity. Differences in wealth and opportunity within our country are not only persistent but also seem to be becoming more extreme. As such, the ideology that we have come to believe may mask the reality of inequality and discrimination and the economic, social, and cultural dominance of a privileged class. It also supports a value system that judges people who fail to achieve success within our supposedly open society as primarily responsible for their own misfortunes.

Class

The measurement of status differences in a class-based society, such as Canada, presents major difficulties because of the complexity and flexibility of the stratification system. A person's class is identifiable mainly according to his or her economic situation, which involves at least two separate factors, income and net worth—that is, the value of assets that a person owns. The difference between these two measures is often substantial. For example, in the United States, Blacks earn about 60 percent of the incomes that Whites do, but their net worth, at 8 percent of the White level, reveals a much deeper inequality (Keister and Moller 2000: 73). Moreover, social as well as economic factors are important in assigning social status. Education is becoming an increasingly important mark of attainment. Similarly, certain occupations, such as those in the professions, are valued more highly than others. People's status may also be evaluated on the basis of their ancestry, race, or ethnic background. Social class patterns are further complicated by the nature of social mobility. In industrial and post-industrial societies, economic growth may create gains for everyone, but the people at the top often improve their lot at a greater rate than those lower down. Lower- and middle-class families may think that they are getting ahead, but the gap between them and the elite may actually be increasing.

Canada is a typical post-industrial society and broadly follows patterns observable in other Western countries that reveal deep and growing differences in wealth and opportunity. One segment of our society earns little or no income, and is subject to severe conditions of poverty, including lack of food, shelter, and other basic necessities. At the other extreme, another segment, including twenty-two billionaires, owns unimaginable wealth and exerts influence in national and international halls of power.

Patterns and trends in such wealth differences can be revealed in a variety of ways. Income inequality is often measured by comparing the earnings of the top ten percent of the population to the bottom ten percent. The most recent figures for Canada indicate that in 2004 families in the highest "decile" earned almost nine times as much as those in the lowest (approximately $170 000 as opposed to $20 000) (Heisz 2007). This ratio compares favourably to that of other Western countries, such as the United States or England, but is nevertheless substantial and, more importantly, has been increasing. In 1989 the ratio was less than seven, and the income difference between the top and the bottom amounted to $100 000. In other words, the well-to-do have increased their earnings by 40 percent, while the incomes of the poorest families have remained stagnant, actually declining by a small amount. Wealth discrepancies have increased on another scale as well. The size of the middle class has declined from 52 percent to 47 percent of the population falling below a critical 50 percent threshold. Thus not only has the gap between haves and have-nots widened, but it has involved a greater degree of polarization between rich and poor.

Even more dramatic trends are visible in wealth ownership. Between 1984 and 2004, a general improvement in wealth for the population as a whole occurred. Average net worth increased from $130 000 to $200 000 per family. However, this bounty was almost exclusively enjoyed by those at the top. The net worth of the top 10 percent rose from $500 000 to $1 200 000. In general terms, this change meant an increase in their ownership of all private assets in Canada from 52 percent to 59 percent. The bottom decile experienced an increase in their own right, from a $2000 to a $9000 debt load (Morisette and Zhang 2006).

Further breakdowns of Canadian wealth distribution reveal other significant trends. In general the worst hit groups have been the young, people without higher education, and the growing population of single mothers. The educational differential is particularly critical since it is related to class mobility. Families in the top quarter of the income scale send their children to university at a much higher rate than those in the bottom quarter (50 percent as opposed to 31 percent), reinforcing differences in opportunity that are most deeply felt among the poorest segments of Canadian society (Frenette 2007).

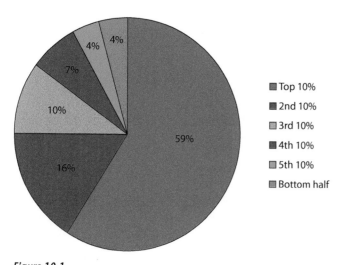

Figure 10.1
Wealth Distribution in Canada.
Source: Adapted from the Statistics Canada, "Perspectives on Labour and Income", Catalogue 75–001, December 2006, vol. 7, no. 12, page 7.

The full weight of inequality within Canada can be appreciated by a consideration of the issue of homelessness, which has become an increasingly serious problem in our major cities. Vancouver is, according to some surveys, the best city in the world to live in. However, between the short period of 1999 to 2003, the number of people living on the street doubled from 600 to 1200, and the use of homeless shelters increased from 500 to 700 people per night (Graves 2004). These figures substantially underestimate the total because many of the homeless may live for short periods with family or friends, occupy abandoned buildings, or simply not be visible to enumerators. In Toronto, the situation is even worse.

Increases in the scale of homelessness have been associated with a widening spectrum of those who find themselves without shelter. The traditional component of alcoholic men has been joined by groups we have already identified as the most vulnerable—young people who cannot find employment or who are working at part-time minimum-wage jobs, and single mothers. Their experiences of transience and life on the street have involved not only discomfort but substantially higher rates of illness, victimization, and death than the general population. While many programs have been initiated to alleviate this condition, the root causes—unemployment, low wages, and limited opportunities—persist. Several other forces aggravate this situation. Governments have reduced support for public housing projects, while the private sector is almost solely engaged in constructing residential units for sale rather than for rent. Media coverage and public attitudes promulgate negative attitudes toward the homeless. Official municipal programs adopt an ambivalent attitude that often views homelessness as a result of deviant behaviour that requires medical and judicial interventions rather than improved access to resources.

Race and Ethnicity

Problems of inequality are compounded by limits on access to resources and opportunities on the basis of culture, national origin, or perceived race. Discriminatory practices have been imposed on these minority groups through barriers to immigration, training, and employment; restrictions on social and political participation; and the imposition of a dominant Eurocentric culture. The severity of these practices has fluctuated in the course of Canadian history, but even in the most liberal periods, ambivalence towards the acceptance of cultural and racial pluralism has typified both personal attitudes and government policy.

Canada's current attempts to celebrate and maintain its diversity emerged only after the 1960s and must be understood in terms of a background of economic, political, and cultural dominance of a White Anglo-Saxon majority during most of our history. British settlement was accomplished through the acquisition of territory from Canada's indigenous people, who were resettled on small isolated reserves under the direct administration of a federal bureaucracy. Lands were seized by force or acquired through treaties signed under direct or indirect coercion. Left without access to their traditional resources or to opportunities within the newly expanding economy, Aboriginal communities languished under conditions of poverty and disease and suffered mortality rates that decimated their populations. They were also subject to many forms of discrimination from the larger society and denied the right to vote. Government policies presumed that Aboriginal cultures were primitive and inferior and encouraged assimilation. Legislation and programs were devised to encourage conversion to Christianity, ban traditional ceremonies, and remove children from their families and communities to attend boarding schools. Training focused on rudimentary skills and was geared towards preparing Aboriginal youth for low-paying, unskilled jobs.

After initial settlement, Anglo-Canadian power, wealth, and dominance was expanded by the conquest of Quebec, whose francophone inhabitants also experienced many forms of discrimination, and by the more recent incorporation of waves of immigrants who supplied the labour to enable Canada's industrial growth during the twentieth century. The treatment of immigrants again reflected many injustices and inequalities. Basic policy focused on the assimilation of newcomers to the dominant Anglo-Canadian culture. Official government practice viewed diverse national groups

? *Do you think that you will fall within the same social class as your parents or do you anticipate an improvement or decline in status or income? What degree of social mobility do you observe in the experiences of your family and friends?*

as expressing unique racial propensities. Those groups whose biological makeup was thought to facilitate the adoption of Canadian values, particularly Northern Europeans, were assigned preferential immigration quotas. Southern and Eastern Europeans, who were deemed biologically and morally inferior and less able to assimilate, were assigned lower priority.

Working class immigrants of all backgrounds were subject to various forms of discrimination and exploitation. During and after World War I, immigrant communities received even worse treatment. Eastern Europeans, Ukrainians in particular, were placed in internment camps because they had migrated from the Austro-Hungarian Empire, with which Canada was at war. Many of them were subsequently deported during the hard economic times of the early 1920s. Internment and deportation of Japanese Canadians during World War II replayed these earlier acts of racism.

The Chinese received particularly horrendous treatment. They were encouraged to immigrate to Canada in the nineteenth century to provide manual labour, particularly for the construction of the Canadian Pacific Railway, and were exploited through the imposition of harsh and dangerous working conditions and payment of wages which were half those of White workers. Later streams of Chinese immigrants were required to pay taxes equivalent to two years wages in order to enter Canada. They were denied citizenship and other rights, including the ability to sponsor the immigration of their wives and children. A number of bizarre regulations were put in place because of anti-Chinese attitudes. For example, the Saskatchewan government banned Chinese business owners from employing White women, obviously because of fears of miscegenation. Official discrimination was accompanied by anti-Chinese sentiment within the general population. The Asiatic Exclusion League opposed Chinese settlement, and anti-Chinese riots occurred in Vancouver and Calgary in the early years of the twentieth century. Racist sentiment culminated in the passing of the *Chinese Exclusion Act*, which cut off almost all immigration from China between 1924 and 1947.

After World War II, Canada's treatment of racial and cultural minorities began to change to advocate for a more open and just society. The reason for the adoption of new attitudes and policies are complex. An expanding globalized economy created a demand

Table 10.1 ETHNIC IDENTIFICATION OF CANADIANS IN THE 2001 CENSUS SINGLE RESPONSES ONLY

English	15.5%	Portuguese	2.7%
French	11.1%	Jewish	2.0%
Chinese	9.8%	Greek	1.5%
Italian	7.6%	Jamaican	1.5%
German	7.4%	Vietnamese	1.3%
Scottish	6.4%	Hungarian (Magyar)	1.0%
East Indian	6.1%	Métis	0.8%
Irish	5.2%	Russian	0.7%
North American Indian	4.8%	Spanish	0.7%
Ukrainian	3.4%	Norwegian	0.5%
Dutch (Netherlands)	3.3%	Danish	0.4%
Filipino	2.8%	Swedish	0.3%
Polish	2.7%	Welsh	0.3%

Source: Adapted from Statistics Canada, "Ethnocultural Portrait of Canada: Highlight Tables, 2001 Census", Catalogue 97F0024XIE2001006, Released January 21, 2003.
Note: This enumeration excludes a large group (40 percent of the population) who identified their ethnic group as "Canadian."

for more open labour, trade, and capital flows across national boundaries. Pressures from international capital were accompanied by demands for recognition and better treatment from minority groups within Canada, especially French Canadians. As a result, disenfranchised groups have been given the vote. Aboriginal communities have gradually received fuller land and resource rights within their localities. Banned traditional practices have been legalized, and children are now educated within their communities rather than in boarding schools. Immigration policies have replaced national quotas with considerations of an individual applicant's training and skills. Legislation now mandates that employers give hiring preference to visible minorities, Aboriginals, and women. Bilingualism and multicultural practices encourage Canadians to experience and value ways of life other than their own.

While Canada's commendable turnaround promises a bright future of co-operation and understanding, we must temper our evaluation of social progress with a consideration that the transformation of our society is only partial and is beset with embedded attitudes and practices that molded race and ethnic relations in earlier periods. Problems of ethnocentrism, discrimination, and racism are still evident in many areas.

Members of immigrant communities that formed the working class in the early twentieth century were generally able to achieve economic success, and subsequent Canadian-born generations have gained acceptance and have been able to improve both income and status in Canadian society. However, racial minorities, who form the largest share of most recent immigration streams, have not fared as well. "Visible minorities" have experienced discrimination in both private and public contexts and in general enjoy a lower standard of living than other Canadians (see Table 10.2). Aboriginal communities have fared even worse.

Discrimination against minorities in Canada occurs in many contexts, including personal interactions, employment decision, service access, media coverage, and in formal government policies. Statistics Canada (2003) has documented that 25 percent of people who are visible minorities feel "uncomfortable or out of place because of their ethno-cultural characteristics all, most, or some of the time." Twenty percent have experienced discriminatory treatment, most usually in the course of applying for work or in work situations. This perception is supported by research that has shown that university-educated people from visible minorities are 40 percent more likely to be unemployed than other Canadians. Among Aboriginal people with community college degrees the rate is twice as high. Even more severe racist treatment is evident in the 300 000 hate crimes that account for over 10 percent of all assaults in Canada each year (Janhevich 2001).

Table 10.2 EARNINGS OF SELECT GROUPS AS A
PERCENTAGE OF AVERAGE CANADIAN
EARNINGS

Ethnic/Racial Group	
Chinese	91%
South Asian	87%
Arab/West Asian	81%
Filipino and South East Asian	80%
Black	79%
Latin American	72%
Aboriginal	68%
Official Languages Spoken	
Both	104%
English only	102%
French only	78%
Neither	58%

Source: Adapted from Statistics Canada, "Earnings of Canadians, 2001 Census", Catalogue 97F0019XIE2001047, Released July 24, 2003.

The most serious aspect of discrimination lies in the force of systemic racism that is embedded in our public policies, legal system, and media coverage. Attitudes and practices that are perpetuated within our institutions not only disadvantage minorities in themselves but support and instill prejudices on the private level. Governmental forms of discrimination can still be seen in immigration policies. Current regulations base immigration decisions on education and skill levels. Unskillled applicants are treated less favourably or are brought in under special programs that deny them the rights and opportunities that other immigrants enjoy. This practice has racial implications, since unskilled workers tend to come from the developing world. We have already discussed the treatment of nannies and maids from the Philippines in the last chapter. Even more restrictive rules are applied to Mexican and Caribbean migrants under the Seasonal Agricultural Workers Program. They are allowed into the country under temporary work permits that are valid only while they are working. They must return to their homelands after the harvest and cannot obtain resident status or citizenship. This situation leaves them with little voice in negotiating their conditions or work, since the terms of their stay in effect deny them the right to strike.

Even broader and more persistent discrimination is embedded in the Canadian government's administration of Aboriginal communities. Reserves have been subject to a colonial system of rule under the Department of Indian and Northern Affairs. Indigenous peoples still have the status of wards of the Crown that are denied the full use of their territories and are not given the same autonomy as the cities and municipalities of other Canadians. They are subject to special provisions of the *Indian Act*, which replace federal and provincial legislation in many areas. For example, an Aboriginal Canadian is not subject to the Marital Property Act and is not allowed to bring a complaint of discrimination before the Canadian Human Rights Commission. This situation is currently in the process of change as a new policy of self-government for reserves is being implemented, but this reversal has proceeded at a slow pace. Full amelioration of the treatment that official government discrimination has imposed on Aboriginal communities will take generations to realize.

In addition to formal discriminatory policies, standard government practices often reflect and encourage racist attitudes. Particular problems are evident within the justice system. Visible minorities are particularly vulnerable to harassment and mistreatment from the police and to prejudicial convictions and sentencing within the courts. Research indicates that Black people in Ontario receive harsher sentences than Whites convicted of the same offence. Aboriginal people have had a particularly difficult experience with their interactions with the police and the courts and, accordingly, are disproportionately represented in the prison population.

A final area of discrimination occurs in the way minorities are represented in the media. While improvements have occurred, the treatment of race and racial issues is still a serious problem. Minorities are given less attention than other sectors of the society and are still often depicted in an unfavourable light. A study by Frances Henry and Carol Tater (2000) of the University of Toronto considered the coverage of three cases in which Black groups raised objections to the way in which their communities and cultures were represented in cultural productions: a protest over an African art display at the Royal Ontario Museum, a protest over the performance of the musical, *Showboat*, and the convening of a conference of writers from racial minorities on the portrayal of races in Canadian literature. Henry and Tator found that these attempts of the Black community to voice their concerns received uniformly and heavily critical treatment in the news media that followed several similar themes. The coverage generally questioned the motivations and authenticity of the organizers of these protests. They were labelled as extremists, militants, leftists, and zealots and were depicted as self-appointed leaders with no support within the wider minority community. Protesters were criticized as being racist in their own right and practising reverse discrimination. In a similar vein they were accused of expressing values that deviated from and contradicted the norms of the dominant culture such as truth, freedom of expression, rationality, and individualism. Other frequently occurring comments "trivialized or dismissed minority concerns about systemic forms of inequality, such as racism in cultural productions, and said that minorities were hyper-sensitive about race" and showed concern over the conflicts and threats to social harmony that the protests had caused. The authors concluded that this hostile reaction attempted to unfairly place the minority representatives in the category of "others," who were situated "outside of the 'imagined

DARK CONTINENT

MUGABE

artizans.com

As this editorial cartoon shows, negative racial stereotypes are still advanced in Canada's media.

community' of Canada" and, in doing so, implicitly denied the presence of any racism in the representations that the protestors found objectionable. It had a significant effect on frustrating the Black community's attempt to obtain a voice in the public forum and led to the withdrawal of funding for the literature conference in question.

The prevalence of racial inequality and discrimination in many public and private contexts brings into question whether Canada has built a more open and tolerant society than other Western countries such as the United States or Britain. Research indicates that our sense of superiority is not well founded. A comparison between Canada and Britain does in fact indicate that Canadian racial minorities receive relatively higher wages than their British counterparts (Reitz 1985). However this difference can be attributed to immigration policy rather than attitudes. As we have seen, Canada has a restrictive immigration policy that accepts people according to educational and skill attainment. Britain has a more open policy that lets in unskilled and less-educated immigrants, particularly if they come from countries within the British Commonwealth. Their wages tend to be lower than those of Canadian immigrants. More incisive measures, such as whether minority applicants were more successful than white applicants with equal qualifications, showed that both societies were equally discriminatory. Whites had a three-to-one advantage in both cases (Reitz). However, the two countries differ in one important way: Canada has less racial conflict. Greater harmony may be attributed to the educational and economic differences between the two sets of minorities. Another explanation can be advanced: Canada's multicultural policy may have a marked effect on minority group leadership patterns that affect levels of militancy. Representatives of ethnic and racial communities are brought into the wider Canadian establishment through the multicultural bureaucracies at different levels of government. As such they become co-opted and tend to pursue cultural retention projects rather than those which involve active demands for the elimination of discriminatory treatment (Reitz). Multiculturalism may have an additional effect on political mobilization. The division of people into numerous distinct subgroups and subcultures creates a "divide and rule" pattern. Parochial identities may work against the formation of coalitions among disadvantaged groups to articulate common demands for fairer treatment. We shall return to a fuller consideration of multicultural politics in Canada in our final chapter.

Chapter Summary

Equality, Inequality, and Social Stratification

- Societies differ in respect to people's access to resources, livelihood, respect, and prestige. In egalitarian societies, all individuals have equal access to whatever resources are available and have equal likelihood of achieving positions of respect and prestige in their cultures. Although people's different skills and talents are rewarded, no one is denied opportunities and the possibilities of achievement. Small foraging societies and some horticultural societies are likely to be egalitarian in their basic social and ethical principles. Egalitarian societies often involve status difference among their members. People can acquire wealth and become a "big man" by utilizing it to achieve influence and prestige through acts of public generosity. The position of a big man is not permanently enshrined. He may lose his status and cannot pass it on to an heir.

- In social systems based on rank, individuals and kinship groups occupy different positions in the social hierarchy. Each position is ranked in relation to all others. Occupying a high rank gives people economic, social, and political advantages. In some ranked systems, high-ranking individuals are freed from subsistence activities. They are supported by the productive work of others through claims that they may make through kinship ties and through the inherent rights of high rank. High-ranking individuals benefit socially by being awarded prestige and by the inherent influence that follows from high rank. And, finally, people of high rank wield political influence through their roles in decision making as leaders of kinship groups and in some cases of territorial units. However, despite the significant privileges of rank, no one is denied a basically decent standard of living, sufficient food, clothing, and housing. In fact, although high-ranking people have rights not granted to others, they also have the responsibility of distributing goods to members of their kin groups. Indeed, generosity is one of the necessary personal attributes of high-ranking people.

- In stratified societies, people are differentiated on the basis of certain attributes that they have at birth. These differences allow some people to have greater access to resources, wealth, and positions of prestige, influence, and power than other people. The granting of privileges and opportunities to some people effectively denies them to others. Many traditional agrarian societies and all modern industrial states are highly stratified. Unlike systems of rank, in stratified societies some people may go hungry, may be poorly clothed, and live in substandard housing or may even find themselves homeless. The gap in the standard of living between rich and poor may be quite wide.

Caste and Class

- A caste is a closed social group whose membership is hereditary. That is, a person is born into a particular caste and remains so for life. Caste membership, then, is an ascribed status. The various castes are ordered hierarchically in relation to one another from highest to lowest. Just as one caste identity is unchangeable, the hierarchical order of castes is also fixed. Mobility is not possible. Members of higher castes have rights and privileges denied to members of lower castes. They have better standards of living, greater opportunities for achievement, and are more likely to occupy positions of influence and power in their society. In India, for example, caste membership not only dictates social group but also regulates marriage, occupation, and area of residence. People must marry members of their own caste. Each caste is associated with a specific set of occupations. And in traditional villages, castes have their own assigned neighbourhoods.

- Some stratified systems are organized into classes rather than castes. Class systems are, at least theoretically, based on achieved factors including education, occupation, and income. However, in practice, access to better education and with it to occupations and income is more readily available to people whose parents have greater wealth and are in higher classes. In addition, although mobility is, at least in theory, a characteristic of class systems, most people do not change their class membership but remain more or less constant in their position within society. In fact, downward mobility is as likely as upward mobility.

Ethnicity

- Ethnicity is a feature of cultural identification. Cultural traits that often are used to define group membership include language, territorial residence, food habits, items of dress, and body ornamentation. In some ways, ethnicity is an ascribed status in that people are born into a cultural group. In other ways, ethnicity is an achieved status because people can choose either to identify with their ethnic group of origin by maintaining the cultural traits associated with it or they can give up identifying cultural behaviours and become assimilated into the mainstream society, however that is defined.

Race

- Race is a social construct, focusing on a particular set of external physical traits but having no biological basis as separate, discrete categories. Physical traits that are used to demarcate the races, including skin colour, hair colour and texture, and facial features, appear in human populations on a continuum, not as consistent markers of groups. But race, once identified on the basis of physical characteristics, becomes projected onto social and personal behaviour. The races then are ranked hierarchically in relation to each other. Obviously, the group that controls the social, economic, political, and ideological structures of society thinks of itself as superior and projects negative qualities on to other groups thought of as inferior.

Class, Race, Ethnicity, and Ideology in Canadian Society

• In Canada, ideology obscures the actual facts of the structure of class and of class privilege. While elites who control policies promulgated by government agencies

obviously act in the interests of their class, barriers are created that hinder the formation of class consciousness among disadvantaged groups. People who are poor, uneducated, unskilled find it hard to move up the social ladder and are blamed, and blame themselves, for their disadvantages instead of recognizing their imposed structural position in a hierarchical system. Other barriers that divide people include racial, ethnic, and gender differences. Trends that have been developing since the 1980s suggest that inequalities in wealth and opportunity have been growing and that the rich and poor segments of Canadian society have become more polarized. Government cut-backs in welfare and income redistribution programs have been a major factor in these developments.

Key Terms

wealth   258
power   258
prestige   258
achieved status   259

ascribed status   259
ranked societies   259
egalitarian societies   259
big man   260

levelling mechanism   260
stratified societies   261
social stratification   261
elites   261

mobility   267
slavery   268
ethnicity   269
race   273

Review Questions

1. What core concepts are used in the analysis of systems of social stratification?

2. What are some ethnographic examples of egalitarian, ranked, and stratified societies? How are these forms of social stratification different?

3. What is the nature of status difference in egalitarian societies? How is the role of the "big man" similar to and different from status holders in ranked and stratified societies.

4. What are three basic theoretical explanations for the existence of systems of social stratification?

5. What are the differences between caste and class? What role does social mobility play in caste and class societies?

6. How can ideologies be used to socialize conformity to the social order, to reinforce the system of social stratification, and to challenge the system?

7. What is class consciousness? How might the pursuit of multiculturalism in Canada limit its development? How might it contribute to it?

8. How are race and ethnicity social constructs? In what contexts can race and ethnicity be seen as a form of caste?

Political Systems

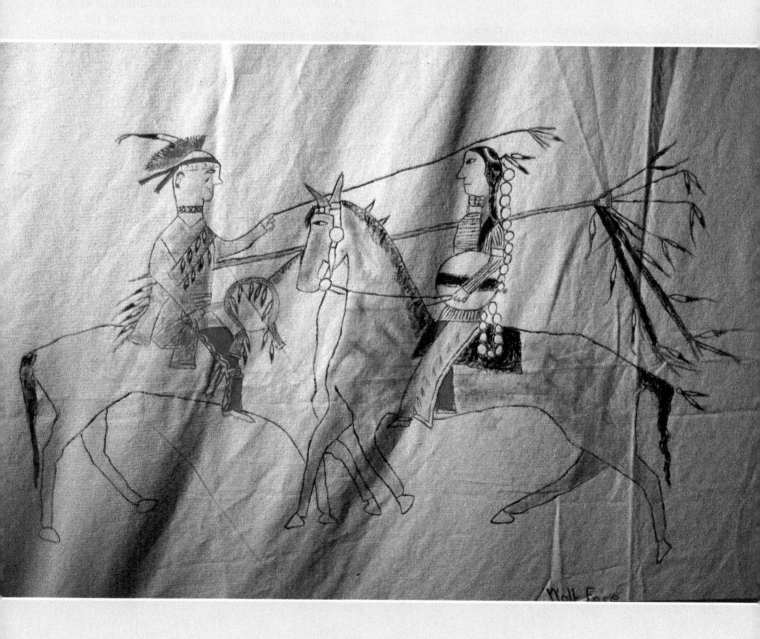

Wolf Face

CHAPTER 11

Preview

1. **What do political anthropologists study, and why?**

2. **What are the four main types of political organization in human societies? How are they different?**

3. **In what ways do different political systems manage and resolve conflict?**

4. **What forces cause political systems to change, and how do those forces operate?**

5. **What are the origins and characteristics of political entities known as states?**

Long ago, a girl named Short Woman lived with her parents and her brother on the plains at a distance from a large *Cheyenne camp. One day the father, named Bull Looks Back, killed his wife and deserted his two young children. The children wandered about for a time trying to find the main camp to seek shelter and food. Finally, they came upon the camp and entered a lodge. There they were told that they were the children of Bull Looks Back, who was then also in the camp. When the father heard that his children had arrived, he said aloud: "Those monstrous children of mine killed their own mother and ate her flesh. That is why I left them. They should be staked to the ground and abandoned."*

And so the people did as he said. The girl and boy were bound by leather ropes and left to die on the plains. But a dog approached at nightfall and chewed on the straps binding the girl. When she got free, she untied her brother and both ran swiftly away. They were met by a stranger who told them that the girl had a power to kill buffalo by looking at them. At first she did not believe the stranger's words, but when a large herd of buffalo appeared, she looked up and they all fell dead.

After she butchered the animals, the girl told a crow to carry some meat to the Cheyenne camp where she and her brother had been abandoned. She said to the crow: "Tell those people the meat is from the children they left on the plains to die." The people then understood that the children were alive and that the girl had special powers.

Then the girl sent for the people to come to her. She told them, "We are going to make chiefs. You know I have been accused of killing my mother. That is not true. Now, we shall make chiefs, and hereafter we shall have a rule that if anyone kills a fellow tribesmember they shall be ordered away from one to five years, whatever the people shall decide."

The girl chose the first chiefs. She told them, "You will swear that you will be honest and care for all the tribe."

The girl told the chiefs how they should act and gave them a pipe of peace to smoke. She taught them songs and prayers to guide and protect them. Then she said, "My brother and I will leave this earth. We may go up into the heavens. Yet I shall always be working for the people. I may be a star."

From *The Cheyennes: Indians of the Great Plains* by E. Adamson Hoebel, pp. 45–49. Copyright © 1978. Reprinted with permission of Wadsworth, a division of Thomson Learning: www.thomsonrights.com. Fax (800) 730-2215.

In this narrative, the Cheyenne of the American plains tell the story of the founding of their system of governance. It tells of the creation of the Council of Forty-four, a council that united the ten Cheyenne bands into a system of tribal government. The council had forty-four members chosen from the ten constituent bands (Hoebel 1978). Members served ten-year terms. They met only during the summer, when the nation as a whole gathered for communal buffalo hunts. Council members were responsible for settling internal disputes and organizing and overseeing communal hunting. As the narrative relates, the members of the council were

political organization
The ways in which societies are organized to plan group activities, make decisions affecting members of the group, select leadership, and settle disputes both within the group and with other groups.

political anthropology
The study of the ways that communities plan group actions, make decisions affecting the group, select leadership, and resolve conflicts and disputes both within the group and with other groups.

selected because they were men of sound judgment and good moral character. The story also relates that wrongdoers were punished by banishment from their communities, a punishment that might have severe consequences because other bands would be reluctant to take in strangers or people who were suspected of antisocial behaviour. Systems of leadership and decision making are mechanisms that help unify and integrate community members into a relatively cohesive society.

POLITICAL ANTHROPOLOGY

In every society, indeed, in every social group, actions need to be planned, decisions need to be made, and procedures for organizing group activities need to be drawn up. Societies differ in the ways in which people organize their interactions and integrate themselves into a cohesive community. In every society, in every social group, different people have different roles to play. Some people have more influence than others when group decisions have to be made and assume leadership responsibilities when actions have to be undertaken. These features of society are the components of each group's **political organization**. Political systems, then, include procedures for making decisions, organizing group actions, choosing leaders, and settling disputes both within the group and with other groups. All societies have some form of political organization, but not all have formal governments familiar to people living in modern states.

Political anthropology is the branch of anthropology that studies these cultural dynamics. Political anthropologists focus on the mechanisms people use to solve the basic problems that confront them as a group. Although every person has individual interests and needs, social groups are formed on principles of cohesion, of sharing, and of reciprocity. People know that, no matter what their individual inclinations, they need to adjust their actions in ways that enable their group to survive and thrive. Political anthropologists are concerned with understanding these mechanisms and with analyzing how they develop and are implemented. They are interested in understanding differences in the degree of influence, authority, or power that leaders may wield in different types of society. Of course, not everyone in any community agrees with group goals or conforms to group wishes, so political anthropologists also study the ways that community decisions are reached and conflicts are resolved. In this chapter, we examine questions of community organization, leadership, and conflict and conflict resolution.

> ### REVIEW
> Political anthropology is the branch of anthropology that studies political organization—the roles and processes that societies have for making decisions, mobilizing action, choosing leaders, settling disputes, and enforcing social norms.

TYPES OF POLITICAL ORGANIZATION

Anthropologists generally describe political systems in terms of a four-part typology of band, tribe, chiefdom, and state. This typology, introduced by Elman Service (1962), is based on distinguishing different kinds of sociopolitical organization according to types of leadership, societal integration and cohesion, decision-making mechanisms, and degree of control over people. Although the typology might seem to make rigid distinctions among societies, it is a useful tool in discussing cultural differences. We must remember, though, that few societies are ideal "types," but features within them overlap from one type to another. It is best to think of the types as constellations of varying features rather than as absolute cases and not to overgeneralize. The different sociopolitical types of societies tend to co-occur with particular kinds of subsistence activities, economic modes, settlement patterns, and kinship systems.

Stateless Societies: Bands and Tribes

Bands and tribes are both typified by a lack of specialized governmental institutions. These stateless societies have no presidents, queens, parliaments, court officials, or police officers. Many social philosophers, including the architects of Western democratic institutions, concluded from the absence of easily identifiable political bodies that such societies represented a "state of nature," which reflected a "war of every man against every man" (Hobbes 1651). However, anthropological treatment of peoples without identifiable governments, such as E.E. Evans-Pritchard's classic study of the Nuer (1940), found that order rather than anarchy prevailed and that conflict and warfare were moderated by regulating forces. Accordingly, they raised a basic analytical issue: the identification of the institutions and processes that defined and maintained a coherent political organization in the absence of formal governmental institutions. The ultimate answer to the question of social order is based on recognition of the political functions of general social institutions, such as kinship, and other types of association based on gender, territory, age, and status that we have considered in previous units.

On June 28, 2004, U.S. Administrator Paul Bremer (left) ceremoniously transferred state sovereignty to Iraq's interim President Ghazi al-Yawar (right), as Bremer's deputy David Richmond applauded. Political anthropologists recognize that the transfer of power in Iraq was delayed by violence and foreign occupation.

Bands and tribes are two forms of stateless society that differ according to size and scale and the complexity of their political structures. **Bands** are small, loosely organized groups of people held together by informal means. **Tribes** are larger systems with some degree of formalization of structure and leadership, including village and intervillage councils whose members regularly meet to settle disputes and plan community activities. The difference in scale and degree of organization is one of degree rather than kind. Bands are often associated with foraging subsistence economies, while tribal forms occur in horticultural and pastoral societies.

Bands

Bands are generally small, loosely organized groups of people. Their leaders are selected on the basis of personal qualities and skills. They lead by example and influence but lack authority to enforce their opinions on the community. Decision making is relatively informal and open to the participation of all competent members. Until a few centuries ago, band societies could be found in many parts of the world, but by the middle of the twentieth century, the remaining band societies were located only in marginal areas of the world, such as the Arctic, the desert regions of Africa and Australia, and the dense forests of South America. Bands generally have (and had) relatively small populations. The smallest groups have perhaps only twenty-five to fifty people, while larger bands might have as many as several hundred members. Individual settlements and populations were generally dispersed throughout a wide territory and frequently relocated according to a pattern of nomadism.

Bands are held together by informal means. Families or households are the significant units of the social order. Membership within one band rather than another is generally based on kinship ties, through either descent or marriage, to other people in the group. Choice of band membership may also be based on loyalty to and approval of the band's leader. But band leadership is also informal. It is based on the personal abilities of the leader, including intelligence, subsistence skills, charismatic personality traits, and in some cases spiritual knowledge. The leader contributes as much as anyone else, and in some cases more, to the band's subsistence. He (or she, although most leaders of bands are men) lives no differently than other members of the band and receives no financial economic rewards.

The reward of leadership is prestige. But leadership also carries with it greater responsibilities because the leader is thought to be responsible for the well-being of the group. While the band's success increases the prestige of its leader, the band's

bands
Small, loosely organized groups of people held together by informal means.

tribes
Societies with some degree of formalization of structure and leadership, including village and intervillage councils whose members regularly meet to settle disputes and plan community activities.

failure is similarly attributed to the leader's weakness or faults. A leader who proves unsuccessful risks losing his position. The band members will simply choose another leader or leave the settlement and relocate to another group. Band leaders, therefore, have only influence, not power. That is, they can use their skills to persuade people to remain with them and to follow their advice, but they have no means of enforcing their decisions. In fact, in many band societies, leaders who even attempt to control the actions of others would immediately disqualify themselves as leaders. Authority roles tend to be limited to the family, and even in that context, the authority of parents over children or of one spouse over the other is generally weak.

In band societies notions of private property are generally weak or absent. Land is never individually owned but is understood to be the common domain of band members. In some bands, specific resources or resource sites may be controlled by kinship groups but never by individuals, and people in band societies do not accumulate significant surpluses of resources or personal possessions. Band societies, and foraging societies generally, are usually egalitarian in their social system. Their egalitarian ethics are reflected in people's equal access to resources, equal potential access to prestige, and equal gender relations.

Tribes

Tribes differ from bands in the scale of the society and the degree of structure and organization contributing to group cohesion and community integration. A number of cultural correlates tend to be associated with tribes, although subsistence patterns vary considerably. Some tribes have economies based on foraging, some on pastoralism, and still others on horticulture. Many tribal societies have mixed economies, combining resources derived from foraging, farming, and animal herding. Settlement patterns and sizes vary as well. Some tribal groups are fully sedentary, remaining in stable villages for many years. Farmers are especially likely to be sedentary, locating near their fields. Foragers and pastoralists are less likely to remain in stable settlements due to the necessity of gathering wild plants and hunting animals or finding grazing land for their animals. Sedentary villages may consist of many hundreds of people, whereas less permanent settlements tend to be smaller.

Concepts of territoriality and private property tend to be more significant in tribal than in band societies. Farming and pastoral people delineate commonly recognized boundaries encompassing their territories. Status differentiation based on wealth occurs in some tribal cultures. However, great imbalances in wealth and standards of living do not develop because tendencies toward accumulation are countered by the values of generosity and hospitality. People aspiring to positions of prestige and influence must co-operate with others and generously give away whatever surpluses they may have. People are especially obligated to help and support their kin materially as well as emotionally. In tribal societies, networks of kin are the primary arena of social action and social responsibility.

Kinship relations in tribal societies are usually organized according to some unilineal principle, either patrilineal or matrilineal. However, some tribal societies reckon descent bilaterally. Where they exist, unilineal kinship groups, such as patriclans, are often corporate political bodies, controlling access to land and resources. Kinship groups may become differentiated on the basis of the amount or value of the resources they control. Some social inequality may arise as members of some kin groups have higher status than members of other groups. Although kinship is the most important factor in organizing social interactions and responsibilities, many tribal societies also develop non-kin sociopolitical **associations** that link people in a community on the basis of shared interests and skills. These associations may have social, economic, ritual, or military functions. Membership may be voluntary or it may be assigned on the basis of specific criteria, and membership may be temporary or permanent. By drawing members from diverse kinship groups, associations integrate people on a basis other than kinship and descent. Modern state societies also have such associations, such as political clubs, religious groups, and hobby groups.

Some tribal societies have a system of age grades or age sets, associations of people of a similar age. An **age grade** is an assigned sociopolitical association—a grouping of

associations
Sociopolitical groups that link people in a community on the basis of shared interests and skills.

age grade (age set)
A sociopolitical association of people of more or less similar age who are given specific social functions.

Ju/'hoansi Foraging Bands

The Ju/'hoansi were traditionally organized within a number of small independent migratory groups typical of a band organization. In the nineteenth century, they were gradually and intermittently affected by and sometimes incorporated into the Tswana chiefdoms on their boundaries. Subsequently, British and South African colonial regimes assumed control over their territories, which are now included in the countries of Botswana and Namibia. Until recently, local political organization remained subject to traditional rules and processes and has been recorded in several ethnographies. We shall investigate the major features of their territorial organization, leadership arrangements, and conflict resolution. Warfare, as such, seems not to have been present in traditional Ju/'hoansi society.

TERRITORIAL ORGANIZATION

Ju/'hoansi are organized into small territories, called *n!ore*, that are usually contained within radii of 15 kilometres and include no more than a few dozen people. These areas and their resources are formally owned by camp members on a collective basis, although they are regularly named after the most prominent group member. Each territory's actual extent is vague, and adjacent units usually overlap. Neighbouring groups generally share resources, but more distant ones will usually have to formally request the use of the resources of another. Few disputes over territory or natural resources occur. Conflict much more frequently arises over sexual misconduct, contested betrothals, and marital strife (Lee 1979:334–338).

LEADERSHIP

Ju/'hoansi leadership arrangements reflect the general patterns of informal non-coercive control that is typical in stateless societies. Each n!ore is nominally owned by a single individual, usually an elder member of the camp that owns the territory. However, his or her influence is strictly limited and must always be applied with care and subtlety. Decisions are made by consultation within the group and general agreement among most of the members. Decisions are never fully binding, and people who are not in agreement with the general consensus always have the option to leave the n!ore and join a new one. In the course of group deliberations, some people's opinions may carry greater weight than others. Precedence is usually dependent upon age, kinship status, oratorical skill, ritual expertise and hunting ability. The attainment of wealth is relatively unimportant and the big man, typical of many other stateless societies, does not come to power. Both men and women can contribute to these public discussions (Lee 1979:343–348).

SOCIAL CONTROL AND CONFLICT RESOLUTION

Conflict and hostility mainly arise over issues relating to sex and marriage, including disagreements over betrothals and marital infidelities. They are expressed in a variety of ways and in different intensities, which can be ranked on a three-stage scale: verbal abuse, hand-to-hand fighting, and fighting with deadly weapons, including poison arrows (Lee 1979:370–400). The level of hostility varies with both the severity of the misdeed and the duration of the argument, as conflicts can escalate as they become protracted. In general, the ease of resorting to self-help in a stateless society and the absence of formal conflict settlement mechanisms has meant that violent recourse is by no means rare among the Ju/"hoansi. Homicides happen with some regularity, at a frequency of 30 per 100 000 that compares to murder rates in some of America's largest metropolitan regions and exceeds those of Canada. However, at a much lower population density of less than one person per km², this statistic translates into only one death every two years within a locality.

The incidence of violence in Ju/'hoansi society is related to the absence of appropriate institutions to forestall and settle disputes. However, one basic factor, nomadic movement, tends to reduce the overall conflict level by providing appropriate occasions for hostile parties to avail themselves of temporary or permanent removal. For example, most of the serious arguments and fights occur when several camps group together in relatively large clusters during the dry season. The problem is partially a consequence of "work stress" that people feel at this time of the year, because greater density translates into longer walks to acquire food. Under these conditions, conflicts usually reach a crisis point, sometimes culminating in a homicide, after which the contending parties settle their differences by breaking up the camp and dispersing into smaller groups. By the next year, tempers have cooled and former combatants can camp together again. If the conflict is too severe, one of the parties may decide to go to a different dry season settlement. An additional conflict resolution institution has been introduced through contacts between Ju/'hoansi and Tswana societies. The foragers have increasingly taken their disputes to the Tswana chiefs for adjudication. The chief acts as a mediator and makes judgments that either party may disagree with but usually accepts in the interest of long-term peace and harmony.

Colonization and integration into national systems have introduced new political structures and issues. The Ju/'hoansi represent tiny and impoverished minorities within the nation states of Botswana and Namibia and have little ability to represent their interests to government bodies. Their main problem has

been to retain access to their traditional territories under the status of an indigenous people. However, private and public interests have led to the loss of almost all their territory, especially after 1997 when the Botswana government expropriated 50,000 km^2 of land to establish the Central Kalahari Game Reserve, an important site of economic investment for both tourism and diamond mining. In 2006, the Ju/'hoansi won a court case to allow them to return to the area. However, the government has used a variety of techniques to frustrate resettlement. It has granted occupation rights to only the 250 people who filed the suit and specified that they can hunt only if they obtain licences (London Daily Telegraph, April 19, 2007).

In spite of many problems, Ju/'hoansi voices have not been totally suppressed. They have been able to represent their interests through a common organization, the First People of the Kalahari, and to raise concerns about their fate in the international forum through indigenous rights organizations, such as Cultural Survival, and communication and cooperation with other indigenous peoples. They have also been represented in a UN discussion that led to the passing of the *Declaration of the Rights of Indigenous Peoples* in 2007 (see Chapter 14).

people of more or less similar ages who are given specific social functions. Members of the same age grade consider themselves to have a kin-like relationship. They are expected to aid one another in times of need, to share resources when necessary, and to give each other emotional support. When disputes arise between members of different age grades, the members of each are expected to rally behind their own.

Conflict and Conflict Resolution in Stateless Societies

Stateless societies have few formal mechanisms for addressing problems that are usually handled by the specialized legal systems of state societies. Establishing behavioural norms, punishing misdeeds, and settling disputes are usually accomplished through customary regulation and practice, reinforced by religious beliefs and sanctions. They are carried out on an ad hoc basis by family and neighbours or, in the more serious cases, by informal leaders. The most serious problems in stateless societies arise as disputes between contending parties and have the potential to cause serious violence or social breakdown. Most adjudicative processes focus on resolving such conflicts to the satisfaction of both parties rather than punishing offenders. Several common mechanisms for dispute settlement include public opinion mobilization, moots, mediation, removal, ostracism, and self help.

Mobilization of Public Opinion. Much behaviour is sanctioned simply by public opinion, especially in small communities where everyone knows everyone else. Gossip is the main mechanism by which public attitudes are established and voiced. It is very important in stateless systems and is also used as an informal social control mechanism in most state societies. The Ibibio of Nigeria have developed a particularly effective form of publicizing and discouraging deviations from community norms in the practice of "singing." This institution involves the composition of satirical songs about offenders and their misdeeds, which people will continually sing in their presence. Some of these works can become particularly popular and eventually assume folksong status so that an offender's misdeeds may even be reported to future generations. The Inuit

Case study

Tribal Organization among the Igbo

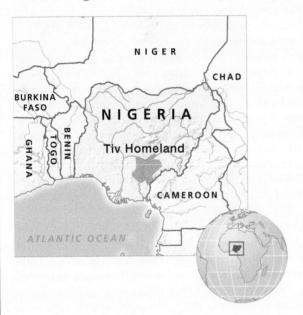

Like the Ju/'hoansi, Igbo political organization prior to British colonization at the turn of the twentieth century followed a stateless pattern and was marked by the absence of formal political institutions with coercive authority. However, the Igbo tribal system displays greater complexities of group and alliance formation that were supported by permanent settlement and larger populations. It also reflects a prominent emphasis on warfare.

TERRITORIAL ORGANIZATION
The Igbo were organized into territorial groupings on three levels: the ward, the village, and the village group. Wards were composed of patrilineal lineages and placed under the authority of lineage heads known as *okpara*. This official was the oldest male within the group. His authority was supported by traditions of descent from family ancestors and his direct connection to them through the performance of sacred rituals.

The village was composed of several wards and ruled by a village council composed of all the adult men. Meetings were held on an ad hoc basis and were led by an inner council composed of the *okpara* and other prominent community leaders, such the higher-ranking members of the title societies. Everyone could have a say in public deliberations, but final decisions were submitted to the inner council. However, they had to be announced to the community at large for final proclamation (Uchendu 1965). Women formed

their own council and could make and enforce their own decisions (see Chapter 9).

Anywhere from a few to a dozen neighbouring villages made up a village group. Its administration was organized according to representation from each constituent village, though most essential decisions and rulings occurred at the village level. Traditionally, there were no coalitions or political units beyond the village group level. Neighbouring groups were usually in an active or potential state of war with one another and travel across village group boundaries was risky for ordinary villagers. However, prominent title holders and religious specialists could be assured of safe passage throughout Igbo territory.

AGE GRADES
The Igbo age grade system complemented the pattern or territorial organization. Beyond a stage of early childhood, Igbo males were successively assigned to three formal age grades: boys, young adults, and elders (Jones 1962). They passed into these grades not as individuals but as members of a cohort or age set. The sets were opened every three years. The bottom set included all the boys of between ten and twelve years old living within the same village. Each grade contained several sets and each set rose separately through the system. Only the oldest set in each grade could be promoted to a higher one. The sets in the junior grade were involved in sports, dancing, and other recreational activities. They completed against rival sets within the village and from different settlements within the village group. Co-operation within the group and rivalry between senior and junior sets and among different villages established a firm basis of friendship and solidarity among age mates. The middle grade was responsible for military service and public works. Its members built and maintained the paths, markets, and public buildings and manned the village watch. The senior grade was made up of the elders, who were in charge of organizing and concluding public deliberations, implementing any decisions reached, and directing the activities of the middle grade. The main features of Igbo age organization facilitated the maintenance of order and created common bonds among members of different descent lines.

LEADERSHIP
Igbo political organization fostered the development of leadership positions in a variety of public arenas, although no formal or specialized offices or hereditary statuses were present. Authority was regularly ceded to older men and to heads of compounds, especially large and wealthy ones, and to the lineage heads.

Other individuals who were not particularly senior within the age and family hierarchies could advance themselves through the acquisition of wealth and the purchase of prestigious titles. Titled men were considered on a par with elders in public deliberations and also held special privileges and authority within powerful title associations. The property and persons of title holders were granted special value and greater fines and restitutions were exacted from individuals who violated them. Title holders also acted as protectors of people accused of crimes and of travellers and other strangers (Meek 1937:174–184).

Generally, leadership was consultative and noncoercive, following the pattern of most tribal societies. Sanctions were imposed through the pressure to stand in good favour with important, wealthy, and influential authority figures within the community. Additional support was added through the religious system. Leaders within the family, age, and wealth hierarchies all possessed special ritual objects and performed sacrifices to powerful spirits who could be invoked to punish malefactors who failed to follow the decisions of the authorities or who otherwise threatened the social order.

SOCIAL CONTROL AND CONFLICT RESOLUTION

As with leadership institutions, the maintenance of social control and resolution of conflicts in Igbo communities followed the general patterns of other stateless societies. Formal police forces, legal codes, court systems, and penal institutions were absent and individuals were often left to their own devices to protect their rights and to exact justice. However, a variety of effective institutions were developed to allow for a modicum of social order. Village councils regularly met to establish rules to protect their members against threats to their security and to set punishments for violators. Acts of theft, sexual misconduct, and violence, as well as failure to repay debts, were discouraged by the weight of public opinion and threat of the gods' displeasure. In addition, leaders regularly held informal moots to hear cases. In particularly difficult cases they might make additional consultations with the gods through the mediation of religious specialists, such as oracles or diviners.

Convicted felons were assessed punishments, such as fines, loss of status and titles, enslavement, and banishment. Corporal and capital punishment were not allowed but a moot could request that a convicted felon, especially in a serious case such as murder or incest, commit suicide. If anyone was not satisfied with publicly made decisions, he or she retained the right to self help and vengeance, and before the imposition of British colonial rule protracted feuds were common. These usually occurred because of disputes between members of separate villages over bride price refunds. If the feuding communities were included in the same village group, combatants were expected to moderate their hostility by the use of machetes rather than guns, which were reserved for warfare between village groups. Protracted conflicts could and did lead to the dissolution of the village group and the rearrangement of alliances.

WARFARE

Hostilities between neighbouring village groups was endemic. Wars were waged between and among communities within the same region. Combatants shared the same culture and very often were related to one another through marriage. Alliances formed, dissolved, and reformed, making friends among former enemies and vice versa. Warfare did not seem to be directly based on the acquisition of territory, although the net effect may have put pressure on some groups to migrate into previously unfarmed areas. Following the pattern of Igbo feuding, it may very well have revolved around issues of marriage and exchange. Igbo warfare patterns also reflected an emphasis on the prestige value of physical combat and success. Victorious soldiers took the heads of their enemies and gained the honour of displaying their skulls in their trophy rooms. They could take defeated enemies captive and add them to their households, thereby enhancing their status as "big compound heads." In the course of the development of the trans-Atlantic slave trade, more mercenary motivations prevailed as war captives were increasingly sold to coastal merchants. In all, Igbo warfare can be viewed as a response to a complex set of political and economic forces that have changed over time.

? *Aside from seeking recourse through formal government institutions, such as the courts, in what ways do Canadians resolve conflicts? How do these techniques compare with the conflict resolution strategies outlined in this section?*

have developed a similar practice in the "song duel," in which each party in a conflict makes up a verse critical of his/her opponent.

Mediation.   The process of mediating a dispute involves the intervention of a third party agreed upon by all the contesting parties. He or she may be simply a mutual friend or ally or may occupy a specific role such as the "leopard-skin chief" among the Nuer. The holder of this position is not a chief in a political sense but a ritual specialist who can assist conflicting parties to reach a settlement but cannot impose a decision. Each party meets with the chief, who proposes a remedy such as payment of compensation to atone for a homicide or theft. If both sides accept and uphold the chief's decision, the conflict is resolved. However, either party may reject a resolution and continue the dispute.

Moots.   A moot, an informal court, constitutes another method of making a judgment on a misdeed or resolving a conflict. In this arrangement an ad hoc jury is convened by the parties involved to decide on a punishment or resolution. Very often, community leaders will preside over the assembly and make a final decision on who is at fault and what the consequences will be.

Removal, Exile, and Ostracism.   In situations where a dispute cannot be settled, a resolution can be reached by the physical removal of the individuals or groups involved. In cases of individuals who repeatedly defy norms or act violently, the usual remedy is ostracism from the community or isolation within it, such as in the Mennonite practice of "shunning." In many instances, this punishment is tantamount to a death penalty. In a similar manner, conflicting parties often resolve their differences by moving away from one another to avoid the continuation of hostilities. This arrangement is especially convenient in stateless societies, in which territorial boundaries tend to be flexible. Among the Ju/'hoansi, conflict and removal have become a patterned feature of the seasonal cycle. The annual concentration into larger settlements during the dry season leads to frequent disputes among neighbours, who alleviate these social tensions by dispersing into smaller units at the arrival of the rains. Following a different arrangement, the Igbo regularly settle conflicts, or at least temporarily remove offenders, through the practice of exiling them to their mother's villages, in which they can claim sanctuary.

Leopard-skin chiefs worked to prevent blood feuds among the Nuer by mediating conflicts.

Self Help.   A common outcome of a failure to punish a misdeed or resolve a dispute is for a concerned party to seek redress by taking direct action. In states, such recourse is considered to be "taking the law in one's own hands" and is strictly forbidden. Stateless societies, however, have no way of monopolizing the use of force and leave their members free to take personal action. One act of retribution usually leads to another and can frequently lead to feuds between the families of the offending parties and victims.

In Medieval Europe, where central institutions were weak, feuds were standard occurrences. Most killings were not considered to be "murders" punishable by the state but as affairs for personal revenge or, where the parties could agree, for compensation payments to the members of a victim's kindred.

Warfare in Stateless Societies

Among Western nations and other centralized political systems, the conduct of war is the exclusive concern of the state and is organized according to national strategic interests and foreign policy. Internal conflicts, such as civil wars, are extraordinary events distinct from normal political processes and can lead to a change in the state's territorial composition and sometimes of its governmental structure. In band and tribal societies, warfare is more difficult to distinguish from internal strife because of the fluid nature of group composition. For example, among the Yanomamo, hostilities between neighbouring alliances of villages was common. Combatants shared a common culture and played by the same rules of engagement. The alliances were unstable. Allied villages often engaged in disputes with each other, which could grow into major conflicts. Alliances would then break up, and each member village would abandon its location and seek out a new alliance to engage its new enemy. A regular cycle of coalition, division, removal, and realignment occured (Chagnon 1997).

The unique character of warfare in stateless societies, such as the Yanomamo and Igbo, suggests the presence of a specific type of conflict, tribal warfare, which differs in many respects from military action in state societies, where hostilities are often geared towards territorial conquest. As such, anthropologists have concluded that warfare is not a necessary feature of the human condition. Its occurrence, severity, and character is affected by social and cultural forces, and in some cases, particularly in foraging societies,

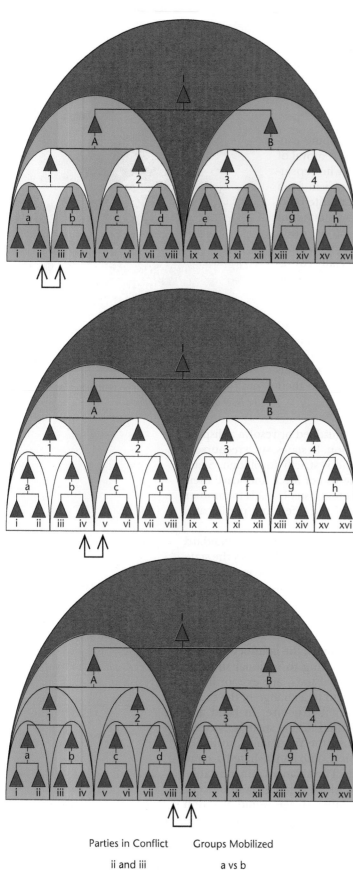

Parties in Conflict	Groups Mobilized
ii and iii	a vs b
iv and iv	1 vs 2
viii and ix	A vs B

Figure 11.1
Segmentary Opposition.

it is rare. Accordingly, tribal forms of warfare have unique characteristics. They tend not to be tied to the acquisition of productive resources, such as land and labour, and are very often directly or indirectly related to the attainment of prestige. Paradoxically, some anthropologists have suggested that these violent acts serve to maintain states of balance in society and its relation to its local environment in clear contrast to more imperialistic forms of war in state societies.

The social balance explanation of warfare maintains that it creates a source of unity and direction within a society by emphasizing the danger imposed by an external enemy. In stateless societies this consolidating process is especially important because of the fluidity of social groups and alliances and the problem of personal resort to force. E.E. Evans-Pritchard's analysis of social order among the Nuer (1940) identifies a particularly intricate system of controlling violence and reinforcing group solidarity in the form of segmentary opposition. This mechanism is based on an underlying segmentary lineage structure (see Chapter 7). Segmentary opposition involves the ordering of cooperation and conflict between territorially situated lineages. Concerted action within the group is mobilized by a dispute between one of its members and someone in an opposing group; that is, the members of each antagonist's group come to his aid in a conflict situation. However, these feuding factions may become united and settle their differences if one of their members comes into conflict with a more distantly related group (see Figure 11.1). According to Evans-Pritchard, this process helps to stabilize local social groups and alliances and reduce levels of violence.

A second approach to tribal warfare emphasizes its effect on ecological rather than social balances and focuses on the demands of a horticultural subsistence pattern prevalent in tribal systems. The low yields of producing fields and the need to keep large areas in fallow creates a situation in which households and settlements must continually make adjustments in the acreage they require for subsistence. Ultimately, therefore, warfare is focused on the redistribution of farmland as victorious groups acquire new plots and losers either make do with lesser amounts or, more usually, occupy new territories. In other words, warfare puts pressure on some communities to relocate and to accordingly reduce the population pressure within the tribal area. Andrew Vayda (1974) extends this argument by noting that tribal communities in a region are reluctant to expand into new farming areas because too much effort is required to clear areas that have never been cultivated before. Accordingly, they prefer to attempt to seize land from neighbouring communities, who must bear the burden of settling new territories. The long-term effect of this process is to balance populations to match environmental resources.

Culture Change

COLONIALISM, NATIONHOOD, AND SEPARATISM AMONG THE IGBO

While tribal systems of government were widespread in the past, colonization and the creation of independent nation states have placed these local forms under the hegemony of national governments and radically modified their forms and functions. Some aspects of traditional political organization may sometimes remain in force on an informal level but have largely been replaced by Western models of local government. Among the Igbo, changes in governmental form and process have entailed changes not only at the village and village group levels but have also involved an active engagement in regional and national politics within the Federation of Nigeria.

Patterns of Igbo political organization began to change at the turn of the twentieth century in the course of British colonization. The British seized control of the territory of what is now Nigeria and set up a colony whose economy was based on the export of agricultural products produced by small-scale indigenous farmers. The colony was divided into three regions: the North, the West, and the East. Each contained a mixture of different cultural groups, among which a single group was numerically dominant: Hausa in the North, Yoruba in the West, and Igbo in the East. British colonial policy focused on "indirect rule," which sought to retain indigenous political systems and integrate them within the colony's administrative hierarchy as local government bodies. In the North, this process was based on a single, highly centralized system of Islamic Emirates, whose rulers cooperated with the British. In the West, smaller and more decentralized chiefdoms were restructured to achieve a similar top-down system of control. However, the Igbo system introduced a problem. Realizing that the Igbo had a democratic and decentralized political order that would be difficult to co-opt, the British appointed warrant chiefs in each village to impose the hierarchical structure that they were familiar with in other parts of the colony. Igbo villagers strongly rejected this coercive authority and the system was replaced by direct administration by British district officers. As Nigeria was granted independence, a system of elected local councils was put in place. These elected bodies reflect the democratic emphasis embedded in the older village council system but have involved major changes. The elected representatives tend to come from the better-educated segments of the population and seldom include women, who have lost much of the voice that they traditionally held in local affairs (see Chapter 9).

In addition to local changes, colonization and independence have introduced the Igbo to political engagement on regional and national levels on a scale well beyond that of indigenous society. Traditionally, the Igbo identified according to membership in localized village groups, with little sense of a wider social or cultural unity. Under the colonial system, they were introduced into regional and national arenas through participation in new institutions and migration to the colonial urban centres, where new opportunities were available. Because of the particular character of indirect rule within regions dominated by a single cultural group, a sense of common ethnic identity developed and pan-Igbo social and political associations were formed. This movement culminated in the formation of an ethnically-based party, the National Conference of Nigeria and the Cameroons (NCNC), which became a strong advocate for Nigerian independence. The Igbo elite felt that they would gain better opportunities under African rule and, unlike the Yoruba and Hausa, did not include traditional rulers who had become dependent on British support.

In 1960 an independent Federation of Nigeria was created. The system of government was based on a British system, with a national parliament and regional parliaments in the North, West, and East. The NCNC won a majority of the seats in the legislature of the Eastern Region, where the Igbo formed a sizable majority. It also won a large enough proportion of seats in the federal parliament to become an important force on the national level. However, Igbo attempts to prevail in the complex ethnic politics that dominated elections in the early independence period were frustrated. The 1965 election involved a struggle between Igbo and Hausa over consolidating support within their own ethnic communities and creating alliances with other ethnic groups. The Hausa party was victorious, but the Igbo party claimed that widespread abuse had occurred prior to and during the election. In 1966, Igbo army officers led a coup that assassinated several prominent Hausa political leaders and their allies. In retribution, mass killings of Igbo occurred in the Northern Region. A counter coup ensued and the Igbo generals were deposed.

In the wake of these tumultuous events, Igbo leaders advocated for separation of the Eastern Region and formed the break-away nation of Biafra, which held all of Nigeria's oil fields, the country's main source of income. In 1967, a civil war ensued, and, after three years of fighting and over one million fatalities, Nigerian forces defeated and reabsorbed the Eastern Region. Administrative changes and attempts at reconciliation since then have discouraged the formation of ethnic political movements and have reduced tensions. However, recent economic problems in Nigeria have led to a renewed ethnic nationalism, especially among the growing body of unemployed youth. Some disaffected Igbos claim that the effect of the civil war has been to marginalize them, and they are envisioning the recreation of Biafra as a solution to their woes. The Movement for the Actualisation of the Sovereign State of Biafra has been formed within Nigeria. It has been opposed by most Igbo leaders in the country but has received significant support from Igbos living abroad (Omeje 2005).

The patterns of change in Igbo political organization and strategy parallel transformations that have occurred elsewhere in the world. Later in this chapter we will review traditional governmental institutions within the Kingdom of Rwanda and how they have changed in the course of the imposition of a colonial regime and the granting of independence. We will also investigate the emergence of conflict and violence in the wake of unresolved problems and the appearance of new forms of competition for power and resources. In Chapter 14 we will investigate the dissolution of the Iroquois chiefdom under Canadian and American hegemony and attempts to revive its institutions to restore autonomy and resources to First Nation communities.

CRITICAL THINKING QUESTIONS

What effect did the British policy of indirect rule have on the development of conflict and civil war in Nigeria? Was the British assumption that Western democratic forms could not be instituted in all cultures and that each society should be ruled according to its own values and institutions valid? Would it be advisable for Canada to apply a modified indirect rule policy to create an Aboriginal self-government arrangement that would incorporate traditional political forms?

Chiefdoms

chiefdoms
Formal governmental systems organized by kinship.

Chiefdoms are political forms that are transitional between tribal and fully centralized state forms. They have specialized organs of government that regulate the use of force, but their powers are decentralized and limited. They are usually organized according to ranked kinship groups. Only high-ranking lineages are entitled to hold the key leadership positions and assign them to their members. These leaders, or chiefs, perform political, economic, and often ritual functions. In some chiefdoms, they are not markedly distinguished from other people except in their social prestige, whereas in other chiefdoms, higher status people have economic, social, and political privileges.

Despite stratification in chiefdom societies, ethics of egalitarian relationships underlie daily interactions and community activities. Although the chief is privileged, notions of equality and kinship obligations remain strong. These ethics are demonstrated in the redistributive networks and functions of the chief. Chiefs know very well that they owe their position to the loyalty of their kin and others in the community. They solidify their support through their generosity, through attending to emergency needs of their subjects, and by showing respect and consideration to all. In essence, then, chiefs are embedded in kinship networks and are burdened with the responsibilities and obligations that come from expectations of reciprocity and fair treatment.

In contrast to band and tribal societies, where leadership is diffuse and spontaneous, chiefdoms have some centralization of authority. However, their political organization systematically involves the division of powers among a council of chiefs or devolution to subchiefs. Chiefdoms, therefore, incorporate many chiefs who may be organized in different ways. Within the Iroquois Confederacy (see the Case Study on page 298), localized clans appointed a total of fifty chiefs to a central council. All could enter into deliberations on an equal footing. Among the Pacific Northwest Coast societies, chiefs from neighbouring communities regularly assembled, interacted, and came to joint decisions. They were ranked in order of importance and influence according to the wealth that they could display during potlatches. The Akan of Ghana had a more formal hierarchy of chiefs. A paramount chief was responsible for a large territory, which was divided into divisions over which divisional chiefs assumed authority. At the bottom level, town chiefs ruled within their districts. Chiefs at each level were chosen from royal matrilineages. Since higher ranking chiefs could neither select nor dismiss their subordinates, local groups retained a good deal of autonomy. Moreover, lower ranking officials had to be included in state councils and deliberations.

Succession to the office of chief is not usually based on a predetermined heir. A number of candidates within a given lineage will compete for the position with varying degrees of intensity. A person aspiring to the position of chief needs the requisite skills, intelligence, and personality traits as well as the support of kin. He may also have to organize an aggressive campaign to gain office. Among the Zulu of South Africa, any one of a chief's sons was eligible to take over after his father's death. During an interregnum period, rival brothers would raise armies against each other to determine who would become the new chief. Even after a succession, an incumbent could be deposed by a brother, as was the most famous Zulu chief, Chaka.

The distribution of goods, both in food and material items, is the special prerogative of chiefs in such societies. As heads of their lineages and clans, chiefs redistribute resources among their members and throughout their local communities. They arrange and host feasts periodically, celebrating harvests, successful hunts, and ceremonial events such as marriages or deaths. They might also host feasts that celebrate victorious raids or sporting competitions. In preparation for feasts, chiefs encourage their kinspeople to work hard to produce surplus crops and to amass large stores of foods. Then entire communities and sometimes neighbouring villages as well are invited to the feasts. The visitors receive part of the bounty of goods produced and collected by the host lineage or clan. They thus benefit economically and also bear witness to the generosity of the chief. The potlatch, described in Chapter 6, is a classic example of the redistributive functions of chiefs and the complex meanings of the feasts that they sponsor.

Because of their role at the centre of redistributive networks, chiefs and their close kin have access to strategic resources not available to other people. In some chiefdoms, the chief and chiefly families do not benefit economically from their position. They work just as hard as other members of the community. In other chiefdoms, the chiefs and their kin are able to retain a disproportionate amount of goods brought in for feasting occasions. They use this surplus for their own economic and social benefit. Their standard of living is higher or more elaborate than that of other people in the community. Their houses are larger, their clothing and ornaments finer, and their foods more exotic. In addition to economic benefits, chiefs and their kin use their access to strategic resources to attract followers. Through their redistribution of goods and their generosity, chiefs ensure the loyalty of their supporters.

A number of other cultural correlates are associated with chiefdom societies. Concepts of territoriality and landownership tend to be well developed. The boundaries between neighbouring chiefdoms are usually marked and recognized by both residents and outsiders. Ownership or control of other resources is also strongly identified. Some types of property might be deemed private and individual and other types might be considered a communal heritage of kinship groups as collective bodies. Where property is held communally, the chief becomes its guardian and titular owner (owner by title). Most chiefdoms have fully sedentary settlements with economies based on farming or pastoralism, although some foraging societies, such as those of the Pacific Northwest Coast, are also organized into chiefdoms.

People in chiefdoms tend to have a strong sense of belonging not only to their own kinship group but to wider political and social associations as well. This sense of identity may promote rivalry and competition. Rivalry may be friendly, expressed in competitive sporting events, or, in some cases, lead to raiding and warfare. Warfare tends to occur more frequently in chiefdoms than in band and tribal societies. The goals of warfare may involve factors relatively rare or unknown in band or tribal warfare, such as looting or confiscating enemy property. Warfare may also include raiding for captives or for the acquisition of new territories and subjects. Warfare in chiefdoms also tends to be more deadly than in band or tribal groups, as killing one's enemies becomes a goal.

A chief's responsibilities are often widespread. He may have a role in leading troops into battle and may assume judicial functions.

Tikopian society is ranked, with chiefs having the highest status. Chiefs of patrilineages (maru) *are elders directly descended from lineage ancestors, while clan chiefs* (ariki) *are descended from the common ancestor of the lineages (Firth 1970).*

Case study

Mohawk Political Organization

Iroquois Territory

Present-Day New York State

The Mohawk were part of the Iroquois Confederacy. Assuming the form of a chiefdom, this polity was the largest and most powerful political organization in pre-colonial Canada and the American Northeast. A union of six nations, among whom the Mohawk were the largest, the Confederacy was formed to ensure peace among its members and pursue a joint project of defense and warfare against neighbouring groups. Within the union, each member was organized at two levels: a national level and a village level. Each of the three tiers of government was ruled by a council of chiefs.

The Mohawk village chiefs were chosen from the settlement's constituent clans. The usual framework was for each of the three main matrilineal clans—Bear,

Wolf, and Turtle—to fill three positions each for a total of nine chiefs for the village council. In addition, one or more special war chiefs was selected in a similar manner. The clan mothers were responsible for choosing the chiefs but had to consult with other family members before making a choice. However, succession generally followed a specific line from mother's brother to sister's son. A chief would formally be invested during condolence ceremonies for the deceased officeholder, whose name he would take. He would also be given a horned cap as an insignia of office. The council met on various issues that confronted the community but had to hold open meetings to consult with the general public. Women usually held their own meetings and communicated their decisions through the clan mother. These women also had a final say in whether the group would go to war and exerted control over a chief's actions through their power to "dehorn" him (Abler 2004).

Mohawk national affairs were governed by an assembly of all the chiefs within the constituent villages. At the Confederacy level, a total of fifty special chiefs were chosen from designated longhouse clans to form a council to decide on public issues. They rose to office in the same way as village chiefs did and could also be deposed. The Confederacy was devoted to settling disputes among its members and waging war against its neighbours. Historical accounts indicate that some of the motivation for warfare was control over the European fur trade. However, one dominant reason was to acquire captives, who would then be adopted and integrated into Mohawk families to maintain and increase their size and strength.

In the course of European settlement of Canada and the United States, the Confederacy was dissolved as First Nations communities were deprived of their traditional lands and settled on small and fragmented reserves directly subject to rule of the Indian affairs bureaucracies in each country. Over the last one hundred years, several attempts have been made to revive the traditional political order, a movement that we shall investigate further in Chapter 14.

Chiefs of various ranks will administer court sessions to hear cases, settle disputes, and mete out punishments. They usually hold ritual and spiritual power, leading ceremonies that help bind members of the community together. In some chiefdoms, the chief may be thought to possess special spirit powers or even to be a descendant of divine beings. Among the Maori of New Zealand, for example, *mana* is a kind of power and knowledge derived from the spirit world that can be controlled and manipulated by human beings and human action (Mataira 2000). A person's control of *mana* is demonstrated by his or her success and achievements. Chiefs, who have the highest status and greatest success, are assumed also to have greater control of *mana*. In some chiefdoms of Polynesia, including Tikopia and Tahiti, contact with a chief's powerful *mana* could cause harm to an ordinary person. Commoners, therefore, were not permitted to approach a chief too closely, to look at him directly, or to speak to him without an intermediary. Such beliefs isolated the chief from ordinary people.

states
Highly organized, centralized political systems with a hierarchical structure of authority.

> **REVIEW**
>
> Foraging societies tended to form small, mobile, loosely defined bands. At the band level of political organization, leadership was informal, temporary, and consensual. The political organization of tribes, whether horticultural, agricultural, or pastoral, was based on kin groups such as clans, which might be ranked. Tribal people also formed groups that crosscut kin ties, based on associations such as warrior societies or age grades. Chiefdoms, such as the Iroquois, incorporated formal and specialized leadership positions, delegated to kinship groups. Selection of chiefs was based on hereditary principals. Chiefs were distinguished according to rank rather than caste or class stratification (see Chapter 10). Land and other productive resources were equally distributed among all members of the community. Chiefs could only control symbolic wealth and had to redistribute surpluses through acts of public generosity.

CHARACTERISTICS OF STATE SOCIETIES

States are centralized social and political systems with formal governments organized into a hierarchical structure of authority. They are similar to chiefdoms but are more centralized and powerful since full and ultimate authority and power rest with the head of state, whether he or she is a king or queen, an emperor, or a president. States are marked by the following features:

1. concentration of power and authority involving the appointment of regional administrators from a single administrative centre

2. specialized bureaucratic departments

3. formal systems of taxation

4. total monopolization of the use of violent force through permanent standing armies and police force under central control.

Based on principles of sovereignty, or self-rule, state systems usually demarcate their territory and divide it into jurisdictions or districts and subdistricts. Each territorial unit is administered by officials appointed by central authorities and responsible to them. These officials are in charge of implementing government policies in their region, acting as conduits for central powers and sometimes as intermediaries between local residents and state officials. Thus, states are based on political unification, often with a national identity, and the centralization and delegation of power within a sovereign territory. Expanding state societies become empires, enlarging their territory and power through conquest.

State societies have much larger populations than bands, tribes, or chiefdoms, and often support some degree of occupational specialization. In addition, state societies have the need for many different kinds of officials and bureaucrats who help organize and run projects that involve many people. Some of these are public works projects, such as construction and maintenance of roads, water delivery systems, and other infrastructure. Some bureaucrats keep track of the populace, taking census and collecting tribute or taxes. Other people work for the state as members of a police force that controls the resident population or as a military force that defends the state from its enemies and conducts offensive warfare to expand the borders or influence of the state. Still other specialists work in commerce, facilitating the flow of raw materials, foods, and manufactured goods from one area of the state to another, as well as to other states. Some members of society are full-time religious practitioners, conducting private and public rituals. Finally, some segments of the state society do no work at all but are fully supported by the labour of others.

Labour specialization intersects with systems of social stratification. All states are hierarchically stratified societies in which some people have greater access than other

terrorism
A criminal act intended or calculated to provoke a state of terror in the general public, a group of persons or particular persons for political purposes.

people to property of all kinds and to other strategic social and economic resources. States are divided into at least two strata: elites and commoners. Elites make up a minority of the population but reap disproportionate wealth and disproportionately occupy positions of social prestige and political power (Mills 1956). Elites have important economic functions in society but rarely enter the labour force as workers. They are sustained directly or indirectly by the tribute, rents, and taxes paid by commoners. For example, elites may own land that is farmed by peasant workers, receiving part of the harvest as rent. State societies usually develop urban areas where populations are concentrated. These urban centres become the seats of centralized government functions. Cities are the sites of monumental architecture that celebrate the power of the state. Large buildings house government and administrative offices. Wealth is displayed in the size and opulence of homes.

Just as in chiefdoms where chiefs manage and organize redistributive networks, elites in state societies control the production and distribution of foods and other resources for consumption. However, unlike chiefs, elites retain the majority of surplus, improving their standard of living as a class while other people live in situations of comparative disadvantage. The degree of inequality between elites and commoners varies in different states. The greater the disparity in wealth, the greater the likelihood that elites will exert coercive control over commoner classes, as commoners may come to resent the fact that the elite lifestyle is supported by their own labour.

In order to maintain a system based on wealth and power imbalances, state governments support ideologies that legitimate the status and privileges that elites receive. Religions often explain social differences as outcomes of divine will. A trained and specialized priesthood may ally itself with civil authorities, both groups benefiting from their consolidation of power. Religious specialists may define right and wrong, encourage obedience to authority, and claim divine origin or sanction for the political system. Many early states were theocracies, ruled by religious leaders or by rulers thought to be divine or divinely sanctioned to rule.

Social Control, Conflict, and Warfare in State Societies

? How is terrorism a factor in the maintenance and expansion of modern states today?

In addition to ideological control, state societies have mechanisms of force that can be brought to bear on an unruly populace. Laws are codified and standardized. They regulate behaviour and declare certain actions criminal offenses punishable by state authorities. Court systems determine the guilt or innocence of individuals accused of crimes and punish those deemed guilty. A police force is used as an agent of social control. State-organized judicial institutions also decide on conflicts between individuals and groups, who are not permitted to resort to personal action to settle grievances. In the codification of rules of conduct and in the punishment of wrongdoing, the state replaces kinship groups as the regulators of social behaviour.

In external relations, the state also monopolizes rights to conduct warfare against others. In the same way that they are not allowed to resort to force within the boundaries of the state, private citizens cannot legitimately take up arms against a foreign country without the cover and sanction of a state-declared war. In fact, we now label such behaviour "**terrorism**." According to the United Nations, terrorism involves "criminal acts intended or calculated to provoke a state of terror in the general public, a group of persons, or particular persons for political purposes" (United Nations 1999). However, it also notes that "The lack of agreement on a definition of terrorism has been a major obstacle to meaningful international countermeasures. Cynics have often commented that one state's "terrorist" is another state's "freedom fighter.'"

Early state societies included the first seats of civilization that were based on intensive agriculture in such places as the Indus Valley, the Fertile Crescent of Mesopotamia, the Nile Valley, and the Yellow River valley of China. State systems also developed in the Americas. Here, the ruins of Machu Picchu mark one of the last sacred outposts of the Inca Empire, conquered in 1535 by Spanish invaders.

INTERNAL POLITICAL CHANGE AND STATE SOCIETIES

State societies are the largest, most complex, and highly centralized political systems. The first states arose in the Middle East in Mesopotamia around 5000 years ago. Other states developed slightly later in the Nile region of Egypt. States also arose independently in the Indus River valley of India, in China, in Meso-America (Mexico and Guatemala), and in the Andes of Peru. Today state societies exist in every part of the world, replacing other kinds of society and dominating the world scene.

Political systems also change through internal processes. State societies, for example, change through factionalism and revolution. Disagreements about community actions occur from time to time in all societies, but they can lead to entrenched **factionalism** as various interest groups vie for control of decision making and leadership roles. If a powerful faction is able to assert its will, this can lead to fundamental social changes. For example, in the early 1900s, two contentious factions developed in the Hopi community of Oraibi in Arizona over whether or not to participate in federal educational programs for Hopi children. Some people believed that knowledge of the English language and American culture would benefit the Hopi, but others feared that any but the most tangential contacts with American culture would lead to the destruction of Hopi lifestyle.

Conflicts between these two factions intensified and grew increasingly bitter, eventually spilling into other issues and even dividing family groups. Finally, in 1906, the Hopi in Oraibi decided that they could not all live together in the same community. Using a "tug-of-war" across a line etched in the dirt, the two sides dramatized their inability to coexist. The group who lost (called the "Hostiles," because of their opposition to American assimilationist policies) was forced to leave, later founding a new village, Hotevilla. The faction known as the "Friendlies" remained at Oraibi and continued their more accommodating approach toward American cultural innovations (Titiev 1992).

In large stratified societies, political change can come about as a result of a **revolution**, which is an attempt to overthrow the existing government. These are complex processes that take different forms in different contexts. In colonial situations, people may decide that they no longer want to live under foreign domination. They may engage in wars of independence to oust their rulers. A successful revolution may enable indigenous people to return to some form of traditional life. Alternatively, as in the United States, colonial settlers may rebel against their country of origin to set up an independent nation. Other revolutions take place within powerful states when a subjugated class, such as peasants or workers, attempts to free itself from the exactions of its rulers. The French Revolution (1789) attempted to eliminate

GLOBALIZATION

In modern times, as weaponry has become increasingly sophisticated and deadly—nuclear warfare and biological warfare—and as wars have embroiled larger numbers of countries, international efforts have been directed at establishing formal mechanisms for conflict resolution. The United Nations and the World Court, formed after World War II, are two international groups that mediate conflicts.

factionalism
The tendency for groups to split into opposing parties over political issues, often a cause of violence and a threat to political unity.

revolution
An attempt to overthrow the existing government.

In the late 1960s, China's Cultural Revolution, under the leadership of Mao Zedong (seen on the banner here), transformed Chinese society from a Soviet-style communist state to a modern "people's republic." This transformation was accomplished through the mobilization of urban Chinese youths into the Red Guards. The Red Guards persecuted teachers, intellectuals, and people who practised traditional arts and ways of life, which were seen as "bourgeois." The Cultural Revolution turned violent as the Red Guards broke into factions, and many people were killed in purges.

In Their Own Voices

Testimony from South Africa's Truth and Reconciliation Hearings of 1998

Following the end of apartheid in South Africa, the newly elected government, led by the African National Congress (ANC), established the Truth and Reconciliation Commission in order to confront and help resolve past tragedies with the goal of uncovering the causes of racial violence and establishing a unified country. The commission held hearings in 1998 to determine whether individuals who had committed politically motivated racial killings and assaults during the decades of civil disturbance deserved amnesty for their crimes. Persons requesting amnesty had to testify at the hearings, confessing their crimes, explaining their motivations, and conveying their remorse. They included members of the police who had been engaged in the violent suppression of all protests among native Africans, and indigenous Africans who had engaged in acts of sabotage and racially motivated killings in resistance to white rule. On the basis of their testimony, putting great weight on their sincerity and their insights into their crimes, members of the commission decided whether or not the person deserved amnesty and release.

The commission was established because South Africans decided that revenge against the perpetrators of racial crimes would create division and hostility for generations to come. In the words of one of the commission's members, "It is natural to want revenge but we need to rebuild a nation."

In these excerpts, perpetrators of racially motivated crimes give testimony, explaining their deeds. In the first, a black South African discusses his role in the killing of Amy Biehl, an American who was in South Africa working in the anti-apartheid movement. In the second excerpt, two white policemen discuss their role in the killing of four members of the African National Congress. The questioners are all members of the Truth and Reconciliation Commission.

Testimony of Ntombeko Ambrose Peni, one of the men who killed Amy Biehl

MR. BRINK: You had absolutely no idea of what Amy Biehl's political views were, isn't that the situation?

MR. PENI: I did not know.

MR. BRINK: And your evidence here was that you participated in this murderous attack because the aims of your organization was to bring back land to the African people. Now what I want to know is, how would the killing of an unarmed, defenseless woman possibly help you to achieve that aim?

MR. PENI: We believed that the minority white people ruling the country would realise that we wanted our land back. We also believed that they were going to give up this land back to the African people.

MR. BRINK: Is it your evidence that by murdering, in the most brutal fashion, Amy Biehl, the African people would get their land back?

MR. PENI: Yes it's my evidence. First of all I would like to rectify something, gender was not significant. Our aim was to attack each white person and go forward.

JUDGE WILSON: But it was not the aim of the PAC at that time to kill every white person they saw, was it?

MR. PENI: It could not happen that every person be killed, but there was one slogan: 'One settler, one bullet'.

JUDGE WILSON: Do you agree it was not the policy of the PAC to kill white persons on sight, which is what you did on this afternoon, do you agree with that?

Mr Peni: It is true that the PAC could not have killed everybody that they saw; however, the PAC was aware that killing each white person the land would come back to the African people.

Mr Brink: Mr. Peni, isn't it the position that on that dreadful afternoon you were involved in a mindless, savage attack on this young woman, and that it was not politically motivated at all?

Mr Peni: Our killing Amy Biehl had everything to do with politics.

Testimony of Mr. Du Plessis, a security police officer, who helped set up and kill the Cradock 4, members of the African National Congress

Mr. Booyens: Did you have anything personal against any of these four persons?

Mr. Du Plessis: I can state this unequivocally, absolutely not.

Mr. Booyens: To the extent that you were involved in the fact that they lost their lives ultimately, why were you involved?

Mr. Du Plessis: Because I felt or had the opinion that it would prevent the anarchy, that it would disempower the state of anarchy. . . . They were definitely members of the ANC. I don't have precise facts about their activities any more, but I know that they were all buried under the flag of communism.

Mr. Booyens: Very well. And for which reason did you personally become involved in these matters?

Mr. Du Plessis: In this case I received an order to become involved. I also felt that it would be the only way to attempt to stop the onslaught.

Mr. Booyens: Mr Du Plessis, today it is almost fifteen years since what happened. How do you feel now about what happened?

Mr. Du Plessis: One is indeed sorry and I am speaking for myself that a person as a result of one's job was compelled to such steps.

For us who believed in the struggle of the National Party, we also believed that if the ANC/SACP alliance were to take over, it would signify the end of the white in Africa.

Right or wrong, that is what we believed. It is a great pity that two political parties such as the NP and the ANC could not sit down and discuss this matter and sort it out. And as a result, some of us and some of them died in the struggle.

I am sorry, especially for the families. I am sincerely sorry, not only for the sake of the families, but for the families of the members of the Security Branch to which we had to give orders.

Chairperson: Do I understand correctly that if it had not been for the nature of the work, that none of this would have happened?

Mr. Du Plessis: I was placed in a situation where I believed that this was the only way out. If I had been in a different position, perhaps I would have regarded the situation differently and believed something different, but I can tell you in all earnestness that that is what I believed to be the only viable solution.

Testimony of Mr. Taylor, another of the policemen

Mr. Potgieter: Was it wrong if black people demanded human rights?

Mr. Taylor: Mr. Chairperson, if you can give the opportunity to answer the question fully. It wasn't a question of the whole black population of South Africa, it was about the activation of radicals and mass activities and this demand for human rights was about the question of housing, schools, accommodation, books, to vote etc., etc. In other words it was part of the whole liberation struggle, yes. And I wish to reiterate that is how I thought and believed in 1985.

Mr. Potgieter: And you thought it was wrong?

Mr. Taylor: Yes.

Mr. Potgieter: But now you think it's right?

Mr. Taylor: Of course.

You must remember that if I have to admit, at that time I had been indoctrinated, I was politicized and for me all of these things were part of the struggle to overthrow the government and at time I thought that way and I felt that way.

The circumstances and the climate of that time, the feelings among the people, all these things have changed and we can see it now in 1998 that everything has changed.

_____

From South African government website: **www.doj.gov.za/trc/ trc_frameset.htm.**

CRITICAL THINKING QUESTIONS

What do the three testimonies have in common? Do you agree with the assertion that events must be interpreted in their historical and cultural contexts? To what extent do you think that public discussion is effective as a means of post-conflict reconciliation?

Case study

The Kingdom of Rwanda: a State Society

While many African kingdoms conform to some degree to the structure of a chiefdom, the kingdom of Rwanda represented a more highly centralized state organization. The kingdom had a complex history involving a long period of Belgian colonialism and a violent revolution in the course of the formation of the nation state of Rwanda.

The precolonial Kingdom of Rwanda was based on a stratification system that differentiated between a wealthy and powerful Tutsi minority and a subordinate majority, the Hutu (Maquet 1961). The Tutsi claimed a distinct ethnic and political status on the basis of conquest. However, both groups spoke the same language and shared a common culture.

The Tutsi formed the ruling class. They maintained their superior status through their ownership of cattle, a primary economic, social, and political resource, and control over agricultural production through the administrative allocation of arable land. Their Hutu subjects undertook all the farm work on lands received from their Tutsi overlords. In return, they had to give them a share of the harvest and a substantial amount of unpaid labour. Hutu farmers could mitigate the severity of a Tutsi superior's demands by moving to the jurisdiction of another land holder who might exact fewer obligations. They could also rise in the system by acquiring cattle and joining the Tutsi aristocracy (Jefremovas 1997).

The administrative framework of Rwanda was organized through the office of the king, who held his position through hereditary right. He exercised strong central authority through his ability to conscript and maintain a standing army of Tutsi warriors and collect taxes in the form of cattle and agricultural products. Territories were administered through appointed officials who held specialized posts in a hierarchical bureaucracy. The king appointed three separate chiefs to each administrative district—an army chief, a cattle chief, and land chief—each of whom was directly and separately accountable to the king. He maintained the authority to dismiss and replace his subordinates, and regularly changed their locations in order to forestall the cultivation of regional power blocks. He also encouraged the chiefs to spy on one another to ensure that they were not plotting against him (Maquet 1961).

At the beginning of the twentieth century, the Belgians assumed colonial control over the kingdom and instituted a system of indirect rule similar to that of the British. The indigenous structure was left intact but was modified to facilitate Belgian control and exploitation of the colony. The major force of Belgian policy was to further stratify and rigidify Tutsi and Hutu distinctions. Each group was redefined as a distinct "race" in a system which eliminated the social mobility that was allowed within the pre-colonial system. However, physical differences between Hutu and Tutsi are not always apparent. The Belgians devised a method for determining who was who, mainly according to height difference, and issued racial identity cards on that basis. Children took on the racial identities of their fathers. Further rigidities were introduced by rescinding Hutu rights to change locations. These new arrangement enabled the Belgians to utilize Hutu subjugation and increase their exploitation by extracting forced labour from them through their Tutsi chiefs (Jefremovas 1997).

In the 1950s, the Belgians started making plans to free their colonies in Africa but did not provide a clear direction for a post-colonial governmental structure. They began to shift their support from the Tutsi to the Hutu, but the Tutsi campaigned for an administrative system that would retain the kingdom. The Hutu forced the situation by staging a violent uprising against their Tutsi masters, killing many and forcing a sizeable component of them into exile in neighbouring countries. Hutu leaders then instituted a national government based on a European democratic model, which they managed to control through their hold on a majority of the population. Throughout the next thirty years, Hutu politicians managed to stay in power in spite of a poor record in alleviating the poverty of the majority of the population. Popular dissatisfaction was regularly quelled by blaming the Tutsi for the country's problems.

In the opening years of the 1990s, two important events happened. The ruling government was forced to open up elections to opposition parties, which posed a clear threat to the leaders of the time. In addition, a Tutsi armed force entered Rwanda with the intention of taking over the country. The new Tutsi threat provided a clear opportunity to stir up ethnic conflict to forestall a possible change of regime. In 1994, the crisis was heightened when the President was killed in an attack on his plane. Blaming the Tutsi, the government then organized an "ethnic cleansing" campaign both directly through the army and presidential guard and indirectly though the mobilization of party militias and the encouragement of ethnic hatred within the Hutu population. Several hundred thousand people were killed, including many Hutu who opposed the regime and the massacres. The violence ended when the Tutsi militia was able to seize power in the country and install their own regime. In the aftermath, the Tutsi were responsible for revenge killings of their own. They also arrested over 100 000 Hutu on suspicion of genocide and could possibly still indict a similar number. The court schedule is so backed up that many defendants could be incarcerated indefinitely.

The Rwandan genocide raises many moral issues as well as a basic anthropological one. Jacques Maquet, the ethnographer who provided the classic monograph on Rwandan political organization (1961), maintained that the traditional system had created a harmonious society and that the Hutu peasants had accepted their status at the bottom of the ladder. This understanding was clearly contradicted by the suddenness and violence of the Hutu uprising, which has been seen as a classic example of a revolution. Many other anthropological analyses have emphasized harmony and stability in indigenous political systems and overlooked the realities of struggles over power and uneven distribution of resources and rewards.

CRITICAL THINKING QUESTIONS

Both Rwanda and Nigeria have experienced civil wars based on ethnic nationalism. Were the causes of these conflicts the same? Could you apply the distinction between factionalism and revolution to understand the differences? What do your observations mean for understanding ethnic conflicts in different cultural contexts?

---

the class privileges of wealthy and aristocratic elites. The lack of full attainment of these goals demonstrates how difficult it is to break completely with the past.

In the twentieth century, new movements for social and political change occurred in many places in the world. The Mexican Revolution of 1910 and the Russian Revolution of 1917 were attempts to change the stratified social systems that created economic and political inequalities. Following the end of World War II, many countries in Africa that had been colonized by Europeans gained their independence. These movements were successful both because of internal resistance to colonial control and external pressure from growing international anti-colonialism.

More recently, movements for internal democratic change have also taken root worldwide as people in stratified societies with imbalances in wealth and power have attempted to claim a more equitable share of their country's resources. Elites do not give up their power and privilege easily, however. They may resist openly by using the police force at their disposal to put down revolutionary movements or by using the legal apparatus to arrest and punish leaders and participants. For example, the apartheid government of South Africa upheld the exclusive wealth, power, and privilege of European settlers through the establishment of a police state. Africans were strictly monitored through the pass laws, which required them to carry detailed identity documents. They were not allowed to organize into unions or political parties or in any way attempt to change their conditions. Violators were arrested and jailed under the *Terrorism Act* of 1967, which defined terrorism as any act that might "endanger the maintenance of law and order" and enabled the police to imprison people indefinitely without trial. Once in jail, detainees were sometimes murdered by the police, as in the renowned case of Steven Biko. Public protests were violently suppressed. In the 1960 Sharpeville Massacre, the police killed sixty-nine unarmed demonstrators who had burned their passes. In 1974 several hundred school children were killed when they rioted over the compulsory use of Afrikaans, the language of the Dutch settlers, rather than English as a language of instruction. Another brutal case of what has sometimes been called "state terrorism" occurred during the Rwandan massacres in 1994. The Hutu-dominated government ordered the police and military to attack Tutsi citizens and created a general sense of hysteria to urge other Hutu to do the same. Hundreds of thousands of casualties occurred (see the Case Study on page 304).

REVIEW

Internal patterns of change in political systems include, among others, factionalism, in which groups split on issues and vie for power, and revolution, in which citizens rebel against their colonial rulers, government, or ruling elites.

Chapter Summary

Political Anthropology

- Political anthropology is the branch of anthropology that focuses on the ways that societies are organized to select their leaders, make decisions affecting the group, provide community functions and services, and resolve conflicts and disputes. These cultural mechanisms help integrate a community and help direct and maintain relations with other communities.

Types of Political Organization

- Bands are generally small, loosely organized groups of people. Communities in band societies usually have relatively small populations, which are dispersed throughout a wide territory. Bands are held together by informal means. Membership within one band rather than another is typically based on kinship ties to other people in the group. Band leadership is also informal, based on the personal abilities of the leader. Such leaders have influence but they do not have power to control the actions of others. Bands are usually egalitarian societies, and individuals' rights to resources and access to positions of influence are respected.

- Tribal societies differ from bands in the degree of structure and organization and in their group cohesion and community organization. Tribal societies may have more formalized organizational procedures, such as highly structured councils whose members regularly meet and deliberate. Tribal chiefs may be selected in more formal ways and may have some ability to reinforce their decisions. However, the powers of tribal chiefs or councils are limited by egalitarian social ethics, and there are often structured ways to ignore or depose leaders who try to exert too much authority.

- Voluntary associations and age-grade or age-set organizations are common in tribal societies. These systems unite people within a community across lines of kinship. Members of the same age grade consider themselves to have a kin-like relationship. When disputes arise between members of different age grades, members are expected to rally behind their group.

- Chiefdoms are hierarchical societies organized by kinship, although the degree of difference among the various strata varies cross-culturally. Chiefs assume positions of leadership according to inherited status within kinship groups. Higher status people generally have economic, social, and political privileges. They have some ability to control economic production and the distribution of resources, but their position and influence depend on the co-operation of their kin groups and communities. Chiefs cannot coerce other people to do their bidding. In chiefdoms, there is some centralization of authority, but there is not one paramount leader. Although a chieftancy is inherited, within a family several people may compete for the position. A candidate needs to have the requisite skills, intelligence, and personality traits to become the recognized heir.

Characteristics of State Societies

- State societies are the largest, most complex, and highly centralized political systems. The first states arose in the Middle East in Mesopotamia around 8000 years ago. Other states developed in the Nile region of Egypt, in the Indus River valley of India, in China, in Meso-America, and in the Andes of Peru. State societies exist in every part of the world, replacing other types of societies and dominating the world scene.

- State governments are organized in a hierarchical structure of authority. Ultimate authority and power rests with the head of state, whether president, king, or emperor. State government systems include procedures for formally selecting leaders and their assistants. State systems usually divide their entire territory under their jurisdiction into districts and have economic systems characterized by labour specialization. Some people produce food and others may work as artisans, traders, bureaucrats, police force, and religious practitioners. States are stratified societies in which some people have greater access to property and resources than other people.

- State societies develop and promulgate ideologies that legitimate the status and privileges that elites receive. In addition, they have mechanisms of force that can be brought to bear upon an unruly populace to maintain the status quo. Laws are codified and standardized, regulating behaviour and assigning punishments to criminal offenses. The state monopolizes the right to control and punish wrongdoers through a system of police and courts. And the state also monopolizes the right to conduct warfare against others. States pursue political and economic ends through warfare by expanding their influence and control of people living in other lands.

Internal Political Change and State Societies

- State societies, like all types of social formations, are subject to change. States are inherently expansionist because of the desire on the part of elites to increase their wealth and power. Therefore, states expand territorially and absorb the population and resources of conquered lands. Change can also result from external pressures as one state conquers another and imposes its political will. State conquest always has cultural components as basic systems of family organization, economic productive relationships, and religion may be altered to conform to the practices and beliefs of the conquering state.

- States may also be transformed from within as various interest groups or factions compete for prominence. Reform movements may develop in response to perceived inequalities and injustices in the system. Revolutionary movements may also develop to effect more fundamental changes in state systems. Attempts at revolutionary transformations may or may not be successful, depending on the support they receive from the populace. Although revolutions are met with state and military resistance initially, some revolutionary movements have proven to be unstoppable. The worldwide movement of decolonization beginning after World War II is one such phenomenon.

Key Terms

political organization 286
political anthropology 286
bands 287

tribes 287
associations 288
age grade (age set) 288

chiefdom 296
states 299
terrorism 300

factionalism 301
revolution 301

Review Questions

1. How might a political anthropologist approach the study of factionalism or domestic terrorism in a present-day state society? What kinds of questions might he or she ask to determine the nature, causes, and consequences of these behaviours and ideologies in the society?

2. How are bands, tribes, chiefdoms, confederacies, and states different? What is a specific ethnographic example of each "ideal" type?

3. What roles do kinship and associations play in each type of political system?

4. Do bands, tribes, chiefdoms, and states represent steps in the development of political systems? If so, how? If not, what determines which form of political organization a society is likely to have?

5. How do the characteristics of state societies relate to social stratification?

6. What have been some impacts of colonization on people's sociopolitical systems? Of globalization?

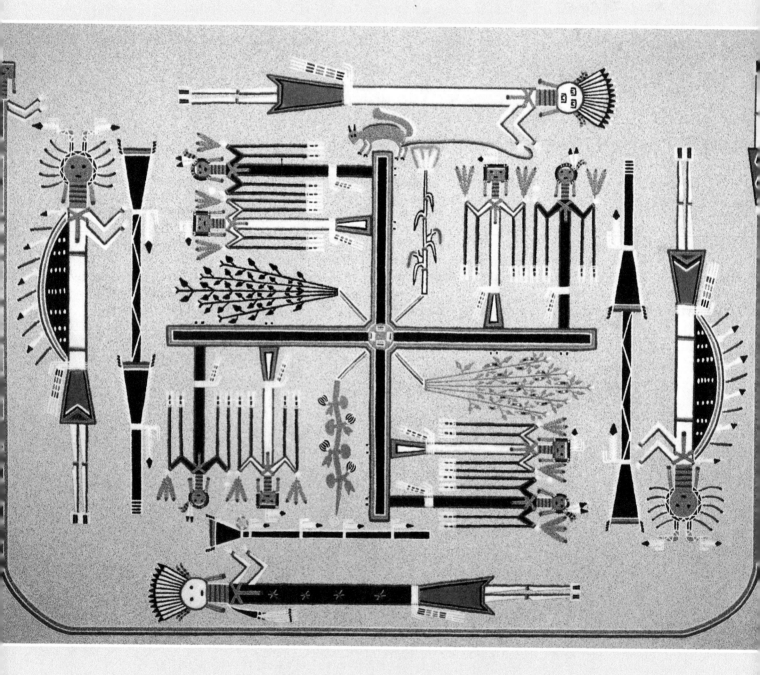

CHAPTER 12

Preview

1. **What is religion?**

2. **What perspectives do anthropologists take in studying religion?**

3. **What types of spirit entities and powers or forces do people believe in?**

4. **Who are religious practitioners, and how do they reflect their society and culture?**

5. **What are the main types of religious practice?**

6. **What are some psychological, social, and cultural sources and functions of religion?**

7. **How do religions help maintain the social order? How do they both instigate and reflect culture change?**

The surface of the fourth world was unlike the surface of any of the lower worlds. For it was a mixture of black and white. The sky above was alternately white, blue, yellow, and black, just as it had been in the worlds below. But here the colours were of a different duration. As yet there was no sun and no moon; as yet there were no stars.

When they arrived on the surface of the fourth world, the exiles from the lower worlds saw no living thing. But they did observe four great snow-covered peaks along the horizon around them. One peak lay to the east. One peak lay to the south. One peak lay likewise to the west. And to the north there was one peak.

It was now evident to the newcomers that the fourth world was larger than any of the worlds below.

Twenty-three days came and went, and twenty-three nights passed and all was well. And on the twenty-fourth night the exiles held a council meeting. They talked quietly among themselves, and they resolved to mend their ways and to do nothing unintelligent that would create disorder. This was a good world, and the wandering people meant to stay here, it is said.

[Eventually the people were visited by the gods or "Holy People" who gave them instructions about how to prepare themselves to live in the fourth world. The Holy People promised to give them advice and to teach them to live properly.]

Proceeding silently the gods laid one buckskin on the ground, careful that its head faced the west. Upon its skin they placed two ears of corn, being just as careful that the tips of each pointed east. Over the corn they spread the other buckskin, making sure that its head faced east.

Under the white ear they put the feather of a white eagle. And under the yellow ear they put the feather of a yellow eagle. Then they told the onlooking people to stand at a distance.

So that the wind could enter.

Then from the east the white wind blew between the buckskins. And while the wind thus blew, each of the Holy People came and walked four times around the objects they had placed so carefully on the ground. As they walked, the eagle feathers moved slightly. Just slightly. So that only those who watched carefully were able to notice. And when the Holy People had finished walking, they lifted the topmost buckskin. And lo! The ears of corn disappeared.

In their place there lay a man and there lay a woman.

The white ear of corn had been transformed into our most ancient male ancestor [First Man] and the yellow ear of corn had been transformed into our most ancient female ancestor [First Woman].

It was the wind that had given them life: the very wind that gives us our breath as we go about our daily affairs here in the world we ourselves live in. When this *wind ceases to blow inside of us, we become speechless. And we die.*

In the skin at the tips of our fingers we can see the trail of that life-giving wind. Look carefully at your own fingertips. There you will see where the wind blew when it created your most ancient ancestors out of two ears of corn, it is said.

From *Diné Bahané: The Navajo Creation Story* by Paul Zolbrod, pp. 45–51. Copyright 1984. Reprinted by permission of the University of New Mexico Press.

Creation stories from various cultures express different ideas about how people were given life and how people relate to their physical and social universe. The stories express different worldviews about the people and their relationships with their environment, other people, and the spirit world. The narrative told by the Diné (or Navajo) describes the physical environment in which the people came to be. It is a world surrounded by four sacred mountains, and it is the fourth world in which people now live. The fact that it is the fourth world surrounded by four sacred mountains is no coincidence. The number four is the sacred number for the Diné and for most Native Americans. When the people emerged into this fourth world, they saw that it was beautiful and well formed. The three previous worlds had also been beautiful and well formed, but the people had made those worlds dangerous and frightening by their own behaviour. Because of their lying, adultery, and greed, they had rendered their worlds uninhabitable. Through their own wrongdoings, they created worlds of disorder. Now, arriving in the fourth world, they hoped, as the narrative says, "to do nothing unintelligent" so that they could live in peace and harmony in this beautiful new world.

The gods, called the "Holy People," created First Man and First Woman out of ears of corn, the most potent and sacred of all Diné symbols of life. These sacred ears of corn, white symbolizing maleness and yellow symbolizing femaleness, came to life through the breath of wind that animates all living things. The narrative is an origin story, explaining why we breathe and why our fingertips have whirls.

The Diné story sets out a physical and moral landscape for the people to live in. They learn the importance of proper behaviour, of goodness, so that the inherent harmony of the world can be maintained. Disorder comes through wrong behaviour, whereas harmony, balance, and order come through ritual and right thinking. It ties the people to a specific place, giving explanations for their surroundings, as well as linking their lives to an ancient and sacred past.

WHAT IS RELIGION?

religion
Beliefs and practices about spirit beings and supranormal and superhuman forces and their relationship to everyday life.

Religion involves a constellation of beliefs and practices about spirit beings and supranormal and superhuman forces and their relationship to everyday life.

Spirits may be thought to inhabit a realm different from our own, or they may be ever-present, although usually unseen. People believe that the spirit world, whether visible or invisible, is connected in some ways to humans, influencing the course of human life and the outcome of human activities. To obtain the help of spirit beings and to

The Creation of Adam shows the bearded figure of God touching the finger of the first man. In the book of Genesis from the Judeo-Christian-Islamic tradition, the first humans are created in the image of God and instructed to "replenish the earth," so that people will live in every habitable place, not one specific locale as in the Diné story. (Michelangelo, "The Creation of Adam," 15-08-1512. Fresco, ceiling (restored), Sistine Chapel, The Vatican, Rome. Photograph © Nippon Television Network Corporation, Tokyo).

harness spirit forces, people show them honour and respect and perform rituals that convey their desires and intentions.

Although we often speak of the spirit world as "supernatural," this term may be misleading and not fitting for all cultures. People in some cultures believe that the spirit realm is ever-present as part of their natural world and informs their daily lives in significant ways.

Religion includes both beliefs and practices. Beliefs are a people's ideas about the spirit world, the kinds of beings and forces that have spiritual power, and the ways in which the universe is created and continues to be. Religions also embody worldviews that teach people ethical values and attitudes. Sacred rituals or practices dramatize people's beliefs and allow them to actively express those beliefs. Through ritual action and speech, people make contact with the spirit world and manipulate spirit power for their own purposes.

Anthropologists analyze religious beliefs and rituals reviewing objective conditions and subjective experiences. What do people's beliefs and practices mean for them? How do people interpret their world and their experience? How does participation in rituals affect them, and what meanings do they ascribe to the rituals? How are people's religious beliefs and practices consistent with other aspects of their culture? How do people's economies and modes of subsistence influence the meanings and actions of their rituals? How do their political systems or social hierarchies frame the ways they structure their beliefs about the spirit world?

Variations in religious practices and beliefs sometimes correlate with other aspects of society. In egalitarian, stateless societies, for example, relationships between deities or spirit beings tend to be egalitarian as well. Just as all individuals have more or less equal access to economic resources and social prestige, they also have the potential to acquire spirit powers. In contrast, in societies with hierarchical social structures, people are more likely to believe in the existence of a ranked pantheon of deities. The Greek and Roman gods and goddesses are a good example of such a system. Zeus (in Greece) or Jupiter (in Rome) stood at the apex of a pyramidal structure of power. Each was allied with a spouse, Hera and Juno respectively, with whom they formed a conjugal unit, a reflection of the household structure of ancient Greece and Rome.

Monotheistic religions with their single supreme deity reflect political systems having central supreme leaders—a king or emperor. In the past, rulers of these societies were thought to be divine or to derive their authority directly from a god. Thus, many of the first state societies are referred to as theocracies, literally, governments by god. The relationships of gods and their activities are thus metaphors for ways of life on earth but on a more heroic, larger-than-life scale.

Religious behaviour is both practical and symbolic. Performing rituals may do something to achieve practical results, but these actions also have symbolic meanings. **Religious speech**—invocations, prayers, prophecies, songs of praise, curses—is a powerful means of transmitting messages about the world, and in doing so shapes the way

religious speech
Invocations, prayers, prophecies, songs of praise, and curses that are powerful means of transmitting messages about the world.

The hierarchical relationships among these Roman gods reflect the social structure of the society that invented and worshipped them.

These gospel singers illustrate the concept of religious speech. The anthropology of religion seeks to understand what people believe; how they embody, structure, and express their spiritual beliefs; and how these beliefs intersect with other aspects of their society and culture.

in which we perceive that world and make it understandable. Religious speech attempts to change a state of being, to exert agency or control over people or over events or natural phenomena. Through both speech and action, people express their ideas about causality, about how things happen and how human and other powers affect the world.

REVIEW

Religion is thoughts, actions, and feelings based on beliefs in the existence of gods, spirit beings, or supernatural forces. Religious beliefs and practices give people ways to contact such beings or forces, to honour and respect them, and to invoke their blessings and protection. Anthropologists analyze religious beliefs and behaviours using the perspectives of comparison and cultural relativism. As social institutions, religions tend to reflect the structure of the societies in which they arise.

SPIRIT BEINGS AND FORCES

Spirit beings and forces are believed to have extraordinary, more than human, powers. They typically are eternal or indestructible; they know more than an ordinary person can know; and they are able to act in ways that humans cannot. Thus, people seek contact with them to gain their protection and aid. Spirits may have the shape of animals, humans, or other, unusual forms and may change their shape at will. Sometimes they imbue inanimate objects with special powers. A supernatural force may be a vague spirit essence that pervades the universe.

Animism and Animatism

One common, nearly universal form of religious belief involves the soul. Souls are considered to be the spiritual and eternal aspect of living things. In some belief systems, such as Judaism, Christianity, and Islam, only human beings have souls, but in many cultures, people believe that animals and plants—all living things—have souls as well. The soul is seen as the animating aspect of living things. It gives life to the body that it inhabits. For example, people with such beliefs might ascribe consciousness and personality to a thunderstorm, a tree, or a rock. When the body dies, the soul is believed to leave and exist eternally in some other form or in a nonmaterial state. The belief in souls is called **animism**.

Animatism is the belief that all things, including men and women, are endowed with a generalized and all pervasive spiritual power. The main example of this complex is the belief in *mana* in many areas of Polynesia. Mana is thought of as a spiritical force that endows natural beings and phenomena with a special power that is both sacred and dangerous. Humans can benefit from it by using magical rites to control it. Leaders, especially hereditary chiefs, are thought to embody a larger amount of mana than ordinary people and derive their political power from it. Another example of this religious form can be drawn from the Christian belief in the special efficacy of the Holy Spirit, especially within Pentecostal traditions. This manifestation of a nominally monotheistic divinity takes the form of a special spiritual agency that has the power to cure and sometimes possesses it adherents.

animism
Belief in the existence of souls.

animatism
Belief that all things, including men and women, are endowed with a pervasive spiritual power.

Gods and Heroes

Some religious traditions have many spirit beings in human form—gods—with specific attributes, powers, and functions. Belief in numerous deities, called **polytheism**, is widespread throughout the world. In Hinduism, with its hundreds of millions of followers, as well as in the belief systems of small subsistence societies numbering in the hundreds, polytheistic spirit worlds are inhabited by multitudes of beings, each with a name, identity, genealogy, history, and domain of influence. In contrast, in **monotheistic religions** people believe in one supreme deity who has powers and knowledge that affect all aspects of life. In addition, monotheistic believers may recognize lesser spirit beings and important mortal heroes. Catholicism allows for the worship of saints, as does Islam (see the Culture Change feature on page 333).

Ancestors, Ghosts, and Demons

Other types of spirit beings include the spirit forms of deceased ancestors. Ancestral spirits have a particular connection to their living descendants, who honour them through prayer and ritual. In return, the spirits bestow blessings, health, and good fortune on their surviving kin. However, if people fail to perform the rituals, ancestor spirits can bring illness and misfortune.

This Japanese woman honours a dead ancestor by presenting offerings at an altar in her home.

In Japan, after a death, especially of a man, his eldest son prepares a mortuary tablet that commemorates his father (Morioka 1984). These tablets are kept in a household altar for at least several generations. They are honoured and given offerings from time to time in commemorative rituals. Eventually, the tablets of the eldest ancestor may be retired, either buried or broken and discarded. This belief is sometimes referred to as **ancestor worship**. In the past, reflecting Japan's patrilineal descent and patriarchal society, tablets for women usually were discarded after only one or two generations, but tablets for men were kept for a longer time. Today, however, a bilateral principle governs ancestor worship, and mothers and grandmothers are honoured along with fathers and grandfathers, and any member of the family, not just the eldest son, can carry out the rituals. These changes reflect shifts in Japanese household composition from extended family to nuclear family forms.

Among the Ju/'hoansi of the Kalahari, ancestral spirits, called *gangwasi*, are thought to cause illness and misfortune. People are wary of their ancestral spirits, avoiding contact with them in the night and hoping to be spared misfortune. They periodically perform dances to prevent ancestral spirits from attacking them and causing harm. Most important is treating people fairly while they are alive so that after death their spirit will not seek out offenders to harm them.

The Hopi of Arizona believe that ancestral spirits join the *kachinas*, powerful beings who bring rain. When a person dies, his or her spirit becomes mist and clouds that return to the people in the form of rain, helping to sustain crops in their arid environment. The Hopi view themselves as eternally linked in cycles of life and death, and they pray to and honour their ancestors so that they will be blessed with rain. Representational wooden carvings of spirits, called kachina dolls, are conduits to the spirit world.

In many cultures, people believe that deceased individuals may return or appear in the form of a ghost. Ghosts may have human shape or they may be only a shadow. Ghosts may be welcomed or feared, and they may return to the living to cause mischief or harm or to transmit messages of great importance. In some societies, ghosts are cast as demons. Among New Guinea natives, for example, village compounds must be ritually protected against wandering demons.

Totems and Taboos

In some cultures of Australia and the Pacific Northwest of North America, people believe that they are the descendants of spirit beings or ancestors, a belief called

polytheism
Belief in the existence of numerous deities that have specific attributes, powers, and functions.

monotheistic religions
Belief systems that hold to the existence of one supreme deity who has knowledge and powers that affect all aspects of life.

? How are ghosts viewed in American popular culture today?

ancestor worship
Belief in the importance of ancestors as they affect the lives of their survivors, protecting their descendants in return for rituals of honour performed to show them respect.

totemism
Belief system in which people believe they are descendants of spirit beings.

secret societies
Organizations that control the use of special objects used in religious rituals.

totemism. Totemic ancestors may have human or animal form. From ancient times, they gave protection or lifesaving advice to human beings in need or in danger. Thus, they are the primordial protectors of the people. Ancestral totems may also be identified as the actual progenitors of the present-day people. In either case, people owe them gratitude and respect and perform rituals in their honour so that they will continue to receive protection and guidance.

Totemism celebrates the solidarity of social groups. Australian Aborigines believe that each clan is descended from a specific animal in the mythic past, which they call "the Dreaming" (Hume 2000). At some time in an earlier realm of existence, the mythic animal ancestor was transformed into a human being and continues to be connected to its human descendants. The descendants honour their animal ancestor, or totem, by performing rituals in its honour and by refraining from eating its flesh. The totemic figure functioned to unite Aborigines, who, because of their nomadic lifestyle and dispersed populations, rarely came into sustained contact. Spirit links among people have survival value, because they create bonds of mutual acknowledgment, interdependence, and obligations to extend hospitality and share resources.

Spirit forces and beings are believed to be dangerous if contacted in the wrong way, in the wrong place, or at the wrong time. Some spirits inhabit particular locales that may be dangerous if entered without spiritual protection. Objects used in rituals also may be dangerous if touched or used when a person is not prepared. Societies that believe in these dangers may have organizations, known as **secret societies**, that control the special places or the use of special objects. For example, among Australian Aborigines and Amazonian Indians, only men may touch special musical instruments or ritual objects. If women come into contact with these objects, they may be seriously harmed or even killed by the spirit forces associated with them. Even to hear the sounds of the music or the singing of the men may be dangerous to women.

Restrictions such as these are called taboos. A tabooed object or place is one that can cause harm if contacted or entered. Its danger derives from its power. A dangerous person, object, or place may not be regarded as evil, however, because spirit power in itself is neither positive nor negative. Rather, it is the use to which the power is put that renders it good or bad. Individuals may use their spirit powers to become healers, fortune-tellers, or other ritual practitioners, serving their communities in important ways. Others, however, may seek to acquire spirit powers to do harm.

An example of taboos is seen in rituals surrounding pregnancy and birth. In many cultures, expectant mothers, and sometimes their husbands as well, avoid eating certain foods or engaging in certain kinds of activities. Many of these restrictions are geared toward ensuring a safe pregnancy and easy delivery. Inuit parents were not to tie their belts tight lest the placenta strangle the baby during birth. Haida mothers refrained from eating sticky substances, such as salmon eggs, to ensure a smooth and quick delivery.

Pregnancy taboos symbolize the dangers of pregnancy and birth and the uncertainty of outcomes. Through taboos, people express their fears and their desires to control essentially unpredictable events. In addition, taboos allow people to explain both positive and negative results. If the birth goes well and the baby is healthy, parents can feel that their behaviour contributed to the happy occasion. However, if the baby is sickly or dies, parents can find the reason for their misfortune by recalling taboos that they failed to observe.

REVIEW

Spirit beings and forces include gods, ancestors, ghosts, demons, totems, mana, souls, and spirit powers that may be evidenced in good or bad luck. Animism is belief that animals, plants, and inanimate objects are endowed with souls or personalities and have special spiritual powers. Animatism is the belief in a generalized and pervasive spiritual force, such as mana. Some religions are monotheistic (one god) while others are polytheistic (many gods). In totemism, living people trace their descent from animal ancestors and observe ritual taboos to protect the ancestral spirits. Potentially dangerous or contaminating spiritual power may be managed through secret societies or through individuals' observations of taboos. Religious rituals and religious speech often are aimed at giving people agency or control over forces and events that affect their lives. Shared religious beliefs and practices also contribute to people's social solidarity.

RELIGIOUS PRACTITIONERS

Most religions have individuals or groups who function as either part-time or full-time specialists or practitioners. Sometimes a person receives a calling from the spirit world to become a religious specialist. The calling could be received in a dream, a waking vision, or an omen or sign. Some societies believe that particular individuals inherit spiritual abilities from one generation to the next. In other cases, a person decides to become a religious practitioner because of his or her interests or experiences or wish to benefit the community through ritual practice. Some people may be drawn to ritual practice because of its creative and aesthetic qualities that give outlet for artistic expression through music, song, dance, and drama. Religious specialists also may enlist others to take the training necessary to become a practitioner. Mediums, healers, shamans, diviners, and priests are all religious practitioners.

Mediums, Diviners, and Healers

Mediums are believed to have special gifts that enable them to make contact with the spirit world and with spirit beings or spirits of the dead. They usually establish a direct relationship with a particular spirit or group of spirits. Through rituals they perform, mediums become conduits or channels between ordinary people and the contacted spirit beings. They often conduct these rituals in a state of trance—an altered state of consciousness in which they are not fully conscious of their surroundings. Trance states can be achieved through various means, including meditation or mental concentration; once in a trance, a medium can pass messages between individuals and members of the spirit world.

Diviners are believed to have the power to predict the future through messages and omens they receive and interpret from the spirit world. They use various divination techniques to obtain the spirit's guidance or answers to specific questions or problems. For example, they may recognize patterns or designs that tell a story, as in reading tea leaves or tarot cards. In some African societies, diviners roll chicken bones to read a person's fortune or examine animal entrails to predict a family's best course of action. In some Central American societies, diviners tell fortunes by throwing corn kernels into a bowl and finding meaning in the pattern the kernels make. In Native North America, diviners threw fruit pits to read patterns in the way they fell. Diviners may also look at the stars or gaze into water to retrieve omens and warnings.

Healers are religious practitioners who acquire spirit power to heal. Their followers believe that healers can diagnose the spirit cause of illness and effect cures through the performance of rituals. In North America, many people heed the advice of "faith healers," some of whom have large followings of enthusiastic believers. Traditional healers usually have some practical knowledge of human anatomy and physiology, pharmacology, and pharmaceutical substances in their environment. Healers may use this practical knowledge in their cures in addition to religious rituals. In some societies, healers may be suspected of sometimes using their control of spirit powers to cause harm rather than to cure illness. Ritual healers are usually called in to treat a patient when the illness is protracted or life-threatening. The following account, related in 1918 by a Fox woman, describes her experience with a healer called to assist her in the difficult birth of her first child.

> When that woman [the healer] came, she at once boiled some medicine. After she had boiled it, she said: "Let her sit up for a while. You must hold her so that she will not fall over." After I was made to sit up, she spat upon my head; and she gave me the medicine to drink. After she had given me the medicine, she began singing. She started to go out singing and went around the little lodge singing. When she danced by where I was, she knocked on the side. "Come out if you are a boy," she would say. And she would again begin singing. When she danced by she again knocked the side. "Come out if you are a girl," she would say again. After she sang four times in a circle, she entered the lodge. And she gave me medicine to drink. "Now it will be born. She may lie down." Lo, sure enough, my baby was born. (Michelson 1920:319)

? How do mediums and diviners practise in your society or community today?

mediums
Persons having special gifts to make contact with the spirit world, often in a state of trance.

diviners
Persons with the power to predict the future through messages and omens from the spirit world.

healers
Religious practitioners who acquire spirit power to diagnose the spirit cause of illness and effect cures.

This female shaman, or mudang, is conducting a kut ceremony in a village in present-day Korea. In a kut ceremony, the shaman summons forth the spirit world to promote harmony, heal, bring messages to the living, or appease the dead. Shamanism was a key feature of the traditional religion of Korea before the arrival of Buddhism, and it continues today in rural areas.

Shamans and Priests

Shamans are religious practitioners who are believed to contact the spirit world through ritual, prayer, and trance. They may use masks that represent spirit beings. Shamans are similar to mediums in many respects, except that they may not channel with a particular spirit being. Rather, they enter trance states to receive visions and messages from the spirit realm. Their work tends to be on behalf of the community as a whole. Shamans may also perform healing rituals or rituals seeking spirit protection, advice, and support. Ecstatic experience, whether through trance, visions, or dreams, is central to the way that shamans make contact with the spirit world. Shamanism may be quite ancient in the origins of religions (Goodman 1990).

Some societies have full-time religious practitioners called **priests**, who lead religious organizations and officiate at rituals but are not necessarily expected to be able to communicate directly with gods or the spirit world. The category of priest includes spiritual and ritual leaders of formally institutionalized religions with places of worship, such as churches, mosques, or synagogues, including ministers, mullahs, and rabbis, in addition to Roman Catholic or Greek Orthodox priests. Priests are often chosen from a select and privileged stratum of the society. In ancient Israel, the priesthood was hereditary with a specific patrilineal group, the Levites (sons of Levi). In the contemporary Catholic Church, it is composed only of men. Priests work on behalf of their religious organization, as well as their community and its members. Priests often preside at rites of passage, such as those that mark birth, puberty, marriage, and death.

> **REVIEW**
>
> Religious practitioners include mediums, healers, diviners, shamans, and priests; for some religious practitioners, these roles may overlap. A shaman, for example, may also be a diviner and a healer. Mediums enter trance states to serve as channels for communication between individuals and the spirit world; diviners tell the future or enter trance states to receive omens or advice from the spirit world. Healers use both spiritual and practical means to treat illness. Priests are full-time specialists who work for religious organizations and lead congregations in religious ceremonies and rituals. Unlike shamans, priests are not expected to have spirit power or communicate directly with divine beings.

shamans
Religious practitioners who are believed to make contact with the spirit world through prayer, ritual, and trance.

priests
Full-time religious practitioners who lead a religious organization and officiate at rituals but are not expected to be able to communicate directly with the spirit world.

rituals
Activities, including religious speech, ceremonies, and behaviours, that are demonstrations of belief.

RELIGIOUS PRACTICE

Religious practices, or **rituals**, are demonstrations of belief, putting belief into action. Rituals may be formal and public with many well-rehearsed participants and performers. They may also be informal and private, carried out by individuals or small groups. Rituals, including those involving religious speech, play a central role in most religions. They are the means by which believers make contact with the gods or spirit world; express honour and respect for spirit beings; obtain blessings, health, prosperity, or success; and achieve particular personal or communal goals. Rituals also can have specific ends, such as purification (spiritual cleansing), sanctification (making something sacred), veneration (worshipping something), or absolution (giving spiritual forgiveness). Individual rituals may be linked together in a ceremonial, a series of interconnected rituals.

Rituals usually involve the visual and performing arts. The aesthetic impact and spiritual meaning of rituals is meant to transport participants to a mental, emotional, and spiritual state of being that is different from their ordinary lives. Participants may adorn themselves with special clothing, masks, or face and body painting. They typically employ special objects made with precious metals, or such objects may be carved and painted or decorated with jewels, feathers, or stone in designs that incorporate religious symbols. Religious art and iconography (the meaning of symbols and design) thus reveal a people's aesthetic values. Rituals also involve poetic language and the arts of music, song, and dance, the subjects of Chapter 13.

Sacred and Secular Rituals

Secular life is full of rituals or ritualized activities, but these are not the same as sacred rituals. **Sacred rituals** are dedicated to the spirit realm and the expression of religious faith. Secular rituals may also be important culturally. For example, secular holidays such as Independence Day (in the United States) and Canada Day (in Canada) are times to display national symbols such as flags, sing national songs, and hear patriotic speeches. Sporting events also may be marked by ritualized protection, such as wearing team insignia or colours and cheering. The players may practise personal rituals to bring success, such as wearing good-luck gear in the game. These behaviours and attitudes involve magical thinking not unlike practices associated with religious beliefs, but their purpose is secular rather than spiritual.

In many societies, seasonal or annual rituals with both sacred and secular elements are held to celebrate the earth's bounty. Celebrations serve both as a thanksgiving for the past year's plants and animals and as a request to the spirits for renewed generation and continued supplies. These are examples of **rites of renewal**, also called rites of intensification.

Prayer and Sacrifice

Prayer is both a private and a public ritual. Through **prayer**, believers transmit messages to the spirit beings or to particular deities or ancestors. Prayers are meant to honour the spirits, ask favours of them, or win future blessings. Some religions

sacred rituals
Activities, places, or objects that are connected to the spirit realm and are imbued with power.

rites of renewal
Rituals performed with the goal of renewing the bounty of the earth.

prayer
Religious speech or thought through which believers transmit messages to spirit beings.

The Nuna and Bwa peoples of Burkina Faso use wooden painted animal masks and dances to make the spirit world come alive, as the butterfly dancer shows here. Geometric patterns in the masks depict moral principles. Zigzag lines, for example, represent the difficult life paths that the ancestors had to follow, and checkerboard patterns represent opposing moral forces, such as knowledge and ignorance.

Flying from the Potala Palace in Tibet, former home of the Dalai Lama, are prayer flags, each representing a blessing to all beings, carried everywhere on the wind. Buddhist sacred texts and symbols are printed or painted on the flags, and colours symbolize aspects of nature. Thus, prayers are sacred messages invoking global peace and harmony that are intended to link each person to the universe. The flags are never removed, but new flags are continually raised to ensure the future.

emphasize the memorization and correct verbatim repetition of prayers. Without correct recitations, prayers may not be effective. Other religions permit or encourage private prayers that individuals make up as they pray.

Believers also may transmit messages to the spirit realm through the **sacrifice** of offerings that honour spirit beings by giving up something important. Offerings may consist of foods that the deities are thought to prefer or valuable objects. People may also fast, refrain from sleep, or subject themselves to some kind of ordeal as a kind of sacrifice. Offerings may also include animals given in rituals of blood sacrifice in which the animals are slaughtered. Societies where people keep domesticated animals may use their stock in sacrificial offerings.

Blood sacrifice centres on the killing of a valuable domesticated animal, but some societies practised human sacrifice. Perhaps the best-known example was the human sacrifice performed by the Aztecs in central Mexico in the fifteenth and sixteenth centuries. Aztecs believed that the sun god (also the war god), called Huitzilopochtli, needed to be fed so that he would have the energy to travel across the sky from sunrise to sunset every day. He was nourished on human blood from daily sacrifices. This practice eventually contributed to the downfall of the Aztec Empire: As the need for more sacrificial victims increased, the priesthood demanded sacrifices from defeated groups forcibly incorporated into the expanding Aztec state. Those groups thus became even more hostile toward the Aztec state and aided the Spanish invasion of the Aztec Empire in the early sixteenth century.

sacrifice
Offerings made to spirit beings in order to show gratitude and honour.

puberty rites
Rituals performed to mark the passage of an individual from childhood to adulthood; also called initiation rites.

? *As an ethnographer, how might you describe a puberty rite, funerary rite, or other rite of passage that you have observed?*

Rites of Passage

As you read in Chapter 4, in most societies, people perform rituals to celebrate socially significant transitions in an individual's life cycle. Such rites of passage are typically conducted to mark birth, puberty, marriage, and death. Rituals may also mark other aspects of the life cycle, such as naming or initiation into an association. According to anthropologist Arnold van Gennep (1961), rites of passage ritualize three aspects of change in life status: separation, transition, and reincorporation. That is, individuals separate from their families, learn new knowledge and skills, and return to their communities as new people. Let us apply this model to two rites of passage: puberty rites and funerary rites.

Puberty Rites. Van Gennep's model can be applied to **puberty rites**, also called initiation rites, which celebrate the transition from childhood to adulthood. In some cultures, puberty rites are held for only girls or only boys; in others, both boys and girls receive

Less extreme than the Aztecs, the North American Plains Indians incorporated sacrificial acts through self-torture by male participants in the Sun Dance. Young warriors, like the one pictured here, sacrificed small parts of their bodies in honour of their spirit protectors. The flesh was pierced on the chest, a long tether was tied to a stretch of skin, and the tether was then attached to a specially dedicated pole. During the all-day Sun Dance, the warrior danced slowly around the pole in an ever-widening circle until strips of flesh were torn from his body. Participants in the ritual were honoured by their communities for their courage and spiritual dedication.

Renewal Rituals in North America

In many Native American cultures, people pay homage to animals by thanking the animals' spirit protectors, the spirit form of the living animals. Among northern Algonquin foragers of eastern and central Canada, for example, killing a bear required special rituals. Hunters addressed the dead bear's spirit with words generally used for kinspeople. Thus, through language, they called forth the reciprocal bonds between humans and animals. They dressed the slain bear in ceremonial clothing and erected a wooden pole nearby on which they hung the bear's skull and offerings of tobacco. After the bear was butchered, its bones were placed on a raised platform so that dogs and other scavengers would not disturb them. Algonquins and others "buried" their deceased kin in the same way.

This practice, showing the animal the same respect as one would show a relative, served as a symbolic link between bears and people. Algonquins believed that the spirits appreciated these signs of respect and responded by allowing more bears to be caught.

As a man from the Saulteaux nation (one of the Algonquin-speaking groups of Ontario) explained:

> The bears have a chief, and the orders of this chief must be obeyed. Sometimes he orders a bear to go to an Indian trap. When offerings or prayers are made to the chief of the bears, he sends more of his children to the Indians. If this were not done, the spirit of the bear would be offended and would report the circumstances to the chief of bears who would prevent the careless Indians from catching more. (Skinner 1911:162)

Farming peoples also perform ceremonies to honour and thank the spirits who gave them the knowledge to grow their crops. These ceremonies are often scheduled to coincide with calendar times for planting and harvesting and are, therefore, referred to as **calendric rituals**. For example, contemporary Mohawks continue to celebrate traditional calendric rituals marking Midwinter, Maple Festival, Strawberry Festival, Green Bean Festival, Green Corn Festival, and Harvest Festival at specific times throughout the year.

Seasonal ceremonies may be held to celebrate renewal of the community, express thanks for good fortune, and create or strengthen solidarity. The Sacred Arrow ceremony of the Cheyenne of South Dakota and Wyoming brought together all of the Cheyenne bands who lived during most of the year in small, dispersed communities. Thousands of people congregated at the annual event to celebrate Cheyenne history, socialize, and symbolically renew the Cheyenne nation. The renewal rite involved unwrapping a sacred "medicine bundle"—a collection of religious objects wrapped in a buffalo skin. The medicine bundle contained four sacred arrows, two with power over buffalos and two with power over human beings. The arrows were cleansed, prayed over, and blessed by a ritual specialist called an Arrow Keeper. Then the Arrow Keeper received small willow sticks given by each family, which he held over a fire burning sweet incense. The smoke purified each stick, thus blessing the family that it represented. On the last day of the four-day rite, the sacred arrows were displayed in a central lodge and viewed by all the boys and men. Through their collective presence and participation, hunters and warriors were ensured success, communal bonds were strengthened, and the well-being of the Cheyenne nation was assured.

ritual recognition. The Jewish and Christian faiths have rituals that mark a child's growth and maturation. The Jewish bar mitzvah (for boys) and bat mitzvah (for girls) incorporate the child into the adult community of believers. In the Christian ceremony of confirmation, children pledge themselves to their faith and join the congregation of their own volition. Children are usually pre-teens or teenagers when they are confirmed, an age associated with cognitive maturation. In various Christian

calendric rituals
Ceremonies performed at specific times during the year, for example, agricultural rituals performed for planting, growing, and harvesting crops.

funerary rites
Rituals performed to mark a person's death and passage to the afterworld.

denominations, christening marks religious as well as social birth, baptism consecrates the person in the faith, and confirmation welcomes the individual into the community of believers. In many African cultures, the transition to manhood is marked by lengthy initiation ceremonies preceded by periods of preparation and training (see the In Their Own Voices feature in Chapter 4).

Funerary Rites.   Funerals, or **funerary rites**, mark the final stage of life and are usually solemn. Death rituals serve purposes both for the living and the dead. According to many belief systems, the proper performance of a funeral allows the soul of the deceased to depart in peace. At death, the soul, which is the activating, invigorating, life-giving aspect of a person, leaves the body and eventually travels to the afterworld. In many cultures, however, it is believed that the soul does not make its final journey until after the funeral, and if the funeral is not properly conducted, the soul may never be fully released. It may hover near the living or wander aimlessly, possibly causing mischief and harm.

After a death, the body is usually cleansed, decorated, and dressed in special clothes by relatives or by specialists hired to perform the task. After a set number of days, the funeral takes place. Cultures vary widely in the degree of elaboration of funerals and the amount of time spent on them. For example, foragers spend less time and resources on funerals than people in settled populations. In some cultures, funerals are a time for the display of solidarity or interdependence among kin. For example, Mohawk funerals were arranged and conducted not by members of the deceased's own clan and moiety but by people belonging to the opposite moiety. Mohawks thought that close relatives of the deceased were too overcome by grief to be bothered with funeral details; but the exchange of roles also symbolized interdependence, unity, and societal balance.

In addition to marking the departure of the deceased, funerals serve to underscore family solidarity and allow for people's expression of sorrow and loss. Funerals are usually followed by a period of mourning during which close relatives of the deceased may wear special clothing, eat or avoid eating certain foods, refrain from engaging in some

Funerary rites in India end in the above-ground cremation of the deceased in a funeral pyre. In the past, widows were permitted or even encouraged to commit suicide (a practice called sati) *by throwing themselves onto the pyre of their deceased husband. Through self-immolation, Hindu widows directly enacted the reality of their low social status and lack of autonomy. Outside of marriage, women essentially had no social identity or even a right to live. Both voluntary and involuntary sati was made illegal by the British colonial government in 1829. However, the practice has not disappeared entirely and has even increased in some areas.*

activities, and act out their grief in culturally prescribed ways. The duration of the mourning period varies widely. In some patriarchal cultures, widows may be expected never to remarry.

Healing or Curing

In every culture, people have theories about health maintenance, causes of disease, and strategies for treatment. In many cultures, health is thought of as a state of harmony or balance. Health depends on the orderly functioning of a person's body, a person's relations with other people, the environment in which a person lives, and the spirit beings and forces with which a person interacts. When this balance is disturbed, illness and misfortune may follow.

A distinction is made in many belief systems between illnesses with natural causes and those caused by spirit beings or forces. Natural illnesses include minor aches and pains, accidents, and transitory ailments such as the common cold. These ailments are typically treated with natural remedies, such as medicinal plants and animal or mineral substances. If problems persist or worsen, spiritual causes may be suspected that call for ritual diagnosis and treatment. Patients then seek the aid of religious specialists who can diagnose the cause and recommend or perform the cure. Diagnosis may be achieved through divination or revelation in a dream or vision. Spirit causes can include soul loss, object intrusion, spirit possession, or the violation of taboos.

Some Hispanic and Latino people living in North, Central, and South America believe that illness may be caused by the sudden departure of a person's soul, a condition known as *susto*. Since the soul is the activating, life-giving part of a person, soul loss is obviously a serious, potentially fatal, illness. Soul loss may cause fearfulness, listlessness, loss of appetite, loss of interest in social activities, and a general lack of enthusiasm and vitality (Rubel 1977). *Susto* is usually triggered by sudden fright resulting from natural disasters, such as earthquakes or thunderstorms, car accidents, or emotional shocks, such as the sudden and unexpected death of a loved one. In treating *susto*, with the help of spirit messages from dreams or visions, a specialist is able to locate the missing soul and coax it back into the patient, thus effecting a cure.

In some parts of the world, object intrusion may be the diagnosis when a person experiences a sudden, localized pain in some part of the body. It is believed that a spirit, witch, or malevolent person somehow shot a foreign object into the patient's body, causing pain and distress. The object may have a specific shape, such as a pebble, grain of sand, feather, or animal tooth, or it could be an amorphous substance or liquid. The specialist ritually extracts the foreign object by "cupping" (pressing with the hands) or by sucking at the site of the pain. After the object is extracted, it is ritually disposed of to prevent further harm.

Spirit possession may be welcomed as a positive experience or spiritual gift or as evidence of faith in some religions. In other religions, it is considered a symptom of illness. In all societies with this belief, signs of spirit possession commonly include convulsions or loss of muscular control, erratic and rapid changes in mood, or insomnia. People possessed by spirits may seek treatment aimed at removing the spirit or enticing it to leave the person's body. Techniques of exorcism range from cajoling, bargaining with, threatening, or punishing the spirit to make it leave.

In Korea, women are most commonly the targets of spirit possession. When such a diagnosis is made, a shaman, also usually a woman, entreats the spirit to leave the afflicted person. The shaman gives offerings and promises that the patient will, in the future, erect a shrine in the spirit's honour and furnish it periodically with food and drink. It is believed that spirits choose to possess women who experience tension in their households, usually from conflicts over their roles as dutiful daughter, wife, and mother. These women may feel burdened by excessive demands, and spirit possession may be an outlet for them to express frustration about their life circumstances, as well as a means of extracting themselves from their daily burdens (Harvey 1979; Kendall 1984). The woman is not blamed for her predicament, but other members of her household may be held responsible for her unhappiness.

In Haiti, some people believe that both men and women may be possessed. Male spirits generally possess women and female spirits possess men. The spirits are attracted

spirit possession
Belief that spirits can enter a person's body and take over their thoughts and actions.

In Their Own Voices

Macumba Trance and Spirit Healing

In these excerpts from the film Macumba Trance and Spirit Healing, *two practitioners talk about their feelings when possessed by several of the macumba* orishas: *the Old Black Slave, the Indian, and the Child. Moisir, a lawyer, and his daughter Beje, a schoolteacher, have been participating in macumba ceremonies for about ten years, attending several times every week. In these group rites, dozens of mediums become possessed by four different spirits in succession. The mediums can then receive messages from the spirit world, giving advice to people who are sick, depressed, or in need. The experiences of Moisir and Beje reflect their direct contact with the spirit world, a contact that gives them emotional release and a prestigious role as healer or advisor in their community.*

MOISIR: Coming out of Senior Tupan (the Indian), my guide is annoyed, then I fall to the floor on the knees with one inside the other. He beats the floor twice with the hand opened and three times with the hand closed. They are strong blows, even violent enough to injure the hand. With this the recovery is complete.

BEJE: I feel that weight. Such a heavy weight. That once I am on my knees, as much as I want to, I can't get up. It's like I'm carrying something on my shoulders. Although the possession of the Old One is easy, coming out of it is a horrible thing. I think my head will leave my body. I begin to feel weak. Now, the Children are another story; they just say goodbye. With the Indian, the entrance and departure are equal. We feel tired to a degree but with a rested head. I have the impression of it being a little like a catharsis, you know, you get everything bad out and bring in a great deal of peace and tranquility.

MOISIR: The possession of the Old Black leaves the person very well. In spite of it being slow and difficult for the medium, it leaves the person feeling very well afterwards. Possession by the Old Black makes me feel very differently from the one by the Indian. In the possession of the Old Black, instead of feeling vibrations in the upper region, I feel it in both of my legs. My legs begin to get cold and a kind of pain comes into the knee and ends up knocking me on the floor. Upon feeling knocked down on the floor, I am nearly unconsciousness. I don't have the ability to reason, to talk for myself, to know people. I have a certain lack of consciousness in my work as the Old Black.

BEJE: The two possessions are totally different, not at all similar. For example, with the Indian, my hand begins to tremble, tremble, it keeps trembling, trembling, trembling until I feel the vibrations and fall to the knees. With the Old Black, I don't feel anything. Bam, bam, I'm on the floor.

MOISIR: As for coming out of the Old Black, it is very difficult. It really hurts when he leaves the medium. After, you feel a pleasant sensation as if you've come out of a sauna. You feel very tranquil, serene, without pain or preoccupations.

I don't like to call these "consultations" because we are not doctors. We simply give advice as to what people should do to better their spiritual and material lives. They look for jobs and they don't know what to do with all this desperation we are experiencing today. So we raise their morale. The Old Blacks have this objective, they are very much alive in material worlds.

From *Macumba Trance and Spirit Healing*, 1984. Written, produced, and directed by Madeleine Richeport. Richeport Films. Distributed by Filmakers Library, New York.

to their targets by physical or personality characteristics. To persuade the spirit to leave the body, the afflicted person may agree to establish a lifelong conjugal relationship with the spirit. In some cases, a formal marriage ceremony is performed between the patient and the possessing spirit. Thereafter, a separate bed is kept to which the patient retires for one or two nights each week to have conjugal visits with his or her spirit spouse (Lewis 1989).

Religious beliefs, such as spirit possession, allow for emotional release. Brazilian practitioners of *macumba*, which combines West African, Roman Catholic, and Native American beliefs and practices, enter a trance induced by a deity or *orisha*, a Yoruba term. In large public gatherings held several times a week, spirit mediums are serially possessed by four different deities. These include the Old Black Slave, the Indian, and two trickster deities, the Child and Eshu, a Yoruba trickster figure. In the macumba belief system, spirits possess people to impart advice and protection to the mediums as

Anthropology Applied

Medical Anthropology and Ethnomedicine

Medical anthropologists apply the holistic and cross-cultural approaches of anthropology to understand and respond to questions of human well-being, health, and disease. How are illnesses caused, experienced, and spread, and how can they be prevented and treated? What healers, healing substances, and healing processes do people use, and what beliefs and values inform those uses? How is human health related to social structure, the health of other species, and the environment?

Medical practitioners use information from medical anthropology in treating their culturally diverse patients. For example, reaching a diagnosis and prescribing effective treatment is not based strictly on the scientific model but involves understanding people's perceptions and interpretations of their bodies and bodily processes and their beliefs about illness. Those perceptions, interpretations, and beliefs are culturally constructed, because what is considered pathological is culturally defined. It is even the case that some diseases are culture-specific.

At a broader level, medical anthropologists may study epidemics, endemic diseases that persist in a society, or disease vectors that cause the spread of disease. They may study the distribution of disease in the world and the disparities in health among different populations. Some focus on the relationships between people's health and health care and the political and economic factors in societies. Others focus on particular problem areas, such as child and maternal health, eating habits and nutrition, or sanitation in a world where 1400 children die each day from diarrhea.

A branch of medical anthropology is ethnomedicine, the study of traditional medicine in cultural groups or in pre-industrial societies. Beliefs and practices in different human groups include ideas about hygiene, disease prevention, and healing properties of objects in their environment. An example is the study of Maasai ethnomedicine based on their use of the tree bark and roots for digestive health (Ryan 2000). The Maasai use an infusion of the bark from a kind of acacia tree to add to food as a stimulant. It is used as a digestive aid during ceremonies that call for the consumption of huge quantities of meat. The Maasai also use the bark from a kind of albizia tree as an emetic. The root can be boiled and mixed with milk to get rid of or prevent intestinal parasites, and they use this drink to de-worm their animals as well.

According to the World Health Organization (2004), 80 percent of the population of Africa relies on traditional medicine to meet daily health requirements. In Asia and Latin America as well, reliance on traditional medicines and practices may be more culturally acceptable and psychologically satisfying than those based on the Western scientific medical model. Modern medicine, which is also the subject of ethnomedical research, may be inaccessible to the majority of people in a developing country. However, traditional medicines and practices may be just as effective; plants that pre-industrial people used to treat illness include the sources of aspirin, morphine, ephedrin, and penicillin.

CRITICAL THINKING QUESTIONS

What are some of your beliefs and values about health and illness? Where do those beliefs and values come from?

well as to their clients. Clients seek help making decisions or finding solutions for problems of illness, social tension, emotional distress, or difficulties such as unemployment. But possession also provides mediums with an outlet for behaviour that would otherwise be deemed inappropriate. When possessed by "the child," for example, adults may act silly, play with toys, perform pranks, giggle for no reason, and in other ways express childish exuberance. It has been suggested (Lewis 1989) that through the ecstatic experience, people give vent to their frustrations in a socially channelled and acceptable form. They are able to air their grievances in a way that does not disrupt or undermine the social order.

Illness may result when a person commits some ritual transgression. For example, people may become ill if they fail to adhere to taboos, trespass on territory protected by spirit beings, or come in contact with powerful ritual objects. To be cured, the patient needs to undergo purification and ritual rebalancing. Most spirit causes of disease are metaphors for imbalance or disorder.

? *How can spirit-caused illnesses give people outlets for expressing their needs for order, balance, and security in their lives? How do healers address those needs?*

imitative magic
Magic that operates on the principle of "like causes like."

contagious magic
Magic that operates on the principle that positive and negative qualities can be transferred through proximity or contact.

Religious, ritual, and practical approaches to illness and health go hand in hand, even in societies with medical treatment models based on modern science. Spiritual and magical treatments are especially effective if people believe in them at the same time as other factors are at work, such as the use of pharmaceuticals, the therapeutic effects of receiving treatment, and the curative passage of time. A critical factor in the efficacy of ritual treatments is the patients' psychological state and beliefs. Patients become the centre of attention of their family and community and benefit psychologically from the knowledge that people care about them and want them to recover. The patient's belief in the healer, whether shaman or physician, and in the treatment also affect the outcome of the cure.

Magic and Witchcraft

In addition to spirit causes of illness, in some cultures witchcraft (also called sorcery) may be suspected in cases of illness, death, or misfortunes such as crop failure or infertility. Witches are defined as people who employ spirit powers to cause harm to others, the opposite of healers. They are usually thought to be motivated by anger, jealousy, or simply the desire to see other people suffer. Their targets may be people with whom they have quarreled, but they may also harm someone randomly. Witchcraft also is used as a form of social control and a means of achieving social justice. It is effective partly because people believe in it. For example, the literature cites many cases of healthy young people sickening and dying upon learning that a sorcerer has placed a curse on them.

Witches employ different forms of magic to produce a specific and connected result. **Imitative magic**, for example, operates on the principle that "like causes like" or that "life imitates art." Thus, depictions and enactments of harmony may predispose a community toward harmony. Manipulating drawings or replicas of individuals may cause good or harm to come to those individuals in life. Witches may use imitative magic by cursing or damaging images or objects that represent their targets.

A practice known as *couvade* is an example of benign imitative magic. In Amazonian cultures, men leave the village when their wives are about to give birth, retiring to the forest. There they imitate the actions of women in labour. They may clutch their abdomens, writhe in pain, and scream out as though in physical distress. These actions are intended to attract evil spirits who lurk about in hopes of attacking newborns. These spirits are lured to the men, allowing the expectant mother to give birth in safety.

Contagious magic operates on the principle that positive and negative qualities can be transferred through proximity or contact, like an infection. Thus, one can become more sanctified or blessed by touching something holy. In pre-Christian Europe, contagious magic was used as a palliative for pain. The cure for toothache, for example, was to nail a strand of one's hair to an oak tree, known for its strength, and then to pull one's head away. The pain of the toothache passed through the hair to the tree, where it remained. Gaining power or immunity by touching or wearing objects made powerful or immune through ritual, such as amulets or shrunken heads, are also examples of contagious magic. Witches may use contagious magic by secretly collecting a victim's nail clippings, hair, urine, or excrement and saying a spell over it to harm their target.

In some cultures, witches are thought to sprinkle harmful substances in people's food or drink, on their bodies while they sleep, or along the thresholds of their houses. People may believe that witches are capable of extraordinary physical feats, making things appear or disappear, transforming themselves into animals to lurk near a victim's house, or transporting themselves great distances in an instant.

Witchcraft may be a vehicle for the conscious or unconscious expression of anger and envy. For example, patterns of witchcraft accusations may follow lines of social tensions. Among the Cewa of Zimbabwe, accusations of witchcraft are usually preceded by quarrels, especially among matrilineal kin (Marwick 1967). Cewa society has formal mechanisms for airing and resolving disputes between matrilineal groups but not within them. When conflict arises between members of the same matrilineal group, accusations about witchcraft may emerge as outlets.

Thus, a belief in witchcraft is also an expression of people's fears, revulsions, and suspicions about the unusual behaviour of others and about the sources or causes of misfortunes. It is also an expression of people's desires and intentions in situations over which they have no direct control. Because of the secrecy of witchcraft, very little is known about its actual frequency.

Magic is not confined to societies with witchcraft. All cultures incorporate principles or practices that can be understood as magic. Bronislaw Malinowski tried to explain the universality of magic in terms of its role in risky, dangerous, and unpredictable undertakings (1954). He maintained that, in these situations, it gives people a sense of control and optimism that actually contributed to their ability to take risks and achieve success. His theory has been applied to explain magical practices among North American groups that face particularly risky situations, such as gamblers, baseball players, and university students. For example, a study at the University of Manitoba found that many students incorporated magical practices in the course of taking examinations (Albas and Albas 1989). Some would wear lucky items of clothing or jewellery. Others would take the pen that they used to take reading and lecture notes into the exam room in hopes that it would remember what it had written. Other strategies included arranging breakfast sausage and eggs to represent the number 100, making a complete circle around the exam building, sitting in the "lucky zone" within the exam room, sitting next to a good student, not cutting one's hair, abstaining from sex, or just praying. While such practices might not have replaced conscientious study as a preparation tactic, they did alleviate the sense of panic that often interferes with concentration and good performance on an exam.

? *Do you practise magic or magical thinking in your daily life? Are there principles or practices in a religion in your society that could be understood as magic?*

REVIEW

Religious practices include ritual, prayer, and sacrifice—ways of mediating between people and their spirit world or spiritual forces. Rituals, both sacred and secular, may include rites of renewal or intensification, calendric rituals, and rites of passage, such as puberty or initiation rites and funerary rites. Rituals are also used in curing ceremonies for illnesses with spirit causes, such as soul loss, object intrusion, spirit possession, or the violation of taboos. Imitative magic or contagious magic may be used in curing ceremonies and in other contexts, such as the couvade. Witchcraft or sorcery, which has complex social and psychological functions, also involves the use of magic.

THE ORIGINS AND FUNCTIONS OF RELIGION

It is impossible to know when or where religious beliefs first appeared in human societies. Archaeologists have discovered ancient human burials and can infer ritual practices that may have had religious meaning, such as the use of red ochre, grave goods, caches of ritual objects, and reliquaries or shrines. But we cannot know what was in the minds of those ancient peoples. Did they have some feeling of community and family ties that made them want to memorialize the burial places of their kin? Did they have some beliefs in an eternal soul that made them want to give their relatives a respectable interment? Did they include grave goods with the burial so that the deceased could use them in an afterlife? Possible evidence of religious practices also comes from ancient cave paintings and rock paintings discovered in France, Spain, southern Africa, and Australia (Peregrine 2003). Most of the paintings in these venues are of animals.

Explaining the World

People often turn to their religion to seek explanations for events whose causes seem unknown or uncontrollable. Their beliefs help them gain some sense of control over what is ultimately unexplainable, unpredictable, and uncontrollable. People may wonder why their efforts are sometimes successful and sometimes not, why the same effort on different occasions may lead to a positive outcome and sometimes not. Why are some hunting expeditions successful while others fail? Why are some babies born healthy while others are sickly? Why do people die? Through ritual, people attempt to impose order and control over the outcomes of their efforts. Through ritual, they

Some researchers suggest that cave paintings such as this one are expressions of magical beliefs (Wallace 1966). The painters drew pictures of animals that they wanted to hunt. Was this imitative magic in the belief that images of desired results would lead to actual occurrences? Others suggest that human beings were not included in paintings because of beliefs that a person could be harmed through their image by contagious magic.

appeal to spirit forces to aid them in their endeavours, to ensure successful outcomes and to avoid misfortune.

The explanatory power of religious beliefs also helps people understand why the world is the way it is, why the earth has the shape it has, why the animals and plants have the form they have, and why people look and act the way they do. Most religions profess a belief in creator or transformer deities who gave the world and all the creatures in it their present shape. These creator deities may also be responsible for imparting knowledge to people, teaching them how to plant, to hunt, and to organize their social life. They may be responsible for the origin of kinship groupings and of political structure. They may be responsible for setting out the kind of work that people do, the roles that men and women fill, and the values and ethics that people live by. In this way, religious beliefs are not only explanatory but also serve to legitimate a particular social or political system. For example, social inequality may be explained as part of a divine plan. A loved one's death may be explained as god's will.

Science and technology serve many of the same functions of explaining, predicting, and attempting to control the world but in science the underlying premises about cause and effect are different. The scientific approach is based on empirical observation or modelling of effects that are believed to have physical causes. Religious interpretations of observations are based on the belief that the ultimate causes are spiritual processes and forces.

Solace, Healing, and Emotional Release

Religious faith provides psychological support in times of anxiety and stress, and religious practices can be emotionally therapeutic for individuals and groups. Confession of wrongdoings enables people to express their remorse, shed their guilt, and feel rehabilitated in their own eyes, in the eyes of their community, and in the eyes of the deities who may see their actions, judge them, and bestow forgiveness or mercy. Psychological functions of religion may be seen, for example, in visionary experiences or spirit quests. The profound emotional catharsis that can result from prayer, participation in rituals, and contact with the spirit world may have a healing effect by comforting a sufferer, releasing tension and worry.

Social Cohesion

Religious beliefs and practices often function to support cohesive communities. Most rituals involve individuals, their family, wider kinship grouping, and social networks that connect them to others. Some rituals, such as seasonal or annual celebrations, unite an entire local population or tribal group.

Religious beliefs and practices can further function to justify the existing social order. Relationships among deities may reflect the sociopolitical nature of the human society. In stratified societies, the leader (whether chief, emperor, or king) may be thought to be a descendant of the divinity, endowed with divine power, or chosen directly by the deities. In the Polynesian chiefdoms, central and southern African kingdoms, European monarchies, and the Inca Empire, the head of state was thought to rule by divine right.

Teachings conveyed by spirits, especially in stories of creation and transformation, also legitimate the existing social order. Gender roles, for example, and the relations between women and men may be mandated through divine teachings or modelled through the relationships of male and female deities. For example, in the Hindu pantheon of deities, gods, and goddesses have important and powerful roles and are equally as likely to be worshipped by believers. However, there is a striking difference in the personalities of married and unmarried goddesses. When married, goddesses are nurturing, benevolent, and trustworthy; when unmarried, they are aggressive, dangerous, and unpredictable.

Pigs for the Ancestors

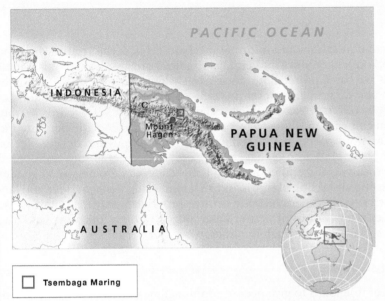

☐ **Tsembaga Maring**

The Tsembaga of New Guinea, numbering about 200 people, participate in an interrelated system of rituals, economic production, social activity, and warfare. The Tsembaga practise a combination of horticulture and animal husbandry. Women are the principal farmers, planting and harvesting yams that feed the people and the many dozens of pigs that each family maintains. The Tsembaga live in balanced competition with neighbouring tribes. Intergroup relations involve mutually beneficial trading exchanges and social interactions that lead to marriage alliances and military support for raids. Raids help balance the ratio of people to land and resources. Raids also function to create buffer zones of uninhabitable land that is left fallow to regenerate. However, too frequent raiding would upset this balance by disturbing people's ability to farm and raise their pigs. Therefore, a complex set of practices has developed to control the frequency of warfare, and these practices are couched in beliefs about people's obligations to their ancestors and the spirit realm.

The cycle of practices may last as long as twenty years. At the end of a period of hostilities, Tsembaga ritually plant a shrub, called a *rumbin*, in their territory. The act of planting the *rumbin* communicates the group's symbolic and real connection to their territory. An elaborate feast is then held, centred around the slaughter of nearly all of the group's pigs. Only juvenile pigs are spared, to ensure future supplies. The pigs are slaughtered as a sacrifice to the ancestors who assisted the group in warfare with its neighbours and helped attain a successful outcome.

No matter how many pigs are sacrificed, however, the people think that the ancestors are not satisfied and obligations to the ancestors remain partly unfulfilled. People then make solemn pledges to the ancestors that they will offer future sacrifices. And until that time, hostilities must cease, because, according to Tsembaga belief, it is improper to renew hostilities until all obligations to the ancestors have been discharged. Thus, episodes of warfare are regulated by the amount of time it takes to increase the pig population to the number needed for a proper sacrifice.

Complex factors are involved in people's judgments about whether or not they have enough pigs to offer to the ancestors. When the pig population is relatively small, the animals can be fed without too much human effort, but after awhile the women gardeners must turn over a good portion of land that would otherwise go into production for human consumption and use it to grow food for the pigs instead. For instance, during Rappaport's fieldwork in the 1960s, about 36 percent of active farmland was used to produce food for the village's 170 pigs.

Eventually, a woman's complaints to her husband about the undue burdens on her labour reach a critical point, and he becomes willing to speak to other men on her behalf. By that time, most of the men in the village are receiving similar complaints from their wives. Once people experience the burdens of maintaining a large number of pigs, they acknowledge their readiness to make sacrifices to the ancestors.

The next episode of the cycle commences with the uprooting of the *rumbin*, signalling the beginning of a year-long festival. During the festival, friendly neighbouring groups are invited to visit the village to socialize and feast on the sacrificed pigs. Social and economic goals may be pursued during these festivals. Pork is distributed to one's allies, and other articles of trade are exchanged. In addition, young men hold dances to signal their interest in and availability for marriage. Eligible young women attend the dances and have a chance to observe the physical and social qualities of eligible men. The young men's presence is also interpreted as a willingness to aid the hosts as military allies in future conflicts.

The final segment of the cycle begins after the festival period has drawn to a close. Raiding one's enemies (one's competitors for scarce land) may now resume. When the hostilities have temporarily resolved underlying tensions, the *rumbin* is replanted, marking the end of one cycle and the beginning of the next.

? *What do texts in a religion with which you are familiar teach about gender roles and relationships? What social order do those teachings tend to support?*

In contrast, Diné **cosmology**—the belief system concerning the origin and nature of the universe—presents many deities as interdependent and complementary male and female pairs. First Man and First Woman are important creator and transformer deities. Twilight Man and Twilight Woman and Dawn Man and Dawn Woman are deities of the daytime cycle. Although they play different roles, male and female deities have similar powers, personalities, and effects on the lives of humans.

Social Control

Rituals often function as formal and informal mechanisms of social control. In some stratified societies, codified criminal and civil laws, judicial processes, and punishments or penal sanctions are based on religious doctrines, customs, or texts. The function of social control can also be subtle, however. In some cultures, for example, the time of puberty is marked by role reversals in which socially disapproved behaviour is permitted briefly in ritual context. Amish teenagers completing high school are permitted to drink beer and have noisy parties before settling down to a serious and devout life, for example. Similarly, central African teenagers are permitted to act in ways considered deviant—publicly speaking obscenities or acting lewd. They may also engage in gender reversals, boys dressing and acting like girls and girls mimicking the behaviour and language of boys. Such ritualized permission to act inappropriately may temporarily ease tensions in societies where norms of proper behaviour are strictly followed. They also serve to highlight social values through the transgression of norms.

Economic Adaptation

Another function of religion is to give people additional means to adapt to their environments and changes in their circumstances. Anthropologists using cultural materialist or ecological perspectives analyze religious practices as means of adapting to one's environment. Recall from Chapter 2, for example, Marvin Harris's interpretation of the sacred cow in India as protection against the slaughter of cattle in light of their central importance in the economy of farmers. In another classic study, Roy Rappaport (1969, 2000) demonstrates how a complex ritual cycle relates to the economy and environment of the Tsembaga of New Guinea.

REVIEW

Whatever their origins, religious beliefs and practices provide explanations for the world as it is, for the way people are, and for major events in people's lives. Religion also helps give people solace in times of trouble and sorrow, allowing for emotional release and providing emotional support. In addition, religious beliefs and practices function to bind communities together into cohesive networks. As ideologies, they can both support and change the existing social order and, as in the case of the Tsembaga, people's adaptations to their environment.

RELIGION AND CULTURE CHANGE

Religious beliefs and practices, like every other aspect of culture, are responsive to changes in society. Social, economic, political, and historical developments have an impact on religions. Changes in other areas of their lives may cause people to think about their relationship with the spirit world in different ways, altering some practices or even abandoning them altogether. People may begin to rethink the roles of religious practitioners, possibly changing the criteria for choosing them or how they are trained. Ritual practice may change as new ceremonies are adopted and older ones are modified or discarded. Although religion seems like a timeless tradition, like any other system of ideology and practice it is subject to transformation.

Religions are dynamic systems, incorporating new ideas either from external sources or from the innovative creativity of believers. Some religions may be inherently more receptive to change. Polytheistic religions, for example, usually do not have a

? *What is an example of a belief or practice in a religion that you know about that has been changed or abandoned?*

cosmology
Religious worldview of a people, including beliefs about the origin of the world, the pantheon of deities that exist, and their relationships to the spirit realm.

single standardized doctrine. They allow for additions of new ideas or ritual elements that appear to be effective and the elimination of those that no longer achieve desired results. New rituals might be borrowed from neighbours or from the religions of more distant people met in travel or trade. People observe each other's rituals, listen to religious narratives, and adopt practices that they find beautiful, compelling, or effective. New deities may be incorporated into a local pantheon as believers find them appealing or useful. This process is more common in religions that lack central texts whose interpretation can be argued or even fought over. People tend to borrow stories and mythic characters readily, often changing details to suit their own circumstances and attitudes. This process of combining and modifying elements from different religions is called **syncretism** and is a process inherent to all religions.

Defeated populations, seeing the conquerors' gods as superior, may willingly adopt their religious systems. In many situations, however, conquered people resist change and resist abandoning their own religious beliefs and practices. They may hold even more tightly to their own traditions, keeping their rituals as acts of resistance and self-empowerment. In this context, new religious traditions may arise that give former practices new meanings and interpretations as discussed in the case study.

Revitalization Movements

A source of new religious traditions is revitalization movements—religion-based responses to societal crises. Revitalization movements arise in times of social and political upheaval, often in situations of invasion, conquest, and control, when people are confronted by a loss of their rights and restrictions on their freedom. Such movements also may arise as a response to increasing social and political inequalities within a society among people who lack rights or advantages. They are aimed at restructuring power relationships within a society or between conquered peoples and their rulers.

Revitalization movements frequently begin after an individual receives direct messages believed to be from the spirit world telling him or her to convey divine teachings to the community. Referred to as **prophets**, such individuals become the conduits for communication between the spirit world and ordinary people. Essentially, the messages tend to point out how people have become demoralized by straying from the right path and abandoning their traditional values and ethics. Although external forces may be causing people's suffering, the people themselves contribute to their troubles. The prophets teach that the people must return to traditional ways, stressing the values of hospitality or civility, generosity, cooperativeness, and solidarity with relatives and community members. Leaders of revitalization movements proselytize others, always seeking to enlarge the community of followers and establish a network of believers.

There are several kinds of revitalization movements. **Nativistic movements** attempt to rid the society of foreign elements, returning to what is conceived to be a prior state of cultural purity. The late nineteenth-century Ghost Dance cult of the Plains Indians (see Chapter 1) is an example of a nativistic movement, as is the longhouse movement among the Iroquois (see Chapter 14). **Revivalistic movements** stress the importance of reviving cultural and religious practices that express core values but have been marginalized or abandoned. **Millinerian movements** incorporate apocalyptic themes, prophesying an abrupt end to the world as we know it by a specific time or date in the future, leading to the establishment of a new way of life or form of existence. **Messianic movements** stress the role of a prophet or messiah as a savior for his or her people. Some religion-based social movements combine aspects of these revitalization themes.

Although revitalization movements are religious, they also have social and political messages. They are always at least potentially revolutionary and can develop into direct challenges to the established order with the aim of transforming or overturning social and political systems. Historical factors affect whether political movements develop. If authorities recognize the political potential of revitalization themes, for example, they may brutally suppress the movement. However, the leaders of the movement may direct people's energies away from political action to protect them from attack. Messages might call for accommodating external situations, or they might postpone the rewards for faith to some distant time in the future, even until after death. These kinds of messages also direct people away from political rebellion.

GLOBALIZATION

Syncretism is a common result of political processes, especially in situations of conquest and colonization. As state societies have expanded throughout history, conquerors have imposed their religious beliefs and practices on defeated populations.

syncretism
The blending of two religious traditions to form a new one.

prophets
Religious leaders who receive divine inspiration, often in a vision or trance.

nativistic movements
Revitalization movements attempting to rid society of foreign elements and return to what is conceived to be a prior state of cultural purity.

millinerian movements
Revitalization movements incorporating apocalyptic themes, prophesying an abrupt end to the world as we know it, leading to the establishment of a new way of life or form of existence.

messianic movements
Revitalization movements stressing the role of a prophet or messiah as a saviour for his or her people.

Case study

First Nations and Christianity

Christianity has been an instrumental force in the colonization and assimilation of Aboriginal peoples in Canada. Missionaries often provided the initial contact between European society and indigenous peoples and served as the gatekeepers through whom European influences were channelled. They advocated for the elimination of indigenous belief and practices and for assimilation into a European Christian culture. Churches ran the residential schools in which generations of children were forced to follow Christian traditions and moral codes. As a consequence, most Aboriginal peoples are currently Christian, and many of their traditional beliefs and rituals have been abandoned and lost. However, they have not necessarily been passive victims in this interchange. Many First Nations peoples and communities willingly accepted Christianity, sometimes with great zeal, and were able to modify orthodox belief and practice to conform to their own cultural meaning systems and serve their needs. Angela Robinson's study of Mikmaq Catholicism (2005) and John Barker's study of the Anglican Church among the Nisgaa (1998) provide two examples.

MIKMAQ

The Mikmaq of Nova Scotia were first introduced into Christianity by the Jesuit Missionaries in the seventeenth century. Over time, they developed a strong attachment to Catholic belief and practice and claimed it as a central part of their tradition and identity. For example, when the British ousted the French in the eighteenth century, they attempted to suppress Catholicism and convert the people to the Anglican faith. The Mikmaq firmly resisted and were able to maintain Catholic observances through indigenous catechists during a two-hundred-year period when priests were banned. Currently Catholicism remains the majority religion although a recent revitalization of indigenous practice has emerged.

Mikmaq Catholicism has incorporated many elements that reflect the retention of pre-contact belief and practice and the addition of innovations in response to specific local experiences and needs. The main vehicle for the expression of local aspects of Catholicism is the veneration of St. Anne, Mary's mother, as the patron saint of the community. As in many other Catholic localities, observances focused on saints allow individual communities to adapt the details of a supposedly universal orthodox tradition to their own circumstances (also see the Culture Change feature on page 233). One specific localized aspect of worship involves the identification of St. Anne as the "grandmother," an important kinswoman in Mikmaq families who is associated with care, wisdom, and

healing. Accordingly, St. Anne is venerated and called upon to cure illnesses and help with emotional distress. St. Anne's shrine on Potlotek Island is an especially sacred location which forms the focus of an annual summer pilgrimage. During a sacred week, thousands of Mikmaq come from both the surrounding communities and from areas to which they have migrated to attend a church service and a procession for the saint. This event closely resembles the summer gatherings of pre-contact times that are typical of yearly congregations within foraging subsistence systems (see Chapter 5). As on other such occasions, people who are otherwise dispersed gather together to engage in a complex of activities including ritual, political consultations, trade, and social networking. For example, Mikmaq chiefs are formally incorporated into church and processional activities and make important political announcements to the celebrants. Family members get an opportunity to catch up on the details of each other's lives. Young people view the pilgrimage as a prime opportunity for courtship.

These various modifications of belief have often disturbed local Catholic clergy, who tend to be non-Aboriginal, but Mikmaq believers strongly adhere to their version of the religion and attempt to "train" their priests to accept it. This process is often direct, as illustrated in words of advice proffered to a new parish priest: "If you want to be happy, you have to change. [We have] four thousand people who will not change, and it's easier for you to change than everyone else (quoted in Robinson 2006:60)."

NISGAA

Barker's work among the Nisgaa of the Northwest Coast reflects a similar bending of official Christian traditions to suit local circumstances. The Nisgaa adopted Anglican Christianity without much apparent resistance, although it threatened to make deep inroads into their traditional beliefs and practices. The most serious issue was the suppression of potlatching, which was tied not only to their ritual cycle but also to the way in which they allocated political office and social status and documented territorial ownership. However, they easily found a way to incorporate their political processes into Christian forms. The main vehicle for status validation became the erection of tombstones. Instead of obtaining a crest or constructing a totem pole through a potlatch (see Chapter 10), a person could obtain a "name" by providing a tombstone and unveiling it at a large feast in honour of a dead chief. Status acquisition was also incorporated into church offices, some of which were assigned to traditional chiefs.

Another way in which the Nisgaa were able to use Anglican practice to serve their own interests was in their relations with the Canadian government. Local priests became somewhat hesitant participants in advancing Aboriginal land claims, which were facilitated through literacy and knowledge of the Canadian court system.

While many earlier priests were ambivalent about the Nisgaa versions of Christianity, the Anglican Church has been trying to achieve a new relationship with local congregations. It now openly endorses the retention and inclusion of indigenous practice, including potlatches, and some priests have even taken names and crests. It has also become a vocal advocate of indigenous causes and assisted in the negotiations that led to the signing of the *Nisgaa Treaty*, a critical event in the recognition of Aboriginal rights and title.

Cargo Cults

A different kind of revitalization movement arose in Melanesia in the early twentieth century. Referred to as **cargo cults**, these movements were a response to British colonial control, the expropriation of native land, and the relegation of indigenous peoples to roles as menial labourers and second-class citizens. Cargo cults arose at various times and in various places in Melanesia, most notably in New Guinea (Worseley 1967, 1968). Prophets were believed to have received spirit messages telling people to perform rituals, based on traditional principles of magical cause and effect, that were supposed to result in the arrival of material wealth ("cargo") for the native people.

Cargo cult followers built loading docks along the coast and, later, landing strips for airplanes in the bush, intending to make landing sites for ships and airplanes. They had seen these vehicles bringing in goods for the colonial Europeans, and they believed that if they acted as if the goods were coming, life would imitate art. On this principle of magic, the people imitated European behaviour that they thought was responsible for the arrival of the cargo: They wore European-style tophats, neckties, and jackets, and sat around tables and scribbled on pieces of paper that they then put into boxes—all in imitation of having meetings and sending orders for goods.

Cargo cult activities appeared foolish to the Europeans, but these activities were consistent with the native worldview. According to Melanesian principles, wealth was obtained by a combination of hard work and ritual. Native people never saw Europeans doing what the Melanesians regarded as work, yet the foreigners received wealth from across the ocean or from the sky, so, clearly, their rituals were powerful. The pre-literate Melanesians imitated what they took to be European rituals involving costumes and actions such as writing. Eventually, rituals were abandoned as they failed to attract cargo, until another prophet came with a new set of instructions on what to do. Waves of cargo rituals emerged and dissipated in the 1930s and 1940s. In contrast to the repressive responses to the Ghost Dance of the American Plains, however, the colonial government in New Guinea ignored the cargo cults because they posed no threat to colonial power. Eventually, the cargo movements dissolved because they failed to achieve the desired results. Note that cargo cults and the imitation of European behaviour also demonstrate the political message underlying revitalization movements.

Role of Founders in Buddhism, Christianity, and Islam

Some of the most widely practised religions in the world today began as revitalization movements. Buddhism, Christianity, and Islam originated with individuals who received divine inspiration. These founders essentially reacted against human suffering and the social and political inequalities in their societies, giving as their message the need for all people to establish freedom, equality, justice, and peace. These messages ultimately became institutionalized in formal religions under the control of ecclesiastical elites who serve as intermediaries and interpreters of divine messages.

Siddhartha Gautama, later referred to as Buddha, or "Enlightened One," was born about 525 BCE in India, the eldest son of a local prince, destined to inherit his father's position. But Gautama rejected the privilege to which he was entitled by birth, choosing instead to leave his parents, wife, and son to seek inner wisdom and the end to

cargo cults
Revitalization movements arising in Melanesia in the early twentieth century with the aim of obtaining material wealth through magical means.

physical and spiritual suffering (Koller 1982). Buddha's message was in part a reaction against inequities in the caste system maintained through Hinduism. That system consigned people at birth to specific inherited occupations, social standing, and degrees of ritual purity. Hinduism also emphasized people's role in an inescapable cycle of reincarnation with its inescapable cycle of suffering. The message of Buddhism is that people can escape caste duty through right thinking and right action to achieve spiritual enlightenment, equality, and oneness with the universe. Eventually, a person can escape the cycle of reincarnation by attaining perfect knowledge and self-control.

Jesus, whose teachings led to the founding of Christianity, was born sometime after the death of Herod in 4 BCE. Biblical scholars have different interpretations of the life of Jesus, and those interpretations reflect the social and political beliefs of the analysts (Meier 1991). Some scholars emphasize Jesus' role as a prophet of "restoration theology," predicting the divine destruction of the imperial order imposed by Rome on Israel and the establishment of a world of justice and mercy (Sanders 1985). In this view, Jesus' spiritual prophecy was central and within the tradition of Jewish law and interpretation. Other scholars emphasize his role as a teacher and somewhat subversive commentator on the life of his times (Mack 1988). Still others stress the social context of Jesus' life and see his message as relating fundamentally to sociopolitical conditions (Borg 1994; Crossan 1994). According to this view, like Buddha, Jesus was appalled by inequalities in the prevailing social system of his day. He was also angered by the cooperation of some members of the inner circles of power in the Hebrew state with their Roman invaders and conquerors. While the common people chafed under increased control and demands for labour and tribute, the local secular and religious elites benefited from their favoured positions as puppets of Roman colonial rule. This dynamic is not unique to that area but, rather, occurs in most colonized societies.

According to one modern interpretation (Crossan 1994), Jesus' critique of his own society focused on inequalities within the family, particularly the privileged role of the father in a patriarchal system of male dominance. Because hierarchical relations begin with lessons on dominance and subordination within the family, Jesus advocated the equality of women and men (Fiorenza 1983). Jesus used the metaphor of "open commensality"—the practice of eating at the same table—to undermine norms that segregated people according to rank and gender (Crossan 1994). The "open table," where everyone—men and women, beggars, lepers, and all types of social outcasts—were welcome and could eat together became a powerful symbol of the egalitarian society Jesus envisioned. In addition, Jesus urged his followers to create the kingdom of God on earth through social and religious transformation.

The founder of Islam, Muhammad, was born in Mecca around 570 CE into a poor family. The Arabian Peninsula at the time was home to many small tribal groups who practised polytheistic religions with an array of nature deities (Guillaume 1986). During a solitary meditation, Muhammad experienced a vision of the angel Gabriel, who told him that God is the one and only God whom people must obey. Muhammad began to preach his message of a monotheistic religion, initially attracting only a small following of mostly slaves and poor people. He was attacked as a sorcerer, but he continued to proclaim his message for all Arabs. His mission, then, was to unite the Arab world under the mantle of one religion with its one God. However, unity came with the price of war: If people did not join the faith on their own, they had to be compelled through force to believe, thus unleashing a holy war of proselytizing religion through conquest.

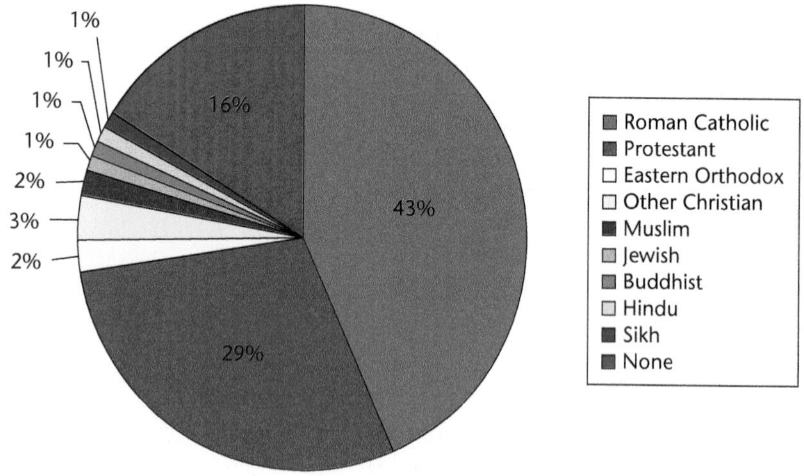

Figure 12.1
Religion in Canada.
In spite of increasing numbers of non-believers and devotees of other faiths, Canada remains a predominantly religious and Christian country. Fifty percent of Canadians attend religious services at least once a month (Statistics Canada 2003). Religion is also embedded directly and indirectly in many of our public institutions. For example, The Charter of Rights and Freedoms asserts a foundation based on "the supremacy of God."
Source: Adapted from Statistics Canada, "Religions in Canada, 2001 Census (Religion and Age Groups for Population)", Catalogue 95F0450XCB2001004, Released May 13, 2003.

Culture Change

WOMEN IN ISLAM IN ETHIOPIA, PALESTINE, AND CANADA

Excluding the large Christian majority, Islam has become the largest religious tradition in Canada with over 600 000 adherents. Its prominence has been based on a large volume of immigration from areas such as the Middle East, Pakistan, and Africa. However, immigrants represent many different ethnic groups and versions of Islamic belief. A comparative study by Camilla Gibb and Celia Rothenberg (2000) looks at local Muslim practice in two regions—Ethiopia and Palestine—and how it has been modified in the course of settlement within Canada. They focus especially on women's roles and experiences.

The Ethiopian case involves migrants from the city of Harar, who form a distinct ethnic group and Islamic community within a predominantly Christian country. Religious and ethnic persecution by the Ethiopian government caused many Harari to flee the country and seek refugee status in Canada and other countries. Islamic practice in Harar took on a dual focus involving relatively orthodox observance within the mosques and a localized tradition involving the worship of saints. While not officially incorporated into Islamic theology, practices revolving around saints are tolerated and common throughout the Muslim world. In Harar, sainthood is granted to the municipal founders, who are thought to be able to intercede with Allah on behalf of their adherents. Many shines are distributed throughout the city and are organized by religious practitioners known as *murids*, who inherit their positions as descendants of the saint to whom they are dedicated. Either men or women can occupy this office, and women are frequently represented in the community of worshippers. Gender inclusiveness in this realm contrasts to the world of the mosque, where men dominate. Observances at the saints' shrines include the normal round of Islamic holy days, such as the prophet's birthday and celebrations at the end of Ramadan. In addition, devotees may petition the saint for help with illness or other personal problems.

Palestinian observance of Islam is similar to patterns in Harar insofar as forms of worship are divided between an orthodox tradition, which is basically a male domain, and a locally distinct set of practices open to women. In this case, the female ritual realm is contained within the household and involves the incorporation of prayer and observance into the daily round of domestic chores. In addition, belief and practice revolve around concern over the *djin*, who are usually thought to be malignant spirits. They can bring misfortune to people and sometimes possess them, bringing on violent fits. They can often be visited upon their victims by malicious neighbours. Gibb and Rothenberg maintain that this belief system serves to empower women. Blaming one's misfortune on the spirit world or on the malice of others can help to fend off accusations of personal responsibility for serious conditions such as infertility. It can also exert pressure on husbands to give serious attention to their wives' problems and on neighbours to ensure that amicable relations are maintained.

The presence of locally and culturally unique traditions within Islamic is well represented in other countries and parallels diversity within other world religions. In many cases these variants are disappearing, and forms of observance are becoming homogenized through various forces of globalization, including international migration. Gibb and Rothenberg suggest that, when Harari and Palestinians settled in Canada, they suppressed many cultural practices out of a concern that they might display a backward and ignorant way of life. People adopted more orthodox beliefs and practices appropriate to a globalized and homogeneous form of the religion. In the process, both groups submerged their ethnic identity in favour of a broader Muslim one and became integrated into Canada's Islamic community. One implication of this trend has been a lessening of women's agency and power. Similar trends towards a globalized religious standardization of Islamic practice are documented in other studies. In the Ivory Coast, localized forms of Islam are declining due to the emphasis on learning Arabic and Islamic knowledge through formalized systems of instruction modelled on European educational institutions (LeBlanc 1999).

In Buddhism, Christianity, and Islam, following the deaths of the founders, disciples or followers began to spread the faith to others. Over the centuries, increasingly centralized "churches" were organized to pull together a body of worship, setting out practices and doctrine. Eventually, ecclesiastical elites took control not only of priestly functions but also of standardized religious doctrines. People who had divergent interpretations of religious texts were deemed dissidents, and at various times in the history of Buddhism, Christianity, and Islam, religious authorities harassed and punished

GLOBALIZATION

In 2003, the number of adherents of Christian religions worldwide was estimated at more than 2 billion, about a third of the world population. European state expansion, missionism, colonialism, economic and political hegemony, and imperialism have contributed to what some observers refer to as the globalization of Christianity. Islam, another strongly proselytizing religion historically associated with state expansion and consolidation and with economic and political domination, has about 1.3 billion adherents worldwide.

proselytism
The attempt to convert a person or group from one religion to another.

fundamentalism
A term coined in the United States in 1920 meaning a commitment to defend traditional religious beliefs.

dissidents as heretics. According to some views, these authorities moved away from the original messages, replacing them with doctrines of obedience to the state, hierarchical family systems, and a controlling priesthood.

Religion and Globalization

As state societies expand their borders and influence throughout many parts of the world far from their centres of origin, they have spread their religious beliefs through proselytism. **Proselytism** is the attempt to convert a person or group from one religion to another. State societies throughout history have brought their religions to the people they have conquered. Various denominations of Buddhism, Christianity, and Islam have gained millions of converts through this process. As missionaries spread their religions to all parts of the world, some locally indigenous religious beliefs and practices have been modified and others have been abandoned and replaced by the new religions. In some cases, people have modified foreign rituals and developed different interpretations of standard beliefs.

Diffusion of beliefs and practices and their absorption by distant peoples have resulted in marked contrasts between local practices and those in the centres of origin. For example, in the Caribbean, Roman Catholic saints are identified with tribal African deities, and rituals dedicated to indigenous deities are merged with Roman Catholic practice. Spirit possession, a phenomenon marginalized in mainstream Roman Catholic doctrine, is given central importance in Haiti, Brazil, and many African indigenous churches. Similarly, First Nations Christians may incorporate traditional beliefs and practices in their observances (see the Culture Change feature on page 333).

Buddhism, Christianity, and Islam, the major proselytizing religions, have been successful in part because their practice is not tied to a specific locale. They can be transplanted anywhere and incorporate local beliefs and practices. This characteristic contrasts with religions whose cosmologies are tied to specific places, such as those of the Diné or Australian Aborigines.

In the world today, as in the past, global economic and political processes have affected religious practices and interpretations of sacred texts. Some revitalization movements within Christianity and Islam have led to an increase in religious fundamentalism. **Fundamentalism**, a term coined in the United States in 1920, means a commitment to defend traditional religious beliefs. In the United States and Canada, members of some Christian fundamentalist movements advocate a return to both religious and social orthodoxy. They keep to a literal interpretation of the Bible and tend to believe in the divine origin of gender roles differentiating the work and family roles of women and men. They also tend to support an ideologically conservative political agenda and to place religious authority above secular authority in life matters. Fundamentalists organize against abortion rights, for example, and against gay marriage. They oppose the teaching of evolution in schools. Some fundamentalist groups have become associated with beliefs in white supremacy.

The fundamentalist movement in Canada has been less prominent than in the United States. However, fundamentalist organizations and lobbies have become an important influence in provincial and federal politics. The former Reform Party, which now forms an important component of the Conservative Party, was founded by Preston Manning, son of an Alberta premier who was also an evangelical preacher. Manning followed in his father's footsteps and brought fundamentalist views on social morality onto the federal scene covering such issues as family law, immigration, individual responsibility, and minority rights (Sigurdson 1994). When the Reform Party merged with its Progressive Conservative rival to form the Conservative Party, it had to compromise on some of its more controversial positions, but its guiding principles have still had an influence on federal policy and practice. Some people anticipate that, if the current Conservative party gains a parliamentary majority, it will be less moderate on some of the issues that its fundamentalist members hold dear (Hedges 2006).

Christian activism has also had an important influence on the other end of the political spectrum. Social gospel activists, most notably Tommy Douglas, were at the forefront of the formation of the Canadian Commonwealth Federation, which was later to become the New Democratic Party (NDP). Douglas was a Baptist minister, who advocated for the farmers and workers and endorsed a socialist agenda. He became the Premier of Saskatchewan and introduced a public health care plan that became the model for Canada's current system. Currently, many religious organizations work for progressive social and political change and are outspoken members of peace and anti-nuclear movements. Within the Roman Catholic Church, clergy and lay workers associated with liberation theology have been in the forefront of movements for social, economic, and political justice and equality, particularly in Central and South America.

Islamic fundamentalism has become increasingly popular and dangerous. In some countries of the Middle East and Africa, Islamic fundamentalists have taken over local or national governments, imposing a strict interpretation of the Qur'an on social and political policies. In Iran, for example, and in several states in Nigeria, public laws must conform to Islamic principles, and crimes and punishments are defined according to sacred texts. Religious authorities double as political leaders, whether by election or proclamation. In other Middle Eastern countries—for example, Iraq—as well as in Indonesia and the Philippines, Islamist movements have contributed to the destabilization of local and central governments and are attempting to overthrow elected or appointed authorities and institute Islamic law.

Some analysts attribute the upsurge in Islamic fundamentalism to the global spread of Western influence, chiefly from the United States. American social behaviours and social values are seen as immoral. Fundamentalist movements have gained popularity as proponents claim to resist American influence on internal affairs and foreign policies (Castells 2004). This resistance has become increasingly violent. Al Qaeda, a terrorist network with cells in more than fifty countries, is an extreme expression of Islamic fundamentalism. Its members are both anti-Western and opposed to Arabic governments that do not espouse its own version of strict Islamic principles. On September 11, 2001, members of Al Qaeda killed more than 3000 people by flying aircraft into the twin towers of the World Trade Center in New York City, the Pentagon in Washington, D.C., and a rural area of Pennsylvania.

REVIEW

Religious practices and beliefs change over time through internal and external forces of transformation. In syncretism, new religions are created by combining parts of older ones. Revitalization movements emphasize core beliefs and values as a means of adapting to undesired changes. Nativistic, revivalistic, millinerian, and messianic movements, as well as cargo cults, are all forms of religion-based adaptations to change. Major world religions such as Buddhism, Christianity, and Islam began as revitalization movements of some kind. Religions have spread through forces of globalization and the practice of proselytism. Religious fundamentalism is a powerful force in the world today.

Chapter Summary

What Is Religion?

- Religion refers to actions and feelings based on beliefs in the existence of spirit beings and supranormal (or superhuman) forces. Religious beliefs and practices give people ways to contact spirit beings and forces and to show them honour and respect, as well as to invoke their blessings and protection. Anthropologists analyze religious beliefs and behaviours using perspectives of comparison and cultural relativism. They try to understand people's ideas about the spirit realm from the people's own point of view. They focus on the ways that religious beliefs and practices are consistent with other aspects of culture. Religions tend to reflect the structure of their society. For example, in societies with hierarchical social structures, people are more likely to believe in the existence of a ranked pantheon of deities.

Spirit Beings and Forces

- Spirit entities and forces are believed to have extraordinary, more than human, powers. They are typically eternal or indestructible. They know more than a person can know, and they are able to act in ways that humans cannot. Thus, people seek contact with them to gain their protection and aid.

- One common, nearly universal, form that spirit takes is the soul—the eternal aspect of living things. In some beliefs, only humans have souls. Souls are seen as the animating aspect of living things. In some belief systems, when the body dies, the soul escapes and exists eternally in some other form or in a nonmaterial state. The belief in souls is called animism; the belief that all things are endowed with some spirit essence is called animatism.

- Some religious traditions have many spirit beings in human form with specific attributes, powers, and functions. Polytheism, belief in numerous deities, is widespread throughout the world. In monotheistic religions, people believe in one supreme deity with powers and knowledge that affect all aspects of life, although there may be other, lesser, spirit beings and important moral heroes as well. Other types of spirit beings include, for example, the spirit forms of deceased ancestors.

- Some peoples believe in mana—a spirit power or essence that endows people, animals, objects, or events with special qualities or powers. In some cultures of Australia and North America, people believe that they are descended from human or animal spirit beings called totems. Totems are the primordial protectors of the people to whom people owe gratitude and respect.

- Spirit beings and forces are believed to be dangerous if they are contacted in the wrong way, in the wrong place, or at the wrong time. Restrictions on places or objects are called taboos. A tabooed object or place can cause harm because the spirit power within it can become dangerous.

Religious Practitioners and Specialists

- Most religions have individuals or groups who function as either part-time or full-time religious specialists. In some cases a person receives a calling from the spirit world to become a religious specialist, or he or she inherits spiritual powers from someone in the previous generation. In other cases, a person decides to become a religious practitioner for personal reasons or because ritual practice gives outlet for artistic expression.

- Mediums are specialists who are believed to make contact with spirit beings or spirits of the dead. Through ritual and trance, they become conduits for messages between ordinary people and the spirit world. Diviners have the power to predict or shape the future through messages and omens they receive and interpret from the spirit world. Healers diagnose the spirit cause of illness and effect cures through the performance of rituals. Shamans are part-time religious practitioners who make contact with the spirit world through ritual, prayer, and trance. They receive visions and messages from the spirit realm and may serve as diviners and healers. Some societies have full-time religious practitioners called priests who lead religious organizations and officiate at rituals but are not expected to be able to communicate directly with the spirit world.

Religious Practice

- Rituals are a fundamental aspect of all religious practices and include prayer, a public and private ritual through which believers transmit messages to spirit beings.

Believers also transmit messages through offerings they make of foods or animals given in rituals of sacrifice. Rituals mark events in religious and secular calendars.

- People also perform rituals to celebrate socially significant transitions in an individual's life cycle. Such rites of passage mark birth, puberty, marriage, and death. Rites of passage ritualize three aspects of a change in life status: separation, transition, and reincorporation. Puberty rites mark sexual maturity and the transition from childhood to adulthood. Funerals mark the departure of the deceased and reinforce family and community solidarity as people share the expression of sorrow and loss.

- People adhere to theories of health maintenance, causes of disease, and strategies for treatment. Health is often thought of as a state of harmony or balance that depends on the orderly functioning of a person's body, relations with others, the health of the environment, and relations with spirit beings and forces. When this balance is disturbed, illness and misfortune may follow. Serious illness is often attributed to spiritual causes needing ritual diagnosis and treatment with the aid of religious specialists. Spirit causes can include soul loss (the sudden departure of a person's soul), object intrusion (a foreign object shot into the patient's body), spirit possession (the invasion of a person's body by a spirit), or the violation of taboos. Curative rituals attempt to restore balance through magic, practical remedies, therapeutic effects, social validation, and the passage of time. In combination, spiritual treatments can be especially effective when people believe in them.

- Witchcraft may be suspected in cases of illness, death, or misfortune. Witches or sorcerers employ spirit powers to cause harm to others. They are usually thought to be motivated by anger, jealousy, or simply the desire to see other people suffer. Witchcraft may be used as a form of social control and a means of achieving social justice. Witches, like healers, employ imitative and contagious magic. Magic is an expression of people's desires and intentions in situations over which they have no direct control.

The Origins and Functions of Religion

- Specific origins of religious beliefs are unknown. Religions give people solace in times of trouble and sorrow, and religious beliefs and practices bind communities together into cohesive networks. They give ideological support for the existing social structures, including family organization, social stratification, and political inequalities. Anthropologists using cultural materialist or ecological perspectives analyze religious practices as a means of adapting to one's environment.

- Social, economic, political, and historical developments have an impact on religions. Changes may cause people to think about their relationship with the spirit world in different ways, altering some practices or even abandoning them altogether. Religions incorporate new ideas from either external sources or the innovations of believers.

Religion and Culture Change

- Revitalization movements are religion-based responses to societal crises. They arise in times of social and political upheaval, often in situations of invasion, conquest, and colonial control. Revitalization movements are aimed at restructuring power relationships within a society or between conquered peoples and their rulers. They are begun by individuals who receive direct messages from the spirit world telling them to convey divine teachings to the community. Nativism is aimed at ridding society of foreign elements, returning to what is thought to be a prior state of cultural purity. Revivalism stresses the importance of reviving cultural and political practices. Millinerian movements incorporate apocalyptic themes and an abrupt end to the present world and establishment of a new world. Messianic movements stress the role of a prophet or messiah as a saviour for his or her people.

- The major world religions have changed many times and continue to change, following local practices and beliefs throughout the world. As times change and social norms are transformed, religions respond by altering their practices and beliefs. These changes can lead to the development of distinctive religious sects and denominations within the world religions, differentiated on the basis of both belief and practice.

- As state societies have expanded their borders and influence throughout the world, they have spread their religious beliefs through proselytism, converting people or groups from one religion to another. Various denominations of Buddhism, Christianity, and Islam have gained millions of converts through this process. Revitalization movements within Christianity and Islam have led to an increase in religious fundamentalism. Particularly in the United States, Christian fundamentalists advocate a literal interpretation of the Bible and tend to support an ideologically conservative political agenda and to place religious authority above secular authority in life matters. Islamic fundamentalism includes terrorism and rejection of Western influences.

Key Terms

religion 310
religious speech 311
animism 312
animatism 312
polytheism 313
monotheistic religions 313
ancestor worship 313
totemism 314
secret societies 314

mediums 315
diviners 315
healers 315
shamans 316
priests 316
rituals 316
sacred rituals 317
rites of renewal 317
prayer 317

sacrifice 318
puberty rites 318
calendric rituals 319
funerary rites 320
spirit possession 321
imitative magic 324
contagious magic 324
cosmology 328
syncretism 329

prophets 329
nativistic movements 329
millenarian movements 329
messianic movements 329
cargo cults 331
proselytism 334
fundamentalism 334

Review Questions

1. What questions do all religions answer?
2. How are animism, animatism, and deism different? What are some examples of ways that these belief systems are expressed?
3. How do different religions define and treat spirits of the dead?
4. What are the differences between a shaman and a priest?
5. What are other types of religious practitioners? What roles and functions do they play in their societies?
6. How do people make distinctions between the sacred and the secular? How are concepts such as mana, taboo, and blessing used to bestow sacredness?
7. In what ways is religion expressed through symbolic culture and religious speech?
8. In what ways is religion expressed through behaviour? What religious concepts do people use to explain human behaviour?
9. What types of secular and sacred rituals do people everywhere perform?
10. What are the different types of magic? Why do people everywhere sometimes use magical thinking?
11. What are some social and cultural functions of sorcery or witchcraft?
12. What are some examples of the relationship between religion and other social systems in a society, such as the political and economic system, system of social control, and system of social stratification?
13. What five basic functions does religion serve for people and their ways of life?
14. How do religions change in response to dynamics of social and culture change?
15. How do syncretisms reveal adaptations to cultural contact and the diffusion of ideas?
16. What are the types and characteristics of revitalization movements?
17. How were the Ghost Dance movement of the North American Plains Indians and the cargo cults of Pacific Islanders similar? How were they different?
18. What is the impact of globalization on world religions?

The Arts

CHAPTER 13

Preview

1. **How do anthropologists define art?**
2. **What can we learn about people by examining their art?**
3. **How is art embedded in culture? How do cultures shape artistic expression and the aesthetic principles on which it is based?**
4. **What are some universal and culturally specific forms of art? How do those forms of art express or create symbolic culture?**
5. **How does art reflect society and social realities?**
6. **What cultural, social, and personal functions does art serve?**

After a long time Mataora became jealous of his elder brother Tau-toru; he saw that he ardently desired his wife. In consequence he thrashed his wife Niwareka; which caused her to flee away to the underworld to the home of her ancestors and parents. A great sorrow fell on Mataora, and he deeply lamented his beautiful wife.

And now Mataora started off to search for his wife. When Mataora arrived at the guard-house of the underworld, he asked of the guard "Did you not see a woman pass this way?" "Ah, yes! She has gone on long ago; she was crying as she came along." Mataora then said, "Cannot I go to where she is?"

Mataora then descended, and went on until he came to a shed, at the village of Ue-tonga, where were many people. He found Ue-tonga engaged in tattooing; he sat down there to see the operation, and saw the blood descending from the cuts in the face. He called out, "Your system of tattooing the face is all wrong! It is not done in that manner up above." Ue-tonga said, "This is the custom below here; that above is quite wrong. That system is called by us 'painted'. That kind of moko [or face tattooing] is used in house building." Mataora replied, "That is called carving with us." Then Ue-tonga placed his hand on Mataora's face and rubbed it—and all the moko came off! The people all burst out laughing, and then Ue-tonga called out, "O ye above! O ye people of above! Ye are quite wrong in calling it carving. Behold the face is quite clean from rubbing. That is only painting."

Mataora now said to Ue-tonga, "You have destroyed the moko on my face; you must tattoo me." Ue-tonga replied, "It is well! Lie down!" Then Ue-tonga called on

the artists to delineate the pattern on Mataora's face. Then Ue-tonga sat down by the side of Mataora with his chisel and commenced to tattoo him. Great was his pain and his groans. He then sang his song:

Niwareka! that is lost, where art thou?
Show thy self, O Niwareka! O Niwareka!
'Twas love of thee that dragged me down here below,
Niwareka! Niwareka! Love eats me up!
Niwareka! Niwareka! Thou has bound me tight.
Niwareka! Niwareka! Let us remain in this world,
Niwareka! Niwareka! Leave behind this underworld,
Niwareka! Niwareka! And thus end my pain.

When Ue-kuru, the younger sister of Niwareka, heard this, she ran off to where Niwareka was engaged in weaving a garment. Ue-kuru said to her sister, "There is a man over there who is being tattooed; a very handsome man; who, whilst the operation was going on, was crying and singing. The words of the song often repeated your name." The female companions of Niwareka all said, "Let us all go and see!"

So Mataora was led off. Then was heard the welcome of Niwareka and her lady companions, who became enamored with the appearance of Mataora. She said to her friends, "His bearing is that of Mataora" When Mataora had sat down on the mats, Niwareka asked, "Art thou Mataora?" He bowed his head and held out his arms towards Niwareka, asking her to draw near. Niwareka then knew it was indeed Mataora.

Mataora now said to Niwareka, "Let us both return to the Earth." She replied, "The customs of the upper world are bad. Rather let us remain below, and gather our thoughts and turn them from the evils of the upper world." So Niwareka told her father and brothers the reason of Mataora's visit—to take her back to the Earth. Upon hearing this, her father said, "You go back, O Mataora! Leave Niwareka here. A custom of the upper world is to beat women, is it not?"

At this, Mataora was consumed with shame. The brother of Niwareka, said to him, "Mataora! Abandon the upper world—the home of evil—altogether, and let us both live down here. Cut off all above and its evil ways, let all below with its better customs be separate."

"Mataora replied, "I will in future adopt your methods in the upper-world." Then the father said to him, "Mataora! Do not let a repetition of the evil repute of the upper-world, reach here below." Mataora replied, "Look on my moko [face-tattoo]; if it had been painted it might be washed off, but as it is a moko cut in the flesh by you it is permanent and cannot be washed out. I will adopt in future the ways of this lower world and its works."

From S. Percy Smith, *The Lore of the Whare-Wananga* (New Plymouth, N.Z., 1913), **www.sacred-texts.com/pac/lww/index.**

In this story, the Maori of New Zealand tell the origin of one of their prominent arts, tattooing on the face and body. According to tradition, the art was learned in primordial times from sacred beings who inhabited the underworld. This story gives a divine license to an artistic and aesthetic style. By the early twentieth century, few Maori were getting tattoos because of pressure from European colonial authorities who regarded the practice as savage. However, by the late twentieth century, the art had become popular again, partly as a sign of ethnic pride and identity.

WHAT IS ART?

Like the word culture, art is a word that we use in everyday speech but for which we have difficulty formulating a precise definition. Even anthropologists often describe the arts of the people they study without defining what they mean by art, taking it for granted that the meaning is understood. In a study of arts and **aesthetics**—philosophies about what has beauty and value in art—anthropologist Richard Anderson (2000:8) proposed a number of key characteristics of art. According to Anderson, works of **art** are

- artifacts of human creation;
- created through the exercise of exceptional physical, conceptual, or imaginative skill;
- intended to affect the senses; and
- share stylistic conventions with similar works.

Let us explore these characteristics. Art objects are made by human beings. This characteristic seems straightforward enough, despite occasional museum exhibitions of the "artwork" of gorillas, chimpanzees, and even elephants. Although it might be said that some paintings done by our primate relatives look similar to the works of modern artists, most would dismiss these as "not art" because of the lack of intentionality, at least as we attribute intentionality to human beings. That is, a human artist produces work intended to be art, with a preconceived plan of working through a specific medium. We assume that other animals lack this type of volition and intentionality, even though they may delight in the process of producing new objects.

Second, art is work stimulated by an exceptional creative concept and produced with exceptional physical skill. This criterion suggests that paintings produced by some people may be defined as art, while paintings made by others may not. The concept of "skill" is embedded in the word art, which derives from the Latin *artem*, meaning "skill of any kind." The fact that art continues to mean skillful or a skill is reflected in such expressions as "the healing arts" or "the evil arts."

Artistic productions appeal to the human senses, stirring our minds and imaginations as well as our feelings. Some arts appeal primarily to the visual senses (painting, sculpture), whereas others appeal to the senses of hearing (music, song, prayer,

aesthetics
Philosophies about what has beauty and value in art.

art
Artifacts of human creation created through the exercise of exceptional physical, conceptual, or imaginative skill; produced in a public medium and intended to affect the senses, sharing stylistic conventions with similar works.

oratory, poetry), touch (sculpture, carvings), and the sense of movement (dance). These sensual characteristics differentiate art objects from mundane utilitarian utensils, tools, or clothing.

Finally, artistic work is influenced by aesthetic conventions that are primarily cultural. In all societies, people have cultural assumptions about the media used to make art and the styles of painting, sculpting, decoration, oral traditions, and dance movements that are considered appropriate. These conventions may be more or less rigid or flexible, depending on cultural attitudes. In certain media, strict adherence to formal conventions may be necessary, while in other realms of artistic work, greater flexibility and latitude are given to the artist or performer. In other words, in every society, people have ideas about what they consider to be art based on their interpretation of the criteria in Anderson's definition. Of course, artistic conventions may change. For example, Western musical styles heard today, both in classical and popular music, are vastly different from those appreciated during earlier centuries or even earlier decades.

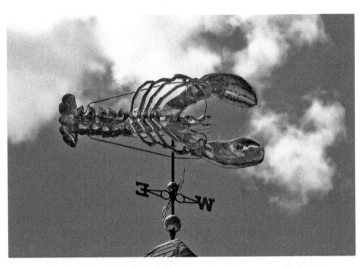

How might the definition of art presented in this chapter be applied to this piece of twentieth-century folk art? North American cultural conceptions of art distinguish folk art *from* fine art. *Other cultures may apply a variety of other criteria to evaluate what is art. In ethnographic research, it is important to know what those criteria are.*

In addition to cultural variability in what is considered art, there are similarities and differences in the meanings attributed to artistic production and the purposes that they serve. In some societies, artistic production is primarily destined to serve ritual or religious purposes. In other societies, secular functions of artistic production are paramount. In both cases, artistic work serves emotional or psychological needs, expressing the creativity of the artist and stimulating emotional responses in the viewers or users of art.

REVIEW

All societies have aesthetic values (ideas about what is beautiful). From an anthropological perspective, art is made by the human hand using exceptional skill. It is intended to affect the senses of people who view it, and it refers in some way to culture-based stylistic conventions. Art has meaning and serves important needs of both individuals and their societies.

CULTURAL AESTHETICS

Not only do cultures differ in the ways in which they express artistic impulses, but they also differ in their aesthetics or philosophies of art. In a cross-cultural study of aesthetic principles, Anderson (1990) demonstrates the variety of cultural attitudes toward art and artists. Although cultural attitudes and philosophies of art are not all the same in his sample of nine societies, many of the foragers and horticulturalists share an understanding of art as a means of improving the world and life experiences or of serving primarily spiritual functions. For example, the Yoruba of Nigeria use art mainly to attract and show respect to spirit beings who then bestow prosperity, happiness, and fertility on the people who honour them.

In Western art, according to one analysis, five aesthetic paradigms or models have developed: mimetic, representational, instrumental, emotionalist, and formalist (Anderson, 2000:201–202). The **mimetic** paradigm focuses on the ability of art to portray the world around us. Art may be **representational**, thus imitating, idealizing, or symbolizing form and experience, or it may be **instrumental**, transforming the world, enhancing our experience, or making the world a better place. In the instrumental

mimetic
Art that portrays the world accurately.

representational
Art that imitates, idealizes, or symbolizes form and experience.

instrumental
Art that attempts to have a beneficial effect on society, enriching people's lives, teaching moral lessons, and providing insights for improving and changing the world.

Case study

Totem Poles as Art, Monuments, and Historical Records

The totem poles of the Pacific Northwest are testaments to the power and imagination of the Aboriginal communities and artists who have constructed them. As such, they are staple installations within Canadian museums, parks, and public buildings. Miniature versions are stock fare at souvenir stands. However, few displays fully explain or do justice to the complex symbols that the poles contain or to the critical role that they play in indigenous societies. Richard Daly provides a deep insight into their meaning and function in the context of Gitksan culture (2004:55–98).

In indigenous practice, totem poles, also known as crest poles, are constructed through the sponsorship of a chief in order to commemorate his ancestors and his House and to display his own wealth and power. Accordingly, a major ritual and a lavish potlatch accompany the raising of the pole. As not every chief can afford to sponsor such an event, it is a rare occurrence. Thus the pole is a preeminent status symbol in itself, while the figures carved into it portray the clan ancestors of the House hosting the event, the "names" of rank to which the House holds title, and the crest of the pole raiser's father's House. It also creates a physical connection between the community and the land and validates the group's occupation of its terri-

tory. It is the "public face of the House and clan . . . [and] . . . faces the main avenue of communication (Daly 2004 67)." Before pole raising was illegalized, rivers or roadways running through a village displayed a line of poles marking the presence of its major Houses.

In addition to the expenses of the commemorative feast, the construction of the pole itself is a formidable undertaking and involves an immense effort and numerous workers to fell and transport an appropriately large and strong cedar, to carve the figures into it, and to raise it. As such it can be considered a monumental artwork comparable to other traditions in which power and status is displayed in massive public constructions. In the Pacific Northwest, the labour force is recruited from within the House itself, from the pole raiser's father's House and from other relatives and dependents. Aside from displaying their loyalty and support, the participants also receive payment from the event's sponsor.

After its installation, the pole has a limited life span and eventually falls over and rots in the course of twenty to thirty years. This process is viewed as a necessary stage in the social cycle, and, rather than trying to preserve an existing pole, a chief will plan to raise a new one to restate his status and the claims of his House. As such the pole is a flexible historical record that is written anew with some modifications in every generation.

View of Totem Poles, Massett

The social and cultural context of the totem pole indicates that it embodies a symbolic code that represents power, status, continuity, ties to the land, and family history that adds a rich depth of meaning to its aesthetic value.

CRITICAL THINKING QUESTION

What political and social functions do art objects and performances serve in Canadian society?

paradigm, art should have a beneficial effect on society, enriching our lives, teaching us moral lessons, and providing us with the insights and abilities to improve and change our world. **Emotionalist** paradigms focus on the role of art to connect to our inner experience and feelings. In this view, art is expressive of the artist's emotions, but it can also serve to release emotions in the viewers of art. In fact, both artists and viewers are linked in the emotional catharsis stimulated by the creative process. And, finally, the **formalist** aesthetic centres on the formal qualities of art—colour, composition, sound, words, or movements. Qualities of form and the medium are more important than a true representation of the subject. Thus, art can be abstract.

emotionalist
Art that attempts to express the artist's feelings or to release the feelings of viewers.

formalist
Abstract art that focuses on the formal qualities of art— colour, composition, sound, words, or movements.

These paradigms may not be foremost in our minds as we view art or as we live our lives in the midst of artworks, but thinking about them can help us understand the different functions of art. Art is part of symbolic culture—that is, art has meaning. Through art, we can learn about the world and be stimulated to make changes in our lives as we understand the messages transmitted through art. Messages may be transmitted through social and political art, for example, which reflects the instrumental potential in artworks, Artistic creations serve as emotional expression for both the artist and the viewer. We are moved when we see paintings and sculptures, when we hear music and song, and when we participate in or watch performances of dance and drama. When we view art, we appreciate that art objects in any medium require skill of execution and conform to principles of style and form that are culturally appropriate in context, time, and place.

Is this urban graffiti art? How might an anthropologist study these artistic expressions? In what sense is this an example of political art?

In Their Own Voices

Bill Reid's Spirit of Haida Gwaii

Bill Reid was an artist of First Nation's ancestry who carved sculptures in a distinctive style based on traditional themes and forms from Haida culture. His skill, power, and creativity brought him into the public spotlight and many of his works are displayed in museums and public locations throughout Canada. His most famous sculpture, the Spirit of Haida Gwaii, is installed in the vestibule of the Canadian Embassy in Washington and appears on the Canadian twenty-dollar bill. According to his own interpretations, his art attempts to document the strength, beauty, and originality of First Nation's culture and to protest Canada's treatment of Aboriginal peoples. The symbolsim in his work is therefore quite complex and reflects several themes in indigenous and Canadian culture and the relationship between them. The political issues surrounding his art are also complex as indicated in the following analysis:

"The Spirit of Haida Gwaii . . . extends Haidaness into the very vortex of western power. . . . But it is also used by the patron that commissioned it, the Canadian government, to represent Canada's embrasure of democracy—a complex and problematical embrasure. In this instance, as in many others, Canada uses aboriginal sensibilities to express Canadian identity to the world. The practice conveniently masks the government's internal policies toward aboriginal peoples. Such tensions between artist and patron are of course hardly unique to this work or this artist. Reid, however, was keenly aware of the tensions and inevitable compromises that result when patrons publicly display art, and his written texts often address in exquisite ways the conflict he anticipated (Martineau 2001)."

So did his actions. He held up completion of his embassy installation until the Canadian and British Columbia governments made concessions on outstanding Haida land claims in 1987. The conflict and ambivalence inherent in the situation of the Aboriginal artist in a colonial context are expressed in the Haida Gwaii sculpture itself as indicated in the following description by the artist:

Here we are at last, a long way from Haida Gwaii, not too sure where we are or where we're going, still squabbling and vying for position in the boat, but somehow managing to appear to be heading in some direction; at least the paddles are together, and the man in the middle seems to have some vision of what is to come.

As for the rest, they are superficially more or less what they always were, symbols of another time when the Haidas, all ten thousand of them, knew they were the greatest of all nations.

The Bear, as he sits in the bow of the boat, broad back deflecting any unfamiliar, novel or interesting sensation, eyes firmly and forever fixed on the past, tries to believe

REVIEW

Art conveys important messages. Mimetic art attempts to portray the world accurately, whereas representational art portrays the world in an ideal or symbolic way. Instrumental art attempts to change the world or people's experiences of the world or to enrich people's lives. Emotionalist art attempts to express the artist's feelings or to release the feelings of viewers. Formalist art is abstract art that focuses on colour, form, texture, medium, or technique rather than on particular subjects, ideas, or feelings.

that things are still as they were. The **Bear Mother**, being human, is looking over his shoulder into the future, concerned more with her children than with her legend. After all, they wandered in from another myth, the one about Good Bear and Bad Bear and how they changed, so she has to keep a sharp eye on them.

Next, doughtily paddling away, hardworking if not very imaginative, the compulsory Canadian content, big teeth and scaly tail, perfectly designed for cutting down trees and damming rivers.

And here she is, still the ranking woman of noble birth, yielding no place to the pretty Bear Mother. In spite of her great cheeks like monstrous scars, her headdress reflecting the pointed shape of the dogfish head, and her grotesque labret—in spite of all these, the most desirable and fascinating woman from myth-time. More magical than the Mouse Woman, as mysterious as the deep ocean waters which support the sleek, sinuous fish from whom she derives her power, **Dogfish Woman** stands aloof from the rest, the enormous concentration of her thoughts smoldering smoke dreams behind her inward-looking eyes.

Tucked away in the stern of the boat, still ruled by the same obsession to stay concealed in the night shadows and lightless caves and other pockets of darkness in which she spends her immortality, the **Mouse Woman** lost her place among the other characters of her own myth, an important part of the Bear Mother story, and barely squeezed in at the opposite end of the boat, under the tail of the Raven. No human, beast, or monster has yet seen her in the flesh, so she may or may not look like this.

Not so the **Raven**. There is no doubt what he looks like in this myth-image: exactly the same as he does in his multiple existences as the familiar carrion bird of the northern latitude of the earth. Of course he is the steersman. So, although the boat appears to be heading in a purposeful direction, it can arrive anywhere the Raven's whim dictates.

A culture will be remembered for its warriors, artists, heroes and heroines of all callings, but in order to survive it needs survivors. And here is our professional survivor, the **Ancient Reluctant Conscript**, present if seldom noticed in all the turbulent histories of men on earth. When our latter-day kings and captains have joined their forebears, he will still be carrying on, stoically obeying orders and performing the tasks allotted to him. But only up to a point. It is also he who finally says, "Enough!" And after the rulers have disappeared into the morass of their own excesses, it is he who builds on the rubble and once more gets the whole thing going.

The **Wolf** of the Haidas was a completely imaginary creature, perhaps existing over there on the mainland, but never seen on Haida Gwaii. Nevertheless, he was an important figure in the crest hierarchy. Troublesome, volatile, ferociously playful, he can usually be found with his sharp fangs embedded in someone's anatomy. Here he is vigorously chewing on the **Eagle**'s wing while that proud, imperial, somewhat pompous bird retaliates by attacking the Bear's paws.

That accounts for everybody except the **Frog** who sits partially in and partially out of the boat and above the gunwales: the ever-present intermediary between two of the worlds of the Haidas, the land the sea.

So there is certainly no lack of activity in our little boat, but is there any purpose? Is the tall figure who may or may not be the Spirit of Haida Gwaii leading us, for we are all in the same boat, to a sheltered beach beyond the rim of the world as he seems to be, or is he lost in a dream of his own dreamings? The boat moves on, forever anchored in the same place.

Source: Reid, Bill. *The Spirit of Haida Gwaii.* Bill Reid Foundation Website: www.billreid.ca/. Accessed on the World Wide Web on September 19, 2007. Used with permission of Martine Reid, William Reid Ltd.

CRITICAL THINKING QUESTIONS

What do some of the figures in the sculpture symbolize? In what ways does the imagery represent the social and political context in which it was produced?

BODY ART

One of the most common media for the display of art is the human body, as in Maori tattooing and Yoruba **scarification**—piercing the skin to make patterns or designs of healed scars. Although societies differ in the degree to which they employ the human body as a canvas, all peoples take pleasure in the use of body decoration, hairstyles, clothing, and jewellery to enhance one's appearance and to display one's personal and cultural identity. Nomadic peoples are particularly likely to emphasize the use of the body in artistic production. Because they do not have permanent settlements and need

scarification
Artistic and ritualistic scarring of the face or other parts of the body in particular designs, commonly used to mark transitions to adulthood.

These Australian Aborigines (c.1910) painted traditional symbols and stylized designs on their bodies as part of their religious rituals. These icons and patterns represented features of a sacred landscape or events from the Dreamtime. The differences in body painting among these men represent their different roles in the ceremonies they were performing. Australian Aborigine artists today use the same imagery.

? Do you practise any body arts? Why?

tattooing
Injecting inks or dyes under the skin to produce designs.

to carry with them whatever objects they own, they keep their possessions to a minimum. The human body in this context becomes a sort of movable canvas for painting, tattooing, or decorating with jewellery.

Aboriginal foraging peoples of Australia used elaborate body painting, especially in ritual occasions when people painted themselves with lines, dots, and other designs as they prepared to participate in ceremonies. Nomadic foragers of the Kalahari Desert in Africa decorated their hair and bodies with beads cut from ostrich eggshells. They also fashioned their hair in decorative styles, cutting the hair in rows and patterns to make lines and other designs, and they used facial tattooing. The Inuit of Arctic Alaska and Canada also used **tattooing**, resulting when ink or dyes are injected under the skin at piercing sites, to enhance their appearance. Inuit tattooing was done mainly on the face, hands, and wrist. In their cold climate, these are the parts of the body that are exposed to the view of other people. Other parts of the body (chest, back, arms, and legs) were nearly always covered with clothing because of the cold temperatures. The fact that the Inuit tattooed those parts of the body exposed to people's view demonstrates one of the uses of personal art, namely, to announce one's identity, embellish one's appearance, and make oneself attractive to others.

In warm climates, where much of the body is routinely exposed, body tattooing may be much more elaborate, as described for the Maori in the narrative that opened this chapter. In Samoa and other South Pacific societies, young men had much of their bodies, including their face, arms, hands, back, chest, and legs, emblazoned with intricate tattoos as they prepared themselves for marriage. The higher the social status of the individual, the more elaborate the tattooing. Tattooing, therefore, was a signal not only of personal inclination and artistic display but was also a validation of one's social status. Differences in tattooing were correlated with a social system that emphasized rank and distinctions in the social standing of people ordered in a hierarchical system of stratification.

Tattooing and other body decoration may be indicators of age and identity. In North American society, tattoos and facial and body piercings have come to be almost necessities for teenagers in some social circles. The practice of multiple piercings may also be a gesture of defiance against parental authority and values. While defying adult standards and practices, it also unites teenagers and reinforces their group identity through conformity to youth culture and values.

Throughout the world, people fashion beads, stones, and metals into jewellery that beautifies their appearance. In societies where there are differences in status and wealth, higher-ranked and wealthier people are able to accumulate more elaborate and more valuable jewellery for display on their bodies. Thus, they enhance their appearance and attractiveness, advertise their social status and identity, and display their wealth. In addition, jewellery may be a repository of wealth, convertible into other goods through trade or sale. Clothing functions in the same way. While clothes are culturally necessary body coverings, the fineness of their materials and intricacies of design serve to transmit messages about social standing and wealth.

Clothing may be used to differentiate ethnic populations within complex, multiethnic societies. Wearing ethnically marked clothing may be a voluntary choice on the part of the wearer. In modern multiethnic states, people may prefer to wear the clothing of their region as a sign of their belonging to an identifiable community. Immigrants may choose to wear clothing typical of their native land to feel comfortable and as a sign of emotional loyalty to their homeland. For example, Indian women living in Canada may continue to wear saris even after otherwise assimilating.

In the past, some state societies used clothing and ornamentation as a means of dramatizing elite power. For example, in the Aztec Empire of Mexico, only high-ranking people were permitted to wear certain kinds of clothing or jewellery (Soustelle 1961:138–139). Denying access to specific types of clothing and ornaments was not simply a matter of wealth, of being able to afford finery, but was a means of formally differentiating the population. Only the emperor was permitted to wear turquoise nose ornaments. Members of the military had the privilege of wearing particular jewels and feather adornments, depending on their rank. They also had the right to wear distinctive high-back sandals. Any man who was caught wearing an ornament or article of clothing to which he had no right was likely to be punished by death.

Hairstyles, body decoration, clothing, and jewellery are also indications of gender identity in nearly all societies. Women and men may wear their hair at different lengths or arrange it in different styles. They may use body painting or tattooing in different places or employ contrasting patterning and designs. Body adornments such as clothing and jewellery are often styled differently for women and men. Although some of these differences in clothing style may be a response to anatomical or practical differences in work roles, they also highlight and dramatize the social roles of gender and gender identity.

artisans
Specialists in the production of works of art.

REVIEW

Body art is universal in humans and includes clothing, jewellery, hairstyles, body painting, body piercing, tattooing, and other alterations of the body. Body art primarily communicates individual identity, group affiliation, and social standing.

ORIGINS AND FUNCTIONS OF ART OBJECTS

In many societies, utilitarian objects are sometimes embellished with colouration, designs, carvings, paintings, or other decoration to enhance their beauty or impart magical or spiritual properties. Objects usually referred to as crafts, such as those made of pottery, basketry, wood, or stone, may have ornamental designs that demonstrate people's aesthetic sense and awareness of the ways that human effort and skill can add to the beauty of the object. In many foraging and small farming societies, nearly everyone is a producer of some kind of tool, utensil, or craft necessary for their work. Some individuals may make such objects with only a utilitarian purpose in mind; other individuals, those more skilled or more imaginative, may add to the basic utilitarian object through the creative use of design and colour. Still other members of the community may collect their work because of its beauty. These **artisans** may become part-time specialists, exchanging their work either in barter or sale to others, thereby raising their status and increasing their wealth.

Societies differ in the degree to which they stress individuality or conformity to artistic styles. While we value originality and denigrate an artist or craftsperson whose work is derivative and imitative, members of other societies appreciate an artist who adheres to particular artistic conventions. Such artists demonstrate their creativity and inspiration by the level of their skill and variation within specific parameters. Therefore, an archaeologist who unearths a clay pot in Mexico can tell by its style whether a Maya or an Aztec made it.

In the Suriname Maroon society of Saramaka, descendants of slaves who escaped from their masters, women carve and decorate the hard surfaces of calabash gourds as they fashion them into bowls, ladles, and other types of dishes. Men decorate the surfaces of covered

This Navajo medicine man is sandpainting as part of a healing ritual. The painting's designs are transformed into the spirits themselves. The sand used in the painting is then no longer just coloured grains but contains the spirit powers of the beings that it represents. When the sand is applied to the patient's body, it is believed that the patient becomes the power itself and is healed.

sandpaintings
Paintings made by sprinkling fine, coloured sand to make stylized representations of spirit beings, in particular for use in Navajo curing ceremonials.

calabash containers, but these containers are also considered to be the property of women. There are gender differences in the equipment used to execute the carvings, and there are differences in features of style and design as well (Price 1984). Men use chisels and compasses that they obtain in the world outside their remote communities, whereas women use pieces of broken glass to etch their designs. Men's work emphasizes symmetry and clear boundaries, but women's designs are more free-flowing and slightly unbalanced, sometimes with marks that disturb a central symmetry. All Saramaka women carve and decorate some of their own calabashes, but some women are known to be experts and others collect their work.

Saramakas have names for various calabash designs. Some styles are traditional, but others are the result of innovation. The people value both conformity to a standard aesthetic and the originality of individual artisans. Regional differences, village by village, are also recognized. These, too, are the result of personal innovations that become popular.

In addition to calabash carvings, women's art includes embroidery and patchwork with which they embellish rectangular cotton capes and cloths. Again, following a traditional aesthetic, both adherence to standard forms and innovation in design are appreciated. Among the compositional principles for these works are bilateral symmetry, sharp contrasts in colours but avoidance of domination by any one colour, and avoidance of combining patchwork pieces taken from different grades of cotton (Price 1984:157).

In most societies, objects used in rituals are embellished with either representational or abstract designs, painting, or beads, feathers, and jewels. These artistic works may add not only to the beauty of the object but also to its effectiveness in ceremonies. Works of art may attract spirit beings, please them, and make them more likely to bestow their blessings on the community. For example, as part of curing rituals performed by Navajo healers, the practitioner may construct a sandpainting to attract spirit beings and gain their beneficial powers. The **sandpaintings** are stylized representations of the Holy People, the Navajos' spirit beings. During the ritual, the practitioner, called a singer, and his or her helpers make a sandpainting on the floor of the ceremonial hogan or house by trickling ground bits of red, yellow, and white sandstone and charcoal through their fingers. The patient sits on one of the figures depicted. The singer then moistens his or her palms with herbal medicines, takes up sand from the painting, and applies it to the corresponding parts of the patient's body. This act identifies the patient with the Holy People and allows the patient to absorb their protective powers and exchange evil for good.

When the ceremonial is completed, the sandpainting is ritually destroyed. The designs are methodically erased, trampled into the dirt by the healer. Once mixed back into the earth, the sand is taken up, removed from the ceremonial house, and disposed of to the north, the direction of power and danger. Although Navajos recognize and appreciate the beauty of the painting, its purpose is not to remain a frozen design but to create power. It is the act of creation and the use to which it is put that makes the painting powerful and effective, but its power also makes it dangerous. Therefore, it must be destroyed in order to protect human beings from the effects of too much contact with too great a spirit force.

The Origins of Art

The earliest known works of art date to about 30 000 to 40 000 years ago in Europe and Africa and to about 30 000 to 50 000 years ago in Australia (Peregrine 2003). Most of these are paintings in caves or on rocks. The most famous European examples come from caves in southern France and northern Spain. There, people used paint to depict animals and hunting gear. Because of the association between the animals and the weapons, anthropologists believe that the paintings were intended to bring about a successful hunt. This is a form of association called imitative magic, discussed in Chapter 12. Perhaps people believed that, by drawing pictures of animals being hunted, they were increasing the likelihood of a successful outcome. Although this is a reasonable hypothesis, it is impossible to know what people living so long ago believed or intended by their actions.

This 10-centimetre-high limestone figurine of a woman was found in Willendorf, Austria, and dates to between 26 000 and 24 000 years ago. What hypotheses have been advanced to explain portable Paleolithic art objects like this figurine? What would we need to know to determine which hypothesis offers the best explanation?

Controversies

Interpreting "Art": The Case of Inca Quipus

Looking at the objects produced by ancient peoples, we may have difficulties understanding their intentions. If we consider sculptures or paintings produced by ancient Egyptians, Aztecs, or Greeks, we may infer that they had representational or symbolic meaning. We assume that the designs used to decorate objects or the paints applied to their surfaces had symbolic or expressive meaning to their creators. We may not be sure what that meaning was, but we generally assume that they intended to produce a work of art. But what about objects such as the Inca quipu?

Quipu, a word meaning "knot" and derived from Quechua, an indigenous Andean language, was a device made out of knotted strings that was used for record keeping in the Inca Empire. All complex state societies need some means of keeping track of their population, of their economic output, trade, military service, and tribute or taxes due or collected from citizens. The Inca quipus served to enumerate objects or people and also served as records of events (Urton 2003).

Looking at quipus today, we are faced with a number of dilemmas. First, archaeologists and historians believe that they understand the counting system used by the Inca in constructing the quipus; however, they do not know what was being counted or recorded. Second, we may find them beautiful, we appreciate the use of colour, texture, and design; what we don't know is whether the people who created them intended them to be works of art as well as utilitarian objects for record keeping. This problem touches on the issues of artistic intentionality and interpretation. Since quipus are no longer used for record keeping, we see them as objects of human creation detached from their utilitarian context. We can value them for their skill and ingenuity of construction and for the beauty created by their textures and colours, but we must reconcile ourselves to the fact that we will never know what was in the minds of their creators. This is a problem that arises in comparing different artistic traditions. If we are studying the aesthetic

Quipus were constructed of strings, thickly spun and interwoven. Main cords contain threads of different colours. The largest known quipu contains more than 1500 pendant strings. The most complex of the quipus have up to thirteen levels of subsidiary strings attached to the core pendant strings. The great majority of quipus are made from spun cotton, although some are made of wool. A small number also contain human hair. Some archaeologists suggest that the quipus containing human hair may have been used to record kinship groups called ayllus.

principles and artistic traditions of living peoples, we can always ask them what they think about their work. With prehistoric cultures, that is obviously impossible.

CRITICAL THINKING QUESTIONS

Were quipus art? What about utilitarian objects in our own society? Would an anthropologist from the distant future consider an automobile, a stapler, or a light switch as art?

Cave paintings and rock paintings of animals have also been discovered in Africa dating to about the same time as those in Europe. Even older examples have been found in Australia. Some of the Australian examples include outline and stick figure drawings of animals and human beings, as well as stenciled outlines of human hands. It is possible that these paintings and etchings, as well as those found in Europe and Africa, may be reflections of images connecting the artists to the spirit world and to experiences of spiritual power obtained through prayer, trance, and shamanic performances. Again, we will never know what these drawings and etchings meant to the people who created them, but we do know that modern Aboriginal Australians intend their paintings and drawings to represent spirit beings alive in the Dreaming, a primordial time when the world was being formed (Hume 2000). These spirits arose from inside the earth and then crossed the Australian continent, performing works and creating features of the landscape as they went. They also created human beings and taught the people important elements of their culture and beliefs.

Ancient stone sculptures have been discovered in Europe, dating to about 30 000 years ago. These sculptures, known as **Venus figurines**, are thought to represent pregnant women with enlarged breasts and hips. As in the case of cave and rock paintings, several theories attempt to explain the meaning of the carvings (Peregrine 2003:15). Some researchers suggest that they were fertility objects, intended through principles of imitative magic to promote human fertility. Others suggest that they were meant as erotic representations of women, and still others analyze them as self-portraits made by women to depict their own bodies (McDermott 1996). All of these views focus on the disproportionate size of the breasts and hips of the sculpted figurines. By emphasizing secondary sexual characteristics, the figurines could be representations of fertility or of erotic sexual pleasure.

Male figurines with enlarged penises have also been found in Europe and elsewhere. These date from earliest farming communities and may, along with female symbols, be representations of generative impulses and powers (Gimbutas 1982).

REVIEW

Art is human and ancient, but we cannot know the intentions of prehistoric artists or distinguish utilitarian art (crafts and decorative arts) from high art or fine art. All art may be seen as utilitarian in some way. Quipus and sandpaintings are examples of art with important practical uses, whereas cave art and fertility figurines suggest the importance of art in magic, religion, and ritual.

THE ARTS OF SOUND AND MOVEMENT

Artistic impulses also find expression in the sounds of music and song. In many cultures, music and singing are means of expressing religious themes or making contact with the spirit world. Through the power of song and sound, people attract spirit beings and transmit messages to the spirit realm. In some societies, religious songs must be sung according to prescribed patterns, but in others, people compose their songs spontaneously as they make direct contact with the spirit world.

Among the Gitksan of British Columbia, songs come spontaneously to people when they are called by the spirits to be healers or other religious practitioners. Isaac Tens, a Gitksan healer, had such an experience when he began to receive messages from the spirit world. In the midst of a vision from an Owl spirit, he reported, "My body was quivering. While I remained in this state, I began to sing. A chant was coming out of me without my being able to do anything to stop it. Many things appeared to me presently: huge birds and other animals. They were calling me" (Barbeau, 1975:5).

Secular songs and spontaneous singing often accompany everyday activities. For example, the Navajos of the American Southwest have "riding songs, walking songs, grinding songs, planting songs, growing songs, and harvesting songs" (Witherspoon 1977). These songs are sung not to entertain the singer but to enhance the beauty and harmony of the activity. According to Gary Witherspoon, Navajos, "count their wealth in songs they know, especially in the songs they have created" (p. 155). It is, therefore, the acts of creation and of artistic expression that make the songs beautiful and meaningful. In the words of a Navajo singer quoted by ethnomusicologist David McAllester, "If it's worthwhile, it's beautiful" (1954:71).

Navajo songs are not meant to last and be preserved but to be created and expressed. The interaction of sound, music, and activity is what makes art meaningful, effective, and powerful. It is what creates *hozho*, or beauty, the goal of every Navajo ritual,

? *Do you ever find yourself singing spontaneously? What are the occasions? What are the songs?*

Anthropology Applied

Ethnomusicology

Ethnomusicologists point out that music is more than expressive or entertaining in the context of popular culture. It can play a central role in people's religious, political, and economic systems. For example, Javanese gamelan ensembles accompany puppet dramas called *wayang*, which are used to transmit stories from the Hindu epics. Gamelan polyphonic music is made with bronze keyed instruments; gongs; xylophone, lute, zither, and flute; and choral and solo voices (Knight 2002). Traditional Mandinka drummers and kora players in Gambia, West Africa, are involved in healing ceremonies, and Tswana boys in Botswana play thumb pianos to calm the family cattle herd. In many societies, music marks rites of passage and is also a medium of social protest and social action (Chernoff 1981).

Some ethnomusicologists study the globalization of music and the emergence of world music. Zouk, for example, like reggae and calypso before it, is French Creole music of the West Indies. A combination of African, Caribbean, and French colonial influences, zouk has gained global popularity (Guibault et al. 1993). Thus, new and emerging music, such as zouk or benga (Kenyan pop), is as much a legitimate subject of study as ancient, traditional, or folk music, such as cajun (southern Louisiana, United States).

CRITICAL THINKING QUESTIONS

What aspect or type of music might you choose to study as an ethnomusicologist, and why? How would you apply an anthropological perspective?

---

daily activity, thought, and speech. In the Navajo language, *hozho* refers to harmony, order, peacefulness, and appropriateness, in addition to its English translation of beauty. *Hozho* resides in the proper functioning of a person's body, mind, and spirit, in people's proper relationship with the holy beings and forces that inhabit the universe, in proper relations with other people, and in the harmony of their environment. Artistic expression is one means of creating and living in beauty and harmony.

The Inuit understand artistic expression in songs as a creative impulse that allows people to convey their inner feelings in ways that ordinary words cannot. As an Inuit man in Arctic Canada explained:

> Songs are thoughts, sung out with the breath when people are moved by great forces and ordinary speech no longer suffices. Man is moved just like the ice floe sailing here and there out in the current. His thoughts are driven by a flowing force when he feels joy, when he feels fear, when he feels sorrow. Thoughts can wash over him like a flood, making his breath come in gasps and his heart throb. And then it will happen that we, who always think we are small, will feel still smaller. And we will fear to use words. But it will happen that the words we need will come of themselves. When the words we want to use shoot up of themselves—we get a new song. (Rasmussen 1929)

Ethnomusicology is the study of music and musical performances, such as dance, in past or present cultural contexts. Ethnomusicologists study music systems, instruments, aesthetic values, symbols (including language), expression (including lyrics and costumes), and communication (including folklore). While ethnomusicology is associated with recording and videotaping traditional or tribal musicians, it is really about studying any music from an anthropological perspective. How do people define, create, and use music in their lives and in the life of their community?

Dance is an art that is truly universal, appearing as a form of individual and group expression in all cultures. As Anya Royce notes, "Dance has been called the oldest of the arts. It is perhaps equally true that it is older than the arts. The human body making patterns in time and space is what makes the dance unique among the arts. Perhaps it explains its antiquity and universality" (1977:3). Furthermore, Royce says, dance shares with other "social dramas" the characteristic of an "intensification or exaggeration of ordinary behaviour. These kinds of events allow an outsider to see values stated forcefully" (p. 27).

In most cultures, dance is a central or key aspect of many rituals. Dance styles and movements may express sacred meanings handed down from ancient traditions or

? *As an ethnomusicologist, how might you design a study of blues, ragtime, country and western, or banjo music?*

ethnomusicology
The study of the musical styles and traditions of a people.

believed to indicate the movements of spirit beings. The intricate hand gestures of Balinese and Indian dancers refer specifically to characters or events in sacred narratives and folktales.

Artistic aesthetics influence styles of dance. The Yoruba emphasis on youthful vitality is reflected in dance as well as in sculpture and music. According to this tradition, dancers must be strong and use all parts of their bodies with equal strength and emphasis. The shoulders, the torso, the hips, and the feet—all are driven by a percussive force that parallels the rhythms of the music and singing, and with this force there is flexibility. All movements are linked together, with an emphasis on central balance. Finally, movements have clear boundaries marking beginnings and endings. Many of these elements, linking together movement, sound, and overall aesthetic design, have been carried into African-American artistic styles, especially in dance and music (Thompson 1983).

Dance is important everywhere as a means of using the human body in the process of creating art. It involves movement of the body in ways not typically found in daily mundane activities. Dance is a complex artistic form because it generally combines many other arts as well. It is usually accompanied by the sounds of music, chanting, or singing. Dancers often adorn their bodies with special paint, costumes, and other body decorations. Dance sometimes tells a story or expresses a narrative either in literal or symbolic form. Participation in or observation of a dance performance, therefore, is not only artistically complex but stimulates an appreciation through many realms of the senses. This appeal is a significant factor for an audience even when observing ritual performances. So, for example, Zuni audiences often request encores of public sacred dances that they find beautiful (Bunzel 1932).

Cultural attitudes vary concerning the kinds of movements and configurations that are properly displayed in dance, and there are cultural norms about the degree of individual innovation permitted to dancers. In some societies, dancers must conform to an already established pattern, contributing very little of their own artistic sense except in some personal aspects of style and performance. In other societies, individual dancers are encouraged to innovate, creating new steps, new movements and new configurations. There are also differences in whether people dance alone, in couples, or in groups. Gender may be a factor influencing the kinds of dancing that people do or even whether they are permitted to dance in public at all.

? *How might you compare and contrast the cultural contexts of a tap dance, a line dance, and a disco dance?*

As in all aspects of behaviour, context is significant. Some dances are reserved for sacred events, others for secular contexts, emphasizing the social element of dance and its entertainment values both for the dancer and the audience. Royce points out that social and recreational dances are usually relatively simple in their steps and movements so that everyone can participate (1977:81). Dances that require greater skill tend to be performed by specialists. These specialized dances are more often restricted to particular contexts and serve other functions. They may celebrate ritual occasions or they may be performed by specialists for an audience's entertainment.

Styles of dance, like all other aspects of culture, are subject to change from innovation and influence. The kinds of social and recreational dance styles popular in North America today differ vastly from their European, African, and other predecessors. Dances today are far removed in pattern and tempo from the courtly dances popular in Europe in the seventeenth and eighteenth centuries. Today popular dancing may be done in groups rather than pairs, and unique movements may be preferred over the set steps of dance styles of the twentieth century, such as jazz and ballroom dancing, which called for specific steps and patterns of movement. Nevertheless, as in all other aspects of our behaviour, as dancers we are influenced by cultural norms that dictate appropriateness in particular contexts. Today's hip-hop dancers conform to contemporary values and expectations just as their parents and grandparents conformed to the practices of their eras.

REVIEW

Music, song, and dance, the subjects of ethnomusicology, are universal in humans and serve critical individual and social functions, such as personal expression, group solidarity, and religious speech. Performances and their meanings must be understood through the cultural contexts in which they occur.

ORAL LITERATURE AND WRITTEN TEXTS

Another universal domain of artistic expression is **oral literature**. All peoples tell stories about their sacred past, their secular histories, and their personal lives. These narratives conform to cultural patterns of content and organization.

Sacred narratives recounting the creation or transformation of the world and the exploits of spirit beings form the central core of oral literature. Sacred stories tell of a primordial world that existed before this one and of the events that led to the formation of our present world. Such narratives present a blueprint for life, giving an understanding of how things are and how things ought to be. They may set out the roles that men and women ought to have, the relationships that people ought to have with other living creatures, and the responsibilities that people have to other members of their communities. Sacred stories present moral issues, giving guidance as to what is right and what is wrong. They may be interpreted to validate or justify the prevailing social order, teaching people their place in society.

Folktales of a secular nature relate events that teach moral lessons or simply entertain. Like sacred narratives, folktales have stylistic features that set them apart. For example, the oral literature of the Zuni begins with the incantation "So'nahchi," a form without a specific translation in English. The stories end with a phrase translated as "lived long ago" (Tedlock 1972, 1983). The recurrence of these phrasings alerts Zuni listeners that they are hearing a particular type of story.

A traditional Zuni performance style sets the stories off as an artistic event. The performance style includes changes in speaking volume from louder to softer, changes in voice quality, such as raspiness, tightness, and breaks, and pausing both within and between words. The dramatic shifts of pause and voice evoke different emotional states, not only on the part of the speaker but also on the part of the listeners.

The narratives of the Western Apaches of New Mexico also have distinct stylistic features that convey cues about the type of artistic event being performed. Apache narratives, referred to as "historical tales," recount events occurring at specific, named places involving people a long time ago (Basso 1990). The stories teach moral lessons by pointing out mistakes that people made in the past and the unfortunate and sometimes humorous consequences that followed. They are morality tales, teaching and transmitting the wisdom of the ancestors and making them relevant to people today. The tales begin and end with the phrase "It happened at (named place)." This device frames the narrative, signalling to listeners both the beginning and ending.

In many African cultures, proverbs are an important repository of traditional advice and admonitions. They, too, adhere to stylistic patterns. Here are some examples.

The eyes of the wise person see through you. (Haya)
If nothing touches the palm leaves, they do not rustle. (Ashanti)
The house-roof fights with the rain, but he who is sheltered ignores it. (Wolof)
His opinions are like water in the bottom of a canoe, going from side to side. (Efik)
A bird is in the air but its mind is on the ground. (Mandinka)
Between true friends even water drunk together is sweet enough. (Zimbabwe)
Words are spoken with their shells; let the wise man come to shuck them. (Mossi)
A family is like a forest; when you are outside it is dense, when you are inside you see that each tree has its place. (Akan)
The hunter in pursuit of an elephant does not stop to throw stones at birds. (Uganda).
Until lions have their own historians, tales of the hunt will always glorify the hunter. (Igbo)
Even the Niger River must flow around an island. (Hausa)
A bird will always use another bird's feathers to feather its own nest. (Southern Sotho)
Where there is no jealousy, a small hare's leather is enough to cover four people. (Burundi)
An egg never sits on a hen (a child is never greater than its parents). (Kiswahili)
If the foot doesn't go (to the place of the quarrel), the mouth won't interfere. (Dagbani)
When they gossip about someone, listen as if it were about you. (Ethiopia)

oral literature
Stories that people tell about their sacred past, their secular histories, and their personal lives.

folktales
Secular stories that relate events that teach moral lessons or entertain listeners.

Everybody, even he who has a bad character, can be softened by kind conversation. (Sumbwa)

If a hen crows, kill it. (Northern Sotho)

All bent things, as days go by, will be straightened. (Kaonde)

Wisdom is like termite hills: each one puts out new earth in its own way. (Luganda)

Where there is no shame, there is no honour. (Congo)

Sticks in a bundle are unbreakable. (Bondei)

He who hates, hates himself. (Zulu)

Proverbs can be used to instruct, amuse, praise, or criticize, their particular meaning dependant on the situation. Among the Akan of Ghana, people can use proverbs to indirectly give advice, make requests, or criticize someone's behaviour. These are all actions that are considered rude if done directly. For example, a mother can ask her adult son to send money home to contribute to the support of his aged parents by reminding him of his familial responsibilities, quoting proverbs from the "elders." In one recorded conversation, the mother admonished her son (the researcher!) by saying "It is the elders who said, 'If someone looks after you when you're teething, you should also look after him when he loses his teeth.' You're aware of your father's illness. Now he's incapable of working. Life is hard these days" (Obeng 1996:532).

Riddles are another way of imparting cultural knowledge and wisdom through an artistic form. Riddles ask questions and provide answers that rely on wordplay, metaphor, and imagery. For example, fifteenth- and sixteenth-century Aztec children and adults tested each other with riddles as a means of both play and instruction. Following are some examples (Carrasco 1998:168–169).

What is a little blue-green jar filled with popcorn? Someone is sure to guess our riddle: It is the sky.

What is a mountainside that has a spring of water in it? Our nose.

What is that which says: You jump so that I shall jump? This is the drum stick.

What is that which is a small mirror in a house made of fir branches? Our eye.

What is it that goes along the foothills of the mountain patting [us] with its hands? A butterfly!

What is it that has a tight shift? The tomato.

What is that which we enter in three places and leave by only one? It is our shirt.

What is a tiny coloured stone sitting on the road? Dog excrement.

What is it that bends over us all over the world? The maize tassel.

Although we more readily think of artistic components of sacred and folk narratives, personal stories may also be produced by gifted storytellers with stylistic features that make them art. For example, in an influential study of the structure of personal narratives told by ordinary people, William Labov collected the following story in response to his question, "Have you ever been in danger of dying? Have you ever said to yourself, 'This is it?'" The storyteller, a man named Harold Shambaugh, told about events that occurred to him when he was in South America. In addition to dialect, his story contains features that produce drama and tension (Labov 1997:398).

Oh I w's settin' at a table drinkin'
And—this Norwegian sailor came over
an' kep' givin me a bunch o' junk about I was sittin' with his woman
An' everybody sittin' at the table with me were my shipmates.
So I jus' turn aroun'
an' shoved 'im
an' told 'im, I said, "Go away.
I don't even wanna fool with ya"
An' nex' thing I know I'm layin' on the floor, blood all over me,
An' a guy told me, says, "Don't move your head.
Your throat's cut."

Shambaugh's story is deceptively short and simple, but it contains all of the basic features of personal narrative. The events are recounted in chronological order with a bare minimum of detail, concentrating on the critical features of context, setting,

? *What proverbs and riddles can you recall from your childhood enculturation? Which folktales may have had the greatest impact on your social or moral development?*

significant characters, and dramatically relevant moments: the arrival of the Norwegian sailor, Shambaugh's responses (physical and verbal), and the result of the Norwegian's actions. But Shambaugh's skill as a storyteller is in his simplification and streamlining of events, with the effect of heightening the drama. He leaves out important details, not describing the Norwegian's actions directly but leaving it to the listener's imagination to reconstruct what happened. Only the violent consequences are stated. We contribute to the narrative ourselves by using our knowledge and imagination to fill in the empty spaces. This involves the listener as an active participant in the construction of the story.

Notice, too, the use of direct quotation: Shambaugh first quotes himself making what he presumably thought was an appropriate response to the Norwegian's accusations but evidently provoking the latter to retaliate. Then Shambaugh quotes a companion who reported the dramatic conclusion of events with the frightening warning, "Don't move your head" because "your throat's cut." Although the narrative recounts an occurrence of undoubtedly intense emotion for Shambaugh, it is told in objective, dispassionate language. The story is the product of a skilled narrator using the art of verbal construction to create a scene that he and his listeners would not soon forget.

Storytellers often have a special role and status in society. West African griots memorized and sang genealogies, local histories, and cultural sagas or myths. Travelling bards and minstrels of medieval Europe recited and sang the news of the day, including what would be known in modern journalism as Op-Ed pieces, commenting on current social and political issues. Fictional storytellers, such as Mother Goose, filled special roles in the socialization of children. Here this storyteller continues this tradition at a Kwanzaa celebration in Chicago.

Written texts also have structural principles that reveal cultural norms and allow readers to follow, and, indeed, to anticipate, the content and the plot's development. When reading novels, for example, we expect certain background facts to be made known to us, such as principal characters, physical settings, and motivations. We generally expect the plot to be about some tension or crisis in the main character's life that he or she confronts, deals with, or resolves. We expect some change in the character's circumstances, thoughts, or attitudes. In other words, we want the story to be about "something" where something "happens." Distinct genres of novels have their own structures and expectations: Think about the differences between Gothic romance, detective stories, and science fiction.

Some written texts are made to be visually beautiful in addition to their verbal content. For instance, ancient sacred texts produced in India combine the elegance of Sanskrit writing and the intricate beauty of illustrations embossed in gold and silver. Illustrated texts describe real as well as imagined events. Several decades after the fall of the Inca Empire, for example, Felipe Guaman Pomo de Ayala, a native Peruvian of the Andes, organized a 1200-page handwritten manuscript around his 400 original drawings of life under the Spanish colonial government. His illustrated manuscript essentially was an account of the Spanish conquest and a letter to King Philip III of Spain asking him to reform the colonial government to save the Andean peoples from destruction (Adorno 2004).

? *What are some examples of skilled narratives you have read or heard? What literary devices contributed to their effectiveness?*

REVIEW

Oral literature includes folktales, fairy tales, riddles, proverbs, poetry, rhymes, recitations of history and myth, and other skilled narratives. Written texts preserve these forms in various genres that reveal the cultural norms, beliefs, values, and styles on which they are based.

ART AND GLOBALIZATION

Global processes have influenced the kinds of artworks produced, displayed, and performed. In some cases, arts originating in one country have become popular in far distant places. When a particular art form or art product is borrowed, it may keep its identification with its source, functioning as a symbol of the original ethnic or national identity. Sometimes people adopt art forms because they are associated with a dominant group and therefore can be interpreted as status symbols, but people also acquire the artwork of small, relatively powerless groups in appreciation of its beauty. In the process of diffusion, art is like any other cultural form, changing both the donor and the receiver. Some indigenous communities have been able to prosper through the sale of pottery, basketry, carvings, and clothing that they formerly made for their own use and currently make for sale as well.

European classical music is taught and played in every country of the world. While maintaining national musical styles, countries such as Japan, India, and China also play European orchestral compositions. Influences on musical traditions are also evident in pop music, as American and British popular songs are sung throughout the world. All over the world people have translated songs and musical styles into their languages from English and have translated their own songs into English.

Performers of dance and music travel around the world, disseminating their styles and influencing each other. The current world music movement brings musicians and dancers from Asia, Africa, the Middle East, and Latin America to North American and European audiences. Not only is the music of a different style than Western forms, but the blending of music, dance, and song takes place in both sacred and secular contexts. In contrast, the performance practices of Western styles, where music is played in large concert halls, often removes ethnic musical traditions from their lived contexts (Shannon 2003). However, audiences can become sensitive to the cultural meanings of the music they hear by being exposed to new sounds and new styles.

Through colonialism and globalization, the arts of Europe and the North America have spread throughout the world. As in all diffusion, art forms carry with them cultural values and practices that contribute to culture change. Western art has also been influenced by the artistic content and styles of other peoples. For example, African music and stylistic features of sound and song for centuries have informed American musical traditions. Gospel singing, jazz, and rock and roll would not be what they are without African melodies and singing styles. African and Asian artistic traditions in music, painting, and sculpture have influenced Western art forms significantly since the nineteenth century.

Contacts between different peoples and cultures have always included introductions to each other's material and performing arts. In the twentieth century, Western art connoisseurs became fascinated with what they referred to as "primitive art," art produced by indigenous or tribal peoples. Such art was unsigned, anonymous to the Western viewer, and often stereotyped as expressing a universal unconscious or innocence that modern "civilized" people have lost (Price 1989). The styles and genres of "primitive art" had a significant influence on the works of many modern painters and sculptors, including Picasso, Gauguin, and Pollock. Together this influence is sometimes referred to as "primitivism" (McEvilley 1992).

Art and Identity

? *What art do you display in your home? What does it say about who you are and the cultural groups you belong to?*

Art objects and art styles can serve as carriers of cultural identity. This is particularly true in multiethnic states where each group strives to maintain its uniqueness. Language, kinship systems, religion, and ethical values may be used to transmit and maintain cultural identity, but the arts, both art objects and performing arts, can also carry meaning by identifying a particular ethnic group. In modern markets for indigenous "primitive art," the people making the art often come to see themselves through their products as symbols that represent them culturally (Graburn 1976). This connection between arts and ethnicity led some colonial and national governments to ban certain arts in order to impose control or enforce unity. For example, the Asmat, of the part of New Guinea now absorbed by Indonesia as the province of West Irian, were forbidden to continue their traditional styles of decorated house building and wood carvings, which incorporated human forms. These were seen as graven images, barred by Islamic principles.

Dance is also a marker of cultural identity. Particular types of dance styles may come to be associated both by in-group members and by outsiders as archetypal or symbolic of that cultural group. For example, we may think of the Mexican hat dance, the Hawaiian hula, and the Plains Indian war dance as representative of their respective cultural groups. This iconic use of a dance style often originates in situations of culture contact, with outsiders looking at "the other" and reinforcing stereotypes. In some situations of culture contact, people may accept others' views of them and associate their art styles with their ethnic identity.

For example, dance style is used to transmit Zapotec ethnic identity in southern Mexico. In the city of Juchitan, Zapotecs are the majority ethnic group (Royce 1977:166). On social occasions where all the participants are Zapotec, people engage in popular Mexican dances of all types. However, when non-Zapotecs are present, especially for celebrations of marriages between Zapotec and non-Zapotec, the Zapotec participants display their own ethnic dance style, emphasizing their Zapotec identity so that "the friends and relatives of the outsider spouse will be impressed with the extravagance and richness of the Zapotec heritage, which can more than hold its own in competition with anything else Mexico has to offer" (p. 170).

Art in the Global Economy

In all times and places, incorporation of indigenous peoples into regional, national, and global networks has an impact on artistic production. Local artisans become specialists, creating particular types of work destined for wider markets. These products then become symbols of their ethnic identity. For example, in Panama, women of the indigenous Kuna communities produce embroidered blouses and other items called *molas*, made of cotton appliquéd and embroidered with bright colours and bold designs. Molas were first made as blouses worn by the artisan and female members of her family. Then, in the 1960s, the influx of tourists visiting Kuna communities helped promote and broaden artistic production. Since then, production of molas has rapidly increased and diversified. Now women may sew and embroider privately in their homes or in cooperative workshops where they produce molas as blouses, wall hangings, table coverings, pillows, and numerous other household and personal items. The designs are often adapted according to market demands. Organizers of the cooperatives have contacts with retail outlets in Panama, North America, and elsewhere. These contacts influence styles and motifs by contracting for particular designs.

Through wide dissemination and popularity inside and outside of Panama, molas have become symbols of Kuna uniqueness and autonomy. The women's incorporation into the global economy helps sustain their families, contributing substantially to their income. An activity that was once part of women's domestic work has now become central to their families' economies. Many Kuna families are able to maintain other aspects of their traditional subsistence patterns and their land base, because the women bring in needed cash to purchase goods that are no longer made at home.

Similarly, in Canada, Inuit sculpture and other artworks are major sources of income in many small communities. Traditional sculptures were made from soapstone and whalebone, carved and etched to represent people, animals, and spirit beings. In the traditional view of artistic creativity, Inuit artists do not create the sculptures from their own imaginations but release the form hidden but inherent in the medium that they are using. Thus, it is the soapstone that releases its form through the work of the artist rather than the artist who imposes his or her creation on the stone. Market forces have led to a diversification of Inuit artwork since the middle of the twentieth century. In addition to sculpture, Inuit artisans now make prints and calendars for sale throughout North America and the world. The artworks and styles of carving and stencilled prints have become iconic symbols of Inuit culture.

Art and Tourism

In conjunction with other global processes linking distant places through trade and communication, tourists from North America, Europe, and Asia have travelled throughout the world looking for new experiences. In addition to visiting major cities that house

The dances and costuming associated with the Plains powwow have spread to the northeast, the southeast, and elsewhere in North America. This dancer is performing in Brooklyn, New York. Dances originally associated with particular rituals or social activities are now performed during the summer as the powwows are held on different reservations throughout the season in what has become known as "the powwow trail" (Brewer 2000:263).

GLOBALIZATION

In the United States and Canada, the Native American powwow has come to symbolize pan-Indian culture and heritage for the participants and for Indian and non-Indian spectators alike. Costumes worn by the dancers and the styles of dancing have spread from reservation to reservation, merging and blending formerly distinctive artistic expressions. Powwows thus symbolize both a local tribal identity and an international native identity.

Culture Change

NAVAJO ART RESPONDS TO MARKET FORCES

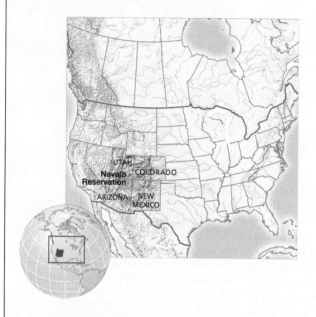

The Navajos of the American Southwest are well known for their skill as weavers of blankets and rugs and as makers of silver and turquoise jewellery. Both of these arts were learned from other peoples, however. When the Navajos' ancestors migrated to the Southwest from western Canada sometime in the fourteenth century, they settled near Pueblo peoples who had lived in the region for many centuries. Many of the Navajo cultural practices were adopted from the Hopis and Zunis.

Although weaving is a man's job among the Pueblo, Navajo women became the weavers in their families. Pueblo cloth was made from cotton, an art originally diffused from the Aztecs. By the time the Navajos learned to weave, sheep had been introduced into the Southwest by Spanish colonizers and settlers, and Navajo weavers began to work with wool. The earliest fragments of woolen blankets date from the late eighteenth and early nineteenth centuries (Kahlenberg and Berlant 1972).

There were no artist specialists among the Navajo but every woman wove blankets for her family's personal use. People draped the blankets over their shoulders as coverings. Women also made dresses, fashioned shirts and leggings for the men in their family, and made saddle blankets, sashes, and cords for their hair. In addition, blankets were thrown on the floor for sitting and sleeping and were hung in doorways to keep out cold and wind. They were not used as decorative rugs, a use that became popular later in non-Indian homes.

In the 1870s, shortly after the Navajos returned to their own territory after four years of forced confinement in New Mexico at an American army base called Bosque Redondo, the people gradually became involved in commerce, trading wool and animal skins. Within a decade, Navajo women were supplying regional markets and Anglo communities with woolen blankets. The Anglo purchasers, including the American military, used the blankets mainly as bed coverings, prompting Navajo women to make larger sizes. This was their first adaptation to market demands.

By the 1880s, Navajo blankets were making their way into national trade networks, finally arriving in the homes of eastern buyers. By that time, aniline dyes provided a new range of colours in addition to the traditional white, black, and brown. A further innovation of the 1880s was machine-spun, dyed yarn that made a weaver's work much easier, since she no longer had to spin the yarn from wool sheared from her own sheep.

Commercial expansion was facilitated by the establishment of trading posts on the Navajo reservation in the nineteenth century. Traders operated as middlemen in the market, buying rugs woven by independent producers and then selling them to the American domestic market. While commercial dyes and machine-made yarn increased production and lightened workload, these innovations also had the effect of cheapening the product. Soon, wholesale houses sprang up and became the primary suppliers of Navajo blankets to American cities (Weiss 1984). At the same time, the market for Navajo commodities diversified; weavers produced blankets, saddle blankets, sash belts, garters, saddle cinches, women's dresses, and knitted socks and leggings.

In addition to the blankets that women wove, men sold silver and turquoise jewellery, an art they learned from Mexican Indians. As the tourist trade grew, national companies became involved in the sale of the jewellery. Several companies sent raw materials (silver, turquoise, and other jewels) to traders on the reservation, who farmed out supplies and gave orders for particular designs. Navajo jewellers were paid by the ounce for the finished product (Weiss 1984). Silverwork included buttons, bracelets, bridle ornaments, concha belts, tobacco cases, and jewellery with turquoise stones (Bailey and Bailey 1986). Silversmithing grew in importance when trading posts on the reservation started accepting silver ornaments in exchange for goods. People began to think of their jewellery as a form of savings. Meanwhile, crafts, such as pottery and basketry, declined because these products had little or no commercial value and could be replaced by store-bought items.

People prospered initially through their integration into the national economy with outlets for the sale of wool, woven products, and silverwork. However, that integration proved disastrous by the end of the nineteenth century, because the people were vulnerable to fluctuations in prices for their goods. A further obstacle to Navajo economic prosperity was the fact that, as the market for artwork expanded, competing non-Indian establishments were opened off-reservation that produced imitation rugs and jewellery. In response, some companies established workshops on the reservation where they oversaw the production process (Weiss 1984). Although this practice aided sales against non-authentic competitors, it undermined the creative and autonomous role of the artists, essentially turning them into wage workers.

By the end of the nineteenth century, traders and other commercial interests had a further impact on Navajo weaving by influencing the choices of colour and design. Early Navajo designs were of plain stripes, a style borrowed from their Pueblo neighbours. New motifs were introduced in the 1880s, most popularly diamond-shaped designs and pictorial representations of horses, cows, birds, bows and arrows, knives and forks, shovels, houses, trains, and alphabet letters (Kahlenberg and Berlant 1972).

Copying from patterns and following instructions conflicted with traditional ways of weaving in which weavers created designs in their own imaginations. Weaving was not just a utilitarian or even artistic act but was seen as a powerful spiritual act as well. Navajo weavers believed that they were expressing their spirituality. The entire process, from building the loom, carding and spinning the yarn, and weaving the pattern, was one of creative enlightenment, reenacting mythic narratives of world creation. According to Navajo sacred narratives,

> Spider Woman instructed the Navajo women how to weave on a loom which Spider Man told them how to make. The cross poles were made of sky and earth, the warp sticks of sunrays, the healds of rock crystal

and sheet lightening. The batten was a sun halo, white shell made the comb. There were four spindles: one stick of zigzag lightning with a whorl of cannel coal; one stick of flash lightning with a whorl of turquoise; a third had a stick of sheet lightning with a whorl of abalone; a rain streamer formed the stick of the fourth, and its whorl was white shell. (Kahlenberg and Berlant, 1972:6)

And then, after Spider Man made the loom, he told the women,

> Now you know all that I have made for you. It is yours to work with and to use following your own wishes. But from now on when a baby girl is born you shall go and find a spider web woven at the mouth of some hole; you must take it and rub it on the baby's hand and arm. Thus, when she grows up she will weave, and her fingers and arms will not tire from the weaving. (p. 19)

Navajo weavers and jewellers now sell their work to retail outlets on the reservation and throughout the United States and the world and via the Internet. However, jewellery makers in particular have become increasingly concerned about the production and sale of imitation jewellery made in foreign countries that is passed off as American Indian products. Federal and state laws are aimed at preventing fraudulent marketing claims by imitation jewellery, but these statutes are rarely enforced. Fake American Indian jewellery seriously undercuts Navajo (and other Native American) markets. They are made cheaply in mass production factories in foreign countries where wages are very low. In comparison, authentic Navajo and other Native American crafts are expensive.

The Navajos and other southwestern native artisans have appealed to federal and state authorities to crack down on the illegal sale of fake jewellery, forming the Council for Indigenous Arts and Culture. In 1990, the U.S. Congress passed the *Indian Arts and Crafts Act* (Public Law 101-644). This law makes it illegal to sell any art or craft product "in a manner that falsely suggests it is Indian produced, an Indian product, or the product of a particular Indian or Indian tribe or Indian arts and crafts organization." The act is aimed at protecting Native American artisans and the authenticity of their work.

museums, theatres, and stores, people increasingly travel to indigenous communities to learn about other cultures and collect unique arts and crafts. Indigenous peoples have taken advantage of this trend in ecotourism to earn money and widen the market for their products. Many indigenous groups benefit economically from allowing tourists to explore their territories and even their homes, but others resent this attention or wish to avoid the risk of being viewed as curiosities. Some indigenous peoples use tourism as an opportunity to educate the public and gain support for political causes.

Arts made or performed for tourists often omit traditional intentions and symbolic meanings. In Hawaii, for example, the female hula dancer has come to symbolize tourist entertainment, a projection of tourists' ideas about the South Pacific: With her

Case study

Tourists among the Toraja

In Indonesia, the Toraja, a farming people of Sulawesi, have attracted foreign visitors who photograph their elaborate funeral rituals and their intricate carved effigies of the dead. Funeral ceremonies can go on for many days and include water buffalo fights, after which the animals, sometimes more than a dozen of them, are killed as sacrifices to the ancestors. Funerary rites are based on animism and ancestor worship, with influences from Christianity derived from Dutch and British colonial agents. After the animal sacrifices, the deceased person is placed in a coffin and interred in a cave hollowed out of a high cliff side containing the remains of Toraja ancestors. Sometimes the remains are suspended from the cliff wall as a hanging grave. Lifelike statues, called Tau-Tau, house the spirits of the ancestors and guard the grave sites, looking out from balconies high over the living.

The Toraja, who number approximately 350 000, have been inundated in the last decade with foreign and domestic tourists. In 1973, only 422 foreigners came to Toraja territory, but by 1991, more than 215 000 foreign and domestic tourists visited the region annually (Adams 1995a, 1995b). The explosion of tourism was prompted by efforts of the Indonesian government to promote Toraja culture to attract foreign dollars. The Toraja are marketed through travel brochures, postcards, T-shirts, hotel promotions, and videos. They themselves purchase these commodities, becoming both viewer and viewed, observer and observed.

As tourism increased, conflict and competition among the Toraja intensified. The Toraja live in a ranked society, with status differences based on three ranks (high, middle, and low). High-status people claim descent from ancestral spirit beings who imparted the charter for Torajan society; middle-status Toraja are tradespeople; and lower-status people, the majority, are farmers and labourers.

With the influx of tourism, lower-status Toraja entered into competition with higher-ranking groups. They began to construct elaborate carved decorations and to perform funeral dances for the public, ignoring or disguising status differences in their society. This trend benefited lower-status Toraja, but it bred dissatisfaction and conflict between elite and non-elite members. The Toraja example demonstrates that outsiders, whether anthropologists or tourists, have an impact on the inner workings of indigenous societies.

dark, flowing hair, warm, sunny smile, and alluring gestures and movements, she entices the tourist into a sensual experience. This imagery distorts Hawaiian culture, however, specifically the movements and purposes of Hawaiian dance. As Haunani-Kay Trask observed, "In the hotel version of the hula, the sacredness of the dance has completely evaporated while the athleticism and sexual expression have been packaged like ornaments. The purpose is entertainment for profit rather than a joyful and truly Hawaiian celebration of human and divine nature" (2001:399). The Hawaiian dance form "hula kahiko" is traditionally dedicated to a celebration of indigenous spirit beings, honouring them for their role in the creation of the Hawaiian Islands and the culture of indigenous peoples. The state of Hawaii has come to rely heavily on income from tourism. By 2000, tourists outnumbered state residents six to one and outnumbered Native Hawaiians by thirty to one (p. 394).

Tourism and the appeal of **ethnic art**—art produced by a particular ethnic group—can make economic changes in people's lives and in village life. An example is the marked increase since the 1980s of interest in wooden carvings called *alebrijes,* produced since the 1950s by villagers in the Oaxacan Valley in Mexico. As tourism has

ethnic art
Art produced by a particular group of people that comes to express and symbolize their ethnic identity.

increased, residents of the towns of Arrazola, San Martin, Tilcajete, and Launion Tejalapan have significantly raised their standard of living through sales of the carvings. The *alebrijes* are fanciful representations of lizards, cats, serpents, panthers, and other animals. Most of them are made of a soft wood, called copal, that is easy to carve but also vulnerable to insect infestations. Some artisans work instead with cedar, which is harder and longer lasting but more costly, thus making the carvings more expensive. Many of the *alebrijes* have elaborate detailed decoration and are painted in dazzling colours.

At first, townspeople sold their work to individual buyers, mostly tourists. Then galleries in Mexico and elsewhere began to send in orders for particular designs. In addition, wealthy collectors and their agents descended on the towns to buy the most intricate and skillful of the carvings. Today, an estimated one-fifth of all of the families in the three major art-producing towns are involved in the work (Do 2004). Men and women, Zapotec Indians and mestizos—all participate. Artwork is often a family affair involving parents and their children. Adults do the carving and decorating, and children help paint the finished product, or different families may cooperate in different phases of the work.

The carved buffalo head on this traditional house in Sulawesi is a symbol of well-being and security.

Whatever the level of sophistication of the artist, the appeal of the *alebrijes* in national and international markets has changed the quality of life in the villages. Individual standards of living have improved as people spend their earnings on enlarging their houses and purchasing household goods that make their lives easier. In addition, the towns spend money on paving roads, bringing in electricity, and building and renovating schools. Fewer families are involved in farming, the traditional occupation and subsistence strategy of Oaxacan villagers. Many are now able to devote their time to producing ethnic arts, an occupation that earns them a greater income and is also less arduous. However, the unpredictability of the tourist art market makes the future of the Oaxacan carvers unpredictable as well. One response has been to diversify. Zapotec weavers incorporate motifs and designs from paintings by European masters such as Picasso and Miró as well as from Navajo blankets.

REVIEW

Ethnic arts have become commodities in the global economy, which influences art forms and alters the relationships between artists and their work as well as between artworks and the life of the community. This is because art responds to market forces and tourist interests, as in the examples of the Navajo and the Toraja. Revenues from sales or performances of art have become important sources of income for indigenous peoples and cultural minorities.

Chapter Summary

What Is Art?

- Anthropologists study arts and artistic principles to understand the ways that artworks are produced, by whom, in what context, and for what purposes. They also study cultural aesthetics, or the philosophies of what has beauty and value in art. In some societies, art has primarily representational functions, meant to imitate or represent the natural world. In other societies, art functions in the context of ritual, used to express spirituality, attract spirit beings, and honour the spirit realm.

Cultural Aesthetics

- In Western art, five aesthetic models have developed: mimetic (the ability of art to portray the world around us), representational (imitating, idealizing, or symbolizing form and experience), instrumental (transforming the world, enhancing our experience, or making the world a better place), emotionalist (art connects to our inner experience and feelings), and formalist (focusing on the formal qualities of art, the use of colour, composition, sound, words, or movements).

Body Art

- One of the most common media for the display of art is the human body. Body art includes body decoration, hairstyles, clothing, and jewellery. Nomadic peoples are particularly likely to emphasize the use of the body in artistic production because their lifestyle makes it necessary to refrain from accumulating possessions that they would otherwise have to carry with them when they move.

Origins and Functions of Art Objects

- The earliest known works of art date to about 30 000 to 40 000 years ago in Europe and Africa and about 30 000 to 50 000 years ago in Australia. Most of these are paintings found in caves or on rocks. Many have been interpreted as making an association between animals hunted and weapons used, possibly a form of sympathetic magic with the desired result portrayed. In addition, ancient stone sculptures, called Venus figurines, have been discovered in Europe from about 30 000 years ago.

The Arts of Sound and Movement

- Artistic impulses also find expression in the sounds of music and song. In many cultures, music and singing are frequent means of expressing religious themes or making contact with the spirit world through the power of song and sound. Secular songs and spontaneous singing also often accompany everyday activities.
- Dance is a universal art, appearing as a form of individual and group expression in all cultures. In most cultures, dance is a central or key aspect of many rituals. Dance is also important as a means of using the human body in the process of creating art.

Oral Literature and Written Texts

- Another universal domain of artistic expression is oral literature. Oral literature includes sacred narratives told about the spirit world or used in the context of ritual performances and secular folktales that teach moral lessons or entertain. Cultures vary in the ways in which sacred narratives and folktales are structured. They may begin or end with a particular phrase that cues the listener, alerting them to the fact that a particular genre of story is being told. Proverbs, riddles, and other wordplay also function to instruct, amuse, advise, praise, or criticize listeners. Finally, there are cultural styles of personal storytelling, allowing speakers to recount events and experiences in their own lives.

Art and Globalization

- Styles of art, including the production of objects, the use of the voice in song, musical instruments, and dance, are, like all other aspects of culture, subject to change both from innovation and influence. Art can also function as a marker of cultural identity. This is particularly true in multiethnic states where each group strives to maintain and dramatize their uniqueness.
- Incorporation of indigenous peoples into regional, national, and global networks has an impact on artistic production. Local artisans have become specialists creating particular types of work destined for wider markets. These products then become symbols of their ethnic identity. Like the production of any goods or services, artworks respond to market forces. Preferences of buyers influence styles, materials used, designs, and colours.
- In conjunction with other global processes linking distant places through trade and communication, tourists travel throughout the world looking for new experiences. Indigenous peoples have become tourist attractions, marketing and selling their products, and sometimes their performances, to a national and international audience. Tourism brings in much needed money to remote and marginalized communities. As particular ethnic art objects become popular, people are able to improve their standard of living, as artisans working to benefit their households and the community as a whole.

Key Terms

aesthetics 340	instrumental 341	tattooing 346	ethnomusicology 351
art 340	emotionalist 343	artisans 347	oral literature 353
mimetic 341	formalist 343	sandpaintings 348	folktales 353
representational 341	scarification 345	Venus figurines 350	ethnic art 360

Review Questions

1. How do anthropologists distinguish among types or categories of art?

2. On what different aesthetic principles can art be based? What are some examples of the expression of aesthetic principles in African and Native American art?

3. How do Venus figurines and Inca quipu illustrate the problems of defining art from an anthropological perspective?

4. How do individuals and groups use art to signify their identity and status?

5. What is body art? What are other universal categories of art forms?

6. What are some social functions of art forms, such as oral literature?

7. How does art relate to social institutions, such as education and religion?

8. What are some ethnographic examples of the use of art in healing?

9. What do ethnomusicologists contribute to our understanding of being human?

10. What is the role and impact of arts and crafts in people's economies?

11. In what ways is art a part of global culture?

12. What forces encourage people like the Toraja of Indonesia to make funerals into performance art?

Living in a Global World

Preview

1. **How is globalization affecting people's lives in different parts of the world?**

2. **How are different types of migration changing national and world demographics today?**

3. **How does migration affect local, national, and global economies?**

4. **How have new nations re-created themselves in the post-colonial era, and how have they adapted to their own cultural diversity?**

5. **In what ways can ethnogenesis reflect both a colonial past and a globalized future?**

6. **What are the characteristics of transnationalism and the emerging "global identity"?**

7. **What is the status of cultural minorities in the world today? How are they threatened, and how can they protect themselves?**

Travis counts himself amongst the thirteenth generation of carvers in his Kwakiutl family. Though he doesn't use a knife (or an axe, or a chainsaw), he expertly uses digital tools of all kinds (and he's pretty handy with a guitar, as well). He sits in front of the computer, his silver copper around his neck, systematically checking lines of code as he talks on his cell phone to Air Canada about his lost luggage. He is a true geek as well as an artist. And as co-founder of Waterstreet Technologies, he is a businessman, too. Travis is the ultimate Urban Aboriginal, as comfortable with these new technologies as his ancestors were with steel.

The focus of the first room is a totem pole, which some may recognize from the days that it stood in front of Brock Memorial Hall on the University of British Columbia campus. Carved by Ellen Neel, Travis's grandmother, circa 1951, it went up in a pole-raising ceremony and became an important symbol of the University, its thunderbird becoming the school's mascot!

Even its football stadium was named Thunderbird Stadium, with permission of the Neel family. Despite its importance, the pole recently was taken down and brought to the conservation department, a victim of negligence and vandalism. The text is from a letter from the University, updating the Neels on the debate about "replacing" the pole.

The sides of the room are bordered by two bars of red, making it seem like a slightly-too-close look at some alternative Canadian flag, one in which the bland maple leaf is substituted for something with a little more cultural pizzazz. A map of the Kwakiutl region blended with an image of a building replaces the area that is usually white. The room is called "Oh Canada."

Travis questions the non-Native embrace of all West Coast art and culture.

Institutions that never included Native people in their policy-making bodies are now clamouring for our art. The Vancouver airport, for example, is totally kitted out in West Coast imagery.

But all is not cynical. Travis's final room, "Music" is the positive take on the theme. There he is, surrounded by performers, fellow crew, and the artistic director of the Vancouver Folk Music Festival, where he has volunteered for fifteen years and which opens each year with an elders blessing. Behind the people is a map of the festival grounds, showing their proximity to the ocean. The blue pattern used to represent the water is actually "digital chaos," as Travis puts it. It is a photo of his PC crashing.

From "A Chatroom is Worth a Thousand Words"
www.cyberpowwow.net/STFwork-tn.html. Used with permission of Tricia Skawennati.

cultural minorities
Members of ethnic or cultural groups who have become minorities in their native lands due to migrations of other peoples into their territories or due to the historical configuration of a nation-state made up of diverse groups.

This text describes a Canadian Aboriginal artist who has experimented with digital technologies to produce art work based on indigenous themes and on his engagement with Canadian urban society. The "rooms" described are computerized images that are accessible on the website, **www.cyberpowwow.net**. This description of Travis cites themes of indigenous rights, urban migration, new technologies, global travel and communications, and new forms of cultural expression and social connectedness that are affecting people throughout the world. In this chapter we investigate some of these contemporary trends.

Processes of culture change have intensified throughout the twentieth and into the twenty-first century. The present-day global economy has introduced an unprecedented pace of technological innovation and economic expansion, transferring investment, goods, services, and peoples from one part of the world to others. Within nation states, employment is shifting from sectors concerned with the production of goods to those that focus on providing services and producing and processing information. Higher education has become the entry level requirement for secure and well-paying employment. People are communicating and interacting across boundaries as they change locations and link into global media. On the international level, migration has brought people far from their homes, some moving voluntarily to seek better employment or educational opportunities, others fleeing oppressive social conditions, political repression, and war. As they settle into their new countries, they adopt new cultural practices, often adapting them to their own values and perspectives, and add cultural diversity and richness to their host communities.

Global networks and influences have expanded the most radically in the economic realm. Large transnational companies are expanding the size and locations of their businesses, establishing branch plants and joint ventures across continents. Coordination and security of investment is increasingly protected by international regulatory bodies such as the International Monetary Fund and the World Trade Organization. Regions have also become linked together to address social, cultural, and humanitarian issues. International organizations, such as the United Nations and the World Health Organization, and many regional groups strive to coordinate activities, formulate policies, and resolve conflicts. The success of these organizations varies greatly. Although in principle countries come together as equals, in practice the voices of smaller and poorer nations are typically drowned out by those of larger, richer, and more powerful ones. Larger countries are able to exert greater influence because they can promise economic rewards, political support, and military aid to those who follow their lead, while they threaten to withdraw aid or retaliate against those who defy it.

As a result of present-day globalization, international organizations and transnational corporations have tremendous impacts on nations and on **cultural minorities** living in those nations, as well as on global interrelationships among nations. All of

The Nenets, Samoyeds of western Siberia, live in an autonomous district as nomadic foragers, fishers, and reindeer herders. Nenets have joined other circumpolar peoples in political action groups to protect themselves and their land from pollution caused by oil drilling, chemical plants, and nuclear plants located in their territories. Nenets inadvertently consume deadly heavy metals from pollution in their meals of mosses and reindeer meat.

these factors are part of the process of globalization. Globalization includes the movement of people and the exchange of cultural practices, goods and services, and attitudes worldwide. Through global exchanges, people learn from each other, obtain goods made elsewhere, and share information through media outlets and technological advances such as the internet. This chapter explores some of the characteristics and consequences of these processes.

THE GLOBAL ECONOMY

Globalization has involved the reorganization of investment, production, and trade as the international market place has been replacing the nation state as the main focus of economic activity. This process has been facilitated by the increase in scale and economic power of transnational corporations and the reversal of government policies that have attempted to contain the flows of capital and goods within national borders. Trends in the globalization of the marketplace can be seen in the development of world trade. Between 1971 and 2006, exports grew at over twice the rate of global production, and in that process trade volumes increased by a factor of more than thirty. World trade is now valued at over 14 trillion dollars, about 30 percent of the world's GNP.

While initiated by broadly based economic changes inherent in the post-industrial social order, globalization has been intensified by specific policies at the international and national levels. The World Bank and the World Trade Organization have established agreements and systems of sanctions and reward that encourage countries to relax or eliminate many of their economic regulations, such as tariffs and state ownership and subsidization of businesses, to free up the flow of capital, goods, and people. The rationale that is put forward to justify such economic reorganization is that a global system operating under free market conditions will lead to high levels of growth and will benefit the majority of the world's people. However, not every one agrees with this premise. Many economic analysts maintain that the wealthier segments of the population, both internationally and nationally, will gain the most from a more competitive world economy and that the less advantaged will either remain poor or even become worse off. Research to determine which of these scenarios is most plausible has produced contradictory results.

According to one reputable source, the Human Development Report, a publication of the United Nations Development Program, trade has indeed stimulated growth around the world. Regions that have adopted aggressive trade strategies, such as Asia, have experienced unprecedented growth, while regions that have not, such as Africa, have lagged behind. However, regional divergence in trade and growth is in itself creating greater inequality between countries and may not be easily corrected by policy changes alone. More importantly, economic growth within a country does not necessarily benefit all of its citizens. We have already seen for Canada that only the top half of the population has enjoyed increased income and wealth and the degree of improvement has risen most substantially at the very top of the ladder. Similar divergence and polarization are evident in other countries. Between 1995 and 2005, fifty-three countries experienced increased wealth inequality, while only nine saw decreases (UNDP 2006).

China provides a good example of some of the disparities that have emerged with rapid growth based on the globalization of investment and trade and the liberalization of government economic policies. During the Maoist period, the government imposed strict controls over the economy to ensure adherence to communist doctrine and to maintain an insulated economy and society. Foreign investment was not welcome and international trade was insignificant. After Mao's death, the new regime undertook to encourage capitalist development based on attracting new investment, mostly from Hong Kong and Taiwan, and to increase exports to acquire more income and create more jobs. Since then, the economy has seen dramatic growth led by the rapid expansion of agricultural and industrial production geared towards international trade. China's exports now amount to almost a trillion dollars per year. It is the world's third largest trading nation, after the United States and Germany, and its second largest economy.

Case study

Women Factory Workers in Guangdong, China

Ching Kwan Lee has provided a detailed look into the lives of the factory workers in the heartland of the "South China Miracle" that has involved the phenomenal growth of industry in Guandong (Canton) Province which surrounds Hong Kong (Lee 1999). Her ethnography of workers within an electronics plant documents working conditions and the lives and aspirations of the young women who make up the bulk of the unskilled labour force.

The factory studied employed a range of workers both male and female, but young women exclusively took up the unskilled jobs on the production line. They were subject to a "despotic" regime of labour management. They had to work at a relentless pace and were frequently required to put in overtime shifts that sometimes doubled their work week. They could take a bathroom break only with the permission of a supervisor and often were not allowed time off to go to a medical appointment or attend to an emergency. Compliance was assured through dockage of pay, which was applied to such infractions as having long finger nails or not conforming to the factory's dress code. If a worker refused to come in for an overtime shift four times in succession, a whole week's pay was forfeited. Pay levels were low, averaging $25 per week, and sometimes paycheques were held up.

Lee observed that the worker's situation gave them little opportunity to organize against the oppressive conditions they faced. While unions have been established in China, they are organized under a state's bureaucracy that has little interest in taking sides with the workers against the factory owners, whose investments form the basis of the economy. Moreover, class solidarity was undermined by divisions occurring because of locality, ethnic, and language differences among the workers, which the factory's management encouraged as an additional means of labour control. In spite of the unfavourable conditions of employment, the workers did make some attempts to secure a better future. They generally saw their move to the city as an improvement over rural life and the reins of familial authority, which could often dictate an arranged marriage. They also used their urban location and employment savings to support projects to take them out of the factory. Marriage offered one escape route, and the city gave single women a chance to meet a wider range of marital partners than they would in the rural village as well as the money needed to pay a dowry. Other avenues included attending evening courses to upgrade educational qualifications and accumulating enough capital to invest in a modest business, usually back in the rural areas. Lee does not give any details on the success of these plans for social mobility but notes that the factory's treatment of its workers is based upon expectations of a high turnover rate, through which new cohorts of young rural migrants are constantly introduced into the workforce.

This new and dynamic order has benefited many sectors of Chinese society, but gains have been unequally distributed. One major divide is evident in differences between rural and urban populations. In the course of liberalization, previously confined rural inhabitants, who had been banned from migrating out of the villages flocked to the cities seeking employment in the new factories. Although this movement was illegal, the government allowed it to occur because of the labour needs of the expanding export sector. It also avoided the extra expense of providing additional urban services by maintaining the locality registration system, which restricted access to education, health care, and a variety of subsidies that the state provided to urban-born residents. This "floating population" of 200 000 000 people now contributes the core unskilled labour force for China's labour-intensive manufacturing economy. In return it receives low wages, poor working and living conditions, and few services (see the Case Study on page 368). The government has started to make some improvement to this situation and has been relaxing the residential registration laws. However, it has counterbalanced this expansion by privatizing its publicly funded health care system.

The fate of China's rural-to-urban migrant is repeated in other parts of the world, where export-led industrialization has accompanied the movement of capital to low wage regions. In Malaysia, for example, rural peasant families send some of their children to work in electronics and other factories owned by transnational corporations, especially from Japan and Korea (Ong 1983). In Mexico, industrial investment has been concentrated in *maquiladoras* along the American border, to which rural migrants have flocked to take on low paying, unskilled jobs. Special exemptions free the transnational corporations that are located there from taxes, collective bargaining, and restrictions on environmental pollution (Fernandez-Kelly 1983).

REVIEW

Globalization has involved the rapid expansion of international trade and investment and the decline of the state's role in protecting national economies and providing services for its citizens. Export sectors have grown in many world regions and have often been based on attracting capital to low-wage regions. Some research suggests that this trend has led to the exploitation of workers in developing countries, the loss of manufacturing jobs in older industrialized regions, and greater inequalities in income and access to services.

MIGRATION

Temporary travel and permanent migration have been features of human life for millennia, but the last several centuries have witnessed an acceleration of these processes both in the numbers of people who leave their native countries and in the distances that they travel. For example, immigration to Canada has been expanding both in magnitude and in the number of countries from whom it is accepting new immigrants. In 2006, it received 250 000 new permanent residents. This influx accounted for almost 70 percent of the country's net population increase and an equal proportion of growth in the workforce. An additional 270 000 entered as temporary residents, including 60 000 students (Citizenship and Immigration Canada 2007). In addition to voluntary migrants, some people become refugees because of war and other turmoil. In 2005, for example, 1.9 million Afghan refugees were reported by seventy-two asylum countries, constituting 22 percent of the global refugee population. Pakistan, Iran, and Saudi Arabia were chief among the asylum countries for people fleeing the war in Afghanistan.

International migration has had a profound effect on people in both the countries of origin and of settlement. Poor countries lose citizens to wealthier countries with better job opportunities. While in

Calling the 800 number of your utility company or other service provider, you might reach someone in one of these cubicles in a business office in India or Malaysia. Outsourcing is another way that transnational corporations take advantage of less expensive foreign labour. Computer and communications technologies make it possible for service workers to be located anywhere in the world.

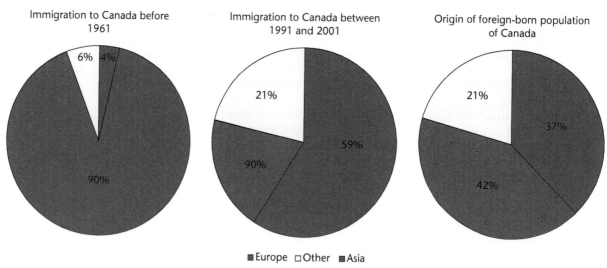

Immigration to Canada before 1961

Immigration to Canada between 1991 and 2001

Origin of foreign-born population of Canada

■Europe □Other ■Asia

Figure 14.1
Foreign-Born Population of Canada.

theory population loss might relieve economic burdens within a poor country, in practice many of the people who leave are among the better educated and more skilled; thus the possibilities of economic recovery are undermined in their home countries. Today's migrants often send a portion of their earnings back to their families, money that makes its way into the local and national economies. Still, the loss of people's skills, experience, and knowledge is more significant and has greater long-term effects than the loss of money alone.

Immigration has regularly played a major role in the dynamics of Canadian society. According to the 2006 census, foreign-born residents now make up 20 percent of the population and 50 percent of the inhabitants of the large "gateway" cities of Toronto and Vancouver. The composition of the immigrant community has changed over the last hundred years. Before 1960, 90 percent of immigrants came from Europe with a heavy emphasis on the United Kingdom (25 percent of all immigration) and other countries in Northern and Western Europe. Between 1991 and 2001, Asia provided Canada with 60 percent of its foreign-born residents, while only 20 percent migrated from Europe and the remaining 20 percent from other world regions (See Figure 14.1). While some consideration has been given to refugees and family members of Canadian residents, over half of all people immigrating within the last forty years have been admitted as economic immigrants who have been selected on the basis of education, skills, and capital resources that are expected to make a positive contribution to the Canadian economy.

In spite of the selective nature of Canadian immigration, many migrants experience problems of adjustment to their new society, particularly when they find themselves marginalized on the basis of racial, linguistic, religious, or cultural differences. Eventually, immigrants form "ethnic groups," based on markers of cultural identity, a process called ethnogenesis. Ethnic groups are also formed because of rejection from members of the dominant culture, creating "a generalized culture of ethnic inequality in which immigrants are perceived in stereotypical terms by the indigenous population, whatever their actual attributes, as a race apart, as primitives" (Worsley 1984:239).

REVIEW

Migration patterns include international or transnational migration to escape persecution, warfare, or poverty; rural-to-urban migration in developing countries; and labour migration to take advantage of new economic opportunities, as in Mexico's *maquiladora* system. Refugee and immigrant groups affect the communities or countries they leave, as well as the ones they join. Often they become tolerated but isolated ethnic minorities.

ETHNOGENESIS AND ETHNIC IDENTITIES

As we have discussed in Chapter 10, ethnic identity is context-bound but changeable, an adaptation to circumstances. Although we may think of an ethnic identity as a single, stable concept, in fact, people can have various identities, depending on the way they see themselves in relation to others. Ethnic groups are formed and transformed in response to interactions with other people. As with other social identities, ethnic labels are applied as conditions arise that favour their use. People may think of themselves as members of groups based on one set of criteria but may find themselves categorized as members of other groups based on others.

Group identity based on a political stance as well as an ethnic or tribal identity complicates social relations, even in comparatively homogeneous societies. An example is Papua New Guinea. Its colonial history began in the nineteenth century, when the British and the Germans divided between themselves the eastern portion of the island of New Guinea. (The western portion was formerly a Dutch colony, invaded and annexed by Indonesia in 1975.) At the end of World War I, the two colonial regions were united under Australian administration as Papua New Guinea, becoming an independent country in 1975. Although independence has led to some detribalization as the central government attempts to form a national identity, other factors led to **tribalization**, or the formation of tribal identities. One of the consequences of the competition for access to political power and economic benefits has been a resurgence of "tribal" warfare, especially in the highlands. Such warfare "has defined and redefined groups in such a way as to re-create, in part, an earlier tribal structure—a structure uncomfortably at odds with its own national government" (Strathern 1992:232).

Even though government agencies have attempted to quell the fighting, people's respect for state authority has declined. Instead, local businessmen vie for economic advantages and political power, very much in the traditional model of the Melanesian big-men. These men attract armed fighters who support them and are in return protected by them. The central government occasionally sends in police and military patrols to keep order, but they are largely unsuccessful in eliminating violence.

Transnationalism

Although migrants adjust to and adapt to their country of settlement, they all do not necessarily focus solely on developing their lives in their new environment; they also maintain emotional and cultural ties with their homeland. Because of increased ease of communication and travel, a new phenomenon of transnationalism is developing. **Transnationalism** is the constellation of "processes by which immigrants build social fields that link together their country of origin and their country of settlement, connecting them to two or more societies simultaneously" (Schiller et al., 1992:1–2). Transmigrants maintain complex social, economic, religious, and political ties linking them to their immigrant communities and to their communities back home.

Transnationalism is a phenomenon in which migrants create new sociocultural networks and identities for themselves that link their country of origin and their country of settlement. Transnationalism, while not new, has redeveloped in the context of the spread of global capitalism, which has shifted populations across borders.

tribalization
A process of identification with one's tribal origins.

transnationalism
Processes by which immigrants maintain social, economic, religious, and political ties to both their immigrant communities and their communities back home.

Pakistani Brahmin immigrants to the United Kingdom who may think of themselves as White and as superior to dark-skinned South Indians are shocked to find out that the British may think of them as "Black" or "Coloured," in the same category as immigrants from the West Indies (Worsley 1984). Similarly, class distinctions that may be relevant in an immigrant's own country may be overlooked by a system of ethnic or racial categorization in the new country that lumps people together on the basis of socially constructed concepts of race and ethnicity.

Case Study

Ethnic Identity in Sudan

In a study of Sudanese agricultural production, Jay O'Brien (1986) details the ways that ethnic identities were formed as different groups of people were incorporated into the work force. Their particular roles in production became linked to their ethnic identity. In the early 1900s, farmers and pastoralists began to work, at least seasonally, on plantations that produced cotton for export. These plantations were located in what came to be known as the Gezira Scheme, a large area of irrigated fields. As elsewhere in the British colonial empire, indigenous people had to pay taxes in cash, but their sources of obtaining money were limited because there were few markets for their subsistence crops, and home craft production was undermined by the importation of manufactured goods sold cheaply.

Sudanese farmers and pastoralists continued to maintain their traditional productive strategies but were available for seasonal work on the plantations when needed during the peak season. They received wages but remained marginal actors in the new economy. Then, as the plantation system expanded, workers from other countries were recruited, especially from Muslim Hausa communities in West Africa. These immigrants were landless and therefore readily available to serve as a pool of cheap wage labour. In addition, other groups of West African Muslims settled nearby and provided seasonal labour. They came from several different ethnic groups with distinct tribal names and spoke different languages, although many learned Hausa as a second language (O'Brien 1986:901).

Nearly as soon as the immigrants arrived, distinctions developed between them and the indigenous people with whom they worked. The immigrants came to be known as *Fellata,* a term with negative connotations that obliterated their own separate tribal distinctions. In response to their new cultural environment, the West Africans adopted some outward traits of their Sudanese neighbours, especially styles of dress and housing. But they also intensified some of their own cultural practices in an attempt to differentiate themselves from the Sudanese, especially emphasizing certain fundamentalist Islamic practices in contrast to the beliefs in spirit possession and trance found among Arabs in North Africa. They began to apply the word *Takari* to themselves, a respectful term signifying "pilgrims." Although they replaced a negative term (Fellata) with a positive one, they essentially accepted the view of themselves as members of an ethnic group different from their hosts. Thus, they participated in the formation of an ethnic identity, initially imposed on them but then taken up as part of their self-definition.

A third group, the Joama, also was incorporated into plantation production. The Joama of central Sudan became known as efficient and hardworking cotton pickers and were actively recruited to help in the harvest. They earned a high reputation and a relatively stable income. Gradually, some migrants from West Africa settled on the outskirts of Joama communities and were hired as seasonal cotton pickers as well. By their own hard work and commitment to the region, they came to refer to themselves and to be referred to as *Joama.* In so doing, they took on an ethnic identity that was theirs only by assertion and by lifestyle. It was an identity that they had to earn.

Transnationalism has developed in the context of the spread of global capitalism that has shifted capital and labour across borders. As capital investments flow from high-wage countries to low-wage regions, labour shifts take place in both developed and developing countries. A transnational identity based on transnational commitments is a sensible and appropriate response to economic vulnerability and possible

The internet features many transnational sites like this one, uniting people culturally whatever their citizenship status. This page for Indians abroad embraces all people with roots in India living anywhere in the world, including those who have become citizens of other countries. An estimated 700 000 Indians live in Canada alone. Transnational groups encourage people to develop social solidarity around a shared cultural identity, which the globalization of internet technologies encourages.

job displacement. In addition, transmigrants are important players in the creation of ethnic identities in their countries of settlement, forming connections among people who identify as a group on the basis of shared activities, values, beliefs, and goals (see the Case Study on page 374).

Nationalism and Pluralism

In addition to analyzing the ways that people create themselves as ethnic groups, anthropologists also look at the ways that ethnic groups are formed as structural features that support social, economic, and political systems. Ethnic groupings are especially significant in state societies composed of peoples of disparate origins and traditions. And they are "inherently political, shaped by and shaping the politics of 'us versus them' in political systems" (Ferguson and Whitehead 1992:15).

At the same time, states also generate nationalistic views of themselves as overriding ethnic differences in the formation of a national identity. Peter Worsley describes nationalism as a form of ethnicity that is the "institutionalization of one particular ethnic identity by attaching it to the State" (1984:247). Nationalism, though, is more than identifying with a state as a political institution. It is also an allegiance to the nation as a symbolic identity, as a people associated with a particular way of life and sets of values. As members of a state develop a national identity, they ignore their differences and concentrate on achieving commonly shared goals and interests. Nationalism also involves the process of selective memory and the construction of a fictive past as the past is formulated according to contemporary values and goals. As Worsley points out, "They project the values of the present onto a past which does not always sustain them" (p. 274).

States, according to Worsley, utilize various processes to resolve relationships between a central identity and disparate ethnic groups. A dominant ethnic group may assert itself as the only legitimate identity, equating the national culture with its own. A state may assert a uniformity of culture, subsuming and homogenizing differences. Finally, a

Case study

Two Transnational Communities in Canada

High rates of immigration have produced communities within Canada whose members maintain numerous and complex contacts with families, groups, and organizations in the regions from which they have migrated and with similar immigrant communities in other receiving countries. The nature of these contacts varies from maintaining ties with family and remitting money to support them, to utilizing international ethnic ties to organize business ventures, to lobbying for Canadian support for political movements in ethnic homelands. In this feature we will consider two different forms of transnational networks: the participation of Croatian Canadians in the Croatian independence movement and the organization of transnational business operations among Chinese Canadians.

CROATIAN NATIONALIST NETWORKS

Croatia is a recently formed country that was previously a region of Yugoslavia. Throughout the twentieth century, it was the source of several immigration streams, and Croatians living abroad in the diaspora are as numerous as those that remain in their homeland. They have been important to the formation of Croatia because of the financial, political, and moral support they have provided for the new country. Daphne Winland's ethnographic research on Croatian-Canadians in Toronto documents the importance of Croatian nationalism to their identity and social relationships within an ethnically focused transnational network as well as the contradictions and tensions that have occurred within it (2002).

Winland's research documented three streams of Croatian immigrants to Canada: a group who arrived at the turn of the twentieth century in response to the labour demands of Canada's growing industries; a group that arrived immediately after World War II as Croatia was being absorbed into Yugoslavia; and a group that arrived in the 1970s when Yugoslavia liberalized its emigration policy. Each stream had different orientations, and some tension developed between the older generation of labourers who were active in socialist movements and the later groups who had immigrated to escape communism. Further ambivalence revolved around the possible role of some of the World War II immigrants in the Nazi-supported regime in Croatia.

The formation of Croatia in 1992 and the attendant war between Croatians and Serbs led to more coherent action within the Croatian diaspora. Overseas communities were mobilized to send financial support and lobby their governments and international agencies to help settle the war, recognize Croatian independence, and provide development aid. The Croatian regime cultivated this support and gave recognition to expatriate communities. Ethnic Croatians living out of the country were given rights to vote for a block of seats set aside for them in the Croatian legislature. Several Croatian Canadians were elected as representatives and one served as a Minister of Defense. Through this process, a strong sense of ethnic nationalism and unity prevailed within both the homeland and the diaspora.

Winland's analysis of the mobilization of expatriate Croatians notes that, while diasporas are often viewed as translocal networks typical of a globalized world, the movement was actually focused on a specific locality, and place and landscape formed a critical element in how the participants expressed their attachment to their homeland. As such, the transnational distribution of the ethnic community and the utilization of global transportation and communications systems were activated to support a clearly nineteenth-century project, the creation of a nation state on the basis of ethnic homogeneity and exclusivity. However, nationalist harmony was soon challenged as independence brought economic and political problems that undermined the new government's credibility. Within the homeland, class and regional divisions encouraged the strengthening of subnational identities. Moreover, Croatians who had remained within the country became critical of those within the diaspora, who were viewed as expressing an antiquated and overzealous nationalism and who were more closely associated with the increasingly unpopular regime. Accordingly, transnational linkages were fragile and ethnic identity became a problematic issue.

CHINESE BUSINESS NETWORKS

China, Hong Kong, and Taiwan have collectively been responsible for the largest single volume of immigrants to Canada over the last twenty years, and the Chinese community in Canada numbers over one million people. Chinese Canadians, however, are quite diverse and represent several different language and cultural groups and have migrated for a variety of different reasons. The component we are considering for this case study comprises a special class of business immigrants who have been admitted to Canada on the basis of the standard point system, which assesses education and skills, and on their ability to invest enough capital to start a viable business, which may be as much as $500 000. Chinese business immigrants from Hong Kong and Taiwan have regularly constituted over 50 percent of this class and have invested billions of dollars in the Canadian economy. They are concentrated primarily in Toronto and Vancouver (Wong 1997).

A survey of 384 business-class Chinese immigrants in Vancouver revealed a detailed pattern of transnational contacts that articulated economic interests and family and ethnic relationships. The enterprises involved included retail, manufacturing, food service, import/export, and real estate and construction. The scale of businesses varied from small business operators who may have owned grocery stores and restaurants to heads of transnational enterprises. In many cases the nature of the business required economic, political, and social linkages back to the immigrants' home countries.

The business investment patterns of Chinese business class immigrants often involved the ownership of multiple operations. An individual might have one branch or independent firm located in Canada, another in his or her country of origin (usually Hong Kong or Taiwan), and another in mainland China or other area of Chinese settlement. Accordingly, over 37 percent of the sample surveyed spent over a month conducting business outside of Canada. Thirty percent spent over two months abroad. In some cases, this dispersed activity indicated an openness to more permanent relocation in another country to start a new operation or devote more time to an existing one.

In many cases, these plans involved allowing one or more family members to remain in Canada to maintain an ongoing presence in the country.

Business contacts and business travel were tied to dispersed family and ethnic ties. Extended family members and friends of Chinese origin were incorporated as business partners in approximately 25 percent of the businesses. Moreover, a large majority of employees were Chinese and constituted a secondary immigrant stream that followed the movement of Chinese investment.

The activities of Chinese business immigrants documented in the Vancouver study suggest an emergent pattern of translocalism that has developed in accord with the globalization of capital. Settlement in Canada is rooted in an investment system with multiple locations that may shift according to economic and political changes and involve transmigrants in multiple relocations of both short- and long-term duration. Accordingly, they become part of what Manuel Castels calls the "network society" in which space has become abstract and delocalized or, as he suggests, a "space of flows" (2000). Denizens of this territory belong to no single country but participate in an international community with its own conventions and ways of life. In the Chinese case, this network retains an ethnic and family base and connects and transfers participants from the major home territories of China, Taiwan, Hong Kong, and Singapore and in overseas Chinese communities throughout the world.

Croatian and Chinese transnationalism both incorporate an emphasis on ethnicity, one of several ways that global networks are formed and expressed. However, ethnicity plays a different role in each case. For the Croatian diaspora it is related to the formation of a localized nation state that takes its definition on a premise of a unitary national culture. The Chinese system is truly delocalized, both economically and ethnically across a variety of investment centres and Chinese polities and communities. Ethnicity plays a critical role in facilitating business relations through establishing a framework of shared business values and practices and a community of trust.

state may maintain a pluralistic attitude toward cultural differences, allowing secondary identities to coexist along with a national one (p. 252).

A state's strategies may change over time. A state often chooses a dominant identity as it embarks on consolidation and expansion, exerting control over its constituent populations. An emphasis on uniformity then becomes prominent as states become secure and attempt to eliminate ethnic boundaries. Recognition of cultural pluralism often emerges with the formation of ethnically diverse nation-states as older colonial empires crumble. The rise of ethnic pluralism, therefore, was often a product of decolonization, giving legitimacy to the strivings of disparate groups within a country for recognition and some degree of social and political autonomy. As in the past, however, newly independent states vary in the approaches that they take to ethnic diversity.

Culture Change

IMPACTS OF INDONESIAN STATE EXPANSION

Indonesia is an instructive example of a central government's attempts to create a national identity that privileges one ethnic group, the Javanese, as the national norm (Perry 1996). Javanese cultural traditions are exported to members of other groups through formal education, the media, and public discourse. Following a process of **Islamization**, the religion of Islam is imposed on others, either obliterating or subsuming local beliefs. A national language called Indonesian (based on a dialect of Malay) is taught throughout the country and used in all public contexts. The Indonesian government has embarked on an aggressive policy of creating and imposing cultural uniformity while giving some recognition to ethnic diversity.

However, for Indonesia, as Bernard Nietschmann (1988) puts it, "nation-building" sometimes is state expansion by "nation-destroying." Authorities developed a program of forced internal migration, sending Javanese people to outlying regions originally inhabited by various tribal groups who, in turn, were forcibly evicted from their homelands and sent to live elsewhere. It is a program of intense, directed culture change in the service of national unity. But it is also an attempt to wrest lands rich in resources from indigenous peoples. The resources can then be exploited by transnational corporations allied with the state government. The Indonesian policy is also aimed at dissipating indigenous resistance movements that were

organized for local autonomy and independence. The army is often deployed to indigenous territories, ostensibly to fight terrorism and militant insurgencies.

Just one year after Indonesia gained its independence from the Netherlands (after a war of independence against allied forces following Japanese occupation during World War II), the central government embarked on policies of state expansion by invading and annexing independent islands. In 1950, the army took over South Moluccas, followed in 1962 by the annexation of West Papua (renamed Irian Jaya), and in 1975 by the invasion of East Timor. West Papua is a rich prize because it now comprises about 22 percent of the total landmass of Indonesia but has only 1 percent of the country's total population (Ballard 2002:40). (The eastern half of the island is the independent country of Papua New Guinea.)

In West Papua, the Indonesian government implemented its program of transmigration to "redistribute overpopulation" by importing five million people from Java (Nietschmann, 1988). In the process, indigenous peoples were displaced and their lands and resources were appropriated to accelerate economic development and national unity. The region is especially rich in timber, various minerals, and offshore reserves of oil. The Indonesian program was financed in part by the World Bank, the United Nations, the Islamic Development Bank, and several countries, including the United States, Germany, France, and the Netherlands. The government also established "assimilation camps" in which cultural minorities were taught the official national Indonesian language and the Muslim religion. These were also called "centres for social development" with the aim of "cultivating national pride and defending the state." People who resisted the imposition of Indonesian political control and cultural hegemony were branded "terrorists," justifying military action against them.

The eastern half of the island of Timor became a battleground where the struggles of the indigenous East Timorese erupted in violence after decades of clandestine resistance. The Indonesian government had forced many East Timorese from their homes, transporting them to Sumatra and other majority Javanese islands while at the same time importing Javanese to East Timor. An estimated 200 000 East Timorese (about one-third of the population) were killed between 1975 and 1990 (Perry 1996:204). But in 1991, the East Timorese resistance movement became a more public armed struggle after the Indonesian military attacked a peaceful funeral procession. For more than two decades after 1975, when the Indonesian army invaded and unilaterally annexed East Timor, the international community (including the influential governments of the United States and Australia) ignored the situation. In the 1990s, world public opinion shifted to support independence for East Timor.

Reactions against Pluralism

In many Western countries, ethnic identities have become significant vehicles for the development, channelling, and recruitment of individuals for social and political action. This rise in cultural identities is coincident with large increases in immigration throughout the twentieth century. Perhaps the worldwide movement toward decolonization since the end of World War II is a contributing factor because it champions political and cultural independence and autonomy.

In addition, large numbers of people immigrating from the same country or region are more likely to maintain ties among themselves. These bonds can create cohesion and solidarity that can be used to achieve social and political goals. They also allow immigrants to resist social and political pressures toward assimilation. For instance, the influx into the United States of people from Central and South America since the 1970s has led to the development of a strong power base wielding political influence both regionally and nationally. In Europe, the rise in immigration from the Caribbean, Africa, and South Asia has brought to the foreground issues of nationality and national identity. For example, the multiracial and multicultural makeup of the populations of the United Kingdom or France must redefine what it means to be "British" or "French."

Cultural pluralism is usually tolerated as long as members of disparate ethnic groups do not attempt to build political power blocs. But at the same time as the complexion

Islamization
The process of imposing the Islamic religion and associated cultural values within a nation to foster cultural uniformity.

On May 20, 2002, these East Timorese celebrated their independence after twenty-four years of Indonesian rule and centuries of Portuguese colonization. Their determination to obtain their independence set an example for others, such as the native peoples of Irian Jaya (West Papua New Guinea), which recently won from Indonesia economic benefits due them from the utilization of their timber, minerals, and oil (Ballard 2002:42).

Controversies

Has Canada's Policy of Multiculturalism Simultaneously Contributed to National Unity and Respect for Cultural Diversity?

In 1971, Canada adopted a multiculturalism policy, which was later given greater emphasis and definition by the *Charter of Rights and Freedoms* of 1982 and the *Multiculturalism Act* of 1988. The Act replaces previous assimilationist policies with an acceptance of cultural pluralism as part of a broad set of changes that purport to create a more open society and extend cultural as well as political rights to marginalized groups such as French Canadians, immigrants, Aboriginal Canadians, and other minorities. It annunciates a need "to recognize and promote . . . multiculturalism . . . [as] a fundamental characteristic of the Canadian heritage and identity," and sets up a bureaucracy and funding base to achieve this goal. In many of its pronouncements, it affirms the basic anthropological endorsement of cultural relativity, maintaining that no culture, including an historically dominant Anglo-Canadian one, should be considered superior to any other and that people should accept and value cultural difference.

Reactions to the ideology and implementation of Canadian multiculturalism have been mixed. Its adherents have been beset from two opposed camps. On one hand, the political right has reiterated an assimilationist position, which fears that the celebration of diversity will lead to disunity and conflict. This position has recently been given new life in a publication by the well known social theorist Robert Putnam, whose research has concluded that increasing ethnic diversity in the United States has led to a weakening of community (2007). On the other hand, left-leaning academics have seen the policy as a ruse designed to give lip service to embracing cultural difference, while continuing a program of excluding minorities and denying them basic rights and opportunities.

Eva Mackey, an anthropologist at McMaster University has carried out a detailed study of Canada's multicultural policies based on her analysis of government documents and fieldwork on summer festivals in small towns surrounding Toronto. She maintains that multiculturalism emerged as part of a project to create and affirm a clear Canadian identity. As such, the celebration of diversity has paradoxically supported a nationalist agenda that affirms a unitary value system based on British traditions. She argues that multiculturalism presupposes a dualistic opposition between a core Canadian value system and those of other cultures. In the process a sense of "Canadianness" becomes defined in terms of a contrast with an "ethnic other," that is, the multicultural community. In the process, cultural values of ethnic groups are understood to be diverse and arbitrary while Canadian culture becomes understood as incorporating core values that are thought to be natural and self-evident, or "just plain Canadian."

(both literally and figuratively) of North American and European countries is changing, internal political movements opposing immigration have strengthened. Members of some anti-immigration movements claim that immigrants threaten national unity because they do not share prevailing heritage, values, and attitudes. These claims are based on a view of a nation that has been mythologized and manipulated for political purposes. In addition, a rise of xenophobic sentiments—the fear and hatred of outgroups—is stimulated by economic shifts and the perceived downward mobility of members of the middle and lower classes who then blame their misfortunes on the newcomers. Thus, xenophobia and anti-immigration movements are two common reactions to cultural pluralism. (See the Controversies feature for a discussion of multiculturalism and nationalism in Canada.)

Malaysia, Singapore, and Indonesia are examples of countries with complex histories that in post-colonial times have led to the establishment of multicultural societies (Hefner 2001). Prior to the European presence in Southeast Asia, these countries had a long history of maritime trade that brought in people from elsewhere, particularly from China and India. Ethnic differences were recognized, but people cooperated in

Ethnic others must conform to these central and dominant principles but are allowed and encouraged to promote superficial and disconnected cultural elements, such as food and dance, as long as they involve no demands for economic or political change. Mackey concludes from her analysis that the "mosaic" model of difference in Canada is misleading. Cultural diversity becomes integrated within a unitary pattern where the dominant culture both opposes and defines a group of marginalized cultures.

Mackey also suggests that politicians have manipulated the dynamic integration of core and marginal cultures to enhance national identity and unity and to facilitate government control over the population. It allows the state to manage and incorporate ethnic communities through its ability to define the nature of ethnicity and incorporate ethnic leaders into patronage networks. It also allows for the appropriation of ethnic culture to add to the repertoire of national symbols. Finally, it provides another focal point for distinguishing Canada from the United States, which is negatively portrayed as pursuing a "melting pot" (assimilationist) rather than a multicultural policy and becomes a second "other" against which Canadian identity is perceived as distinct.

In spite of criticism from both ends of the political spectrum, some academics support the continuation and evolution of Canadian multiculturalism. David Ley maintains that over time the policy has shifted away from supporting expressive culture to minority rights and welfare (2007). He notes that, in contrast to the American assimilationist model, Canadian multicultural policy has resulted in better support for immigrants. For example, multicultural programs have led to a higher level of citizenship and enfranchisement. While naturalization rates among immigrants in the two countries were similar at the start of the 1970s, they have since risen to 70 percent in Canada and fallen to 35 percent in the United States. He also claims that respect for ethnic difference has mediated a potentially divisive situation in the relationship between Asian- and Anglo-Canadian residents in Vancouver. At the beginning of the 1990s, Asian immigrants who had established successful businesses began to purchase older homes on well-treed lots and tear down existing structures and vegetation to construct what have been called "monster homes." The old line Anglo-Canadian families objected to a change in the character of the neighbourhood and began to petition the city to restrict new construction. A series of hearings were held in which both sides represented their positions. An eventual compromise was reached which allowed new construction as long as the houses didn't exceed a fixed size and trees on the lot were allowed to stand. Ley believes that this model of compromise and accommodation will continue to ensure that different groups and values systems can coexist.

CRITICAL THINKING QUESTIONS

With which of the three positions articulated above do you agree? Do you think that Canada is following a sensible multicultural program or should it be doing more, or less, to support ethnic diversity?

Do you think that in pursuit of a truly multicultural society we should legalize practices such as polygyny, clitorectemy, or sharia (Islamic) law that appear to contradict Canadian core values?

What light does a consideration of cultural politics surrounding multiculturalism and the debates that it has raised shed on the culture concept as discussed in Chapter 1?

the formation of pluralistic societies. However, the Dutch and the British treated the inhabitants as segregated groups in order to assert control and foster competition for access to influence and rewards. When the countries became independent in the mid-twentieth century, their constituent ethnic groups then vied for control of the newly emerging states. Competition for the benefits of economic development programs contributed to inter-group tensions.

Ancestors of these nomadic Rom "Gypsies" originated in northern India in the Punjab and were victims of xenophobia in every country they entered on their long-distance treks. Slated for extermination by the Nazis, the Rom survived their dispersal throughout Europe and North America, where they continue to face xenophobic reaction and social isolation.

In Malaysia and Indonesia, social and political distinctions were maintained between indigenous peoples and the ethnic Chinese descended from merchants who prospered from trade even before European colonial powers came to dominate the region. However, treatment of the Chinese differs in Malaysia and Indonesia. In Malaysia, the Chinese have been permitted to send their children to Chinese-language schools if they wish and to maintain their culture. Still, Malaysian political parties are organized along ethnic lines, and although pluralism is part of the social and political fabric of society, ethnic Malays have ascendancy over people of Chinese, Indian, and other origin. Also, while religious differences are protected, Islam is the state religion of Malaysia. In Indonesia, however, the Chinese have faced discrimination despite official statements of ethnic inclusion and pluralism. Cultural and religious distinctions are used to promote Javanese interests and claims to power over those of the Chinese and other groups.

Anthropologists and other social scientists have been studying the global marketplace as a kind of borderless society. The shared beliefs, values, expectations, and behaviours of members of this society constitute a global culture. This culture has emerged as a result of rapid changes in technology and the political and economic process known as globalization. Researchers seek to make sense of what may be called a global culture of consumerism.

Globalization and Cultural Identities

Globalization is popularly thought of as an economic and cultural process that spreads wealth and investment throughout the world. But, as in the past, wealth and investment are concentrated regionally and in the hands of elites. Today much of the world's wealth comes from Europe and the United States, but investment increasingly goes elsewhere, such as Asia and the Pacific Rim.

These economic shifts have contributed to what some theorists see as the re-creation of an international or **global identity** based on social class. In North America and Europe, regions that Jonathan Friedman (1999) calls "declining hegemonies," members of elite classes have a global identity that links them to elites in other countries on the basis of class. Characteristics include sharing privileges, interests, leisure activities, locations, and tastes. This global identity is different from the global popular culture in which the world's middle classes increasingly participate, in which they eat food from McDonald's, watch the same movies, listen to the same music, discuss the same topics on the internet, and buy the same books and other consumer goods.

A global identity has developed as middle and lower classes have tended to fragment along ethnic lines, with groups asserting their own interests. In addition, the power of the state to "manufacture consent" (to use the term from Herman and Chomsky [1988]) and to create and transmit a national identity tends to decline as the nation's economic and political elites focus their activities elsewhere. At the same time, immigrants tend to remain identified with their countries of origin or with emigrants residing in other countries. Thus, some theorists see both a rise in ethnic pluralism and an increasing gap between the classes as major factors in the process of globalization and the invention of a global identity.

The mass media contribute to, and reflect, a growing global identity. People throughout the world watch many of the same movies and television programs, listen to much of the same music, and read the same magazines translated into dozens of languages. These sources of information and entertainment disseminate people's activities, attitudes, and tastes, contributing to shared experiences and frames of reference. Although there are and will continue to be local variations, the media provide outlets for creating global identities. The internet also is a powerful and increasingly utilized forum through which people in many countries can communicate, learn from each other, and share ideas. The global spread of the English language, now the most common second language of the world, helps facilitate this exchange. An estimated 75 percent of all mail and 80 percent of computer data sent worldwide are written in English (Baron 1990).

global identity
An identity of shared interests, practices, and values across international borders, uniting people worldwide.

REVIEW

Ethnogenesis involves a group's creation of a new ethnic identity through both self-definition and definition by other groups in the society. Proliferating identities can stimulate conflict in new nations, sometimes leading to tribalization rather than national unity. In transnationalism, however, groups identify across nationalities, based on their shared country or culture of origin. Nationalism calls for minimizing differences between groups to achieve national rather than group unity and loyalty. In pluralistic or culturally diverse societies, ethnic minorities may become marginalized or forced to conform to majority culture, as in the Islamization of Indonesia. Ethnic minorities, like immigrant groups, are also often victims of xenophobic reactions against out-groups or outsiders, and conflicts between groups based on their cultural identities can lead to genocide. Some theorists suggest that in this post-colonial era, a global identity is developing, based on social class.

CULTURE MINORITIES AND INDIGENOUS PEOPLES IN A GLOBAL WORLD

The mid- and late twentieth century saw a revitalization of indigenous communities in many countries and a new energy and focus in their struggles for self-determination. An estimated half of the world's conflicts are now fought over lands and resources of foragers, horticulturalists, and pastoralists (Nietschmann 1988). The term *indigenous* refers to comparatively homogeneous peoples or small-scale societies who share the same culture and are "native" to their territory or have occupied it for a long time. Defining who is indigenous is a complex matter, however, and depends also on historical and cultural contexts. In countries with a history as a settler colony (the United States, Canada, Australia, New Zealand, Mexico, and all the countries of modern Central and South America), the term *indigenous* refers to the peoples who lived in these regions prior to the arrival of Europeans, beginning in the late fifteenth century. In these countries, descendants of the original settlers and later immigrants now dominate. The following sections survey the state of indigenous peoples in the Americas.

? *Are you or any of your friends members of cultural minorities or indigenous peoples?*

United States and Canada

Both countries have a similar history of conquest and colonization of the Aboriginal peoples. Indigenous peoples were evicted from their lands and settled on reserves (reservations in the United States) that occupied small, scattered patches of territory, usually in isolated regions. These communities were placed under federal jurisdiction under the control of a government bureaucracy, The Department of Indian and Northern Affairs in Canada and the Bureau of Indian Affairs in the United States. Under special legislative acts, such as the Canadian *Indian Act*, they were held as wards of the state. These provisions allowed them some rights, such as freedom from taxation, but denied them others, such as political representation and local self-government. Further arrangements to forfeit territory and agree to federal jurisdiction were framed according to treaties. Government policies towards Aboriginal communities were based on assimilation, which was forcefully instituted through illegalization of indigenous cultural practices and residential schools in both countries. During the 1960s the United States and Canada began to move towards a more liberal policy of settling land claims to provide the reserves with more territory and to institute systems of self-government that would provide communities with greater control over their own policies and services. Each country has implemented this process in a different way.

In 1975, the United States Congress passed the *Indian Self-Determination and Education Act*, establishing principles of self-government for native reservations. Indian tribes have used these principles to broaden their claims of sovereignty and to extend tribal jurisdiction in planning and implementing educational, medical, and social services, as well as to gain control over their territories, economic development plans, and tax immunity.

In the state of Hawaii, some Native Hawaiians are asking for recognition of their claims to ancestral territories and their desire to have a legal status somewhat comparable to that of Native Americans living in the other forty-nine states. In 1978, the state created an Office of Hawaiian Affairs with responsibility for administering 1.8 million acres of royal land held in trust for Native Hawaiians. This land was exempt from annexation when Hawaii became a state. The office collects revenues generated by the natural resources, minerals, and use of these lands for the benefit of Native Hawaiians. It also formulates policies regarding social, economic, and health services applicable to native people.

In Canada, the *Constitution Act* of 1982 included a short section that affirmed the aboriginal rights of the country's indigenous peoples. Subsequently, both the federal and provincial governments concluded government-to-government agreements with native reserves covering and expanding indigenous control over health, education, and social services, as well as economic development. In 1995, the Department of Indian and Northern Affairs issued a policy statement on Aboriginal self-government to initiate a process of freeing local bands from the provisions of the *Indian Act* and giving them autonomous powers equivalent to those of other local governments. To date, only a small percentage of the six hundred reserves in the country have negotiated final agreements. The agreements retain the fragmented band structure that was set up when the reserves were originally established. However, many are linked to land settlements that provide the bands with additional territory or compensation funds or both. They uniformly contain clauses that bind bands to provisions of federal and provincial law.

Land claims and resource rights have been the most significant issue in negotiations between Aboriginal communities and the Canadian government. Beginning with the Calder decision in 1973, landmark cases have returned some land or compensation to a number of reserves and a large number of cases are still pending. The most comprehensive land claims have been awarded to Inuit communities in Nunavut, the largest of which was signed in 1993 and awarded over 350 000 square kilometres of territory. Other notable awards have included the Nisgaa treaty. Signed in 2000, it gives the Nisgaa control over 8 percent of the territory that they originally inhabited and recognizes Nisgaa self-government. Resource rights cases have been fought over whether Aboriginal peoples have a right to fish, hunt, or extract lumber and other valuable resources on their territories or on crown land without licenses and to sell their harvests. The most important has been the Marshall decision in 1999. In this case, the Supreme Court ruled that Donald Marshall's right to fish for eel on a commercial basis was guaranteed under Miqmak treaty rights in Nova Scotia.

While progress has been made on restoring Aboriginal resource, political, and cultural rights, many problems remain to be solved. The pace at which settlements have been made has been exceedingly slow. For example the Delgamuukw case, which we discussed in Chapter 2, was first heard in the 1980s and dragged on for ten years before the Supreme Court made a ruling. Moreover, the Court's decision was to turn the case back to the provincial court with the provision that it had to accept oral tradition as evidence of indigenous rights. The case has not been heard, and the Gitksan claim in question is still outstanding as are over fifty other land claims cases in British Columbia. Even after cases have been concluded, governments have been slow to honour them or to implement new practices. As a consequence, Aboriginal groups often claim that Ottawa and the provinces are implicitly refusing to honour their commitments. In many instances, frustration over the lack of significant response to Aboriginal concerns has lead to more militant action. Beginning with the Oka incident (see the Case Study on page 383), First Nations communities have on occasion blockaded roads or railway lines to put pressure on the settlement of outstanding claims. While confrontation may be deplorable, it has sometimes led to quicker and more concrete results than pursuing claims through formal bureaucratic channels.

Mexico and *Indigenismo*

The Mexican government, like several in South America, has vacillated in its policies toward indigenous peoples throughout its history since independence from Spain

Mohawk Revival and Resistance

Many indigenous peoples have suffered a common fate in the wake of European colonial expansion over the past five hundred years. They have been subject to the rule of a foreign power to which they have lost some or all of their autonomy. Such empires as the Aztecs and Inca were completely destroyed and their traditions lost. In other cases, such as the Buganda, Rwanda, and Ashanti kingdoms, the colonizing power retained their structures and personnel for purposes of local administration. In Canada, Aboriginal government models have followed the same assimilationist emphasis that has been applied to other aspects of indigenous culture. The federal government, through the *Indian Act* and the offices of the Department of Indian Affairs, pursued a policy of setting aside all traditional forms of government and administering Aboriginal communities on a reserve-by-reserve basis. It imposed a uniform model of local government based on Western practice. However, unlike other Canadian municipalities, the band councils established on the reserves have had only limited powers and have been subject to the direct review and control of the federal bureaucracy. In this feature, we look at the experience of Mohawk communities and the ways in which their political structures and processes have changed over time.

COLONIAL HEGEMONY

The establishment of British and Canadian rule over Mohawk land and people occurred over four centuries and culminated in the passage of the *Indian Act* and the establishment of the band council system. Colonization involved changes for the Mohawk on many fronts, including drastic population decline, land and resource loss, the ceding of autonomy, internecine strife, conversion to Christianity, and the disappearance of many cultural traditions and practices.

Changes in land ownership and tenure had a particularly significant effect on Mohawk society and culture. The loss of territory reduced the resource base on which indigenous communities depended. Moreover, Westernization involved the transformation of ownership from collective to private forms. This change weakened the clan and matrilineal family system on which the political structure was based and created wealth differences among Mohawks.

A final and decisive blow to indigenous institutions was introduced at the end of the nineteenth century with the passage of the *Indian Act,* under which the Canadian government instituted a standardized system of Aboriginal local government. Its provisions took away recognition of hereditary Mohawk chiefs and

During the 1992 Oka crisis Mohawk warriors and their supporters set up barricades to block the building of a golf course on lands which they claimed as theirs. A seventy-eight day standoff resulted.

those of other nations within the different levels of the Iroquois Confederacy (see Chapter 11) and set up standardized, elected band councils with substantially reduced powers and direct responsibility to the Department of Indian Affairs though the local Indian agent. While put forward as an attempt to improve Aboriginal government, federal policies applied direct coercion to take away the resources and sovereignty of local communities and encouraged the abandonment of institutions that had given meaning to life. It also dismantled a political order that had once united communities into powerful alliances, replacing it with a fragmented system of small local governments that could garner little power to oppose colonial policies and projects.

RESISTANCE AND REVIVAL

The implementation of the band council system met with immediate resistance within Mohawk communities. In Kahnawake, an important Mohawk settlement near Montreal, the community became divided between wealthy landowners who supported the elected council system and those who had little or no land, who wanted to retain the traditional chiefs. Each party sent petitions to Ottawa to argue for their position. However, once the system was established, the traditionalists participated in council elections and at times were able to place people sympathetic to their cause in power. This expression of popular will caused alarm within the federal bureaucracy, and the Superintendent General of Indian Affairs vetoed many of the bylaws that the more militant members of the band council attempted to enact. The council responded by attempting to have the federal parliament amend the Indian Act to grant local autonomy to Aboriginal governments. Relevant legislation was proposed before the House of Commons but was defeated (Reid 2004).

Further factional struggles, petitions to Ottawa, and land claims suits within the courts marked Mohawk political activity during the early years of the twentieth century. After World War I, frustration with Ottawa's refusal to accommodate Aboriginal interests and demands led to a widespread movement to end the council system and reinstitute the "old rules" of selecting hereditary life chiefs and to restore the Iroquois Confederacy. Mohawk traditionalists began to form longhouse groups that attempted to reintroduce indigenous religious and political practices. Chiefs were elected according to system of clan representation and formed parallel councils to the band governments, dividing the community into supporters and opponents of the *Indian Act* structure. The Grand Council of the Iroquois, located on the Six Nations Reserve in Ontario, was reconstituted.

The longhouse movements and the Grand Council took up the fight to pressure Ottawa to allow the re-establishment of indigenous political forms and to grant autonomy to Aboriginal governments, not only at the band level, but also to the larger Confederacy. Their argument for the more comprehensive proposal was that the Iroquois had been allies of the British and had never been conquered or ceded land or sovereignty to Canada or the United States. Consequently, the Confederacy remained an independent nation that had been illegally occupied. As such, it should be allowed to reoccupy seized lands, re-amalgamate with American Iroquois groups, and be recognized as a nation that would communicate with Canada through an ambassadorial delegation on the same terms as any other foreign power. This theme has been consistently reaffirmed until the present and has been the basis for both legal suits and acts of civil disobedience geared towards reclaiming land and asserting Aboriginal rights. It has led to confrontations with the government and with neighbouring communities and to divisions over objectives and strategies within Mohawk communities themselves. The split between band council supporters and longhouse groups has been further compounded by divisions within longhouses

between those who have adopted a policy of peaceful resistance and the Warrior Movement, which advocates more radical action.

Mohawk activism was prominently highlighted during the Oka crisis of 1990, one of Canada's most serious incidents of civil unrest. Members of the Kahnesetake Mohawk community attempted to block the expansion of a golf course into lands to which it claimed title and which it had used as a burial ground. Originally a blockade was set up on the road to the contested site. When the Quebec police arrived to disperse the protestors, they were met by resistance from armed Warriors. The standoff spanned seventy-eight days, in the course of which hundreds of federal army troops were called in to face a growing body of protestors as Warriors from other Mohawk reserves and from other parts of Canada, as well as more moderate Mohawks, joined their ranks. Volleys of gunfire were exchanged and a police officer was killed. In the wake of the incident, the federal government purchased the contested land and gave it to the Kahnesetake band. Further attempts to meet Mohawk demands have involved additional land concessions and movement towards more autonomous band councils. However, the broader issues of major land and resource concessions to impoverished communities, rights to set up tax free or gambling outlets on reserves, and recognition of a sovereign Mohawk or Iroquois nation remain contested (York and Pindera 1991).

CRITICAL THINKING QUESTIONS

With due regard to the principles of cultural relativism, answer the following questions.

Do you think that land and other resource rights should be granted to Aboriginal groups on the basis of occupation prior to European settlement?

Should provisions of self government for reserves allow for the reinstitution of indigenous forms of government, such as clan based hereditary chieftaincies? If so, what provisions should be made for residents who have opted for assimilation and wish to develop their communities by working through the current system of Aboriginal administration?

Should the Iroquois Confederacy be granted the status of an independent nation controlling all or some of the territory it traditionally occupied in Quebec, Ontario, and New York State?

in 1821. Some indigenous peoples have had recognized rights to land that they held communally, but at other times these rights have been ignored and the state has appropriated Indian land. The constitution of 1993 acknowledged the rights of indigenous peoples in a policy known as *indigenismo* that guarantees protection of native customs. However, the actual living conditions of native peoples have not improved, particularly in the southernmost state of Chiapas with its majority Maya population. There, some Indians maintain their traditional land-use patterns, holding their land communally in *ejidos*. Others have been forced off their land by intruding settlers and transnational companies. Some have retreated farther into the highlands, where they have cleared new farmland, many growing coffee for sale and export.

In the early 1990s, the Mexican government embarked on policies to exploit its vast oil deposits. As an adjunct to this strategy, the government abandoned its stated intentions to grant additional Indian groups the right to their communal *ejidos*. The government also eliminated price supports to small farmers, another policy that harmed the Maya farmers of Chiapas, and allowed wealthy ranchers to expand their holdings, buying up the land of poor farmers. In addition, public projects to develop and generate electricity from hydropower led to the flooding of Indian lands. Finally, the Mexican government has begun to develop biodiversity projects, concluding agreements with pharmaceutical companies for the exploitation of forests and plants for research into the manufacture of drugs. As a result of these policies, the Maya

In March 2001, the Zapatista high command was honoured in Mexico City, where they were lobbying to implement the San Andreas peace accords. In April 2004, Mexican militias took action against Zapatistas protesting lack of access to water in Zinacantan, a continuation of decades of conflict. Zapatistas have gained international support for their struggle. Their ultimate goal is to gain autonomy in their region, where they constitute a majority of the population.

often become landless wage workers, but their wages are so low that they need to maintain links to strong family networks in traditional communities in order to survive (Barreda and Cecena 1998).

The Maya suffer discrimination because they have become a cultural minority within their traditional territories. They are outnumbered by Ladino settlers whose incomes and levels of education far exceed those of the Maya. The Ladinos—an ethnic term for Mexicans with an appearance, language, and identity that are more Spanish than Indian—feel justified in their negative attitudes toward the Maya, because the Indians are poor and lack the education or job skills that would suit them for the modern sector. But the Indians' poverty is a result, not a cause, of their marginalization.

The issue of indigenous rights in Mexico became nationally and internationally visible because of the efforts of a group of Mayas in Chiapas to mobilize for their collective rights in land and resources. Their organization, called the Zapatista Army for National Liberation (named after the Mexican revolutionary leader Emiliano Zapata), burst upon the world scene on January 1, 1994, when they took up arms against the Mexican military, a move that was timed to coincide with the implementation of the North American Free Trade Agreement, or NAFTA, signed by the United States, Canada, and Mexico.

The Zapatistas have been particularly effective in utilizing sophisticated communication technologies, especially the internet, to publicize their movement and to forge alliances with other indigenous and marginalized groups striving for social, economic, and political justice. They have also used these communication channels to gain international support.

Brazil and the "Indian Problem"

Due to the establishment of plantations by the Portuguese in the seventeenth century, the immigration of many Portuguese and Spanish settlers, and the importation of millions of African slaves, the indigenous population of Brazil is relatively small, currently about 300 000 people, only 0.2 percent of the total population. Estimates of the number of inhabitants in 1500 range from one million to six million, but while enormous population losses occurred in the early centuries of European colonization, about one hundred indigenous nations disappeared in the first seventy years of the twentieth century (Ribeiro 1971). Most remaining Indian communities are located in isolated regions in the Amazon. They are generally small settlements, each consisting of a few hundred residents.

Brazil's "Operation Amazonia" was a direct response to the global economy and the globalization of industries that exploit natural resources. To encourage economic development, this government program granted tax credits to foreign companies and exempted them from paying import or export duties.

Brazil's policies toward its indigenous peoples have wavered between protecting Indian lands and cultures and allowing intrusions into Indian territories by ranchers, settlers, and transnational corporations exploiting their resources. Earlier in the twentieth century, the Brazilian government established a federal Indian agency to protect Indian rights to maintain their lands and their cultures. The agency was to be guided by the motto of "Die if need be, but never kill" (quoted in Maybury-Lewis 1997:22). But in the 1960s, the government changed course and instituted aggressive efforts to develop remote regions. Settlers and ranchers took this as permission to go into indigenous territories and either push out or kill the residents. Although the government did not officially condone their actions, it did little to stop them. In fact, it permitted cattle ranchers in particular to invade the region in large numbers and clear the forests for their herds.

Operation Amazonia. In a program called Operation Amazonia, the Brazilian government granted tax credits and exempted companies from paying import or export duties. By 1980, more than $1 billion had been invested in cattle ranching in the Brazilian Amazon (Schmink 1988:168). Forest timber and minerals, especially tin, copper, uranium, iron, gold, and diamonds, have been found in rich deposits as well. Brazil and the other countries that share the Amazon have recently attracted investment in biodiversity projects; of the estimated 500 000 species of plants currently existing in the world, about 16 percent (35 000 to 50 000 species) are located in the Amazon (Tyler 1996:7).

In order to develop these resources, the Brazilian government has set aside some fourteen "extractive reserves," together containing more than three million hectares of land. These reserves are defined as "forest areas inhabited by extractive populations granted long-term usufruct rights to forest resources which they collectively manage" (Elisabetsky 1996:403). The term *extractive populations* refers to rubber tappers, miners, timber workers, and settlers, but the territories set aside are often also claimed by indigenous peoples, groups whose use of the land is not protected. Instead of protecting Indians' interests in their resources, officials drew up policies aimed at "civilizing" them, attempting to solve the "Indian problem" through assimilation, with the hope of eventually phasing out the government's national Indian Service that oversees Indian land.

However, despite the efforts of the Brazilian government to assimilate Indian nations, from time to time formerly unknown communities of indigenous peoples are "discovered." About five years ago, a group known as the Korubu was found deep in the Amazonian region of northwestern Brazil, near the borders with Colombia and Peru. Brazilian officials have documented at least fifty sites of Indian habitation that were previously unknown (Schemo 1999). When new groups are found, authorities working for the National Foundation for the Indian (FUNAI) attempt to have further contact by placing tools, utensils, and clothing in forest clearings. This is done with the assumption that the Indians will continue to return to the clearings to obtain more goods and can eventually be convinced to leave the region or settle in supervised communities. Lands claimed by indigenous peoples can then be opened for development of their timber, mineral, and pharmaceutical resources.

Guarani Indians in Paraguay and Brazil today focus on establishing strong communities based on village life. This Guarani Indian family rides a horse-drawn cart on one of the ranches they "repossessed," claiming it as ancestral land.

Yanomami at Risk. Because of pressure exerted on the Brazilian government by indigenous peoples and their advocates, a number of reservations have been

Anthropology Applied

FUNAI Anthropologists

Anthropologists work both for the Brazilian government and for indigenous communities in efforts to protect or extend Indian rights while at the same time furthering government policies and national goals—a balancing act that often is difficult to maintain. Anthropologists have played crucial roles in mapping aboriginal lands to support Indian claims to ancestral territories; contacting new groups deep in the Amazon to help them prepare for inevitable contact with the outside world; reporting government and civilian abuses of Indians to the world community; representing Indians in disputes with settlers, prospectors, and government agents; educating indigenous communities about their political and economic rights and interests; and spearheading advocacy efforts on behalf of indigenous peoples of the Amazon.

In March 2003, for example, indigenous leaders from across Brazil, politicians, anthropologists, and officials from the National Indigenous Foundation (FUNAI) met in Brasilia to discuss indigenous rights. Topics included proposals to improve the quality of life of indigenous populations and strategies to prevent the invasion of indigenous lands. They also discussed the corruption of some FUNAI officials and the murder of indigenous leaders (Radiobras, 3/18/03, **http://forests.org/articles/reader.asp?linkid=21266**).

In 2004, anthropologists' interventions helped prevent bloodshed when 3000 Guarani Indians invaded fourteen ranches on land near the Paraguayan border that they claim as part of their ancestral land. In negotiations through FUNAI, the Guaranis agreed to leave eleven of the farms but continued to occupy the three largest ranches in an effort to press FUNAI to expand their tribal reserve by incorporating the land on which the ranches are located.

Anthropologists say that, under the Brazilian constitution, the indigenous community has a legitimate ancestral claim to the property in question. Rubem Almeida, one of the two anthropologists who wrote the report that will serve as the basis for FUNAI's demarcation of the Guarani territory, said the Guaranis are legally entitled to the land. Almeida presented testimony and material evidence that the Guaranis traditionally lived on the property in question, as well as "specific documents from 1927" that confirm their legal claim to the land. Despite the ranchers' protests, under the Brazilian constitution the local indigenous community has a right to that land, which cancels out the land titles held by the ranchers. The anthropologists suggested that the state should pay compensation to the ranchers (Mario Osava, Inter Press Service News Agency, 2/3/04, **http://ipsnews.org/interna.asp?idnews=22228**).

CRITICAL THINKING QUESTIONS

Why is being a government anthropologist a balancing act in Brazil? How might this compare with being a government anthropologist in the Department of Indian and Northern Affairs in Canada?

set aside where lands are under indigenous control and given government protection. The largest of these, and, indeed, the largest indigenous reservation in the world, is an area of 8.3 million square hectares inhabited by some 23 000 Yanomami, the largest indigenous nation in the Amazon (Schemo 1999:72).

Traditional Yanomami territory had been made vulnerable in the early 1980s, when the Brazilian government permitted road construction cutting through their lands. Although the road was never completed, the initial projects brought a number of deadly diseases to the people, including measles, influenza, and malaria. These diseases killed many hundreds of Yanomami, decimating 90 percent of some communities (Gorman 1991). The government also conducted aerial surveys that revealed valuable deposits of gold, tin, and radioactive materials.

In particular, gold has brought about 50 000 miners to the region. They have illegally built some 120 airstrips hidden in the jungle and dammed dozens of rivers to obtain water pressure to make prospecting easier. In addition, the use of mercury in gold prospecting has polluted many of the rivers, contaminating the fish that the Yanomami eat, in turn leading to birth defects and nerve disorders (Gorman 1991). New waves of epidemic diseases have stricken the communities. The miners killed hundreds of people, burned their houses, and destroyed forestland (Wiessner 1999:77).

? *As an anthropologist, to what extent do you think you would get involved in the political, economic, or medical problems or struggles of the people you were studying? What ethical dilemmas would you face in deciding this question?*

Infringements on their lands, the spread of diseases, and competition over resources had the further effect of creating or exacerbating internal conflicts between neighbouring Yanomami settlements and within the communities as well (Ferguson 1992). Therefore, what might look to an outsider as endemic warfare was actually, at least in part, a response to turmoil caused by external forces.

The plight of the Yanomami came to international public awareness in 1987, when four Indians and one miner were killed in a clash (Gorman 1991). Brazilian authorities then drew up plans to reduce the size of Yanomami lands, giving the Indians nineteen separate "islands of habitation" and creating state parks and national forests in which gold mining was permitted. However, an indigenous advocacy group called Survival International brought a lawsuit to the Brazilian High Court, which ruled the government's plan to be unconstitutional and instead ordered the expulsion of the gold miners. In the following year, the government reached a compromise that would return most of the confiscated land to the Yanomami, keeping about 4800 square kilometres for mining operations.

The establishment of reservations grants the Indians the right to control their own destinies, living according to their own cultural norms and absorbing as much external influence as they choose. However, despite the intentions of FUNAI, ranchers and resource developers continue to encroach on Indian lands. They often operate in remote regions far from contact with government officials. In addition, although reservation lands are formally protected, most have unclear and unmarked boundaries, making it difficult for Indians to assert claims over particular acreage. So far, about 80 percent of the lands in Brazil officially defined as indigenous territory have been mapped, although even their boundaries are vulnerable to encroachment by settlers, miners, and resource companies (Wiessner 1999:79).

Brazil's "Urban Indians." In addition to the indigenous communities officially recognized by the Brazilian government, there are many more self-identified Indian people who live in small villages, towns, and cities throughout the country, even in the densely settled northeast. Some estimates suggest that urban Indians account for about one-quarter of Brazil's Indian population (Warren 2001:16), and their numbers are increasing. In Brazil, as in the United States and Canada, the number of people who self-identify as Indian has steadily risen in the last several decades. Part of the increase can be explained on the basis of natural growth, but the numbers far exceed that process. Most of the increase results from the easing of people's reluctance to identify themselves as indigenous because of prevailing racism and social stigma.

Many Indians living in rural or urban settings are oriented to indigenous traditions that have been transformed or destroyed over the past five centuries. Still, they "define indigenous ancestral roots as essential to [their] identity, to make them the anchor of [their] dreams and future, and to work toward their recovery" (Warren 2001:21). They have an orientation that is "post-traditional" in the sense that they look to traditions but also mold and adapt these traditions in a way that is meaningful today. Many face negative attitudes held in Brazilian society toward Indians and "Indianness." Some are denied social recognition as Indians because they are the products of racial mixtures, and their appearance does not conform to stereotypical images of Indians. Their behaviour similarly combines practices and attitudes of their multiple ancestries, but while they recognize their complex past,

Advocates for the Yanomami, including anthropologists from the world community, objected to the Brazilian government's plan to restrict the size of Yanomami territory and to permit gold prospecting by outsiders. They feared that any presence of miners would spread disease, such as mercury poisoning and tuberculosis. Finally, in 1991, a new Brazilian president banned all outsiders from the region and put into motion procedures that established a protected reservation. Here a Brazilian doctor aids the Yanomami.

they gravitate most toward their Indian identity. They feel most comfortable associating with other Indians, living in Indian communities or neighbourhoods, and decorating their homes with symbols of their indigenous heritage (Warren 2001:254–259).

Brazilian Indians and their supporters are active in forming organizations that advocate for their lands and their rights. Some of these organizations are backed and funded by members of the Catholic clergy espousing "liberation theology," which looks to the church to ally itself with the struggles of indigenous and other poor people who are fighting for social, economic, and political justice (Ramos 1997). While they do not represent the dominant or mainstream church, they do constitute a vocal and active faction. In addition, Brazilian Indians forge alliances among themselves, as well as with other indigenous peoples in South, Central, and North America, learning from each other's experiences and working together to accomplish their common goals.

Costs of Economic Development in Ecuador and Bolivia

Indigenous peoples in Ecuador and Bolivia are in the forefront of movements to organize opposition to government policies that encroach on their lands, harm their environments, and destroy their cultures. Both countries have a majority population of indigenous people, the descendants of powerful and complex societies. Today, their territories are the targets of oil exploration and extraction. In Ecuador, for example, the government is focusing on oil as the basis of its projected economic development. Ecuador has the largest petroleum reserves in Latin America, equal to those of Mexico and Nigeria (Forero 2003). Most of the oil is located in remote areas of the Amazon inhabited primarily by indigenous communities. Many of these communities oppose the oil companies because of the environmental pollution and destruction that follow oil drilling and pipelines, interfering with the people's ability to maintain their traditional economies that rely on horticulture and foraging. In addition, the people do not receive monetary benefits from the resources because profits from the oil are rarely reinvested in their communities. Instead, the resources benefit wealthy investors and consumers elsewhere in Ecuador, as well as in foreign countries.

Indians have organized protests against government policy and have also occasionally sabotaged the drilling equipment and pipelines. The Ecuadorian government responded by sending military patrols to protect oil company gear and personnel. In addition, representatives of the indigenous Kichwa, Achuar, and Shuar have sent delegations to the capital, Quito, and to meetings of the Organization of American States and of petroleum company shareholders. They have also forged coalitions with environmental groups. Although some indigenous people favour the development, hoping that they will reap economic benefits, the majority oppose petroleum extraction.

In Bolivia, indigenous peoples led protests against government policies in 2003 that eventually led to the resignation of the president, Gonzalo Sanchez de Lozada (Rohter 2003). In 2005, they organized protests calling for nationalizing oil and gas resources. The proportion of indigenous peoples in Bolivia is the highest of all in South America, constituting 55 percent of the total population (Wiessner 1999:83). Since the 1980s, Indians in Bolivia have gained recognition of their rights to land, obtaining ownership of one million hectares of territory in the Andes. In 1994, an addendum to the Bolivian constitution officially designated the country as a "multiethnic, pluricultural society" (p. 84). However, despite favourable political and legal status, indigenous peoples occupy the lowest stratum economically and socially.

Developments in Africa

The situation for indigenous peoples in Africa shares some similarities with, and yet differences from, that of peoples in North and South America. Most European colonial efforts in Africa did not include large numbers of settlers. Therefore, in contemporary Africa, the delineation of who is "indigenous" or "tribal" is more complex than in the settler colonies of the Americas and Australia. After former colonies gained their independence, the new countries developed policies that affected various groups within their borders. In general, members of large and powerful groups came to dominate the governments and benefitted from political, economic, and social policies, whereas

? *Do you think the indigenous people of Ecuador have the right to block oil drilling on their property? How would you resolve the conflict of interest in this situation?*

members of small, isolated groups received far fewer advantages. In many cases, they remain marginalized in their own countries and face various forms of discrimination and control. These factors are reflected in various definitions of "indigenous" proposed by scholars of international law. However, a consensus summary states that

> Indigenous communities are best conceived of as peoples traditionally regarded, and self-defined, as descendants of the original inhabitants of lands with which they share a strong, often spiritual bond. These peoples are, and desire to be, culturally, socially and/or economically distinct from the dominant groups in society, at the hands of which they have suffered, in past or present, a pervasive pattern of subjugation, marginalization, dispossession, exclusion and discrimination. (Wiessner, 1999:115)

Central governments in the East African countries of Sudan, Kenya, and Tanzania have continued colonial policies aimed at encouraging or forcing nomadic pastoral societies to become sedentary farmers or wage workers. Colonial and post-colonial governments prefer sedentary citizens because they are more easily supervised and controlled. In addition, nomadic pastoralists rely on large tracts of land to graze their animals. Gaining access to these lands allows national governments to proceed with economic development projects. Also, the governments often phrase their policies in terms of building national unity through cultural uniformity. In some cases, pastoralists are forced to change their economic systems by the unilateral confiscation of their territory. For example, in the 1970s, the Sudanese government undertook the construction of canals on the Nile River that would control flooding but disrupted the traditional economies of the Dinka, cattle pastoralists of southern Sudan (Lako 1988).

Sudan and the Dinka.   The Dinka rely on floodwaters to irrigate pastureland for their cattle, but the Sudanese authorities claim that such use of water is wasteful. Instead, the government diverts floodwaters for the use of farmers and urban dwellers in the populous northern Sudan. There are political implications of these choices as well since Sudanese society is split between the predominantly Muslim north and the predominantly Christian south. The two regions are frequently at odds, a conflict that periodically erupts in sectarian violence. The government's plan was to build the Jonglei Canal at a part of the Nile that is in the heart of Dinka territory. They claimed that the Dinka would benefit from the changes as the people became incorporated into the modern economy. The authorities tried to convince the Dinka that they would be able to maintain their cattle as sedentary ranchers rather than as nomadic pastoralists. They held out the promise of health care, educational services, and agricultural training as incentives to living in stable villages. In response to the Dinka's complaints that the canal would disrupt animal migration routes, the government established crossing points on the canal, but the crossing points created a further problem because animals would be concentrated in these areas, leading to depletion of resources through heavy use. In addition, the amount of fish available to the Dinka would be diminished, curtailing an important source of food.

Given their awareness of the potential negative effects, most Dinka feared the loss of their traditional way of life. But, although they objected to the presence of the canal in their territory, opposition was relatively weak, and a minority of canal supporters, consisting mainly of traders, businessmen, and civil servants, proved to be more vocal. The Jonglei Canal project uncovered latent class distinctions and contrasts in class interests in Dinka society. Many Dinka were forced to move, although they did receive some financial compensation.

Kenya and Tanzania: The Maasai and the Barabaig.   The Maasai, a group of fourteen independent tribal entities of about 375 000 people, have seen their grazing lands in Kenya and Tanzania decreased, first by actions of British and German colonial authorities and then by post-colonial governments. In the early nineteenth century, European settlers encroached on Maasai lands, taking about half of their acreage (Fratkin and Wu 1997). In the mid-twentieth century, additional land was taken by the Kenyan and Tanzanian governments to create wildlife parks and reserves. In addition, the Maasai have lost grazing territories to small-scale independent farmers and large-scale corporate estates. Governments and international funding sources claim that the

Maasai and other pastoralists are inefficient utilizers of the land, which could be better used for producing cash crops and commercial beef (Fratkin and Wu 1997). In Tanzania, Maasai grazing lands have been confiscated to make way for commercial rice farms and irrigation projects.

However, the Maasai are no longer willing to see their way of life deteriorate. In Kenya, the Loita Maasai have organized the Loita Naimina Enkiyio Conservation Trust to help protect their legal rights to lands in Narok County against a plan to turn some of their acreage into a wildlife reserve that would include the construction of roads and a hotel for tourists.

In Tanzania, the Barabaig, a group of cattle pastoralists numbering about 30 000, are fighting government and private projects that will turn much of their land into commercial wheat farms. In an important decision, the Tanzanian High Court supported the Barabaig suit on the basis of customary use rights. The decision was overturned in 1986, however, after the government filed an appeal on the grounds that not all of the plaintiffs in the case were "native" according to official definitions because some were not indigenous Barabaig but instead were descendants of Somali immigrants.

The Kenyan and Tanzanian governments took thousands of square kilometres of land from the Maasai when they created one of the world's largest and most visited wildlife reserves and national parks. When the British originally established the Serengeti National Park in 1929, the Maasai lost resource-rich grazing and farming territory. In response to protests, the British granted the tribes access to the nearby Ngorongoro Conservation Area (NCA). However, by 1975, the Kenyan government prohibited farming in the NCA, even though the Maasai had come to rely on maize as a necessary supplement to their shrinking herds. Malnutrition is becoming an increasingly serious problem. Restrictions on access to lands now turned into game parks have also created and exacerbated inter-tribal tensions as various groups compete for scarcer territories and resources.

Nigeria and the Ogoni.   Indigenous lands are confiscated elsewhere in Africa so that economic development can proceed apace. For example, the Nigerian government has granted licenses to the Shell Oil Company for drilling on land claimed by the Ogoni, a group of about 500 000 people (Beveridge 2003:9). Most of the oil drilled in Nigeria is located in Ogoni territory, land that has been harmed by toxic emissions and oil leakages from ruptured pipelines. A group of eight Ogoni activists and one of their supporters, the internationally known writer Ken Saro-Wiwa, were arrested, charged with murder, and executed in 1995 despite vigorous protests from the United Nations and from many countries in the world.

Biodiversity prospecting is becoming big business in parts of Africa, as in Asia and the Pacific (Reid et al. 1996), but the issue of ownership is a contentious problem in many countries (Iwu 1996). Africa, for example, is rich in plants and animals containing medicinal properties that could be used to treat many ailments. A research project in Nigeria identified several plants that could be used for the treatment of viral infections, and other agents that have antiparasitic, antiplaque, and antifungal properties, as well as a greaseless body oil (Iwu 1996:243). Management of these and other resources is complicated by competing needs. Conservation of biodiversity resources is critical to their continuation but, at the same time, the intense poverty suffered by many Africans drives the governments to allow rapid harvesting even though future supplies are threatened by this policy.

? *What do you predict for the future of pastoralism as a mode of human subsistence?*

REVIEW

In the United States, issues have centred on indigenous peoples' control of land and resources and gaming, while in Canada, efforts have also focused on achieving sovereignty. In Mexico, the policy of *indigenismo* has granted rights to natives, but cultural minorities such as the Maya continue to struggle for independence. South American governments vacillate between protecting Amazonian Indians and exploiting the natural resources in their homelands. Bolivian and Ecuadoran Indians also protest resource exploitation on their lands. In Africa, pastoralists such as the Dinka and Barabaig struggle to retain grazing land, while people such as the Ogoni of Nigeria take action to keep commercial oil interests at bay.

Case study

Papua New Guinea's Customary Law

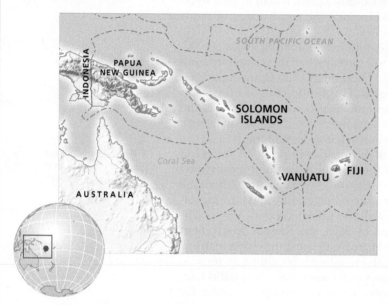

The history of legal practice in Papua New Guinea has vacillated between formal jurisprudence and customary procedures. Although Papua New Guinea consists of numerous and diverse populations, the traditions of most communities stress the responsibility of kin groups to redress wrongs committed against their members, either by demanding compensation or by physical retaliation against the perpetrators. People resort to personal problem solving with or without the approval of informal councils who hear complaints and attempt reconciliation. These councils have only the force of public opinion; they have no coercive authority. Before taking direct action, kinship groups may try to facilitate agreements through negotiation and compromise with the ultimate aim of resolving problems and reconstituting social harmony.

During most of the colonial period, British and, later, Australian authorities did not recognize customary practices in state legal settings. The adversarial system of due process was imposed through the courts and the laws, but in the villages, away from official view, people continued to seek resolution of disputes through traditional means, either by consulting village councils or by calling on their kinship groups to act as mediators. In the 1960s, colonial jurisprudence began to recognize Papuan customs by accepting defenses or reducing sentences based on customary practices and attitudes.

The courts nevertheless regarded customary law as illegitimate, a product of the "primitive culture and environment of the accused, which made it impossible for the accused to understand and accept Australian values" (Ottley and Zorn 1983:265). For example, people accused of assault, manslaughter, or murder might offer a defense of provocation, claiming that cultural expectations led them to commit the offense after they had been provoked by a prior act of the victim. The court often accepted such a defense. If the accused were a member of a remote community where traditional practices and attitudes prevailed, she or he might be acquitted or receive a light sentence; if the accused were, in the court's judgment, sufficiently assimilated, cultural defenses might not be accepted.

In addition, the Australian Supreme Court denied defenses based on retaliation for sorcery, even though beliefs in sorcery are widespread throughout Papua New Guinea. The court did not acknowledge that Papuans consider a belief in sorcery to be "reasonable" but imposed their own cultural and legal standards. The court would allow Australian defendants to plead insanity for killing someone they believed was a sorcerer, but Papuans were not allowed to plead insanity in the same situation. In the court's opinion, "In Papua New Guinea, although most people believe in sorcery, and most sane people do so, no reasonable person would" (Ottley and Zorn 1983:276).

Following independence, the Papua New Guinea Law Reform Commission formulated a system of law emphasizing customary law consistent with traditional principles of conflict resolution (Ottley and Zorn 1983). These principles were based on provisions of the new constitution that aimed to legitimate customary practices where possible. However, customary principles and procedures have been only marginally and inconsistently incorporated into the country's legal system. Decisions rendered by the Supreme Court in cases involving customary practices rely heavily on colonial statutes. For example, the court ruled as unconstitutional a statute called the *Inter-Group Fighting Act,* passed in 1973 in response to a perceived escalation of fighting in tribal areas. That statute was consistent with customary attitudes that hold each member of a group responsible for the actions of the group as a whole. The act was aimed at limiting fighting by permitting the legal system to punish all members of a group engaged in fighting even though each person may not have been involved in a particular incident. In declaring the act to be unconstitutional, the Supreme Court referred to the Western tradition of individual responsibility rather than the Papuan tradition of collective responsibility for criminal acts. In addition, the court continues to base its judgments on rulings made prior to independence, again impeding the establishment of customary law.

The actions of the Papua New Guinea courts highlight resistance to custom as a legitimate source of judicial and political processes. This resistance suggests the desire of the state to retain control over competing local interests. Central control and consistency are not possible if communities have the right to develop their own mechanisms of solving disputes and punishing wrongdoers. The post-independence government also is concerned with establishing a national identity distinct from its colonial past and with attracting foreign investment. At the same time, it sees customary law not as an aspect of society that is uniquely Papuan but as a threat to its power.

LEGAL RIGHTS AND INTERNATIONAL RECOGNITION

To protect themselves and their lands, indigenous peoples have formed coalitions to place their concerns on the agendas of international organizations. In the international forum, the question of who is "indigenous" becomes politically and legally significant. Self-identification and community cohesiveness are some of the relevant factors, but historical changes, migrations of individuals and groups, and intermarriage with members of other communities blur identities and social cohesion. In 1993, a United Nations working group proposed a *Declaration on the Rights of Indigenous Peoples* that contains forty-five articles outlining international recognition of their rights. Among these are the right to self-determination (to determine their political status and identity), to maintain their cultures, and to be protected from genocide, ethnocide (cultural genocide), or forced relocation. In addition, the document recognizes indigenous peoples' right to practise, develop, and teach their traditions, histories, languages, and religions. They have the right of access to all forms of media, and they are protected in their rights to fully participate in the development of policies and decisions that affect them through their own chosen representatives.

In economic spheres, indigenous peoples have the right to own and control "the total environment of their traditional territories," including the conservation, development, and protection of their lands and resources. In politics, indigenous peoples have the right to autonomy or self-government, to maintain their own systems of justice and conflict resolution, to maintain "traditional relationships with peoples across international borders," and to protect their rights agreed in treaties. Finally, the United Nations is charged with creating a special indigenous body to oversee implementation of the declaration (United Nations 1993). In 2007, the UN General Assembly passed the Declaration. Only four countries voted against it: Australia, New Zealand, the United States, and Canada (See In Their Own Voices feature).

International law supports the claims of indigenous peoples to their lands, resources, and cultural heritage. In North America, treaties signed between representatives of native peoples and European or American colonial powers have the force of international law. Since treaties are documents signed by sovereign countries, they either explicitly or implicitly recognize the basic sovereignty of native nations. The fact that subsequent governments in the United States and Canada have unilaterally abrogated provisions of these treaties does not alter the underlying principles of international law.

This park ranger is an Aborigine working at Ayers Rock (Uluru) in Australia. The rock is sacred to the Aborigines.

In Their Own Voices

Canada Votes Against the UN Declaration of the Rights of Indigenous Peoples

Statement by Ambassador McNee to the General Assembly

New York, September 13, 2007

Canada has long demonstrated our commitment to actively advancing indigenous rights at home and internationally. We recognize that the situation of indigenous peoples around the world warrants concerted and concrete international action. We have strongly supported the establishment and ongoing work of the Permanent Forum on Indigenous Issues and the Special Rapporteur on the situation of the fundamental freedoms and human rights of indigenous peoples and have promoted consideration of indigenous issues within a variety of international conferences. We have a constructive and far-reaching international development program, targeted specifically at improving the situation of indigenous peoples in many parts of the world. Canada continues to make further progress at home, working within our constitutional guarantees for Aboriginal and treaty rights, and with our negotiated self-government and land claims agreements with several Aboriginal groups in Canada. Canada also intends to continue our active international engagement, both multilaterally and bilaterally. It is therefore with disappointment that we find ourselves having to vote against the adoption of this Declaration as drafted.

Since 1985, when the United Nations expert Working Group on Indigenous Populations decided to produce a Declaration on indigenous rights, Canada has been an active participant in its development. Canada has long been a proponent of a strong and effective text that would promote and protect the human rights and fundamental freedoms of every indigenous person without discrimination and recognize the collective rights of indigenous peoples around the world. We have sought for many years, along with others, an aspirational document which would advance indigenous rights and promote harmonious arrangements between indigenous peoples and the States in which they live.

However, the text that was presented at the Human Rights Council in June 2006 did not meet such expectations and did not address some of our concerns. This is why we voted against it. We also expressed dissatisfaction with the process.

Canada's position has remained consistent and principled. We have stated publicly that we have significant concerns with respect to the wording of the current text, including the provisions on lands, territories and resources; free, prior and informed consent when used as a veto; self-government without recognition of the importance of negotiations; intellectual property; military issues; and the need to achieve an appropriate balance between the rights and obligations of indigenous peoples, member States and third parties.

For example, the recognition of indigenous rights to lands, territories, and resources is important to Canada. Canada is proud of the fact that Aboriginal and treaty rights are given strong recognition and protection in its Constitution. We are equally proud of the processes that have been put in place to deal with Aboriginal claims respecting these rights and are working actively to improve these processes to address these claims even more effectively. Unfortunately, the provisions in the Declaration on lands, territories, and resources are overly broad, unclear, and capable of a wide variety of interpretations, discounting the need to recognize a range of rights over land and possibly putting into question matters that have been settled by treaty.

Similarly, some of the provisions dealing with the concept of free, prior, and informed consent are unduly restrictive. Provisions such as Article 19 provide that the State cannot act on any legislative or administrative matter that may affect indigenous peoples without obtaining

REVIEW

To protect themselves and their lands, indigenous peoples have formed transnational coalitions to place their concerns on the agendas of international agencies and nongovernment organizations. International law supports the claims of indigenous peoples to their lands, resources, and cultural heritage, as well as to basic human rights.

their consent. While we in Canada have strong consultation processes in place, and while our courts have reinforced these as a matter of law, the establishment of a complete veto power over legislative and administrative action for a particular group would be fundamentally incompatible with Canada's parliamentary system.

We regard it as particularly unfortunate that a number of States, like Canada, with significant indigenous populations, cannot solidly support the adoption of this particular text as a meaningful and effective United Nations Declaration on the Rights of Indigenous Peoples.

Yet let me reiterate that regardless of the Declaration, Canada will continue to take effective action, at home and abroad, to promote and protect the rights of indigenous peoples based on our existing human rights obligations and commitments. Such effective action, we must be clear, would not be undertaken on the basis of the provisions of this Declaration.

By voting against the adoption of this text, Canada puts on record its disappointment with both the substance and process. For clarity, we also underline our understanding that this Declaration is not a legally binding instrument. It has no legal effect in Canada, and its provisions do not represent customary international law.

Madam President, Canada will vote against adoption of this text.

Permanent Mission of Canada to the United Nations website (http://geo.international.gc.ca/canada_un/new_york/whats_new/default-en.asp?id=10382&content_type=2), Foreign Affairs and International Trade Canada, 2008. Reproduced with the permission of Her Majesty the Queen in Right of Canada, represented by the Minister of Foreign Affairs, 2008.

AFN National Chief Applauds Today's Passage of the UN Declaration on the Rights of Indigenous Peoples—Recognizing 30 Years of Work in the Making

The National Chief of the Assembly of First Nations called today an important day for Indigenous people around the world, including First Nations in Canada.

"While the Declaration is not perfect, it is a step toward setting minimum standards for the survival, dignity and well-being of Indigenous people everywhere. It's a day to celebrate.

"This recognition was a long time coming," National Chief Phil Fontaine said. "The Declaration recognizes our collective histories, traditions, cultures, languages, and spirituality. It is an important international instrument that supports the activities and efforts of Indigenous peoples to have their rights fully recognized, respected and implemented by state governments."

However, the National Chief said he is gravely concerned that the Government of Canada chose to vote against the UN Declaration and, in effect, opposes fundamental human rights protections for Indigenous peoples. Canada lobbied hard to convince other countries to not support the Declaration. It is the first time Canada voted against an international human rights instrument. Despite Canada's efforts, many countries decided to vote in favour of the United Nations Declaration.

"The Assembly of First Nations and other representatives of Indigenous peoples in Canada offered to work with the government to address the concerns it had and to come to a solution, but that offer was refused," National Chief Phil Fontaine said. "Canada prides itself as a protector of human rights. It is a member of the UN Human Rights Council, yet it is disappointing today to see this government vote against recognizing the basic rights of Canada's First Peoples. This is a stain on the country's international reputation."

First Nations Chiefs and First Nations representatives invested an enormous amount of work into the Declaration over the last thirty years.

www.afn.ca/article.asp?id=3772. Used with permission of the Assembly of First Nations.

CRITICAL THINKING QUESTIONS

How would you distinguish between indigenous rights, human rights, and treaty rights with regard to how they apply to indigenous peoples in Canada?

What is the basis for each set of rights?

In what ways might these sets of rights conflict? If so, which should have precedence?

How might anthropological concepts of culture and cultural relativity assist in arguing for the validity of indigenous rights?

Do you think that Canada was justified in rejecting the UN Declaration?

Chapter Summary

The Global Economy

- The internationalization of trade and investment has been expanding rapidly since the end of World War II.
- Cross border flows of capital and goods has been supported by the elimination of many state controls on the economy.

- Export sectors have grown in many countries and have often been based on attracting capital to low-wage regions.
- Some research suggests that these trends have led to the exploitation of workers in developing countries, the loss of manufacturing jobs in older industrialized

regions, and greater inequalities in income and access to services.

Migration

- Processes of transformation and cultural interaction have intensified throughout the twentieth and into the twenty-first century. The global economy accelerates the pace of transferring goods, services, and peoples from one part of the world to others. International migration has brought people far from their homes, contributing their labour, spending money, and adding cultural diversity worldwide. Political processes have also strengthened ties among countries.

- Processes of internal migration have also accelerated, often because people are mobile, seeking job opportunities where they are available. Urban centres attract people from rural areas in particular. The establishment of factories run by transnational corporations in development or free trade zones in many countries in Asia and Latin America has contributed to the increase in internal migration. Young women make up the majority of the work force in labour-intensive factories that produce electronics and garments.

- International migration has shifted populations from poor countries to wealthier countries with better job opportunities. As transnational migrants, people are increasingly maintaining ties with their native countries and communities at the same time that they are establishing themselves in their new countries. A transnational identity is made more likely with the ease of transportation and communication.

- While many international migrants assimilate into their new countries, many others develop an identity based on their origin and ethnicity. But ethnic identities are not immutable. Instead, they are context-bound and adaptable to circumstances. People may think of themselves as members of groups based on one set of criteria but may find themselves categorized as members of other groups based on different criteria. Ethnic groups may develop strong political influence on the basis of their relative numbers and their relative cohesiveness as a social and political community.

Ethnogenesis and Ethnic Identity

- States utilize various processes to develop a national identity. In multiethnic states, various strategies may be employed to resolve relationships between central identities and disparate ethnic groups. One ethnic group may assert itself as dominant and legitimate, equating national culture with its own. A state may assert a uniformity of culture, homogenizing ethnic differences, or a state may maintain a pluralistic attitude toward cultural differences, allowing secondary identities to coexist along with a national identity. Ethnic strife, resulting from economic and political forces, may lead to tension and conflict internally within a multiethnic country. In some cases, cultural pluralism may spawn xenophobic sentiments leading to hostility and even violence against immigrants.

- An international or global identity based on social class has developed. Members of elite classes have a global identity that links them to elites in other countries on the basis of class, sharing privileges, interests, leisure activities, and tastes with other elites. A popular global culture has also developed as people throughout the world eat the same foods, watch the same movies, listen to the same music, and purchase the same types of consumer goods.

Cultural Minorities and Indigenous Peoples in a Global World

- Since the middle of the twentieth century, indigenous communities in many countries have gained a new energy and focus for their struggles in self-determination. Policies toward indigenous peoples vary considerably in different countries. In the United States and Canada, native peoples have legally defined rights based on treaties signed between their representatives and the federal governments. These treaties and subsequent court rulings support some limited sovereignty for indigenous communities, including some degree of self-government, tax immunity, and rights to control economic, educational, and social programs. In Mexico, federal policies have vacillated between recognizing the land rights of indigenous peoples and ignoring those rights in the interest of national economic development. In other countries of Latin America, governments have followed similar variations in policy. While indigenous communities have gained some recognition to rights to land and resources and their rights to continue cultural practices, their lands have also been the target of resource extraction, especially oil and minerals, and, more recently, biodiversity research.

- The situation for indigenous peoples in Africa differs somewhat from that of peoples in the Western Hemisphere. In Africa, there were relatively few European colonial settlers and, therefore, the delineation of "indigenous" or "tribal" is more complex than in American or Australian settler colonies. In many African states, as in other countries, indigenous peoples remain marginalized and face various forms of discrimination and control. In Sudan, Kenya, and Tanzania, national governments have attempted to force nomadic pastoralists to adopt a sedentary lifestyle, phrased in the interest of a national culture and economic development.

Legal Rights and International Recognition

- To protect themselves and their land, indigenous peoples have formed coalitions to assert their rights under international law. The United Nations is in the process of formulating a *Declaration on the Rights of Indigenous Peoples* outlining legal, economic, social, and cultural rights.

Key Terms

cultural minorities   366   transnationalism   371   Islamization   377   global identity   380
tribalization   371

Review Questions

1. What are the distinguishing features and effects of forced migration, urban migration, and labour migration?

2. How is Mexico's *maquiladora* system an example of the role of transnational corporations in labour migration? What might be some other examples?

3. What are the main difficulties that transnational migration can cause for cultural minorities? In what ways might they participate in a culture of transnationalism?

4. What is the process of ethnogenesis? What are some examples of the creation of new ethnic and political identities in newly independent states, such as Sudan and Papua New Guinea?

5. How have post-colonial states treated cultural minorities in the process of nation building, for example, in Indonesia or Malaysia? How did colonialism influence these outcomes?

6. How has globalization been expressed in both cultural identities and consumerism?

7. What challenges do cultural minorities face in every part of the world? How do situations in Canada, Brazil, Nigeria, and other countries show how those challenges play out in specific cultural contexts?

8. How has the law worked both against and for the interests of cultural minorities?

Glossary

acculturation Process by which a group adjusts to the influence of a dominant culture, while at the same time maintaining its original cultural identity.

achieved status A social position attained by a person's own efforts and skills.

aesthetics Philosophies about what has beauty and value in art.

affines People related through marriage.

age grade (age set) A sociopolitical association of people of more or less similar age who are given specific social functions.

agency The way in which an individual reacts to and acts upon his or her culture and society.

agriculture A subsistence strategy focusing on intensive farming, investing a great deal of time, energy, and technology.

alliance theory Theory that maintains that the major function of marriage is to bind groups together into a larger social system.

ambilineal descent Principle of descent in which individuals may choose to affiliate with either their mother's or their father's kinship group.

ancestor worship Belief in the importance of ancestors as they affect the lives of their survivors, protecting their descendants in return for rituals of honour performed to show them respect.

animatism Belief that all things, including men and women, are endowed with a pervasive spiritual power.

animism Belief in the existence of souls.

anthropology The study of humanity, from its evolutionary origins millions of years ago to its current worldwide diversity.

applied anthropology An area of anthropology that applies the techniques and theories of the field to problem solving outside of traditional academic settings.

archaeology The study of past cultures, both historic cultures with written records and prehistoric cultures that predate the invention of writing.

arranged marriages Marriages that are arranged by the parents or other relatives of the bride and groom.

art Artifacts of human creation created through the exercise of exceptional physical, conceptual, or imaginative skill; produced in a public medium and intended to affect the senses, sharing stylistic conventions with similar works.

artisans Specialists in the production of works of art.

ascribed status A social position that a person attains by birth. A person is born into an ascribed status.

assimilation Wholesale acceptance of the entire value and meaning system and abandonment of one's own beliefs and values. Often occurs under pressure from the domination of a more powerful group over a subjugated one.

associations Sociopolitical groups that link people in a community on the basis of shared interests and skills.

avoidance relationships Patterns of behaviour between certain sets of kin that demonstrate respect and social distance.

avunculocal residence Patterns of residence after marriage in which the couple lives with or near the husband's mother's brother.

balanced reciprocity Exchange of goods and services of a specified value.

bands Small, loosely organized groups of people held together by informal means.

barter An exchange of products in which one person gives one type of product in exchange for another type of product.

berdaches Male Two-Spirits in some Native North American societies who adopted some of the economic and social roles of women.

big man A status within egalitarian societies that places people in leadership positions based on personal wealth and influence over supporters.

bilateral descent Principle of descent in which people think of themselves related to both their mother's kin and their father's kin at the same time.

bilocal residence Patterns of residence after marriage in which the couple alternates between living with the wife's kin and the husband's kin.

biological or physical anthropology The study of human origins and biological diversity.

body language The meanings people communicate through their posture, stance, movements, expressions, gestures, and proximity to other communicants.

brideservice A period of months or years before or after marriage during which the husband performs labour for his wife's parents.

bridewealth Presents given by the husband's family to the wife's kin before, during, or after the wedding ceremony.

calendric rituals Ceremonies performed at specific times during the year, for example, agricultural rituals performed for planting, growing, and harvesting crops.

call systems (signal systems) Animal communication systems that consist of a relatively small number of sounds to express moods and sensations, like fear, delight, contentment, anger, or pain.

capital goods Items that are produced for the purpose of producing other goods rather than for production.

capitalism An economic mode of production in which the goal is to amass wealth in the form of money in order to gain control over the means of production and then use this control to accumulate even greater wealth.

cargo cults Revitalization movements arising in Melanesia in the early twentieth century with the aim of obtaining material wealth through magical means.

carrying capacity The number of people who can be sustained by the resources and environment in which they live.

caste Social grouping whose membership is determined at birth and is generally inflexible.

chiefdoms Formal governmental systems organized by kinship.

child-rearing practices Methods used to take care of infants and young children, including ways of feeding, playing with, carrying, and sleeping arrangements.

clans Named groups of people who believe that they are relatives even though they may not be able to trace their actual relationships with all members of their group.

code-switching Changing from one dialect or language to another according to the context in which one is speaking.

cognates Words in different languages that are derived from the same word in their parent language.

colonialism Policies in which countries establish colonies in distant places in order to exploit their resources and labour and possibly to establish settlements of their own citizens abroad.

commodity A product that can be sold or traded in return for money or other products.

comparative perspective An approach in anthropology that uses data about the behaviour and beliefs in many societies to document both cultural universals and cultural diversity.

complex foragers Foraging societies that have developed permanent settlements, territorial exclusiveness, property accumulation, and social stratification on the basis of food storage technologies.

componential analysis A technique of analyzing the similarities and contrasts among words in a particular category, such as kinship terms or animal names.

consanguines People related by blood.

consumerism Culture of consumption of goods and services.

contagious magic Magic that operates on the principle that positive and negative qualities can be transferred through proximity or contact.

contract archaeology The application of archaeology to assess the potential impact of construction on archaeological sites and to salvage archaeological evidence.

cosmology Religious worldview of a people, including beliefs about the origin of the world, the pantheon of deities that exist, and their relationships to the spirit realm.

counterculture An alternative cultural model within a society that expresses different views about the way that society should be organized.

courtship Period prior to marriage when a couple tests attraction to and compatibility with each other.

creole A language that has historic roots as an amalgamation of vocabulary and grammar derived from two or more independent languages.

cross-cousin A child of one's mother's brother or of one's father's sister.

Crow system Kin terms used by some matrilineal peoples that extend the term for father and father's sister to include cross-cousins on the paternal side.

cult of domesticity Constellation of beliefs popular in the late nineteenth and early twentieth centuries that women were, by nature and biology, suited to the domestic tasks of nurturing and caring for their husbands and children.

cultural anthropology The study of cultural behaviour, especially the comparative study of living and recent human cultures.

cultural constructs Models of behaviour and attitudes that a particular culture transmits to its members.

cultural ecology A theory which analyzes culture as the means by which people adapt to their local environment.

cultural evolution Theory which classifies and explains culture according to standard technologies of food acquisition and production.

cultural hegemony The use of cultural beliefs to justify and support social hierarchy and political domination.

cultural integration The tendency for people's practices and beliefs to form a relatively coherent and consistent system.

cultural minorities Members of ethnic or cultural groups who have become minorities in their native lands due to migrations of other peoples into their territories or due to the historical configuration of a nation-state made up of diverse groups.

cultural relativism An approach that stresses the importance of analyzing cultures in their own terms rather than in terms of the culture of the anthropologist.

cultural resource management (CRM) The application of archaeology to preserve and protect historic structures and prehistoric sites.

culture-specific psychological disorders Psychological disorders that seem to occur with some frequency in certain cultures but are rare or absent in others.

culture contact Direct interaction between peoples of different cultures through migration, trade, invasion, or conquest.

culture shock The feeling an anthropologist may have at the start of fieldwork of being out of place in unfamiliar surroundings.

culture The values, beliefs, technological knowledge, and rules of conduct acquired by learning and shared to some extent by the members of a society that govern their interaction with their environment, their ties with one another, and their thinking about themselves and the world.

deviance Behaviours that violate cultural norms and expectations.

dialect A variety of a language spoken by a particular group of people, based on regional differences or social differences such as gender, class, race, or ethnicity.

diffusion Spread of ideas, material objects, and cultural practices from one society to another through direct and indirect culture contact.

diffusionism View that similarities in culture could be explained by borrowing from a common source.

displacement The ability to communicate about something that is not happening at the moment.

diviners Persons with the power to predict the future through messages and omens from the spirit world.

double descent Kinship principle in which people belong to kinship groups of both their mother and father.

dowry Gifts given by the wife's family to the married couple or to the husband's kin before, during, or after the wedding ceremony.

duality of patterning The independent ordering of speech at two levels: sound and meaning.

ecological anthropology Specialization within anthropology that focuses on subsistence strategies and how people exploit and adapt to their environments.

economic system Methods of allocating resources, and the production, distribution, consumption, and exchange of goods and services.

egalitarian societies Societies in which all members have equal access to valued resources, including land, social prestige, wealth, and power.

elites Members of a social group in a stratified society who have privileges denied to the majority of the population.

emblems Nonverbal actions with specific meanings that substitute for spoken words.

emic Subjective, based on insiders' views, as in explanations people have for their own cultural behaviour.

emotionalist Art that attempts to express the artist's feelings or to release the feelings of viewers.

enculturation (A) Process of learning one's culture through informal observation and formal instruction. (B) The process by which children acquire their culture.

endogamy Marriage principle in which people marry members of their own group.

Eskimo system Kin tems making distinctions between the nuclear family and all other types of relatives and on gender.

ethnic art Art produced by a particular group of people that comes to express and symbolize their ethnic identity.

ethnicity Social category based on a complex mix of ancestry, culture, and self-identification in the context of a wider pluralistic and often stratified society.

ethnocentrism A set of misunderstandings and prejudices based on the idea that one's own belief system provides the only accurate and moral view of the world.

ethnography Observing and documenting peoples' ways of life.

ethnography of communication Study of communication as it occurs within a particular cultural context, considering such features as settings, participants, and participants' attitudes and goals.

ethnology Building theories about cultural behaviours and forms.

ethnomusicology The study of the musical styles and traditions of a people.

ethnosemantics An approach that uses linguistic methods to reveal a culture's meaning system by analyzing the words it uses to name and classify items in the real and imagined worlds.

etic Objective, based on outsiders' views, as in explanations of people's behaviour by anthropologists or other observers.

evolutionism View that cultural variation can be accounted for by different degrees of intellectual progress, leading to different levels of cultural achievement.

exogamy Marriage principle in which people cannot marry members of their own lineage or clan but instead must forge alliances with members of other groups.

extended family Family formed with three or more generations, for example, parents, children, and grandparents.

factionalism The tendency for groups to split into opposing parties over political issues, often a cause of violence and a threat to political unity.

family A married couple or other group of adult kinfolk who co-operate economically and in the upbringing of children, all or most of whom share a common dwelling.

fictive kin Unrelated individuals who are regarded and treated as relatives.

fieldwork In anthropology, living and interacting with the people or group under study.

folklore Texts that relate traditional stories, the exploits of cultural heroes and characters handed down from generation to generation.

folktales Secular stories that relate events that teach moral lessons or entertain listeners.

food producers Users of a subsistence strategy that transforms and manages the environment in order to obtain food.

foragers Peoples whose subsistence pattern is hunting and gathering.

forensic anthropologists Biological anthropologists who analyze human remains in the service of criminal justice and families of disaster victims.

formalist Abstract art that focuses on the formal qualities of art—colour, composition, sound, words, or movements.

fundamentalism A term coined in the United States in 1920 meaning a commitment to defend traditional religious beliefs.

funerary rites Rituals performed to mark a person's death and passage to the afterworld.

gender The roles that people perform in their households and communities and the values and attitudes that people have regarding men and women.

gender construct (gender model) The set of cultural assumptions about gender roles and values and the relations between the genders that people learn as members of their societies.

gender equality A constellation of behaviours, attitudes, and rights that support the autonomy of both women and men.

gender gap The difference in wages and income earned by men and women for comparable work.

gender identity The way that people think about themselves in terms of their sex, how they present themselves as men or women.

gender inequality The denial of autonomy and equal rights to one group of people based on their gender.

gender relations Norms of interaction between men and women, which may reflect differences in the relative status, prestige, and power of women and men.

gender roles Constellations of rights, duties, attitudes, and behaviours that are culturally associated with each gender.

general purpose money Money that can be used to acquire any of the resources, goods, and services within an economic system.

generalized reciprocity The exchange of goods and services without keeping track of their exact value but often with the expectation that their value will balance out over time.

Ghost Dance movement Nineteenth-century revitalization movement of the Plains Indians of North America.

ghost marriage Marriage practice among the Nuer of Sudan in which a widow marries her dead husband's brother and in which the children ensuing from the second marriage are said to be the children of the dead husband.

global culture A constellation of technologies, practices, attitudes, values, and symbols that spread internationally from one broad cultural origin, most prominently from the Anglo-European-American cultural complex.

global identity An identity of shared interests, practices, and values across international borders, uniting people worldwide.

globalization The process in which the exchange of products, investment, and people across national and regional boundaries increases.

Hawaiian system Kin terms making distinctions only of generation and gender.

healers Religious practitioners who acquire spirit power to diagnose the spirit cause of illness and effect cures.

historical linguistics The study of changes in language and communication over time and between peoples in contact.

historical particularism The theory that each way of life is a unique result of its particular historical conditions.

holistic perspective The way in which anthropologists view culture as an integrated whole, no part of which can be completely understood without considering the whole.

horticulture A subsistence strategy that focuses on small-scale farming using a relatively simple technology.

household A group of people occupying a common dwelling.

imitative magic Magic that operates on the principle of "like causes like."

incest taboo A ban on sexual relations or marriage between parents and their children and between siblings.

independent self Concepts of individuals as self-contained, independent agents with a focus on their own thoughts, feelings, and achievements.

indigenous cultures Comparatively homogeneous peoples or small-scale societies who share the same culture and are "native" to their territory or have occupied it for a long time.

Indigenous knowledge system Body of classification, folklore, observation, and practice that local people have developed to adapt to their local environment.

initiation rites Rituals that mark a person's transition from childhood to adulthood.

instrumental Art that attempts to have a beneficial effect on society, enriching people's lives, teaching moral lessons, and providing insights for improving and changing the world.

intercultural communication The communication of meanings between people of different languages and cultures.

interdependent self Concepts of individuals as connected to others, related to other people, with a focus on group needs rather than individual inner feelings, opinions, and attitudes.

interpretive anthropology View that cultural differences can be understood as complex webs of meaning.

Iroquois system Kin terms that emphasize the difference between one's parents' same-sex siblings and parents' opposite-sex siblings, classifying parallel cousins with one's own siblings.

Islamization The process of imposing the Islamic religion and associated cultural values within a nation to foster cultural uniformity.

jargons Specialized or technical words and expressions spoken by people who share a particular occupation or interest.

joking relationships Patterns of behaviour between certain kin that involve reciprocal joking, teasing, and playfulness, sometimes taking the form of flirtation and sexual innuendo.

judgment sample A sample of research informants selected according to how well they represent the larger population rather than on a random basis.

key informants Research subjects who are well versed in local cultural knowledge and representative of the larger community.

kin terms The set of names that people use to designate and address their relatives.

kindred Kinship group consisting of known bilateral relatives with whom people interact and socialize, and on whom they rely for economic and emotional assistance.

kinship system System of determining who one's relatives are and what one's relationship is to them.

language Any form of communication that involves symbols, displacement, and productivity.

language family A group of languages that are historically related, descendants of a common ancestral form.

levelling mechanism A custom, such as a feast, in which individuals give away their wealth to obtain prestige.

levirate Marriage preference rule in which a widow marries her deceased husband's brother.

liberalization policies Policies that attempt to eliminate national government controls on investment, imports and exports, currency rates, and many other practices that were considered to constrain trade.

lineage A set of relatives tracing descent from a known common ancestor.

lingua francas Languages used in particular areas by speakers of many different languages in order to communicate with each other.

linguistic anthropology The study of language and communication and the relationship between language and other aspects of culture and society.

loanwords Words borrowed from one language into another.

male dominance A constellation of behaviours and attitudes that grant men access to roles of prestige and reward and deny the same to women.

market economy Economic system in which products are traded in impersonal exchanges between buyers and sellers using an all-purpose currency.

marriage A socially recognized, stable, and enduring union between two adults that publicly acknowledges their rights and obligations and forms a new alliance between kin groups.

Marxism Theory that views culture as an aspect of a mode of production, particularly in the way it upholds and sometimes challenges class differences based on the ownership of productive resources.

Marxist theory Theory that analyzes society and culture in terms of class divisions and class conflicts.

material culture The tools people make and use, the clothing and ornaments they wear, the buildings they live in, and the household utensils they use.

matriclans Clans formed through descent and inheritance from women of their group.

matrilineal Descent system in which kinship group membership and inheritance pass through the female line.

matrilocal residence Pattern for residence after marriage in which the couple lives with or near the wife's family.

mediums Persons having special gifts to make contact with the spirit world, often in a state of trance.

messianic movements Revitalization movements stressing the role of a prophet or messiah as a saviour for his or her people.

millinerian movements Revitalization movements incorporating apocalyptic themes, prophesying an abrupt end to the world as we know it, leading to the establishment of a new way of life or form of existence.

mimetic Art that portrays the world accurately.

mobility A principle that people can move from membership in one social group to another.

mode of production Social type that is defined by the way in which society is divided into classes based on ownership of the "means of production."

moieties Groups of linked clans that divide a society into two halves, usually exogamous.

monogamy Marriage rule that stipulates a union between two people.

monotheistic religions Belief systems that hold to the existence of one supreme deity who has knowledge and powers that affect all aspects of life.

morpheme A unit of sound and meaning, either a separate word or a meaningful part of a word.

morphology The study of the internal structure of words and the combination of meaningful units within the words.

national character A constellation of behaviours and attitudes thought to be characteristic of a modal personality type prevalent in a particular country.

nativistic movements Revitalization movements attempting to rid society of foreign elements and return to what is conceived to be a prior state of cultural purity.

naturalized concepts Ideas and behaviours so deeply embedded in a culture that they are regarded as universally normal or natural.

negative reciprocity Exchange of goods and services in which each party seeks to benefit at the expense of the other, thus making a profit.

neolocal residence Pattern of residence after marriage in which the couple establishes a new, independent household separate from their relatives.

nomads People who do not have permanent homes but travel to sources of food as the food becomes seasonably available.

nonverbal communication Communication through gestures, facial expressions, body posture, use of space, and touch.

norms Sets of expectations and attitudes that people have about appropriate behaviour.

nuclear family Family consisting of parents and their children.

Omaha system Kin terms used by some patrilineal peoples that extend the term for mother and mother's brother to include cross-cousins on the maternal side.

oral literature Stories that people tell about their sacred past, their secular histories, and their personal lives.

paleoanthropology The study of the fossil record, especially skeletal remains, to understand the process and products of human evolution.

parallel cousin A child of one's mother's sister or of one's father's brother.

pastoralism A subsistence strategy focusing on raising and caring for large herds of domesticated animals.

patriarchy Social system in which men occupy positions of social, economic, and political power from which women are excluded.

patriclans Clans formed through descent and inheritance from men of their group.

patrilineal Descent system in which kinship group membership and inheritance pass through the male line.

patrilocal residence Pattern of residence after marriage in which the couple lives with or near the husband's relatives.

peasants Rural agriculturalists who are partly enmeshed in a larger social and economic system. Part of their production is devoted to supporting the larger system and its dominant elite.

personality A constellation of behavioural traits and dispositions. Some features of personality emerge at birth while others are acquired in the process of enculturation and psychological and cognitive growth.

phoneme A minimal unit of sound that differentiates meaning in a particular language.

phonemics Analysis of the use of sounds to differentiate the meanings of words.

phonetics Study of the articulation and production of human speech sounds.

phonology Study of sound systems in language, including phonetics and phonemics.

phratries Groups of linked clans that are usually exogamous.

pitch Phonemic use of rising and falling speech cadences.

political anthropology The study of the ways that communities plan group actions, make decisions affecting the group, select leadership, and resolve conflicts and disputes both within the group and with other groups.

political organization The ways in which societies are organized to plan group activities, make decisions affecting members of the group, select leadership, and settle disputes both within the group and with other groups.

poll taxes Taxes levied on households.

polyandry Marriage between a woman and two or more men.

polygamy Marriage in which the marital unit consists of three or more people.

polygyny Marriage between a man and two or more women.

polyphony The many voices of people from all the different segments and groups that make up a society; a quality of ethnographic writing today that presents multiple views of a culture.

polytheism Belief in the existence of numerous deities that have specific attributes, powers, and functions.

post-industrialism An economic order based on the expansion of the service economy, especially within the knowledge sector, and on globally organized corporations and institutions.

power The ability to exert control over the actions of other people and to make decisions that affect them.

prayer Religious speech or thought through which believers transmit messages to spirit beings.

prestige A social resource reflected in others' good opinions, respect, and willingness to be influenced.

priests Full-time religious practitioners who lead a religious organization and officiate at rituals but are not expected to be able to communicate directly with the spirit world.

private self One's inner feelings and concepts of oneself.

productivity The ability to join sounds and words in theoretically infinite meaningful combinations.

prophets Religious leaders who receive divine inspiration, often in a vision or trance.

proselytism The attempt to convert a person or group from one religion to another.

psychological anthropology A subfield of cultural anthropology that studies the psychological motivations of behaviour and the personality types prevalent in a society.

puberty rites Rituals performed to mark the passage of an individual from childhood to adulthood; also called initiation rites.

public self The self that one projects in public, in interactions with others.

race A cultural category that groups people according to so-called "racial" distinctions.

ranked societies Societies in which people or, more usually, kinship groups are ordered on a continuum in relation to each other.

reactive adaptation Coping response of captive, conquered, or oppressed peoples to loss and deprivation.

reciprocity Principles of mutual gift giving.

redistribution The gathering together and reallocation of food and resources to ensure everyone's survival.

redistributive networks Economic systems in which food and other goods are amassed by an organizer and then distributed to community members or guests at large public gatherings.

reflexive anthropology The anthropology of anthropology, which focuses on the cultural and political bias in ethnographic research, the impacts of anthropologists on the people they study, and professional ethics.

religion Beliefs and practices about spirit beings and supranormal and superhuman forces and their relationship to everyday life.

religious speech Invocations, prayers, prophecies, songs of praise, and curses that are powerful means of transmitting messages about the world.

representational Art that imitates, idealizes, or symbolizes form and experience.

residence rules Rules that stipulate where a couple will reside after their marriage.

revitalization movement Type of nonviolent reactive adaptation in which people try to resurrect their cultural heroes and restore their traditional way of life.

revolution An attempt to overthrow the existing government.

rites of passage Rituals that mark culturally significant transitions throughout the life cycle, including birth, puberty, marriage, and death.

rites of renewal Rituals performed with the goal of renewing the bounty of the earth.

rituals Activities, including religious speech, ceremonies, and behaviours, that are demonstrations of belief.

rules of descent Social rules that stipulate the nature of relationships from one generation to another.

sacred rituals Activities, places, or objects that are connected to the spirit realm and are imbued with power.

sacrifice Offerings made to spirit beings in order to show gratitude and honour.

same-sex marriage Marriage between two men or two women.

sandpaintings Paintings made by sprinkling fine, coloured sand to make stylized representations of spirit beings, in particular for use in Navajo curing ceremonials.

Sapir-Whorf hypothesis The assertion that the form and content of language influence speakers' behaviours, thought processes, and worldview.

scarification Artistic and ritualistic scarring of the face or other parts of the body in particular designs, commonly used to mark transitions to adulthood.

secret societies Organizations that control the use of special objects used in religious rituals.

sedentism A settlement pattern involving long-term, permanent settlements.

segmentary lineages Lineages organized in a hierarchical structure, ranked according to the number of generations they encompass.

self-concepts Attitudes that people hold about themselves.

semantics Study of systems of meaning in language.

serial monogamy Marriage pattern that stipulates that a person can be married to only one person at a time, although individuals may have two or more spouses during their lifetime. Subsequent marriages may be formed after the death of one spouse or after divorce.

settlement pattern The way people distribute themselves in their environment, including where they locate their dwellings, how they group dwellings into settlements, and how permanent or transitory those settlements are.

sex Biological differences between males and females.

shamans Religious practitioners who are believed to make contact with the spirit world through prayer, ritual, and trance.

single-parent family Family consisting of one parent (either mother or father) and her or his children.

slash-and-burn (swidden) cultivation A farming technique for preparing new fields by cutting down trees and bushes and then burning them in order to clear the land and enrich the soil with nutrients.

slavery An ascribed status forced on a person upon birth or through involuntary servitude.

social birth Social recognition of the transition to personhood.

social capital Bonds of reliable friendship and support that a person can call on to achieve a goal.

social culture The rules and practices that regulate membership and participation in social groups and networks.

social fatherhood The status of a man who fulfills the responsibilities of parenting, a role that may or may not be the same as biological paternity.

social reproduction The care and sustenance of people who will be able to contribute productively to society.

social stratification Divison of society into two or more groups, or strata, that are hierarchically ordered.

social structure The integrated assemblage of formal groups and social roles that make up a society.

socialization A similar process to enculturation that emphasizes social rather than cultural factors in learning one's culture.

societies Populations of people living in organized groups with social institutions and expectations of behaviour.

sociolinguistics Study of the impacts of socioeconomic and cultural factors, such as gender and class, on language and communication within a society.

sororal polygyny Marriage between a man and two or more women who are sisters.

sororate Marriage between a widower and his deceased wife's sister.

special purpose money Money that can be used for only a limited range of transactions.

spirit possession Belief that spirits can enter a person's body and take over their thoughts and actions.

Standard English The dialect of English chosen as normative, a reflection of the social, economic, and political standing of its speakers.

states Highly organized, centralized political systems with a hierarchical structure of authority.

status The position or rank that one occupies in a group or society that carries certain role expectations.

stratified societies Societies in which people have differential access to valued resources, including land and property, social prestige, wealth, and political power.

stress Phonemic use of accented sounds or syllables.

structural functionalism The theory that social structure determines people's thought and behaviour and that culture functions primarily to uphold the unity and continuity of society.

subculture A group whose members and others think of their way of life as in some significant way different from that of other people in the larger society.

subsistence patterns   Methods of obtaining food using available land and resources, available labour and energy, and technology.

Sudanese system   Kin tems that give separate terms for all kin relationships.

surplus value   The amount of value produced by workers in capitalist production that is greater than the wage paid to them.

survey research   Use of formal questionnaires administered to a random sample of subjects, eliciting social data that can be analyzed statistically.

symbol   A word, image, or object that stands for cultural ideas or sentiments.

symbolic culture   The ideas and knowledge people have about themselves, others, and the world, and the ways that people express these ideas.

syncretism   The blending of two religious traditions to form a new one.

syntax   The rules that generate the combination of words to form phrases and sentences.

taboos   Norms specifying behaviours that are prohibited in a culture.

tattooing   Injecting inks or dyes under the skin to produce designs.

terrorism   A criminal act intended or calculated to provoke a state of terror in the general public, a group of persons or particular persons for political purposes.

totem   An animal or plant believed by a group of people to have been their primordial ancestor or protector.

totemism   Belief system in which people believe they are descendants of spirit beings.

transhumance   The practice among pastoralists of moving to new pastureland on a seasonal basis.

transnationalism   Processes by which immigrants maintain social, economic, religious, and political ties to both their immigrant communities and their communities back home.

tribalization   A process of identification with one's tribal origins.

tribes   Societies with some degree of formalization of structure and leadership, including village and intervillage councils whose members regularly meet to settle disputes and plan community activities.

Two-Spirits   In Native North American societies, males who adopted some of the social and economic roles of women, and females who adopted some of the social and economic roles of men.

unilineal descent   Principle of descent in which people define themselves in relation to only one line, either their mother's line traced back through a series of women or their father's line traced back though a series of men.

universal grammar   Abstract rules that underlie the structure of phrases and sentences in all languages, generally thought to be an innate capacity of human thought.

uxorilocal   Living with or near the wife's parents.

Venus figurines   Sculptures made in Europe about 30 000 years ago, thought to represent pregnant women.

virilocal   Living with or near the husband's parents.

wealth   Economic resources, whether in land, goods, or money.

worldview   Culture-based, often ethnocentric, way that people see the world and other peoples.

References

Aberle, David. 1961. "Matrilineal Descent in Cross-Cultural Perspective." In *Matrilineal Kinship* (Eds. D. Schneider and K. Gough). Berkeley: University of California Press, pp. 655–727.

Abler, Thomas 2004. "Seneca moieties and hereditary chieftainships: The early-nineteenth century political organization of an Iroquois nation." *Ethnohistory* 51:459–488.

Abrahams, Roger. 1983. *African Folktales*. New York: Pantheon.

Abu-Lughod, Lila. 1986. *Veiled Sentiments*. Berkeley: University of California Press.

Abu-Lughod, Lila. 1990. "The Romance of Resistance: Tracing Transformations of Power through Bedouin Women." *American Ethnologist* 17:41–55.

Adams, Kathleen. 1995a. "Cultural Commoditization in Tana Toraja, Indonesia." *Cultural Survival Quarterly* 14:31–36.

Adams, Kathleen. 1995b. "Making Up the Toraja? The Appropriation of Tourism, Anthropology and Museums for Politics in Upland Sulawesi, Indonesia." *Ethnology* 34: 143–154.

Adorno, Rolena. 2004. *Nueva corónica y buen gabierno* (c. 1615) by Pomo de Ayala, Felipe Gauman. Yale University. **http://base.kb.dk/pls/hsk_web**. Accessed August 24, 2004.

Ahmadu, Fuambai. 2000. "Female Circumcision." In *Africa: Culture, Controversy, and Change* (Eds. B. Shell-Duncan and Y. Hernlund). London: Lynne Rienner.

Albas, Daniel and Cheryl Albas. 1989. "Modern magic: The case of examinations." *The Sociological Quarterly* 30:603–613.

Alexander, Alex E. 1975. *Russian Folklore: An Anthology in English Translation*. Belmont, CA: Nordland.

Ambert, Anne-Marie. 2005. *Same-Sex Couples and Same-Sex-Parent Families: Relationships, Parenting, and Issues of Marriage*. Ottawa: Vanier Institute of the Family.

Anderson, Richard. 1990. *Calliope's Sisters: A Comparative Study of Philosophies of Art*. Upper Saddle River, NJ: Prentice Hall.

Anderson, Richard. 2000. *American Muse: Anthropological Excursions into Art and Aesthetics*. Upper Saddle River, NJ: Prentice Hall.

Armstrong, Sue. 1991. "Female Circumcision: Fighting a Cruel Tradition." *New Scientist* 2:42–47.

Arnold, Fred, and Liu Zhaoxiang. 1986. "Sex Preference, Fertility, and Family Planning in China." *Population and Development Review* 12:221–246.

Asad, Talal. 1973. Anthropology and the Colonial Encounter. London: Ithaca Press.

Bailey, Garrick, and Roberta Bailey. 1986. *A History of the Navajos: The Reservation Years.* Santa Fe, NM: School of American Research Press.

Bakhtin, Mikhail. 1981. *The Dialogic Imagination, Four Essays.* Austin: University of Texas Press.

Balick, M., and P. Cox. 1996. *Plants, People, and Culture: The Science of Ethnobotany.* New York: Scientific American Library.

Ballard, Chris. 2002. "The Denial of Traditional Landrights in West Papua." *Cultural Survival Quarterly* 26 (3):40–43.

Barbeau, Marius. 1975. "The Career of a Medicine Man." In *Teachings from the American Earth* (Eds. D. Tedlock and B. Tedlock). New York: Liveright, pp. 3–12.

Barber, Pauline. 1990. "Culture, Capital and Class Conflicts in the Political Economy of Cape Breton." *Journal of Historical Sociology* 3:362–378.

Barber, Pauline. 2000. "Agency in Philippine women's labour migration and provisional diaspora." *Women's Studies International Forum* 23:399–412.

Barker, John. 1988. "Tangled Reconciliations: The Anglican Church and the Nisga'a of British Columbia." *American Ethnologist* 5:433–451.

Bartlett, Peggy. 1989. "Industrial Agriculture." In *Economic Anthropology* (Ed. S. Plattner). Palo Alto, CA: Stanford University Press, pp. 253–291.

Baron, Dennis. 1990. *The English-Only Question.* New Haven, CT: Yale University Press.

Barreda, Andres, and Ana Cecena. 1998. "Chiapas and the Global Restructuring of Capital." In *Zapatista! Reinventing Revolution in Mexico* (Eds. John Holloway and Eloina Pelaez). London: Pluto Press, pp. 39–63.

Barth, Frederick. 1964. *Nomads of South Persia.* Oslo: Universitetsforlaget.

Basso, Keith. 1990. *Western Apache Language and Culture: Essays in Linguistic Anthropology.* Tucson: University of Arizona Press.

Beaupré, Pascale, Pierre Turcotte and Anne Milan. 2006. "When is junior moving out? Transitions from the parental home to independence." *Canadian Social Trends* 82:8–14.

Benedict, Ruth. 1934. *Patterns of Culture.* Boston: Houghton Mifflin.

Benedict, Ruth. 1946. *The Chrysanthemum and the Sword.* Boston: Houghton Mifflin.

Beneria, Lourdes, and Gita Sen. 1986. "Accumulation, Reproduction, and Women's Role in Economic Development: Boserup Revisited." In *Women's Work: Development and the Division of Labor by Gender* (Eds. E. Leacock and H. Safa). Cambridge, MA: Bergin & Garvey, 141–157.

Bennett, John W. 1976. *Northern Plainsmen: Adaptive strategy and agrarian life.* Arlington Heights, Ill: AHM Publishing Corporation.

Berch, Bettina. 1982. *The Endless Day: The Political Economy of Women and Work.* New York: Harcourt Brace.

Beveridge, Sydney. 2003. "Human Rights Commission Condemns Mistreatment of Ogoni." *Cultural Survival Quarterly* 26 (3):9.

Blackman, Margaret. 1982. *During My Time: Florence Edenshaw Davidson, a Haida Woman.* Seattle: University of Washington Press.

Blackman, Margaret. 1989. *Sadie Brower Neakok: An Inupiaq Woman.* Seattle: University of Washington Press.

Boas, Franz. 1897. *The Social Organization and the Secret Societies of the Kwakiutl Indians.* Report of the U.S. National Museum of 1895. Washington, DC, pp. 311–738.

Boas, Franz. 1966. *Kwakiutl Ethnography* (Ed. H. Codere). Chicago: University of Chicago Press.

Boddy, Janice. 1982. "Womb as Oasis: The Symbolic Context of Pharaonic Circumcision in Rural Northern Sudan". American Ethnologist 9:682–698.

Boddy, Janice. 2001. "Spirit Possession and Gender Complementarity: Zar in Rural Northern Sudan." In *Gender in Cross-Cultural Perspective,* 3rd ed. (Eds. C. Brettell and C. Sargent). Upper Saddle River, NJ: Prentice Hall, pp. 397–408.

Bodenhorn, Barbara. 1988. "Whales, Souls, Children, and Other Things That Are 'Good to Share': Core Metaphors in a Contemporary Whaling Society." *Cambridge Anthropology* 13 (1):1–19.

Bodenhorn, Barbara. 1993. "Gendered Spaces, Public Places: Public and Private Revisited on the North Slope of Alaska." In *Landscape: Politics and Perspectives* (Ed. B. Bender). Providence, RI: Berg, pp. 169–203.

Bones, Jah. 1986. "Language of the Rastafaris." In *Language & the Black Experience* (Eds. D. Sutcliffe and A. Wong). London: Blackwell.

Bonvillain, Nancy. 1980. "Iroquoian Women." In *Studies on Iroquoian Culture* (Ed. N. Bonvillain). *Man in the Northeast.* Occasional Publications in Northeastern Anthropology No. 6, pp. 47–58.

Bonvillain, Nancy. 2001. *Native Nations: Cultures and Histories of Native North America.* Upper Saddle River, NJ: Prentice Hall.

Bordo, Susan. 2004. *Unbearable Weight: Feminism, Western Culture, and the Body,* rev. ed. Berkeley: University of California Press.

Borg, Marcus. 1994. *Jesus in Contemporary Scholarship.* Valley Forge, PA: Trinity Press International.

Boserup, Ester. 1970. *Women's Role in Economic Development.* London: Allen & Unwin.

Boudreau, Annette and Chantal White. 2004. "Turning the Tide in Acadian Nova Scotia: How Heritage Tourism is Changing Language Practices and Representations of Language". *Canadian Journal of Linguistics* 49:27–351.

Bourdieu, Pierre. 1991. *Language and Symbolic Power.* Cambridge, MA: Harvard University Press.

Brewer, Terri. 2000. "Touching the Past, Teaching Ways Forward: The American Indian Powwow." In *Indigenous Religions: A Companion* (Ed. Graham Harvey). New York: Cassell, pp. 255–268.

Briggs, Jean. 1982. "Eskimo Women: Makers of Men." In *Many Sisters* (Ed. C. Matthiason). New York: Free Press, pp. 261–304.

Brooke, James. 2003. "Dowry Too High, Lose Bride and Go to Jail." *New York Times,* February 3.

Brown, Judith. 1975. "Economic Organization and the Position of Women among the Iroquois." In *Toward an Anthropology of Women* (Ed. R. Rieter). New York: Monthly Review Press, pp. 235–251.

Bunzel, Ruth V. 1932. "Introduction to Zuni Ceremonialism." *Bureau of American Ethnology, Annual Report No. 47.* Washington, DC, pp. 467–544.

Burger, Richard L. 1992a. *Chavin and the Origins of Andean Civilization.* London: Thames & Hudson.

Burger, Richard L. 1992b. "The Sacred Center of Chavín de Huantar." In *The Ancient Americans, Art from Sacred Landscapes* (Ed. Richard F. Townsend). Art Institute of Chicago/Prestel Verlag, Munich.

Callender, Charles, and Lee Kochems. 1983. "The North American Berdache." *Current Anthropology* 24:443–470.

Canadian Press. 2007. "Many boomers not saving enough to retire." *Globe and Mail.* June 15, 2007. **www.reportonbusiness. com/servlet/story/RTGAM.20070614. wretirement0614/BNStory/robNews/ home**

Carrasco, David. 1998. *Daily Life of the Aztecs: People of the Sun and Earth.* Westport, CT: Greenwood Press.

Castells. Manuel. 2000. *The Network Society.* Oxford: Blackwell.

Castells, Manuel. 2000. *The Rise of the Network Society,* second edition. Oxford. Blackwell.

Castells, Manuel. 2004. *The Power of Identity: The Information Age—Economy, Society and Culture,* Volume II. Oxford: Blackwell.

Center for Strategic and International Study. 2003. HIV/AIDS Task Force. "Botswana's Strategy to Combat HIV/AIDS, Empowering Women and People Living with HIV/AIDS," November 12.

Chagnon, Napoleon. 1973. "The Culture-Ecology of Shifting Cultivation among the Yanomamo Indians." In *Peoples and Cultures of Native South America* (Ed. D. Gross). New York: Doubleday/Natural History Press, pp. 126–142.

Chagnon, Napoleon. 1997. *Yanomamo: The Fierce People,* 5th ed. New York: Holt, Rinehart & Winston.

Chambers, J. K. 1995. "The Canada–U.S. border as a vanishing isogloss: the evidence of chesterfield." *Journal of English Linguistics* 23:156–66.

Chance, Norman. 1990. *The Inupiat and Arctic Alaska: An Ethnography of Development.* New York: Holt, Rinehart & Winston.

Chawla, Raj K. and Ted Wannell. 2005. "Spenders and savers." *Perspectives and labour and income* 6:5–13.

Chernoff, J. M. 1981. *Aesthetics and Social Action in African Musical Idioms.* Chicago: University of Chicago Press.

Cheshire, Jenny. 1982. "Linguistic Variation and Social Function." In *Sociolinguistic Variation in Speech Communities* (Ed. S. Romaine). London: Edward Arnold, pp. 153–166.

Chitnis, Suma. 1988. "Feminism: Indian Ethos and Indian Convictions." In *Women in Indian Society* (Ed. R. Ghadially). Newbury Park, CA: Sage, pp. 81–95.

Chouinard, Craig. 1994. "A Tale of Two Synagogues: Culture, Conflict and Consolidation in the Jewish Community of Saint John, 1906–1919." *Canadian Jewish Studies* 2:19.

Chomsky, Noam. 1968. *Language and Mind.* New York: Harcourt Brace Jovanovich.

Citzenship and Immigration Canada. 2007. *Facts and figures 2006: Immigration overview: Permanent and temporary residents.* **www.cic. gc.ca/ english/resources/statistics/facts2006/ index.asp**. Accessed October 12, 2007.

Clancy, Patricia. 1986. "The Acquisition of Communicative Style in Japanese." In *Language Socialization across Cultures* (Eds. B. Schieffelin and E. Ochs). Cambridge: Cambridge University Press, pp. 213–250.

Clark, Warren and Susan Cromption. 2006. "Till death do us part? The risk of first and second marriage dissolution." *Canadian Social Trends* 81:23–33.

Clifford, James, and George Marcus (Eds.). 1986. *Writing Culture: The Poetics and Politics of Ethnography.* Berkeley: University of California Press.

Codere, Helen. 1961. "Kwakiutl." In *Perspectives in American Indian Culture Change.* (Ed. E. H. Spicer) Chicago: University of Chicago Press, pp. 431–516.

Collard, Chantal. 1988. "Enfants de Dieu, enfant du peche; Anthropologie des crèches quebecoise de 1900 à 1960". *Anthropologie et societé* 12:97–123.

Cooke-Reynolds, Melissa and Nancy Zukewich. 2004. "The feminization of work." *Canadian Social Trends* 72:24–29.

Condon, Richard. 1990. "The rise of adolescence: social change and life stages dilemmas in the Central Canadian Arctic." *Human Organization* 49:266–279.

Cordain L. 2006. "Implications of Plio-Pleistocene Hominin Diets for Modern Humans." In *Early Hominin Diets: The Known, the Unknown, and the Unknowable.*

(Ed. P. Ungar). Oxford: Oxford University Press.

Council on Foreign Relations. 2005. *Building a North American community: report of an independent task force.* New York: Council on Foreign Relations.

Counts, Dorothy and David Counts. 1996. *Over the Next Hill: An Ethnography of RVing Seniors in North America.* Peterborough, Ontario: Broadview Press.

Croll, Elizabeth. 1982. "The Sexual Division of Labor in Rural China." In *Women and Development: The Sexual Division of Labor in Rural Societies* (Ed. L. Beneria). New York: Praeger, pp. 223–274.

Crossan, John. 1994. *Jesus: A Revolutionary Biography.* New York: HarperCollins.

Cushing, Frank H. 1979. *Zuni: The Selected Writings of Frank Hamilton Cushing.* Lincoln: University of Nebraska Press.

Daly, Richard. 2005. *Our Box is Full: An Ethnography for the Delgamuukw Plaintiffs.* Vancouver: UBC Press.

D'Anglure, Bernard Saladin. 1984. "Inuit of Quebec." In *Arctic,* Vol. 5, *Handbook of North American Indians.* Washington, DC: Smithsonian Institution Press, pp. 476–507.

Darnell, Regna. 1997. "Changing patterns of ethnography in Canadian anthropology: a comparison of themes." *Canadian Review of Sociology and Anthropology* 34:269–296.

Davis, Reade. 2006. "All or nothing: Video lottery terminal gambling and economic restructuring in rural Newfoundland." *Identities: Global Studies in Culture and Power* 13:503–531.

Demos, John. 1994. *The Unredeemed Captive: A Family Story from Early America.* New York: Vintage.

Denny, J. P. 1982. "Semantics of the Inuktitut (Eskimo) Spatial Deictics." *International Journal of American Linguistics* 48:359–384.

Deveson, Morris. (1995). "The history of agriculture in Manitoba 1812–1995." (online) **www.mts.net/~agrifame/histormb.html**

Diamond, Jared. 1995. "The Worst Mistake in the History of the Human Race." In *Peoples of the Past and Present.* (Ed. J.-L. Chodkiewicz). New York: Harcourt Brace, pp. 114–117.

Diamond, Norma. 1975. "Collectivization, Kinship and the Status of Women in Rural China." In *Toward an Anthropology of Women* (Ed. R. Reiter). New York: Monthly Review Press, pp. 372–395.

Dirks, Nicholas. 2001. *Castes in Mind: Colonialism and the Making of Modern India.* Princeton, NJ: Princeton University Press.

Do, Anh. 2004. "Art Brings Creature Comforts to Villages." **http://kicon.com/anhdo/ artbrings.html**

Dorson, Richard. 1975. *Folktales Told around the World.* Chicago: University of Chicago Press.

Draper, Patricia. 1975. "!Kung Women: Contrasts in Sexual Egalitarianism in Foraging and Sedentary Contexts." In *Toward an Anthropology of Women* (Ed. R. Reiter).

New York: Monthly Review Press, pp. 77–109.

DuBois, W. E. B. 1903/1995. *The Souls of Black Folk.* New York: Signet Classics.

Dunk, Thomas. 2000. National culture, political economy and socio–cultural anthropology in English Canada. *Anthropologica* 42:131–145.

Dusenbery, Verne. 1997. "The poetics and politics of recognition: diasporan Sikhs in pluralist polities." *American Ethnologist* 24:738–762.

Egan, Fred. 1950. *Social Organization of the Western Pueblos.* Chicago: Chicago University Press.

Eiselen, W. M. 1934. "Christianity and the Religious Life of the Bantu." In *Western Civilization and the Natives of South Africa* (Ed. I. Schapera). London: Rutledge, pp. 65–82.

Elisabetsky, Elaine. 1996. "Community Ethnobotany: Setting Foundations for an Informed Decision on Training Rain Forest Resources." In *Medicinal Resources of the Tropical Forest: Biodiversity and Its Importance to Human Health* (Ed. M. Balick et al.). New York: Columbia University Press, pp. 402–408.

Ember, Carol. 1981. "A Cross-Cultural Perspective on Sex Differences." In *Handbook of Cross-Cultural Human Development* (Eds. Ruth H. Munroe, Robert L. Munroe, and Beatrice B. Whiting). New York: Garland, pp. 531–580.

Erikson, Thomas. 1993. *Ethnicity and Nationalism: Anthropological Perspectives.* London: Pluto Press.

Ervin-Tripp, S. M., M. C. O'Connor, and J. Rosenberg. 1984. "Language and Power in the Family." In *Language and Power* (Eds. M. Schulz and C. Kramerae). Belmont, CA: Sage, pp. 116–135.

Esposito, Anita. 1979. "Sex Differences in Children's Conversation." *Language and Speech* 22 (3):213–220.

Etienne, Mona, and Eleanor Leacock (Eds.). 1980. *Women and Colonization.* New York: Praeger.

Evans-Pritchard, E. E. 1940. *The Nuer.* Oxford: Oxford University Press.

Evans-Pritchard, E. E. 1955. *Kinship and Marriage among the Nuer.* Oxford: Clarendon.

Farnell, Brenda. 1995. "Movement and Gesture." In *Encyclopedia of Cultural Anthropology* (Eds. D. Levinson and M. Ember). New Haven, CT: Human Relations Area Files.

Ferguson, R. Brian. 1992. "A Savage Encounter: Western Contact and the Yanomami War Complex." In *War in the Tribal Zone: Expanding States and Indigenous Warfare* (Eds. R. Ferguson and N. Whitehead). Santa Fe, NM: School of American Research Press, pp. 199–227.

Ferguson, R. Brian, and Neil Whitehead. 1992. "The Violent Edge of Empire." In *War in the Tribal Zone: Expanding States and Indigenous Warfare* (Eds. R. Ferguson and N. Whitehead). Santa Fe, NM: School of American Research Press, pp. 1–30.

Fernandez-Kelly, Maria. 1983. "Mexican Border Industrialization, Female Labor Force Participation, and Migration." In *Women, Men, and the International Division of Labor* (Eds. J. Nash and M. Fernandez-Kelly). Albany: State University of New York Press, pp. 205–223.

Fiorenza, Elisabeth. 1983. *In Memory of Her: A Feminist Theological Reconstruction of Christian Origins.* New York: Crossroad Press.

Firth, Raymond. 1970. *Rank and Religion in Tikopia.* London: Allen & Unwin.

Forbes, Jack. 1990. "Undercounting Native Americans: The 1980 Census and the Manipulation of Racial Identity in the United States." *Wicazo Sa Review* 6:2–26.

Forero, Juan. 2003. "Seeking Balance: Growth vs. Culture in the Amazon." *New York Times,* December 10.

Forte, Maximillian. 2006. "The Political Economy of Tradition: Sponsoring and Incorporating the Caribs of Trinidad and Tobago." *Research in Economic Anthropology* 24:329–358.

Foster, George, and Barbara Anderson. 1978. *Medical Anthropology.* New York: Wiley.

Foucault, Michel. 1976. *Madness and Civilization: A History of Insanity in the Age of Reason.* New York: Pantheon.

Foulks, Edward. 1972. "The Arctic Hysterias of the North Alaskan Eskimo." *Anthropological Studies* No. 10. Washington, DC: American Anthropological Association.

Fournier, Suzanne. 1997. Stolen from our embrace : the abduction of First Nations children and the restoration of aboriginal communities. Vancouver: Douglas & McIntyre.

Fox, Robin. 1984. *Kinship and Marriage: An Anthropological Perspective.* New York: Cambridge University Press.

Fratkin, Elliot, and Tiffany Wu. 1997. "Maasai and Barabaig Herders Struggle for Landrights in Kenya and Tanzania." *Cultural Survival Quarterly* 21 (3).

Freese. 2006. *Pork powerhouses 2006.* **www.agriculture.com/ag/pdf/06PorkPowerhouses.pdf.** Retrieved on August 23, 2007.

Frenette, Marc. 2007. *Why Are Youth from Lower-income Families Less Likely to Attend University? Evidence from Academic Abilities, Parental Influences, and Financial Constraints.* Analytical Studies Branch Research Paper Series. Ottawa: Statistics Canada.

Fried, Morton. 1967. *The Evolution of Political Society.* New York: Random House.

Friedl, Ernestine. 1975. *Women and Men.* New York: Holt, Rinehart & Winston.

Friedman, Jonathan. 1999. "Class Formation, Hybridity and Ethnification in Declining Global Hegemonies." In *Globalisation and the Asia-Pacific* (Eds. Kris Olds et al.). London: Routledge, pp. 183–201.

Gadsby, Patricia. 2004. "The Inuit Paradox: How can people who gorge on fat and rarely see a vegetable be healthier than we are?" *Discover* 1/10/04.

Gagnon, Marie. 2001. "Crime comparisons between Canada and the United States". *Juristat* Vol 21. No. 11.

Gailey, Christine. 1980. "Putting Down Sisters and Wives: Tongan Woman and Colonization." In *Women and Colonization* (Eds. M. Etienne and E. Leacock). New York: Praeger, pp. 294–322.

Gailey, Christine. 1987a. "Evolutionary Perspective on Gender Hierarchy." In *Analyzing Gender* (Eds. B. Hess and M. Ferree). Newbury Park, CA: Sage, pp. 32–67.

Gailey, Christine. 1987b. *Kinship to Kingship: Gender Hierarchy and State Formation in the Tongan Islands.* Austin: University of Texas Press.

Geertz, Clifford. 1973. *The Interpretation of Cultures.* New York: Basic Books.

Ghadially, Rehana, and Pramod Kumar. 1988. "Bride Burning: The Psycho-Social Dynamics of Dowry Deaths." In *Women in Indian Society* (Ed. R. Ghadially). Newbury Park, CA: Sage, pp. 167–177.

Gibb, Camilla, and Celia Rothenberg. 2000. "Believing Women: Harari and Palestinian Women at Home and in the Canadian Diaspora." *Journal of Muslim Minority Affairs* 20:243–259.

Gibbs, James. 1965. "The Kpelle of Liberia." In *Peoples of Africa* (Ed. J. Gibbs). New York: Holt, Reinhart & Winston, pp. 197–240.

Gimbutas, Marija. 1982. *Goddesses and Gods of Old Europe: 6500–3500 BC.* Berkeley: University of California Press.

Gleason, Jean. 1987. "Sex Differences in Parent-Child Interaction." In *Language, Gender and Sex in Comparative Perspective* (Eds. Susan Philips et al.). New York: Cambridge University Press, pp. 189–199.

Glick, J. 1975. "Cognitive Development in Cross-Cultural Perspective." In *Review of Child Development Research* (Ed. F. D. Horowitz). Vol. 4, pp. 595–654. Chicago: University of Chicago Press.

Goodman, Felicitas. 1990. *Where the Spirits Ride the Wind: Trance Journeys and Other Ecstatic Experiences.* Bloomington: Indiana University Press.

Goody, Jack. 1983. *The development of the family and marriage in Europe.* Cambridge: Cambridge University Press.

Gorman, Peter. 1991. "A People at Risk: The Yanomami of Brazil." *Culture-Crossroads,* November, pp. 670–681.

Gough, Kathleen. 1968. "Anthropology, Child of Imperialism." *Monthly Review* 19(11): 12–27.

Gough, Kathleen. 1975. "The Origin of the Family." In *Toward an Anthropology of Women* (Ed. R. Reiter). New York: Monthly Review Press, pp. 51–76.

Government of Canada. 1982. *Charter of Rights and Freedoms.*

Graburn, Nelson. 1969. *Eskimos without Igloos: Social and Economic Development in Sugluk.* Boston: Little, Brown.

Graburn, Nelson (Ed.). 1976. *Ethnic and Tourist Arts: Cultural Expressions from the Fourth*

World. Berkeley: University of California Press.

Graves, J. 2004. *Administrative Report.* Vancouver: Vancouver City Council. www.city.vancouver. bc.ca/ctyclerk/cclerk/20040224/rr1b.htm. Accessed October 10, 2007.

Gray, Andrew. 1990. "Indigenous Peoples and the Marketing of the Rainforest." *The Ecologist* 20 (6):223.

Green, M.M. 1964. *Ibo village affairs.* New York: Praeger.

Gruenbaum, Ellen. 1993. "The Movement against Clitoridectomy and Infibulation in Sudan: Public Health Policy and the Women's Movement." In *Gender in Cross-Cultural Perspective* (Eds. C. Brettell and C. Sargent). Upper Saddle River, NJ: Prentice Hall, pp. 411–422.

Guibault, J., G. Averill, E. Benoit, and G. Rabess. 1993. *Zouk: World Music in the West Indies.* Chicago: University of Chicago Press.

Guillaume, Alfred. 1986. *Islam.* New York: Viking/Penguin.

Hafner, Katie. 1999. "Coming of Age in Palo Alto." *New York Times,* June 10.

Hall, Judith. 1984. *Non-Verbal Sex Differences: Communication, Accuracy and Expressive Style.* Baltimore: Johns Hopkins University Press.

Halperin, Rhoda. 1990. *The Livelihood of Kin: Making Ends Meet (The Kentucky Way).* Austin: University of Texas Press.

Hancock, Robert L.A. 2006. "Toward a historiography of Canadian anthropology." In Julia Harrison and Regna Darnell, eds. 2006. *Historicizing Canadian Anthropology.* Vancouver: UBC Press.

Hardman, Charlotte. 2000. "Rites of Passage among the Lohorung Rai of East Nepal." In *Indigenous Religions* (Ed. G. Harvey). London: Cassell, pp. 204–218.

Harris, Marvin. 1964. *Patterns of Race in the Americas.* New York: Walker and Company.

Harris, Marvin. 1974. *Cows, Pigs, Wars and Witches: The Riddles of Culture.* New York: Random House/Vintage.

Harrison, Julia and Regna Darnell. 2006. "Historicizing traditions in Canadian anthropology." In Julia Harrison and Regna Darnell, eds. 2006. *Historicizing Canadian Anthropology.* Vancouver: UBC Press.

Harrison, Julia and Regna Darnell, eds. 2006. *Historicizing Canadian Anthropology.* Vancouver: UBC Press.

Hartmann, Heidi. 1979. "Capitalism, Patriarchy, and Job Segregation by Sex." In *Capitalist Patriarchy and the Case for Socialist Feminism* (Ed. Z. Eisenstein). New York: Monthly Review Press, pp. 206–247.

Harvey, Youngsook Kim. 1979. *Six Korean Women: The Socialization of Shamans.* St. Paul, MN: West.

Hassrick, Royal. 1964. *The Sioux, Life and Customs of a Warrior Society.* Norman: University of Oklahoma Press.

Hathaway, Debbie. 1982. "The Political Equality League of Manitoba." *Manitoba History* 3.

Hedges, Chris. 2006. "Letter From Canada: The New Christian Right." *The Nation.* November 27, 2006 issue.

Hefner, Robert. 2001. "Multiculturalism and Citizenship in Malaysia, Singapore and Indonesia." In *Politics of Multiculturalism: Pluralism and Citizenship in Malaysia, Singapore and Indonesia* (Ed. R. Hefner). Honolulu: University of Hawaii Press, pp. 1–58.

Heider, Karl. 1996. *The Grand Valley Dani. Peaceful warriors.* 3rd edition. Belmont, CA: Wadsworth Publishing.

Heine, S. J., et al. 1999. "Is There a Universal Need for Positive Self-Regard?" *Psychological Review* 106 (4):766–794.

Heisz, Andrew 2007. *Income Inequality and Redistribution in Canada: 1976 to 2004.* Ottawa: Statistics Canada.

Henley, Nancy. 1977. *Body Politics: Power, Sex and Non-Verbal Communication.* Englewood Cliffs, NJ: Prentice Hall.

Henry, Francis and Carol Tater. 2002. "The role and practice of racialized discourse in culture and cultural production." *Journal of Canadian Studies* 35:120–137.

Henshaw, Anne. 2006a. "Winds of Change: Weather Knowledge Amongst the Sikusilarmiut." In Rick Riewe and Jill Oakes, eds. *Climate Change: Linking Traditional and Scientific Knowledge.* Winnipeg: Aboriginal Issues Press and University of Manitoba.

Henshaw, Anne. 2006b. "Pausing along the Journey: Learning Landscapes, Environmental Change, and Toponymy Amongst the Sikusilarmiut" *Arctic Anthropology* 43: 52–66.

Herman, Edward, and Noam Chomsky. 1988. *Manufacturing Consent: The Political Economy of the Mass Media.* New York: Pantheon.

Hill, A. 2002. "Tryptamine Based Entheogens of South America." **http://students.whitman. edu/~hillap/tryptamine%20based %20Entheogens.htm**.

Hill, Polly. 1963. *Migrant cocoa farmers of Southern Ghana: Studies in rural capitalism.* Cambridge: Cambridge University Press.

HimRights. "International Himalayan Human Rights Monitors (INHURED)." **www.inhured.org/download/HimRights brochure.pdf**. Accessed November 2, 2004.

Hoebel, E. Adamson. 1978. *The Cheyennes: Indians of the Great Plains.* New York: Holt, Rinehart & Winston.

Holtzman, J. 2000. *Nuer Journeys, Nuer Lives.* Boston: Allyn & Bacon.

"Honoring Native Languages, Defeating the Shame." 2000. *Tribal College Journal of American Indian Higher Education.* Spring.

Hou, Feng and John Myles. 2007. *The Changing Role of Education in the Marriage Market: Assortative Marriage in Canada and the United States since the 1970s.* Ottawa: Statistics Canada.

Howes, David. 2006. Constituting Canadian anthropology. In Julia Harrison and Regna Darnell, eds. 2006. *Historicizing Canadian Anthropology.* Vancouver: UBC Press.

Hudon, Marie-ve. 2007. Language Regimes in the Provinces and Territories. Ottawa: Parliamentary Information and Research Service. **www.parl.gc.ca/information/library/ PRBpubs/prb0638-e. htm#table1** Accessed October 3, 2007.

Hume, Lynne. 2000. "The Dreaming in Contemporary Aboriginal Australia." In *Indigenous Religion* (Ed. G. Harvey). London: Cassell, pp. 125–138.

Hymes, Dell. 1974. *Foundations in Socio-Linguistics: An Ethnographic Approach.* Philadelphia: University of Pennsylvania Press.

Hytek Ltd. 2007. www.hytekmb.com. Accessed August 23, 2007.

Itoh, Shinji. 1980. "Physiology of Circumpolar People." In *The Human Biology of Circumpolar Populations* (Ed. F. A. Milan). Cambridge: Cambridge University Press.

Iwu, Maurice. 1996. "Resource Utilization and Conservation of Biodiversity in Africa." In *Medicinal Resources of the Tropical Forest: Biodiversity and Its Importance to Human Health* (Eds. M. Balick et al.). New York: Columbia University Press, pp. 233–250.

Janhevich, Derek. 2001. *Hate Crime in Canada: An Overview of Issues and Data Sources.* Ottawa: Statistics Canada.

Jefremovas, Villia. 1997. "Contested Identities: Power and the Fictions of Ethnicity, Ethnography and History in Rwanda." *Anthropologica* 39:91–104.

Johnson, Allen. 1978. "In Search of the Affluent Society." *Human Nature,* September, pp. 50–59.

Jolly, Alison. 1985. *The Evolution of Primate Behavior,* 2nd ed. New York: Macmillan.

Jones, Barbara. 1998. "Infighting in San Francisco: Anthropology in Family Court, Or: A Study in Cultural Misunderstanding." *High Plains Applied Anthropologist* 18 (1):37–41.

Jones, G.I. 1962. "Ibo age organization with special reference to the Cross River and North Eastern Ibo." *Journal of the Royal Anthropological Institute* 92:191–210.

Kahlenberg, Mary, and Anthony Berlant. 1972. *The Navajo Blanket.* New York: Praeger/Los Angeles County Museum of Art.

Katz, Richard. 1982. *Boiling Energy: Community Healing among the Kalahari !Kung.* Cambridge, MA: Harvard University Press.

Kehoe, Alice. 1989. *The Ghost Dance: Ethnohistory and Revitalization.* New York: Holt, Rinehart & Winston.

Keister, Lisa and Stephanie Moller. 2000. "Wealth inequality in the United States." *Annual Review of Sociology* 26:63–81.

Kellman, Shelly. 1982. "The Yanomamis: Their Battle for Survival." *Journal of International Affairs* 36:15–42.

Kelly, Raymond. 1976. "Witchcraft and Sexual Relations: An Exploration in the Social and Semantic Implications of the Structure of Belief." In *Man and Woman in the New Guinea Highlands* (Eds. P. Brown and G. Buchdinder). Special Publication No. 8.

Washington, DC: American Anthropological Association, pp. 36–53.

Kendall, Laurel. 1984. "Korean Shamanism: Women's Rites and a Chinese Comparison." In *Religion and the Family in East Asia* (Eds. G. DeVos and T. Sofue). Berkeley: University of California Press, pp. 185–200.

Knight, R. 2002. "Ethnomusicology." **www.oberlin.edu/faculty/rknight/**. Accessed November 18, 2004.

Koller, John. 1982. *The Indian Way*. New York: Macmillan.

Koso-Thomas, Olayinka. 1992. *The Circumcision of Women: A Strategy for Eradication*. London: Zed Books.

Krauss, Michael. 1992. "The World's Languages in Crisis." *Language* 68:4–10.

Kumar, Radha. 1995. "From Chipko to Sati: The Contemporary Indian Women's Movement." In *The Challenge of Local Feminisms: Women's Movement in Global Perspective* (Ed. A. Basu). Boulder, CO: Westview.

Kuper, Adam. 1982 *Wives for cattle: Bridewealth and marriage in South Africa*. London, Routledge and Kegan Paul.

Labov, William. 1972. *Sociolinguistic Patterns*. Philadelphia: University of Pennsylvania Press.

Labov, William. 1997. "Some Further Steps in Narrative Analysis." *Journal of Narrative and Life History* 7:395–415.

Lacey, Mark. 2004. "Genital Cutting Shows Signs of Losing Favor in Africa." *New York Times*, June 8.

Lafitau, Joseph. 1974 (1724). *Customs of the American Indians*. Toronto: Champlain Society.

Lako, George. 1988. "The Impact of Jonglei Scheme on the Economy of the Dinka." In *Tribal Peoples and Development Issues* (Ed. J. Bodley). Mountain View, CA: Mayfield, pp. 137–150.

Lakoff, George, and Mark Johnson. 1980. *Metaphors We Live By*. Chicago: University of Chicago Press.

Lamphere, Louise. 2001. "The Domestic Sphere of Women and the Public World of Men: The Strengths and Limitations of an Anthropological Dichotomy." In *Gender in Cross-Cultural Perspective*, 3rd ed. (Eds. C. Brettell and C. Sargent). Upper Saddle River, NJ: Prentice Hall, pp. 100–110.

Laurendeau, Paul. 1992. "Socio-historicité des français non conventionnels': le cas du JOUAL (Québec 1960–1975)". *Grammaire des fautes et français non conventionnels*, Presses de l'École Normale Supérieure, Paris, pp. 279–296.

Leacock, Eleanor. 1954. "The Montagnais 'Hunting Territory' and the Fur Trade," Vol. 56, No. 5, Pt. 2, Memoir No. 78. Washington, DC: American Anthropological Association.

Leacock, Eleanor. 1981. *Myths of Male Dominance*. New York: Monthly Review Press.

LeBlanc, Marie Nathalie. 1999. "The Production of Islamic Identities through Knowledge Claims in Bouaké, Côte d'Ivoire." *African Affairs* 98:485–508.

Lee, Ching Kwan. 1998. *Gender and the South China Miracle*. Berkeley: University of California Press.

Lee, Richard. 1972. "Work Effort, Group Structure, and Land Use in Hunter-Gatherers." In *Man, Settlement, and Urbanism*, Peter Ucko, Ruth Tringham and G.W. Dimbleby (eds.), London: Duckworth.

Lee, Richard. 1982. "Politics, Sexual and Nonsexual, in an Egalitarian Society." In *Politics and History in Band Societies* (Eds. E. Leacock and R. Lee). New York: Cambridge University Press, pp. 37–60.

Lee, Richard. 2003. *The Dobe Ju/'hoansi*, 3rd ed. New York: Harcourt Brace.

Leibowitz, Lila. 1983. "Origins of the Sexual Division of Labor." In *Women's Nature: Rationalizations of Inequality* (Eds. M. Lowe and R. Hubbard). Elmsford, NY: Pergamon, pp. 123–147.

Levine, Nancy E. 1988. *The Dynamics of Polyandry. Kinship, Domesticity, and Population on the Tibetan Border*. Chicago: University of Chicago Press.

Lévis-Strauss, Claude. 1949. *Elementary Structures of Kinship*. Paris: Presses Universitaires de France.

Lewis, I. M. 1989. *Ecstatic Religion: A Study of Shamanism and Spirit Possession*, 2nd ed. London: Routledge.

Ley, David. 2007. "Post-multiculturalism?" In B. Ruble, ed. *Renegotiating the City: Concepts of Immigration and Integration in Urban Communities*. Washington, DC: Woodrow Wilson International Center Press.

Leyton, Elliot. 2005. *Hunting humans: The rise of the modern multiple murderer*. Toronto: McClelland & Stewart.

Lindenbaum, Shirley. 1979. *Kuru Sorcery: Disease and Danger in the New Guinea Highlands*. Palo Alto, CA: Mayfield.

Lindenfeld, Jacqueline. 1969. "The Social Conditioning of Syntactic Variation in French." *American Anthropologist* 71:890–898.

Lindfors, Bernth, and Oyekan Owomoyela. 1973. "Yoruba Proverbs: Translation and Annotation." *Papers in International Studies: Africa Series No. 17*. Athens: Ohio University Center for International Studies.

Lizot, Jacques. 1971. "Remarques sur le vocabulaire de parente Yanomami". *L'Homme* 11:25–38.

Lockwood, Victoria. 1997. "The Impact of Development on Women: The Interplay of Material Conditions and Gender Ideology." In *Gender in Cross-Cultural Perspective*, 2nd ed. (Eds. C. Brettell and C. Sargent). Upper Saddle River, NJ: Prentice Hall, pp. 504–517.

London Daily Telegraph April 19, 2007. "Botswana betrays the outcast Bushmen."

Mack, Burton. 1988. *A Myth of Innocence: Mark and Christian Origins*. Philadelphia: Fortress Press.

Mackey, Eva. 1999. *The house of difference: Cultural politics and national identity in Canada*. Toronto: University of Toronto Press.

Malinowski, Bronislaw. 1922. *Argonauts of the Western Pacific*. London: Routledge & Kegan Paul.

Malinowski, Bronislaw. 1954. *Magic, science, and religion and other essays*. Garden City, N.J.: Doubleday.

Maple Leaf Foods Inc. 2007. **www.mapleleaf.ca** Accessed August 23, 2007.

Maquet, Jacques. 1961. *The premise of inequality in Ruanda: A study of political relations in a central African kingdom*. London: Oxford University Press.

Marable, Manning. 1995. "Beyond Racial Identity Politics: Towards a Liberation Theory for Multicultural Democracy." In *Race, Class, and Gender*, 2nd ed. (Eds. M. Andersen and P. Collins). Belmont, CA: Wadsworth, pp. 363–366.

Markus, Hazel R., and Shinobu Kitayama. 1991. "Culture and the Self: Implications for Cognition, Emotion, and Motivation." *Psychological Review* 98 (2):224–253.

Marmen, Louise and Jean-Pierre Corbeil. 2004. *Languages in Canada: 2001 Census*. Ottawa: Statistics Canada.

Marshall, Katherine. 2006. "Converging gender roles." *Perspectives on Labour and Income* 7(7):5–17.

Martineau, Joel. 2001. "Autoethnography and Material Culture: The Case of Bill Reid." *Biography* 24:242–258.

Marwick, M. G. 1967. "The Sociology of Sorcery in a Central African Tribe." In *Magic, Witchcraft, and Curing* (Ed. J. Middleton). New York: Natural History Press, pp. 101–126.

Mataira, Peter. 2000. "Mana and Tapu: Sacred Knowledge, Sacred Boundaries." In *Indigenous Religions* (Ed. G. Harvey). New York: Cassell, pp. 99–112.

Matthaei, Julie. 1982. *An Economic History of Women in America*. New York: Schocken.

Maybury-Lewis, David. 1997. *Indigenous Peoples, Ethnic Groups, and the State*. Boston: Allyn & Bacon.

McAllester, David. 1954. *Enemy Way Music*. Cambridge, MA: Peabody Museum.

McDermott, LeRoy. 1996. "Self-Representation in Female Figurines." *Current Anthropology* 37:227–275.

McElroy, Ann and Patricia Townsend. 1989. *Medical Anthropology in Ecological Perspective*. Boulder, CO: Westview.

McEvilley, Thomas. 1992. *Art and Otherness: Crisis in Cultural Identity*. Kingston, NY: McPherson.

McWhorter, John. 1997. "Wasting Energy on an Illusion." *Black Scholar* 27 (1):9–14.

Meggers, Betty. 1971. *Amazonia: Man and Culture in a Counterfeit Paradise*. New York: Free Press.

Meek, C. K. 1937. *Law and authority in a Nigerian tribe: a study in indirect rule*. Oxford University Press.

Meier, John. 1991. *A Marginal Jew: Rethinking the Historical Jesus*. New York: Doubleday.

Meillassoux, Claude. 1972. "From Reproduction to Production: A Marxist Approach to

Economic Anthropology", *Economy and Society* 1:93–105.

Mencher, Joan. 1965. "The Nayars of South Malabar." In *Comparative Family Systems* (Ed. M. E. Nimkoff). Boston: Houghton Mifflin, pp. 162–191.

Menkis, Richard. 2002. "Negotiating Ethnicity, Regionalism and Historiography: Arthur A. Chiel and The Jews in Manitoba: A Social History." *Canadian Jewish Studies* 10:1–31.

Michelson, Truman. 1920. *Autobiography of a Fox Woman*. Fortieth Annual Report of the Bureau of American Ethnology for the years 1918–1919, pp. 291–349. Washington, DC.

Milan, Anne. 2000. "One hundred years of families." *Canadian Social Trends* 56:1–12

Milan, Anne and Brian Hamm. 2004. "Mixed unions." *Canadian Social Trends* 73: 2–6.

Mills, Antonia. 1994. *Eagle down is our law: the Witsuwit'en law, feasts, and land claims*. Vancouver : UBC Press.

Mills, C. Wright. 1956. *The Power Elite*. New York: Oxford University Press.

Mintz, Sydney. 1996. *Tasting Food, Tasting Freedom: Excursions into Eating, Culture, and the Past*. Boston: Beacon Press.

Mooney, James. 1965. *The Ghost Dance Religion and the Sioux Outbreak of 1890*. Chicago: University of Chicago Press.

Moore, Henrietta. 1988. *Feminism and Anthropology*. Minneapolis: University of Minnesota Press.

Morelli, G. A., et al. 1992. "Cultural Variation in Infants' Sleeping Arrangements: Questions of Independence." *Developmental Psychology* 38:604–613.

Morgan, Lewis Henry. 1877. *Ancient Society*. Cambridge, MA: Harvard University Press.

Morioka, Kiyomi. 1984. "Ancestor Worship in Contemporary Japan: Continuity and Change." In *Religion and the Family in East Asia* (Eds. G. DeVos and T. Sofue). Berkeley: University of California Press, pp. 201–216.

Morissette, Rene and Xuelin Zhang. 2006. "Revisiting wealth inequality." *Perspectives on Labour and Income* 8:5–16.

Munroe R. M., and R. H. Munroe. 1975. "Levels of Obedience among U.S. and East African Children on an Experimental Task." *Journal of Cross-Cultural Psychology* 6:498–503.

Murphy, Jane. 1981. "Abnormal Behavior in Traditional Societies: Labels, Explanations and Social Reactions." *Medical Anthropology*, pp. 809–826.

Namias, June. 1995. *White Captives: Gender and Ethnicity on the American Frontier*. Chapel Hill: University of North Carolina Press.

Nanda, Serena. 1990. *Neither Man Nor Woman: The Hijras of India*. Belmont, CA: Wadsworth.

Navajo Nation. 1972. *The Navajo Ten Year Plan*. Windowrock, AZ: The Navajo Tribe.

Neihardt, John. 1961. *Black Elk Speaks: Being a Life Story of a Holy Man of the Oglala Sioux*. Lincoln: University of Nebraska Press.

Nietschmann, B. 1988. "Third World Colonial Expansion: Indonesia, Disguised Invasion of Indigenous Nations." In *Tribal Peoples and Development Issues* (Ed. J. Bodley). Mountain View, CA: Mayfield, pp. 191–208.

Nock, David. 2006. "The erasure of Horatio Hales contributions to Boasian anthropology." In Julia Harrison and Regna Darnell, eds. 2006. *Historicizing Canadian Anthropology*. Vancouver: UBC Press.

Norris, Mary Jane. 1998. "Aboriginal languages in Canada: Emerging trends and perspectives on second language acquisition". *Canadian Social Trends* 83:19–27.

Norris, Mary Jane. 2007. "Aboriginal languages in Canada: Emerging trends and perspectives on second language acquisition". *Canadian Social Trends* 83.

Novek, Joel. 2003. "Intensive hog farming in Manitoba: transnational treadmills and local conflicts." *Canadian Review of Sociology and Anthropology* 40:3–26.

Obeng, Samuel Gyasi. 1996. "The Proverb as a Mitigating and Politeness Strategy in Akan Discourse." *Anthropological Linguistics* 38:521–549.

O'Brien, Jay. 1986. "Toward a Reconstitution Ethnicity: Capitalist Expansion and Cultural Dynamics in Sudan." *American Anthropologist* 88 (4):898–907.

Ochs, Elinor, and Caroline Taylor. 1995. "The 'Father Knows Best' Dynamic in Dinnertime Narratives." In *Linguistic Anthropology: A Reader* (Ed. A. Duranti). Malden, MA: Blackwell, pp. 431–449.

Offert, M. Rose. "ND Farming." In *The Encyclopedia of Saskatchewan*. esask.uregina.ca/entry/farming.htm Accessed August 23, 2007.

Omeje, Kenneth. 2005. "Enyimba enyi: The comeback of Igbo nationalism in Nigeria." *Review of African Political Economy* 32:628–635.

Ong, Aihwa. 1983. "Global Industries and Malay Peasants in Peninsula Asia." In *Women, Men, and the International Division of Labor* (Eds. J. Nash and M. Fernandez-Kelly). Albany: State University of New York Press, pp. 426–439.

Ottenberg, Phoebe. 1965. "The Afikpo Ibo of Eastern Nigeria." In *Peoples of Africa* (Ed. J. Gibbs). New York: Holt, Rinehart & Winston, pp. 3–39.

Ottenberg, Simon, and Phoebe Ottenberg. 1962. "Afikpo Market 1900–1960." In *Markets in Africa* (Eds. P. Bohannan and G. Dalton). Evanston, IL: Northwestern University Press, pp. 117–169.

Ottley, Bruce, and Jean Zorn. 1983. "Criminal Law in Papua New Guinea: Code, Custom and the Courts in Conflict." In *American Journal of Comparative Law* 31:251–300.

Patrick, Donna. 2005. Language Rights in Indigenous Communities: The Case of the Inuit of Arctic Québec. Journal of Sociolinguistics 9/3, 2005:369–389.

Peregrine, Peter. 2003. *World Prehistory: Two Million Years of Human Life*. Upper Saddle River, NJ: Prentice Hall.

Perry, Richard. 1996. "From Time in Memorial: Indigenous Peoples and State Systems." Austin: University of Texas Press.

Piquemal, Natali and Bret Nickels. 2005. "Cultural Congruence in the Education of and Research With Young Aboriginal Students: Ethical Implications for Classroom Researchers." *Alberta Journal of Educational Research* 51:118–134.

Polanyi, Karl. 1966. *Dahomey and the slave trade: An analysis of an archaic economy*. Seattle: University of Washington.

Poulin, Denis and Attah Boame. 2003. *Mad cow disease and beef trade*. Ottawa: Statistics Canada.

Price, Sally. 1984. *Co-wives and Calabashes*. Ann Arbor: University of Michigan Press.

Price, Sally. 1989. *Primitive Art in Civilized Places*. Chicago: University of Chicago Press.

Province of Manitoba. 2006. "Farm cash receipts estimates." January–December 2005, 2006. **www.gov.mb.ca/agriculture/statistics/pdf/farmcashreceiptsjandecember2006.pdf** Accessed August 23, 2007.

Putnam, Robert D. 2007. "E Pluribus Unum: Diversity and community in the twenty-first century." *Scandinavian Political Studies* 30:137–174.

Raheja, Gloria Goodwin, and Ann Grodzins Gold. 1994. *Listen to the Heron's Words: Reimagining Gender and Kinship in North India*. Berkeley: University of California Press.

Ramos, Alcida. 1997. "The Indigenous Movement in Brazil: A Quarter Century of Ups and Downs." *Cultural Survival Quarterly* 21 (2).

Rappaport, Roy. 1969. "Ritual Regulation of Environmental Relations among a New Guinea People." In *Environment and Cultural Behavior* (Ed. A. Vayda). Garden City, NY: Natural History Press, pp. 181–201.

Rappaport, Roy. 2000. *Pigs for the Ancestors: Ritual in the Ecology of a New Guinea People*, 2nd ed. New Haven, CT: Yale University Press.

Rasmussen, Knud. 1929. *Intellectual Culture of the Iglulik Eskimo*. Vol. 7, No. 1, of the Report of the Fifth Thule Expedition, 1921–1924. Copenhagen: Clydendalske Boghandel.

Rathje W., and Murphy C. 1992. "Five Major Myths about Garbage and Why They're Wrong." *Smithsonian*, July.

Reid, Gerald. 2004. *Kahnawá:ke : factionalism, traditionalism, and nationalism in a Mohawk community*. Lincoln: University of Nebraska Press.

Reid, Walter, et al. 1996. "Biodiversity Prospecting." In *Medicinal Resources of the Tropical Forest: Biodiversity and Its Importance to Human Health* (Eds. M. Balick et al.). New York: Columbia University Press, pp. 142–173.

Reitz, Jeffrey. 1985. "Less Racial Discrimination in Canada, or Simply Less Racial Conflict?: Implications of Comparisons with Britain." *Canadian Public Policy* 14:424–441.

Rensberger, Boyce. 2001. "Racial Odyssey." In *Anthropology: Contemporary Perspectives,*

8th ed. (Ed. P. Whitten). Boston: Allyn & Bacon, pp. 81–89.

Ribeiro, Darcy. 1971. *The Americas and Civilization.* New York: Dutton.

Richeport, Madeleine. 1984. *Macumba Trance and Spirit Healing.* Richeport Films. Written, produced, and directed by Madeleine Richeport.

Richmond, John. 1986. "The Language of Black Children and the Language Debate in the Schools." In *Language and the Black Experience* (Eds. D. Sutcliffe and A. Wong). Oxford: Blackwell, pp. 123–135.

Rickford, John. 1997. "Unequal Partnership: Sociolinguistics and the African American Speech Community." *Language in Society* 26:161–198.

Robinson, Angela. 2004. *Ta'n teliktlamsitasit (ways of believing): Mi'kmaw religion in Eskasoni.* Toronto: Pearson.

Rodman, Margaret. 1993. "Keeping Options Open: Copra and Fish in Rural Vanuatu." In *Contemporary Pacific Societies: Studies in Development and Change* (Eds. V. Lockwood et al.). Upper Saddle River, NJ: Prentice Hall, pp. 171–184.

Rogoff, Barbara, and Morelli, Gilda. 1989. "Perspectives on Children's Development from Cultural Psychology." *American Psychologist* 44 (2):343–348.

Rohrlich-Leavitt, Ruby, et al. 1975. "Aboriginal Woman: Male and Female Anthropological Perspectives." In *Toward an Anthropology of Women* (Ed. R. Reiter). New York: Monthly Review Press, pp. 110–126.

Rohter, Larry. 2003. "Bolivia's Poor Proclaim Abiding Distrust of Globalization." *New York Times,* October 17.

Rosaldo, Michelle. 1974. "Women, Culture and Society: A Theoretical Overview." In *Women, Culture and Society* (Eds. M. Rosaldo and L. Lamphere). Stanford, CA: Stanford University Press, pp. 17–42.

Roy, Sylvie. 2004. "Language Varieties as Social Practices: Evidence from Two Minority Francophone Communities in Canada". *Canadian Journal of Linguistics* 49: 353–373.

Royce, Anya. 1977. *The Anthropology of Dance.* Bloomington: Indiana University Press.

Rubel, Arthur. 1977. "The Epidemiology of a Folk Illness: Susto in Hispanic America." In *Culture, Disease, and Healing: Studies in Medical Anthropology* (Ed. D. Landy). New York: Macmillan, pp. 119–128.

Ryan, K. 2000. "Edible Wild Plants as Digestive Aids: Ethnoarchaeology in Maasailand. Science and Archaeology." *Expedition* 42 (3):7–8.

Sahlins, Marshall. 1961. "The Segmentary Lineage: An Organization of Predatory Expansion." *American Anthropologist* 63:332–345.

Sahlins, Marshall. 1970. "Poor Man, Rich Man, Big-Man, Chief: Political Types in Melanesia and Polynesia." In *Cultures of the Pacific* (Eds. T. Harding and B. Wallace). New York: Free Press, pp. 203–215.

Sakajiri, N. 2004. "Japan Cited in Human Trafficking. *Asahi Shimbun,* June 16.

Sanday, Peggy. 1981. *Female Power and Male Dominance.* New York: Cambridge University Press.

Sanders, E. P. 1985. *Jesus and Judaism.* Philadelphia: Fortress Press.

Sapir, Edward. 1949. "Language and Environment." In *Selected Writings of Edward Sapir* (Ed. E. Mandelbaum). Berkeley: University of California Press, pp. 89–103.

Sasson, Jack. 1995. *Civilizations of the Ancient Near East, I-IV.* New York: Scribner's.

Shaienks, Danielle et al. 2006. *Follow-up on Education and Labour Market Pathways of Young Canadians Aged 18 to 20—Results from YITS Cycle 3.* Ottawa: Statistics Canada.

Schemo, Diana. 1999. "The Last Tribal Battle." *New York Times Magazine,* October 31, pp. 70–77.

Scheper-Hughes, Nancy. 1989. "The Human Strategy: Death without Weeping." *Natural History Magazine,* October, pp. 8–16.

Scheper-Hughes, Nancy. 1992. *Death without Weeping: The Violence of Everyday Life in Brazil.* Berkeley: University of California Press.

Scheper-Hughes, Nancy. 2004. *Parts Unknown: Undercover Ethnography of the Organs-Trafficking Underworld.* Thousand Oaks, CA: Sage.

Schiller, Nina Glick, et al. 1992. "Transnationalism: A New Analytic Framework for Understanding Migration." In *Towards a Transnational Perspective on Migration: Race, Class, Ethnicity, and Nationalism Reconsidered* (Eds. N. G. Schiller et al.). Annals of the New York Academy of Sciences, Vol. 645, pp. 1–24. New York: New York Academy of Sciences.

Schmink, Marianne. 1988. "Big Business in the Amazon." In *People of the Tropical Rain Forest* (Eds. Julie Denslow and Christine Padoch). Berkeley: University of California Press, pp. 163–174.

Schmink, Marianne, and Charles Wood. 1992. *Contested Frontiers in Amazonia.* New York: Columbia University Press.

Schneller, Raphael. 1988. "The Israeli Experience of Cross-Cultural Misunderstanding: Insights and Lessons." In *Cross-Cultural Perspectives in Non-Verbal Communication* (Ed. F. Poyatos). Lewiston, NY: C. J. Hogrefe, pp. 153–171.

Seattle Times. 1996. "British Agree to Destroy Beef in Mad-Cow Scare, Europeans to Help Pay for Industry Losses." April 3, p. A3.

Segall, Marshall. 1979. *Cross-Cultural Psychology: Human Behavior in Global Perspective.* Monterey, CA: Brooks/Cole.

Seligman, Charles. 1930. *Races of Africa.* London: Thornton and Butterworth.

Service, Elman. 1962. *Primitive Social Organization: An Evolutionary Perspective.* New York: Random House.

Shannon, Jonathan. 2003. "Sultans of Spin: Syrian Sacred Music on the World Stage." *American Anthropologist* 105:266–277.

Shostak, Marjorie. 1983. *Nisa: The Life and Words of a! Kung Woman.* New York: Vintage.

Sigurdson, Richard. 1994. "Preston Manning and the Politics of Postmodernism in Canada." *Canadian Journal of Political Science* 27:249–276.

Siskind, Janet. 1973. "Tropical Forest Hunters and the Economy of Sex." In *Peoples and Cultures of Native South America* (Ed. D. Gross). New York: Doubleday/Natural History Press, pp. 226–240.

Skinner, Alanson. 1911. *Notes on the Eastern Cree and Northern Saulteaux.* Anthropological Papers, Vol. 9, Pt. 1. New York: American Museum of Natural History.

Smith, S. Percy. 1913. "The Lore of the Whare-Wananga." New Plymouth, N.Z., **www.sacredtexts.com/pac/lww/index**.

Smitherman, Geneva, and Sylvia Cunningham. 1997. "Moving Beyond Resistance: Ebonics and African American Youth." *Journal of Black Psychology* 28:227–232.

Sofue, Takao. 1984. "Family and Interpersonal Relationships in Early Japan." In *Religion and the Family in East Asia* (Eds. G. DeVos and T. Sofue). Berkeley: University of California Press, pp. 201–216.

Soustelle, Jacques. 1961. *Daily Life of the Aztecs: On the Eve of the Spanish Conquest.* Stanford, CA: Stanford University Press.

Southwold, Martin. 1965. "The Ganda of Uganda." In *Peoples of Africa* (Ed. J. Gibbs). New York: Holt, Rinehart & Winston, pp. 81–118.

Spencer, Robert. 1984. "North Alaska Coast Eskimo." In *Arctic,* Vol. 5, pp. 320–337. *Handbook of North American Indians.* Washington, DC: Smithsonian Institution Press.

Spradley, James. 1972. *Guests Never Leave Hungry: The Autobiography of James Sewid, a Kwakiutl Indian.* Montreal: McGill–Queen's University Press.

Stack, Carol. 1975. *All My Kin: Strategies for Survival in a Black Community.* New York: Harper Torchbooks.

Statistics Canada. 1996. *Census of Population.*

Statistics Canada. 2001. *Census of Population.*

Statistics Canada. 2003. *Ethnic Diversity Survey: Portrait of a Multicultural Society.*

Statistics Canada. 2006. *Spending Patterns in Canada,* 2005.

Statistics Canada. 2007a. "Census of Agriculture counts 44,329 farms in Saskatchewan." www.statcan.ca/english/agcensus2006/media_release/sk.htm Accessed August 23, 2007.

Statistics Canada. 2007b. *Hog Statistics* 6 (3):34–36. www.gov.mb.ca/agriculture/statistics/pdf/hogsjuly07. pdf Accessed August 23, 2007.

Story, G. M. 1990. *Dictionary of Newfoundland English.* St. John's, Newfoundland: Breakwater Books.

Strathern, Andrew. 1992. "Let the Bow Go Down." In *War in the Tribal Zone: Expanding States and Indigenous Warfare* (Eds. R. Ferguson and N. Whitehead). Santa Fe, NM: School of American Research Press, pp. 229–250.

Tedlock, Dennis. 1972. *Finding the Center: Narrative Poetry of the Zuñi Indians.* Dennis Tedlock, trans.; from performances in the Zuñi by Andrew Peynetsa and Walter Sanchez. Lincoln: University of Nebraska Press.

Tedlock, Dennis. 1983. *The Spoken Word and the Work of Interpretation.* Philadelphia: University of Pennsylvania Press.

Thom, Brian 2003. "Aboriginal Rights and Title in Canada After Delgamuukw: Part One, Oral Traditions and Anthropological Evidence in the Courtroom". Native Studies Review. 14:1–2.

Thompson, Robert. 1974. *African Art in Motion.* Berkeley: University of California Press.

Thompson, Robert. 1983. *Flash of the Spirit: African and Afro-American Art and Philosophy.* New York: Random House.

Thwaites, R. G. (Ed.). 1906. *Jesuit Relations and Allied Documents, 1610–1791.* 73 vols. Cleveland, OH: Burrows Brothers.

Titiev, Mischa. 1992. *Old Oraibi: A Study of the Hopi Indians of Third Mesa.* Albuquerque: University of New Mexico Press.

Trask, Haunani-Kay. 2001. "Lovely Hula Hands: Corporate Tourism and the Prostitution of Hawaiian Culture." In *Native American Voices: A Reader,* 2nd ed. (Eds. Susan Lobo and Steve Talbot). Upper Saddle River, NJ: Prentice Hall, pp. 393–401.

Triandis, Harry. 1989. "The Self and Social Behavior in Differing Cultural Contexts." *Psychological Review* 96 (3):506–520.

Tronick, Edward, et al. 1992. "The Efe Forager Infant and Toddler's Pattern of Social Relationships: Multiple and Simultaneous." *Developmental Psychology* 28 (4):568–577.

Trudgill, Peter. 1972. "Sex, Covert Prestige and Linguistic Change in the Urban British English of Norwich." *Language in Society* 1:179–195.

Trudgill, Peter. 1974. *The Social Differentiation of English in Norwich.* New York: Cambridge University Press.

Tyler, Varro. 1996. "Natural Products and Medicine: An Overview." In *Medicinal Resources of the Tropical Forest: Biodiversity and Its Importance to Human Health* (Eds. M. Balick et al.). New York: Columbia University Press, pp. 3–10.

Tylor, Edward Burnett. 1871. *Primitive Culture.* London: J. Murray.

UNDP. 2006. *Human Development Report.* NY: Palgrave Macmillan.

United Nations. 1993. *Draft Declaration on the Rights of Indigenous Peoples.* New York.

United Nations. 2006. *Definitions of Terrorism.* **www.unodc.org/unodc/terrorism_definitions.html.** Accessed September 18, 2007.

United Nations. *Department of Economic and Social Affairs.* 2004. **www.unstats.un.org/unsd/cdb.**

United Nations, *Division for the Advancement of Women.* 2000. **www.unstats.un.org/unsd/cdb.**

Urton, Gary. 2003. *Quipu Knotting Account in the Inka Empire.* Santiago: Chilean Museum of Pre-Columbian Art.

van den Broeck, Jef. 1977. "Class Differences in Syntactic Complexity in the Flemish Town of Maaseik." *Language in Society* 6:149–181.

van Gennep, Arnold. 1961. *Rites of Passage.* Chicago: University of Chicago Press.

Vanover, Raymond. 1980. *Sun Songs: Creation Myths from around the World.* New York: New American Library.

Vayda, Andrew. 1961. "Expansion and Warfare among Swidden Agriculturalists." *American Anthropologist:* 63:346–358.

Wa, Gisday. 1989. *The spirit in the land : the opening statement of the Gitksan and Wet'suwet'en hereditary chiefs in the Supreme Court of British Columbia.* Gabriola, B.C.: Reflections.

Wallace, Anthony F. C. 1956. "Revitalization Movements." *American Anthropologist* 58:264–281.

Wallace, A. F. C. 1966. *Religion: An Anthropological View.* New York: Random House.

Warren, Jonathan. 2001. "Racial Revolutions: Antiracism and Indian Resurgence in Brazil." Durham, NC: Duke University Press.

Watson, Ruby. 1986. "The Named and the Nameless: Gender and Person in Chinese Society." *American Ethnologist* 13 (4): 619–631.

Weber, Max. 1968. *Max Weber on Charisma and Institution Building* (Ed. S. N. Eisenstadt). Chicago: University of Chicago Press.

Weber, Max. 1981. *General Economic History.* New York: Collier Books.

Weiss, Lawrence. 1984. *The Development of Capitalism in the Navajo Nation: A Political-Economic History. Studies in Marxism,* Vol. 15. Minneapolis: MEP Publications.

Wellington, John. 1967. *South West Africa and Its Human Issues.* Oxford: Clarendon/Oxford University Press.

Whiting, John W. M., and Irvin L. Child. 1953. *Child Training and Personality.* New Haven, CT: Yale University Press.

Whorf, Benjamin. 1956. "The Relation of Habitual Thought and Behavior to Language." In *Language, Thought and Reality* (Ed. J. B. Carroll). Cambridge, MA: MIT Press, pp. 134–159.

Wiessner, Siegfried. 1999. "Rights and Status of Indigenous Peoples: A Global Comparative and International Legal Analysis." *Harvard Human Rights Journal* 12:57–128.

Williams, Robert. 1997. "The Ebonics Controversy." *Journal of Black Psychology* 23: 208–213.

Williams, Walter. 1986. *The Spirit and the Flesh: Sexual Diversity in American Indian Culture.* Boston: Beacon Press.

Wilson, Gilbert. 1981. *Waheenee: An Indian Girl's Story Told by Herself to Gilbert L. Wilson.* Lincoln: University of Nebraska Press.

Winland, Daphne. 2002. "The politics of desire and disdain: Croatians between 'Home' and 'Homeland'." *American Ethnologist* 29:693–718.

Winslow, Donna. 1997. *The Canadian Airborne Regiment in Somalia : a socio-cultural inquiry : a study prepared for the Commission of Inquiry into the deployment of Canadian Forces in Somalia.* Ottawa: The Commission : Canadian Government Publishing.

Witherspoon, Gary. 1977. *Language and Art in the Navajo Universe.* Ann Arbor: University of Michigan Press.

Wolf, Arthur P.1980. *Marriage and adoption in China, 1845–1945.* Stanford: Stanford University Press

Wolf, Eric. 1982. *Europe and the People without History.* Berkeley: University of California Press.

Wolf, Marjorie. 1974. "Chinese Women: Old Skills in a New Context." In *Women, Culture and Society* (Eds. M. Rosaldo and L. Lamphere). Stanford, CA: Stanford University Press, pp. 157–172.

Wong, Aline. 1974. "Women in China: Past and Present." In *Many Sisters* (Ed. C. Matthiasson). New York: Free Press.

Wong, Aline. 1986. "Planned Development, Social Stratification, and the Sexual Division of Labor in Singapore." In *Women's Work: Development and the Division of Labor by Gender* (Eds. E. Leacock and H. Safa). Cambridge, MA: Bergen & Garvey, pp. 207–223.

Wong, L. 1997. "Globalization and transnational migration: A study of recent Chinese capitalist migration from the Asia Pacific to Canada." *International Sociology* 12:329–51.

World Health Organization. *Traditional Medicine Fact Sheet.* **www.who.int/mediacentre/factsheets/fs134/en.** Accessed November 18, 2004.

Worseley, Peter. 1967. "Millenarian Movements in Melanesia." In *Gods and Rituals* (Ed. J. Middleton). Garden City, NY: Natural History Press, pp. 337–352.

Worseley, Peter. 1968. *The Trumpet Shall Sound: A Study of Cargo Cults in Melanesia.* New York: Schocken.

Worseley, Peter. 1984. *The Three Worlds: Culture and World Development.* Chicago: University of Chicago Press.

Yap, P. M. 1969. "The Culture-Bound Reactive Syndromes." In *Mental Health Research in Asia and the Pacific* (Eds. W. Caudill and T. Y. Lin). Honolulu: East-West Center Press, pp. 33–53.

York, Geoffrey and Loreen Pindera. 1991. *People of the Pines: the Warriors and the legacy of Oka.* Toronto: McArthur and Company.

Zolbrod, Paul. 1984. *Diné Bahane: The Navajo Creation Story.* Albuquerque: University of New Mexico.

Index

A

abnormal behaviour, 105–10
Aboriginal cultures, 274–75, 277, 280, 330–31. *See also* indigenous people
  ceremonies of, 24–25
  Christianity and, 330–32
  education and, 100–101
  land claims and, 11, 50–52
  languages of, 7, 21, 24, 64–66
  renewal rituals in, 319
  residential schools and, 21 , 24
Aborigines, 183, 314, 346, 350
absolution, 316
Academie Française, 71, 75
accent, 68, 69
acculturation, 24, 25
achieved status, 259, 261, 267
adaptation, 9–10
  carrying capacity and, 115–16
  culture and, 16–17
  kuru and mad cow disease, 17–18
  reactive, 25
Adesanya, Aderonke, 42
admixture, 34
adoption, 120, 176–77
adultery, 229, 240
aesthetics, 340–45, 352
affines, 172, 198
Africa. *See also individual countries*
  indigenous people in, 389–90
African-Americans
  education and, 101
  English of, 70, 101
Afro-Lingua dialect, 19
Agbaje-Williams, Babatunde, 42
age
  power and prestige and, 259
  socialization, 91–92, 116
  work and, 116
age grades, 288–89, 291
agency, 41
age set, 288–189
agriculture, 114–15, 133–34.
     See also horticulture
  in Africa, 190
  ancient, 16
  in Canada, 135–38, 140–41
  child labour and, 89
  gender and, 114, 243

  horticulture *vs.*, 133
  land and resources and, 146
  malnutrition and, 134
  percent population involved in, 157–58
  warfare and, 294
Ahmadu, Fuambai, 36–37
Akan culture, 147, 175, 178–81, 191, 354
  matrilineal kinship in, 190
alebrijes, 360–61
Algonquin people, 108, 319
alliance theory, 205
Al Qaeda, 335
Amazonian culture, 314, 324
ambilineal descent, 188
American Anthropological Association, 199
Americanist tradition, 47
American Sign Language, 57
Amish culture, 328
amok, 107
ancestor worship, 313
Anderson, Richard, 340
Andes, 9, 11, 14, 301, 355, 389
animatism, 311–12
animism, 311–12
anorexia, 108
anthropologists, 3–4
  biases of, 37–38
  careers of, 6
  early, 34–35
  economic, 159
  as expert witnesses, 203
anthropology, 3–4, 6–9
  applied, 9–11
  archaeology as, 8–9
  biological, 9–10
  in Canada, 47
  cultural, 6–7
  ecological, 114
  history of, 34–36, 37–38
  interpretive, 38
  linguistic, 7–8, 62–72
  medical, 323
  methodology of, 44
  political, 286
  psychological, 101–5
  reflexive, 48–49
Apache people, 8, 353
apartheid, 20–22, 267, 302

Credits